Starting a Business
ALL-IN-ONE

FOR DUMMIES®

A Wiley Brand

Starting a Business
ALL-IN-ONE

FOR DUMMIES
A Wiley Brand

by Kathleen R. Allen, PhD, Peter Economy,
Paul and Sarah Edwards, Lita Epstein,
Alex Hiam, Greg Holden, Peter Jaret,
Jim Muehlhausen, JD, Bob Nelson, PhD,
Steven Peterson, Barbara Findlay Schenck,
Michael Seid, Dave Thomas, John A. Tracy,
Tage C. Tracy

FOR DUMMIES
A Wiley Brand

Starting a Business All-In-One For Dummies®

Published by:
John Wiley & Sons, Inc.,
111 River Street, Hoboken,
NJ 07030-5774,

www.wiley.com

Copyright © 2015 by John Wiley & Sons, Inc., Hoboken, New Jersey

Published simultaneously in Canada

For general information on our other products and services, please contact our Customer Care Department within the U.S. at 877-762-2974, outside the U.S. at 317-572-3993, or fax 317-572-4002. For technical support, please visit www.wiley.com/techsupport.

Wiley publishes in a variety of print and electronic formats and by print-on-demand. Some material included with standard print versions of this book may not be included in e-books or in print-on-demand. If this book refers to media such as a CD or DVD that is not included in the version you purchased, you may download this material at http://booksupport.wiley.com. For more information about Wiley products, visit www.wiley.com.

Library of Congress Control Number: 2014957354

ISBN 978-1-119-04910-4 (pbk); ISBN 978-1-119-04908-1 (ebk); ISBN 978-1-119-04907-4 (ebk)

Manufactured in the United States of America

10 9 8 7 6 5 4 3 2 1

Contents at a Glance

Introduction *1*

Book I: From Idea to Reality *5*

Chapter 1: Your Business in Context 7
Chapter 2: Refining and Defining Your Business Idea 27
Chapter 3: Creating a Business Model 45
Chapter 4: Finding Your Target Market 63
Chapter 5: Considering a Franchise 79

Book II: Planning for Your Business *97*

Chapter 1: Writing a Business Plan 99
Chapter 2: Finding the Funding 115
Chapter 3: Setting Your Franchise's Wheels in Motion 135
Chapter 4: Starting a Home-Based Business 163
Chapter 5: Creating a Website for Your Business 191
Chapter 6: Starting with the Right Legal Structure 221

Book III: Managing Your Finances *235*

Chapter 1: Setting Up the Books 237
Chapter 2: Understanding Your P&L 263
Chapter 3: Working with Cash Flow and Staying Solvent 287
Chapter 4: Controlling Costs and Budgeting 321
Chapter 5: Satisfying the Tax Man 357

Book IV: Managing Your Business *363*

Chapter 1: Tackling the Hiring Process 365
Chapter 2: Setting Goals 383
Chapter 3: Embracing Corporate Social Responsibility 395
Chapter 4: Managing with Technology 405
Chapter 5: Developing Employees Through Coaching and Mentoring ... 415
Chapter 6: Delegating to Get Things Done 431

Book V: Marketing and Promotion 443

Chapter 1: Optimizing Your Marketing Program 445
Chapter 2: Strengthening Your Marketing Strategy 461
Chapter 3: Taking Stock of Your Business Image 477
Chapter 4: Forging Your Brand 491
Chapter 5: Creating Marketing Communications That Work 507
Chapter 6: Social Marketing: Facebook, Pinterest, Twitter, and Blogs ... 525

Index 537

Table of Contents

Introduction *1*

About This Book 1
Foolish Assumptions... 2
Icons Used in This Book 2
Beyond the Book 3
Where to Go from Here... 3

Book I: From Idea to Reality *5*

Chapter 1: Your Business in Context 7

An Overview of Feasibility Analysis 8
    Executive summary 8
    Business concept 9
    Industry analysis... 9
    Market/customer analysis 10
    Genesis or founding team analysis 10
    Product/service development analysis............................. 10
    Financial analysis 10
    Feasibility decision 11
    Timeline to launch 11
Understanding Your Industry 11
    Using a framework of industry structure......................... 12
    Deciding on an entry strategy 15
Researching an Industry... 15
    Checking out the status of your industry 16
    Competitive intelligence: Checking out the competition 17
Defining Your Market Niche 20
    Narrowing your market... 21
    Developing a niche strategy 23
Zeroing-in on a Brand New Product 23
    Become an inventor.. 24
    Team up with an inventor.. 24
    License an invention.. 25

Chapter 2: Refining and Defining Your Business Idea.............27

Recognizing the Power of a Good Idea 27
    Knowing the difference between passion and profitability............ 28
    Turning a gig into a business 29

Planning ahead: Great ideas take time...............................30
Checking out the competition..31
Brainstorming New Business Ideas...32
Using the do-it-yourself idea blender...............................33
Inspiring team creativity (with or without donuts or bagels) 36
Finding business ideas within your work environment...............39
Identifying Business Opportunities..40
Listening to what customers have to say..........................40
Spotting changes that open up new opportunities.....................40
Testing your business ideas...41
Doing Your First Reality Check..42
Getting a second opinion..42
Conducting a self-appraisal...43

Chapter 3: Creating a Business Model...........................**45**
Evolution of Business Models...46
Business Models Are a Hot Topic..46
Who Needs a Business Model?..47
Common Aspects of All Business Models 47
Business Models in Their Simplest Form 49
Examples of Business Models 49
Finding Success with a Business Model 53
Your secret sauce for making money..................................54
Same industry, different business models............................57
How your business model sets you apart from the
competition...58
Considering your competitive advantage..............................59
Obtaining your competitive advantage................................59
Enhancing your competitive advantage 61

Chapter 4: Finding Your Target Market..........................**63**
Gauging the Target Market..63
Determining Industry Attractiveness......................................64
Finding the best industry...66
Working in unserved or underserved markets..........................67
Case study: Software versus airlines................................68
Looking for Niche Attractiveness...69
The power of a good niche...69
Unlimited niches exist..70
Markets have a habit of splitting...................................71
Find unserved or underserved markets................................73
Checking Out Customer Attractiveness.....................................74
Finding Your Place on the Industry Value Chain...........................76

Chapter 5: Considering a Franchise **79**

So What Is a Franchise, Anyway? 79
The effects of franchising on modern business 80
The success of franchising for business owners 80
What's the Deal with Brands in Franchising? .81
The Two Types of Franchises 82
Product distribution franchises 82
Business format franchises 83
The Roles and Goals of Franchisors and Franchisees 84
Looking at the world through franchisor lenses 85
The franchisee's end of the bargain 86
Franchise Relationships 87
Flying solo: Single-unit franchises 87
Growing a family, one franchise at a time 88
Multi-unit or area developers 89
Playing in the big leagues: Master franchising 91
The hired gun: Area representatives 92
Pros and Cons of Franchising 92
Advantages of franchise ownership 93
Disadvantages for franchisees 94

Book II: Planning for Your Business **97**

Chapter 1: Writing a Business Plan **99**

Selling Yourself on the Importance of Planning 99
Tallying up the benefits of having a plan 100
Knowing what can go wrong without a plan 101
The Anatomy of a Business Plan 101
Business-plan contents from beginning to end 102
Frequently asked business-plan questions 103
Understanding Your Starting Position 104
Planning for a startup 105
Planning for a solo business 105
Planning to address changing conditions 106
Planning to seize growth opportunity 106
Setting Out Your Planning Objectives 106
Identifying Target Audiences and Key Messages 107
Your audience 108
Your message 108
Business planning as a test drive 109
Establishing Your Plan's Time Frame 109
Committing to a schedule 110
Defining milestones 110

Preparing for the Real World 111
    Locating informative resources 112
    Seeking expert advice... 113

Chapter 2: Finding the Funding **115**
Starting with a Plan 116
    When you're financing a traditional business................... 116
    When you're financing for e-commerce 118
Tapping Friends, Family, and Lovers 119
Finding an Angel 120
    How to spot an angel.. 120
    How to deal with angels 121
Daring to Use Venture Capital 122
    Calculating the real cost of money 123
    Tracking the venture capital process 124
Selling Stock to the Public: An IPO.. 126
    Considering the advantages and disadvantages
        of going public 127
    Deciding to go for it 128
Finding Other Ways to Finance Growth................................. 130
Guarding Your Interests 132
    Contracts.. 132
    Non-disclosure agreements 132

Chapter 3: Setting Your Franchise's Wheels in Motion **135**
Surveying Your Options for Locale.. 135
    Common site options 136
    Opting for alternate, or off-street, sites 138
    Working from home.. 139
    Landing near another franchise: Dual branding 140
Setting Up Shop: Finding Your Franchise's Habitat 141
    Finding out what constitutes a good site........................ 141
    Using the franchisor as your compass............................ 142
    Use drive time to evaluate a site on your own............... 144
Avoiding Encroachment 145
Securing Your Space After Finding Your Piece of Heaven 147
    Understanding and signing a lease.................................. 147
    Building a location 148
Getting the Goods: Merchandise and Supplies...................... 149
    Knowing whom to buy from when your franchisor
        is involved 150
    Finding your own suppliers and goods............................ 154
Receiving Merchandise.. 154
    Receiving deliveries... 155
    Checking the goods after they're in your location 155
    Verifying invoices 156

Maintaining Inventory 156
    Back of the house 157
    Front of the house 158
Getting Good Training Before and After You Open Your Franchise 159
    Getting good initial training 160
    Ensuring that you receive effective ongoing training 162

Chapter 4: Starting a Home-Based Business **163**

Looking at the Basics of Home-Based Business 164
    Determining the kind of business you want to have 164
    Managing your money 166
    Avoiding problems 167
    Moving ahead 167
    Leaving your full-time job for your part-time business 168
Examining the Good News and the Bad 169
    Good reasons to start a home-based business 169
    The pitfalls of owning your own home-based businesses 170
Taking the Home-Based Business Quiz 172
Starting Something from Scratch 174
    Examples to inspire you 175
    Doing what you've been doing in a job 176
    Doing something new and different 178
Transitioning into Your Home-Based Business 178
    Knowing what to do before leaving your day job 180
    Understanding what you have to do to start your
        own home-based business 181

Chapter 5: Creating a Website for Your Business **191**

Feng Shui-ing Your Website 192
Creating Content That Attracts Customers 195
    Following the KISS principle: Keep it simple, sir (or sister) 196
    Striking the right tone with your text 197
    Making your site easy to navigate 197
    Pointing the way with headings 200
    Becoming an expert list maker 201
    Leading your readers on with links 202
    Enhancing your text with well-placed images 203
    Making your site searchable 204
Nip and Tuck: Establishing a Visual Identity 206
    Choosing an appropriate background 207
    Using web typefaces like a pro 208
    Using clip art is free and fun 209
    A picture is worth a thousand words 210
    Creating a logo 213
Inviting Comments from Customers 214
    Getting positive email feedback 214

Web page forms that aren't offputting.................................216
Blogs that promote discussion 216
Chit-chat that counts...218
Moving from Website to Web Presence..................................219

Chapter 6: Starting with the Right Legal Structure **221**
Deciding on the Best Legal Form for Your Business.............................222
Going It Alone: The Sole Proprietorship.....................................224
Advantages of sole proprietorships 225
Disadvantages of sole proprietorships 225
Choosing a Partner: The Partnership 226
Forming a partnership...226
The partnership agreement......................................227
Going for the Gold: The Corporation 228
Enjoying the benefits of a corporation........................229
Weighing the risks 230
Where and how to incorporate 230
Looking for Flexibility: The S Corporation, the LLC,
and the Nonprofit Corporation 231
Sizing up the S Corporation....................................231
Comparing the S Corporation with the LLC 232
Making profits in a nonprofit organization....................233
Benchmarking Your Best Choice...234

Book III: Managing Your Finances **235**

Chapter 1: Setting Up the Books **237**
Bookkeepers: The Record Keepers of the Business World...................238
Wading through Basic Bookkeeping Lingo..................................239
Accounts for the balance sheet 239
Accounts for the income statement 240
Other common terms 240
Pedaling through the Accounting Cycle 241
Tackling the Big Decision: Cash-Basis or Accrual Accounting 243
Waiting for funds with cash-basis accounting 243
Recording right away with accrual accounting 245
Seeing Double with Double-Entry Bookkeeping 245
Differentiating Debits and Credits...247
Outlining Your Financial Roadmap with a Chart of Accounts 248
Starting with the Balance Sheet Accounts 250
Tackling assets 250
Laying out your liabilities 254
Eyeing the equity 255
Tracking the Income Statement Accounts 256

Recording the money you make 257
Tracking the Cost of Sales 258
Acknowledging the money you spend 258
Setting Up Your Chart of Accounts 260

Chapter 2: Understanding Your P&L 263
Getting Intimate with Your Profit and Loss Report..............................264
Measuring and Reporting Profit and Loss......................................268
Accounting for profit isn't an exact science..............................269
Your accounting records may have errors 269
Selecting the accounting methods for recording revenue
and expenses 270
Recording unusual, nonrecurring gains and losses 270
Keeping the number of lines in your P&L relatively short 271
Profit-neutral business transactions 271
Including more information on inventory and purchases............272
Presenting the P&L Report for Your Business................................273
Figuring out the reasons for your profit improvement................276
Knowing how your expenses behave.......................................279
Breaking Through the Breakeven Barrier 281
Improving Profit..282
Improving markup 283
Improving sales volume 285

Chapter 3: Working with Cash Flow and Staying Solvent 287
Sorting Out Your Sources of Cash...288
Avoiding Confusion Between Profit and Its Cash Flow.........................290
Deciding How to Have Cash Flow Information Reported to You...........291
Appending cash flow to your P&L report 292
Reporting differences of cash flows from sales revenue
and expenses in the P&L...293
Introducing the Statement of Cash Flows.....................................296
Running down the balance sheet from the cash flow
point of view 298
Doing a quick calculation of cash flow from profit.......................299
Classifying cash flows in the statement of cash flows 300
Presenting the statement of cash flows 301
Summing Up the Critical Importance of Cash Flow from Profit............303
Liquidity and Business Solvency..303
Business Solvency Measurements Tools.......................................307
Liquidity Measurements Tools 309
Liquidity Traps 311
Asset investment..312
Inappropriate use of debt...314
Excessive growth rates 315

Untapped Sources of Liquidity 316
    Asset liquidations 316
    Lending sources..317
    Unsecured creditors...318
    Equity and off-balance sheet sources 319
Financial Leverage: The Good, the Bad, and the Ugly 320

Chapter 4: Controlling Costs and Budgeting 321

Getting in the Right Frame of Mind 322
Getting Down to Business..322
    Putting cost control in its proper context 323
    Beginning with sales revenue change 324
    Focusing on cost of goods sold and gross margin 326
    Analyzing employee cost 328
    Analyzing advertising and sales promotion costs.......................329
    Appreciating depreciation expense...330
    Looking at facilities expense 331
    Looking over or looking into other expenses 332
    Running the numbers on interest expense....................................333
    Comparing your P&L with your balance sheet 334
Looking into Cost of Goods Sold Expense..336
    Selecting a cost of goods sold expense method 336
    Dealing with inventory shrinkage and inventory write-downs 338
Focusing on Profit Centers 339
Reducing Your Costs..341
Deciding Where the Budgeting Process Starts 341
Honing In on Budgeting Tools..343
    CART: Complete, Accurate, Reliable, and Timely.......................343
    SWOT: Strengths, Weaknesses, Opportunities, and Threats 344
    Flash reports 345
Preparing an Actual Budget or Forecast 347
Understanding Internal Versus External Budgets 350
Creating a Living Budget...351
Using the Budget as a Business-Management Tool..................................354
Using Budgets in Other Ways 355

Chapter 5: Satisfying the Tax Man 357

Tax Reporting for Sole Proprietors 357
Filing Tax Forms for Partnerships 358
Paying Corporate Taxes..359
    Reporting for an S Corporation...359
    Reporting for a C Corporation...359
    Reporting for Limited Liability Companies (LLC)........................360
Taking Care of Sales Taxes Obligations...361

Book IV: Managing Your Business............................. 363

Chapter 1: Tackling the Hiring Process 365
Starting with a Clear Job Description 366
Defining the Characteristics of Desirable Candidates 367
Finding Good People 368
   Going through traditional recruiting channels 369
   Leveraging the power of the Internet................................... 371
Becoming a Great Interviewer 372
   Asking the right questions.. 372
   Following interviewing do's 374
   Avoiding interviewing don'ts 375
Evaluating Your Candidates 376
   Checking references 376
   Reviewing your notes 378
   Conducting a second (or third) round................................ 378
   Checking employment eligibility 379
Hiring the Best (and Leaving the Rest).. 379
   Being objective... 380
   Trusting your gut 380
   Revisiting the candidate pool.. 381

Chapter 2: Setting Goals 383
Knowing Where You're Going... 384
Identifying SMART Goals 386
Setting Goals: Less Is More... 388
Communicating Your Vision and Goals to Your Team 389
Juggling Priorities: Keeping Your Eye on the Ball 391
Using Your Power for Good: Making Your Goals Reality 393

Chapter 3: Embracing Corporate Social Responsibility 395
Understanding Socially Responsible Practices 396
   Figuring out how you can employ CSR 396
   Enjoying net benefits of socially responsible practices 397
   Developing a CSR strategy for implementation 398
Doing the Right Thing: Ethics and You.. 400
   Defining ethics on the job.. 400
   Creating a code of ethics 401
   Making ethical choices every day...................................... 402

Chapter 4: Managing with Technology 405
Weighing the Benefits and Drawbacks of Technology
  in the Workplace... 406
   Making advances, thanks to automation 406

Improving efficiency and productivity.................................407
Taking steps to neutralize the negatives 408
Using Technology to Your Advantage 409
Know your business 409
Create a technology-competitive advantage..................410
Develop a plan..410
Get some help...412
Getting the Most Out of Company Networks 413

**Chapter 5: Developing Employees Through Coaching
and Mentoring...415**

Why Help Develop Your Employees?....................................416
Getting Down to Employee Development............................418
Taking a step-by-step approach.....................................419
Creating career development plans 420
Coaching Employees to Career Growth and Success 422
Serving as both manager and coach 422
Identifying a coach's tools...424
Teaching through show-and-tell coaching 426
Making turning points big successes 426
Incorporating coaching into your day-to-day interactions 427
Finding a Mentor, Being a Mentor 429

Chapter 6: Delegating to Get Things Done.................431

Delegating: The Manager's Best Tool....................................431
Debunking Myths about Delegation 433
You can't trust your employees to be responsible 433
You'll lose control of a task and its outcome................434
You're the only one with all the answers 434
You can do the work faster by yourself.........................435
Delegation dilutes your authority....................................435
You relinquish the credit for doing a good job.............436
Delegation decreases your flexibility 436
Taking the Six Steps to Delegate...437
Sorting Out What to Delegate and What to Do Yourself.........438
Pointing out appropriate tasks for delegation 438
Knowing what tasks should stay with you 440

Book V: Marketing and Promotion........................... **443**

Chapter 1: Optimizing Your Marketing Program..................445

Know Yourself, Know Your Customer 445
Asking the right question..446
Filling the awareness gap...448

Focusing on your target customer 449
Identifying and playing up your strengths 450
Discovering the best way to find customers 450
Finding Your Marketing Formula 453
Analyzing your Five P's 453
Refining your list of possibilities 455
Avoiding the pricing trap 455
Controlling Your Marketing Program 456
Refining Your Marketing Expectations 457
Projecting improvements above base sales 457
Preparing for (ultimately successful) failures 458
Revealing More Ways to Maximize Your Marketing Impact 459

Chapter 2: Strengthening Your Marketing Strategy 461
Finding and Riding a Growth Wave 461
Measuring the growth rate of your market 462
Responding to a flat or shrinking market 462
Growing with a Market Expansion Strategy 463
Offering more products 463
Riding a bestseller to the top 464
Specializing with a Market Segmentation Strategy 465
Gauging whether specializing is a good move 466
Adding a segment to expand your market 466
Developing a Market Share Strategy 467
Choosing a unit 467
Estimating market share 467
Understanding where your product fits in the market 468
Knowing your competitors 470
Studying market trends and revising if need be 470
Designing a Positioning Strategy 471
Envisioning your position: An exercise
in observation and creativity 471
Writing a positioning strategy: The how-to 472
Considering Other Core Strategies 473
Simplicity marketing 473
Quality strategies 474
Reminder strategies 474
Innovative distribution strategies 474
Selling Innovative Products 475
Writing Down and Regularly Reviewing Your Strategy 476

Chapter 3: Taking Stock of Your Business Image 477
Making First Impressions 477
Encountering your business through online searches 478
Arriving at your website 480
Managing email impressions 481

Arriving by telephone...482
Approaching your business in person........................484
Auditing the Impressions Your Business Makes 488
Surveying your marketing materials and communications.........488
Creating an impression inventory 489
Improving the impressions you're making....................490

Chapter 4: Forging Your Brand...........................491

What Brands Are and What They Do 491
Unlocking the power and value of a brand...................492
Tipping the balance online 493
Building a Powerful Brand..493
Being consistent to power your brand 494
Taking six brand-management steps........................494
Your Market Position: The Birthplace of Your Brand 496
Seeing how positioning happens 496
Determining your positioning strategy....................497
Conveying Your Position and Brand through Taglines 498
Balancing Personal and Business Brands 500
Maintaining and Protecting Your Brand........................501
Staying consistent with your brand message
and creative strategy...502
Controlling your brand presentation 503

Chapter 5: Creating Marketing Communications That Work.......507

Starting with Good Objectives 508
Defining what you want to accomplish......................508
Putting creative directions in writing......................509
Developing Effective Marketing Communications 514
Steering the creative process toward a "big idea" 515
Brainstorming...516
Following simple advertising rules 517
Making Media Selections 518
Selecting from the media menu 518
Deciding which media vehicles to use and when.........520
The Making of a Mass Media Schedule............................521
Balancing reach and frequency..............................521
Timing your ads 523
Evaluating Your Efforts..523

**Chapter 6: Social Marketing: Facebook, Pinterest,
Twitter, and Blogs 525**

Developing a Business Presence on Facebook...................526
Attracting "likers" to your Facebook page 527
Getting your customers excited...............................528
Creating a Facebook "kiosk".................................529

Sharing Your Images with Pinterest..............................531
Building a Fan Base with Twitter...................................532
    Setting up a Twitter presence 533
    Signing up and posting..533
Using Your Blog for Profit . . . and Fun.........................534
    Choosing a host with the most for your posts..........534
    Adding ads to your blog..535
    Achieving other business benefits.........................535

Index *537*

Introduction

Welcome to *Starting a Business All-in-One For Dummies!*

It's a good bet that you share the popular dream of starting your own business and being your own boss. Increasingly, this dream is becoming more relevant to the challenges of the economy that's emerging today. It's not just a pie-in-the-sky dream anymore; starting a business is a reality that has created opportunity and satisfaction for many people who decided to take the plunge — just as it can for you.

This book presents and explains a very wide variety of information, all aimed at enlightening you on what you need to know and ensuring your success. Whether you need know-how and advice on turning your idea into reality, creating a business plan and business model, finding funding, picking a legal structure, setting up your books, or marketing and promoting, you'll find the help you need here. Most of this book is applicable to you whether your business is a local business, startup corporation, franchise, or based out of your home.

The aim of this book is to provide you with the very best ideas, concepts, and tools for starting and successfully operating your business. Using the info here, you should be able to create exactly the kind of business you've always dreamed of and find exactly the level of success you've always wanted.

About This Book

This book is a generous conglomeration of material from a number of Dummies business books, carefully selected with an eye toward getting the new business owner/entrepreneur up and running. Your current level of business experience (or lack thereof) doesn't matter. Don't worry about not having years of management experience under your belt or about not knowing the difference between a *balance sheet* and a *P&L*.

For a fraction of the amount you'd pay to get an MBA, this book provides you with an easily understandable road map to today's most innovative and effective business techniques and strategies. The information you find here is firmly grounded in the real world. This book isn't an abstract collection of theoretical, pie-in-the-sky mumbo-jumbo that sounds good but doesn't work when you put it to the test. Instead, you'll find only the best information, the best strategies, and the best techniques — the same ones that top business schools teach today.

This book is also meant to be at least a little fun — running a business doesn't have to be a bore! In fact, maintaining a sense of humor can be vital when facing the challenges that all new business owners face from time to time.

Within this book, you may note that some web addresses (URLs) break across two lines of text. If you're reading this book in print and want to visit one of these web pages, simply key in the web address exactly as it's noted in the text, pretending as though the line break doesn't exist. If you're reading this as an e-book, you've got it easy — just tap the web address to be taken directly to the web page.

Foolish Assumptions

This book makes a few assumptions about you. For example, you have at least a passing interest in starting your own business. (Duh.) Maybe you've already started a business and are looking for tips to refine the techniques you're already developing. Or perhaps it's something you think you may want to try and are looking to read up on it before you make your move. Either way, you've come to the right place.

It's also safe to assume that you can — or believe you can — produce and deliver products or services that people will be willing to pay you for. These products and services can be most anything. You're limited only by your imagination (and, of course, your bank account, about which you'll soon be reading quite a bit). Finally, this book assumes you're eager to scoop up and implement new tips and tricks and that you're willing to acquire some new perspectives on the topic.

Icons Used in This Book

Icons are handy little graphic images that are meant to point out particularly important information about starting your own business. Throughout this book, you find the following icons, conveniently located along the left margins:

This icon directs you to tips and shortcuts you can follow to save time and do things the right way the first time.

Remember the important points of information that follow this icon, and your business will be all the better for it.

Danger! Ignore the advice next to this icon at your own risk!

This one points out slightly advanced material that you can safely skip if you're in a hurry. But by all means, read these if you want to stretch yourself a bit.

Beyond the Book

In addition to the material in the print or e-book you're reading right now, this product also comes with some access-anywhere goodies on the web. No matter how hard you work at creating your business, you'll likely come across a few questions where you don't have a clue. Check out the free Cheat Sheet at www.dummies.com/cheatsheet/startingabusinessaio for helpful tips on getting inspired to start your own business, how to succeed at it, and how to handle your business's money.

You'll also find a handful of articles online at www.dummies.com/extras/startingabusinessaio. These freebies cover stuff that wouldn't quite fit inside these covers, such as questions you should answer before completing your business plan, ways of boosting your web sales, and financial management rules for small business survival.

Where to Go from Here

If you're new to starting a business, you may want to start at the beginning of this book and work your way through to the end. A wealth of information and practical advice awaits you. Simply turn the page and you're on your way! But you can start anywhere. If you already own and operate a business and are short of time (and who isn't?), feel free to use the table of contents and index to zero in on particular topics of interest to you right now.

Regardless of how you find your way around this book, the sincere hope of this endeavor is that you'll enjoy the journey.

Book I
From Idea to Reality

getting started
with

starting a
business

Contents at a Glance

Chapter 1: Your Business in Context 7

An Overview of Feasibility Analysis 8
Understanding Your Industry 11
Researching an Industry 15
Defining Your Market Niche 20
Zeroing-in on a Brand New Product 23

Chapter 2: Refining and Defining Your Business Idea 27

Recognizing the Power of a Good Idea 27
Brainstorming New Business Ideas 32
Identifying Business Opportunities 40
Doing Your First Reality Check 42

Chapter 3: Creating a Business Model 45

Evolution of Business Models 46
Business Models Are a Hot Topic 46
Who Needs a Business Model? 47
Common Aspects of All Business Models 47
Business Models in Their Simplest Form 49
Examples of Business Models 49
Finding Success with a Business Model 53

Chapter 4: Finding Your Target Market 63

Gauging the Target Market 63
Determining Industry Attractiveness 64
Looking for Niche Attractiveness 69
Checking Out Customer Attractiveness 74
Finding Your Place on the Industry Value Chain 76

Chapter 5: Considering a Franchise 79

So What Is a Franchise, Anyway? 79
What's the Deal with Brands in Franchising? 81
The Two Types of Franchises 82
The Roles and Goals of Franchisors and Franchisees 84
Franchise Relationships 87
Pros and Cons of Franchising 92

Chapter 1

Your Business in Context

In This Chapter

▶ Analyzing the feasibility of your business idea

▶ Figuring out your industry

▶ Doing research on your industry

▶ Determining where you fit in

▶ Targeting a new product for the market

*T*his chapter starts at the very beginning, looking at how to step back and see a potential start-up business in the context within which it operates. If you've already started your business and are committed to it, or if you know exactly what kind of business you want to run and nothing will change your mind, or if your idea is to start rather small, with a modest idea that doesn't require finding much funding to get you going, you can skip this chapter. Good luck to you. But it could be to your advantage to stick around anyway, because the fact is, not every business is a good idea at the time and place where it is born. You could save yourself some heartache by examining the external factors that will affect your business whether you like it or not. If you choose the right business at the right time and the right place, your chances of success are much higher.

Every successful business operates inside an environment that affects everything it does. The environment includes the industry in which the business operates, the market the business serves, the state of the economy, and the various people and businesses the business interacts with. Your business doesn't exist in a vacuum. Now, more than ever before, understanding your industry is a critical component of the success of your business venture.

If you position your company well inside a growing, healthy industry, you have a better chance of building a successful venture. By contrast, if your business niche is a weak position in a hostile, mature industry, your fledgling business may be doomed.

Conducting a feasibility analysis can be a good way to get a clear picture of the landscape. The first section of this chapter provides an overview of this process.

An Overview of Feasibility Analysis

Feasibility analysis consists of a series of tests that you conduct as you discover more and more about your opportunity. After each test, you ask yourself if you still want to go forward. Is there anything here that prevents you from going forward with this business? Feasibility is a process of discovery, and during that process you will probably modify your original concept several times until you get it right. That's the real value of feasibility — the way that it helps you refine your concept so that you have the highest potential for success when you launch your business.

Today, you can often go for financing on the strength of a feasibility study alone. Certainly in the case of Internet businesses, speed is of the essence. Many an online business has gotten first-round financing on its proof of concept alone and *then* done a business plan before going for bigger dollars in the form of venture capital. But even if your business is a traditional one, feasibility can help you avoid big early mistakes.

Executive summary

The executive summary is probably the most important piece of a feasibility analysis because, in two pages, it presents the most important and persuasive points from every test you did during your analysis. An effective executive summary captures the reader's attention immediately with the excitement of the concept. It doesn't let the reader get away; it draws the reader deeper and deeper into the concept as it proves your claim that the concept is feasible and will be a market success.

The most important information to emphasize in the executive summary is your proof that customers want what you have to offer. This proof comes from the primary research you do with the customers to find out what they think of your concept and how much demand there is. The other key piece to emphasize is your description of your founding team. Even the greatest ideas can't happen without a great team, and investors put a lot of stock in a founding team's expertise and experience.

For an online business, you may want to prepare what's called a *proof of concept*. This is essentially a one-page statement of why your concept will work, emphasizing what you have done to prove that customers will come to your site. That may be in the form of showing hits to your beta site or a list of customers signed up and ready to go when the site is finished. Similarly, if you're developing a new product, your proof of concept is your market-quality prototype.

Business concept

In this first part of the body of your feasibility analysis, you are developing your business concept. Essentially you are answering these questions:

- ✔ What is the business?
- ✔ Who is the customer?
- ✔ What is the value proposition?
- ✔ How will the benefit be delivered?

It's important to be able to state your business concept in a few clear, concise, and direct sentences that include all four of the components of the concept. This is what is often called your *elevator pitch* — a conversation that begins when the elevator door closes and ends when the door opens at your floor. That means you have only a few seconds to capture your listener's attention, so you better be able to get it all out quickly and confidently. If you're preparing a feasibility analysis that will be shown to investors, you should to state your business concept right up front in the concept section. Then you can elaborate on each point as a follow-up. Here's an example:

> Rural Power Tools is in the power equipment business, providing contractors and developers solutions to power needs in remote areas through rental equipment outlets.

As you find out more about your business concept, you'll also want to consider the various spin-off products and services you may be able to offer.

One-product businesses often have a more difficult time becoming successful than multi-product/service companies. You don't want to put all your eggs into one basket if you can help it, and you want to give your customer choices.

Industry analysis

Testing whether or not the industry in which you will be operating will support your concept is an important part of any feasibility analysis. Here you look at the status of your industry, identify trends and patterns of change, and look at who the major players in terms of competitors may be. Also, don't forget that one way to *find* a great opportunity is to study an industry first. More details on how to do an industry analysis are covered in the section "Researching an Industry," later in this chapter.

Market/customer analysis

Here you will be testing your customer. Ideally, inside your industry, you find a market segment appropriate to your business. Then you identify a niche that is not being served so that you have an entry strategy with the lowest barriers possible and the highest probability of success. In this part of the analysis, you also look at what your potential customer wants and what the demand for your product/service is. You will also consider a variety of different distribution channels to deliver the benefit to the customer. To find out more, see the section "Defining Your Market Niche," later in this chapter.

Genesis or founding team analysis

Investors look very carefully at the founding team because even the best concept won't happen without a team that can execute. In this part of the analysis, you want to consider the qualifications, expertise, and experience of your founding team, even if that consists of only yourself. Be aware that today's business environment is so complex and fast-paced that no one person has all the skills, time, and resources to do everything him- or herself.

Product/service development analysis

Whether you're planning to offer a product or a service or both (and that's usually the case), it's going to take some planning. Consider which tasks must be accomplished to prepare the product or service for market, whether that be developing a product from raw materials and going through the patent process or developing a plan for implementing a service concept. Identify these preparatory tasks and figure out a realistic timeline for completion of them. Put that timeline in your analysis.

Financial analysis

In this part of the feasibility analysis, you figure out how much money you need to start the business and carry it to a positive cash flow. You also distinguish among the types of money, which will be important in defining your financial strategy. You can find out more about finding funding in Book II Chapter 2.

Feasibility decision

After you have gone through all the various tests that comprise the feasibility analysis, you are ready to make a decision about going forward. Of course, throughout the process of doing the tests, you may have decided to stop — because of something you found out from analysis of the industry, market, product/service, and so forth. But if you're still on the mission, now's the time to define the conditions under which you go forward.

Timeline to launch

You always need to end a feasibility analysis with an action plan so that you're sure that at least something will happen. Establishing a list of all tasks to be completed and a time frame for completing them will increase the probability that your business will be launched in a timely fashion. The research you have done along the way will help you make wise decisions about the length of time it takes to complete everything and open the doors to your business.

Understanding Your Industry

New industries emerge on a regular basis. In fact, with e-commerce holding so much of the attention of young businesspeople today, you may well ask, "Is e-commerce an industry?" That's a great question. If you define an industry as a group of related businesses, then all e-commerce businesses have one thing in common: the Internet. But retail businesses, manufacturers, wholesalers, and service companies are all on the Internet, so every member of the value chain is found in one location.

All retail businesses have retail in common, and all manufacturers have manufacturing in common. Are retail and manufacturing industries as well? Within retail, you find clothing retailers and book retailers among many others. Is clothing an industry? Is publishing an industry? The answer to all these questions is yes.

Actually, there are layers of industries, starting with the broadest terms and working down to the more specific terms. Take an e-commerce business that almost everyone knows: Amazon.com. If you consider e-commerce to be an industry, a grouping of like businesses, then Amazon is definitely part of that industry. Within e-commerce, Amazon is also a retail business that happens to be using the Internet as its marketing/distribution channel. Within retail, it operates in the publishing, music, toys, and video industries, among others. What this means to you is that when you study Amazon's industry, you're really looking at three distinct industries, and it's important to understand what's going on in each.

You need to study the industry you have chosen for your feasibility study. Start at the broadest level of industry definition and work your way down to the segment that includes the product or service that you are providing.

Using a framework of industry structure

One way to begin to look at the industry you're interested in is to use a common framework. One useful framework is based on the work of W.H. Starbuck and Michael E. Porter, two experts on organizational strategy. This framework steps you through analyzing your potential industry by assessing the outside forces that work upon it and then assessing the countermeasures that you'll need to implement against those outside forces. According to Starbuck and Porter, new businesses must be constantly on the lookout for forces that affect them in every area.

The business environment, especially the entrepreneurial environment, often looks like a battlefield. But for every threat there's a countermeasure. The first step is to look at what these outside forces really are.

Carrying capacity, uncertainty, and complexity

This first environmental factor explains why so many industries today are changing, moving more rapidly, and making it more difficult for businesses to succeed. *Carrying capacity* refers to the extent to which an industry can accept more businesses. Industries can become oversaturated with too many businesses. When that happens, the capacity of businesses to produce their products and services exceeds the demand for them. Then it becomes increasingly difficult for new businesses to enter the industry and survive.

Uncertainty refers to the predictability or unpredictability of the industry — stability or instability. Typically volatile and fast-changing, modern technology industries produce more uncertainty. But these same industries often produce more opportunities for new businesses to take advantage of.

Complexity is about the number and diversity of inputs and outputs in the industry. Complex industries cause businesses to have to deal with more suppliers, customers, and competitors than other industries. Biotechnology and telecommunications are examples of industries with high degrees of complexity in the form of competition and government regulation.

Threat to new entrants

Some industries have barriers to entry that are quite high. These barriers come in many forms. Here are the main ones:

- ✔ **Economies of scale:** These are product volumes that enable established businesses to produce goods more inexpensively than a new business can. A new business can't compete with the low costs of the entrenched firms. To combat economies of scale, new firms often form alliances that give them more clout.

- ✔ **Brand loyalty:** If you're a new business, you face competitors that have achieved brand loyalty, which makes it much more difficult to entice customers to your products and services. That's why it's so important to find a market niche that you can control — a need in the market that is not being served. That will give you time to establish some brand loyalty of your own. Later in this chapter you'll find out more about niches, and Book V Chapter 4 covers branding in detail.

- ✔ **High capital requirements:** In some industries, you encounter high costs for the advertising, R&D (research and development), and plants and equipment you need to compete with established firms. Again, new companies often overcome this barrier by outsourcing expensive functions to other firms.

- ✔ **Buyer switching costs:** Buyers don't generally like to switch from one supplier to another unless there's a good reason to do so. That's why once a person invests the time to learn and use the Windows environment, for example, he or she is reluctant to start all over with a different platform. Entrepreneurs must match a need *that is not being met with the current product on the market* to get the customer to switch.

- ✔ **Access to distribution channels:** Every industry has established methods for getting products to customers. New companies must have access to those distribution channels if they are going to succeed. The one exception is where the new business finds a new method of delivering a product or service that the customer accepts — for example, the Internet.

- ✔ **Proprietary factors:** Established companies may own technology or a location that gives them a competitive advantage over new companies. However, new ventures have often entered industries with their own proprietary factors that enable them to enjoy a relatively competition-free environment for a brief time.

- ✔ **Government regulations:** In some industries, a long and expensive governmental process, such as FDA approval for foods and drugs, can be prohibitive for a new business. That's why many new ventures form strategic alliances with larger companies to help support the costs along the way.

✓ **Industry hostility:** In some industries, rival companies make it difficult for a new business to enter. Because they typically are mature companies with many resources, they can afford to do what it takes to push the new entrant out. Again, finding that niche in the market where you're giving the customer what your competitors are not helps your company survive, even in a hostile industry.

Threat from substitute products/services

Remember that your competition comes not only from companies that deal in the same products and services that you do, but also from companies that have substitute products. These products accomplish the same function but use a different method. For example, restaurants compete with other restaurants for consumer dollars, but they also compete with other forms of entertainment that include food. You could go out to dinner at a restaurant, take in a movie, and stop off at a pub for a nightcap. But there are movie theaters now where you can do all three of these things.

Threat from buyers' bargaining power

Buyers have the power to force down prices in the industry when they are able to buy in volume. Established companies, if they are worth their salt, have this kind of buying power. New entrants can't purchase at volume rates; therefore, they have to charge customers more. Consequently, it's more difficult for them to compete.

Threat from suppliers' bargaining power

In some industries, suppliers have the power to raise prices or change the quality of products that they supply to manufacturers or distributors. This is particularly true where there are few suppliers relative to the size of the industry and they are the primary source of materials in the industry. Don't forget that labor is also a source of supply, and in some industries such as software, highly skilled labor is in short supply; therefore the price goes up.

Rivalry among existing firms

Highly competitive industries force prices down and profits as well. That's when you see price wars, the kind you find in the airline industry. One company lowers its prices and others quickly follow. This kind of strategy hurts everyone in the industry and makes it nearly impossible for a new entrant to compete on price. Instead, savvy new businesses find an unserved niche in the market where they don't have to compete on price.

Deciding on an entry strategy

The structure of your industry will largely determine how you enter it. Failing to consider the structure of your industry can mean that you spend a lot of time and money only to find that you have chosen the wrong entry strategy. By then, you may have lost your window of opportunity. For the most part, new ventures have three broad options as entry strategies: differentiation, niche strategy, and cost superiority.

Differentiation

With a *differentiation* strategy, you attempt to distinguish your company from others in the industry through product/process innovation, a unique marketing or distribution strategy, or through branding. If you are able to gain customer loyalty through your differentiation strategy, you will succeed in making your product or service less sensitive to price because customers will perceive the inherent value of dealing with your company.

Niche strategy

The *niche* strategy is perhaps the most popular strategy for new ventures. It involves identifying and creating a place in the market where no one else is — serving a need that no one else is serving. This niche gives you space and time to compete without going head to head with the established players in the industry. It lets you own a piece of the market where you can establish the standards and create your brand.

Cost superiority

Being the low-cost leader is typically difficult for a new venture because it relies heavily on volume sales and low-cost production. A new venture can take advantage of providing the lowest-cost products and services when it's part of an emerging industry where everyone shares the same disadvantage.

Researching an Industry

Getting to understand your industry inside and out is critical to developing any business strategies you may have. Yes, it's a lot of work, but it will pay off many times over.

Today, it's much easier than it used to be to research an industry because of all the sources available on the Internet. Of course, not everything posted on a website is necessarily true or from a creditable source. Anyone can easily put up a website, tout that he or she is an expert in whatever, and if you don't do any checking, you may end up relying on an unreliable source. So, how do you check on your sources? Here are some things you can do:

- ✔ Ask yourself whether the site or author is a recognized expert in the field.

- ✔ Ask people who are familiar with the industry you're researching whether they've ever heard of that site or that person.

- ✔ Compare what that site or person has said with what others are saying. If you find a number of sources that seem to agree, you're probably okay. Of course, don't assume that just because many people are saying something, it's necessarily true — that's how rumors get started.

By the way, when you present information to potential lenders or funders that you've gathered from someone else's research in your feasibility study (see earlier in this chapter) or business plan (see Book II Chapter 1), you need to give credit to that person with a full citation of the title, author, source, date, and page. Things become a bit trickier with websites because sometimes all they give is the URL. Great sites like Inc. Online and BusinessWeek Online always attribute articles to their authors and the hard copy source. Be wary of sites that don't do this. Always be aware that not all sites archive information, so what you find one week may be gone the next. That's why it's important to have a citation that includes more than just the URL.

When it's time to analyze your industry, you'll find a wealth of information out there. One good place to start is with the Standard Industrial Classification Index at www.wave.net/upg/immigration/sic_index.html. This site lets you search for your industry and industry segment and then gives you the 4-digit SIC code that represents that portion of the industry. This code can prove useful for finding information at many sites you may choose.

Checking out the status of your industry

As you begin to do your research, you will probably find yourself overwhelmed with data and unsure which is important and which is not. Here's a list of questions to guide you in defining the critical information about your industry:

- ✔ **Is the industry growing?** Growth can be measured in many ways: number of employees, revenues, units produced, and number of new companies entering the industry.

- ✔ **Who are the major competitors?** You want to understand which companies dominate the industry, what their strategies are, and how your business is differentiated from them.

✔ **Where are the opportunities in the industry?** In some industries, new products and services provide more opportunity, whereas in others, an innovative marketing and distribution strategy will win the game.

✔ **What are the trends and patterns of change in your industry?** You want to look backward and forward to study what has happened over time in your industry to see if it foreshadows what will happen in the future. You also want to see what the industry prognosticators are saying about the future of the industry. But the best way to find out about the future of your industry is to get close to the new technology that is in the works yet may not hit the marketplace for five years.

✔ **What is the status of new technology and R&D spending?** Does your industry adopt new technology quickly? Is your industry technology-based or driven by new technology? If you look at how much the major firms are spending on research and development of new technologies, you'll get a pretty good idea of how important technology is to your industry. You'll also find out how rapid the product development cycle is, which tells you how fast you'll have to be to compete.

✔ **Are there young and successful companies in the industry?** If you see no new companies being formed in your industry, it's a pretty good bet that it's a mature industry with dominant players. That doesn't automatically preclude your entry into the industry, but it does make it much more expensive and difficult.

✔ **Are there any threats to the industry?** Is there anything on the horizon that you or others can see that makes any part of your industry obsolete? Certainly, if you were in the mechanical office equipment industry in the early 1980s, you should have seen the writing on the wall with the introduction and mass acceptance of the personal computer.

✔ **What are the typical gross profit margins in the industry?** The *gross profit margin* (or *gross margin*) tells you how much room you have to make mistakes. Gross margin is the gross profit (revenues minus cost of goods sold) as a percentage of sales. If your industry has margins of 2 percent, like the grocery industry has (sometimes even less), you have little room for error, because 98 percent of what you receive in revenues goes to pay your direct costs of production. You only have 2 percent left to pay overhead. On the other hand, in some industries gross margins run at 70 percent or more, so you end up with a lot more capital to expend on overhead and profit.

Competitive intelligence: Checking out the competition

One of the most difficult tasks you'll face is finding information about your competitors. Not the obvious things that you can easily find by going to a competitor's physical site or website (although of course you should do those things), but the really important stuff that can affect what you do with your business concept. Things like how much competitors spend on customer service, what their profit margins are, how many customers they have, what their growth strategies are, and so forth.

If you're in competition with private companies (which is true most of the time), your task is that much more difficult because private companies don't have to disclose the kinds of information that public companies do.

Here's some of the information you may want to collect on your competitors:

- The management style of the company
- Current market strategies — also what they've done in the past because history tends to repeat itself
- The unique features and benefits of the products and services they offer
- Their pricing strategy
- Their customer mix
- Their promotional mix

With a concerted effort and a plan in hand, you can find out a lot about the companies you'll be competing against. This section provides a step-by-step strategy for attacking the challenge of competitive intelligence.

Pound the pavement

If your competition has brick-and-mortar sites, visit them and observe what goes on. What kinds of customers frequent their sites? What do they buy, and how much do they buy? What is the appearance of the site? How would you evaluate the location? Gather as much information as you can through observation and talking to customers and employees.

Buy your competitors' products

Buying your competitors' products helps you find out more about how your competition treats its customers and how good its products and services are. If you think that it sounds strange to buy your competitors' products, just remember, as soon as yours are in the marketplace, your competitors will buy them.

Rev up the search engines

Go to the Internet and hit the search engines. Just type in the names of the companies you're interested in and see what comes up. True, this is not the most effective way to search, but it's a start, and you never know what you'll pull up that you otherwise may not have found.

Try to go beyond Google. In addition to Google (www.google.com), you might try Bing (www.bing.com), Yahoo! (www.yahoo.com), DuckDuckGo (www.duckduckgo.com), and Ask (www.ask.com). And be sure to check out your competition's social media activity on sites like Facebook (www.facebook.com), Pinterest (www.pinterest.com), and Twitter (www.twitter.com). Finally, see if anyone is saying anything about your competitors on the customer review site Yelp (www.yelp.com).

Check information on public companies

In most industries, public companies are the most established companies and often the dominant players, so it's a good idea to check them out. They can also serve as benchmarks for best practices in the industry. There are a host of online resources related to public companies. Here are two to get you started:

- ✔ **Hoover's Online** (www.hoovers.com): This source provides detailed profiles of more than 2,500 public companies. Visit the site to find out about current pricing.

- ✔ **U.S. Securities & Exchange Commission** (www.sec.gov): This site contains the SEC's EDGAR (Electronic Data Gathering, Analysis, and Retrieval) database about companies. It's not terribly user friendly but has great information. Try Free Edgar, www.freeedgar.com, which is a good place to research public companies and those that have filed to go public.

Use online media

Here are some great online sources that you may want to check out:

- ✔ **Inc 500** (www.inc.com): This database of the fastest-growing private companies in the U.S. contains information you won't find elsewhere on revenue, profit-and-loss percentages, numbers of employees, and so forth for the past eight years.

- ✔ **The Electric Library** (www.elibrary.com): This is a great site if you're looking for articles, reference works, and news wires. You can try it for 30 days free; check the site for current pricing. If you are near a local university, you may be able to access it from the university's library computers.

- ✔ **ProfNet** (www.profnet.com): This site provides a direct link to experts at universities, colleges, corporations, and national laboratories. You may be able to find an expert in your industry and contact that person. Check the site for current pricing.

- ✔ **The Competitive Intelligence Guide** (www.fuld.com): This site gives you advice on how to seek competitive intelligence and has many links to information on specific industries.

Troll for data at government websites

You will find an extensive network of government sites with mostly free information on economic news, export information, legislative trends, and so forth. A good place to start your search is at FedWorld, online at at `fedworld.ntis.gov`.

You may also want to go directly to many other often-used sites like the following:

- ✔ **U.S. Department of Commerce** (`www.commerce.gov`): Here you'll find everything you ever wanted to know about the U.S. economy.
- ✔ **U.S. Census Bureau** (`www.census.gov`): This is the home of the stats based on the census taken every ten years. The amount of information available here is very impressive.
- ✔ **Bureau of Labor Statistics** (`www.bls.gov`): This is another site full of information on the economy, in particular, the labor market.

Go offline for more research

The Internet is not the only place you can find important information. Here are two offline options you ought to consider:

- ✔ **Industry trade associations:** Virtually every industry has its own trade association with a corresponding journal or magazine. Trade associations usually track what's going on in their industries, so they are a wealth of information. If you are serious about starting a business in your particular industry, you may want to join a trade association, so you'll have access to inside information.
- ✔ **Network, network, network:** Take every opportunity to talk with people in the industry. They are on the front lines on a daily basis and they will give you information that is probably more current than what you'll find in the media or on the web.

Defining Your Market Niche

Markets are groups of customers inside an industry. Take a look at Figure 1-1 and you can see that in conducting your feasibility analysis (see the overview of feasibility analysis earlier in this chapter), you work your way down from the broad industry to the narrower market niche.

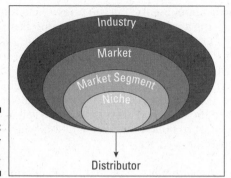

Figure 1-1:
Finding your
niche.

Narrowing your market

Within each broad market are segments. For example, the broad market of people who buy books contains segments of customers for

- Travel books (or any other broad category of books).
- Kids' books.
- Books appealing to seniors.
- Audiobooks.

Within a market segment, you can find niches — specific needs that perhaps aren't being served — such as

- Travel books geared toward people with disabilities.
- Kids' books that target minorities.
- Books that teach seniors how to deal with technology.
- Audiobooks that provide current journal articles to professionals.

Market niches provide a place for new businesses to enter a market and gain a foothold before bigger companies take notice and begin to compete. Having a niche all to yourself gives you a quiet period during which you alone serve a need of the customer that otherwise is not being met. As a result, you get to set the standards for the niche. In short, you're the market leader.

As you zero in on your market, take care that the niche you ultimately choose is big enough to allow your business to make money. The niche you select must have enough customers willing to buy your product from you, enabling you to pay your expenses and turn a profit.

Defining your target market is about identifying the primary customer for your products or services — the customer most likely to purchase from you. You want to identify a target market because creating customer awareness of a new product or service is time-consuming and costly, requiring lots of marketing dollars — dollars that few startups have at their disposal. So, instead of using a shotgun approach and trying to bag a broad market, aiming at the specific customers who are likely to purchase from you is far more effective. More important still, going to the customer who's easiest to sell to helps you gain a foothold quickly and start to build brand recognition, which makes selling to other potential customers easier.

Your first definition of a target customer will probably be fairly loose — an estimate. For example, suppose your target customers are "professional women." That's a fairly broad estimate. But as you conduct market research, you come to know your primary customer well. In this example, the picture may emerge of "a woman in law, medicine, or business, between 35 and 55 years of age, married, with children."

The basic questions to answer about your potential customers are:

- ✔ What are their demographics: age, education, ethnicity, income level?

- ✔ What are their buying habits? What do they buy? When? How?

- ✔ How do customers hear about your products and services? Do your customers buy based on TV ads, magazines, social media, web advertising, word-of-mouth, referrals?

- ✔ How can your new business meet customers' needs? What customer need is your product now meeting?

Where do you find the answers to these important questions? Your market research — actually talking with potential customers — provides answers.

Not all customers are individuals; many are other businesses. In fact, the greatest dollar volume of transactions conducted on the Internet today is business-to-business. If a distributor, wholesaler, retail store, or manufacturer is paying you, your customer is a business, not an individual consumer. Businesses as customers can be described in pretty much the same way that you describe a person. Businesses come in a variety of sizes and revenue levels. Like consumers, they also have buying cycles, tastes, and preferences.

Don't forget that if your customer is another business, that business may not be the actual end user of your product or service. So then you also have an end user to deal with. The *end user* is the ultimate consumer, the person who uses the product or service. For example, here is a typical channel for distributing a product:

Manufacturer > Distributor > Retailer > Consumer

If that distribution channel is filled with your products — refrigerators, for example — who is your customer? It's the distributor who purchases the fridge from you to distribute to retailers. The retailer, in turn, is the distributor's customer. The consumer, who actually uses the fridge, is the retailer's customer and your end user. (The easiest way to identify the customer is to find out who pays you — follow the money.)

Just because the end users aren't technically your customers doesn't mean that you can ignore them. You need to know as much about the end user as you do about the customer, because you must convince the distributor that a market for the product exists and that the end user will buy enough product so that the distributor and retailer can make a profit. Thus, you must conduct the same kind of research on the end user that you do on the distributor.

Developing a niche strategy

One primary reason to define and analyze a target market is to find a way into the market so that you have a chance to compete. If you enter a market without a strategy, you're setting yourself up for failure. You are the new kid on the block. If customers can't distinguish you from your competitors, they're not likely to buy from you. People generally prefer to deal with someone they know.

Niche strategy is probably the premier strategy for entrepreneurs because it yields the greatest amount of control. Creating a niche that no one else is serving is the key. That way, you become the leader and can set the standards for those who follow. Niche strategy is important because, as the sole occupant of the niche, you can establish your business in a relatively safe environment (the quiet period) before you develop any direct competitors. Fending off competitors takes a lot of marketing dollars, and when you're a startup company, you have numerous better uses for your limited resources.

How do you find a niche that no one else has found? By talking to customers. The target market from which your business opportunity comes also holds the keys to your entry strategy. Your potential customers tell you what's missing in your competitors' products and services. They also tell you what they need. Fulfilling that unmet need is your entry strategy.

Zeroing-in on a Brand New Product

Many entrepreneurs would like to deal in products, but they're not quite sure how to get started. Of course, you could import products from other countries or buy your products from domestic manufacturers. But if you like the idea of manufacturing and distributing a brand-new technology or other type of product, then you have three choices: invent something, team up with an inventor, or license an invention.

Become an inventor

If you're the kind of person who likes to tinker and play around with new ideas that might become inventions, then your role might be to invent a new product. Most entrepreneurs and startup businesspeople, however, are not inventors — not because they don't have the ability to invent, but because their focus is elsewhere.

The mindsets of businesspeople and inventors tend to be quite different, and it's unusual to find both in the same person. Not only are the mindsets different, but the skills required by each are very different. In general, pure inventor types aren't interested in the commercial side of things. They invent for the love of invention. Unless an entrepreneur comes along and points out an opportunity, many inventors never see their inventions reach the marketplace.

Many types of inventors — engineers, scientists, and so forth — would rather spend their time in the laboratory than consider business issues like markets and customers. You have to ask yourself what role feels right to you and do that. You can always find the other talents in someone else.

Team up with an inventor

Entrepreneurs often team up with inventors to commercialize a new product. Often the opportunity to pair up with an inventor comes out of the industry in which you're working. You hear about someone who's working on something; you investigate and discover an interesting invention.

Don't hesitate to approach an inventor, but remember a couple important things:

1. Inventors are paranoid about their inventions. They are sure that someone is out to steal their ideas.

2. Inventors typically aren't business oriented and don't want to become business people. Their love is inventing, so don't expect them to be partners in a business sense.

Be sure your attorney structures a beneficial arrangement with your inventor that doesn't hamstring your efforts to commercialize the invention. You are each bringing something very important to the mix, so be sure you can work together well. For much more on the details of inventing, check out *Inventing For Dummies* by Pamela Riddle Bird and Forrest M. Bird (John Wiley & Sons, Inc.).

License an invention

Companies, universities, the government, and independent inventors are all looking for entrepreneurs to commercialize their inventions. You gain access to these inventions through a vehicle known as licensing. *Licensing* grants you the right to use the invention in an agreed-upon way for an agreed-upon time period. In return, you agree to pay a royalty to the inventor, usually based on sales of the product that results from the invention.

The government owns many core technologies developed for the military and the aerospace program, among others. You can license these core technologies and create a new application for use in a different industry. For example, with the NASA QuickLaunch licensing tool at `https://quicklaunch.ndc.nasa.gov`, you can easily find technologies that are available to license.

Alternatively, visit the technology licensing office of most major research universities and you'll find more opportunities. For example, the Stanford University Office of Technology Licensing (`http://otl.stanford.edu`) evaluates, markets, and licenses technology owned by Stanford University. Universities are a gold mine of new technology you can tap into.

Chapter 2

Refining and Defining Your Business Idea

In This Chapter

▶ Developing great ideas

▶ Brainstorming alone or in a group

▶ Deciding which ideas are worth pursuing

▶ Putting your ideas through a reality check

Almost all successful businesses begin with a good idea. The idea may be to present a new product or service, or plan to introduce an existing product or service into a new niche. Great business ideas are born when someone figures out a better way to make something or to provide customers what they want. Successful business ideas don't have to be world-shaking. No matter how modest or extensive they are, they're an important and new way to improve efficiency, cut costs, or deal with a critical business challenge.

Count on this chapter to fuel your idea-generating process with tips and tools for taking stock of your personal resources, asking others for advice, brainstorming ideas alone or in a group, putting your possibilities through a make-it-or-break-it reality check, and, finally, weighing the likelihood that investors, customers, and colleagues will want to buy into your business proposition.

Recognizing the Power of a Good Idea

Facebook started with a good idea. So did Google. Toyota had a pretty good idea when it developed a hybrid engine. Apple did, too, when the company decided to build a touchscreen device big enough to read, draw, and write on. Good ideas aren't limited to major companies. The young couple who decides to open a doggy day care in a town where a lot of people commute to work may have a great idea, too — one that could make them an impressive profit. When coming up with a business idea, keep these five key characteristics of a *good* business idea in mind:

- ✔ It meets a real need or desire.
- ✔ It offers something new (or at least a little different).
- ✔ It's grounded in reality, not wishful thinking.
- ✔ It can generate money.
- ✔ It's something you want to do.

Read on to begin the process of evaluating your business idea to make sure it's both realistic and practical.

Knowing the difference between passion and profitability

Plenty of successful businesses owe their success to a personal passion. A baker who starts a successful bakery, a musician who opens a recording studio, and a teacher who starts a tutoring service all have passion in common. That's great. Excitement and confidence are crucial to making a business a success.

But so is a good dose of reality.

Being excited about what you want to do is no guarantee of success, after all. Businesses that begin with passionate optimism often go belly-up. Personal passion can carry you away, blinding you to the hard realities that any business faces in making it in today's highly competitive world. The bottom line of all for-profit businesses is ultimately — you guessed it — profit. If you're hoping to turn a personal passion into a successful business, you need to ask yourself a simple question: Can it make a profit?

The question may be simple. Answering it isn't always easy.

Before you head over to Book II Chapter 1 to write a business plan for your knock-'em-dead idea, give it a test run. Use the questions in Figure 2-1 to begin to evaluate whether the idea you're excited about can turn a profit.

Great Business Idea Evaluation Form
You can easily get swept up in the excitement of a new idea. To begin the process of evaluating your business idea, answer these twelve questions.
1. Does the idea meet a real need or desire?
2. What's new or different about the idea?
3. Who are your customers likely to be?
4. What do you offer your customers that no one else does?
5. How much are they willing to pay?
6. Who are your competitors?
7. What's the best thing about the idea?
8. What's the biggest weakness?
9. What will be the biggest challenge you face in turning your idea into a reality?
10. How long will it take to get a company up and running?
11. Is this idea scalable, meaning can you provide more to meet demand, and if so, how?
12. Is this something you really want to do?

Figure 2-1: Use this form to begin the process of evaluating your business idea.

© John Wiley & Sons, Inc.

Turning a gig into a business

Most successful entrepreneurs will tell you that they were surprised to discover what goes into making a business work. Often, the surprise is how little they knew about the nuts and bolts of operating a business. Consider the example of a woman who developed her baking skills at home and then started a highly successful Northern California bakery. She knew the craft of baking. She knew the equipment she needed to go from home baking to commercial baking. What she wasn't prepared for was managing a staff. In the first year, personnel problems plagued her bakery and almost scuttled her business.

If you're thinking of turning something you love to do into a business, take time to ask yourself some basic but important questions. Figure 2-2 has some questions you can use to begin the process of exploring what you'll need to turn passion into profitability.

Turning a Gig into a Business

Making money by doing something you love to do sounds great. But turning a passion into a business requires a realistic evaluation of your capabilities and the market you hope to serve. Use this form to begin answering the hard questions that will ultimately make the task of turning a gig into a business a little easier.

1. What is your product or service? (Be as specific as possible.)

2. How will you make money? (Be as specific and creative as possible.)

3. How will you reach your customers or clients?

4. Where will you conduct your business?

5. Will you need employees? How many? What jobs will they do?

6. What kinds of equipment will you need to get started?

7. How much money will you need to get up and running?

8. What are your monthly operating expenses likely to be?

9. How much money will you need to earn each month to be successful?

10. What are your biggest strengths when it comes to starting this business?

11. What are your greatest weaknesses?

12. What can you do to turn those weaknesses into strengths (or at least work around them)?

13. Who are your competitors? What are their strengths and weaknesses?

14. What are the potential risks a business like this faces? How can you minimize the risks?

Figure 2-2:
Use this form to explore whether you can turn a passion into a profitable business.

© John Wiley & Sons, Inc.

Planning ahead: Great ideas take time

Most businesses — even those built on a great idea fueled by passion — take time to become successful. A musician who decides to go professional needs to find gigs (and probably music students). An accountant who decides to leave her company and start her own business needs to set up an office and line up clients. An inventor of the next big thing needs to arrange for manufacturing and marketing. These actions all take time.

The more realistic you are about how much time you'll need, the better prepared you'll be. To help, create a timeline for your proposed business. Even in the early stages of evaluating a business idea, a timeline tells you what you need to accomplish and when in order to succeed. Looking ahead obviously requires a fair amount of guesswork. Write down what you want to achieve. Be as realistic as possible about when you'll be able to reach each benchmark.

Checking out the competition

The saying goes that there's nothing new under the sun. It also applies to most new businesses. Chances are a similar business to the one you're planning to launch already exists. One easy way to test your new idea is to check out how other people doing roughly the same thing are faring. In some cases, all you have to do is ask. Unless people perceive you as a competitive threat, they're usually willing to share details about their businesses. If not, you can uncover information in other ways, such as the following:

✔ **Check websites for information about products and services, including pricing.** If appropriate, review any online customer reviews of your competitors, which can provide invaluable tips on how you can do better.

✔ **Search the web for business articles about the kind of business you're planning.** Be sure to check publication dates, because business reports can go out of date quickly. If you don't find what you need online, make a beeline to your local library to browse the periodical shelves.

✔ **Investigate how similar businesses market their goods or services.** If you're starting a local business, check out the phone book and local newspapers. Check out the competition's online presence. If you're going after a national or international market, analyze how other companies use major media and their own websites to market themselves.

✔ **Check out the local Chamber of Commerce.** Most cities and even small towns have Chambers of Commerce, and almost all of them have websites. If you don't find what you need there, make a visit to the bricks-and-mortar office to talk to a representative.

✔ **Talk to prospective customers.** If you're starting a local business, ask friends and family what they consider important as prospective customers. If you're planning a retail business, visit similar stores and observe how customers move through the aisles and what they buy. No matter what kind of business you're planning, check out websites for customer reviews, which have become an invaluable way of listening to customers.

If your new idea is product-based, your business will face special challenges, such as who will make and distribute the product and what kind of service will it require (see Figure 2-3).

New Product Innovation Checklist
New isn't always better. Product innovations have to meet a real need or desire, and they have to be practical to implement. To begin assessing a business idea based on product innovation, use the following questions.
1. What's already out there on the market?
2. What will your innovation offer?
3. Will it meet a real customer need or desire?
4. How much are customers willing to pay for your innovation?
5. Will it be practical to produce?
6. How will customers hear about your new product?
7. How will they buy it?
8. What kinds of service will be required?
9. Who are your current competitors in this marketplace?
10. How easy will it be for new competitors to enter the market?
11. What are the key weaknesses in your innovation?
12. What are the key strengths?
13. How can you leverage your strengths and offset your weaknesses?

Figure 2-3:
Use this form to begin addressing some of the special considerations involved in product innovation.

© John Wiley & Sons, Inc.

Brainstorming New Business Ideas

Not all new businesses start with an idea. Some begin with a group of talented people in search of an idea. Others begin when an individual decides to join the self-employed ranks and begin to think, "But what will I do?"

Plenty of would-be entrepreneurs have caught themselves thinking, "Why didn't I think of that?" or "How in the world did they come up with that idea?" Great ideas may look lucky or random, but when you look a little closer, you're likely to find that considerable time and effort went into making them happen.

Those visionaries everyone admires were able to foresee market needs and respond with precisely matched product and service solutions.

Brainstorming isn't just for when you're starting out. Even after you're off and running, you must constantly stay on the lookout for ways to revitalize existing offerings or add new products or services to stay ahead of the competition. That's especially true these days, with the accelerating pace of technological change.

These sections can help you generate brand-new ideas to build a business around and possibly be the next visionary. They provide you with tried-and-true methods for revving your creative engine — whether alone or in a group — and snaring great ideas for your next business venture.

Using the do-it-yourself idea blender

Humans are a creative bunch. They've invented hoes, fiddles, eyeglasses, the airplane, bendable straws, computers, the sports bra, skateboards, light bulbs, the jitterbug, disposable diapers, safety pins, and *Star Wars*. Motives for invention vary from person to person:

- ✔ **Humans invent to save lives.** The polio vaccine, air bags, laser surgery, and fat-free cheesecake

- ✔ **Humans invent to express deepest thoughts.** Poetry, painting, filmmaking, dance, and music

- ✔ **Humans invent for fun.** Game shows, smartphone apps, rollerblades, Suduko, and professional wrestling

The best thing about creativity is that no one holds a monopoly on great ideas. You may not become a creative genius overnight, but with a little time and effort and by following a few basic steps, you can become a lot more creative than you may have thought!

To see what you can accomplish on the creativity front all by yourself, put the *idea blender* to the test. Take the following easy steps:

1. **Grab a couple of sheets of paper and use Figure 2-4 as a model.**

2. **Fill out the rows as follows:**

   - In the first column, list your personal strengths — for example, "I work well with people," "I'm very detail-oriented," or "I'm not afraid to try something new."

   - In the second column, list things you like to do. Include hobbies like playing videos, listening to classical music, skydiving, refinishing antiques, or reading.

   - In the third column, list cool products or services that you enjoy using. Maybe you're really into smartphones, personal organizers, doggy day care, GPS devices, or stair machines.

   - In the fourth column, make a wish list of the things you'd do if you won the lottery and no longer had to worry about making a living — things like moving to a tropical island, buying your own private jet, traveling, or going back to school.

My Favorite Things			
My Personal Strengths	*Things I Like to Do*	*Products or Services I Really Like*	*What I'd Do If I Won The Lottery*
1. Work well with people	1. Play jazz piano	1. Hybrid cars	1. Write a novel
2. Very detail-oriented	2. Explore new Internet sites	2. Computer-based music programs	2. Retire to Hawaii
3. Not afraid to try something new	3. Get together with friends to play cards	3. www.craigslist.com	3. Create an educational foundation to teach music in schools
4. Work well under deadlines	4. Travel	4. GPS devices	4. Travel
5. Creative, especially when it comes to software design	5. Shop at garage sales and flea markets	5. e-books	5. Travel some more

Figure 2-4:
Identify your
personal
traits and
interests.

3. Blend the items from the rows.

See what you come up with, either by plugging items into a chart like the one in Figure 2-5 or by circling the items.

- Choose an item in the first column, such as "Creative, especially when it comes to software design."

- Choose an item in the next column. You can simply choose randomly or pick an item that seems to fit with your first choice, such as "Explore new Internet sites."

- Do the same thing in column three: Select an item that corresponds. Say that you choose "Computer-based music programs." Don't worry if you don't see an obvious match. We encourage you to make connections, even ones that feel offbeat. The process will get you thinking *out of the box* and allow you to see yourself and your prospects in completely new ways.

- Select an item from column four — "What I'd Do If I Won The Lottery."

- Look over the items you've chosen. Use them to brainstorm three business ideas. Be creative. Entertain ideas you've never considered, such as starting a nonprofit organization.

Figure 2-5 shows an example.

Bright ideas often sound a bit peculiar when first expressed. (Think of online auctions and mood rings, for example. And who would've jumped at the notion of a pet rock?) Yet many creative ideas emerge by combining familiar pieces of the world around you in new and different ways. (Think of TV dinners, car radios, and smartphones, for example.)

4. **Try to pull at least three promising business ideas out of this process.**

Figures 2-4 and 2-5 show the idea blender at work. In this case, the combination of an ability to do creative software design, a love of playing piano, and interest in teaching music suggest three pretty good ideas for business ventures. Not bad for a first run. Choose random combinations to see where they lead. Not all blender concoctions will be winners. "Work well under deadlines," "Hybrid cars," and "Retire to Hawaii" may not lead to a great business idea. (Although who knows, maybe you could start an environmentally-friendly car rental agency on the island.) But "Not afraid to try something new," "Love to travel," and "GPS devices" may be just the inspiration you need to create GPS-based tour guides of leading tourist destinations.

The idea blender is a great way to get an idea for a new business. But it can be equally effective at dreaming up new products or services for existing businesses. Some people we know have used it to find direction as they contemplate changing careers.

The Idea Blender

A personal strength:	*Creative, especially with software design*
Something I really like to do:	*Play jazz piano*
Product or service I really like:	*Computer-based music programs*
If I won the lottery, I'd:	*Create an educational foundation for music in schools*

Three business ideas:
1. *Create a computer game to inspire kids to compose music on their own.*
2. *Develop a web-based program that grade-school teachers can use to teach music.*
3. *Establish a nonprofit organization to bring professional musicians from the community into local schools.*

Figure 2-5:
Mix your
interests
to form
business
ideas.

Boost your personal creativity quotient

Where do creative ideas originate? As part of an informal survey, innovative individuals named their top idea-generating activities. The most frequently cited answers lead off the following list:

In the shower	Commuting	Going to sleep
Just waking up	During quiet moments	Actively thinking
Exercising	Meditating	Walking
Talking with friends	While vacationing	During the night
During a business meeting	Reading	Sitting at the desk
While under pressure	Napping	Dreaming
At a business seminar	Lunching with colleagues	In the classroom

Identify the activities that get your creative juices going, and over the next few weeks, devote a little more time to those pursuits. Watch for a boost in your creativity as a result.

Inspiring team creativity (with or without donuts or bagels)

Not all creative thinking is done alone. Put a few heads together, and you may whip up a mental hurricane. The outcome depends on the nature of the group of individuals you assemble (the more dynamic, inspired, freewheeling, and innovative, the better) and the communication skills that the session leader brings into the room.

The quickest way to kill an idea is to say anything akin to any of the following:

- ✔ It won't work.
- ✔ We're not ready for that.
- ✔ It isn't practical.
- ✔ It's already been done.
- ✔ That's just plain stupid.

The group you assemble needs to remain open to all ideas presented in order to develop a healthy idea-generating environment.

Applying the LCS system to nurture new ideas

To nurture brand-new ideas and allow them to grow, use the three-part *LCS system:*

- **✔ L is for *likes*,** as in, *"What I like about your idea. . . ."* Begin with some positive comments to encourage people to let loose with every creative idea that comes to mind. Not every idea will work. But even zany ideas can spark more practical and effective ones.

- **✔ C is for *concerns*,** as in, *"What concerns me about your idea. . . ."* Sharing concerns begins dialogue that opens up and expands the creative process. As you point out a concern, someone else in the group is likely to offer a creative solution.

- **✔ S is for *suggestions*,** as in, *"I have a few suggestions. . . ."* Offering suggestions moves the brainstorming session along and may lead to the generation of a brand-new set of ideas.

Assembling a brainstorming session

With the LCS system fresh in your brains, your group can take on a brainstorming session following these steps:

1. **Start with a small group of people you trust and admire.**

   You can turn to friends, relatives, or professional acquaintances — anyone you think may contribute a new and useful perspective.

2. **Invite a couple of ringers.**

   Consider inviting a few people who can stretch the group's thinking, challenge assumptions, and take the group in new and unexpected directions, even if these individuals may make you feel a bit uncomfortable.

3. **Choose the right time and place.**

   The same old places can lead to the same old thinking, so be inventive. To inspire creativity, change the scene. Larger companies often hold brainstorming sessions at off-site retreats. If you're a small company or sole proprietor, you can still meet in a place that inspires creativity, such as a park or local coffeehouse (as long as it's not too crowded or noisy). Whatever location you choose, be sure to have everything you need for brainstorming — from an old-fashioned scratchpad to an iPad or digital voice recorder — handy.

4. **Establish ground rules.**

   Explain what you want the group to achieve. Introduce the LCS system (see the previous section) so that participants have a tool that allows them to make positive contributions to the session. Emphasize the fact that at this stage in planning, there are no bad ideas. The group should be encouraged to be as freewheeling as possible.

5. **Act as the group's conductor.**

   Keep the process moving without turning into a dictator. Use these tactics:

   - Encourage alternatives: *How else can we do that?*
   - Stimulate visionary thinking: *What if we had no constraints?*
   - Invite new perspectives: *How would a child see this?*
   - Ask for specifics: *What exactly do you mean?*
   - Clarify the next steps: *How should we proceed on that?*

6. **Record the results.**

   Designate a person to take notes throughout the session or record the session to review later. Remember, the best ideas are often side comments, so capture the offbeat comments as well as the mainstream discussion. Every idea, even ones that seem zany, can lead to something useful. Assign someone the task of taking digital pictures of whiteboards. Sometimes a great idea passes by so quickly that people only later say, "Hey, what was that idea we had?"

7. **Review your notes and thoughts while they're still fresh.**

   Set aside time after the brainstorming session to distill the discussion down to three or four ideas that you want to continue working on.

Tweaking a good idea to make it even better

A successful business doesn't necessarily require an original idea.

When touchscreen phones and tablets came along, a clever entrepreneur created a cool new app that lets people paint digitally with a fingertip. The software wasn't really new; digital art programs for desktops had been around for years. What the innovation did was make digital art available on mobile devices. The new program was a runaway success — until other app developers came along and began making even better drawing and painting programs for touchscreens. By now dozens exist, some more popular than the original app.

Putting your personal stamp on an existing idea can be as bold as designing a better app or as simple as transplanting a successful business concept into your market area, like the couple who started a doggy day care in a town that didn't have one.

Think about the do-it-yourself pottery painting studios that you see practically everywhere these days. The idea migrated from do-it-yourself porcelain painting, which was born out of necessity by a young housewife who reportedly couldn't afford matching china. She decided to paint her own and wanted to help others do the same. Entrepreneurs adapted the idea into a range of do-it-yourself pottery-painting businesses, including hobby shops; ceramics cafes; party businesses; glass, tile, and mosaic studios; and even pottery-painting books and online stores.

Finding business ideas within your work environment

A survey of 500 of the fastest-growing companies in the United States showed that nearly half grew directly out of the founders' previous work environments. In other words, the founders created these companies after looking around at what they were doing and saying, "There *has* to be a better way to do this." Solutions to challenges also often come from within. After all, who knows a business better than its employees?

Many companies require employees to sign non-compete agreements. These agreements usually prohibit former employees from engaging in competitive businesses for a set period of time. If you've signed a non-compete agreement, make sure your new venture doesn't violate its terms.

Although people inside the company are an invaluable source of new ideas, you can find many examples of companies that recognized the challenges they faced but were completely unable to come up with effective strategies to meet them. The reason: People inside a company, who are used to the way things work, often have trouble thinking outside the box. Even sole proprietors and small business people run into the same problem. They're so close to the company and its way of doing business that they can't see the forest from the trees.

When considering new business possibilities, keep in mind that 99 percent of all businesses (both old and new) fall into one of three broad categories:

✔ **Products for sale:** Consider the range of products that your industry offers.

- Can you think of innovative ways to make them better?

- Can you imagine a product that completely replaces them?

- What new product would knock you out of business if the competition offered it first?

✔ **Services for hire:** Consider the services that your industry offers.

- Do you notice problems with consistency that you could remedy?

- What isn't being done that should be?

- What do customers complain about?

- What new services would threaten your business if the competition offered them first?

✔ **Distribution and delivery:** Ask yourself similar questions about your distribution and delivery systems.

- What are the most serious bottlenecks?
- Can you think of clever ways to improve distribution?
- Can you envision a radically new delivery system?

Identifying Business Opportunities

According to Thomas Edison, "Genius is 1 percent inspiration and 99 percent perspiration." The same goes for business. Coming up with the idea is the inspiration part. When you begin to think about how to turn it into a business, that's when you begin to sweat. These sections provide some tips to assist you in recognizing opportunities.

Listening to what customers have to say

The Internet — and specifically online review sites — can be an excellent source of inspiration for new business opportunities. Customers, it turns out, have very strong opinions about what they've bought, and they're not afraid to voice them. Just look at the reviews on Amazon and Yelp. Those reviews, good and bad, can tell you exactly what customers like, what they don't like, and what they'd like to see in products and services. Their input is a gold mine of information.

Say that you're interested in designing and producing a computer program that will make it easier for people to compose their own songs. Several such programs already exist. Go onto music sites that sell them, and you'll find plenty of chatter from satisfied and unsatisfied customers. Their likes and dislikes can help you decide what your product needs to offer in order to compete with products already in the marketplace.

Spotting changes that open up new opportunities

Many fledgling businesses succeed by jumping on new opportunities that arise through technological, social, policy, or other changes. Change can be scary, but it can also open new doors. Spotting that door — and being the first to open it — requires skill and a little daring. For example, when Apple launched the iPad, a whole new industry of apps sprang into existence, created by developers daring enough to plunge into a new technology and a new marketplace.

As Internet bandwidth increased and the potential for streaming video appeared on the horizon, companies like Amazon and Netflix seized the opportunity, establishing themselves as leaders and leaving some competitors — remember Blockbuster Video? — in the dust. Today, with baby boomers retiring, a host of companies are looking for ways to strike gold by opening high-end retirement communities, providing health care consulting services, or offering products and services that promise to keep people youthful even as they age. Any time the government breaks up a monopoly, new arenas for competition arise. As part of your brainstorming, ask your team to consider ongoing or likely changes that could open up new opportunities.

Keep in mind that new opportunities don't have to mean re-inventing the wheel. To be sure, many companies succeed by creating a brand-new product or service to sell to existing customers. But opportunities also exist for selling existing products or services to new customers. If you're already in business, spend some time thinking about opportunities for expanding your market by reaching more customers.

 These days, many companies prosper by finding clever ways to make people's personal or working lives easier or more efficient. Think no-iron shirts. Think parking garages that offer car washes. Think dictation software that does away with the need to type. Evaluate your promising business idea to see whether you can take advantage of new opportunities to improve the efficiency or effectiveness of your customers' lives.

Testing your business ideas

After some combination of brainstorming, market analysis, and a few random flashes of brilliance, you may accumulate a drawer full of promising business ideas. Following are two guidelines to help you separate the real opportunities from the fluff:

- **Focus on the ideas that you're really excited about.** Your passion is what will keep you motivated on the road to success.

- **Pursue ideas that you can follow through on.** If you feel you don't have the means or the drive to take an idea from the drawing board to the real world, scrap it.

Doing Your First Reality Check

Asking questions like "Is this really such a good idea?" and "Who am I kidding, anyway?" doesn't mean you lack confidence. What asking these types of questions does mean is that you've come to the time to step back and make sure that the road you're on is leading you where you want to go. In short, you need a reality check.

In many ways, writing a business plan is a series of reality checks (see Book II Chapter 1 for much more on writing business plans). By making you carefully think through every aspect of your business — from the product or service you offer to the competitors you face and the customers you serve — the business-planning process brings you face to face with the realities of doing business. Read on for tips on bouncing your ideas around with people who may be able to help refine them, as well as useful ways to appraise your personal strengths and weaknesses when it comes to carrying out your ideas.

Getting a second opinion

To help determine whether or not you're on solid ground, discuss your business idea and preliminary plans with someone well respected in your line of work. What you're really seeking is a *mentor* with most or all of the following characteristics:

- ✔ Someone who has experience in the business area you're considering, or at least experience in a similar business.

- ✔ Someone with the courage to tell you the truth, whether it's "That's a great idea. Go for it!" or "If I were you, I'd take a little more time to think this over."

- ✔ Someone you admire and from whom you can take candid criticism without feeling defensive.

Consider turning to colleagues you've worked with in the past, other small business owners, teachers or professors, friends from college, or other associates.

Friends and family members sometimes can offer the advice and perspective you need, but emotional ties can get in the way of absolute honesty and objectivity. If you go this route, set some ground rules in advance. Ask for suggestions, comments, and constructive criticism and be prepared to hear both the good and the bad without taking what you hear personally.

In addition to a mentor, consider designating someone to act as the devil's advocate to guarantee that you address the flip side of every issue that you're considering. This person's task is to be critical of every idea on the table — not in a destructive way, but in a skeptical, show-me-the-money, I'll-believe-it-when-I-see-it kind of way. You may accomplish this goal by creating two teams similar to the brainstorming team you gathered previously (see "Assembling a brainstorming session" earlier in this chapter) — one to defend the idea and the second to criticize it. Ask the opposing team members to think of themselves as a competing firm looking to find weaknesses in the new venture.

Conducting a self-appraisal

If you run a small business or are a sole proprietor of your own business — even if you're an entrepreneur hoping to create the next Facebook — you still have one very important question to answer: "Do I have what it takes to turn this opportunity into a success story?"

You see some common traits among the CEOs who were multimillionaires before they turned 25 and the entrepreneurs cruising around in sports cars issuing orders on their cellphones while the value of their stock options soar: talent *and* hard work. To succeed, you must exhibit both, and to be a high-flyer or, for that matter, to be self-employed, you need discipline, confidence, and the capacity to live with the uncertainty that's part and parcel of being out on your own.

Not all personal strengths and weaknesses are equal contributors to business success. For example, if you plan to be a sole proprietor who works mostly alone, the ability to manage a staff doesn't matter much, but self-motivation is absolutely essential. Or, if your business will depend on face-to-face customer service, interpersonal skills will be indispensable.

Just because you may be weak in an important area doesn't mean you don't have what it takes to turn your idea into a business, but it does unveil areas that will require extra work and compensation on your part. For example, if you aren't good with details, but details are important to the success of your business, you may need to hire a personal assistant or cajole a colleague into tying up all the loose ends.

Write your personal strengths and weaknesses into your daily organizer or post a list of them near your computer. Having it close by constantly reminds you of who you are, the strengths you can draw on, and the areas you need to bolster as you begin the challenge of planning your business.

Chapter 3

Creating a Business Model

In This Chapter

▶ Examining advanced entrepreneurship, also known as business models

▶ Harnessing your business model to execute your business plan

▶ Considering how competitive advantage fits into your business model

▶ Finding out what all business models have in common

▶ Perusing popular business models

So what is a business model, anyway? Is it the way you make money? Yes, in part. Is it competitive advantage? Yes, in part. Is it your business plan? Not really. Simply put, a *business model* is your profit formula. It's the method you use to acquire customers, service them, and make money doing so. You can break down a business model into three primary areas: Offering, monetization, and sustainability. What is your offering? How will you monetize the offering? How will you sustain it?

Many businesspeople mistakenly believe that a business plan and a business model are one and the same. They're not. Your business model is the core concept upon which you build your business plan. Therefore, your business model should be a significant portion of your business plan. Too many business plans gloss over the business model in favor of lengthy financial projections and operational details that go along with business plans. Without a solid business model, though, these projections and details are likely premature. (Book II Chapter 1 is devoted to business plans.) In today's turbulent environment, having a strong business model is more important than ever. This chapter outlines an accessible way to refine the essence of your business.

Ideally, you should consider your business model before even starting to plan how your business will accomplish what it aims to accomplish. That's why business models are discussed in this Book, which focuses on the foundations of your business idea, and business plans are discussed in Book II, where you start up your business.

Evolution of Business Models

The notion of a business model may be relatively new, but the study of business in general has been going on for centuries. The notion of a business plan has been around since the late 1800s. Since then, business planning has grown from a mere notion to a science. Colleges offer courses in business planning. Software and templates have been created, and the general business public is well skilled in the practice.

Next came the concept of entrepreneurship. If you look at the rise of entrepreneurship, you see that it's grown from a vague concept in the 1960s to a major discipline in which you can now get a business degree. If you talk to recent college graduates about careers, a significant and growing percentage of them want to work for an entrepreneurial company or want to start a company of their own one day. Never before has entrepreneurship been celebrated the way it is today — both in the real world and in the academic world, where special programs and degrees are offered in entrepreneurship.

The study of business models can be called *advanced entrepreneurship*. The business model picks up where entrepreneurship leaves off and may well become the next wave of interest within the business community.

Business Models Are a Hot Topic

Aside from simple evolution in business thinking, business models are a hot topic for one reason: quicker profit. There used to be an old saying in business, "It takes 15 years to become an overnight success." The gist of this saying was that a business owner needed to toil in anonymity for 15 years before becoming tremendously successful. Today, business moves much faster, and tremendous profitability can be achieved almost overnight. Commerce is worldwide and moves significantly faster now, creating better opportunities for better businesses. There's simply no need to slog it out for 15 years.

As businesses became very successful quickly, people started to ask, "How can this happen?" The only logical answer was superior business models. With financial stakes resembling lottery winnings, business models gained more and more attention.

Business models aren't a fad. A strong business model is at the heart of a strong business and is the key to its profitability. Business models take all the complexity of a multibillion dollar business and boil it down to an easy-to-communicate profitable essence.

Who Needs a Business Model?

Why is a business model suddenly necessary? People have operated successful businesses for centuries without a business model — or have they?

Sun Tzu (author of *The Art of War*) is widely believed to have provided Napoleon with a quantum shift in thinking, which led to the development of the model through which Napoleon's early successes were won. It's argued that when he moved away from the fundamentals of his business model and started to rely heavily on plans that didn't take into account the sustainability of his actions, he was defeated. The one thing Sun Tzu espoused loudly and often was to consider all aspects and influences of the job at hand. This concept elevated management to a high art. Sun Tzu believed it was critical not only to lay a great plan but also to be flexible and make excellent decisions when things became fluid.

Whether you're an army general or a donut shop owner, every organization has and needs a business model. Schools have business models. Not-for-profit organizations have business models. Families have business models. Even governments have business models.

For your organization to operate at maximum effectiveness, an up-to-date and innovative business model is a necessity.

Common Aspects of All Business Models

Whether your business model is cutting edge or based on 100-year-old principles, all business models answer the following questions:

- ✔ **What problem are you trying to solve?** People don't need a new widget; they need the new widget to solve a problem. No one asked for an ATM. Customers wanted additional banking hours. The ATM solved this problem. Start with the job the customer is trying to accomplish, but without a good solution. These unserved or underserved markets provide the best opportunity for a great business model.

- ✔ **Who needs this problem solved?** The answer to this question is the customer you'll be serving. In the case of the ATM, the market is very large — everyone with a bank account. In the case of pet cloning, the market is much smaller — people with $50,000 who loved their deceased pet enough to re-create it.

✔ **What market segment is the model pursuing?** A *market segment* is a group of prospective buyers who have common needs and will respond similarly to your marketing. Nike makes shoes for many market segments, among them running, basketball, aerobics, and hiking. Traditional marketing focuses on demographic segments while modern marketing focuses on buyer behaviors.

✔ **How will you solve this problem better, cheaper, faster, or differently than other offerings?** Duluth Trading Company offers "ballroom jeans" that offer extra room in the right places so you can crouch without the ouch. Clever, unique offerings like these are superior to a better mousetrap.

✔ **What is the value proposition?** What problem do you solve for the customer in relation to what you charge to fix it? Ballroom jeans have a clever niche and solve a problem for a defined segment, but if the price is $250 per pair, the value proposition is weak. Your product solves a problem for the customer. Hopefully, the customer values the solution and will pay you much more than it costs you to make the product. The larger this spread, the greater your value proposition.

✔ **Where does your offer place you on the value chain?** Many creative business models — like Skype, ProFlowers, and eBay — have redefined the value chain by eliminating or shifting the partners that contribute to the final offering.

✔ **What is your revenue model?** Factors such as how you'll charge for the product, how much you'll charge, and which portions of your offerings will be the biggest money makers all determine your revenue model. For instance, most airlines have radically changed their revenue models to charge separately for items that used to be bundled into the ticket price, effectively making them free. Items like checked bags, extra legroom, in-flight food, and even carry-on bags now generate billions of dollars in revenue for airlines.

✔ **What is your competitive strategy?** You don't want to just jump into the shark tank. You need a plan to differentiate yourself from competition — via marketing, sales, and operations — that allows you to effectively outshine the competition.

✔ **How will you maintain your competitive edge?** After you distance yourself from competitors, how will you hold off their attempts to copy your winning strategies? The best business models create barriers to maintain their hard-earned competitive advantage.

✔ **What partners or other complementary products should be used?** Henry Ford was famous for creating companies to make everything included in his cars. Toyota relies on a partner network to engineer and manufacture most of the components for its cars. Savvy relationships with partners can enhance your business model.

✔ **What network effects can be harnessed?** If you owned the only fax machine, it wouldn't be worth much because you couldn't send or receive a fax. Network effects enhance the value of everyone's purchase when the network of users grows. Nightclubs and Facebook rely on their large network of users to increase the value of their offer.

The best business models aren't merely an idea. A great business model solves problems for customers creatively and generates more profit than was previously thought possible.

Business Models in Their Simplest Form

You have an overwhelming number of factors and concerns to consider when creating a business model. It can be daunting. Here's a simple three-part method to break down a model:

✔ **What is the offering?** Are you selling roses on the side of the road or fractional use of private jets? Why do customers need your offering? How is it different from customers' other options to solve their problem? Are you selling your product to the best market and in the best niche? Book I Chapter 4 talks more about the basics of creating a powerful offering.

✔ **How will you monetize the offering?** Twitter has a powerful offering providing hundreds of millions of users valuable communication tools. However, Twitter has struggled to turn this offering into money. You must have more than just a product people want. You must be able to charge a price that generates significant margin and be able to sell it. Sharper Image was a company whose products were priced at a level that afforded high margins; however, not enough customers bought them. You must be able to execute your sales strategy in order to complete the monetization of the offering.

✔ **How will you create sustainability?** Blockbuster Video had an exceptionally profitable business model for nearly two decades, but the company was unable to sustain it once it missed the digital video streaming boat. Factors such as maintaining/growing competitive advantage, the ability to innovate, and avoiding pitfalls affect the sustainability of the business model.

Examples of Business Models

There are business models hundreds of years old and models only a handful of years old, such as Internet freemium models. Some of the most profitable companies didn't invent new business models; they borrowed a business model from another industry. The Gillette razor and blades model has been highly profitable for Hewlett-Packard's inkjet printer business and Verizon's cellphone business. The cheap chic business model works for Trader Joe's in the grocery business and IKEA in the home furnishing business. Sometimes, one little tweak to an existing business model can yield powerful results in a new industry.

Table 3-1 shows a partial list of common business models. These examples should get your creative juices flowing as you begin to create your business model. Review the list for small ideas you can work into your model rather than copying a model lock, stock, and barrel.

Table 3-1	**Types of Business Models**	
Type of Model	*Description*	*Example Companies and Products*
Razor and blades	Consumer purchases a low-margin item like a razor handle or inkjet printer. Sale of necessary consumables such as replacement blades or ink are sold at a very high markup.	Gillette, Hewlett-Packard printers, Kuerig coffeemakers
Inverted razor and blades	Initial purchase has a high margin, but consumables are sold at a low margin to entice initial purchase or contrast to razor and blade competitor.	Kodak inkjet printers, Apple iPod & iTunes combination. Apple makes very low margins on iTunes but high margins on hardware.
Cheap chic	Marketing of stylish but inexpensive merchandise. Typically allows for high margins because merchandise sells at low price points but has an expensive feel.	Target, Trader Joe's, IKEA
Bricks and clicks	Extension of in-store shopping to include online ordering with in-store pickup or items found exclusively online.	Best Buy, local mystery bookstore with online shop
Multilevel marketing	Leverage friends, family, and other personal networks to recommend products and act as a sales force. Works best for products needing recommendation to facilitate purchase.	Avon, Mary Kay, Amway

Type of Model	Description	Example Companies and Products
Franchise	Sell the right to use the business model in exchange for a percentage of revenues.	McDonald's, Holiday Inn, NFL
Anticipated upsell	High percentage of buyers ultimately purchase more than they expected. For instance, most new home buyers end up spending 1.2 times the base price of the home after extras.	Homebuilders, car dealerships, steel fabricators
Loss leader	This model offers velocity items for a very low margin in anticipation of additional sales at a higher margin.	Gas stations, $1 menus
Subscription model	One of the more popular models because of recurring revenue. Typically involves creating a significant asset and renting a piece of it.	Health clubs, software as a service
Collective	Similar to a franchise. Involves many businesses coming together for purchasing, marketing, or operational purposes but with looser ties than a franchise. Typically, collectives aggregate buying power and don't pay ongoing royalties like a franchise.	Ace Hardware, CarQuest
Productization of services	Standardizing a predetermined bundle of services typically bought together and selling for a fixed price similar to a product. Many times it includes an element of flat-fee pricing as well.	A consultant charges $5,000 for a business plan analysis rather than charging $200 per hour, prepaid legal plans
Servitization of products	Making a product part of a larger service offering.	Rolls-Royce sells aircraft engines, not as distinct components but as complete solutions based on aviation miles. All operations and maintenance functions are included in this "Power by the Hour" plan.

(continued)

Table 3-1 *(continued)*

Type of Model	Description	Example Companies and Products
Long tail	Based on Chris Anderson's famed 2004 *Wired* magazine article. Selecting a tiny niche and serving it in ways mass marketers can't. Hopefully, the tiny niche grows into a much larger one.	Fat Tire beer, YouTube bands, left-handed online store, micro-breweries
Direct sales	Bypass the traditional sales channels to target end users. Methods include door-to-door sales and company-owned stores.	Kirby Vacuums, Girl Scout cookies, outlet mall stores
Cut out the middle man	Removal of intermediaries in a supply chain, such as by skipping the warehouse distributor in the traditional three-step distribution chain.	AutoZone, Dell Computer, farmer's markets
Freemium business model	Product is offered for free. Typically 8% of users upgrade to become paying customers of virtual goods or to get expanded access.	Angry Birds, shareware software, McAfee security
Online auctions	Create a community of buyers and sellers by using an auction-type selling process versus a set sales price.	eBay, Arriba
Hotel California model	Create a must-have product that traps customers into buying unrelated high-profit items.	Concessions at amusement parks, sporting events, movie theaters
Network effect	Create a product in which the value to each user becomes higher as more people use it.	Fax machines, social networks
Crowdsourcing	Leveraging users to co-create products and sell to other users.	Cafepress.com, Frito Lay new flavors, YouTube, Angie's List
Users as experts	Gives users access to technology and tools typically reserved for company employees. Users then create their own designs or versions of the product.	Cook-your-own-steak restaurants, LEGO

Type of Model	Description	Example Companies and Products
Premium	Offer high-end products that appeal to brand-conscious consumers.	Tiffany, Rolls-Royce
Nickel and dime	Price the most cost-sensitive item as low as possible and then charge for every little extra.	Airlines
Flat fee	The opposite of nickel and dime. Most or all incidental purchases are bundled into one fee.	Sandals Resorts, Southwest Airlines

Finding Success with a Business Model

In its simplest form, a business model is your profit formula. It's the method you use to acquire customers, service them, and make money doing so.

Every business has a business model, in fact, even if nobody ever bothers to write it down. That's because the business model is the basic structure of the business — what service it provides or what product it creates or sells to make money.

Generally, business models focus on the creation of profitable revenue and the delivery required to keep the revenue flowing. Most operational, finance, and human resource issues are peripheral to the creation of profitable revenue, and so they're separate from the business model. Here are some examples of business models in action:

✔ Domino's focuses on inexpensive pizza, delivered fast. Jimmy John's has used a similar model in the sandwich business.

✔ Toyota began the push of manufacturers leveraging lean manufacturing in order to produce better quality cars at a lower cost. After Toyota proved the model successful, many other companies followed Toyota's lead.

✔ Walmart strives to consistently lower purchasing and operating costs and then pass the savings on to consumers. As this business model wooed customers away from established retailers, many retailers and non-retailers have imitated Walmart's model.

✔ Zappos.com did what most thought impossible. It created an online business (selling shoes) where physically handling the product was important and virtualized it online. Zappos has set a new standard of online customer service by allowing customers to have several pairs of shoes delivered to their door, try them on in the convenience of their home, and send any or all of them back at no charge.

✔ Dollarshaveclub.com has ignited a monthly club business model craze for everything from the monthly delivery of socks and t-shirts to baby clothes and feminine hygiene products. Even Walmart has jumped onto the monthly club bandwagon.

✔ Zipcar competes with other car rental companies by renting cars by the hour in busy metropolitan areas for quick trips. Cars can be returned to any Zipcar drop-off location.

✔ Crowdspring.com uses a unique business model for graphic design by leveraging crowdsourcing. Rather than pick vendors based upon the quality of their previous work, the customer posts how much she will pay for the project and vendors actually complete the design. Low-resolution samples are shown to the buyer, and then a winner is chosen.

Your secret sauce for making money

At its most basic level, your business model is the formula that allows you to make money. You can think of it as the combination of everything you do — your secret sauce — to provide your customers with value and make a profit doing so. The more differentiated and proprietary your combination is, the more profitable you'll be.

Set yourself apart through differentiation

Differentiated business models offer customers products, services, or other value that stands out from the competition. Consider the following examples:

✔ **BigBelly Solar** doesn't just make trash containers; BigBelly's trash containers harness solar power to compact trash five times more than a typical container. This capability allows cities like Chicago, Philadelphia, and Boston to collect trash far less often and save fuel, manpower, and vehicle wear and tear.

✔ **Camp Bow Wow** offers more than kenneling or dog-sitting. Dogs play together much like children at recess. Customers pay a premium for their dogs to have a good time rather than be cooped up all day.

✔ **The Huffington Post** is an Internet-only news outlet.

✔ **Southwest Airlines** offers customers more direct flights than other airlines, plus it has a fun-loving staff. Operationally, Southwest flies only 737s to keep operating costs at a minimum, doesn't use fee-based outside reservation systems, and uses a faster boarding system with no assigned seats.

✔ **Tesla** makes only high-performance electric automobiles.

✔ **Walk-In Lab** doesn't accept insurance. Instead, the company provides low-cost medical testing to the uninsured.

Make your model difficult to copy

A proprietary business model is a differentiated model that's difficult or impossible for a competitor to emulate. Typically, proprietary models create methods to

- ✔ **Deliver products and services better, cheaper, or faster through a business process known only to that company.** Examples include the following:

    - Toyota's lean manufacturing process.

    - Appliance retailer H.H. Gregg's radically realigned retail and operational systems to allow for same-day delivery.

    - Walmart's heavy investing in technology during the 1980s to create a logistical system that brought goods to market significantly more cheaply than its competitors.

- ✔ **Create a closed ecosystem where ongoing use of your product is highly desirable or required.** A powerful ecosystem attracts new customers and discourages old customers from leaving. Here are some examples of successful closed ecosystems:

    - The iTunes ecosystem (iPod, iPhone, iCloud, and iTunes) that created a proprietary business model for Apple.

    - Amazon's Kindle, which created a large library of books on the proprietary format, making it difficult for customers to purchase any other product.

- ✔ **Find a way to serve customers others thought were unprofitable.** Consider the following:

    - Vistaprint attacked the micro business printing market thought unprofitable by most competitors. The combination of an Internet sales process and large-scale combining of orders allowed Vistaprint to grow rapidly in a contracting market.

    - Microfinance company SKS (www.sksindia.com) lends small amounts to remote villagers in India. At the end of 2011, the company had outstanding loans of $925,844,433 to more than six million active borrowers. Because SKS lends money to those whose only lending option is loan sharks, the company can charge a much higher interest rate than banks charge large corporations.

    - SafeAuto offers minimum coverage to drivers the big insurers deem too risky and too financially unstable to cover.

✔ **Do business in way competitors thought was unprofitable or impractical.** Your business model can be well protected if your competitors think you're nuts for trying. Here are some business models that had competitors shaking their heads:

- For decades, Southwest Airlines served second-tier cities at second-tier airports and insisted on flying only Boeing 737s. Most large airlines were happy to let Southwest serve these less-than-desirable markets with their small airplanes. However, as cost pressures continued to grind upon the industry, it became clear that Southwest had spent 20 years creating a low-cost model that the large airlines couldn't duplicate or compete well with.

- FedEx started as a Yale business school project for founder Fred Smith. Everyone, including Smith's professor (who gave the project a C), thought delivering packages overnight was an awful idea. Not dissuaded, Smith pursued the concept and spent years building the infrastructure to deliver packages efficiently and quickly. By the time it was clear that overnight package delivery was a good business model, Smith had a ten-year head start.

- Nearly every computer maker attempted a tablet computer and failed. It was well known that tablet computers were a niche product for hospitals and a select few customers. Apple ignored the gloom and doom and launched the iPad anyway. The product was a huge success and left competitors scrambling to create their own tablet computers.

✔ **Create a product or service that's patented, trademarked, or difficult to duplicate.** Consider these examples:

- The Xerox 914 copier used a proprietary process to duplicate documents. It's quite possible that Xerox wouldn't have grown to become a Fortune 500 company if it had simply sold the 914 machine outright. Renting the machines was a much better business model. It cost Xerox around $2,000 to build one machine. Instead of selling it, Xerox rented the machines for $95/month plus five cents per copy for each one over the first 2,000/month. Large customers like General Motors were copying up to 100,000 documents per month (that's a $4,995 rental per month).

- NoChar (nochar.com) makes an unpatented polymer that turns nasty liquid spills of anything from diesel fuel to nuclear waste into a solid. The proprietary product isn't patented because the company doesn't want to reveal the formula, even to the patent office. NoChar has built a successful business based on a product its competitors simply can't figure out how to copy.

Becoming the absolute best in your field creates a product or service that's difficult to duplicate. If you're having brain surgery or a cavity filled, you want the most talented person performing the function. The same holds true for any skilled trade. People always want the best, and they're willing to pay a premium for it.

Same industry, different business models

McDonald's, Wendy's, and Burger King are all in the fast-food hamburger business. However, the three burger joints have very different business models. Because of their different business models, the methodologies, psychologies, ideologies, and profit formulas of these businesses differ greatly.

Each of these burger businesses uses a different "secret sauce" — not on its burgers, but on its business model. For instance, McDonald's owns more corner lots than any other company in the world. Clearly, its business model entails acquiring valuable real estate in addition to selling hamburgers.

Wendy's focuses on freshness and more upscale customers than McDonald's mass customer approach, and Wendy's charges accordingly. Wendy's business model focuses on maximizing margin per customer. Like McDonald's, Wendy's is currently focused on a single brand. In the past, Wendy's grew its business by adding new brands, such as Tim Horton's, Baja Fresh, and Arby's. Eventually, Wendy's sold or spun off these businesses.

In recent years, Burger King has struggled with its business model and place in the market. Many years ago, competitors took away Burger King's primary

DuraFlame burns the competition

Most proprietary business models are simply a series of excellent business practices well executed. In the late 1960s, California Cedar Company needed a way to discard shavings from its pencil factory. Through research and development, the company discovered a process to turn these unwanted scraps into the DuraFlame log, a product that today generates $250 million in annual revenue. However, California Cedar Company didn't stop at the invention of this product. The true genius of the business model wasn't how to make the first artificial log; it was using waste to make it. In the 1970s, sawmills had to *pay* to haul off their sawdust. California Cedar went to virtually every sawmill on the Pacific coast and significantly undercut its sawdust waste hauling contract in exchange for a long-term commitment. California Cedar created a business model in which it was paid to accept its primary raw material.

differentiator of making its burgers exactly the way customers want them ("Hold the pickle, hold the lettuce"). Now Burger King is struggling to find a business model that works. Burger King recently closed hundreds of stores and fell to third place behind McDonald's and Wendy's in sales despite having thousands more stores than Wendy's. It seems that Burger King's issues are with its own business model and not the hamburger business in general. While Burger King has struggled, several other hamburger chains have thrived; examples include Red Robin, Rally's, Checker's, In-N-Out, and Five Guys.

How your business model sets you apart from the competition

Your business model is at the core of your business's capability to make profit. Many of the factors that differentiate your business flow directly from your business model. For instance, Walmart and Target sell similar products to similar customers. However, their business models differ significantly.

At the core of Walmart's business model is its "always low prices" promise. To deliver on this promise, Walmart must maintain low costs in all aspects of its business:

- ✔ Low-cost employees
- ✔ Low-cost health insurance
- ✔ Low-cost real estate
- ✔ Low-cost purchasing by creating custom products or beating up vendors for the best deal
- ✔ Logistical efficiencies that lower costs

Walmart's business model aims to be the low-cost provider. The company's desire to provide goods at the lowest cost cascades into many aspects of its operations. Because the chain is focused on the lowest cost, its stores may not be as modern or attractive as those of Target, and its products may not be as trendy as what you can find at Target. Walmart also has a reputation for paying lower wages than Target. The company's business model decisions keep costs at the absolute minimum but have caused significant human resource issues, including potential unionization, lawsuits, and negative publicity. Walmart's business model dictates that keeping costs low always comes first.

Target, on the other hand, has chosen a business model that can be summed up as *cheap chic*. Target spends its organizational energy trying to find hip but inexpensive products for its customers. Of course, Target must remain cost competitive, but the niche it has carved out doesn't require that it charge the lowest possible cost on all items. The money that Walmart makes with sheer volume of transactions, Target makes in higher margin per item. Just think for a second how much the $10 potato peeler with the designer handle in a choice of trendy colors actually costs Target.

Just like Target and Walmart, your business model differentiates you from the competition. The stronger your business model, the stronger your capability to make outstanding profits.

Considering your competitive advantage

Competitive advantage allows a firm to perform at a higher level than others in the same industry or market — or with anyone competing for the customer's limited budget. Competitive advantage can serve as a powerful catalyst for your business. Competitive advantage allows you to outsell, outprofit, and outperform others in the same industry or market. When you're analyzing the strength of a business, if you look only at competitive advantage, your analysis will be incomplete.

People often mistakenly use the term *competitive advantage* as a synonym for the term *business model.* The reality is that competitive advantage is a portion of your business model, but not all of it. A business model is more encompassing than your competitive advantage. For instance, you can have excellent competitive advantage but still have a weak business model. If Starbucks's decided to maximize coffee poundage sales by lowering the price of a cup of coffee to $0.50, its competitive advantage may rise slightly. However, the lower price would result in a significantly different, and worse, business model for Starbucks's.

Obtaining your competitive advantage

According to Michael Porter, the Harvard professor responsible for the concept, competitive advantage is obtained through cost leadership, differentiation, and/or focus.

Cost leadership

Cost leadership means your firm has the capability to deliver similar goods or services as your competitors for a lower cost. This doesn't mean a lower sales price, but a lower cost of goods sold. If one firm has the capability to deliver a widget at a cost of $8 and it costs another firm $10 to deliver a similar widget, the first one has a cost advantage. If your cost advantage is the best in your industry, you have cost leadership. You can gain cost leadership in countless ways; here are just a few:

- **Access to natural resources:** Middle Eastern oil or Chinese cheap labor are examples.
- **Scale:** Walmart can buy Pampers cheaper than anyone else.
- **Vertical integration:** Intel designs, fabricates, and markets chips.
- **Technological leverage:** Many analysts attribute Walmart's rise in the 1980s to technological superiority in logistics.
- **Proprietary processes:** Rolls-Royce uses a secret metallurgy process to make super-durable jet engine blades.

Differentiation

Differentiation means that the customer feels your product has superior and different attributes than the competition's. Customers pay much more for a cup of Starbucks's coffee than for a cup of joe at the diner because they view Starbucks's coffee as a differentiated product. Many times, you can charge extra for the differentiated attributes of your offering, creating additional margin. Businesses can create differentiation by using any of the following tactics:

- **Superior branding** (Coach, Tiffany's, Rolex)
- **Unique supplier relationships** (Eddie Bauer Edition Ford Explorer)
- **First mover advantage** (iPad, Walkman, Crest toothpaste)
- **Location** (remember the retail mantra "location, location, location"?)
- **Scale** (not many companies can build an airplane or a skyscraper)
- **Intellectual property** (iPod circular controls, Hemi engines, Intel Inside)

Focus

You can also gain competitive advantage through your focus. A business can't serve too many masters. You can translate intense focus on a market, niche, or attribute into a significant advantage. Examples include the following:

- Tesla's focus on only electric automobiles
- Taiwan Semiconductor's exclusive focus on fabrication
- Amgen's focus on biopharmaceuticals (rather than all types of drugs)
- Starbucks's focus on coffee rather than becoming just another restaurant
- Rally's focus on drive-through hamburgers
- A doctor's focus on heart surgery

Enhancing your competitive advantage

To fully leverage a strong competitive advantage, you must shore up the other aspects of your business model as well. The following sections detail several other factors that a strong business model must take into account. As a savvy businessperson, you must go further than competitive advantage analysis and explore all aspects of the business model. By doing so, you can unleash the maximum potential of the business.

Innovation

You need to take into account your company's capability to innovate in order to fully evaluate its business model. Without innovation, your competitive advantage will weaken or disappear. Do you think Apple will continue to dominate the tablet market for ten more years? Already there are signs of weakness in iPad sales. Without future innovation, competitors will catch Apple and eat into its market share. Not that long ago, BlackBerry had a dominant share of the cellphone market. A few years later, BlackBerry was teetering on bankruptcy.

Customer segments

What customer segment will the product attack? Competitive advantage is somewhat generic in regard to who the customer will be. It assumes that you'll find the right one. However, chasing the wrong customers or market segment can destroy an otherwise solid business model.

Targeting your competitive advantage to the right customer or market segment makes a big difference, as the following examples demonstrate:

- Motorola had a product well suited for the military market in the Iridium satellite phone, but the company blew billions trying to market it to non-military consumers who were unwilling to buy a $3,000 phone.

- The U.S. military took five years to purchase 50,000 Hummers. In 2006 alone, General Motors sold 70,000 nonmilitary Hummers to the public.

- After NASA was exposed for purchasing $129 pencils for space missions, Paul Fisher took it upon himself to invent a pen that would write in space. He succeeded, calling his invention the Space Pen. For many years, Fisher sold his pen to NASA for $4 (it cost him $1.98 to manufacture). However, the market for the space pen as a collectible item turned out to be much larger for Fisher. The pen sells many more units today for $20 than it did to NASA for $4.

- Ivan Getting conceived of the GPS system in the 1950s. It took nearly 50 years and $12 billion to create a system for tracking military personnel, missiles, ships, tanks, and the like. The consumer electronics industry sold more than one billion GPS-enabled devices in just 15 years.

Pricing

What will you charge for the product? How high or low will the margin be? The answers to these questions are critical factors of the business model, but they aren't addressed directly in competitive advantage. For example, Amazon has competitive advantage in its capability to distribute product conveniently and efficiently. However, what will happen when Amazon is forced to charge sales tax and prices rise? What would happen if Amazon focused on the convenience of the online experience but charged 15 percent more than brick- and -mortar competitors? No one knows the answer, but these factors would affect Amazon's competitive advantage.

Capability to sell

Without a proven and repeatable sales process, most business models fail. Unfortunately, the world doesn't care if you have a better mouse trap. All products and services must be *sold*. It's easy to forget this inconvenient truth as you look at the long line outside the Apple store with customers clamoring to buy. However, don't forget all those iPhone and iPad commercials on television, the publicity, paid product placements on shows like *Modern Family,* and countless other efforts to drive demand. All these things help to create that long line of eager buyers.

In order to finalize the marketing process, someone must purchase your product. A solid sales and marketing system must be used to realize the full potential of your offering.

Potential pitfalls

Competitive advantage doesn't take potential pitfalls into account. Taser pioneered the stun gun business, holds many patents, owns the best brand in the business, and gets sued for $1 million nearly every week. Taser has a good business model despite this pitfall. However, if you look only at Taser's competitive advantage without regard to pitfalls, Taser's business looks much more attractive than it actually is.

Continuity

A significant issue for mid-sized and small businesses is the capability to operate without the day-to-day input of the owner. If the business falls apart without the owner in the building, the business model is weak and the owner will never be able to sell the business.

Let's say Tom has a business that nets him $900,000 per year. The business has significant competitive advantage as witnessed by its profitability. However, the instant Tom stops showing up, the business nets $0. Many doctors, lawyers, accountants, architects, and other professionals face the same issue. The competitive advantage of these businesses is strong, but the business model still needs some work.

Chapter 4

Finding Your Target Market

· ·

In This Chapter

▶ Picking the right industry

▶ Getting the niche right

▶ Gauging the most attractive customers

▶ Choosing the best spot on the industry value chain

· ·

*T*he most important step toward creating a great business is creating a product or service that customers want and will buy. This is called a *powerful offering*. The first step in creating a powerful offering is selecting the right market. Picking the combination of industry attractiveness, niche attractiveness, and customer attractiveness creates the best market for your product.

By combining industry attractiveness, niche attractiveness, and customer attractiveness, you can understand the overall market potential. This chapter refers to this combination as the *market attractiveness* from this point forward. Market attractiveness is one of the most important aspects of your business. It's difficult to imagine a strong business that sells to lousy customers in a bad industry and small niche market.

Gauging the Target Market

You should find a profitable and sufficiently large market segment. However, in order to have a successful and durable business, you need to find a large market that's unserved or underserved. Finding this underserved market is paramount.

Anyone can find huge markets to attack. Hey, let's sell coffee! The market is large and growing, right? However, several large and successful companies already own pieces of this market. In general, it's unwise to attack an established competitor in the exact same market segment. Traditionally, the first mover or incumbent wins.

If you want to go after the coffee market, you need to find a viable market segment that's unserved or underserved by Starbucks and similar companies. You can break down the target market into four pieces to make things easier:

✔ **How attractive is the industry itself?** For instance, software companies tend to be more profitable than construction companies. Professor Scott A. Shane conducted research for his book *The Illusions of Entrepreneurship: The Costly Myths That Entrepreneurs, Investors, and Policy Makers Live By* (Yale University Press). That research offers significant data that some industries are more viable and profitable than others. Of course, the other areas of the business model have great effect on the overall profitability; however, if you're looking for the best model, software development is a better choice than an airline (see the later section "Case study: Software versus airlines").

✔ **How attractive is the niche within the industry?** Typically, packaged software developers are more profitable than custom software developers. You want to pick a niche that offers the best potential profitability.

✔ **How attractive is the customer segment?** The high-end customer targeted by Starbucks is more profitable than the customer targeted by McDonald's. An attractive customer doesn't have to be a wealthy customer. An attractive customer is the one who can make your business model work best. For instance, many profitable business models are being created for the unbanked (people without checking accounts).

✔ **Is the niche big enough to provide a good opportunity for you to enter it and sell enough product or services, at a price point that will allow you to create a viable business?** Prosthetic limbs for pet dogs may seem like a great idea, but can you sell enough of them at a high enough price to be able to make any money doing it?

Determining Industry Attractiveness

An *industry* is the broadest category or definition of the business you'll be in. Examples of industry include the following:

✔ Automotive aftermarket manufacturing

✔ Business consulting

✔ General contracting

✔ Home remodeling

✔ Lawn and garden distribution

✔ Legal services

✔ Medical

✔ Pet care

✔ Residential landscaping

✔ Software development

Within a broad industry are often-defined industry segments that further refine the offering. Here are some examples:

✔ The vehicle manufacturing industry has segments for heavy-duty trucks, electric automobiles, recreational vehicles, and more.

✔ The restaurant industry has segments for fast food, fine dining, casual dining, and so on.

✔ Clothing manufacturers have segments for athletic wear, men's suits, lingerie, women's business attire, and bridal gowns, among others.

✔ The medical doctor industry has segmentation for general practitioners, surgeons, podiatrists, holistic practitioners, ophthalmologists, and hundreds more.

✔ The HVAC (heating, ventilation, and air conditioning) industry has segments for light-duty, boilers, and heavy-duty systems.

You're much more likely to be successful in a "good" industry than a "bad" one. In a good industry, most companies are successful; examples include software development, mineral extraction, and insurance. In a bad industry, margins are historically low and/or competition is overly intense; examples include airlines and construction. However, you can find numerous examples of companies that entered unattractive industries and were successful because their business model was strong in other areas. Examples include Waste Management (garbage), Apple (computer hardware), Nike (shoes), and Vistaprint (commercial printing).

You have a much greater chance of success if you pick an attractive industry. Consider these factors:

✔ Is this industry, as a whole, growing or shrinking?

✔ Will this industry be strong in ten years?

✔ How many incumbents are in this industry, and how strong are they?

✔ Do you see an opportunity for this industry to overlap into a different existing market (convergence)?

✔ Could the industry provide powerful synergies with an existing part of your business?

What's the difference between a market and an industry?

Many businesspeople use the term *market* as a catch-all for the combination of *industry, segment, niche,* and *customer* (in other words, who will pay you for your product). Although simply referring to *the market* is easier, it's better to break things down into more discreet pieces so you can gain additional insight into your model. These concepts, however, do bleed into one another. If your industry niche is electric cars, your customer segment is probably dictated by the fact that you make electric cars. The two complement and bleed into each other.

Market is best used when *industry, segment, niche,* or *customer segment* simply doesn't fully cover all the bases. *Industry* should refer to the industry and the industry segment.

Book I Chapter 1 talks more about researching your chosen industry.

After you identify an attractive industry, identify the best subset of that market, or niche, and then identify the best customers to serve within that niche. Working in an attractive industry is helpful, but it isn't a prerequisite. Many great business models have been created in bad industries by carving out attractive customer segments, niches, or both.

Vistaprint created an excellent business model serving customers no one wanted (microbusinesses) in an industry no one wanted to be in (printing). Vistaprint succeeded by leveraging a highly differentiated sales, distribution, and cost model.

There's an old saying, "Everyone thinks they know how to run a restaurant because they know how to eat." Every industry and business can be learned. However, if you're unfamiliar with an industry, count on some hard work to get up to speed.

As you choose your industry, keep in mind that the business landscape is always changing. Gas stations used to fix cars; now they sell donuts and sandwiches. If you look into the future, it can help you determine whether your chosen industry has peripheral growth opportunities or potential threats.

Finding the best industry

Picking an attractive industry for your business model may seem simple. The key lies in research (see Book I Chapter 1 for more ideas on how to conduct your research). One thing you should do is gather as much independent information as possible regarding current and future trends. By doing so, you're able to make the best choice of industry for your model. Here are some places to find industry data and trends:

- Paid services such as Gartner (www.gartner.com) and Forrester Research (www.forrester.com)
- General business publications like *Business Week* (www.businessweek. com), *Inc.* (www.inc.com), *Barron's* (barrons.com), and *Money* (http://money.cnn.com)
- Books
- Futurists such as Faith Popcorn, author of many books on business trends, including *Clicking: 17 Trends That Drive Your Business — And Your Life* (HarperBusiness)
- Industry trade publications

Watch out for bias when using trade publications as a resource. Such publications put the most positive spin on the industry. For instance, travel industry trade publications were likely still positive on the industry in 2000 even though Internet sites like Priceline.com and Expedia.com were beginning to destroy portions of the business.

- Industry associations
- Personal experience
- IRS or state government (Look for the number of businesses in an industry starting or filing bankruptcy.)

Without proprietary information, you're picking your industry with the same data as your competition. Business is inherently risky. No amount of research is a substitute for time in the marketplace. At some point, you will have done your homework and taken your best guess, and you will need to take the leap.

Working in unserved or underserved markets

Unserved or underserved markets offer significantly better opportunities than most. Underserved markets have growth potential and less competition. Position yourself in an underserved market and your business model will be much stronger. Markets are underserved because

- **The market is growing and too few vendors serve the market.** Most new businesses chase this classic market. Markets like Android application development, social media platforms, 3D printing, and passenger space travel are examples of markets expected to have explosive growth.

- ✔ **The market is stagnant or shrinking and vendors flee.** An overcorrection by competition can create opportunities.

- ✔ **The market is considered unattractive.** Some possible reasons:

  - **Perceived profitability.** Rent-a-Center profits in a market others consider too dicey.

  - **Perceived size.** Walmart found a market serving towns under 20,000 in population while competitors focused on large cities.

  - **Being unsexy.** Markets like portable toilets, paper manufacturing, and salt mining have far less sex appeal than iPhone application development and can offer opportunities because of this lack of appeal.

Some markets are underserved for a reason. Carefully examine the market opportunity, take off the rose-colored glasses, and be brutally honest with yourself — and then pick based on all the criteria.

Case study: Software versus airlines

It's quite difficult to make money in some industries. Case in point is the airline industry. All major U.S. carriers except Southwest Airlines have filed for bankruptcy protection. Yes, all of them. Southwest is not only the top performing airline, but also well respected globally as an outstanding company.

Southwest is an exceptionally well-run company; Southwest is the top performer in its industry by light-years; and Southwest earns net profit around 2 percent of sales. So the best performer in the industry can look forward to a dismal 2 percent net profit and a 1.8 percent return on assets? Wait, that doesn't sound too bad with sales in the billions. What does it take to get into the airline business? First, go hire tens of thousands of employees (46,128 to be exact): flight attendants, pilots, mechanics, ground crews, and so on. Then go purchase a few billion dollars' worth of airplanes, and you're set.

Contrast the airline industry to the software industry. Unlike an airline, the software industry doesn't require massive capital investment, nor does it require tens of thousands of employees. Typically, the software industry offers better margins, higher net profits, fewer employee issues, and higher returns on assets.

Intuit, the maker of Quicken software, is a high-performing company but isn't the top performing company in the software industry. How does it compare to Southwest Airlines? Intuit was able to generate profits of $634 million in

2011 with only 8,500 employees versus Southwest's net profit of $178 million the same year. Intuit earned net profit of 18.48 percent versus Southwest's 1.98 percent.

Nothing against Intuit, but Southwest is the better-run company. Southwest is the best in its industry, by far. Southwest is a revered company. What is Southwest's reward for outstanding performance in the airline industry? Well, the reward stinks! Because Southwest is in a lousy industry, Southwest can perform only to a certain level.

Heed the lessons in this example: If you pick the right industry, your business model will be much better than if you pick poorly. In other words, please don't start an airline.

Looking for Niche Attractiveness

After you pick an attractive industry for your business model (see the preceding section), it's time to find an attractive niche. Your niche market is a subset of the overall market you participate in. Discovery Networks International participates in the broadcast television industry, but its niche is infotainment. Shows like *MythBusters, Dirty Jobs,* and *Deadliest Catch* entertain with an educational bent. The shows on Discovery Networks' channels attract a certain type of audience. This niche has proven to be a good one. Discovery Networks has grown steadily to reach more than 300 million international subscribers.

The power of a good niche

Picking the right niche may be more important than picking the right industry. Vistaprint was founded in 1995 when the traditional printing business was getting crushed. Thousands of printers went out of business during the 1990s and early 2000s. During that time, Vistaprint grew into a billion-dollar business. How could Vistaprint grow when other printers were dramatically shrinking? Vistaprint targeted micro and small businesses considered too small for traditional printers. Combined with ingenious leverage of technology, Vistaprint turned unprofitable small customers into one of the most profitable printing operations in the world.

Unlimited niches exist

Good news! You can find unlimited niches within any market. At the core of many successful companies' strategies was the creation or refinement of a new niche. Here are some examples:

- **Panera Bread:** Healthier, higher-quality sandwiches aimed at the fast-food industry.

- **Häagen Dazs:** High-end ice cream at triple the price versus other ice creams in the frozen dessert industry.

- **Starbucks:** Not just a cup of joe — an experience. You could argue that Starbucks is in the restaurant industry, and it is. However, Starbucks also competes against convenience stores for coffee sales. The niche in either case is the customer who wants the full Starbucks coffee experience.

- **McDonald's:** Fast, consistent food. This niche in the restaurant business is mature and crowded today, but when McDonald's started, it was a new and untapped market. By catering to customers who wanted consistency in fast food, McDonald's dominated this niche.

- **Coach:** Everyday luxury. Coach bags are more stylish than a department store brand but priced much more reasonably than high-fashion brands. This half high-fashion, half department-store niche has worked well for Coach and other everyday luxury brands.

- **iPad:** An email and Internet toy. Apple found a great niche between a laptop, Gameboy, and smartphone.

How many different niches can the hamburger business support? A lot more than anyone expected. The hamburger was invented around 1890, and the first hamburger restaurants began appearing in the 1920s. Since then, dozens of spins on making a hamburger have appeared. Here's a partial list of hamburger chains and their niches.

Chain	*Niche*
McDonald's	The kids' burger chain
Wendy's	The adults' burger chain
Red Robin	Gourmet burgers
White Castle	Craveable sliders
Rally's	Drive-through only
Steak 'n Shake	Sit-down burgers with a diner feel
Five Guys	Simple, fresher burgers and fries

Markets have a habit of splitting

As markets mature, they tend to split into more and more niches. Niches that used to comprise a small portion of the market can become huge. Fifty years ago, abrasive cleaners such as Comet dominated the household cleaner market. In 1977, the Clorox Company introduced the niche cleaner Soft Scrub. The product had a limited market for those looking for an occasional alternative to hard abrasives. Over time, cream cleaners became the largest segment of the household cleaner market. Now you can find niche cream products such as CeramaBryte Stovetop cleaner for specialty uses.

If you think of the overall market as a bell curve in which the largest market exists in the fat portion of the bell curve, the best niches exist on the fringes of the market. Think of the left fringe as low-cost options and the right edge as high-cost options. Figure 4-1 shows bell curves for the household cleaner market.

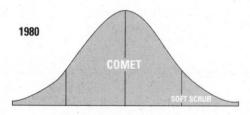

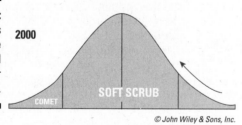

Figure 4-1: Bell curves for the household cleaner market.

© John Wiley & Sons, Inc.

At one time, dry cleaners like Comet held the bulk of the market. Soft Scrub entered the market as a liquid specialty cleaner on the right fringe of the market. Soft Scrub garnered customers who didn't want the harsh abrasive in a dry cleaner. Over time, the appeal of liquid cleaners versus dry cleaners grew, and Soft Scrub replaced Comet as the main portion of the market (the fat part of the bell curve). Comet was relegated to the least attractive portion of the market (the left fringe), appealing to cost-sensitive customers willing to use old-fashioned cleaners.

Both edges of the bell curve offer a variety of niches. Walmart found a niche on the left fringe by providing buyers in small towns a low-cost department store. Today, Walmart represents the fat part of the bell curve, and dollar stores have carved out a niche on the left fringe.

Generally, your business model should *not* attempt to enter a market in the fat portion of the bell curve. These established markets have strong, established players that are typically tough to beat at their own game. Instead, find a fringe to attack (shown in Figure 4-2). Most likely, the established players won't want to leave their large markets to mess with your little niche . . . yet.

Figure 4-2:
Entering the
market on
the fringes.

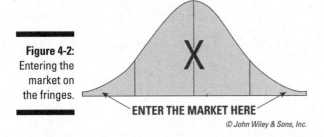

© John Wiley & Sons, Inc.

Niche markets aren't always logical

Creating a niche may be easier than you think. Take the iPad for example. The iPad should *not* have worked for lots of reasons:

- Tablet computers had been tried by dozens of companies, including Apple, without success.

- Smartphones do more than an iPad does.

- An iPad isn't quite a laptop and doesn't allow easy typing.

- Smartphones are portable; an iPad is much less portable.

- Isn't an iPad just a giant iPod?

One hundred million iPads later, all these reasons don't matter. Apple's secret with the iPad was niching the product differently than all the previously failed tablet computers. Previous tablets tried to be computers in tablet form. The iPad is *not* a personal computer — it's a giant iPod. The iPad does many things well, but being a PC isn't one of them. Apple was smart enough to see the unmet demand for unserved customers looking for fast-boot Internet, easy e-mail access, a screen big enough to read, enough portability to be acceptable, and a cool factor to create a brand-new niche.

In Jack Trout's classic marketing book, _The 22 Immutable Laws of Marketing_ (HarperBusiness), he says that your goal as a marketer is to create a Kleenex or Jell-O type brand. Kleenex is a tissue. Jell-O is gelatin. Xerox is a photocopier. These brands created new niches and dominated the niche to such an extent that the market renamed the category after the brand. This is the gold standard of niche creation.

Find unserved or underserved markets

The best way to create a good niche is to find an unserved or underserved market. All blockbuster products do this. To paraphrase Strategyn founder Tony Ulwick, "We don't buy products for their features and benefits; we buy them to help do specific jobs." No one bought a cellphone for what it was; people bought it for what it _did_ — made them feel safer and more productive while driving, for example. The underserved market for cellphones wasn't one for better phones; it was for the capability to communicate in situations where it was previously impossible.

What does _underserved_ mean? If the market was obviously underserved, an existing player in the market would fill the void. Some guesswork is involved in predicting what underserved means. You have to use your business judgment and then guess. Only the market knows what's needed, and the only way to find out is to take it to the market.

Sometimes it's easy to identify an underserved market. A fast-growing suburb needs gas stations, restaurants, and services in prime retail locations. Exponential growth in the use of smartphones creates users faster than the applications needed to serve them.

If you choose a niche in an easy-to-identify growth area, keep in mind that competitors can easily find this niche, too. Count on lots of competition.

Instead of going for the obvious niche, be willing to take some chances and pick a less obvious niche. If everyone is chasing mobile phone growth by writing iPhone and Android apps, take a chance on Microsoft apps. For smaller companies, having a less competitive niche can be far more advantageous than being a very small fish in the big pond.

How can you find these elusive unserved or underserved markets?

✔ **Personal experience:** Many great products and companies have been created by an entrepreneur's discontent with the status quo. Fred Smith wondered why letters couldn't be delivered overnight when he conceived FedEx. While traveling in Italy, Starbucks's Howard Schultz wondered why European-style cafes wouldn't work in America.

- ✔ **Friends and relatives:** If you aren't the cutting-edge type, look to friends who are. What products and services are they buying and why? What problems do they wish they could solve?

- ✔ **Research trends:** You don't need to catch a trend to find a great niche; however, catching a trend can make your niche much better because the growth is built-in.

- ✔ **Hired experts:** Professional business plan writers, business model consultants, futurists, or other gurus can help you find a niche.

- ✔ **Luck:** Popular website Angie's List was founded in 1995 when the Internet didn't exist for very many people. Angie's List was simply a monthly booklet sent to members with reviews of home contractors. Its popularity was concentrated in historic neighborhoods where repairs were frequent and expensive. Angie's List was a nice little business that never envisioned the tidal wave that would carry it to become the leader in its niche. When the Internet turned the Angie's List business model upside down, it also made it better. Instead of a localized printer of recommendation booklets, Angie's List became a social media powerhouse.

Checking Out Customer Attractiveness

You can create an attractive market niche (see the preceding section), but have it destroyed by bad customers. *Attractive customers* have a strong need for your offering, value the solution to their problem more than your product costs (that's a *strong value proposition*), have disposable income to spend on your offering, pay their bills on time, and exist in sufficient numbers to make your venture profitable.

Most business models have customers that are neither exceptionally attractive nor exceptionally unattractive. Most business models don't need to focus on customer attractiveness for long because the old mantra "all customers are good customers" is true most the time. However, you do have to study customer attractiveness.

The most prominent example of gaining the most attractive customer is the retail mantra "location, location, location." What does an outstanding retail location get you? Outstanding customers, that's what. A high-end retail mall has the same industry attractiveness and niche attractiveness regardless of where it's located. Whether the mall is located in the hottest new suburb or the middle of farmland, the industry and niche attractiveness remain the same. However, the high-income customers available in the hot new suburb are typically viewed as more attractive than those in rural locations.

Rent-A-Center is in the same industry as Best Buy. The two companies have some niche overlap, but they serve significantly different customers. Best Buy serves customers who can afford to purchase a television in full. These customers have either cash or pre-arranged financing like a credit card. Rent-A-Center caters to customers with lesser credit availability. Rent-A-Center extends credit to buyers deemed undesirable by traditional retailers like Best Buy. Rent-A-Center accepts monthly or weekly payments from customers until the item is paid in full. Due to the differences in the customer segments they serve, Rent-A-Center's business model is significantly different from Best Buy's:

✔ Best Buy serves a larger number of buyers who are more financially stable and makes money with a traditional retail business model — buying and selling merchandise.

✔ Rent-A-Center is closer to a specialty finance company that happens to sell appliances. Because Rent-A-Center doesn't collect payment in full upfront, the company has many profit areas that Best Buy doesn't have. Finance fees, high interest rates on loans, repossession fees, and more account for the bulk of Rent-A-Center's profit.

Many businesses would consider the customers of Rent-A-Center less than desirable. However, Rent-A-Center has created a profitable business model selling to these supposedly less-than-desirable customers. Because the Rent-A-Center model accounts for sporadic and occasional nonpayment, it's a workable business model.

More affluent customers don't make a market segment more attractive. Typically, more affluent customers can afford to pay a higher price for goods and services. High margin typically follows these higher prices, but may well be set off by higher overheads and lower volumes owing to a higher degree of exclusivity. Simply chasing affluent customers isn't always the best strategy. Remember the old adage, "Sell to the masses, live with the classes. Sell to the classes, live with the masses."

If you meet ten business owners in the construction industry, you'll probably meet someone whose business was destroyed by a slow-paying or nonpaying customer. A workable business model can be destroyed by the wrong customers.

As a businessperson, you must eliminate or account for bad customers in your business model.

Interestingly, you can have a customer niche within your customer niche. Your products are marketed to target a certain segment or niche. However, customers within any niche, no matter how tight, are widely varied. Coach bags fill a niche between the everyday bags you can find at JCPenney's and the high-end bags you can find in Paris. Within this niche you can find Louis Vuitton customers slumming it a bit and middle-class folks looking for a bit of everyday luxury.

The question you need to answer is which of the sub-segments the marketing is directed to. In the case of Coach bags, the marketing is clearly directed at the middle-class buyer looking for everyday luxury.

Starbucks attracts the most affluent and desired customers in the coffee industry. However, within Starbucks's niche are buyers who stretch themselves financially to buy a $5 latte and buyers who spend hundreds of dollars every month at Starbucks. The niche Starbucks markets to is customers who want Starbucks as a lifestyle choice rather than just a cup of coffee.

Finding Your Place on the Industry Value Chain

You want to find the best place on the industry value chain. Every firm involved in getting a product from initial creation to purchase and consumption by the end consumer adds value in the form of activities, incurs costs, and has a resulting margin. Some positions in this value chain offer a greater opportunity than others.

Different industries value the places on this value chain differently. For instance, clothing retailers enjoy a more profitable position on their value chain than the clothing manufacturers. In automobiles, retailers tend to make less than the manufacturers. In some industries, no desirable places on the value chain are available, making the overall market less attractive for your business.

Consider a cup of coffee. Several operators add value to your daily cup of joe. However, the market rewards some activities much more richly than others. If your business model is to be the most successful, you want to assume a position on the value chain that offers the best potential profits. Table 4-1 shows the value chain for coffee.

Coffee prices go up and down, but the principles involved don't change. At the time of writing, whole green Columbian coffee beans sell for $1.97 a pound. Assume the farmer has costs equal to about half that. The farmer's margin is 98.5 cents per pound of coffee. The roaster buys the coffee from the farmer for $1.97 a pound and transports it, roasts it, and grinds it. The cost of logistics and transportation is around 2 cents per pound. The roaster

Table 4-1	Value Chain for Coffee	
Firm	*Value Added*	*Key Activities*
Coffee bean grower	Operations	Farming
Shipper	Logistics	Transportation and logistics
Coffee roaster	Operations	Converting beans into drinkable coffee
Marketers (Folgers, Starbucks)	Sales	Branding, sales, customer service
Retailer	Sales	Merchandising

then sells it to a coffee service, consumer products company, or retail outlet. Unbranded wholesale coffee sells for around $5 per pound. If the coffee roaster's cost of operations is about half the $3.03 per pound value added, then the coffee roaster makes a margin of around $1.51. If the coffee is branded (Starbucks, Folgers, Seattle's Best), add a dollar or two to the value added. Note that almost all the value added by branding drops to profit/margin. Finally, a company like Starbucks, Folgers, Kroger, or a coffee service delivers the coffee to the consumer. Folgers coffee sells for a $9.99 a pound (Starbucks $13.95 per pound). Therefore, the retail seller of Folgers has added about $4 of value (mostly margin). This comprises the entire value chain for a one-pound bag of coffee.

Table 4-2 shows the value added by each function and the approximate margin. Note that the marketing and sales related functions are much more handsomely rewarded than the functions that make the product.

Table 4-2	Value Added for Coffee		
Firm	*Cost Added per Pound*	*Margin Earned per Pound*	*Total Value Added*
Coffee bean grower	$0.985	$0.985	$1.97
Shipper	$0.015	$0.005	$.02
Coffee roaster	$1.52	$1.51	$3.03
Marketers (Folgers, Starbucks)	$0	$2	$2
Retailer	$2	$2	$4

Some places on the coffee value chain are much more profitable than others. To maximize the effectiveness of your business model, find the most profitable portion of the value chain. Usually, the closer you are to the end user or consumer, the greater the opportunity for margin. Don't misconstrue this statement. The best business models may not be retail models. But as manufacturing has shifted to low-wage countries, the value add for manufacturing and related activities has gone down dramatically. As the capability to add value for manufacturing has decreased, the capability to add value through sales, distribution, and branding has increased. This shift has provided opportunities for savvy entrepreneurs.

Savvy entrepreneurs have also created new positions on the value chain to carve value away from existing players. For example, in the field of law, several new players have emerged to carve out a portion of the value chain traditionally owned by lawyers. Law firms in India specialize in large-scale complex research only. Some firms audit bills from law firms in an attempt to save their clients money. Both of these industries used to be part of the law firm value chain.

Ironically, there seems to be very little correlation between the amount of work or the difficulty of work and the amount of value added in the value chain. As you can see from the coffee example, the hardest work is done by the farmer. The farmer takes the risk of bad weather, has the highest number of employees, and puts in the most hours proportionately. However, the farmer makes the least amount of money on the value chain.

Certain portions of the value chain tend to add more value than others. Note that value added is the difference between sales price and cost. An item may have a large percentage of the total sales price to the end consumer, but add little value on the chain.

Chapter 5

Considering a Franchise

In This Chapter

▶ Figuring out what a franchise is

▶ Learning the types of franchises

▶ Finding out about franchise relationships

▶ Going through the pros and cons of franchising

Franchising is the engine that drives much of the world's entrepreneurial train. Today, you can't drive down any major street anywhere in the world and not pass by businesses that are part of a franchise network, and those businesses can be in any of more than 120 distinct lines of business. This chapter looks at franchising, not by looking at any particular franchise but by looking at how well you may fit in as a franchisee or maybe as a franchisor. It explores what franchising is and what the franchise relationship is all about. It also introduces you to different types of franchising and examines the pros and cons to help you make an informed decision.

So What Is a Franchise, Anyway?

Franchising is a system for expanding a business and distributing goods and services — and an opportunity for you to operate a business under a recognized brand name. It's also a relationship between the brand owner and the local operator. For example, Wendy's doesn't franchise hamburgers, and Midas doesn't franchise car mufflers. They franchise *business systems* that provide hamburgers and mufflers to customers — with consistent delivery of products, services, and customer experience.

A franchise occurs when a business (the *franchisor*) licenses its trade name (the brand, such as Wendy's or Midas) and its operating methods (its system of doing business) to a person or group (the *franchisee*) who agrees to operate according to the terms of a contract (the *franchise agreement*).

The franchisor provides the franchisee with support and, in some cases, it exercises some control over the way the franchisee operates under the brand.

In exchange, the franchisee usually pays the franchisor an initial fee (called a *franchise fee*) and a continuing fee (known as a *royalty*) for the use of the trade name and operating methods.

The effects of franchising on modern business

Consumers everywhere love the consistency that comes from shopping in a franchised business. From the cleanliness of the rooms at a Courtyard by Marriott to the fun children have at a Pump It Up, people know what they will get when they purchase under a franchisor's brand. The number of industries bringing goods and services to customers through franchising is growing, limited only by the imagination of the businesspeople who are beginning to understand the potential of this ancient method of distribution. Franchising creates opportunities for business ownership and personal wealth — both part of the foundation for the growth of peace and democracies.

What most people don't realize is the sheer size and impact franchising has on the economy in the United States. Franchising generates nearly 14 percent of private sector employment. Indeed, in the gambling capital of the world, Nevada, 20 percent of its private sector workforce is employed because of franchising. More than 760,000 franchised businesses exist in the United States, generating a total economic output of more than one and a half trillion dollars, or nearly 10 percent of the U.S. private sector economy.

The success of franchising for business owners

For years, the International Franchise Association (IFA) kept statistics on the success of franchising. However, many of the studies that those widely published statistics were based on, including those claiming that franchisees have a success rate of 95 percent versus a failure rate of 85 percent for nonfranchised startups in their first five years in business, turned out to be inaccurate and usually misleading. The IFA no longer publishes those statistics and has asked its member companies to not refer to them any longer. You should be wary of any franchisor that still uses these claims of franchise industry success statistics.

What's the Deal with Brands in Franchising?

Brand is the franchise system's most valuable asset. Consumers decide what and whether to buy at a particular location based on what they know, or think that they know, about the brand. Unless they have a relationship with the local franchisee, they probably don't give any thought to who owns the business. In their minds, they're shopping at a branch of a chain.

In the consumer's mind, brand equals the company's reputation — the experience they expect to get. Franchisors spend a lot of time, energy, and money developing their brands so that consumers know what to expect before they even come in the door. A good brand communicates a message to the customer. When you see an advertisement for a Wendy's hamburger, you immediately associate it with your experience of ordering and eating a Wendy's hamburger. You may think of a "Cheddar Lovers Bacon Cheeseburger," or maybe a baked potato or the freshness of the product. Maybe you think that the line moves just a bit faster, that the service is better, or the staff is friendlier. You may remember seeing the redheaded girl in that last commercial or think back to when Dave Thomas appeared in the ads. The experience of visiting a Wendy's, supported by the message in its advertising, communicates to the public just what Wendy's *is*. You can visualize and almost taste the experience.

The same can be said for other companies, such as Meineke. When you see an ad for the brake services that Meineke offers, you can almost feel your car stopping safely at the light. That's the power of a brand.

Brand recognition is part of what a franchisee hopes to get when purchasing a franchise. A good brand is immediately familiar in consumers' minds. With a well-known brand, you don't have to build brand awareness in your market. The franchisor and the other franchisees have taken care of that for you. This is one of the major advantages of investing in a larger, well-established franchise system. Smaller systems with limited brand recognition can't deliver that until you help them grow.

Ongoing advertising and marketing programs help ensure that the brand remains strong and growing. And if the franchise system is successful in making the brand mean something positive to the consumer, that success means possible increased sales for you.

Brands are not born fully grown. Almost every startup franchisor begins with some local brand recognition (it may be only a neighborhood) and has to grow that brand to achieve regional or national status.

A company can provide the best dry cleaning in town, have a system for one-hour service, be loved by its customers, and yet only be known locally. For startup franchisors with limited brand recognition outside their home market, that's an issue. Franchisees in markets where the franchisor's brand has little or no consumer recognition use advertising and promotions provided by the franchisor to build brand recognition in their market. Those franchisees that must build brand recognition need to spend more on advertising and promotion and may require a different message than franchisees who enter a market in which the franchisor's brand is well known.

The Two Types of Franchises

Two types of franchises exist:

- ✔ Product distribution franchises
- ✔ Business format franchises

In *product distribution franchising,* the most important part is the product the franchisor manufactures. The products sold by a product distribution franchisee usually require some presale preparation by the franchisee before they are sold (such as you find with Coca-Cola, where the franchisee manufacturers and bottles the soda) or some additional postsale servicing (such as you find at a Ford dealer with your periodic maintenance programs). But the major difference between the two types of franchising is that in the product distribution variety, the franchisor may license its trademark and logo to its franchisees, but it typically does *not* provide them with an entire system for running their businesses. Providing a business system is the hallmark of *business format franchising.*

Product distribution franchises represent the largest percentage of total retail sales coming from all franchises, but the majority of franchises available today are business format opportunities. More than 80 percent of the franchised businesses in the United States are the business format type.

Because most franchisees buy a business format franchise, that's the type of franchise this chapter focuses on. However, you will get a glimpse into the world of product distribution franchises in the following section.

Product distribution franchises

In a product distribution franchise, the franchisee typically sells products that are manufactured by their franchisor. The industries where you most often find product distribution franchising are soft drinks, automobiles and trucks, mobile homes, automobile accessories, and gasoline. For example, Coca-Cola, Goodyear Tires, Ford Motor Company, and John Deere distributors are all product distribution franchises.

Product distribution franchises look a lot like what are called supplier-dealer relationships — and they are. The difference between a product distribution franchise and a supplier-dealer is in the degree of the relationship. In a product distribution franchise, the franchisee may handle the franchisor's products on an exclusive or semi-exclusive basis, as opposed to a supplier-dealer who may handle several products — even competing ones. With the growth in auto dealerships that sell multiple brands, this distinction is getting a bit clouded. The franchisee in a product distribution franchise, though, is closely associated with the company's brand name and receives more services from its franchisor than a dealer would from its supplier. Supplier-dealer relationships often exist in business opportunities relationships (which are covered in the following section).

Business format franchises

The business format franchisee gets to use the parent company's trade name and logo just as the product distribution franchisee does, but more importantly, it gets the complete system for delivering the product or service and for doing business. It's this system that produces consistency — and consistency is a franchise's foundation for success. Wendy's, Pump It Up, Dunkin Donuts, Wing Zone, and HouseWall are all great business format franchises. Even ExxonMobil has a business format franchise: Its franchisees have convenience stores called On the Run. The business structure offers a detailed plan that explains how to do almost everything from the ground up. A franchisee is trained to manage the construction of the building, order the right equipment, and even hang the signs.

The confidential operating and procedures manuals (the how-to guides of every great franchise) generally give such specific information as how to market and advertise; open the front door; recruit, hire, train, and dress the staff; and greet customers. To ensure quality and consistency, most franchisors provide business-specific information in the manuals on how and where to order inventory, how to prepare products, and how to present them to customers. The franchisor sometimes even includes procedures for taking out the garbage, turning out the lights, and closing up at night. All these components are part of a business format franchise's unique system. And in a good system, the franchisor prepares and then supports the franchisee to ensure that when you shop in one of their locations, you get the same brand experience each and every time.

Conversion franchising

Although not truly a third type of franchising, *conversion franchising* is a modification of the standard franchise relationships. In conversion franchising, an independent operator in the same business as the franchisor adopts the franchisor's service marks or trademarks, and its system. In many cases, the new franchisee, who is likely an experienced operator, is reluctant to make all the changes or conversions required to make it identical to all other locations in the system, and the franchisor may not be able to require those changes. However, the franchisee adopts the system's service marks or trademarks, advertising programs, buying relationships, training, and the critical customer service standards. Examples of industries that have used conversion franchising extensively are real-estate brokers, florists, and the trades (home remodeling, plumbing, electricians, and so on).

Each franchise system is different, each franchisor does not prescribe identical levels of controls, and each does not strive for the same level of consistency. But most franchisors do have standards that define the minimum levels of service and operations required from the franchisee. Every location — whether it's owned by a franchisor or a franchisee — no matter where it is in the world, should look and feel the same; in restaurants, the food should taste the same. Ever wonder why every Courtyard by Marriott always has a coffeepot in the room and a bar of soap and bottle of shampoo in the bathroom? It's one of the brand requirements set by the franchisor. In other words, with some minor variations and even if the menu is a bit different in different areas of the country or the world, your experience at every location should be the same. Every well-managed franchise system strives to achieve a high degree of consistency so that the buying public knows what they will get just by looking at the brand.

The Roles and Goals of Franchisors and Franchisees

The owner of a franchising company — the entity that grants the franchisee the right to operate the business under the franchise system's trademarks and service marks — is called a *franchisor*. The *franchisee* is the person or entity that becomes the licensee of the franchisor. The franchisee runs the day-to-day business using the franchisor's brand and the franchisor's system of doing business. This section lays out both sides of the coin

for you; however, because you are likely looking to buy into an already
established franchise, the focus is mostly on the franchisee's point of view.

Looking at the world through franchisor lenses

Franchisors may be companies founded by individuals with a great deal of
experience (such as Dave Thomas) or by individuals with little or no experience and who are just concluding an arrangement with the company's first
franchisee. Consider the following points regarding franchise sizes and franchisor levels of experience:

- ✔ Often, the owners are large public or private companies with their
  founders still at the helm, such as John Schnatter of Papa John's.

- ✔ Sometimes, the franchisors are former franchisees who bought the
  companies from the founders (as Tom McDonnell did with U-Save Auto
  Rental, Jack Hollis did with Computer Renaissance, and Abe Gustin did
  with Applebee's before it went public).

- ✔ Sometimes, the franchisors are huge conglomerates (such as Yum,
  which owns Pizza Hut, Taco Bell, KFC, A&W, and Long John Silvers and
  operates restaurants all over the world).

- ✔ Sometimes, the franchisors are small and relatively new to offering franchises (such as Save It Now, Firehouse Subs, or Oogles n Googles).

- ✔ Sometimes, the franchise system is large but seems almost brand new
  (such as Quiznos or Panera Bread Company).

A good franchisor gives its new franchisees the system and training they
need to run their business without having to figure out everything on their
own. The franchisor has already made most, if not all, of the mistakes.
Franchisees get the benefit of the franchisor's experience, so they can take
a shortcut through the minefields that startup businesses usually face. The
franchisee purchases the right to use the franchisor's expertise, brand name,
experience, methods, and initial and ongoing support.

Businesses don't usually fail because their products or services are of low
quality — they usually fail because the owners aren't prepared and make
mistakes from which they can't recover. Great franchisors have already made
the mistakes — and survived. Their survival is the basis for the road map
they provide, and that map is part of what franchisees pay for when they buy
a franchise.

Franchisors aren't providing all this assistance out of the kindness of their hearts. The franchisor wants the whole system to grow, prosper, and turn profits. So the goal of a great franchisor is to provide a great system. If it does, the franchisees make money, stay in business, expand, and pay fees. And the franchisor's brand value grows as more people shop at their branded outlets and more people want to become franchisees. The franchisor is relying on the franchisee to manage the local business well so that each location will contribute to the entire system's success.

The franchisee's end of the bargain

You need to understand the following distinction: When you buy a franchise, you don't own the business. You own the rights to do business using the franchisor's trademark, brand name, product or service, and operating methods. What you typically own are the physical assets, the land, and the building and equipment, but not the brand or systems. In many systems, in fact, the franchisor may even have the right to buy the assets you do own if the relationship ends. Doesn't sound like much of a deal? Here's what you do get when you join a well-established franchise system:

- ✔ A proven and successful way of doing business

- ✔ A nationally known brand name

- ✔ A complete training program with advanced training and updates

- ✔ Research and development into new products and services

- ✔ Professionally designed local, regional, and national advertising and marketing programs

- ✔ Often a chance to own more than one franchise

- ✔ A shortcut around the common mistakes of startup businesses

- ✔ Frequently a buying cooperative or negotiated lower costs from suppliers for many of the things you need to run and operate the business (ingredients, advertising, insurance, supplies, and so on)

- ✔ Your fellow franchisees as a network of peer advisors

- ✔ Thorough and ongoing field and headquarters support

- ✔ Often, a protected market or territory

Franchisors often give their franchisees an area around their location in which no other company-owned or franchisee-owned location is allowed to operate. This is called a *protected market* or *protected territory*. Protected territories may be defined by the following:

✔ A radius or area around the franchisee's location

✔ A number of households or businesses in an area

✔ A number of people who live in an area

✔ Zip codes

✔ Boundaries using highways and streets

✔ Any method that defines the area in which no other same-branded location may be established

If the territory is too large, the total market won't contain enough locations to achieve brand recognition. If it's too small, or other locations are too close, there may not be enough customers to support the business. The goal in a good franchise system is to establish the right number of units in the right locations to ensure that consumers see the brand frequently, which is known as *brand penetration*. When too many units are close by, and that proximity negatively affects unit sales, it's called *encroachment*.

Not all territorial rights are permanent, and the franchisor may only be providing you with those rights for a limited period of time. You may also have to reach certain levels of performance to keep those rights. Also, when a franchisor provides you with a radius around your location, your radius and another franchisee's radius may and usually will overlap. The franchisor will not, however, establish another location within your protected area. Make sure you read and understand your contract, and consult with a lawyer to make certain that you do.

Franchise Relationships

Franchising is an ideal way for individuals, investor groups, and business entities to become business owners because of the variety of opportunities. The number of franchisors, the variety of types of industries represented in franchising, and the range of investments available create opportunities for the smallest single-unit mom-and-pop operator to the large multimillion-dollar investor group looking to add a franchise investment to its portfolio.

Flying solo: Single-unit franchises

A *single-unit* or *direct-unit franchise* is just what it says it is. A franchisee obtains the rights from a franchise system to operate one franchise. This franchise relationship is the simplest form.

Most franchise systems have grown, one franchise at a time, over the years. Owning one franchise is the classic and, until recently, the most common type of relationship in franchising. As people looked for a way to get to their dream of independence through business ownership, franchising became their vehicle. In a single-unit franchise, the franchisee generally supervises the business.

While a single-unit franchise is the classic method for franchise system growth, it does have some weaknesses for franchisors:

✔ Franchisors generally experience slower growth, and the growth can be more costly on a unit basis because they have to locate a new franchisee for each location.

✔ The franchisor has more franchisees to work with, and those franchisees may be less sophisticated and more wary of taking business risks than larger, multi-unit franchisees.

✔ Because an individual owns and operates each location, servicing a franchise system dominated by single-unit franchisees tends to be more expensive for the franchisor than if the same franchisee owned and operated multiple locations.

Growing a family, one franchise at a time

More and more often, as the classic single-unit franchisees prosper, they acquire another franchise from the same franchisor. They know their franchisor, have established a relationship with the franchise system, and can predict what they can earn from investing in additional units. Because they already know how to operate the business, the initial training they took when they opened their first location may not be necessary, and some of the key employees they have in their first location may be perfect to become managers in their second and third locations.

Acquiring additional franchises is a terrific way to grow, because the franchisees' knowledge of the business and the franchise system makes their risk lower than when they made their initial franchise decision.

Except for the added burden — or, possibly, joy — of operating additional locations, the franchise relationship between the franchisor and franchisee is substantially the same. A franchisee that acquires one location at a time is a bit different than the franchisee that planned to operate multiple locations from the beginning (which is described in the next section). Generally, a franchisee that added units one at a time doesn't receive any reduction in fees and often has to share a market with other franchisees. The franchisee simply has multiple single-unit agreements. With more units and more money invested in the franchise system, a single-unit franchisee that establishes additional franchises tends to be noticed more often than a single-unit operator would by the franchisor and its staff. The franchisor is hoping that the franchisee will continue to grow and grow and grow.

Franchisors periodically update their franchise agreements. The franchisor may modify some of the fees, require additional equipment or investment in new technology, change some of the obligations between the parties, or make other significant and often material changes. Franchisees who acquire additional franchises over time are likely to find variations between their original contract with the franchisor for the first unit and the new franchise agreement for later units. Additionally, many franchise agreements provide for what is called a *cross-default*. This provision allows the franchisor to consider a violation of one of the agreements to be a violation of all the agreements. As with all franchise agreements, you should have a franchise attorney review the franchise agreement and other documents provided to you by your franchisor.

Multi-unit or area developers

A *multi-unit* or *area development agreement* is a relationship that grants a franchisee the right and the obligation to open more than one location. It differs from a multiple single-unit relationship primarily because the multi-unit franchisee agrees up front to open a specific number of locations during a defined period of time and usually within a specified area.

For example, say you want to open ten haircutting shops in your town. You can go to the franchisor and buy one franchise at a time (see the preceding section), but you have certain risks:

- ✔ You may have to share the market with other franchisees from the system.

- ✔ The franchisor may have sold all the other available franchises for your market before you were ready to invest in them.

- ✔ Other franchisees that came after you may already have opened in the best locations.

To avoid these risks, you can enter into a multi-unit or area development agreement. This agreement means that you agree to open and operate the ten units over a defined period — say, five years — and the franchisor grants you exclusive rights for the development of locations in your area.

Make sure your development agreement gives you *market exclusivity,* which ensures that you're the only one using your brand looking for locations in your area. In some franchise systems, a development agreement may not grant you exclusivity, and that can cause real trouble down the road.

When you go this route, you typically pay the franchisor a fee for the development rights and sign an area development or multi-unit development agreement obligating you to open the ten locations during the five years (in following with the hair-salon example). The opening dates are usually specified, and you may have staggered dates, such as January 1, July 1, and so on, to open each location.

Regarding the fee you pay for the development rights, nothing is typical; it varies from company to company. As you identify each location, you will usually sign a single-unit franchise agreement. What you pay and how the franchisor applies the fee will vary, depending on the agreement:

✔ You may pay a full, initial franchise fee for the new location.

✔ The initial franchise fee for the new location may be a reduced fee from the franchisor's standard fee.

✔ Your franchisor may have a different royalty fee for multi-unit developers than it has for single-unit operators.

✔ A portion of the fee you paid for the development rights may be credited to the initial franchise fee you owe for each location.

Each franchise system is different. As with every contract you sign, you need to review the agreements with your lawyer.

This type of relationship usually has significant advantages for both the franchisor and the multi-unit franchisee, including but not limited to the following:

✔ Because each multi-unit franchisee is opening more than one location, the cost of acquiring a franchisee on a per-unit basis is lower.

✔ Because fewer franchisees exist, the cost of serving a multi-unit franchisee is generally lower on a per-unit basis.

✔ A multi-unit franchisee is obligated to grow the market, and controlled growth leads to better planning for advertising and better leveraging when negotiating with suppliers and other vendors.

✔ The area developer franchisee can often control the market he is in, so coordination of local advertising and promotions is easier than having to work with all the other franchisees.

✔ The franchisee often can shift personnel from one location to another depending on where the staff is needed.

✔ If the franchises are in a food industry, they can often combine some of the preparation of products into a central commissary or kitchen.

✔ The franchise may save on freight and other costs by buying in greater quantities at a lower cost and storing its inventory into a centralized warehouse.

Why have two agreements — an area development agreement and a franchise agreement? Because they serve two different purposes. Simply put, the area development agreement gives you the right and the obligation to open all of those units and obligates the franchisor to allow you to complete your development schedule. The franchise agreement gives you the right to operate each location as a franchise of the system.

Keep in mind, though, that if you fail to meet the development schedule, the franchisor typically has the right to cancel the development agreement and keep the area development fee. So make sure that the market you select can handle the number of locations you've committed to opening and that you have the financial backing to live up to the agreement if the first store gets off to a slower start than anticipated.

Playing in the big leagues: Master franchising

A *master franchise relationship* is similar to an area development agreement, with one significant variation: The master franchisee, in addition to having the right and obligation to open and operate a number of locations in a defined area, also has the right — and sometimes the obligation — to offer and sell franchises to other people looking to become franchisees of the system. You become sort of a franchisor to those people who buy franchises through your master franchise.

As a master franchisee, you will probably be required to own and operate at least one or two locations yourself. After you open those locations, you can then sell the rights to open additional locations to other franchisees — often called *subfranchisees* — who want to open and operate your franchise in your market.

When you sign the master franchise agreement, you pay a *master franchise fee.* Your subfranchisees then pay a franchise fee and a royalty, both of which you typically share with the franchisor. The percentage of each that you share with the franchisor varies widely depending on the system and the type of master relationship you enter into.

The master franchise relationship comes in several variations:

- ✔ The subfranchisee may execute a franchise agreement directly with the franchisor or with you as the master franchisee.

- ✔ The franchisor may have the right to approve the new subfranchisee, or you may hold that right.

- ✔ The subfranchisee may receive training and continuing support from the franchisor, the master franchisee, or a combination of both.

- ✔ The subfranchisee may pay fees directly to you, to the franchisor, or to a combination of both.

Every master franchise relationship may have variations from others, and again, you should enlist the help of a qualified franchise attorney.

Of all the types of franchising relationships, the master franchise or subfranchise relationship is the most complex for all the parties: the franchisor, the master franchisee, and the subfranchisee.

The hired gun: Area representatives

The role of an *area representative* in a franchise system is fairly unique. This person is the commissioned franchise salesperson and also the commissioned field support person for the franchisor in a geographic area. For each franchise the area rep sells, the franchisor pays the rep a commission, usually based on a percentage of the franchise fee paid to the franchisor, and then the rep provides opening and continuing support to the franchisees, earning a percentage of the royalty paid to the franchisor. Just like a master franchisee, the area representative pays the franchisor a market development fee for the opportunity of developing and servicing a specific minimum number of units, during a specified time period in a defined territory. The difference between the two relationships is that the master franchisee signs an agreement with his subfranchisee, whereas the area representative doesn't enter into a contractual relationship with the franchisees. Those franchisees sign their agreement with the franchisors as in the normal single- and multi-unit development agreements.

Pros and Cons of Franchising

For many years, the U.S. Department of Commerce, the Small Business Administration, franchisors, the trade press, and the franchise associations fueled the perception that franchising was a surefire method of expansion for business and a safe investment for franchisees. Although a well-designed franchise program can be an exceptional method of expansion, poorly designed and cookie-cutter franchise systems or businesses that are not well managed are not. This isn't just a franchise reality — it's a business reality.

Before you consider whether you're cut out to become a franchisee, you need to understand some of the advantages and disadvantages of franchise ownership.

Advantages of franchise ownership

Your chance of success in franchising can only be as strong as the franchise you select. Mature, well-operated franchise systems generally possess the following traits.

Overall competitive benefits

The public has become accustomed to a certain level of quality and consistency from branded locations. A *branded location* is a business that the public thinks of as a chain because each location has the same name, decor, products, services, menu items, and so on, and the customer experience is the same regardless of the location. Whether a company's product is superior or mediocre, if its locations are successful, the secret for its success will likely be in its consistency.

One of the secrets of being a good businessperson is not accepting a poll of one: Just because you find a product or service outstanding or mediocre doesn't mean the rest of the world does.

Regardless of where they are, consumers believe they understand the level of quality they will receive when they shop at a branded location. Because of this perception about branded chains, new franchisees often have an established customer base on the day they open. Branding enables franchises to compete with the well-established, independent operators and even against other franchised and nonfranchised chains. The advantage of brand recognition also extends to national accounts. Companies look at a system that has a network of locations and trust that each will operate at the same level of consistency and commitment. That type of system can service their needs wherever the franchise has a location.

Pre-opening benefits

Although the cost of entrance into a franchise system includes a franchise fee, which is often cited as a disadvantage, the franchisee benefits from the franchisor's having tested operating systems, initial and advanced training for management and staff, operations manuals, marketing and advertising programs, site-selection tools, store design, construction programs, the reduced cost of equipment, and the other necessary support required to successfully launch their business. Additionally, franchisees can ask their franchisor — a seasoned partner — questions, and they have a network of other franchisees in the system who can also be of assistance.

Ongoing benefits

Franchisees benefit from the home-office and field-consulting assistance most franchisors provide. Franchisees enjoy the purchasing power that comes from joining with others, which often results in a reduced cost of goods. They benefit from professionally designed point-of-sale marketing material, advertising, grand-opening programs, and other marketing materials that independents could never afford. Franchise systems can also afford to modernize through ongoing research and development and by test marketing new products and operating systems.

Each franchisee's spending power is combined with the spending power of all the other franchisees in the local market and in the rest of the system. This combined spending power — on advertising, for example — coupled with targeted strategic growth can result in market critical mass. Establishing critical mass enables franchise systems to not only dominate local markets and the established independents but also to compete effectively against large, established chains.

Disadvantages for franchisees

Franchising is not right for every person, and you need to understand some of the disadvantages in a franchise relationship:

- **Loss of independence:** For some people, one of the most serious disadvantages of becoming a franchisee is loss of independence. If you want to make all your own decisions, franchising may be the wrong choice. Franchise systems are structured in such a way that the franchisor sets many of the rules; the franchisee is required to operate the business according to the franchisor's manuals and procedures.

- **Over-dependence on the system:** Loss of independence, if taken to extremes, leads to a further disadvantage: over-dependence on the franchise system. Franchising succeeds when financial and emotional risks motivate franchisees. When franchisees rely totally on the system for their success, their over-dependence can cause problems. Franchisees have to balance system restrictions with their personal ability to manage their own businesses. For example, when a franchisee depends on national advertising exclusively and doesn't invest in local marketing, she's shortchanging her business by relying too greatly on what the franchisor is bringing to the party.

✔ **Other franchisees that are "bad apples":** The principal reason for the success of franchising is the public's perception of quality and consistency throughout the system. When the public receives great service at one location, the assumption is that the system has great service. This consumer expectation is also one of the potential major frailties of any chain, including franchising. Franchisees are not only judged by their performance, but they are also judged by the performance of other franchisees. Poorly performing fellow franchisees or company-owned locations damage a franchisee's business even where they do not share the same market. If the hotel room is dirty in one location or, even worse, if the press were to report that the hotel had rodents, the public assumes the problem exists throughout the system.

✔ **Income expectations:** Although good franchisors try to prevent it, some franchisees have unrealistic expectations about the income they are going to earn. If their expectations are unrealistic, they will regret their investment in dollars, time, and effort and may become a negative influence on the system. Having realistic expectations is important to any investment decision.

✔ **Franchising inelasticity:** Franchise systems are bound together through legal agreements between franchisors and franchisees. Often, these agreements contain restrictions that potentially impact the franchisor's ability to make strategic decisions. For example, if a nonfranchisor finds a perfect location for a new store, it is free to do so. In a franchise system, the franchisor must first look to the legal agreements between itself and the franchisees in the market. If the franchisor has granted the franchisees protected territories, and the potential location is in one of those territories, the franchise system loses that market opportunity — often to a competitor who does not have the same restrictions. A similar situation can arise with e-commerce sales over the World Wide Web if the franchisor has provided the franchisee with those rights in the agreement.

Because of the potential loss of market opportunities, many franchisors are reducing the size of the territory they are granting franchising today, and others are granting exclusivity for a short period of time or eliminating protected territories altogether. In the long run, having a market fully developed is a benefit to the franchisee and the franchisor, although it may have an impact on a particular unit's sales.

The restrictions of franchising can be a double-edged sword — they can make franchising successful but can also be disadvantages to some franchisees. The restrictions may be on the product and services they are allowed to offer; limitations on size and exclusivity of their territory; the possibility of termination for failure to follow the system; the added investment often required for reimaging, remodeling, or new equipment as a condition of renewal; the cost of transfer and renewal; and restrictions on independent marketing. Also, the added costs for royalties, advertising, additional training, and other services potentially reduce a franchisee's earnings.

There are special rules relating to how certain franchise costs are written off for tax purposes. There are also special rules relating to leasehold improvement. Tax treatment depends on the agreements and circumstances, but a franchisee should not automatically assume that the total upfront franchise costs will be totally deductible in the first year. More than likely some costs will be written off over several years. Be sure to consult an accountant or a tax attorney with a lot of experience in what is tax deductible for your franchise.

Book II
Planning for Your Business

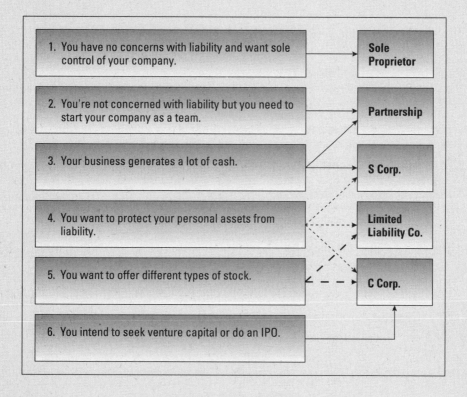

1. You have no concerns with liability and want sole control of your company.	**Sole Proprietor**
2. You're not concerned with liability but you need to start your company as a team.	**Partnership**
3. Your business generates a lot of cash.	**S Corp.**
4. You want to protect your personal assets from liability.	**Limited Liability Co.**
5. You want to offer different types of stock.	**C Corp.**
6. You intend to seek venture capital or do an IPO.	

When you think you have your business plan all done and ready, head over to www.dummies.com/extras/startingabusinessaio for a list of last-minute questions you need to ask yourself.

Contents at a Glance

Chapter 1: Writing a Business Plan 99

Selling Yourself on the Importance of Planning 99
The Anatomy of a Business Plan 101
Understanding Your Starting Position 104
Setting Out Your Planning Objectives 106
Identifying Target Audiences and Key Messages 107
Establishing Your Plan's Time Frame 109
Preparing for the Real World 111

Chapter 2: Finding the Funding 115

Starting with a Plan 116
Tapping Friends, Family, and Lovers 119
Finding an Angel 120
Daring to Use Venture Capital 122
Selling Stock to the Public: An IPO 126
Finding Other Ways to Finance Growth 130
Guarding Your Interests 132

Chapter 3: Setting Your Franchise's Wheels in Motion 135

Surveying Your Options for Locale 135
Setting Up Shop: Finding Your Franchise's Habitat 141
Avoiding Encroachment 145
Securing Your Space After Finding Your Piece of Heaven 147
Getting the Goods: Merchandise and Supplies 149
Receiving Merchandise 154
Maintaining Inventory 156
Getting Good Training Before and After You Open Your Franchise 159

Chapter 4: Starting a Home-Based Business 163

Looking at the Basics of Home-Based Business 164
Examining the Good News and the Bad 169
Taking the Home-Based Business Quiz 172
Starting Something from Scratch 174
Transitioning into Your Home-Based Business 178

Chapter 5: Creating a Website for Your Business 191

Feng Shui-ing Your Website 192
Creating Content That Attracts Customers 195
Nip and Tuck: Establishing a Visual Identity 206
Inviting Comments from Customers 214
Moving from Website to Web Presence 219

Chapter 6: Starting with the Right Legal Structure 221

Deciding on the Best Legal Form for Your Business 222
Going It Alone: The Sole Proprietorship 224
Choosing a Partner: The Partnership 226
Going for the Gold: The Corporation 228
Looking for Flexibility: The S Corporation, the LLC,
    and the Nonprofit Corporation 231
Benchmarking Your Best Choice 234

Chapter 1

Writing a Business Plan

In This Chapter

▶ Recognizing the value of a business plan

▶ Understanding what goes into a plan

▶ Creating a map for your business

▶ Getting your message to your plan's audience

▶ Setting your business time frame and milestones

*T*he fact that you're reading this chapter means the task of writing a business plan has made it onto your to-do list. That's a big step in the right direction. Now come the questions. What exactly is business planning? What should it include? Where do you start the process of writing your business plan?

This chapter should confirm your hunch that business planning is essential — when you start your business and at every growth stage along the way. It helps you think about the audience for your plan, what its key components should be, and roughly how long you'll need to put it together.

Writing a business plan is not exactly a breeze. It takes time and thought. This chapter provides a quick and easy overview to get you oriented and on your way to business-planning success.

Selling Yourself on the Importance of Planning

Nearly all business experts agree on one thing: the importance of drafting a business plan. Yet plenty of companies plunge into the competitive arena without a formal plan. Why? Plenty of excuses have posed as reasons. A lot of new businesses are carried away and figure their passion and optimism are enough to build a successful company. Others say they were just too busy to develop a formal business plan. But operating without a plan can prove even more time-consuming in the long run. This section aims to clarify in plain English the importance of having a business plan.

Tallying up the benefits of having a plan

The time you invest in your business plan will pay off many times over. Here are some of the most obvious benefits you can gain from business planning:

- An opportunity to test out a new idea to see if it holds real promise of success
- A clear statement of your business mission and vision
- A set of values that can help you steer your business through times of trouble
- A blueprint you can use to focus your energy and keep your company on track
- Benchmarks you can use to track your performance and make midcourse corrections
- A clear-eyed analysis of your industry, including opportunities and threats
- A portrait of your potential customers and their buying behaviors
- A rundown of your major competitors and your strategies for facing them
- An honest assessment of your company's strengths and weaknesses
- A roadmap and timetable for achieving your goals and objectives
- A description of the products and services you offer
- An explanation of your marketing strategies
- An analysis of your revenues, costs, and projected profits
- A description of your *business model,* or how you plan to make money and stay in business (see Book I Chapter 3 for more on business models)
- An action plan that anticipates potential detours or hurdles you may encounter
- A handbook for new employees describing who you are and what your company is all about
- A résumé you can use to introduce your business to suppliers, vendors, lenders, and others

Knowing what can go wrong without a plan

The many benefits of having a business plan should be enough to convince you. But in case you're still wavering, consider what can go wrong if you don't take time to plan. Here's what you risk:

✔ Running out of cash before you open your doors because you haven't anticipated your startup costs

✔ Missing sales projections because you don't really know who your customers are or what they want

✔ Losing customers because your quality or service falls short

✔ Becoming overwhelmed by too many options because you never took the time to focus on a mission and vision for your company

✔ Going bankrupt because you don't have a rational business model or a plan for how to make money

Time spent putting together a solid business plan is time well spent. In fact, the more time you spend, the better prepared you'll be. But don't be overwhelmed at the prospect. The basic components of a business plan are fairly simple.

The Anatomy of a Business Plan

Written business plans are as varied as the companies that compile them. Some plans run almost 100 pages. Others barely fill a few sheets. Some plans start with executive summaries, and others plunge right into detailed descriptions of products and services. Here you can discover the basic components of a business plan and adapt yours to meet your needs.

A business plan is your detailed description of how your particular business will succeed. A business model describes the underlying economic rationale for why any business like yours can work. For more on business models, see Book I Chapter 3.

Book II

Planning for Your Business

Business-plan contents from beginning to end

Although business plans come in all shapes, sizes, and formats, they typically share a similar framework. The following components, presented in the order they generally appear, are common elements in most business plans:

- **Table of contents:** This element is a guide to the key sections in your business plan and is especially useful if your plan exceeds ten pages.

- **Executive summary:** This section is a summary of the key points in your business plan. You should incorporate it if your plan runs more than ten pages and you want to convey important information upfront. You want to keep it clear, captivating, and brief — in fact, try to keep it to two pages or less.

- **Company overview:** This section describes your company and the nature of your business. It may include your company's mission and vision statements as well as descriptions of your values, your products or services, ways your company is unique, and what business opportunities you plan to seize.

- **Business environment:** This section includes an analysis of your industry and the forces at work in your market; an in-depth description of your direct and potential competitors; and a close look at your customers, including who they are, what they want, and how they buy products or services. It describes everything that affects your business that's beyond your control.

- **Company description:** In this section, include information about your management team, your organization, your new or proprietary technology, your products and services, your company operations, and your marketing potential.

- **Company strategy:** This section brings together the information about your business environment and your company's resources and then lays out a strategy for going forward.

- **Marketing plan:** This section is where you describe how you plan to reach prospects, make sales, and develop a loyal clientele.

- **Financial review:** This section includes a detailed review of dollars and cents, including the state of your current finances and what you expect your financial picture to look like in the future. It typically contains financial statements, including an income statement, your balance sheet, and a cash-flow statement.

- **Action plan:** Here you detail the steps involved in implementing your business plan, including the sequence of actions and how they align with your goals and objectives.

✔ **Appendixes:** This section includes detailed information that supports your business plan. It may include analyses, reports, surveys, legal documents, product specifications, and spreadsheets that deliver a rounded understanding of your business plan but which are of interest to only a small number of your readers.

As you get down to the business of writing your plan, use the items in that list as your checklist, ticking off the major components as you complete them.

There is no single textbook example of a written business plan. This chapter only provides information on how to develop each of the major components, advice for how business plans tend to work for different kinds of businesses, and ways you can organize and present materials in your written plan. It shows you examples from real-life business plans, including mission statements, goals and objectives, financial statements, and business models. How you put them all together in your plan depends on the nature of your business and what you hope to achieve.

Frequently asked business-plan questions

If you're like most people who get this far into the business-planning process, you have questions, likely including the following:

✔ **Do I really need to include all these sections?** Nope. Your business plan should include only what's important to you and your company. If your plan is short — or written mostly for your own purposes — you can dispose of the executive summary, for example. And if you're a company of one, you probably don't need a section describing the organization of your business (unless you need a little help in getting organized!).

For most businesses, however, the more complete your business plan is, the better off you are. If yours is a one-person operation, for example, you may figure you can do without the company overview section because you already know what your business is all about, right? Well, you may find that by compiling that section — by putting your mission, vision, values, product offering, and unique attributes into words — you uncover new ideas about what you really plan to do with your business. And that exercise can be extremely valuable for any company, no matter how big it is.

✔ **Do I really need to write it all down?** Yep. Creating a written plan forces you to face tough issues that you may otherwise ignore. When you put your thoughts down on paper, you give each question the attention it deserves. For example, when you write your business plan, you define your customers and your strategy for reaching out to them; you also analyze your competition and how your offerings compare to theirs; you uncover market opportunities to seize and threats to buffer yourself against; and you establish a set of goals and objectives — along with your action plan for achieving success. And when you're done, you have it all in writing for quick, easy, and frequent reference.

✔ **How long should my plan be?** As long as it needs to be and not a single word longer. A business plan as thick as a Stephen King novel doesn't impress anyone. In fact, a plan that size is likely to scare people off. What really impresses investors, clients, employees, and anyone else who may read your plan is clear, straightforward, and to-the-point thinking. Don't go overboard in the cutting room or leave anything important out of your plan purely for the sake of keeping it brief, but do condense every section down to its most important points. Even comprehensive plans usually fit on 20 to 30 pages, plus appendixes. And that makes many 100-page business plans about 75 pages too long!

✔ **Is an economic downturn any time to start a business?** Financial bubbles have risen and burst. The economy has climbed to historic highs and undergone unprecedented slumps. Those ups and downs have created a business environment of great uncertainty. In a slow recovery to recession, a reasonable question to ask is, "Is this a good time to plan a new venture?" In fact, it may be one of the best times. Any business that competes on price can expect to fare well during slow economic times. High-end restaurants may suffer, for example, but pizza chains flourish. A downturn is precisely the right time to begin planning for when the economy turns around. Career consulting firms that recruit top-notch talent when the economy is slow can expect sizzling business when hiring picks up.

Understanding Your Starting Position

Every business comes to the planning process with different issues and goals. Most startup businesses understand the importance of business planning. Without a plan, they usually can't get funding.

But business planning is an ongoing process for all businesses — or at least it should be. Effective planning keeps established companies on track. It serves as a guide for companies that plan to launch a new product or service or introduce a new marketing program to seize new business opportunities. A plan is also essential for companies in trouble that want to chart an effective turnaround. Even companies that are looking to go out of business need a plan if they intend to put themselves up for sale or merge with another business.

The purpose and the process of business planning, in other words, are different, depending on your starting position. The following sections describe some of the most common starting positions.

Planning for a startup

A startup company begins with a new idea and high hopes. A business plan helps these new ventures evaluate their new idea, potential market, and competition. The critical questions that a business plan for a startup must address are

- ✔ Does this new venture have a good chance of getting off the ground?
- ✔ How much money will the business need to get up and running?
- ✔ Who are your customers, and what's the best way to reach them?
- ✔ Who are your competitors, and what's the best way to outrun them?
- ✔ Why will customers choose your new product or service instead of your competitors'?

Planning for a solo business

Millions of people work for themselves in businesses called sole proprietorships. They range from accountants and attorneys to artists and musicians. Many never consider drafting a business plan, which is too bad. For people who want to be their own boss, a business plan helps zero in on several key questions:

- ✔ Are you prepared for running a company of one?
- ✔ How can you turn something you love to do into a profitable business?
- ✔ What resources will you need to get your business of one off the ground?
- ✔ How much should you charge for your product or service?
- ✔ What opportunities or partnerships could you explore to deliver more business?

Book II Chapters 4 and 5 provide valuable information on home-based and online businesses, popular examples of sole proprietorships.

Planning to address changing conditions

Especially during rocky economic times, many existing businesses try to retool themselves. The critical questions a business plan must address are

✔ What are the economic realities you face?

✔ How can you reshape the company and its products or services to compete in the new economic environment?

✔ What steps do you need to take to reach the goal of achieving those changes?

Planning to seize growth opportunity

Even successful companies can't rest on their laurels. To remain successful, they have to continue to compete. For many, that means recognizing and seizing opportunities to grow their businesses. For companies charting a strategy to grow, a business plan must address several key questions:

✔ Where do the best opportunities for growth lie?

✔ Who are your competitors in this new market?

✔ Can you take advantage of technological innovations?

✔ How can you best compete to grab new market share?

Setting Out Your Planning Objectives

With a thousand issues clamoring for the precious hours in your day, committing time to plan your company's future isn't easy. But operating without a plan is even harder — and even more time-consuming in the long run. There are dozens of good reasons to plan.

Two steps can help you get started. The first is to define your business situation and how a business plan can help you move your business from where it is to where you want it to be. The second is to list the ways that a business plan can heighten your company's odds of success.

To get your business where you want it to go, you need a map to follow, which is what your business plan is all about. It starts with a description of your current situation; describes your future plans; defines your opportunities; and details the financial, operational, marketing, and organizational strategies you'll follow to achieve success.

Imagine that your company is a ship about to set sail on an ocean voyage. Your business plan defines your destination and the route that you'll follow. It details the supplies and crew you have on board as well as what you still need to acquire. It forecasts the cost of the voyage. It describes the weather and sea conditions you're likely to encounter along the way and anticipates the potential dangers that may lurk over the horizon. Finally, your business plan identifies other ships that may be attempting to beat you to your destination.

The same kind of planning is necessary back on dry land. To navigate a new course for your company, you need to start with an assessment of where your business is right now. You may be putting your business together for the first time. Or your business may be up and running but facing new challenges. Or perhaps your business is doing well and about to launch a new product or service. When you assess your current situation, you need to define where you want to arrive and what strategies you'll follow to get there.

Setting out your priorities in the form of a business-planning wish list can help you focus your efforts. With a completed plan in hand, you can return to this list to make sure that it achieves everything on your list of priorities.

Book II

Planning for Your Business

Identifying Target Audiences and Key Messages

Your business plan is the blueprint for how you plan to build a successful enterprise. It's a comprehensive document that covers a lot of territory and addresses all sorts of issues. To help focus your efforts, consider which groups of people will have the greatest impact on your success. Those groups will be the primary audiences for your business plan.

For example, if you need capital investment, investors will be your primary audience. If you need to build strategic alliances, you want to address potential business partners. You and your team are another key audience for the plan, of course, because it will serve as your guide. Be sure to keep that fact in mind as you fine-tune the messages you want to convey.

After you know *whom* you want to reach with your business plan, you can focus on what those readers will want to know and what message you want them to receive. These sections help you define your audience and your message before you begin to assemble your plan.

Your audience

All the people who have an interest in your business venture — from investors and lenders to your employees, customers, and suppliers — represent different *audiences* for your business plan. Depending on the situation you face and what you want your company to achieve through its plan, certain audiences will be more important than others:

- ✔ If your company seeks investment capital, your all-important target audience is likely to be filled with potential investors.

- ✔ If your plan includes the introduction of stock options (possibly in lieu of high salaries), your current and prospective employees will be a primary target audience.

- ✔ If you're launching a business that needs clients, not cash, to get up and running — the sooner the better — potential customers will comprise your plan's primary audience.

- ✔ If you're a self-employed freelancer, your plan may be for you and you alone to focus your efforts, chart your course, and anticipate problems before they arise.

Make a list of groups that you think will be most important to your business success, given your current situation.

Your message

After you target the audiences for your plan, the next step is to focus on the key messages you want each group to receive. People with different stakes in your business will read your business plan with different interests and values. For example:

- ✔ A person who owns shares in a company wants to read about growth plans.

- ✔ A banker considering a loan request wants to see proof of strong revenue and profit prospects.

- ✔ Employee groups want to see how they'll benefit from the company's growth and profits.

- ✔ Regulators focus on operational and financial issues.

But for now, do some preliminary planning:

1. **Identify the three most important audiences you intend to address with your business plan.**

   Refer to the list of groups you jotted down in the last section.

2. **Jot down key points you need to make to each target audience.**

   Writing down your key points doesn't require fancy prose; just get your ideas down on paper so you can refer to them when you begin writing your business plan.

Business planning as a test drive

Business planning sets the course that you intend to follow. But a good business plan also functions as a kind of test drive. It allows you to think about all the parts you need to have in place to make your company run at peak performance.

A good business plan is also your chance to anticipate bumps or sharp turns that may lie ahead — including economic uncertainties, competitors on the same racetrack, and your particular strengths and weaknesses. Many companies discover that business planning allows them to conduct a virtual test of a new product or service idea or a proposed strategy for a turnaround. Along the way, they get to work out the kinks and avoid problems that, in the real world, may have left them broken down on the shoulder of the road. Many companies end up retooling their product, service, or strategy as a result of the business planning process.

Establishing Your Plan's Time Frame

Your *time frame* represents how far out into the future you want to plan. You want your business to grow successfully for years and years into the future, but that goal doesn't mean your current business plan goes all the way to forever. Each business plan covers a unique planning period. Some are designed to get a company to a defined sales level, a funding objective, or the achievement of some other growth goal. A good business plan covers a time frame that has a realistic start and finish, with a number of measurable checkpoints in between. This section can help you determine how far into the future your plan should extend. It also encourages you to identify the important milestones that will be used to chart your progress.

Committing to a schedule

How far out should your planning horizon go? Your answer depends on the kind of business you're in and the pace at which your industry is moving. Some ventures have only six months to prove themselves. At the other end of the spectrum, organizations that have substantial endowments, such as nonprofits, are in for the long haul with business plans that look at five- or ten-year horizons. Typical business plans, however, tend to use one-year, three-year, or five-year benchmarks. (Odd numbers are popular, for some reason.)

Business planning is an ongoing process. From year to year — and sometimes more often than that — companies review, revise, and even completely overhaul their plans. As you establish your time frame, don't worry about casting it in cement. Instead, think of your schedule as something you commit to follow unless and until circumstances change and you make a conscious decision to revise it.

Defining milestones

Setting goals and establishing measurable objectives is a critical part of business planning. (Take a look at Book IV Chapter 2 for more on setting goals and objectives.) But knowing your goals and objectives isn't enough. You can't just say you'll get around to achieving them; you need to establish and hold yourself accountable to a schedule that includes specific milestones along the way.

Figure 1-1 shows how a retail store specializing in digital equipment (cameras, recorders, and other devices) answered five basic questions in order to establish a reasonable time frame for its expansion plans. Based on their answers, the owners determined that the business would need one year to open new stores and achieve profitability. Over that year-long planning period, they defined a number of milestones:

- ✔ **Month 1:** Complete business plan.
- ✔ **Month 2:** Secure business loans.
- ✔ **Month 3:** Begin search for retail space.
- ✔ **Month 5:** Lease and develop retail space; begin hiring.
- ✔ **Month 7:** Open shops; run holiday ads.
- ✔ **Month 8:** Holiday shopping season begins.
- ✔ **Month 12:** New stores become profitable.

Business Plan Time Frame Questionnaire

1. Identify three milestones that represent essential steps you need to take to get your business off the ground or to the next level of achievement. Estimate a time frame for each.

- **Milestone 1:** Secure business loans. (2 months)
- **Milestone 2:** Lease and develop four locations. (5 months)
- **Milestone 3:** Get all shops up and running. (8 months)

2. Is the success of your business tied to a major business trend? If so, what is the time frame?

The emerging market for digital devices — already underway, with new products scheduled for release every quarter (5 months)

3. Is your business seasonal in nature? When do you need to have your product or service available to take advantage of the peak season?

Holiday sales represent 50 percent of our revenue. (8 months)

4. How soon do you need to make your product or service available to stay ahead of your competition?

Consumer electronics is extremely competitive. (ASAP)

5. When do you absolutely need to start making a profit or meet your profit projection?

Moderate financial pressure on the company. (Within 1 year)

© John Wiley & Sons, Inc.

Figure 1-1:
The questions here help determine an appropriate time frame for your business plan.

Book II

Planning for Your Business

To establish a time frame for your business plan, look over the questions in Figure 1-1 and answer the ones that are relevant to your situation. Your responses will help you set a time frame that includes your key milestones and takes into account your business trends and cycles and the competitive and financial realities of your business.

Preparing for the Real World

You're about ready to dive into the business-planning process. By now you're pretty certain about the purpose and benefit of your plan, and you have a fairly clear idea of whom you want to read your opus when it's ready and what you want them to find out and do as a result. You may even have a preliminary idea of your planning timeline. (If any of that sounds like Greek, look back at the preceding sections in this chapter.)

This section talks about resources you can turn to for additional tips and tools along the way.

Locating informative resources

You're certain to have questions as your business planning gets underway. For example, you may want to find out about trends in your industry or marketplace or obtain information on your customers or competitors. Maybe you need more information before you develop your marketing plan or need help with your finances. Luckily, you have plenty of places to turn to for help. Here's a list of the places you can check out for more information:

- ✔ **The Internet:** You can dig up information on markets, customers, competition — you name it. The challenge of the Internet these days is wading through the abundance of material to find what you need from reliable sources. Check out reputable industry or government sources, as well as sites vetted by colleges or universities.

  Many companies have discovered that customer reviews on websites are one of the best places to turn for information about what customers like and don't like about products and services already on the market. Every complaint you see on a website represents a potential business opportunity.

- ✔ **Your local college or university library:** The periodical section of your library has business journals and other useful publications, and the reference shelves contain books on market demographics, industry trends, and other factual resources.

- ✔ **A nearby business school:** Many schools offer seminars or night classes open to the public, and professors are usually happy to answer your questions.

- ✔ **Industry trade journals:** Yes, the subscriptions are sometimes pricey, but they're often well worth the investment.

- ✔ **Newspapers:** No matter what your business, *The New York Times, The Wall Street Journal,* and a local paper keep you on top of issues you should follow.

- ✔ **Trade shows and industry symposiums:** These gatherings are usually great places to get news about products, services, customers, and your competitors — all under one roof.

- ✔ **U.S. Small Business Administration (SBA):** A rich resource for just about everything you want to know about starting and running a small business. Look online at www.sba.gov.

- ✔ **Search and research companies:** Using these resources comes with a price, but sometimes a LEXUS/NEXUS search or a market-research study is the only place to find must-have data.

- ✔ **Professional groups:** Almost every profession has a professional group, from the American Medical Writers Association to the Society of Wetlands Scientists. Find the group that serves your business arena and check out the website and membership requirements.

- ✔ **Local business networking groups:** These groups are comprised of members with experience, insights, and even business referrals to share.

- ✔ **Your local chamber of commerce:** This organization is a good vehicle for networking and staying abreast of local and state issues and can serve as a resource for all sorts of business and regional information.

Seeking expert advice

Book II

Planning for Your Business

When you can't find the answers to specific questions, ask for advice. For example, if you're thinking of starting a retail business in town, ask other retailers to fill you in on what you need to know. If you want to break away from the corporate grind and go into business for yourself, schedule a lunch with someone who has made a similar move to discover what it takes. You're sure to get an earful of useful firsthand advice to implement in your business planning.

As you interview industry contacts — or people with experience in similar businesses — follow these steps:

- ✔ **Prepare your questions in advance.** With a little advance planning, you won't forget to discuss something really important.

- ✔ **Explain exactly why you're asking for help.** You can't expect people to be open with you if you aren't honest with them.

- ✔ **Be prepared to listen.** Even if you hear something you don't want to know, listen anyway. Anybody who warns you about potential obstacles is doing you a big favor.

- ✔ **Keep the conversation open-ended.** Always ask whether you should be thinking about other issues or addressing other topics.

- ✔ **Build your network of contacts.** Ask for introductions to others who may be helpful or for suggestions for sources of useful information.

- ✔ **Be grateful.** Pick up the lunch or dinner tab. Write a quick thank-you note. Who knows, you may need to turn to the same people later for additional advice or help.

Chapter 2

Finding the Funding

. . . .

In This Chapter

▶ Making a money plan

▶ Using your own money first

▶ Looking for an angel this side of heaven

▶ Using venture capital

▶ Selling stock through an IPO and finding other sources of capital

▶ Protecting your business plan

. . . .

*T*wo common attitudes about startup funds make the search for funds much more difficult. They are

✔ The more money I get, the better. I can use as much as I can get.

✔ My business plan numbers are just estimates — the investor will tell me what I need.

If you're thinking like this, stop right now. First of all, why seek more investment money than you absolutely need? Every bit of capital invested in your business costs you some equity (ownership) in your company. Besides, having too much money may lead you to make poor decisions because you don't think as carefully as you should about how you spend that money.

Secondly, although it's true that your business plan financials are estimates, they had better be *good* estimates based on your research. Your investor may discount your estimate of rapid sales growth, but he or she wants to know that you've carefully considered all of your numbers and that they make sense.

In this chapter, you see how to raise capital for your business the smart way — and you start with a plan.

Starting with a Plan

Before you talk to anyone — even your grandmother — about money, have a plan in place, a set of strategies for targeting the right amount of money from the right sources. Here are some guidelines for putting together a plan that works:

- Seek what you actually need, not what you think you can raise.
- Look at how your company grows and define the points when you'll most likely need capital.
- Consider the sources of money available to you at each stage.
- Make sure that the activities of your business let you tap into the correct source of money at the right time. For example, if you know that you are planning an initial public offering (IPO) in three years, start putting in place the systems, controls, and professional management that you'll need before the IPO takes place.
- Monitor your capital needs as you go so that you don't have to return to the trough too many times. Every time you go back for another round of capital, you give up more stock in your company, and the percentage you own declines.

You can come out a winner if you prepare for your future capital needs. Just follow the lead of one technology company that produces custom productivity and e-commerce applications. This company keeps itself in a good position to raise capital by

- Creating value in the form of long-term customers and great products.
- Running a profitable business.
- Keeping cash flow positive.

If you do these three things, you will probably not have difficulty raising growth capital whenever you need it. If you have a startup venture, strive to achieve these goals from day one.

When you're financing a traditional business

Traditional businesses (non-Internet businesses) typically follow fairly predictable financing cycles. Take a look at Figure 2-1 to see the stages of financing for a typical business.

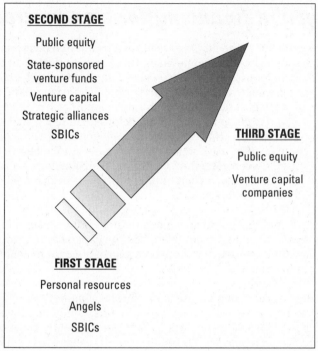

SECOND STAGE

Public equity

State-sponsored
venture funds

Venture capital

Strategic alliances

SBICs

THIRD STAGE

Public equity

Venture capital
companies

Figure 2-1:
Three
stages for
financing
the typical
business.

FIRST STAGE

Personal resources

Angels

SBICs

© John Wiley & Sons, Inc.

Book II

**Planning
for Your
Business**

First-stage funding is about getting seed capital to finish preparing the product and the business for launch. It's also the stage where you seek funding to begin operations and reach a positive cash flow. In the second stage, you're usually looking for growth capital. Your business has proven its concept and now you want to grow. Alternatively, your customers have demanded that your company grow to meet their needs (that's a nice thing when it happens). To successfully use second-round financing, you need to be out looking for capital in advance of needing it.

Third-stage funding generally results in an acquisition or a buyout of the company. It's the harvest stage for the entrepreneur who wants to take his or her wealth out of the business and possibly exit, or for investors who want to exit. In general, if you take on *venture capital* (a professionally managed pool of money), you are probably looking at a buyout or IPO within three to five years. That's because a buyout or IPO provides the cash your investor needs to get out of the investment.

When you're financing for e-commerce

It's pretty easy to look at the funding stages of a traditional business, but the Internet has brought about some business models that don't fit those stages well, if at all. Internet-based businesses (whose primary location is the Internet) require a strategy that is part formula and part artistic achievement. Such a strategy is ill defined at best. And sometimes it's difficult to judge which concept is going to get funding before it launches, and which will have to bootstrap for a while to prove its concept. Drugstore.com is an example of a company that was funded on the concept alone before it went live on the Internet. By contrast, the founders of WebSideStory, a provider of Web-based audience analysis, had to prove their business model online before they received outside funding.

Grabbing early brand recognition from competitors online takes a lot of money, a professional management team, and the capability to grow in a hurry. If that's your business, here are some suggestions for maneuvering through the capital maze:

- ✔ **Don't take the easy money.** You want the smart money. It's okay to fund a traditional business with money from friends, family, and lovers. Doing so isn't a good idea, however, when you're seeking early stage capital for an Internet concept. Who is funding your business is as important as how much they're giving you. Be sure that you associate with people who attract the right kind of money to your venture.

- ✔ **Get an introduction to the money source through one of your advisors.** Be sure you exercise due diligence (fancy words for doing your homework — investigating the money source) on the investor to find one that has worked with your type of business before and has compatible firms in its portfolio that provide synergies with yours.

- ✔ **Don't get married on the first date.** Large quantities of money are available for great Internet concepts. If you have such a concept, you may have more *term sheets* (agreements listing what an investor is willing to do) than you know what to do with. It's tempting to grab the first term sheet under the assumption that the first is always the best. The agreement may be for the most money, maybe not, but the investor may not be the most compatible with your business. Compatibility is even more important than money, because the money source has a lot to say about what happens to your business. So, consider all your options before selecting one. Remember that the most important person to get to know in any potential investment firm is the partner you will be dealing with. If you don't have a good feeling about that person, you may want to look elsewhere.

✔ **Take the deal that moves you on to the next stage.** The biggest deal doesn't always win. What you're looking for is enough money to get you comfortably to the next round of financing and an investment firm that adds value to what you're doing in the form of introductions, contacts, advice, and so forth.

✔ **Get your website up as quickly as possible.** Don't wait for the perfect site. Get up and running and start receiving feedback from potential customers. You need to keep the momentum going and collect data on the people who visit your site. This is important information to have when you talk to your investor.

✔ **Buy the best management you can get with your capital.** Investors are practically unanimous: The management team is more important than the business concept itself. When you obtain money, invest in the best management you can get. If you have to bootstrap with your own funds, seek a strategic alliance with a company whose great management you can leverage.

Tapping Friends, Family, and Lovers

The majority of entrepreneurs — well over 70 percent — start their businesses with personal savings, credit cards, and other personal assets like the proceeds from second mortgages and sale of stock portfolios. Why is that? With all the venture capital and private investor money out there for the taking, why do you have to use your own resources? The answer is simple: Your new company is just too big a risk — it's unproven; you don't know for certain if the market will accept it. The only people who'll invest in your business at this point are you and people who know and believe in you.

But what if you don't have a network of friends and family willing to give you money, or from whom you prefer not to take money? What do you do then? One thing you do is *bootstrap* — beg, borrow, and barter for anything that you can from products to services to an office site. One way to bootstrap is to avoid hiring employees as long as possible (employees are typically the single biggest expense of any business). Here are some other tips:

✔ Look for an office suite where you can share facilities and equipment with other tenants.

✔ Share office space with an established company that is compatible with yours. You may even be able to barter or trade services.

✔ To reduce cash needs, consider leasing rather than buying equipment.

✔ Barter with established companies for services.

✔ Get your customers to pay quickly. Sometimes a new company can get customers to pay a deposit up front, providing capital for the raw materials you need to make the product.

✔ Ask your suppliers for favorable payment terms, and then pay on time. Those relationships become important to your business as it grows. You may find it necessary to request smaller amounts of credit from several suppliers until you establish your business.

If you do decide to take money from friends and family, do it in a business-like manner. That is, have an attorney draw up a contract that protects both sides. Investing in a business venture is a risk and should only be undertaken by people who can bear to lose their investment, should that occur.

Family money is the most expensive money you'll ever use because you pay for it for the rest of your life!

Finding an Angel

The second most common source of capital for starting and growing a business is an angel, also known as a private investor. Angels are members of the informal risk capital market — the largest pool of capital in the United States. So, how do you find one of these gift-givers from heaven? Unfortunately, that's the hard part because angels tend to keep a lower profile than any other type of investor. Entrepreneurs typically find angels through referrals from someone else. That's why networking with people in your industry is so important when you begin thinking about starting a business. You need to build up a personal network to tap when it's time to look for private investment capital.

How to spot an angel

There was a time when angels were into the investment for the long haul. Times have changed; angel investors have, too. Today, angel investors look a lot like professional venture capitalists. Angels typically ask you for the same credentials that a venture capitalist wants:

✔ A business plan

✔ Milestones

✔ A significant equity stake in the business

✔ A seat on the board of directors

The similarity between an angel and a venture capitalist came about because of the long bull market in the late 1990s when venture capital funding reached astronomical levels. Flush with cash, the venture capitalist stopped looking at deals that were less than $3 million to $5 million, leaving the playing field wide open for angels to step in, with the promise of a quicker turnaround.

Angels used to be characterized as middle-aged, former entrepreneurs who generally operated solo and invested near their homes. They usually funded deals for less than a million dollars and stayed in the investment for several years. Today, angels come in all ages, even turning up among the twenty-something Internet crowd who hit it big with their first ventures. Angels also band together to increase the size of their investment pools and take on larger deals. Networks like The Tech Coast Angels and Berkus Technology Ventures, based in Los Angeles, California, consider themselves to be seed venture capitalists. They have become as sophisticated in their investment methods as any professional venture capitalist — exercising more due diligence and sometimes looking for a quicker return on their investment, often to the detriment of the business. In other words, they need to be cashed out of their investment before the growing business is in a position to do so. Entrepreneurs typically work with longer growth and performance horizons than venture capitalists and many of the new breed of angels. So their goals are often in conflict.

Book II

Planning for Your Business

How to deal with angels

In many ways, you deal with angels the same as you deal with professional venture capitalists. You start with a good referral from someone who knows the angel well. Then:

- ✔ **Make sure your goals and your angel's goals are the same.** Otherwise, you may risk the goals you've set for the business. Try to avoid an angel who wants to get in and out in three years or less. You can't build an enduring business in that timeframe. Besides, you need to find a way to buy out the investor at that point, and that may mean selling the business or offering an IPO, which may not have been your original plan.

- ✔ **Exercise your own due diligence (investigation, background check) on the angel.** Don't be afraid to ask for references from other companies the angel has invested in. Talk to those entrepreneurs to find out what their experience was.

- ✔ **Look for an angel who provides more than money.** You want contacts in the industry, potential board members, and strategic assistance for your business. These things are as important as money.

- ✔ **Get the angel's commitment to help you meet certain business milestones that you both agree on.**

Getting ready to deal

One of the more important rules about negotiation is, "He who has the most information wins." Negotiating the best funding deal really is about 1) understanding the needs of the other party, 2) knowing what you want, and 3) knowing your alternatives if you can't come to an agreement. Here's a checklist of information you should have at your fingertips when you negotiate for funding:

1. How much money do you need for startup and years one through five?

2. How will you use the funds?

3. What sources of money will you seek and why?

4. If you seek debt funding, what will you use as collateral?

5. Are you willing to personally guarantee the debt?

6. What funds have been invested to date and by whom? Are these funds debtor equity?

7. If you have received outside investment capital, what did the investor receive in return for the investment?

8. Which outside investors have you approached or will you approach? What were the results?

9. Under what legal form is the company organized and how does this help the principals and investors?

10. What tax benefits does the legal structure provide for the company, the principals, and the investors?

11. What is the financial vehicle being offered to the investors?

12. What is the payback period for the investor and the projected return on investment (ROI)?

13. What is the proposed exit strategy for the investors? The principals?

14. Have your financial projections been reviewed by an accountant?

15. What leases and loan agreements do you currently have?

Daring to Use Venture Capital

Venture capital is a professionally managed pool of funds that usually operates in the form of a limited partnership. The managing general partner pulls together a pool of investors — individual and institutional (pension funds and insurance companies, for example) — whose money he or she invests on behalf of the partnership. Typically, venture capitalists invest at the second round of funding and are looking for fast growth and a quick turnaround of their investment. Consequently, their goals often conflict with the entrepreneur's goals for the company.

In the late 1990s, it appeared that all the rules about what a good investment is changed as venture capitalists began focusing on Internet companies and investing in ideas rather than intellectual property. They rushed to invest in companies like Amazon.com, Buy.com, and e-Toys, companies that weren't projecting profits for several years. But as stock valuations of these companies plummeted to near zero levels in late 1999 and early 2000, venture capitalists began rethinking their strategies. They didn't stop investing in Internet companies; they just started doing a better job of evaluating the opportunities.

What is still true about venture capital is that it funds less than 1 percent of all new ventures, mostly in technology areas — biotechnology, information systems, the Internet, and computer technology. To see how you may be able to use venture capital to your advantage, you first need to understand the cost of raising capital and the process by which it happens.

Book II

Planning for Your Business

Calculating the real cost of money

Raising money for your business, whether private or venture capital, is a time-consuming and costly process. That's why many entrepreneurs in more traditional businesses (non-high-tech or non-Internet) opt for slower growth, using internal cash flows as long as they can. But if you've decided to speed up your startup or growth rate with outside capital, you need to have reasonable expectations about how that can happen. Here's what you need to know:

- ✔ Raising money always takes longer than you planned, at least twice as long. Count on it.

- ✔ Plan to spend several months seeking funds, several more months for the potential investor to agree to fund your venture, and perhaps six more months before the money is actually in your hands.

- ✔ Use financial advisors experienced in raising money.

- ✔ Understand that raising money takes you away from your business a lot, probably when you most need to be there. So be sure to have a good management team in place.

Start looking for money before you need it!

Investors are fickle

Once you've found what you think is the ideal investor — you're compatible, you have the same goals for the future of the company, and you genuinely like each other — the investor may back out of the deal. That's right, after you've spent months trying to find this investor and even more time exercising due diligence (yours and the investor's), the investor may change his or her mind. Perhaps the investor stumbled across something unfavorable; more likely, he or she couldn't pull together the capital needed to fund your deal.

Always have a backup if you sense that the deal may be going sideways.

Investors often want to buy out your early investors, including your friends and family, typically out of the belief that first-round funders have nothing more to contribute to the venture. Investors also don't want to deal with a bunch of small investors. A buyout like this can turn into an awkward situation if you haven't explained to your early funders that it's a possibility. And if you don't agree to the buyout of the first round, understand that your investor may walk away from the deal.

It takes money to make money

It takes money to make money. Truer words were never spoken. The costs of finding your investor, including preparing and printing the business plan, travel, and time, all are paid up front by you. If you're seeking a lot of money — several million — you probably need to have your financials prepared or reviewed by a CPA, and you need to prepare a prospectus, an offering document spelling out the risks and rewards of investing in your business opportunity. Again, these are costs you bear up front.

Once you receive the capital, the cost of maintaining it, ranging from paying interest on loans to keeping investors apprised of what's going on with your business, can usually be paid out of the proceeds. You'll also have back-end costs if you are raising capital by selling securities (shares of stock in your corporation). These costs include investment-banking fees, legal fees, marketing costs, brokerage fees, and any fees charged by state and federal authorities. The total cost of raising equity capital can reach 25 percent of the total amount of money you're seeking. You see it definitely takes money to make money.

Tracking the venture capital process

The process that venture capitalists go through to analyze your deal, decide to make the deal, put together a term sheet, and exercise their due diligence can be quite complex and vary from firm to firm. In general, the process follows a predictable pattern, however. But first, consider what venture capitalists are looking for.

A venture capitalist invests in your company for a specified period of time (typically five years or less) with the expectation that at the end of that time, he or she gets the investment back plus a substantial return, in the neighborhood of 50 percent or more. The amount of return is a function of the risk associated with your venture. In the early stages, the risk is high, so the venture capitalist wants a higher return. Later, when your business has proven itself and you're looking for second-round financing, the risk is less, so you have more clout in your negotiations.

The venture capitalist also probably wants a seat on your board of directors — a say in business strategy and policy.

Approving your plan

The first thing venture capitalists do is scrutinize your business plan, particularly to see if you have a strong management team consisting of people experienced in your industry and committed to the launch of this venture. Then they look at your product and market to ensure the opportunity you've defined is substantial and worth their effort and the risk they're taking. If you have a unique product that is protected through patents, you have an important barrier to competitors that is attractive to the venture capitalists, who also look at the market to ensure a significant potential for growth — that's where they make their money, from the growth in value of your business.

If the venture capitalists like what they see, they'll probably call for a meeting at which you may be asked to present your plan. They want to confirm that your team is everything you say it is. The venture capitalists may or may not discuss initial terms for an agreement at the meeting. It is likely they'll wait until they've exercised due diligence.

Doing due diligence

If you've made it past the meeting stage, and the venture capitalists feel positive about your concept, it's time for them to exercise due diligence, meaning they thoroughly check out your team and your business concept (or business, as the case may be). Once they're satisfied that you check out, they'll draw up legal documents detailing the terms of the investment. But don't hold your breath waiting. Some venture capitalists wait until they know they have a good investment opportunity before putting together the partnership that actually funds your venture. Others just take a long time to release the money. In any case, you can certainly ask what the next steps are and how long they'll take.

One more surprise lies in store: It's unlikely that the money will be released to you in one lump sum. Study your term sheet carefully: it probably states that the money will be released in stages triggered by your achieving certain predefined goals.

Crafting the deal

Always approach a venture capitalist from a position of strength. If you sound and look desperate for money, you won't get a good deal. Venture capitalists see many business concepts, but most of them aren't winners. Your power at the negotiating table comes from proving that your concept is one of the winners.

Every deal is comprised of four parts:

1. The amount of capital to be invested

2. The timing and use of the money

3. The return on investment to the investors

4. The level of risk

The amount of capital the venture capitalist provides reflects need. However, it also depends on the risks involved, how the money will be used, and how quickly the venture capitalist can earn a return on the investment (timing). The amount of equity in your company that the venture capitalist demands depends on the risk and the amount of the investment.

Selling Stock to the Public: An IPO

The aura and myths surrounding the IPO (selling stock in your company on a public stock exchange) have grown with the huge IPOs undertaken by upstart dot-com companies that don't have an ounce of profit to their names. The glamor of watching your stock appear on the exchange you've chosen and the attention you get from the media make you forget for a moment all the hard work that led to this point and all the hard work that you can expect to follow as your company strives every quarter to satisfy stockholders and investment analysts that you're doing the right things.

It's no wonder so many naïve entrepreneurs announce their intention to go public within three years (if not sooner) of starting their businesses. If they knew more about what it's really like to launch a public company, these starry-eyed adventurers would think twice. You need to be doing your homework — reading, talking to people who have done it — before making the decision to do an IPO. Once you decide to go ahead, you set in motion a series of events that have a life of their own. Yes, you can stop the IPO up to the night before your company is scheduled to be listed on the stock exchange, but doing so will cost you a lot of money and time, not to mention bad publicity.

An IPO is really just a more complex version of a private offering. You file your intent to sell a portion of your company to the public with the Securities and Exchange Commission (SEC) and list your stock on one of the exchanges. When you complete the IPO, the proceeds go to the company in what is termed a *primary offering.* If, later on, you sell your shares (after restrictions have ceased), those proceeds are termed a *secondary distribution.*

Considering the advantages and disadvantages of going public

The real reason that many entrepreneurs choose to take their companies public is that an IPO provides an enormous source of interest-free capital for growth and expansion. After you've done one offering, you can do additional offerings if you maintain a positive track record. Other general advantages that companies derive from becoming publicly held are

- ✔ More clout with industry types and the financial community.

- ✔ Easier ways for you to form partnerships and negotiate favorable deals with suppliers, customers, and others.

- ✔ The capability to offer stock to your employees.

- ✔ Easier ways for you to harvest the wealth you have created by selling some of your shares or borrowing against them.

But becoming a public company also has several disadvantages that you should carefully consider. Some of them include

- ✔ The cost exceeds $300,000, and that doesn't include the commission to the underwriter (the investment bank that sells the securities).

- ✔ The process is extremely time-consuming, taking most of your week for more than six months.

- ✔ Everything you and your company do becomes public information.

- ✔ You are now responsible first and foremost to your shareholders, not to your customers or employees.

- ✔ You may no longer have the controlling share of stock in your company.

- ✔ Your stock may lose value because of factors in the economy even if you're running the company well.

- ✔ You face intense pressure to perform in the short term so that revenues and earnings rise, driving up stock prices and dividends to stockholders.

- ✔ The SEC reporting requirements are a huge and time-consuming burden.

Deciding to go for it

If you've weighed all the advantages and disadvantages and still want to go forward with an IPO, you need to have a good understanding of what happens during the months that precede the offering. In general, the process unfolds in a fairly predictable fashion.

Choosing the underwriter

You need to choose an underwriter that serves as your guide on this journey and, you hope, sells your securities to enough institutional investors to make the IPO a success. Like meeting a venture capitalist, you need to secure an introduction to a good investment banker through a mutual acquaintance and investigate the reputation and track record of any investment banker you're considering. Many disreputable firms out there are looking for a quick buck. You also want to find an investment banker who'll stay with you after the IPO and look out for the long-term success of the stock.

Once chosen, the investment banker drafts a letter of intent stating the terms and conditions of the agreement. The letter includes a price range for the stock, although this is just an estimate because the going-out price won't be decided until the night before the offering. At that point, if you're unhappy with the price, you can cancel the offering. You will, however, be responsible for some costs incurred.

Satisfying the SEC

You file a registration statement with the SEC. Known as a *red herring,* this prospectus presents all the potential risks of investing in the IPO and is given to anyone interested in investing. Following the filing of the registration statement, you place an advertisement, known as a *tombstone,* in the financial press announcing the offering. Your prospectus is valid for nine months after the tombstone is published.

You need to decide on which stock exchange your company will be listed. Here are the three best known in the U.S.:

- American Stock Exchange (AMEX)
- National Association of Securities Dealers Automated Quotation (NASDAQ)
- New York Stock Exchange (NYSE)

The NYSE is the most difficult to qualify for listing. The NYSE and AMEX are auction markets where securities are traded on the floor of the exchange so that investors trade directly with one another. By contrast, the NASDAQ is a floorless exchange that trades on the National Market System through a system of broker-dealers from respected securities firms.

You may also want to look at regional exchanges like the Pacific Exchange and the Boston stock exchange. They are generally less expensive alternatives.

Taking your show on the road

Many consider the *road show* to be the high point of the entire IPO process. It is exactly what it sounds like, a whirlwind tour of all the major institutional investors over about two weeks. The entrepreneur and the IPO team present the business and the offering to these potential investors, whom they hope to sign on. The goal is to have the offering oversubscribed so that it can be sold in a day.

One of the more important skills you need to have or develop if you intend to go the IPO route (or seek money from any source) is how to talk to money people. These people have seen so many presentations from so many people begging for their resources that they are jaded. You have to work hard to capture their attention, and that's not an easy thing to do.

Here are some suggestions based on the lessons taught by Jerry Weissman, whose company, Power Presentations, has been behind some of the most famous IPOs in history — Cisco, Yahoo!, and Compaq, to name a few:

- ✔ **Tell a great story.** Investors want to hear why this is the best investment opportunity they've ever seen. In short, they want to know what's in it for them, their return on investment. Entrepreneurs, by contrast, are more focused on what's in it for the customer.

- ✔ **The entrepreneur must tell the story.** Not only must the entrepreneur/ CEO tell the story, but he or she needs to write it as well. No one has the passion for the business that the founder does, and that passion means a higher valuation for the business. So, tell your own story, and tell it with energy and passion.

- ✔ **Don't exaggerate your story.** Remember that investors have heard it all, so you need to tell them what makes your company stand out from the crowd. And don't hide potential problems or negatives your business may have. Recognize them and then tell investors what you intend to do about them.

- ✔ **Get their attention.** You can grab attention in many ways, but one of the best is to show your audience that you have a solution to a problem they're experiencing. For example, Scott Cook of Intuit (Quicken, Quickbooks) started his story with a question: "How many of you balance your own checkbooks?" Every investor raised his or her hand. "How many of you like doing it?" Not one hand was raised. He explained that millions of people around the world dislike that task, but he had a product that would solve the problem. That approach definitely caught the investors' attention.

Dealing with failure

Once in a while, even when you've done all the right things, the IPO can fail, like the Texas company that developed a computer that would stand up to the toughest environments — places like machine shops and hot restaurant kitchens. When the founder decided to raise money through a first registered stock offering on the Internet, it was a long and costly undertaking (more than $65,000) to secure the necessary approvals from the SEC. But finally the company began selling shares through its website, its sights set on raising between $1.5 million and $9.9 million. The offering period was 90 days, and at the end of that time the company had raised only about $300,000. Attempts to do a traditional offering failed as well, and the company filed for Chapter 7 bankruptcy. The total bill for the IPO was about $250,000, for which the company received nothing.

Just because you start an IPO doesn't guarantee that you'll finish it. Many entrepreneurs cancel their IPOs the night before they come out because they are unable to raise sufficient capital during the road show.

Finding Other Ways to Finance Growth

Equity is not the only way to finance the growth of your business. Debt vehicles — IOUs with interest — are another way to acquire the capital you need to grow. When you choose this route, you typically hand over title to a business or personal asset as collateral for a loan bearing a market rate of interest. You normally pay principal and interest on the note until it's paid off. Some arrangements, however, combine debt and equity. For example, a *debenture* is a debt vehicle that can be converted to common stock at some predetermined time in the future. In the meantime, the holder of the debenture receives interest on his or her loan to the company.

Here are some of the more common sources of debt financing for growth.

- ✔ **Commercial banks:** Banks are better sources for growth capital than for startup capital, because by the time you come to them, your company has, in all likelihood, developed a good track record. Banks make loans based on the Five C's: character of the entrepreneur, capacity to repay the loan, capital needed, collateral the entrepreneur can provide to secure the loan, and condition of the entrepreneur's overall financial health and situation. For entrepreneurs with new ventures, character and capacity become the overriding factors.

- ✔ **Commercial finance companies:** Also known as *asset-based lenders,* these companies are typically more expensive to use than commercial banks by as much as 5 percent above the prime interest rate. But they are also more likely to lend to a startup entrepreneur than a commercial bank is. And when you weigh the difference between starting the business and not starting because of money, a commercial lender may not be that expensive.

✓ **Small Business Administration:** For over 60 years the SBA (www.sba.gov) has provided many forms of financial assistance to small businesses. This assistance includes grants, counseling, and loan guarantees. SBA loan programs are designed to help small businesses obtain funding when they can't obtain suitable financing through traditional means. The SBA doesn't directly make loans to small businesses. Instead, it provides a guarantee to banks and other authorized lenders for loans provided to qualifying businesses.

This guarantee protects the lender by promising to repay a portion of the loan in the event the borrower defaults. Therefore an SBA loan application is not submitted directly to the agency but rather through an authorized lender. Note that not all lenders offer SBA loans, and authorized lenders may not offer all of the several types of SBA loans. Because the SBA is a government agency, its programs frequently change based upon current fiscal policy. The following are three of the more typical SBA loan programs currently being offered:

- **SBA 7(a) loans:** This is the SBA's traditional loan program. Currently, 7(a) loans have a maximum of $5 million and no minimum. In fiscal 2012, the average 7(a) loan was $337,730. The SBA guarantees 75–85 percent of the loan, depending on the loan amount. In the fiscal year ending September 30, 2014, the SBA had approved 52,044 7(a) loans for nearly $20 billion.

- **SBA Express:** A relatively new program, SBA Express aims to reduce all the paperwork associated with a traditional SBA loan. If you qualify at a bank, you can borrow up to $350,000 without going through the standard SBA application process. In fact, this program promises to give you a decision within 36 hours. Because the Small Business Administration only guarantees these loans to 50 percent of their face value, not all the SBA-qualified lenders have signed on to the program.

- **Microloan program:** This is another newer program that provides up to $50,000 to help small business with funding for various needs, such as working capital, inventory, and equipment acquisition. The SBA provides funds to specially designated intermediary lenders — nonprofit, community-based organizations with experience in lending and providing other technical and management assistance. These intermediaries administer the microloan program for eligible borrowers.

- Each intermediary lender establishes its own credit requirements. Often these lenders require some sort of collateral as well as the personal guarantee of the business owner. The average microloan is about $13,000.

Guarding Your Interests

Trade secrets generally include sensitive company information that can't be covered by patents, trademarks, and copyrights. Business plans are often considered trade secrets. The only method of protecting trade secrets is through contracts and non-disclosure agreements that specifically detail the trade secret to be protected. No other legal form of protection exists. If you have any concerns about sharing your business plan with anyone outside your circle of trust, including employees or investors, consider creating a contract or a non-disclosure agreement.

Contracts

A contract simply is an offer or a promise to do something or refrain from doing something in exchange for consideration, which is the promise to supply or give up something in return. So you are asking your employees to not reveal your company's trade secrets in exchange for having a job there (and not getting sued if they do reveal them).

In addition to using contracts with employees and others who have access to your trade secrets, make sure that no one has all the components of your trade secret. For example, suppose you develop a new barbecue sauce that you intend to brand and market to specialty shops. If you're producing in large volumes, you obviously can't do all the work yourself, so you hire others to help. To avoid letting them know how to reproduce your unique barbecue sauce, you can do three things:

- Execute a contract with them binding them to not disclose what they know about your recipe.
- Provide them with premixed herbs and spices so they don't know exactly what's in the recipe.
- Give each person a different portion of the sauce to prepare.

Non-disclosure agreements

Many entrepreneurs and small business start-ups try protecting their ideas through a non-disclosure agreement (NDA). An NDA is a document that announces the confidentiality of the material being shared with someone and specifies that the person or persons cannot disclose anything identified by the NDA to other parties or personally use the information. Providing an NDA to anyone you are speaking to in confidence about your business plan, or any other trade secret, is a good idea. Without it, you have no evidence that you provided your proprietary information in confidence; therefore, it can be considered a public disclosure — that is, no longer confidential.

You definitely want to work with an attorney when you construct your NDA, because it must fit your situation. Generic NDAs do not exist. If you want an NDA to be valid for evidence purposes, it must include the following:

- *Consideration,* or what is being given in exchange for signing the document and refraining from revealing the confidentiality.
- A description of what is being covered (be sure this is not too vague or broad).
- A procedure describing how the other party will use or not use the confidential information.

Whom should you have sign an NDA? Anyone who will become privy to your trade secret.

- **Immediate family:** Spouses, children, and parents do not usually require NDAs, but it wouldn't be a bad idea to have them sign one anyway.
- **Extended family and friends who will not be doing business with you:** To meet the consideration requirement for the NDA, you typically offer $1 in compensation.
- **Business associates or companies with which you might do business:** Consideration, in this case, is the opportunity to do business with you. For example, if you show your business plan to a potential investor or creditor, the consideration is the stake in the business or the return on investment.
- **Buyers:** Buyers typically don't sign non-disclosures because doing so may preclude them from developing something similar, or they may already be working on a similar concept. For example, toy manufacturer Mattel Inc. will not sign NDAs from inventors because they have a large R&D department that continually works on new ideas for toys. Chances are they're working on something that will be similar enough to potentially infringe on an inventor's product.

The truth is, an NDA is only as good (and reliable) as the person who signs it. Fighting a violation of an NDA in the courts is difficult and expensive, so when you're ready to talk about your business plan with outsiders, sometimes the best thing you can do is be careful whom you talk to.

Book II

Planning for Your Business

Chapter 3

Setting Your Franchise's Wheels in Motion

In This Chapter

▶ Evaluating and choosing a location for your franchise

▶ Keeping an eye out for encroachment

▶ Buying, receiving, and storing goods and supplies

▶ Getting good training before and after you open your franchise

*F*ranchising is most successful when each and every location in the chain operates in a way that ensures customers a consistent level of quality and service, regardless of which location they're visiting.

But being consistent isn't an easy thing to do (in the business realm, that is). The location's design has to feel right to the customers, and the business needs to be placed where it's convenient for customers to shop. The quality of the products and services you deliver to the customers can't vary much at all from their last experience — they're coming for the experience of shopping with you, which requires your management and staff to be up to the task of delivering on your brand's promise to them. Giving customers that level of reliability is what franchisees do (or should, anyway) every day.

To reach that level of delivery you have to know where you should place your business and how to build it; find the vendors that have the products you need; and understand how to recruit, train, motivate, and manage your staff. Great franchisors teach you how to do all these things. In short, great franchisors share their formula for success.

Surveying Your Options for Locale

Depending on your franchise, you will be confronted with a host of different types of locations in which to establish your business. Good franchisors look closely at successful operations in the system and provide franchisees with profiles of what they consider ideal locations. Some franchisees rent office space in high-rise office buildings; others work from home; but most select from an ever-growing list of options, covered in this section.

Common site options

Here are some of the types of locations you typically will be looking at for your franchise:

- **Malls:** In case you've been living on the moon for the past 50 years, malls are large, enclosed shopping facilities anchored by two or more major retail stores and servicing a large geographic area. A mall is typically easily accessible by automobile via major arteries or interstate highways and surrounded by parking.

  Selecting a well-developed mall requires a franchisee to balance the benefits and the drawbacks. The principal drawback is the cost, which includes not only the rent but a host of additional expenses, such as common-area maintenance — your share of caring for the public space. Malls also charge merchants association fees, which are used for advertising for all the tenants in the mall. You also usually have to operate during the hours that the mall is open. On the plus side, malls are natural draws and attract large numbers of potential customers from as far as 25 or more miles away, depending on traffic patterns and competing malls. You can expect that some malls will include a percentage of your sales as rent in addition to your base rent. In addition to your franchisor having a say on what your location looks like, the better malls may restrict your capability to reimage. You should discuss with your franchisor any restrictions the mall may place on you.

- **Neighborhood centers:** A supermarket typically anchors a neighborhood center with a variety of convenience-oriented small retail and service stores. These centers usually provide the most reasonable rents, and they draw from a trade area of from one to three miles, depending on population access and concentration. Most neighborhood centers have few restrictions on signage — although the upscale centers or those in upscale towns can be as tough as the regional malls on signage and decor and are the type of location that many retail and service franchise systems target for their franchisees.

- **Community centers:** These centers are also convenient for local populations. They usually have two or more anchors, a supermarket, a drugstore, and other general merchandise retailers. They serve local populations up to six or seven miles away, depending on ease of travel and accessibility. They have appeal similar to the neighborhood centers but are much larger and hence may have more signage limitations for their on-street pole signs.

These are the types of centers that most often have available *out-parcels,* which are spaces for smaller freestanding buildings out on the parking lot. The quick service restaurant business uses out-parcels, as do other businesses that need to be closer to the street to be seen by passing motorists.

✔ **Lifestyle centers:** Usually found near affluent residential communities, these open-air centers feature upscale national specialty chain stores, dining and entertainment, and fountains and other ambient design elements that make browsing the internal, uncovered walkways enjoyable — whenever the weather permits. In these setups, traditional anchor stores typically aren't dominant the way they are at the malls. Multiplex cinemas, small department stores, large bookstores, and large-format specialty retailers are usually the biggest individual draws. These centers combine some lower-priced, impulse-purchase vendors trading off of the high traffic counts along with higher-priced, destination-type merchants.

Often, these centers have parking at each of the retail stores and sometimes larger parking lots as well. They will draw from up to 12 or 13 miles, depending on traffic patterns and convenience.

Be careful in choosing a site in a lifestyle center. They are excellent venues for compatible concepts, but they can be expensive mistakes if your concept isn't a good fit with the lifestyle of the majority of its visitors. Most of the time, your franchisor will know whether these centers are a good bet for you or not.

✔ **Power centers:** Power centers are open air and usually located near a regional or super-regional center. They include at least three "big boxes" or "category killers," such as Walmart, Target, and Home Depot. Power centers draw customers from a five-mile radius. A trend in many markets is to convert some of the underproducing regional centers to power centers, because people like the convenience of the regional centers but prefer the option of parking in front of the store of their choice.

✔ **Other centers:** Constantly evolving variations of developments exist where retailing, entertainment, employment, tourism, bargain hunting, and other activities come together. Theme/festival centers are heavy on entertainment and restaurant businesses for leisure and tourist activities. Outlet centers have great bargains and sometimes draw busloads of people from very far away. Mixed-use centers combine many activities in the same area: retail, restaurants, employment, transportation, sports, recreation, office, hotel, cultural, and other activities in various integrated combinations. Specialty centers can focus on restaurants, car care, off-price, and other specific types of businesses on a planned development parcel.

Book II

Planning for Your Business

As with the more typical centers just listed, you want to be part of or nearby these centers to take advantage of the customer flows that they create.

✔ **Shopping areas:** A concentration of stores serving a local community is considered a shopping area. Downtown, also know as a central business district (CBD), is a shopping area that benefits from the traffic from office workers, visitors to downtown, and people who live in the downtown area. Because of the traffic and their prime locations, in some cities, these sites can be expensive and often suffer from lack of customer parking. Because most of the traffic in the downtown areas is usually created by office workers, the hours during the weekdays are busiest, with most customers coming in before work, during lunch, and after work. This inconsistent traffic pattern makes staffing a bit problematic. Except for a few cities that have re-created their downtowns as entertainment destination areas or festival marketplaces for residents from the suburbs — as Baltimore has done — these areas are quiet in the evenings and on weekends and holidays.

✔ **Off-street sites:** Airports, universities, ballparks, and co-branded locations are all types of sites that are usually not easily accessible to customers just driving or walking down the street. These locations represent significant opportunities for many franchisees today and have been a growing trend in franchising. See the next section, "Opting for alternate, or off-street, sites" for more info on this option.

✔ **At-home sites:** Although home locations aren't sites in the traditional sense, more and more franchisees are choosing this option, where the franchisor allows them to work out of their homes. See the later section "Working from home" for more details.

Opting for alternate, or off-street, sites

Many franchisors are able to expand their systems by opening locations in off-street venues or captive-audience venues. These locations are popping up wherever people congregate — gas stations; convenience stores; hospitals; airports; train and bus stations; colleges; large department stores; offices; factories; and movable kiosks at seasonal and recreation locations, sporting arenas, parks, and malls. The idea is to provide your products or services to customers where and when they might want them. Franchisors and franchisees have gotten pretty creative in developing variations of their concepts to fit into more and more venues where people gather.

The strength of captive-audience locations is that the operations benefit from customers drawn to the location by something other than the product you are offering, such as the baseball game at the stadium or to college students between classes. The biggest drawback is that your business success is tied to the ebb and flow of people in the host environment. In other words, when the ballplayers go out on the road or when the season ends, you're out of luck. Colleges are governed by the academic calendar, so get ready to twiddle your thumbs a bit during summer vacation, unless many students attend summer school.

If you visit a convenience store when you purchase gasoline, you are also visiting a captive-audience location. Gas stations operated, for example, by ExxonMobil often share space with quick service restaurants (QSRs). Some may even have a small branch of a service franchise, where you can cash checks or mail packages, for example. The traffic from customers buying gas helps the franchise sell more product and services, and the traffic generated by the franchise helps sell more gas.

Single- or multi-unit operators can operate from these locations. The franchisees can be either the dealer who operates the gas station or another person or entity that simply is renting space from the dealer. Sometimes, the operator may even be the franchisor.

So has a captive-audience site caught your eye? Many of the same criteria you use to check out an on-street site apply here — and then some. Are there signage restrictions? Is it heavily traveled? Is it visible to patrons? If an airport location opens up, you'll see a lot more road warriors in a main terminal, concourse, or food court as opposed to a terminal for the smaller, less traveled carriers, in small regional airports. Not every mass gathering opportunity is the same — you need to do your homework. Where would you rather be, in a sports stadium where the home team fills the stadium each game or in a sports stadium where the home team can invite the spectators to share the bench with them — and still have room? You get the point.

Working from home

Many franchise systems, especially smaller service franchises that never have customers coming to their offices — for example, carpet cleaning, janitorial, maintenance, and repair services — not only allow their franchisees to work from their homes but actually encourage it.

Working at home reduces a franchisee's cost of doing business and is convenient. For many franchisees, working at home is perfect. They can get up early, do their paperwork, and plan their day — all before taking a shower and getting dressed. In the evening, after dinner, they can relax in their office, watch some TV, and prepare for the next day. And because they don't have any other office, they can deduct the costs associated with their home office on their tax returns. (You should check with your accountant and tax preparer to determine what is deductible.)

Landing near another franchise: Dual branding

Another type of arrangement you see frequently where more than one business uses the same premises is called *dual branding:* two or more franchises with different concepts that set up shop next to one another or within the same location, offering customers a one-stop shopping experience.

In this setup, your franchise shares common space with another brand in, for example, a food court at a mall. If your business brings in traffic in the morning hours and is less busy during the afternoon, partnering with another brand that has a heavy afternoon business but a weak morning business may make sense.

Yum! Brands, the parent company of KFC, Pizza Hut, Taco Bell, A&W, and Long John Silver's, often places two or three of its brands in one location. So does ExxonMobil, which often combines its gasoline stations with its On The Run convenience stores with various sandwich, doughnut, other food, quick oil change, or car wash businesses (often with multiple brands all at once).

A dual-branded location may be able to use labor and real estate more efficiently because, if done well, it expands a location's *daypart*. (In the restaurant industry, breakfast, lunch, and dinner are called dayparts.) For example, doughnut chains usually are busiest during the breakfast daypart and slow down during the lunch and dinner dayparts. Other concepts are slow during the breakfast daypart but are busier during the lunch or dinner daypart. By dual branding a location, the operator hopes to capture traffic generated by the other product offering and use the location more fully.

If you choose one of these dual-branded sites, you're still paying an initial franchise fee, paying royalties, and remaining accountable to the same standards. Make sure that your franchisor offers equipment, signage, and design specifications to fit these new locations. Compare the costs — and sales/profit potential — with those of single-branded locations. These sites are usually tucked inside another location and take up less square footage. The smaller space usually means less staff and possibly lower overhead. Some of these franchises operate seasonally. But just because they're smaller doesn't mean they're cheaper. Some — such as limited-access highway travel centers — are on prime properties, and the bidding can be fierce.

Setting Up Shop: Finding Your Franchise's Habitat

Finding a good retail or restaurant location in today's market isn't always easy. Many of the best spots have already been taken, and competition for the available real estate is brisk. Given rapidly changing consumer traveling patterns, opening your franchise in the right location does matter, because if your operations and your location are great, you have the best of both worlds.

 Keep in mind, though, that having a good location is important, but having a good, or even a great, location won't make up for a bad operator. Given the choice between that old tired chant of "location, location, location" and an equally one-dimensional chant of "operations, operations, operations," you should opt for neither — but lean toward the latter.

Exploring your location options is a big part of your franchise research. Startup costs for a home office versus a freestanding site — and everything in-between — can vary by hundreds of thousands of dollars. How's that for hitting you in the pocketbook? Defining your location is also a vital part of your business plan. Anyone who's financing your venture — even your moneybags uncle — will want to know where the cash is going, what the site will look like, why it will attract customers, how much customer traffic will pass the site, and who your competitors are. This section can help you find a site to suit your fancy.

You may luck into a site just by driving through town on the lookout for "For Sale" or "For Lease" signs. Or you may opt to use a commercial real estate broker. You will find that many, or most, of the better sites never have "for sale" or "for lease" signs on the property. The local brokers will become aware of them or dig them out for you based on their business networks and experience. Another resource is the exhibitions where shopping center developers lay out their construction plans. Contact the International Council of Shopping Centers at its website at `www.icsc.org`.

Finding out what constitutes a good site

First, you need to establish the criteria that are important for your type of business. You may think the best place to open your doors is where the crowds are right now, such as in a shopping mall or adjacent to a busy highway. You may be right — for now. But with all the acquisitions, mergers, and market pullouts happening with major retailers and grocers, that major draw your business is dependent on may go away and take with it your customers.

Book II

Planning for Your Business

No one can offer a stock definition of a good site because different businesses require different kinds of locations. Some generalities do hold up, however. If you're investing in a retail franchise, focus your search on a location that gets in your customers' faces. If it's in the path of people commuting to work, near an entertainment arena, or in an office complex, customers can see your business, recognize your brand, and more easily come in to buy your products and services.

For some businesses, however, getting the best corner in town with high visibility and terrific customer access — in a strong, anchored shopping center, for example — is not only unnecessary but also the path to rapid disaster. Carpet cleaners, janitorial services, building repair services, direct mail companies, lawn care services, pest control businesses, moving companies, tool delivery services, and home inspection services, among other service providers, don't usually need high-visibility retail space (and can't afford it, either). Their needs run more to good-looking trucks, delivery access, access to postal facilities, highway access, warehouse facilities, and good telephone service than to locations where their customers shop. After all, most of these service providers go to their customers; the customers don't come to them. Bottom line, if you don't need to be at the corner of Main and Main, you most likely will have more options to choose from, lower rent, and a more accommodating landlord.

As you look for a site, keep your eyes peeled for any red flags. A location that keeps turning over or that has been on the market for a long time should raise your eyebrows. If anything — and we mean anything — smells fishy, investigate further before you sign a lease. Don't let your desire to find a site and open your store trap you into selecting a substandard location. Jim McKenna, president of McKenna Associates, Corp., a Milton, Massachusetts consultant specializing in franchise real estate issues, says that you need to be aware of other site detractors, too. If your customers would be turned off by bad odors from neighboring businesses (perhaps literally smelling fishy), or bad sounds or any negative factors, you may have to reject an otherwise strong site. Consider whether you would leave your children at a beautiful landscaped and convenient day care center if a halfway house for criminals were next door.

Using the franchisor as your compass

When you're dealing with location issues, most franchisors can offer one big advantage: experience. The staff at a mature franchisor can help you identify the kinds of locations that usually work — and those that don't. For example, staff members know whether a franchise can be effectively home-based initially or even long term, whether an office attracts more business in a generic, white, two-story building or with a Park Avenue address, or whether a retail franchise fares better tucked inside a mall or flaunted center stage on a main thoroughfare. So your first step in the process of selecting a location is to discuss viable options with your franchisor. The company may allow a variety of locations, or it may stick to only one type.

You still need to double-check any information the franchisor supplies against your own research. Think of this as a check-and-balance. You check on the accuracy of the data, and your information provides a balance to what the franchisor offers.

A good franchisor points you in the right direction. The franchisor's staff can fill you in on demographic secrets, especially the chain's target market — the profile of your potential customers. How many customers do you need, say, of a particular age and income that can drive to your business in a certain amount of time? How long are customers willing to travel to buy your goods or services? How much are they willing to pay for what you sell?

Many franchisors bombard new franchisees with site criteria — a list that spells out specifications for a particular franchise — inside and out, so that the site meets the franchise system's standards. You may be required to have x number of parking spaces, x number of seats, x number of grills, and so on. Retail and restaurant franchisors, especially, expect their franchisees to comply with their design standards — without variation. On the other hand, an office-based franchise may not care whether you have wood floors or carpeting, mahogany desks or oak. A consistent look at each of the locations may not be important to franchisors, as long as the locations meet their overall quality standards.

Will your franchisor actually help you find this crown jewel of a site? Some franchisors provide considerable help, some provide guidance only, and some leave you on your own. The more hands-on support the franchisor provides in site selection, the better your chances of finding a successful site. Look at your franchise agreement to find out what your franchisor will do for you. Ask the other franchisees in the system how good the franchisor's site-selection assistance actually was.

Franchisors usually educate you about their site criteria, provide you with site criteria forms, and ask you to find the location and do the required research — before you present the site package to them for review. They will then evaluate your information and possibly visit the location before approving or disapproving your choice. Other franchisors — especially

Book II

Planning for Your Business

startup franchisors — may physically accompany you on your site hunting; the staff may jump in the car with you, plot demographics, and talk to landlords.

Check your franchise agreement to see whether and how the franchisor must approve a franchisee-selected site and the time limit for the franchisor to render a decision. Standard contracts allow a franchisor to accept or reject your request to open at a particular location. This decision, like everything else in franchising, reflects the need for consistency.

In almost every franchise agreement, the franchisor is only approving or rejecting a site, not guaranteeing it. This is true even if the franchisor found the location for you — you didn't have to accept it, did you? The franchisor's approval indicates only that the site is acceptable. Ultimately, the selection of the site is your responsibility.

Typically, the franchisor will approve a general area for your location and expect you to search within those boundaries for a location, unless the franchisor already has a site in mind. Some franchisors may already have located the site, built the building, outfitted it with equipment and fixtures, and made it available for you to buy or lease.

Use drive time to evaluate a site on your own

Most demographic studies today can present information based on census tracts, block groups, Zip codes, a radius measured in miles from a center point, drive-time polygons, and many other configurations. For retail and restaurant franchises, the drive times are usually best (except for walk-up locations) because most people will drive to your business — either coming from someplace or while going someplace else. Given a specified amount of time (3 minutes, 5 minutes, 20 minutes, and so on), a computer program can draw an irregular polygon based on vehicle speeds on the various roads and highways and then provide demographic and employment information for the contained area. These polygons usually vary dramatically from the comparable circles of 1, 5, 10, or 20 miles. The size of an area you should measure is most important. If your customers are quick-lunch types who typically drive no more than 3 or 4 minutes each way to get lunch and return to work, measuring the employment population 10 minutes out won't help you. The franchisor usually can give you assistance in determining the size of your *trading area* (the area where you draw the majority your customers).

Getting a landlord on board

Many times a landlord may be unfamiliar with your business, or worse, may have a negative perception of your business. He may simply be naïve, have bad information, or possibly have had a bad experience with a past tenant who offered similar services or goods. Explain why your business is different, who your customers are, and the benefits the other tenants will receive from your business. If your concept is national in scope, give the landlord a sense of the prestige his center will receive by being part of the system.

When you're looking for sites, think of yourself as the seller, not the buyer. Your job is to sell the potential landlord on the merits of your business. Your franchisor should provide you with marketing materials to give to landlords. Give landlords a reason to pick you over other businesses competing for the same space.

Avoiding Encroachment

One thing that gets people talking in franchising is *encroachment*. You need to understand this concept before, not after, you sign your franchise agreement.

Suppose that your franchisor has granted you a protected territory stretching one mile around your location or for a specific trade area outlined on a map. The franchisor then is prohibited from allowing another franchisee or company-owned location from opening closer than one mile from your store or within the boundaries.

With that agreement in hand, you open a franchise on the corner of Fifth and Main. A year or five years later, another franchisee from the same system opens a franchise on Fourth and Main. The new franchise is so close you can see your customers going in and out of the new location. That's encroachment.

As in this example, encroaching can come from another franchisee or company-owned location opening in your protected territory. But it can also happen if the franchisor begins to sell products in other locations — such as a supermarket or a convenience store within your protected territory. It can also happen if the franchisor allows others to offer the same services you sell in your neighborhood.

Encroachment can also occur through catalog sales (from catalogs mailed into your market) or through the Internet, if customers can buy through e-commerce the same products you sell in your location. It depends on what the franchise agreement says about your protected territory and whether the franchisor can sell its products over the web.

Encroachment is like someone stepping on your toes — only the person doing the stepping is your franchisor, who you thought was your partner. Ouch, that can hurt! On the other hand, you don't want to be the only one of your brand in the market. Left all alone, you will be vulnerable to competitors who will have no problem with opening next door to you, especially if you are part of a weak brand with little penetration and unable to advertise sufficiently. Good franchisors try to achieve a balance to create brand recognition in the marketplace and therefore more demand for the products and services of the franchised brand so that everyone in the chain can benefit.

Obviously, encroachment can potentially have an adverse impact on your business. Carefully examine the language of your franchise agreement. Are you getting a protected territory, or do you have no territorial rights? If your franchise grants you only a site address franchise (your protected territory is no bigger than the four walls of your store), the franchisor could conceivably establish other locations nearby that will compete with you. Some contracts specifically state that a franchisor may establish other units and/or sell items through other channels of distribution in direct competition with a franchisee. Because Internet sales don't require the establishment of a location, e-commerce may not legally be encroachment, unless specified in the agreement. Don't assume you have rights not provided in the agreement.

You need to know — before you sign the franchise agreement — whether the franchisor will be able to open locations in your market area. Joyce G. Mazero, lead franchise attorney at Haynes & Boone in Dallas, Texas, cautions, "Contracts normally tell you what the franchisor is granting, such as the right to operate a site, but don't always plainly tell you what it is not granting — such as no right to exclusivity outside of the site, no right to conduct business on the Internet, and no right to prohibit the franchisor or another franchisee from operating from a site close to your site. What you are getting is just as important as what you are not getting."

Don't rely on a franchise salesperson's statements about what the system generally does or doesn't do regarding its locations. Even if the salesperson makes sense when saying that the franchisor would never open a location so close to you that it would adversely affect your business, get the necessary language in writing in the franchise agreement (as with everything else that's important).

Even where the franchise agreement allows the franchisor to establish new locations close to an existing franchisee, some franchisors establish procedures — adopted internally or with their franchisee advisory councils — to review the impact of encroachment on existing units. If the encroachment seems that it will cause a prolonged and material adverse impact, they may decide not to allow the development of the new location. If the encroachment appears that it will cause a minor or temporary impact, they may allow the unit to be developed but may also assist the affected franchisee to make up for the lost sales.

Other franchisors simply cite the terms of the affected franchisee's agreement and allow the unit to open — regardless of the extent of the impact.

Find out what the franchisor's policies and practices are concerning protected territories and encroachment impact before signing the franchise agreement. Read your franchise agreement; speak to other franchisees in the system, and talk to your attorney.

Securing Your Space After Finding Your Piece of Heaven

After you find the perfect location, the real work begins: convincing the landlord to give you a lease you can live with, and then selecting contractors who will build out the location.

Understanding and signing a lease

When you're about to sign a lease, you've already decided on a location. You should be in the process of contacting the real estate or mall management company that manages the property to determine space availability and specific occupancy costs and lease terms, and to complete your site review package for your franchisor.

Does the center have an adequate amount of space available for your business? Although you don't want to squeeze into a space that's too small, you also don't want to pay for space that you will never need. Square foot costs can vary with overall size; often, the larger the space, the lower the square foot cost. However, even with a lower per-foot cost on a larger space, the maintenance and development costs will be higher. Evaluate size based on your needs.

There's far more involved in signing a lease than this chapter has room for. For all the gritty details, check out *Negotiating Commercial Leases & Renewals For Dummies* by Dale Willerton and Jeff Greenfield (John Wiley & Sons, Inc.).

Building a location

Sometimes the only site you can find in the area that is perfect for your franchise is an empty lot. What do you do now? Build.

Building your own location can be tedious and demanding. But if you select the site based on your franchisor's criteria, plan the job, select your contractor carefully, and monitor the job closely, you will have the exact location that you need.

If building a site is going to be your choice, make sure you touch base again with the local zoning board and building department before you even close on the property and certainly before you move that first shovel of dirt. You want to be in compliance with everything — down to local ordinances that set the hours you can hammer and saw to your heart's content. You also want to determine whether the town needs to approve any variances (which give you permission to do something on the land that's different than the zoning rules allow) for the property and whether the site will support your needs for utilities, parking, and the like. Early discussion with the municipality is important. Even where your use is permitted, the planning board can have some unusual requirements that could make the site unworkable for you. Sometimes green-space setbacks or water-retention basins, while nice for the ducks, can push your building out of sight of approaching traffic. If your business relies on impulse purchases, you're in a tough spot.

Although your contractor or architect usually does the pre-groundbreaking legwork, seeing that it all gets done is your responsibility — not the franchisor's.

Your contractor needs to obtain the following:

- ✔ **Permits:** For construction, utilities, signs, curb cuts (those indentations in the sidewalk that let the cars in), and environmental matters
- ✔ **Variances:** If you need the town to approve some specific violation of the zoning requirements for your site
- ✔ **Certificates of occupancy:** Allow you to occupy the location

You also have to prepare preliminary plans and specifications for site improvement and construction, and usually — big surprise! — submit them to your franchisor for approval. Your banker or lender will also want to see these plans.

Understanding the layout

Every retail and restaurant franchisor has a floor plan (footprint) that is excruciating in its exactness. Even if you think that a counter should be two inches longer on the left side, you have to follow the franchisor's plans — or get the franchisor's permission for a change. Even if you know for a fact that menu signs are more readable if they're placed 12 inches lower to the floor than the required 90 inches, you still have to follow the plans. You need to get these specifications and standards so that you can review them with your architect and contractor.

Franchisors usually provide prototype plans for every location. Your architect must develop plans for your site that meet local ordinances and codes as well as the franchisor's standards. Don't assume that you can add improvements to the design, such as a bigger back of house (the kitchen and storage area). Check with your franchisor before making expensive changes you may have to reverse.

All these specifications from the franchisor are intended to ensure consistency, which is great, but what if your particular community has some type of restriction that runs counter to your franchisor's building plans? Make sure that you notify your franchisor so that you can discuss the required changes. If the changes are important, the franchisor often personally contacts the builder or city planner to discuss the changes.

Selecting the contractor

You're probably groaning by now, remembering the last time you hired a contractor to insulate your crawlspace or enclose the patio. But selecting a reputable commercial contractor who has experience with meeting deadlines and the quality requirements of a franchisor isn't difficult. And doing so is only common sense.

Getting the Goods: Merchandise and Supplies

In this section, we look at the way franchisees purchase and maintain inventory and supplies. One of the main benefits you are looking for in a good franchise system is the capability to combine your purchases with those of the franchisor and the other franchisees. Working together, you hope that you can get the best price, the best products, the best equipment, and the best service from suppliers. A good franchisor has also made certain that the suppliers want to participate in this beneficial relationship simply because it's good for their business, too.

Book II

Planning for Your Business

The benefits from the buy

When you're looking at different franchise opportunities, you can tell in advance what methods the franchisor uses by reviewing the franchisor's Uniform Franchise Offering Circular. The UFOC tells you which methods the franchise system uses and whether the franchisor earns any income on the franchisees' purchases. Finding out in advance is important, because some systems with a lower royalty rate may actually cost you more money than a system with a higher royalty rate, because the difference may be more than offset by the income the franchisor earns from your purchases. (In case you're wondering, the *royalty* is your payment to the franchisor that allows you to continue in the franchise system — it's usually based on your total sales.)

Nothing is wrong with a system that earns money every time you purchase goods from a supplier. After all, setting up and maintaining these supplier relationships costs the franchisor. And franchisees need to have a financially strong franchisor who can provide them the services they need and want. However, in a perfect world, you want to find a franchise system in which the "blended" costs of being a franchisee (royalty and other costs) are the lowest, and the services provided by the franchisor are the highest.

Probably no benefit is more important to a franchisee than the potential strength in numbers the system brings to controlling the quality, consistency, availability, and exclusivity of the equipment, supplies, merchandise, and raw materials used by its franchisees.

All franchises need merchandise and supplies of some kind. Some franchise systems require franchisees to buy certain goods direct from the franchisor. Some systems specify that franchisees must purchase from approved suppliers. And some systems allow franchisees to choose their own vendors. The method or combination of methods depends on the type of industry, the products or ingredients the franchise uses, the size of the system, the size of the region the franchisor serves, and the available delivery methods.

Knowing whom to buy from when your franchisor is involved

Suppose you've purchased a maid service franchise. You've hired a first-rate staff, and they're ready to get busy scouring, wiping, dusting, and polishing. But elbow grease isn't enough; they need cleaning products. You may not have the option of hopping over to the local warehouse store and loading up a cart. Your franchisor may require you to purchase products directly from the company. Or your franchise agreement may specify that you use only franchisor-approved suppliers or authorized products. These rules ensure that the supplies you use meet the franchisor's standards. A bonus to you is that, because the franchise system may buy in large volume, prices may be lower. This section explores some of the more common arrangements on how franchisors can enforce system standards by ensuring consistent ingredients and supplies for the franchised network.

Buying goods direct from your franchisor

When franchisors elect to be the exclusive suppliers to their franchisees, the requirement usually extends only to items that are proprietary (read: secret recipes) or that contain certain key ingredients. These products may be ordered directly from the company, or in most systems, the franchisor has provided the products to the distributors that serve the system.

Book II

Planning
for Your
Business

Nonproprietary merchandise and supplies are another matter. Even if the franchisor distributes the goods, they usually aren't the exclusive suppliers, and franchisees have the option of making their purchases from either approved suppliers or from their own chosen vendors. (Sometimes, the purchases must meet standards or specifications set by the franchisor.)

Many of the legal disputes over the past two decades have resulted from franchisees' perception that they are getting gouged — that is, the products they must purchase from the franchisor are excessively marked up, making the franchisee less competitive. Rupert Barkoff, Partner at Kilpatrick Stockton LLP in Atlanta, Georgia, warns, "Beware of franchisors who require that certain products be purchased through them. It is easier for a franchisee to digest the franchisor's decision that products must be purchased from the franchisor when the product sales are not a profit center for the franchisor."

Although the methods the franchisor uses for supplying products are in the UFOC, the franchisee usually gets additional information on supplier relationships at training.

Getting merchandise and supplies from approved and required suppliers

Rather than inventory all the merchandise required for a network of franchisees, some franchisors give franchisees a list of approved suppliers from whom they can buy their items directly. As long as the approved suppliers sell only the merchandise approved by the franchisors — without unauthorized substitutions — franchisors can maintain control over the quality of the products sold under their brand.

A good franchisor is the keeper of the brand. In that role, the franchisor's representatives identify, screen, and approve suppliers to the system. Suppliers come in all shapes and sizes, and your franchisor has hopefully sifted through the best of them for you. Before you chafe over having to use only a franchisor's choice of suppliers, curb your entrepreneurial spirit and read on.

A good franchisor wants to keep your operational costs as low as possible to help you make as much money as you can. If a franchisor has gone to the trouble — and expense — of finding good suppliers for you, take advantage of that effort! Of course, ask your fellow franchisees whether they're happy with their suppliers. (Make sure you ask this question before you buy the franchise. You don't want to be surprised.) If they are, be thankful that finding good suppliers is one less item on your to-do list.

Franchisors worth their salt negotiate with manufacturers for the lowest net prices on goods, for marketing support, and for other benefits. Check with your franchisor about the way rebates are handled in your system. The procedure is far from uniform among franchisors or among suppliers. Also, if you discover that a supplier in your area meets your franchisor's criteria and is less expensive than the franchisor's authorized suppliers, make sure to pass the information on to the franchisor's headquarters.

Supplying goods the Wendy's way

Wendy's franchisees can take advantage of arrangements the franchisor makes with suppliers. Programs set up by the purchasing department can help make sure that products meet their quality standards and are available when their franchisees need them. At the same time, their franchisees can buy at a lower price because of volume buying. The franchisor provides the purchasing service free of charge to its franchisees — it's not a profit center for them. It's another way they ensure consistency in the Wendy's brand. A good franchisor should offer this service for the franchisees, simply because it's the right thing to do.

Wendy's has a whole staff of people who go into the suppliers' operations and audit their facilities. Staff members check on the entire production line and make sure that the company is doing everything the way they want it to. They even check their products by pulling them from the suppliers' facilities and the distribution centers around the country and sending them off to an independent laboratory for evaluation. Wendy's wants to make sure that all the food safety measures are in place and being used. With all the recalls in the food industry, you have to be aware of exactly what the suppliers are doing, what's going on at their production facilities, and what environment your products are being produced in.

Buying products authorized by the franchisor

All franchisors — big, small, or in-between — require consistency in the products sold under their brands. Product standards and specifications are one of the keys to controlling product consistency.

Franchisors set product standards and specifications, which means that they tell their franchisees what type and quality of products to buy. As long as franchisees follow these rules, they can choose their own vendors. This practice is common in small franchise systems, but even big franchisors often allow franchisees to buy items locally, as long as those products meet the standards.

Buying goods through cooperatives

Several franchise systems use *cooperatives,* or buying groups, to purchase products, marketing, advertising, insurance, leasing, credit, and other goods or services.

Cooperatives are by no means uniform in how they function and whom they represent. Many are started by franchisees, and the franchisor isn't part of the buying group. Other cooperatives include both company-owned and franchisee-owned locations. Still others represent members from several franchise systems.

The value of joining a cooperative is that group purchasing lowers prices. This method gives you a competitive advantage over those who can't buy as cheaply. Also, large buying groups often get better access to new products, better allocation when products are scarce, and better service from suppliers when things go wrong.

Franchisees and/or franchisors purchase membership in the cooperative and commit to buying a certain percentage of their requirements through the cooperative. Cooperatives are controlled by the members, typically on a one-member, one-vote basis, with members determining the officers, directors, policies, and procedures adopted by the cooperative.

Cooperative members may also share in what are called *patronage dividends,* which, like stock dividends, are distributions of the earnings of the cooperative. However, patronage dividends differ from stock dividends in one major way: Stock dividends are based on the number of shares you own, whereas patronage dividends are based on the amount of your purchases from the cooperative. The more you buy, the more you get back in patronage dividends.

Of course, when you purchase through a cooperative, you still must meet the standards and specifications your franchisor has set for your location.

Book II

Planning for Your Business

Finding your own suppliers and goods

One key advantage of buying a franchise is that you can be part of a larger network that includes your franchisor, fellow franchisees, and regional support staff. But if you're one of the first franchisees in a system, or your franchisor isn't large enough to have national or regional distributors, you may have to do some of the relationship building with suppliers that a franchisor in a larger system would do for you.

If your franchisor doesn't provide you with a list of authorized suppliers, you're going to have to choose your own vendors.

Work with your field consultant and your franchisor's purchasing department to see whether they can help you identify suppliers in your markets. Visit other similar businesses and ask what suppliers they use. Your local chamber of commerce may also have a list of suitable suppliers.

When you review bids and quotations from vendors, make sure that you understand the total charges. Some vendors quote a low price on a product but make up the loss with additional handling and delivery charges. Look for these hidden charges when you compare pricing.

Price is certainly one of the prime considerations in selecting a vendor. However, basing your decision solely on price can be a mistake. A good price on items constantly out of stock or a good price from a vendor who is continuously trying to dump outdated merchandise won't help you build your business.

Receiving Merchandise

If you own a franchise, one thing you have to figure out is how to manage your *receipt of merchandise.* You must properly check, log in, and store all merchandise entering the store. You can negotiate lower prices for your merchandise, but you won't save any money if you don't notice unacceptable quality or shortages in shipments. To avoid these losses, you or the store manager must establish a regular receiving routine for your store. Having a routine helps to monitor vendors and reduces the chance of shortage.

Your franchisor should provide you with a list of recommendations and procedures for maintaining your inventory. Follow it. If your franchisor doesn't provide inventory procedures, the following sections offer useful guidelines.

Receiving deliveries

Suppose you've just purchased a convenience store franchise. The new site has been built, and you're standing inside your brand-new building. The only problem is that the shelves are empty. Soon you'll need to begin scheduling and receiving deliveries, but you may not have any experience in this process. Follow these general tips for receiving merchandise at any type of franchise:

- ✔ Make sure suppliers schedule their deliveries in advance. Accept deliveries only during specified hours. When the location is open and operating, you want the merchandise to come during off-peak hours so that you can concentrate on accepting the delivery.

- ✔ Don't allow vendors to park in front of your business. Require vendors to park in an out-of-the-way spot. The front of your business is for customers.

- ✔ Have the delivery driver bring all products into the building before you check the items. (Some systems want their own employees to bring merchandise into the store.)

- ✔ Make sure that the merchandise you receive is for your business.

- ✔ Watch helpers. Some vendors have helpers whose main job is to distract you during the check-in process.

- ✔ Immediately put away all perishable products.

Checking the goods after they're in your location

A truck pulls up at the back door of your franchise, and a flurry of activity follows. Suddenly, you're surrounded by boxes. The driver is completing the paperwork for your signature. This situation doesn't have to be scary if you know what to do. Check the quality and condition of the merchandise before accepting it. Here are some additional tips:

- ✔ Examine every box for obvious signs of damage, such as tears, broken or crushed cardboard, signs of tampering, rattles, damp or wet cardboard, bad odors, dented cans, substitutions of standard items, and so on.

- ✔ Before signing for the boxes, open any cartons that have been opened and resealed or that you suspect have internal damage. Note any damages on the receiving record.

✔ Always check the date code on the product when it is delivered. Make sure that the product is within the code and that you can reasonably expect to sell it before the code expires.

Verifying invoices

Attending to paperwork may be the least entertaining part of franchise ownership, but in the case of delivery receipts, it can be rewarding. You can avoid financial losses by ensuring that you're getting what you pay for. Check out these tips:

✔ Before accepting delivery, check each item on the delivery receipt against the product that has been delivered and then compare against the product ordered. Check quantities received against quantities ordered. Count the number of cartons delivered and compare this number to the number on the driver's record or freight bill. Never sign for more cartons than you receive. Note any discrepancies on the freight bill or receiving record or correct the errors before the vendor leaves the store.

✔ Never give the delivery receipt back to the vendor. Obtain the delivery receipt when the vendor walks in and under no circumstances return it to the vendor. Manipulating the delivery receipt is one of the most common ways that some vendors steal from franchise locations.

✔ If the vendor made a substitution, call your franchisor's field consultant to verify that the substitution is valid and acceptable. Inform the driver and note on the invoice that substitutions not approved by your franchisor are subject to return for full credit.

✔ If you don't receive an item appearing on the delivery receipt, have the driver clearly mark the item "short" along with the quantity not received. The driver must then sign the delivery receipt before you sign it.

Maintaining Inventory

Your franchise training manuals teach you all about maintaining your inventory. Procedures vary widely, depending on the type of franchise you own. Your franchise may not even have any inventory, and in that case, you can skip this section. (Nobody but you will know.)

Back of the house

The back of the house is also known as the stockroom. It's literally in the back area of your business, and it's where you keep all the items not currently in use. If you need more vitamins, you go to the back of the house — or the back room or stockroom — and get them. Back of the house is also where you store perishables or frozen items, which means that it can also be the location of a refrigerator or freezer. You'll be expected to know what you have in the back, too. But again, franchisors already do a lot of the work by providing a plan-o-gram for the back of the house, just as they do for the front.

Your franchisor should provide detailed back-of-the-house storage procedures. Follow them. If your franchisor doesn't provide information on back-of-the-house arrangements and procedures, the following sections provide some procedures to consider.

Book II

Planning for Your Business

Dry storage practices

Dry storage is a term used for items that don't require refrigeration. If you're a health food franchisee, your vitamins and sports drinks are both dry storage items. The following are some dry storage practices:

✔ Store products at least 6 inches off the floor on clean, nonporous surfaces to permit the cleaning of floor areas and to protect from contamination and rodents.

✔ Don't store products under exposed sewer or water lines, or next to sweating walls.

✔ Store all poisonous materials — including pesticides, soaps, and detergents — away from food supplies, in designated storage areas.

✔ Store all open packages in closed and labeled containers.

✔ Keep shelving and floors clean and dry at all times.

✔ Schedule cleaning of storage areas at regular intervals.

✔ Date all merchandise upon receipt and rotate inventory on a first-in-first-out basis (place the oldest products in front of the newly received merchandise).

✔ Locate most frequently needed items on lower shelves and near the entrance.

✔ Store heavy packages on low shelves.

✔ Don't store any products above shoulder height.

Refrigerated storage practices

If you have items needing refrigeration, place them into your cold storage as soon as you can. Here are some tips for storing your refrigerated items:

- Enclose any food or other product removed from its original container in a clean, sanitized, covered container and properly identify it.
- Don't store foods in contact with water or undrained ice.
- Check refrigerator and freezer thermometers regularly.
- Store all foods to permit the free circulation of cool air on all surfaces.
- Never store food directly on the floor.
- If you're a business that needs to store products under refrigeration, make certain that the temperature setting is appropriate for the product.
- Schedule cleaning of equipment and refrigerated storage at regular intervals.
- Date all merchandise upon receipt and rotate inventory on a first-in-first-out basis (place the oldest products in front of the newly received merchandise). Doing so is particularly important with refrigerated products because their shelf life is usually short.
- Establish preventive maintenance programs for equipment.

Front of the house

The *front of the house* is everything that's not the back of the house. This is the area that customers see when they enter your store. Obviously, how the front of the house looks is more important for locations that are frequented by customers and less important for locations that customers never see.

If you're a retail location, you will handle your merchandise differently than if you were a restaurant. Still, at all times, the front of the house is your showcase — it's what customers see every time they visit your store.

Retailers need to place merchandise on shelves so that it's attractive to customers and induces them to buy. Restaurants and other businesses that sell food also need to keep their locations attractive. If you have reach-in refrigeration accessible to your customers, or if you have items on display, how you display them is just as important to you as it is to a retailer. Your franchisor should provide you with a plan-o-gram for that purpose.

In order to keep the front of your store in tip-top shape, make the following a priority:

✔ Follow your system's plan-o-gram.

✔ Keep your shelves and merchandisers (displays for your merchandise) stocked, clean, and dust free.

✔ Use proper product rotation by placing the oldest product in front of the newly received merchandise (first-in, first-out).

✔ Price identical items the same. One benefit of modern point-of-sale technology is that you don't have to reprice each item when prices change — all you have to do is change the price in the computer and on the shelf's price tag.

✔ Allow adequate space between displays, as required by your local code.

✔ Use only signage that is acceptable in your system. If your franchisor requires you to use professionally prepared signage, don't use hand-written signs. As important, make sure to keep your signage current. (Remove the Christmas posters before Labor Day!)

✔ Keep your floor area free of empty boxes, unless they're part of your design concept.

Book II

Planning for Your Business

The Americans with Disabilities Act requires that you keep your store arranged in a manner that makes it usable for individuals with disabilities. As a general rule, provide enough space for easy passage of a wheelchair throughout the store, make certain that the lines to your registers are accessible, and don't display merchandise in a way that makes it difficult for people with disabilities to shop. If you have no choice about how you merchandise the store, make certain that your staff is actively available to any customers who may need assistance. Remember, complying with all federal and local laws is the franchisee's responsibility.

Getting Good Training Before and After You Open Your Franchise

A good franchisor insists that you learn the business and that you keep learning as the system changes and market conditions evolve. Most franchisors train at their offices, at established operations, or at franchisee locations. Follow-up support is usually handled through the area field representative, who acts as the liaison between you and the home office.

A right way and a wrong way

Training your staff is the most important thing a franchisor/-ee does. And the training never ends. You even need to teach them how to clean the tables. Believe it or not, there's a right way and a wrong way to teach even these mundane tasks.

Also, franchise systems vary widely in their use of technology in training. If you're considering a franchise that is new or recently launched, you may find use of online training to be very limited, because more sophisticated online training requires large investments by the franchisor. A hard copy of the operations manual and a new franchisee training class are commonly the only training vehicles (and may be adequate depending on other support) in a startup franchise company.

Getting good initial training

Expect to cover a lot of ground during your initial training. Initial training should be aimed at teaching you and your staff how to produce and deliver the franchisor's product or service the same way every time. But good training is more than simply learning how to make the product.

Franchisees should learn the following:

- ✔ Standards and operating procedures
- ✔ Food safety and storage (if the franchise is a restaurant or a store selling food products)
- ✔ Technical operations on products and services (nonfood franchise)
- ✔ Leadership and business management
- ✔ Problem solving
- ✔ Tips for understanding the customer experience
- ✔ Brand positioning (how the franchisor wants the public to think and feel when they hear the brand name)
- ✔ Merchandising and pricing methods
- ✔ Marketing and advertising
- ✔ Labor management, including recruitment, supervision, and motivation
- ✔ Techniques for training staff
- ✔ Cleaning and maintenance

✔ Safety and security

✔ Vendor relations, purchasing, receiving, stocking, and inventory management

✔ Financial management and business plan development

✔ MIS/POS systems

   A management information system (MIS) is the computer system used to manage business matters (accounting, payroll, and so on); a point-of-sale system (POS) is used to manage sales activities (cash registers, pricing, and inventory).

✔ Communications, both internal and external

✔ Site selection, construction, landscaping, and store design

Good training instills in the franchisee the franchisor's brand philosophy; teaches franchisees everything they need to know — from opening the business in the morning to closing at night; and gives them the sources for additional or emergency support.

Most franchise systems begin training after you sign the franchise agreement and pay your initial fee. Many provide training in segments such as the following:

✔ Initial training to assist you in site selection and development

✔ Training for both you and your management personnel

✔ Training for your initial staff

✔ Continual training that introduces your staff to new products and services

✔ Replacement staff training when employees leave the franchise

How much training you can expect depends on the industry, the complexity of the business, and especially on the franchisor.

If the industry historically has high staff turnover — and the franchisor requires you to send your staff to the franchisor's training program and then charges you to train your replacement staff — you will incur additional training costs. These costs are a good inducement to recruit and *retain* good employees.

In some systems, you can expect only a few days of training, and often this time is spent working in operating locations. In others, you can spend months in training, both in class and on the job in training locations, and then the franchisor provides continual training for innovations, new products, and your replacement personnel. The Uniform Franchise Offering Circular, or UFOC, details the length and scope of the training you will receive. Make sure you feel confident that the training is sufficient for you to operate your business.

Ensuring that you receive effective ongoing training

In larger franchise systems, field support is usually provided from one of the franchisor's regional offices. Smaller franchise systems may use the headquarters staff to provide you with your training and ongoing support.

Operating a franchise in today's economic climate means staying on your toes all the time. You can't do that by yourself. As a franchisee, you should expect the franchisor to provide you with more than initial training. After your franchise is open, expect the franchisor's field staff to show up armed with operational, marketing, and organizational support.

You should also expect the company's help with the rollout of innovations, such as the preparation of new products or the operation of new equipment. The hallmarks of great franchisors are offering new products, updating research, implementing new-product development, installing state-of-the-art technology, introducing better methods of customer service, and repositioning franchises in the market. These services keep a company more than one step ahead of the competition.

Chapter 4

Starting a Home-Based Business

In This Chapter

▶ Understanding the basics of home-based businesses

▶ Looking at the pros and cons of having a home-based business

▶ Beginning your business from nothing

▶ Making the transition

There are nearly 30 million businesses in the United States today. Of these businesses, 99.7 percent are *small businesses* (which the government defines as businesses with fewer than 500 employees). Of these, a little more than half — 52 percent — are home-based businesses. Now that's a *lot* of home-based businesses!

Owning your own home-based business may be the most rewarding experience of your entire life — and not just in a financial sense (although many home-based businesspeople find the financial rewards to be significant). Having your own home-based business is also rewarding in the sense of doing the work you love and having control over your own life.

Of course, every great journey begins with the first step. This chapter looks at the basics of home-based business — including getting started, managing your money, avoiding problems, and moving ahead. It also considers some of the good news — and the bad — about starting your own home-based business and explains how to know when it's time to make the move. It talks about starting your business from scratch and ends up with some advice on making the transition to working at your home-based business.

Looking at the Basics of Home-Based Business

Not surprisingly, a *home-based business* is a business based in a home. Whether you do all the work in your home or you do some of it on customers' or third-party premises, whether you run a franchise, a direct-sales operation, or a business opportunity, if the center of your operations is based in your home, it's a home-based business.

Determining the kind of business you want to have

After you decide you're going to start your own home-based business, you have to answer two questions:

- ✔ What kind of home-based business do you want to start?
- ✔ What's the best way to market your products or services?

You basically have two types of home-based businesses to choose from: businesses you start from scratch and businesses you buy. The latter category is further split into three types: franchises, direct-selling opportunities, and business opportunities. Whether you prefer to march to your own drum and start your business from the ground up or get a business-in-a-box depends on your personal preferences.

The advantage of a business you start from scratch is that you can mold it to fit your preferences and the existing and emerging markets, which provides you with a boundless variety of possibilities. Businesses started from scratch account for the majority of viable, full-time businesses — in other words, they tend to be more successful over the long run than businesses you can buy.

In their book *Finding Your Perfect Work* (Tarcher), Paul and Sarah Edwards provide characteristics of more than 1,500 self-employment careers, along with hundreds of examples of unique businesses that people have carved out for themselves.

Each type of home business that you can buy, on the other hand, has its own spin. The following sections illustrate how the three types are different from one another.

Franchise

A *franchise* is an agreement in which one business grants another business the right to distribute its products or services. Some common home-based franchises include the following:

- Aussie Pet Mobile (mobile pet grooming)
- Jani-King (commercial cleaning service)
- Jazzercise (dance/exercise classes)
- ServiceMaster Clean (cleaning service)
- Snap-on Tools (professional tools and equipment)

Check out Book I Chapter 5, which covers franchising in detail.

Direct selling

Direct selling involves selling consumer products or services in a person-to-person manner, away from a fixed retail location. The two main types of direct-selling opportunities are

- **Single-level marketing:** Making money by buying products from a parent company and then selling those products directly to customers
- **Multi-level marketing:** Making money through single-level marketing and by sponsoring new direct sellers

Some common home-based direct-selling opportunities include the following:

- Shaklee (household cleaning products)
- The Pampered Chef (kitchen tools)
- Green Irene (green products and consulting)
- Longaberger Company (baskets)
- Mary Kay, Inc. (cosmetics)
- Fuller Brush Company (household and personal-care products)

Business opportunity

A *business opportunity* is an idea, product, system, or service that someone develops and offers to sell to others to help them start their own, similar businesses. With a business opportunity, your customers and clients pay you directly when you deliver a product or service to them. (Another way to think of a business opportunity is that it's any business concept you can buy

Book II

Planning for Your Business

from someone else that isn't direct selling or franchising.) Here are several examples of business opportunities that you can easily run out of your home:

- ✔ Astro Events of America (inflatable party rentals)
- ✔ Debt Zero LLC (debt settlement)
- ✔ ClosetMaid (storage and organizational products)
- ✔ Vendstar (bulk-candy vending machines)

Interested in how to find more companies and how to get in touch with them? Entrepreneur Media (www.entrepreneur.com) and www.gosmallbiz.com have extensive information on business opportunities you can buy. You can also do a search on Google or your favorite search engine, using the keywords *business opportunity*.

After you decide on a business, you have to find the money to get it started (see Book II Chapter 2 for more on finding funding). Then you have to market your products or services and persuade people to buy them (the chapters in Book V cover the marketing gamut). You can choose conventional methods of promotion, such as advertising and public relations, or you can leverage new selling opportunities, such as the Internet, to your advantage. Or you can (and probably should) do both. It's your choice — you're the boss!

Managing your money

Money makes the world go 'round, and because you're talking about your financial well-being here, it's very important that you have a handle on your business finances. To get the handle you need, do the following:

- ✔ **Find the money you need to start your business.** The good news is that many home-based businesses require little or no money to start up. If you decide to buy a franchise or business opportunity from someone else, however, you definitely need some amount of startup funding. To find this funding, consider all your options, including friends and family, savings, credit cards, bank loans, and more.

- ✔ **Keep track of your money.** In most cases, keeping track of your money means using a simple accounting or bookkeeping software package (such as Quicken) to organize and monitor your business finances.

- ✔ **Set the right price for your products and services.** If you set your prices too high, you'll scare customers away; if you set them too low, you'll be swamped with customers, but you won't make enough money to stay afloat. Be sure to charge enough to cover your costs while generating a healthy profit.

✔ **Obtain health insurance, and plan for your retirement.** When you have your own business, you're the one who needs to arrange for health insurance and set up IRAs, 401(k)s, or other retirement plans for the day when you're ready to hang up your business and stroll off into the sunset.

✔ **Pay taxes.** As someone famous once said, "The only things you can count on in life are death and taxes." Well, taxes are a definite, so make sure you pay all the taxes you owe for your home-based business.

Avoiding problems

Eventually, every business — home-based or not — runs into problems. Whether the problems are being late on a delivery or hitting a snag with the Internal Revenue Service, as the owner of your own business, you need to avoid problems whenever possible and deal with them quickly and decisively when you can't avoid them. Some of the problems you may deal with include the following:

✔ **Legal issues:** After a good accountant, the next best friend of any business owner is a good attorney. Keep one handy to help you deal with legal issues when they inevitably arise.

✔ **Issues with support services:** Finding skilled and reliable outside support services — lawyers, accountants, bankers, business consultants, and insurance brokers — isn't necessarily an easy task, especially if your business is in a small town where you're pretty much stuck with what's down the road. See the section "Consult outside professionals," later in this chapter, for more information on support services.

✔ **Scams and rip-offs:** More and more home-based business scams seem to appear every day, so don't rush into any business opportunity. Take your time and fully explore every opportunity before you sign on the dotted line. And remember, if it looks too good to be true, it probably is.

Moving ahead

One of the best things about owning your own business is watching it develop, mature, and grow. After all, a growing business is the gift that keeps on giving — all year round, year after year. To keep your business moving ahead, consider doing the following:

✔ **Make the web work for you.** Doing business and generating sales and interest in your business via the Internet is practically a given for any home-based business today. You can make the web work for you in any number of ways, from starting a blog or website to networking with others through online forums or social networking sites, such as Twitter, Facebook, and LinkedIn.

✔ **Maintain a serious business attitude.** Just because your business is located at home instead of in a big office building downtown doesn't mean you shouldn't treat it like the business it is. Although you can have fun and work all kinds of creative schedules, don't forget that the business part of your business is important, too; you have to treat your business like a business if you hope to be successful.

✔ **Look for ways to grow.** For many businesses, growth can turn an operation that is doing well financially into an operation that is doing *great!* Growth allows you to take advantage of economies of scale that may be available only to larger businesses, to serve more customers, and to increase profits. For these reasons and more, growing your business should always be on your agenda.

Leaving your full-time job for your part-time business

An important, basic consideration that many fledgling, part-time home-based business owners face is whether or not to leave a full-time job in favor of a home-based business. Before you give up your full-time job, ask yourself these questions:

✔ Has there been a steadily growing flow of new customers in your home-based business?

✔ Has your business, even though it's only been part-time, produced a steady flow of income through seasonal or other cycles typical of the business?

✔ Are you turning away business because of limits on your time? If not, do you think business would increase if you had the time to market or take on more customers?

Being able to answer at least two of these questions in the affirmative is a good sign that it would be safe to leave your full-time job. Of course, you should also be aware of any developments that could worsen the outlook for your business to grow, such as pending legislation, new technology, the movement of the kind of work you do outside the U.S. (*outsourcing* or *cloud computing*), or the decline of an industry your business depends on.

If your day job has been providing you the contacts you've needed to build your part-time business, you need to find ways to replace them before you leave your job.

Breaking the umbilical cord of a paycheck is an uncomfortable step for most people. So the closer the current income from your business is to the amount of money you need to pay your basic business and living expenses, the more confident you can be.

Examining the Good News and the Bad

Anyone can start a home-based business. You can be 10 years old or 100, male or female, rich or poor or somewhere in between, experienced in business — or not. According to a recent study by the Ewing Marion Kauffman Foundation, the median age of company founders is 40 years old, the majority (69.9 percent) were married when they started their first business, and more than half (51.9 percent) were the first in their families to start a business.

Book II

Planning for Your Business

So how do you know if starting a home-based business is right for you? Like most things in life, starting your own home-based business has both advantages and disadvantages, but the good news is that the advantages probably outweigh the disadvantages for most prospective home-business owners. So in the spirit of putting your best foot forward, start with the good news.

Good reasons to start a home-based business

When you start a home-based business, you may be leaving behind the relative comfort and security of a regular career or 9-to-5 job and venturing out on your own. Or you may be entering the world of work again after devoting many years of your life to raising a family. How far out you venture on your own depends on the kind of home-based business you get involved in. For example, many franchises provide extensive support and training, and *franchisees* (the people buying the franchise opportunities — you, for example) are able to seek advice from experienced franchisees or from the *franchisor* (the party selling a franchise opportunity) when they need it. This support can be invaluable if you're new to the world of home-based business.

At the other end of the spectrum, some business opportunities offer little or no support whatsoever. If you're a dealer in synthetic motor oil, for example, you may have trouble getting the huge, multinational conglomerate that manufactures the oil to return your calls, much less send you some product brochures. And you won't find any training or extensive, hands-on support if you run into the inevitable snags, either.

This wide variety of home-based opportunities brings us to the good news about starting and running your own home-based business:

- ✔ **You're the boss.** For many owners of home-based businesses, just being their own boss is reason enough to justify making the move out of the 9-to-5 work world.

- ✔ **You get all the benefits of your hard work.** When you make a profit, it's all yours. No one is going to try to take it away from you (except, perhaps, the tax man — see Book III Chapter 5).

- ✔ **You have the flexibility to work when and where you want.** Are you a night owl? Perhaps your most productive times don't coincide with the standard 9-to-5 work schedule that most regular businesses require their employees to adhere to. And you may find that — because interruptions from co-workers are no longer an issue and the days of endless meetings are left far behind — you're much more productive working in your own workshop than in a regular office. With your own home-based business, you get to decide when and where you work.

- ✔ **You get to choose your clients and customers.** The customers may always be right, but that doesn't mean you have to put up with the ones who mistreat you or give you more headaches than they're worth. When you own your own business, you can fire the clients you don't want to work with. Sounds like fun, doesn't it?

- ✔ **You can put as much or as little time into your business as you want to.** Do you want to work for only a few hours a day or week? No problem. Ready for a full-time schedule or even more? Great! The more effort you put into your business, the more money you can make. As a home-based business owner, you get to decide how much money you want to make and then pick out the kind of schedule that will help you meet your goal.

These reasons to start your own home business are just the tip of the iceberg. But when you add up everything, you're left with one fundamental reason for owning your own home-based business: freedom.

The pitfalls of owning your own home-based business

Starting a home-based business isn't the solution to every problem for every person. Although many home-based businesses are successful and the people who started them are happy with the results, more than a few home-based businesses end up causing far more headaches than their owners anticipated. Some home-based business owners even go bankrupt as a direct result of the failure of their businesses. Starting your own business is hard work, and there are no guarantees for its success.

So the next time you're lying on your sofa, dreaming of starting your own home-based business, don't forget to consider some of the potential pitfalls:

- ✔ **The business is in your home.** Depending on your domestic situation, working in your own home — a home filled with any number of distractions, including busy children, whining spouses or significant others, televisions, loaded refrigerators, and more — can be a difficult proposition at best.

- ✔ **You're the boss.** Yes, being the boss has its drawbacks, too. When you're the boss, you're the one who has to motivate yourself to work hard every day — no one's standing over your shoulder (except maybe your cat) watching your every move. For some people, focusing on work is very difficult when *they* are put in the position of being the boss.

Book II

Planning for Your Business

- ✔ **Health insurance may be unavailable or unaffordable.** If you've ever been without health insurance for a period of time, or if you've been underinsured and had to make large medical or dental payments, you know just how important affordable health insurance is to your health and financial well-being. According to a recent study, 62.1 percent of all bankruptcies are medical related, and 92 percent of these debtors had medical debts of more than $5,000. Unfortunately, when you work for yourself, finding good health insurance isn't a given. In fact, it can sometimes be downright difficult, depending on where you live and work.

The Affordable Care Act (Obamacare) may provide some relief, if not in the form of subsidized health insurance, then at least in showing you your options in the marketplace — if you haven't already, check out `www.healthcare.gov` to see your options.

- ✔ **A home-based business is (usually) a very small business.** As a small business, you're likely more exposed to the ups and downs of fickle customers than larger businesses are. And a customer's decision not to pay could be devastating to you and your business.

- ✔ **You may fail or not like it.** No one can guarantee that your business is going to be a success or that you're going to like the business you start. Failure may cost you dearly, including financial ruin (no small number of business owners have had to declare bankruptcy when their businesses failed), destruction of personal relationships, and worse. However, not all small businesses close because of financial problems. The Small Business Administration has found that at the time of closing, one out of three businesses is financially sound.

Regardless of these potential pitfalls, starting a home-based business remains the avenue of choice for an increasing number of people. Are you ready to join them?

Taking the Home-Based Business Quiz

Many people talk about starting home-based businesses, and many dream about becoming their own bosses. Making the transition from a full-time career to self-employment, however, is a big change in anyone's life. Are you really ready to make the move, or should you put the idea of having your own home-based business on the back burner for a while longer?

To help you decide, take the following home-based business quiz. Circle your answer to each of these questions, add up the results, and find out if you're ready to take the plunge!

1. How strong is your drive to succeed in your own home-based business?

    A. I can and will be a success. Period.

    B. I'm fairly confident that if I put my mind to it, I will succeed.

    C. I'm not sure. Let me think about it for a while.

    D. Did I say that I wanted to start my own business? Are you sure that was me?

2. Are you ready to work as hard as or harder than you have ever worked before?

    A. You bet — I'm ready to do whatever it takes to succeed!

    B. Sure, I don't mind working hard as long as I get something out of it.

    C. Okay, as long as I still get weekends and evenings off.

    D. What? You mean I'll still have to work after I start my own business? Isn't that why I hire employees?

3. Do you like the idea of controlling your own work instead of having someone else control it for you?

    A. I don't want anyone controlling my work but me!

    B. That's certainly my first choice.

    C. It sounds like an interesting idea — can I?

    D. Do I have to control my own work? Can't someone control it for me?

4. Have you developed a strong network of potential customers?

    A. Yes, here are their names and numbers.

    B. Yes, I have some pretty strong leads.

    C. Not yet, but I've started kicking around some ideas with potential customers.

    D. I'm sure that as soon as I let people know that I'm starting my own business, customers will line up.

5. Do you have a plan for making the transition into your home-based business?

    A. Here it is — would you like to read the executive summary or the full plan?

    B. Yes, I've spent a lot of time considering my options and making plans.

    C. I'm just getting started.

    D. I don't believe in plans — they crimp my style.

6. Do you have enough money saved to tide you over while you get your business off the ground?

    A. Will the year's salary that I have saved be enough?

    B. I have six months' expenses hidden away for a rainy day.

    C. I have three months' worth.

    D. I'm still trying to pay off my college student loans.

7. How strong is your self-image?

    A. I *am* self-esteem!

    B. I strongly believe in my own self-worth and in my ability to create my own opportunities.

    C. I feel fairly secure with myself; just don't push too hard.

    D. I don't know — what do you think?

8. Do you have the support of your significant other and/or family?

    A. They're all on board, are an integral part of my plan, and have been assigned responsibilities.

    B. They're in favor of whatever makes me happy.

    C. I'm pretty sure they'll support me.

    D. I'm going to tell them about it later.

9. If it's a necessary part of your plan, will you be able to start up your home-based business while you remain in your current job?

    A. Sure — in fact, my boss wants in!

    B. If I make a few adjustments in my schedule, I can't see any other reason why I can't.

    C. Would you please repeat the question?

    D. Maybe I'll be able to work on it for a couple of hours a month.

10. **What will you tell friends when they ask why you quit that great job?**

    A. I'm free at last!

    B. That the benefits clearly outweigh the potential costs.

    C. I don't know; maybe they won't ask.

    D. I'll pretend that I'm still working for my old organization.

Give yourself 5 points for every A answer, 3 points for every B, –3 for every C, and –5 for every D. Now tally up the numbers, and compare your results with the ranges of numbers below.

By comparing your total points with the points contained in each of the six following categories, you can find out whether you're ready to jump into your own home-based business:

25 to 50 points: Assuming you were honest with yourself as you answered the preceding questions (you were, weren't you?), you're ready! You just need to decide whether to drop your day job or work into your new business gradually.

1 to 24 points: You're definitely warming up to the idea of starting your own home-based business. Consider starting your own business in the near future, but make sure to keep your day job until you have your venture well under way.

0 points: You can go either way on this one. Why don't you try taking this test again in another month or two? Read this book in the meantime.

–1 to –24 points: Unfortunately, you don't appear to be quite ready to make the move from career to home-based business. You should read this book and then take this test again in a few months. Maybe working for someone else isn't the worst thing that can happen to you.

–25 to –50: Forget it. You were clearly born to work for someone else.

Are you ready to make the move to starting a home-based business? If the quiz indicates otherwise, don't worry — you'll have plenty of opportunities in the future. When you're ready for them, they'll be ready for you. If you're ready now, congratulations!

Starting Something from Scratch

You probably find a certain amount of pleasure in making something out of nothing with your own two hands. It's the same pleasure a sculptor gets from creating a beautiful piece of art. You may not get it right the first time — after all, it took Thomas Edison hundreds of tries before he hit on the right material for a successful light bulb filament — but when you do find the right formula for success, the feeling of satisfaction you experience is hard to beat.

Perhaps the quickest and least expensive way to start your own home-based business is to do so from scratch. No need to fill out a bunch of applications, save up money to buy into a franchise, or take weeks or months to learn some complex, proprietary way of doing business. If you really want to, there's no reason why you can't start your own business from scratch — right now. Your friends, relatives, neighbors, and co-workers are doing it, and you can, too.

Book II

**Planning
for Your
Business**

Examples to inspire you

If you decide to start a home business from scratch, you're in good company. Did you know that some of today's largest, most successful companies were originally home-based businesses? Here are a few notable examples:

- **Hewlett-Packard:** With $538 in working capital, Bill Hewlett and David Packard started their fledgling company in Packard's garage in Palo Alto, California. Today Hewlett-Packard is a multinational corporation with sales in excess of $118 billion a year.

- **Apple Computer:** In 1976, two members of Palo Alto, California's Homebrew Computer Club — Steven Jobs and Stephen Wozniak — raised $1,300 by selling Jobs's Volkswagen van and Wozniak's Hewlett-Packard programmable calculator to launch Apple Computer. The company, which began life in the garage of Steven Jobs's parents' home, today has annual revenues of more than $170 billion.

- **Amazon.com:** Jeff Bezos, founder and CEO of Amazon.com, started his business in his rented, two-bedroom house in Bellevue, Washington. To make room for his new home-based business, Bezos converted his garage into a workspace. And to save money — of which he had precious little in those early days — he converted three wooden doors into desks, using some boards and a handful of metal brackets. The cost? Sixty dollars per desk. Today Amazon.com rakes in more than $75 billion a year — enough to pay for all the desks that Jeff Bezos would ever want to buy.

Of course, these home-based business success stories are exceptional, but many home-based business owners find exactly the level of success they're seeking — while paying the bills, doing exactly the work they want to do, spending more time with loved ones, and serving the customers they want to serve. The real beauty of owning your own home-based business is that it's first and foremost *your* business. When you start a business from scratch, you write the rules, and you decide what's important. You may grow your business into the next Apple Computer, or you may simply enjoy a bit of extra income to supplement your earnings from a full-time career or other sources.

Here are some more people who found exactly the level of success they were looking for by starting their own home-based businesses:

- Dan Dorotik of Lubbock, Texas, started his own successful business, Career Documents, a résumé-writing service, when he left his job to move to a different city with his fiancée and found himself out of work. "When I saw the money coming in, I realized that if you're really good at something — and if you're smart at the business and marketing side of it while maintaining the quality of the work — you can make a very good living for yourself," said Dan.

- Former door-to-door fax machine salesperson Sara Blakely cut the feet off a pair of pantyhose to "look smashing" in a pair of slacks. A year later, she was awarded a patent for her footless body-shaping panty-hose, and by the next year had created her own business — Spanx — with $5,000 in personal savings in the back of her apartment in Atlanta, Georgia. After earning scads of celebrity endorsements, including Oprah Winfrey, Drew Barrymore, Valerie Bertinelli, Marsha Cross, and others, Spanx now sells more than $250 million worth of its products a year.

- In high school and pregnant, Alexis Demko knew that she'd have to find some way to support herself and her child. So she started her El Cajon, California–based business — Demko Demolition Warehouse — which specializes in recycling and selling items such as light fixtures and cabinets salvaged from building demolition projects. She has done so well with her business that at just age 20, she was named entrepreneur of the month by *CosmoGIRL!* magazine.

When starting a business from scratch, you can use one of two main approaches: Choose to do the same kind of work you've been doing in your regular job or career, or choose to do something totally different. This section takes a closer look at each approach and the advantages each one offers you.

Doing what you've been doing in a job

As you consider the different options available to you in starting your own business, one of your first thoughts will undoubtedly be to do what you've already been doing in your full-time job.

Ten home-based business opportunities

Entrepreneur magazine (`www.entrepreneur.com`) keeps track of the hottest ideas for new businesses (all of which, coincidentally, can be home-based). Here are some ideas:

✔ College planning consultants

✔ Crafts and handmade goods

✔ Green apparel

✔ Green business services

✔ In-home nonmedical care

✔ Senior services

✔ Solar energy products

✔ Specialty lingerie

✔ Tech training and enrichment courses

✔ Upscale cupcakes

And why not? You know the job, you're already experienced in the business, and you know exactly what to expect. You also know what your customers want and how to give it to them. You may even have a network of potential customers waiting to sign up for your products and services. Not surprisingly, doing what you've been doing has several advantages, including the following:

✔ You can start up your business more quickly (like right *now*) and more easily than if you choose to do something you've never done before.

✔ You don't have to spend your time or money on training courses or workshops, and you don't have to worry much about a learning curve.

✔ You'll be much more efficient and effective because you've already discovered the best ways to do your job, along with time-saving tricks of the trade.

✔ You can capitalize on your good reputation, which may be your most important asset.

✔ You can tap in to your network of business contacts, clients, and customers (when ethically appropriate) and generate business more quickly than when you start something new and different.

For many people, doing something they've been doing is the best choice. So because doing what you've been doing is often the quickest and least expensive avenue for starting your own home-based business, be sure to take a close look at this option before you consider any others.

Doing something new and different

Although doing what you've been doing in a job offers many advantages, doing something new and different has its own set of high points. If you're burned out on your current job and you dream of making radical changes in your career or lifestyle — for example, trading your high-pressure career as an attorney for a much more relaxing home-based massage business — doing something new and different may well be exactly what the doctor ordered.

The following are some key advantages of doing something new and different:

- ✔ Getting a fresh start in your career can be an extremely energizing experience with positive repercussions for every aspect of your life, opening up exciting new possibilities and opportunities for you along the way.

- ✔ Tapping in to new career options allows you to find work that may not have even existed when you first started your career — for example, designing smartphone apps or computer-network consulting.

Many successful home-based business owners have created businesses that have nothing to do whatsoever with what they'd been doing in their full-time jobs. If you're sufficiently motivated, nothing can stand between you and success, no matter which business you choose. If you're looking to shake up the status quo or to make a break from the past, doing something completely new may well be the best option for you.

Transitioning into Your Home-Based Business

Starting your own business is exciting. For those people who have spent all their working lives employed by someone else, it's often the culmination of a dream that's lasted for years or even decades. Imagine the power and personal satisfaction you'll feel when you realize you're the boss and you call the shots — from setting your own work schedule, to deciding how to approach your work, to choosing your computer and office furniture. It's a feeling you won't soon forget.

But there's a right way and a wrong way to make the move. Your goal is to make sure you maintain a sufficient supply of cash to pay the startup costs of your business while paying for the rest of your life — the mortgage or rent, the car loans, the health insurance, the gas and electric, your daughter's piano lessons, and the list goes on and on.

The fact is, few businesses — home-based or otherwise — within the first six months of operation bring in all the money necessary to get them off the ground and keep them going for a prolonged period of time. In other words, you need *a lot of cash* — from a job, your spouse or partner's job, your savings, or loans from friends, family, or a bank — to keep both your business and your personal life going until the business generates enough revenue to take over.

Although you have to decide for yourself exactly what schedule to follow while transitioning into a home-based business, unless you're unemployed or retired, it's best to start your business on a part-time basis while you continue to hold down your regular full-time job. Why? For a number of reasons, including the following:

✔ You can develop and test your new business with virtually no risk — you still have your regular job to fall back on if your new business doesn't work out (and remember, no matter how great your business idea is, there's a chance it won't work out).

✔ You aren't under the intense pressure to perform and show the results that you'd have to show if your new business were your only source of income.

✔ You can keep your established health insurance, retirement plan, time off, and other benefits. Given the difficulty and expense of securing a decent health care plan when you're on your own and not under the umbrella of your employer, health care alone may be reason enough to keep your day job while you start your own business.

✔ You have a steady source of income you can use to pay your bills while you establish your new business.

✔ You may be able to take advantage of tax benefits, like the capability to write off early losses against income.

✔ You have a stronger basis for obtaining bank loans and other financing for your new business.

Of course, the decision is ultimately up to you. When starting a home-based business, follow your heart and make sure the transition fits into your schedule and your life.

This section looks at steps you need to take before you leave your regular job to devote all your time and energy to being your own boss. It also walks through the different steps involved in the process of establishing your home-based business.

Book II

Planning for Your Business

Knowing what to do before leaving your day job

After you're consistently earning enough income from your part-time, home-based business to cover your bare-minimum living and business expenses, you're ready to make the jump to a full-time commitment of your time and attention. Before you turn in your resignation, however, take the following six steps:

1. **Find out when any company benefit plans you have will vest or increase in value.** If you have a 401(k) or other retirement plan to which your employer has been contributing, it may not be fully available to you until you've served a particular number of years of service. Finding out this information may help you determine the best time to resign. It'd be a shame, for example, if you quit two weeks before the value of your retirement benefits was set to jump from 80 to 100 percent of your current salary.

2. **Find out when you can expect to receive any bonus money or profit sharing.** You may, for example, be slated to receive an annual performance bonus or profit sharing a month after the end of the company fiscal year. This information can help with the financial planning for your home-based business because it lets you know when you'll have the money available to help you get your business off the ground.

3. **Get all annual health exams, have all routine procedures done, and fill all prescriptions while you and your family are still covered by your medical/dental/vision insurance.** Check to see whether you can convert your group coverage to an individual policy at favorable rates or what other health coverage options are open to you. (Some group plans can be converted, but be very careful about changes in coverage, co-pays, and deductibles that may actually end up costing you much more money in the long run.)

Don't forget that if you work in the U.S., you're likely covered by COBRA (the Consolidated Omnibus Budget Reconciliation Act of 1985), which requires your employer to allow you to continue your identical group health coverage for a period of 18 months or more. However, qualified individuals may be required to pay the entire premium for coverage up to 102 percent of the cost to the plan.

The American Recovery and Reinvestment Act of 2009 (ARRA) provides for premium reductions and additional election opportunities for health benefits under COBRA. Eligible individuals pay only 35 percent of their COBRA premiums and the remaining 65 percent is reimbursed to the coverage provider through a tax credit.

The Affordable Care Act, signed into law in 2010, may serve to help make your health insurance more portable and provides a marketplace where you can shop for new insurance on your own. Be sure to find out the latest on the law at `www.healthcare.gov`.

4. **If you own a house and you need some extra cash to help you through the transition, consider taking out a home equity line of credit or other loan before leaving your current job.** Having a line of credit or loan to draw upon can be invaluable during the first two years of your new business, and your chances of getting approved for it are much greater while you're employed in a regular job. That's right — after you leave your job, you probably won't qualify for a line of credit or other loans for your business until your business has been successful for two or more years.

5. **Pay off or pay down the balance on your credit cards while you still have a steady job.** Doing so helps your credit rating (always a good thing) and provides you with another source of potential funds to help you finance various startup costs (and depending on the nature of your business, you may have plenty of those).

6. **Take advantage of training and educational opportunities, conferences, and meetings that can result in preparation or contacts that will prepare you for your own business.** Doing so enables you to hit the ground running when you decide it's time to start your own business.

Don't make your announcement or submit your resignation until you're really ready to go. Some companies are (sometimes justifiably) paranoid about soon-to-be former employees stealing ideas, proprietary data, or clients, which can make for a very hasty exit, with a personal escort, when you do resign.

After completing these steps, you're ready to take what may well be one of the most significant steps forward you'll ever take in your life: starting your own home-based business.

Understanding what you have to do to start your own home-based business

This section goes through exactly what you need to do to start up your own home-based business.

Your odds of success are better than you think

A lot of bad information about how long businesses (including home-based businesses) can be expected to survive after founding has circulated throughout the business community. Almost everyone has heard this particular stat: 95 percent of the businesses started in any given year will be gone within five years.

Guess what? It's not true. In reality, most home-based businesses survive for five years or more after their founding. According to surveys conducted by IDC/LINK, an average of only 5 percent of home-based businesses drop out each year. So after five years have gone by, only 25 percent of home-based businesses have dropped out — far less than the average for all businesses, which can be over 50 percent! How, then, can you ensure that your home-based business thrives and doesn't become an unfortunate statistic?

The Small Business Administration (SBA) has uncovered four key indicators of business success. They are

- ✔ **Sound management practices:** Including an ability to manage projects, handle finances, and communicate effectively with customers

- ✔ **Industry experience:** Including the number of years you've worked in the same kind of business you intend to start and your familiarity with suppliers and potential customers

- ✔ **Technical support:** Including your ability to seek and find help in the technical aspects of your business

- ✔ **Planning ability:** Including an ability to set appropriate business goals and targets and then create plans and strategies for achieving them

If you, or the combination of you and a partner, possess all four traits, the probability of your business succeeding is much higher than if you're missing one or more of these traits. If you're missing any of these traits, find people who can help you fill in the gaps.

Develop a business plan

Despite what you may read on many small business websites or blogs, many home-based business owners can get by without drafting a business plan. Indeed, just the thought of having to draft a 50-page tabbed and annotated, multipart business plan is enough to scare many potential home-based business owners away from their dreams. Truth be told, most business owners today use their business plans to obtain financing from third parties, such as banks or investors, and many successful businesses — home-based or not — have been started without one.

That said, the process of drafting a business plan can be very beneficial — both to you as a business owner and to your business. Taking the time to draft a plan helps you do the right things at the right time to get your business off the ground; plus, it forces you to think through what the challenges will be and what you can do about them before they overwhelm you.

In essence, a good business plan

- ✔ Clearly establishes your goals for the business
- ✔ Analyzes the feasibility of a new business and its likelihood of being profitable over the long haul
- ✔ Explores the expansion of an existing business
- ✔ Defines your customers and competitors (very important people to know!) and points out your strengths and weaknesses
- ✔ Details your plans for the future

Even if you think your business is too small to have a business plan, it's really worth your time to see what it's all about — the process of developing the plan for your business will produce a clarity of thought that you can't find any other way.

See Book II Chapter 1 for details on developing an effective business plan.

Book II

Planning for Your Business

Consult outside professionals

As a new home-based businessperson, you need to consider establishing relationships with a number of *outside professionals* — trained and experienced people who can help you with the aspects of your business in which you may have little or no experience. By no means do you have to hire someone from each category described in this section. But if you run into questions that you can't easily answer yourself, don't hesitate to call on outside professionals for help as you go through the business startup process.

Any professional advice you get at the beginning of your business may well save you heartache and potentially expensive extra work down the road.

Here are just some of the outside professionals you may choose to consult as you start your home-based business:

- ✔ **Lawyer:** An attorney's services are an asset not only in the planning stages of your business, but also throughout its life. An attorney can help you choose your legal structure, draw up incorporation or partnership paperwork, draft and review agreements and contracts, and provide information on your legal rights and obligations. Look for an attorney who specializes in working with small businesses and startups. See Book II Chapter 6 for details on starting your business with the right legal structure.
- ✔ **Accountant:** Consult an accountant to set up a good bookkeeping system for your business. Inadequate bookkeeping is a principal contributor to the failure of small businesses. Regardless of how boring or

intimidating it may seem, make sure you understand basic accounting and the bookkeeping system or software you're using, and don't forget to closely review all the regularly produced financial reports related to your business (and make sure you actually receive them!). See Book III Chapter 1 for the basics of setting up your books.

- ✔ **Banker:** The capital requirements of a small business make establishing a good working relationship with a local banker absolutely essential. For example, bankers can approve immediate deposit of checks that would normally be held for ten days. They're also good sources of financial information — and for obtaining cash to tide you over when times are tough or financing expansion of your business when times are good.

Establish a relationship with your banker *before* applying for a loan, not after you decide to initiate the loan process. This relationship may make the difference between getting approved for the loan you need and being turned down.

- ✔ **Business consultant:** Every person has talents in many areas, but no one can be a master of everything. Consultants are available to assist in the areas where you need expert help. You can use business, management, and marketing consultants; promotion experts; financial planners; and a host of other specialists to help make your business more successful. Don't hesitate to draw on their expertise when you need it.

- ✔ **Insurance agent/broker:** Many kinds of insurance options are available for business owners, and some are more necessary than others. An insurance agent or broker can advise you about the type and amount of coverage that's best for you and your business. The agent may also be able to tailor a package that meets your specific needs at reasonable rates.

The relationships you establish with outside professionals during the startup phase of your business can last for years and can be of tremendous benefit to your firm. Be sure to choose your relationships wisely. In the case of outside professionals, you often get what you pay for, so be penny-wise but don't suffer a poor-quality outside professional simply to save a dollar or two.

Choose the best legal structure for your business

Most home-based businesses begin as either sole proprietorships or partnerships because they're the easiest business structures to run and the least expensive. But as these businesses grow, many explore the transition to another kind of legal entity. Before you decide what kind of business you want yours to be, consider the pros and cons of the following legal structures:

- ✔ **Sole proprietorship:** A *sole proprietorship* is the simplest and least regulated form of organization. It also has minimal legal startup costs, making it the most popular choice for new home-based businesses. In a sole proprietorship, one person owns and operates the business and is responsible for seeking and obtaining financing. The sole proprietor (likely you) has total control and receives all profits, which are taxed as personal income. The major disadvantages include unlimited personal liability for the owner (if the business is sued for some reason, the owner is personally liable to pay any judgments against the company) and potential dissolution of the business upon the owner's death.

✔ **Partnership:** A *partnership* is relatively easy to form and can provide additional financial resources. Each partner is an *agent* for the partnership and can borrow money, hire employees, and operate the business. Profits are taxed as personal income, and the partners are still personally liable for debts and taxes. Personal assets can be attached if the partnership can't satisfy creditors' claims. A special arrangement called a *limited partnership* allows partners to avoid unlimited personal liability. Limited partnerships must be registered and must also pay a tax to the appropriate authorities in their jurisdiction. On the plus side, partnerships allow people to combine their unique talents and assets to create a whole greater than the sum of its parts. On the other hand, though, partnerships can become sheer living hell when partners fail to see eye to eye or when relationships turn sour.

When entering into any partnership, consult a lawyer, and insist on a written agreement that clearly describes a process for dissolving the partnership as cleanly and fairly as possible.

✔ **Limited liability company:** A *limited liability company* (LLC) is often the preferred choice for new operations and joint ventures because LLCs have the advantage of being treated as partnerships for U.S. income tax purposes while also providing the limited liability of corporations. However, LLCs have the disadvantage of generally being more expensive to set up than sole proprietorships or partnerships. Owners of limited liability companies, called *members,* are comparable to stockholders in a corporation or limited partners in a limited partnership. To create a limited liability company, articles of organization are filed with the secretary of state. The members must also execute an operating agreement that defines the relationship between the company and its members. Note that all 50 states and the District of Columbia have enacted LLC statutes.

✔ **Corporation:** As the most complex of business organizations, the *corporation* (also known as a *C Corporation*) acts as a legal entity that exists separately from its owners. Although this separation limits the owners from personal liability, it also creates a double taxation on earnings (the corporation pays tax on net taxable income, and the shareholders pay tax on dividends distributed). A corporate structure may be advantageous because it allows the business to raise capital more easily through the sale of stocks or bonds; plus, the business can continue to function even without key individuals. The corporation also enables future employees to participate in various types of insurance and profit-sharing plans.

Book II

Planning for Your Business

Costs to incorporate vary from state to state — contact your secretary of state for more information.

A special type of corporation, an *S Corporation,* allows eligible domestic corporations to overcome the double taxation problem. Qualifying corporations can elect to be treated as an S Corporation under the rules of Subchapter S of the tax code. Making this election allows small corporations to be generally exempt from federal income tax. Similar to partnerships, all items of income, deduction, credit, gain, and loss are passed through on a pro rata basis to the individual S Corporation shareholders. In this way, the S Corporation passes its items of income, loss, deduction, and credits through to its shareholders to be included on their separate returns.

With C Corporations, you need to be careful you aren't erroneously classified by the government as a *professional service corporation,* which is treated much less advantageously than other C Corporations. Professional service corporations are corporations in which the owners (who are licensed professionals) substantially perform certain personal services, including accounting, actuarial science, architecture, consulting, engineering, health, veterinary services, law, and performing arts.

As you set up your new home-based business, take time to carefully think through the ramifications of your business's legal structure. Each option has many potential advantages and disadvantages for your firm, and each can make a big difference in how you run your business. If you have any questions about which kind of legal structure is right for your business, talk to an accountant or seek advice from an attorney who specializes in small businesses. Book II Chapter 6 discusses these legal structures in much more detail.

Decide on a name

Naming your business may well be one of the most enjoyable steps in the process of starting up your own home-based business. Everyone can get in on the action: your friends, your family, and especially your clients-to-be.

Consider your business name carefully — you have to live with it for a long time. Your business name should give people some idea of the nature of your business, it should project the image you want to have, and it should be easy to visualize. Names can be simple, sophisticated, or even silly. Try to pick one that can grow with your business and not limit you in the future.

Along with a name, many businesses develop a logo, which provides a graphic symbol for the business. As with your name, your logo needs to project the image you want, so develop it carefully. Spend a few extra dollars to have a professional graphic artist design your logo for you.

After you come up with a name, register it with your local government to make sure it isn't already in use. (See Book II Chapter 6 for more details.) If you don't check first, you may have to throw out your stationery and business cards and redesign your logo and website when you eventually find out that another company has your name — and registered it 15 years before you did!

Take care of the red tape (and it will take care of you)

Taking care of all the local, state, and federal government legal requirements of starting up a business is something that too many budding home-based entrepreneurs put off or ignore. Unfortunately, ignoring the many legal requirements of going into business may put you and your business at risk.

Getting through the maze of government regulations can certainly be one of the most confusing aspects of starting up and running a business. But even though this process can be intimidating, you have to do it — and do it correctly — because noncompliance can result in costly penalties and perhaps even the loss of your business. Consider this step as one that fortifies the professionalism of your business at the same time that it helps you rest easy at night, knowing that you're following the rules. Do you want people to take you seriously? Then you need to establish your business in a professional way.

Even very small or part-time businesses have certain requirements. It's your responsibility to adhere to any and all regulations that apply to your business. Fortunately, a lot of people and organizations — government small business development centers, chambers of commerce, and sometimes lawyers and certified public accountants — are willing and eager to answer questions and help you with this task. For your sake — and the sake of your business — don't hesitate to ask someone for help when you need it.

Get the insurance you need

In today's expensive, litigious world of business, insurance isn't really an option — it's essential. Without it, all your years of hard work can be lost in a minute because of a catastrophic loss.

So what kinds of insurance do you need for your business? You should talk to an insurance agent and discuss your business and its needs with him or her. Some of the most common kinds of business insurance include the following:

- ✔ **Health insurance:** Includes medical, dental, vision, and other coverage designed to maintain and promote employee health and wellness and to protect employees against catastrophic loss in case of injury or illness

- ✔ **Basic fire insurance:** Covers property losses due to fire and sometimes covers loss of business, as well

- ✔ **Extended coverage:** Protects against conditions not covered by fire insurance, including storms, explosions, smoke damage, and various other disasters

- ✔ **Liability insurance:** Covers claims against your business for bodily injury incurred on the business's premises

- ✔ **Product liability coverage:** Covers liability for products manufactured or sold by your business

- ✔ **Professional liability and/or errors-and-omissions insurance:** Protects the business against claims for damages incurred by customers as a result of your professional advice or recommendations

- ✔ **Vandalism and malicious mischief coverage:** Covers against property losses resulting from vandalism and related activities

- ✔ **Theft coverage:** Protects your business from burglary and robbery

- ✔ **Vehicle insurance:** Covers collision, liability, and property damage for vehicles used for business

- ✔ **Business interruption insurance:** Covers payment of business earnings if the business is closed for an insurable cause, such as fire, flood, or other natural disaster

- ✔ **Workers' compensation:** Provides disability and death benefits to employees and others who work for you, as defined by your state law, who are injured on the job

A homeowner's policy isn't usually enough insurance for a home-based business for a couple of reasons. First, your typical homeowner's policy provides only limited coverage for business equipment and doesn't insure you against risks of liability or lost income. Second, your homeowner's policy may not cover your business activities at all.

Insurance is the kind of thing you don't think about until you need it. And in the case of insurance, when you need it, chances are you *really* need it! Take time to set up proper coverage now — before it's too late. Call your insurance company and talk through the options it may have for your to convert or supplement your homeowner's policy to cover your business.

Decide on an accounting system

Accounting is one of those topics that makes people nervous (with visions of IRS audits dancing in their heads), but keeping books doesn't have to be complicated. In fact, simplicity is the key to a good system for home-based businesses. Keep in mind that your records need to be complete and up-to-date so that you have the information you need for business decisions and taxes.

When you establish an accounting system, pick up one of the excellent computer software programs dedicated to this purpose. Programs such as QuickBooks, Freshbooks, and Sage One do everything your home-based business will ever need — and more.

The two basic bookkeeping methods are *single entry* and *double entry*. Single entry is simpler, with only one entry required per transaction. This is probably the best method for most home-based businesses, and the vast majority can operate very well with the single-entry system. Book III Chapter 1 covers bookkeeping in detail.

You can also choose between two methods to keep track of the money coming in and going out of your business: *cash* or *accrual*. Most small businesses use the cash method, in which income is reported in the year it's received and expenses are deducted in the year they're paid. Under the accrual method, income is reported when it's earned, and expenses are deducted when they're incurred, whether money has changed hands yet or not.

The accounting methods you use depend on your business. You may want to talk to an accountant for help in setting up your system. Even with the support of a professional, however, you need to understand your own system thoroughly.

Many home-based businesses can get by without detailed financial reporting or analysis — after all, if you can keep up with your bills and perhaps have a little bit of money to sock away in your savings account, you must be making money, right? If you really want to understand your business's financial situation, however, you need some basic financial reports.

The following financial statements are the minimum necessary to understand where your business stands financially. With them in hand, you can review your business's financial strengths and weaknesses and make accurate plans for the future.

- ✔ **Balance sheets:** *Balance sheets* show the worth of your business — the difference between its assets and its liabilities. Your balance sheet can tell you whether or not you'd have any cash left over if you shut down your business today and paid off all your bills and loans and liquidated your assets.

- ✔ **Profit-and-loss statements:** *Profit-and-loss (P&L) statements* show you the difference between how much money your business is bringing in *(revenue)* and how much money it's spending *(expenses)*. If you're bringing in more money than you spend, you have a profit. If you're spending more money than you bring in, you have a loss. Book III Chapter 2 covers P&L in detail.

- ✔ **Cash-flow projections:** Cash-flow projections tell you where your money is going and whether or not you're likely to have sufficient money each month to pay your bills and operate the business. For many startup companies — especially those with employees, rent, and other significant recurring expenses — a cash-flow projection is the most important financial statement of all. Check out Book III Chapter 3 for more on staying solvent.

Develop a marketing plan

If you want to be successful, you can't just start a business and then patiently wait for customers to walk in your door. You have to let potential customers know about your new business, get them in to have a look, and then encourage them to buy your product or service. Marketing is all of this and more. Your specific approach to marketing depends on your business, your finances, your potential client or customer base, and your goals.

Marketing sells your products and services, which brings in the cash you need to run your business. Marketing is so important to the survival (and success) of your business that it deserves a plan of its own. A *marketing plan* helps evaluate where your business currently is, where you want it to go, and how you can get there. Your marketing plan should also spell out the specific strategies and costs involved in reaching your goals. You can integrate it into your business plan as one comprehensive section. As with the business plan, you should refer to it regularly and update it as necessary.

Successful marketing for a small or home-based business doesn't happen all by itself. It requires a lot of work and careful analysis and is a terrific opportunity to use your creativity and hone your business sense. For a lot more information on marketing your home-based business, be sure to check out the chapters in Book V.

Seek assistance when you need it

An almost unlimited number of organizations and agencies — private, public, and not-for-profit — are ready, willing, and able to help you work through the process of starting up your home-based business. Check out the websites of each of the following organizations for an incredible amount of free information and help, and know that this list is only the beginning:

- **Small Business Development Centers:** www.sbaonline.sba.gov/sbdc
- **Service Corps of Retired Executives (SCORE):** www.score.org
- **U.S. Chamber of Commerce:** www.uschamber.com
- **Minority Business Development Agency:** www.mbda.gov
- **Federal Business Opportunities:** www.fbo.gov
- **National Business Incubation Association:** www.nbia.org
- **U.S. Patent and Trademark Office:** www.uspto.gov

Chapter 5

Creating a Website for Your Business

In This Chapter

▶ Establishing your business presence(s)

▶ Organizing an easy-to-navigate business website

▶ Optimizing type and images to build a graphic identity

▶ Promoting trust with concise, well-designed web page content

▶ Inviting interaction through forms, email, and more

*N*o matter what you sell or where you sell it — on the web, in a brick-and-mortar store, or even on Facebook — you need to have a home base on the web, a *presence*. Not so long ago, a "home base" on the web automatically meant a website. A website is important, but you can sell online without one. Hence, the term *presence*.

It's a subtle but significant difference. A presence can include a blog, ads on Craigslist, exposure for your app on iTunes, or storefronts on a variety of marketplaces.

Wherever you do business, the same basic principles work on the web just as well as they do in the brick-and-mortar world. Attracting customers is important, but real success comes from establishing relationships with customers who come to trust you and rely on you for providing excellent products and services.

This chapter focuses on creating an organized website as part of an overall presence to attract not only first-time but also return customers. In this chapter, you explore ways to achieve these goals, including making your site easy to navigate, creating compelling content, optimizing your images so they appear quickly, and building interactivity into your site so customers want to return on a regular basis.

There is, of course, a lot more to creating, launching, tweaking, and maintaining a website — so much so that a number of different *For Dummies* books are devoted to it. For further coverage, check out *Starting an Online Business For Dummies* and *Building a Web Site For Dummies,* both published by John Wiley & Sons, Inc.

Feng Shui-ing Your Website

Feng Shui is the art of arranging objects in an environment to achieve (among other things) success in your career, wealth, and happiness. If that's true, try practicing some Feng Shui with your business environment — that is, your website.

Although you may be tempted to jump right into the creation of a cool website, take a moment to plan. Whether you're setting off on a road trip across the nation or building a new addition on your house, you'll progress more smoothly by first drawing a map of where you want to go. Dig down into your miscellaneous drawer until you find pencil and paper and make a list of the elements you want to have on your site.

Look over the items on your list and break them into two or three main categories. These main categories will branch off your *home page,* which functions as the grand entrance for your business site. You can then draw a map of your site similar to the one shown in Figure 5-1.

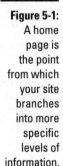

Figure 5-1:
A home page is the point from which your site branches into more specific levels of information.

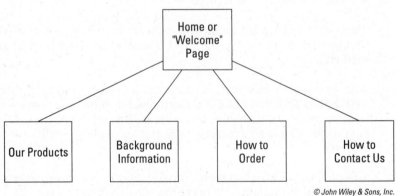

© John Wiley & Sons, Inc.

Note: The page heading Background Information is a placeholder for detailed information about some aspect of your business. You can write about your experience with and your love for what you buy and sell, or anything else that personalizes your site and builds trust.

The preceding example results in a very simple website. But there's nothing wrong with starting out simple. Many businesses start with a three-layered organization for their websites. This arrangement divides the site into two sections — one about the company and one about the products or services for sale, as shown in Figure 5-2.

Book II

Planning for Your Business

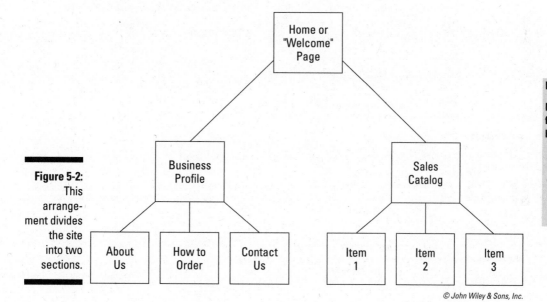

Figure 5-2: This arrangement divides the site into two sections.

© John Wiley & Sons, Inc.

Think of your home page as the lobby of a museum, where a friendly person at the information desk hands you a list of the special exhibits you can visit that day and shows you a map so you can figure out how you're going to get from here to there. Remember to include the following items on your home page:

- The name of the store or business
- Your logo, if you have one
- Links to the main areas of your site or, if your site isn't overly extensive, to every page
- Links to your presences online — your Facebook or Twitter page, or any storefronts you have
- Contact information, such as your email address, phone/fax numbers, and (optionally) your business address so that people know where to find you in the Land Beyond Cyberspace

A mobile version of a website strips away most or all of the images and colors and simply presents the content. The presentation needs to be as straightforward as possible so that pages load quickly on a mobile device. Forget about animations or multiple columns. Isolate your most important links in a single one-column page that is easy to read on a smartphone. For full coverage on creating mobile websites, check out *Mobile Web Design For Dummies* (John Wiley & Sons, Inc.). Figure 5-3 shows a possible mobile website arrangement.

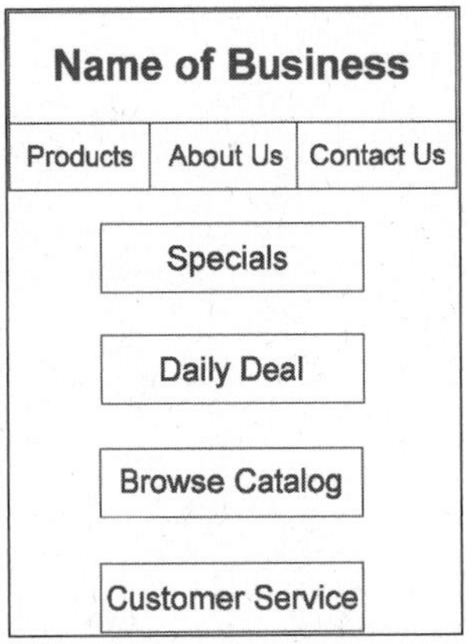

Figure 5-3:
A mobile site's home page needs to be simple and load quickly.

© John Wiley & Sons, Inc.

Some sites are "smart" enough to present a limited amount of content depending on whether a touch-enabled device such as an iPad is being used. For example, go to http://touch.groupon.com to see a version of Groupon's mobile site that has fewer links than Groupon's desktop home page (www.groupon.com) and only one column. Then go to http://m.groupon.com to see an even simpler version with fewer images.

Making them fall in love at first site

First impressions are critical on the web, where shoppers can jump from site to site with a click of their mouse. A few extra seconds of waiting for videos and whatnot to download can cause your prospective buyer to lose patience and you to lose a sale. (Keeping your site simple is especially important for mobile device users.)

How do you make visitors to your welcome page feel like they're being greeted with open arms? Here are some suggestions:

✔ **Less is more.** Don't overload any one page with more than half a dozen images. Keep all images 50KB or less in size. You do this by saving images with a resolution of 72 dpi (dots per inch), as described in "A picture is worth a thousand words," later in this chapter.

✔ **Find a fast host.** Some web servers have superfast connections to the Internet, and others use slower lines. Test your site; if your pages take more than 5 seconds to appear, ask your host company why and find out whether it can move you to a faster machine. These days, cable connections of 30–60 Mbps are fairly easy to find.

✔ **Offer a bargain.** Nothing attracts attention as much as a contest, a giveaway, or a special sales promotion. If you have something you can give away, either through a contest or a deep discount, do it.

✔ **Provide instant gratification.** Make sure your most important information appears at or near the top of your page. Visitors to the web don't like having to scroll through several screens' worth of material to get to the information they want.

Creating Content That Attracts Customers

What sells on the web? Look no further than the search engine you probably use on a regular basis: Google. Google proves that information sells online. Making information easy to find and organizing much of the web's content in one place has helped make this one of the most successful businesses of recent years. When it comes to a business website, you need to present the *right* content in the *right* way to make prospective clients and customers want to explore your site the first time and then come back for more. What, you ask, is the "right" content? The "right" content

✔ Helps people absorb information fast.

✔ Makes it easy for visitors to find out who you are and what you have to offer.

✔ Is friendly and informal in tone, concise in length, and clear in its organization.

✔ Helps develop the all-important one-to-one-relationship with customers and clients by inviting dialogue and interaction, both with you and with others who share the same interests.

Begin by identifying your target audience. Envision the customers you want to attract and make your site appear to speak directly to them, person to person. Ask around and try to determine what people want from your website. Speak informally and directly to them, by using *you* rather than *we* or *us,* and make sure your site has plenty of action points — links to click, forms to fill out, or product descriptions to view. And follow the general principles outlined in the sections that follow.

Consider doing what professional marketing consultants do and write detailed descriptions of the individuals you're trying to reach. Make your customer profiles complete with fictitious names, ages, job descriptions, type of car they drive, and so on. The more detailed you get, the better you can tailor your content to those people.

Following the KISS principle: Keep it simple, sir (or sister)

Studies of how information on a web page is absorbed indicate that people don't really read the contents from top to bottom (or left to right, or frame to frame) in a linear way. In fact, most web surfers don't *read* in the traditional sense at all. Instead, they browse so quickly you'd think they have an itchy mouse finger. They "flip through pages" by clicking link after link. More and more Internet users are swiping their index fingers on tablets, smartphones, and even cars with Internet-ready computer systems. Because your prospective customers don't necessarily have tons of computing power or hours' worth of time to explore your site, the best rule is to *keep it simple.*

People who are looking for things on the web are often in a state of hurried distraction. Think about a TV watcher browsing during a commercial or a parent stealing a few moments on the computer while the baby naps. Imagine this person surfing while standing on a platform waiting for a train. He isn't in the mood to listen while you unfold your fondest hopes and dreams for success, starting with playing grocery-store cashier as a toddler. Attract him immediately by answering these questions:

- ✔ Who are you, anyway?
- ✔ What is your main message or mission?
- ✔ What do you have here for me?
- ✔ Why should I choose your site to explore?

When it comes to web pages, it pays to put the most important components first: who you are, what you do, how you stand out from any competing sites, and your contact information.

People who visit a website give that site less than a minute (in many cases, only 20 seconds).

If you have a long list of items to sell, you probably can't fit everything you have to offer right on the first page of your site. Even if you could, you wouldn't want to: It's better to prioritize the contents of your site so that the "breaking stories" or the best contents appear at the top, and the rest of what's in your catalog is arranged in order of importance.

Think long and hard before you use features that may scare people away instead of wow them, such as a splash page that contains only a logo or short greeting and then reloads automatically and takes the visitor to the main body of a site. Don't overdecorate your home page with Flash animations or Java applets that take your prospective customers' browsers precious seconds to load or that might not appear on an iPad, which doesn't support Flash.

Book II

Planning for Your Business

Striking the right tone with your text

Business writing on the web differs from the dry, linear report writing of the corporate world. So this is your chance to express the real you: Talk about your fashion sense or your collection of salt and pepper shakers. Your business also has a personality, and the more striking you make its description on your web page, the better. Use the tone of your text to define what makes your business unique and what distinguishes it from your competition.

Satisfied customers are another source of endorsements. Ask your customers whether they're willing to provide a quote about how you helped them. If you don't yet have satisfied customers, ask one or two people to try your products or services for free, and then, if they're happy with your wares, ask permission to use their comments on your site. Your goal is to get a pithy, positive quote that you can put on your home page or on a page specifically devoted to quotes from your clients.

Making your site easy to navigate

Imagine prospective customers arriving at your website with only a fraction of their attention engaged. Making the links easy to read and in obvious locations makes your site easier to navigate. Having a row of clickable buttons at the top of your home page, each pointing to an important area of your site, is always a good idea. Such navigational pointers give visitors an idea of what your site contains in a single glance and immediately encourage them to click a primary subsection of your site and explore further. By placing an interactive table of contents up front, you direct surfers right to the material they're looking for.

The links to the most important areas of a site can go at or near the top of the page on either the left or right side. The `Dummies.com` home page, as shown in Figure 5-4, has a few links just above the top banner, but also sports links down *both* the left and right sides. (Note that this web page, like almost any web page, may look different by the time you read this.)

Navigation can help with marketing: If you want to be ranked highly by search engines (and who doesn't?), you have another good reason to place your site's main topics near the top of the page in a series of links. Some search services index the first 50 or so words on a web page. Therefore, if you can get lots of important keywords included in that index, the chances are better that your site will be ranked highly in a list of links returned by the service in response to a search.

On a tablet or other mobile device, you need to arrange the most important links without flashy graphics. Look at the mobile version of the same Dummies.com home page in Figure 5-5. You don't have to design a simplified mobile version of your home page from scratch (although you can do so at `www.strikingly.com`). The marketplace or hosting service you choose should automatically create a mobile version of your site for you. (If you haven't chosen a marketplace or hosting service yet, you'll find a ton of advice on doing so in *Starting an Online Business For Dummies* (John Wiley & Sons, Inc.).

Figure 5-4:
Putting at least five or six links near the top of your home page is a good idea.

Source: Dummies.com

Figure 5-5:
Simple
navigation
on a mobile
site helps
you reach
visitors
who are on
the go.

Source: Dummies.com

How do you get links in there in the first place? You can do it yourself using website creation software. For example, using Dreamweaver, the powerful and popular website creation software by Adobe, you open the web page you want to edit and follow these steps to create links to local files on your website:

1. **Select the text or image on your web page that you want to serve as the jumping-off point for the link.**

2. **Choose Insert⇨Link or press Ctrl+L.**

   The Properties dialog box appears, as shown in Figure 5-6.

3. **In the box in the Link Location section, enter the name of the file you want to link to if you know the filename.**

   If the page you want to link to is in the same directory as the page that contains the jumping-off point, enter only the name of the web page. If the page is in another directory, enter a path relative to the web page that contains the link. Or click the Choose File button, locate the file in the Open HTML File dialog box, and click the Open button.

4. **Click OK.**

   You return to the Composer window. If you made a textual link, the selected text is underlined and in a different color. If you made an image link, a box appears around the image.

Figure 5-6:
Enter the
name of
the file you
want to
link to.

Source: Greg Holden

Presenting the reader with links up front doesn't just help your search engine rankings, it also indicates that your site is content-rich and worthy of exploration.

Pointing the way with headings

Every web page needs to contain headings that direct the reader's attention to the most important contents. This book provides a good example. The chapter title should pique your interest first. Then the section headings and subheadings direct you to more details on the topics you want to read about.

Most graphics designers label their heads with the letters of the alphabet: A, B, C, and so on. In a similar fashion, most web page–editing tools designate top-level headings with the style Heading 1. Beneath this, you place one or more Heading 2 headings. Beneath each of those, you may have Heading 3 and, beneath those, Heading 4. (Headings 5 and 6 are really too small to be useful.) The arrangement may look like this (the following headings are indented for clarity; you don't have to indent them on your page):

```
Miss Cookie's Delectable Cooking School (Heading 1)
    Kitchen Equipment You Can't Live Without (Heading 2)
    The Story of a Calorie Counter Gone Wrong (Heading 2)
    Programs of Culinary Study (Heading 2)
        Registration (Heading 3)
        Course Schedule (Heading 3)
            New Course on Whipped Cream Just Added! (Heading 4)
```

You can energize virtually any heading by telling your audience something specific about your business. Instead of "Ida's Antiques Mall," for example, say something like "Ida's Antiques Mall: The Perfect Destination for the Collector and the Crafter." Instead of simply writing a heading like "Stan Thompson, Pet Grooming," say something specific, such as "Stan Thompson: We Groom Your Pet at Our Place or Yours."

Becoming an expert list maker

Lists are simple and effective ways to break up text and make your web content easier to digest. They're easy to create and easy for your customer to view and absorb. Suppose you import your own decorations and want to offer certain varieties at a discount during various seasons. Rather than bury the items you're offering within an easily overlooked paragraph, why not divide your list into subgroups so that visitors find what they want without being distracted by holidays they may not even celebrate?

Lists are easy to implement. Here's a look at how in another web page creator — this time, in Microsoft Expression Web (a free trial version is available at `www.microsoft.com/en-us/download/details.aspx?id=36179`). You open your web page in the program and follow these steps:

Book II

Planning for Your Business

1. **Type a heading for your list and then select the entire heading.**

   For example, you might type and then select the words *This Month's Specials.*

2. **Choose a heading style from the Style drop-down list.**

   Your text is formatted as a heading.

3. **Click anywhere in Design View (the main editing window) to deselect the heading you just formatted.**

4. **Press Enter to move to a new line.**

5. **Type the first item of your list, press Enter, and then type the second item on the next line.**

6. **Repeat Step 5 until you enter all the items of your list.**

7. **Select all the items of your list (but not the heading).**

8. **Choose Format⇨Bullets and Numbering.**

   The List Properties dialog box appears.

9. **Choose one of the four bullet styles and click OK.**

   A bullet appears next to each list item, and the items appear closer together onscreen so that they look more like a list. That's all there is to it! Figure 5-7 shows the result.

Most web editors let you vary the appearance of the bullet. For example, you can make the bullet a hollow circle rather than a solid black dot, or you can choose a rectangle rather than a circle.

Titling your web page: The ultimate heading

When you're dreaming up clever headings for your web pages, don't overlook the "heading" that appears in the narrow title bar at the very top of your visitor's web browser window: the *title* of your web page.

The two HTML tags `<title>` and `</title>` contain the text that appears within the browser title bar. But you don't have to mess with these nasty HTML codes: All web page–creation programs give you an easy way to

enter or edit a title for a web page. Make the title as catchy and specific as possible, but make sure it's no longer than 64 characters, including spaces. An effective title refers to your goods or services while grabbing the viewer's attention. If your business is Myrna's Cheesecakes, for example, you might make your title "Smile and Say Cheese! with Myrna's Cakes" (40 characters, including spaces).

Figure 5-7:
A bulleted list is an easy way to direct customers' attention to special promotions or sale items.

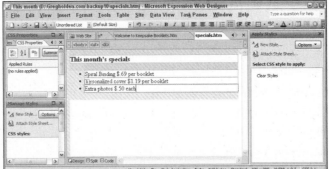

Source: Greg Holden

Leading your readers on with links

You should do anything you can to lead your visitors to your site and then get them to stay long enough to explore individual pages. You can accomplish this goal with a single hyperlinked word that leads to another page on your site:

More . . .

You see this word all the time on web pages that present a lot of content. At the bottom of a list of their products and services, businesses place that word in bold type: **More . . . .**

Magazines use the same approach. On their covers you find phrases that refer you to the kinds of stories you find inside. You can do the same kind of thing on your web pages. For example, which of the following links is more likely to get a response?

Next

Next: Paragon's Success Stories

Whenever possible, tell your visitors what they can expect to encounter as a benefit when they click a link. Give them a tease — and then a big payoff for responding.

Enhancing your text with well-placed images

You can add two kinds of images to a web page: an *inline image,* which appears in the body of your page along with your text, or an *external image,* which is a separate file that visitors access by clicking a link. The link may take the form of highlighted text or a small version of the image — a *thumbnail.* You see lots of thumbnails when you do a search for images on Google Images (http://images.google.com).

The basic HTML tag that inserts an image in your document takes the following form:

```
<img src="URL">
```

This tag tells your browser to display an image (<img>) here. "URL" gives the location of the image file that serves as the source (src) for this image. Whenever possible, also include width and height attributes (as follows) because they help speed up graphics display for many browsers:

```
<img height=51 width=48 SRC="target.gif">
```

Most web page editors add the width and height attributes automatically when you insert an image. Typically, here's what happens:

1. **Click the location in the web page where you want the image to appear.**

2. **Click an Image toolbar button or choose Insert➪Image to display an image selection dialog box.**

3. **Enter the name of the image you want to add and click OK.**

    The image is added to your web page.

A well-placed image points the way to text that you want people to read immediately. Think about where your own eyes go when you first connect to a web page. Most likely, you first look at any images on the page; then you look at the headings; finally, you settle on text to read. If you can place an image next to a heading, you virtually ensure that viewers read the heading.

For more on HTML, the language of the web, check out *Beginning HTML5 & CSS3 For Dummies* (published by John Wiley & Sons, Inc.).

Making your site searchable

A search box is one of the best kinds of content you can put on your website's opening page. A *search box* is a simple text-entry field that lets a visitor enter a word or phrase. Clicking a button labeled Go or Search sends the search term or terms to the site, where a script checks an index of the site's contents for any files that contain those terms. The script then returns links to documents that contain the search terms in the visitor's browser window.

Search boxes are not only found, but are expected to be found on virtually all commercial websites. You usually see them at the top of the home page, near the links to the major sections of the site. Dummies.com, shown in Figure 5-8, includes a search box on the left side of the page.

Figure 5-8: Many surfers prefer using a search box to clicking links.

Source: Dummies.com

Search boxes let visitors instantly scan the site's entire contents for a word or phrase. They put visitors in control right away and get them to interact with your site. They're popular for some very good reasons.

Search boxes require someone with knowledge of computer programming to create or implement a program called a CGI script to do the searching. Someone also has to compile an index of the documents on the website so that the script can search the documents. An application such as Adobe's ColdFusion works well, but it's not a program for beginners.

But you can get around having to write CGI scripts to add search capabilities to your site. Choose one of these options:

- **Let your web host do the work.** Some hosting services do the indexing and creation of the search utility as part of their services. Nearly all shopping carts and e-commerce storefront hosting services do.

- **Use a free site search service.** The server that does the indexing of your web pages and holds the index doesn't need to be the server that hosts your site. Some services make your site searchable for free. In exchange, you display advertisements or logos in the search results you return to your visitors.

- **Pay for a search service.** If you don't want to display ads on your search results pages, pay a monthly fee to have a company index your pages and let users conduct searches. FreeFind (www.freefind.com) has some economy packages, a free version that forces you to view ads, and a professional version (see the site for the latest pricing). SiteMiner (http://siteminer.mycomputer.com) charges $99 per year and lets you customize your search box and re-index your site whenever you add new content.

Book II

Planning
for Your
Business

Make a map of your website

When it comes to your e-commerce website, a map can make your site easier to navigate. A *site map* is a graphical representation of your website — a diagram that graphically depicts all the pages in the site and how they connect to one another. Some web page–editing programs, such as the now-defunct Microsoft FrontPage, had a site map function built into them.

You don't have to invest in a fancy (and expensive) software program to create a site map. You can create one the old-fashioned way, with a pencil and paper. Or you can draw boxes and arrows using a computer graphics program. The point is that your site map can be a useful design tool for organizing the documents within your site.

(continued)

(continued)

> If your sales are sluggish, make sure your customers can actually find what they're looking for. Take a typical product in your sales catalog and then visit your own site to see how many clicks someone would need to make to find it. Then see how many clicks that person would need to make to complete the purchase. Eliminating any unnecessary navigational layers (such as category opening pages) makes your site easier to use.

Nip and Tuck: Establishing a Visual Identity

The prospect of designing a website may be intimidating if you haven't tried it before. But it really boils down to a simple principle: *effective visual communication that conveys a particular message.* The first step in creating graphics is not to open a painting program and start drawing, but to plan your page's message. Next, determine the audience you want to reach with that message and think about how your graphics can best communicate what you want to say. Some ways to do this are

- ✔ **Gather ideas from websites that use graphics well.** Award-winning sites and sites created by designers who are using graphics in new or unusual ways can help you. To find some award winners, check out The Webby Awards (www.webbyawards.com) and the WebAward Competition (www.webaward.org).

- ✔ **Use graphics and colors consistently from page to page.** You can create an identity and convey a consistent message.

- ✔ **Know your audience.** Create graphics that meet visitors' needs and expectations. If you're selling fashions to teenagers, go for neon colors and out-there graphics. If you're selling financial planning to senior citizens, choose a distinguished and sophisticated typeface.

How do you become acquainted with your customers when it's likely you'll never actually meet them face to face? Find newsgroups and mailing lists in which potential visitors to your site discuss subjects related to what you plan to publish on the web. Read the posted messages to get a sense of the concerns and vocabulary of your intended audience.

Choosing an appropriate background

The technical term for the wallpaper behind the contents of a web page is its *background*. Most web browsers display the background of a page as light gray or white unless you specify something different. In this case, leaving well enough alone isn't good enough. If you choose the wrong background color (one that makes your text hard to read and your images look like they've been smeared with mud), viewers are likely to get the impression that the page is poorly designed or the author of the page hasn't put a great deal of thought into the project.

Most web page–creation programs offer a simple way to specify a color or an image file to serve as the background of a web page. For example, in the free editor Komodo Edit, you Ctrl-click the value next to the background-color command in the style sheet for the page you're working on (the section between the `<style>` and `</style>` tags). When the Color dialog box opens, click the color you want and then click OK. The hexadecimal code for your chosen color is added to the style sheet.

Color your website effective

You can use background and other colors to elicit a particular mood or emotion and convey your organization's identity on the web. The right choice of color can create impressions ranging from elegant to funky.

The basic colors chosen by the United Parcel Service website (www.ups.com) convey to customers that it is a staid and reliable company, and the U.S. Postal Service (www.usps.com) sticks to the patriotic choice of red, white, and blue. In contrast, the designers of the more-than-20-years-old HotHotHot hot sauce site (www.hothothot.com) combine fiery colors to convey a site that sizzles.

The colors you use must have contrast so that they don't blend into one another. For example, you don't want to put purple type on a brown or blue background, or yellow type on a white background. Remember to use light type against a dark background and dark type against a light background. That way, all your page's contents show up.

Tile images in the background

You can use an image rather than a solid color to serve as the background of a page. You specify an image in the style sheet code of your web page, and browsers automatically *tile* the image, reproducing it over and over to fill the current width and height of the browser window.

The fact is that few, if any, professional designers use background images any more. Background images worked only when they were subtle and didn't interfere with the page contents. Often, they were distracting. The emphasis these days is on easily accessible and readable content. Focus on that and make sure the background complements rather than interferes with your page's design. Choose an image with no obvious lines that create a distracting pattern when tiled. The effect you're trying to create should literally resemble wallpaper. Go to Google Images (http://images.google.com) and search for examples of background images that add something to a page's design.

Using web typefaces like a pro

If you create a web page and don't specify that the text be displayed in a particular font, the browser that displays the page uses its default font — which is usually Times New Roman or Helvetica (although individual users can customize their browsers by picking a different default font).

If you want to specify a typeface, the simplest option is to pick a generic font that is built into virtually every computer's operating system. This convention ensures that your web pages look more or less the same no matter what web browser or what type of computer displays them. A few choices available to you are Arial, Courier, Century Schoolbook, and Times New Roman.

However, you don't have to limit yourself to the same-old/same-old. As a web page designer, you can exercise a degree of control over the appearance of your web page by specifying that the body type and headings be displayed in a particular nonstandard font. You have to own the font you want to use; you save it on your computer and identify the font and location in the cascading style sheets (CSS) for your website.

 You can copy unusual fonts from dafont.com (www.dafont.com). Its creators sometimes ask for donations for their work. You can generate CSS commands for such typefaces with the aid of Font Squirrel's Webfont Generator (www.fontsquirrel.com/tools/webfont-generator). You then copy and paste the CSS into the style sheet for your page so you can use the font for either headings or body text.

Where do you specify type fonts, colors, and sizes for the text? Again, special HTML tags or CSS commands tell web browsers what fonts to display, but you don't need to mess with these tags yourself if you're using a web page creation tool. The specific steps you take depend on what web design tool you're using. In Dreamweaver, you can specify a group of preferred typefaces rather than a single font in the Properties inspector, as shown in Figure 5-9.

If the viewer doesn't have one font in the group, another font displays. Check the Help files with your own program to find out how to format text and what typeface options you have.

Not all typefaces are equal in the eye of the user. Serif typefaces, such as Times New Roman, have been traditionally considered more readable (at least, for printed materials) than sans-serif fonts, such as Helvetica. However, many claim the sans serif font Arial (which is basically Helvetica) is more readable on a web page than Times New Roman.

If you want to make sure that a heading or block of type appears in a specific typeface (especially a nonstandard one that isn't displayed as body text by web browsers), scan it or create the heading in an image-editing program and insert it into the page as a graphic image. But make sure it doesn't clash with the generic typefaces that appear on the rest of your page.

Book II

Planning for Your Business

Using clip art is free and fun

Not everyone has the time or resources to scan photos or create original graphics. But that doesn't mean you can't add graphic interest to your web page. Many web page designers use clip-art bullets, diamonds, or other small images next to list items or major web page headings that they want to call special attention to. Clip art can also provide a background pattern for a web page or highlight sales headings, such as Free!, New!, or Special!.

Figure 5-9: Most web design tools let you specify a preferred font or fonts for your web page in a dialog box like this.

Source: Greg Holden

Back in the day, you had to buy catalogs of illustrations, literally clip out the art, and paste it down. It's still called clip art, but now the process is different. In keeping with the spirit of exchange that has been a part of the Internet since its inception, some talented and generous artists have created icons, buttons, and other illustrations in electronic form and offered them free for downloading.

Here are two suggestions for tried-and-true sources of clip art on the web:

- Clipart.com (`www.clipart.com/en`)
- Clip Art Universe (`http://clipartuniverse.com`)

 If you use Microsoft Office, you have access to plenty of clip art images that come with the software. In Word, choose Insert➪Clip Art to open the Insert Clip Art dialog box. If these built-in images aren't sufficient, you can connect to the Microsoft Clip Gallery Live website by clicking the Clips Online toolbar button in the Insert Clip Art dialog box. Many web page editors — such as CoffeeCup HTML Editor — come with their own clip art libraries, too.

 Be sure to read the copyright fine print *before* you copy graphics. All artists own the copyright to their work. It's up to them to determine how they want to give someone else the right to copy their work. Sometimes the authors require you to pay a small fee if you want to copy their work, or they may restrict use of their work to nonprofit organizations.

A picture is worth a thousand words

Some customers know exactly what they want from the get-go and don't need any help from you. But most customers love to shop around or could use some encouragement to move from one item or catalog page to another. This is where images can play an important role.

Even if you use only some basic clip art, such as placing spheres or arrows next to sale items, your customer is likely to thank you by buying more. A much better approach, though, is to scan or take digital images of your sale items and provide compact, clear images of them on your site. Here's a quick step-by-step guide to get you started:

1. **Choose the right image to capture.**

    The original quality of an image is just as important as how you scan or retouch it. Images that are murky or fuzzy in print are even worse when viewed on a computer screen.

2. Preview the image.

Digital cameras let you preview images so that you can decide whether to keep or delete individual pictures before downloading to your computer. If you're working with a scanner, some scanning programs let you make a quick *preview scan* of an image so that you can get an idea of what it looks like before you do the actual scan. When you click the Preview button, the optical device in the scanner captures the image. A preview image appears onscreen, surrounded by a *marquee box* (a rectangle made up of dashes), as shown in Figure 5-10.

Figure 5-10:
The marquee box lets you crop a preview image to make it smaller and reduce the file size.

Marquee box

Source: Greg Holden

Book II

Planning for Your Business

3. Crop the image.

Cropping means that you resize the box around the image to select the portion of the image that you want to keep and "crop off" the parts of the image that aren't essential. Cropping an image is a good idea because it highlights the most important contents and reduces the file size. Reducing the file size of an image should always be one of your most important goals — the smaller the image, the quicker it appears in someone's browser window.

Almost all scanning and graphics programs offer separate options for cropping an image and reducing the image size. By cropping the image, you eliminate parts of the image you don't want, and this *does* reduce the image size. But it doesn't reduce the size of the objects within the image. Resizing the overall image size is a separate step, which enables you to change the dimensions of the entire image without eliminating any contents.

4. **Select an input mode.**

   Tell the scanner or graphics program how you want it to save the visual data — as color, line art (used for black-and-white drawings), or grayscale (used for black-and-white photos).

5. **Set the resolution.**

   Digital images are made up of little bits (dots) of computerized information called *pixels.* The more pixels per inch, the higher the level of detail. When you scan an image, you can tell the scanner to make the dots smaller (creating a smoother image) or larger (resulting in a more jagged image). This adjustment is called *setting the resolution* of the image. (When you take a digital photo, the resolution of the image depends on your camera's settings.)

   When you're scanning for the web, your images appear primarily on computer screens. Because many computer monitors can display resolutions only up to 72 dpi, 72 dpi — a relatively rough resolution — is an adequate resolution for a web image. Using this coarse resolution has the advantage of keeping the image's file size small. Remember, the smaller the file size, the more quickly an image appears when your customers load your page in their web browsers. (Alternatively, many designers scan at a fine resolution such as 300 dpi and reduce the file size in a graphics program.)

6. **Adjust contrast and brightness.**

   Virtually all scanning programs and graphics editing programs provide brightness and contrast controls that you can adjust with your mouse to improve the image. If you're happy with the image as is, leave the brightness and contrast set where they are. (You can also leave the image as is and adjust brightness and contrast later in a separate graphics program, such as GIMP, which you can try out by downloading it from the Corel website, www.gimp.org.)

7. **Reduce the image size.**

   The old phrase "Good things come in small packages" is never truer than when you're improving your digital image. You can reduce an image to make it smaller and easier to transport — whether it's from your camera to your computer or your computer to your hosting service. Even more important, it appears more quickly in someone's web browser.

8. **Scan away!**

   Your scanner makes a beautiful whirring sound as it turns those colors into pixels. Because you're scanning only at 72 dpi, the process shouldn't take too long.

9. Save the file.

Now you can save your image to disk. Most programs let you do this by choosing File⇨Save. In the dialog box that appears, enter a name for your file and select a file format. Because you're working with images to be published on the web, remember to save your images either in GIF, JPEG, or PNG format.

Be sure to add the correct filename extension. Web browsers recognize only image files with extensions such as `.png`, `.gif`, `.jpg`, or `.jpeg`. If you name your image product and save it in GIF format, call it `product.gif`. If you save it in JPEG format and you're using a PC, call it `product.jpg`. On a Mac, you can call it `product.jpeg`.

Creating a logo

An effective logo establishes your business's graphic identity in no uncertain terms. A logo can be as simple as a rendering of the company name that imparts an official typeface or color. Whatever text it includes, a *logo* is a small, self-contained graphic object that communicates the group's identity and purpose. Figure 5-11 shows an example of a logo.

A logo doesn't have to be a fabulously complex drawing with drop shadows and gradations of color. A simple, type-only logo can be as good as gold. Pick a typeface, choose your graphic's outline version, and fill the letters with color.

Figure 5-11: A good logo effectively combines color, type, and graphics to convey an organization's identity or mission.

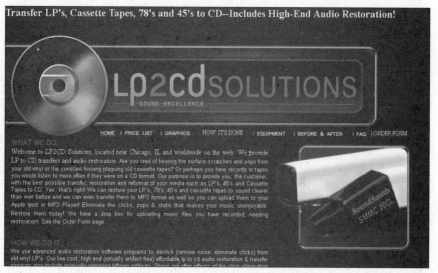

Source: Greg Holden

GIF, JPEG, and PNG

Website technology and HTML may have changed dramatically over the past several years, but for the most part, there are still only three types of images as far as web pages are concerned: GIF, JPEG, and PNG. All three formats use methods that compress computer image files so that the visual information contained within them can be transmitted easily over computer networks. PNG, designed several years ago as a successor to GIF, is now popular and is far superior in terms of compression and image quality, especially when it comes to photos.

GIF (pronounced either *jiff* or *giff*) stands for Graphics Interchange Format. GIF is best suited to text, line art, or images with well-defined edges. Special types of GIF allow images with transparent backgrounds to be *interlaced* (broken into layers that appear gradually over slow connections) and animated. JPEG (pronounced *jay-peg*) stands for Joint Photographic Experts Group, the name of the group that originated the format. JPEG is preferred for large photos and continuous tones of grayscale or color that need greater compression.

If you have a choice, try PNG (Portable Network Graphics). Its images are ideal for the web. The quality is so good you can blow up images, print them on a color inkjet printer, and put them on the wall of your office. And PNG is supported by all the major browsers, so you'll have no problem getting your visitors to enjoy them.

Inviting Comments from Customers

Quick, inexpensive, and *personal:* These are three of the most important advantages that the web has over traditional printed catalogs. The first two are obvious pluses. You don't have to wait for your online catalog to get printed and distributed. On the web, your contents are published and available to your customers right away. Putting a catalog on the web eliminates (or, if publishing a catalog on the web allows you to reduce your print run, dramatically reduces) the cost of printing, which can result in big savings for you.

But the fact that online catalogs can be more personal than the printed variety is perhaps the biggest advantage of all. The personal touch comes from the web's potential for *interactivity*. Getting your customers to click links makes them actively involved with your catalog.

Getting positive email feedback

Playing hide-and-seek is fun when you're amusing your baby niece, but it's not a good way to build a solid base of customers. In fact, providing a way for your customers to interact with you so that they can reach you quickly may be the most important part of your website.

Add a simple `mailto` link like this:

Questions? Comments? Send email to: `info@mycompany.com`

A `mailto` link gets its name from the HTML command that programmers use to create it. When visitors click the email address, their email program opens a new email message window with your email address already entered. That way, they have only to enter a subject line, type the message, and click Send to send you their thoughts.

Most web page–creation programs make it easy to create a `mailto` link. For example, if you use Dreamweaver, follow these steps:

1. **Launch and open the web page to which you want to add your email link.**

2. **Position your mouse arrow and click the spot on the page where you want the address to appear.**

   The convention is to put your email address at or near the bottom of a web page. A vertical blinking cursor appears at the location where you want to insert the address.

3. **Choose Insert ⇨ Email Link.**

   The Insert Email Link dialog box appears.

4. **In the Text box, type the text that you want to appear on your web page.**

   You don't have to type your email address; you can also type **Webmaster, Customer Service,** or your own name.

5. **In the Email box, type your email address.**

6. **Click OK.**

   The Insert Email Link dialog box closes, and you return to the Dreamweaver Document window, where your email link appears in blue and is underlined to signify that it is a clickable link.

Other editors work similarly but may not give you a menu command called Email Link. In that case, you have to type the `mailto` link manually. In the WordPress editor, for example, select the text you want to serve as the link and click the link toolbar icon. When the Insert/Edit Link dialog box opens, in the URL box, after `http://` (which is pre-entered), type **mailto:name@emailaddress**.

The drawback to publishing your email address directly on your web page is that you're certain to get unsolicited email messages (commonly called *spam)* sent to that address. Hiding your email address behind generic link text (such as `Webmaster`) may help reduce your chances of attracting spam.

Book II

Planning
for Your
Business

Web page forms that aren't offputting

You don't have to do much web surfing before you become intimately acquainted with how web page forms work, at least from the standpoint of someone who has to fill them out to sign up for web hosting or to download software.

When it comes to creating your own website, however, you become conscious of how useful forms are as a means of gathering essential marketing information about your customers. They give your visitors a place to sound off, ask questions, and generally get involved with your business.

Be clear and use common sense when creating your order form. Here are some general guidelines on how to organize your form and what you need to include:

- **Make it easy on the customer.** Whenever possible, add pull-down menus with pre-entered options to your *form fields* (text boxes that visitors use to enter information). That way, users don't have to wonder about things such as whether you want them to spell out a state or use the two-letter abbreviation.

- **Validate the information.** You can use a programming language — for example, JavaScript — to ensure that users enter information correctly, that all fields are completely filled out, and so on. You may have to hire someone to add the appropriate code to the order form, but the expense is worth it to save you from having to call customers to verify or correct information that they missed or submitted incorrectly.

- **Provide a help number.** Give people a number to call if they have questions or want to check on an order.

- **Return an acknowledgment.** Let customers know that you have received their order and will be shipping the merchandise immediately or contacting them if more information is needed.

As usual, good web design tools make it a snap to create the text boxes, check boxes, buttons, and other parts of a form that the user fills out. The other part of a form, the computer script that receives the data and processes it so that you can read and use the information, is not as simple. And programs like WordPress provide you with a host of add-on applications — *plugins* — that create both the text entry elements and the scripts for you.

Blogs that promote discussion

Most blogs give readers the chance to respond to individual comments the author has made. This is a standard feature to give readers the opportunity to comment on what you've written.

On blogs that attract a wide following, comments by multiple authors generate long discussions by a community of devoted readers. The comments that appear at the end of an article or blog post have replaced what web designers used to call a *guestbook* — a place where visitors signed in so they could feel that they're part of a thriving community. If you use WordPress to create and manage a blog or website, you can easily give visitors the capability to comment on an article. If you have created a blog, each post is automatically "commentable." That's one of the many nice things about WordPress. You just have to make sure commenting is turned on.

Log in to WordPress and click Settings under the heading Admin Options in the narrow column on the left side of the editing window. Then click Discussion, as shown in Figure 5-12, and select the Allow check box so people can post comments on new articles.

To enable comments on an individual page, follow these steps:

1. **Click Pages in the Admin settings in the narrow column on the left side of the editing window.**

   The list of pages in your WordPress site appears.

2. **Click the page you want, and if necessary, click Quick Edit.**

   The Quick Edit window for your page opens.

3. **Scroll down to the Discussion section and select the Allow check box.**

After you allow comments, be sure to log in to your site regularly to moderate them. You'll probably have to delete spam comments left by *bots* (programs that perform automated functions such as "scraping" web pages for contents)

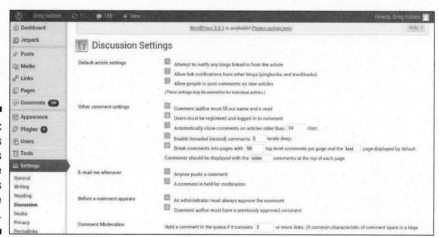

Figure 5-12: WordPress easily lets you manage comments for an entire site.

Source: Greg Holden

that post them automatically and respond to legitimate comments that actual human beings have left. And more and more, the comments left on websites of all types seem to be getting more and more outrageously inappropriate. You must look at your comments and make sure nothing offensive is allowed to just sit there.

Chit-chat that counts

After visitors start coming to your site, the next step is to retain those visitors. A good way to do this is by building a sense of community by posting a bulletin board–type discussion area.

A discussion area takes the form of back-and-forth messages on topics of mutual interest. Each person can read previously posted messages and either respond or start a new topic of discussion. The comments areas discussed in the preceding section are the most popular ways of promoting this sort of interaction. For a more elaborate example of a discussion area that's tied to an business, visit the EcommerceBytes (www.ecommercebytes.com) discussion areas, one of which is shown in Figure 5-13. EcommerceBytes is a highly regarded site that provides information about the online auction industry. Its discussion boards give readers a place to bring up questions and issues in a forum that's independent from those provided by auction sites like eBay.

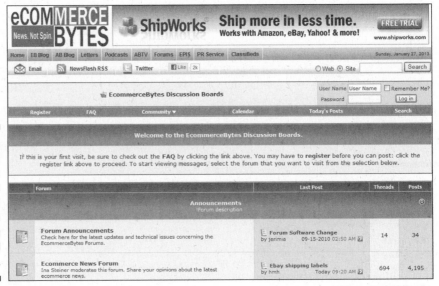

Figure 5-13:
A discussion area stimulates interest and interaction among like-minded customers.

Source: eCommerceBytes.com

The talk doesn't have to be about your particular niche in your business field. In fact, the discussion is livelier if your visitors can discuss concerns about your area of business in general, whether it's flower arranging, boat sales, tax preparation, clock repair, computers, or whatever.

How do you start a discussion area? The basic first step is to install a special computer script on the computer that hosts your website. (Again, discussing this prospect with your web hosting service beforehand is essential.) When visitors come to your site, their web browsers access the script, enabling them to enter comments and read other messages.

Here are some specific ways to prepare a discussion area for your site:

✔ Copy a bulletin board or discussion-group script from either of these sites:

- eXtropia.com (hwww.extropia.com/applications.html)
- Matt's Script Archive (www.scriptarchive.com)

✔ Start your own forum on a service such as vBulletin (www.vbulletin.com), which is used by the aforementioned EcommerceBytes.

Moving from Website to Web Presence

After you have established a visual identity through colors, images, and a logo, you can "brand" yourself by "popping up" in as many web venues as possible. Make no mistake about it: Tending to your image and building a name for yourself takes time and effort. It might take one, two, or more hours every day. And once you start blogging and building an audience, you need to keep at it every few days, if not *every* day. Otherwise, those fickle web visitors you worked so hard to cultivate will flit away to someone else's website or blog or Facebook page.

How do you "pop up" in places where people will find you? You'll find suggestions throughout this book. Here are a few ideas:

✔ Start up a blog and use it to comment on your area of interest.

✔ Tweet as much as possible (www.twitter.com); short tweets can advertise new products or sales you have running.

✔ Get on Facebook (www.facebook.com) and start cultivating a circle of friends. Use Facebook to point them to your website — and your blog, your tweets, and so on.

When in doubt, hire a pro

Part of the fun of running your own business is doing things yourself. You can discover how to create websites by reading books or taking classes on the subject. But in many cases, the initial cost of hiring someone to help design your business can be a good investment. After you pay someone to help you develop a look, you can probably implement it in the future more easily yourself. For example:

✔ If you need business cards, stationery, brochures, or other printed material in addition to a website, hiring someone to develop a consistent look for everything at the beginning is worth the money. You, then, can maintain that look.

✔ You can pay a designer to get you started with a logo, color selections, and page layouts. Then you can save money by adding text yourself.

✔ If you're artistically impaired, consider the benefits of having your logo or other artwork drawn by a real artist.

Most professional designers charge $40 to $60 per hour for their work. You can expect a designer to spend five or six hours creating a logo or template, but if your company uses that initial design for the foreseeable future, you're not really paying that much per year.

(See Book V Chapter 6 for much more on using Twitter and Facebook to market your business.)

✔ Open a storefront on eBay (www.ebay.com) or on a free site like eCRATER (www.ecrater.com).

The art of having a web presence means using *all* these sites to point to one another, so no matter where you are, shoppers are directed to your products or services, or at least prompted to find out more about you.

Chapter 6

Starting with the Right Legal Structure

In This Chapter

▶ Finding the right legal form for your business

▶ Using the sole proprietorship

▶ Choosing the partnership

▶ Electing the corporate form

▶ Selecting the best legal structure

Choosing the legal form for organizing your business is one of the important decisions you must make before launching the business. Because of changing laws, entrepreneurs today have many more choices regarding how to structure their companies. Your need for capital and protection from liability are just two reasons why understanding the options available to you is so essential.

Those changing laws are also a good reason for seeking the advice of a good attorney or CPA to make sure you're making the best choice for you and your type of business.

This chapter gives you a solid background on what you need to think about before choosing a legal form of business and what you need to understand about of the various forms available to you.

Deciding on the Best Legal Form for Your Business

All companies operate under one of four broad legal classifications:

- ✔ Sole proprietorship
- ✔ Partnership
- ✔ Corporation
- ✔ Limited Liability Company (LLC)

Many entrepreneurs assume that the best entity is always one that lets profits pass through to the owners at their personal tax rate. They further assume that incorporating in your home state is always best. These assumptions can be wrong for some entrepreneurs and for some businesses.

For example, if you know that you want to do an IPO (initial public offering) within two years, you should probably form as a C Corporation, because that form is required to go public. If you're going to use venture capital, you probably also want a C corporate form, and you may want to incorporate in California or Delaware. Why? Those states have a substantial body of law in the area of corporate governance. Choosing the wrong entity when speed is of the essence (consider the case of Internet startups) can mean costly delays and lost opportunities.

Understanding the various factors that come into play when you choose a particular form of legal structure is important. Seven factors affect your choice of structure. A summary comparison of these factors appears in Figure 6-1.

Here the factors are presented in the form of questions you can ask yourself:

1. **Who will be the owners of the company?**

   If more than one individual owns the company, you can eliminate sole proprietorship as an option. If many people own the company, the C Corporation form is often the choice because it has an unlimited life and free transferability of interests. If you intend to have many employees, the C Corporation also lets you take advantage of pension plans and stock option plans.

Issues	Sole Proprietorship	Partnership	S Corp.	Limited Liability Company	C Corp.
Number of owners	One	No limit	100	No limit	No limit on shareholders
Liability	Owner liable for all claims against business	General partners liable for all claims. Limited partners only to amount of investment.	Limited liability	Members liable as in partnerships.	Shareholders liable to amount invested. Officers may be personally liable.
Life of Business	Dissolution on the death of the owner	Dissolution on the death or separation of a partner unless otherwise specified in the agreement. Not so in the case of limited partners.	Continuity of life	Continuity of life	No effect
Transfer of Interest	Owner free to sell	General partner requires consent of other generals to sell interest. Limiteds' ability subject to agreement.	Subject to agreement	Free transferability of interests subject to agreement.	Shareholders free to sell unless restricted by agreement.
Distribution of Profits	Profits go to owner	Profits shared based on partnership agreement.	Profits go to owners.	Profits go to members.	Paid to shareholders as dividends according to agreement and shareholder status
Management Control	Owner has full control	Shared by general partners according to partnership agreement	Shared by owners/ shareholders	Rests with management committee (owners or those shareholders)	Rests with the board of directors appointed by the shareholders

Figure 6-1:
This chart shows a summary comparison of legal forms of business organization.

© *John Wiley & Sons, Inc.*

Book II

Planning for Your Business

2. **What level of liability protection do you require, especially for your personal assets?**

Some forms protect you; others do not. It's a sad fact that too many businesses ignore the risks they face and don't acquire the correct forms of insurance. Just as you want to seek the advice of an attorney and accountant as you develop your business, you also want to consider the advice of an insurance broker.

3. **How do you expect to distribute the company's earnings?**

   If you choose an entity allowing pass-through income and losses (partnership, S Corporation, or LLC), tax items at the entity level are allocated immediately without additional taxation, although cash may or may not be distributed. But in a C Corporation, only a salary or other forms of compensation are paid out pretax from the company to an owner.

4. **What are the operating requirements of your business and the costs of running the business under the particular form in question?**

   If you own a manufacturing company that uses a lot of machinery, you have different liabilities than a service company.

5. **What are your financing plans?**

   How attractive is the form to potential investors? Are you able to offer ownership interests to investors and employees? In general, as already mentioned, if you're going to use venture capital, you need a corporate form. Most venture capitalists raise their money from tax-exempt entities such as pension funds, universities, and charitable organizations. These organizations can't invest in companies that have pass-through tax benefits.

6. **What will be the effect on the company's tax strategy and your personal tax strategy?**

   This includes everything from minimizing tax liability, converting ordinary income to capital gain, and avoiding multiple taxation to maximizing the benefits of startup losses.

7. **Do you expect the company to generate a profit or loss in the beginning?**

   If you think your company will lose money for the first few years (this is often true with biotech or other companies developing new products), then a pass-through option can be justified because you get to deduct your losses on your personal tax return.

Going It Alone: The Sole Proprietorship

Most businesses operating in the United States are sole proprietorships. A *sole proprietorship* is a business where the owner essentially *is* the business; that is, he or she is solely responsible for the activities of the business and is the only one to enjoy the profits and suffer the losses of the business.

Why do so many businesses start this way? Sole proprietorship is the easiest and least expensive way to form a business. If you're using your own name as the name of the business, all you need is a business license, some business cards, and you're in, uh, business.

Deciding to use another name for your business is only slightly more complex. For example, in the case of ABC Associates, you apply for a DBA, which is a certificate of Doing Business under an Assumed name. You can secure a DBA at your local government office. Securing a DBA ensures that two businesses don't operate in the same county with the same name.

Advantages of sole proprietorships

Besides being the easiest to start and least expensive form of organization, sole proprietorship also gives the owner complete control of the company. You make all the decisions and suffer all the consequences, but the income from the business is yours and you're taxed only once at your personal income tax rate.

Many professionals, such as consultants, authors, and many home-based business owners, operate as sole proprietors.

Disadvantages of sole proprietorships

For many entrepreneurs, the sole proprietorship form of organization is not satisfactory, for several reasons:

- ✔ As a sole proprietor, you have unlimited liability for any claims against the business. In other words, you are putting your personal assets at risk — your home, car, bank accounts, and any other assets you may have. So, having business liability and errors and omissions insurance is extremely important. If you're producing a product, you'll need product liability insurance to protect you against lawsuits over defective products. If your company does work for other people (such as a construction company), you may be required to have bonding insurance to ensure that you complete the work specified in your contract. Because there are so many areas of liability and so many different types of insurance, you should talk to a good insurance broker.

- ✔ Raising capital is difficult, because you're relying only on your financial statement. You are, for all intents and purposes, the business, and most investors don't like that situation.

- ✔ You probably won't have a management team with diverse skills helping you grow your business. You may have employees, but that isn't really the same thing. Putting together an advisory board of people with skills you need may help compensate for the skills you lack.

> ✔ Because the survival of your company depends on you being there, if something happens to you or a catastrophe strikes, the company doesn't survive. Legally, if the sole proprietor dies, so does the business, unless its assets are willed to someone.

If you intend to really grow your business, organizing as a sole proprietorship may not be a good idea, unless you're taking advantage of income and control benefits during the early stages of your business — for example, through product development.

Choosing a Partner: The Partnership

A *partnership* is two or more people deciding to share the assets, liabilities, and profits of their business. Partnering is often an improvement over the sole proprietorship because more people are sharing the responsibilities of the business and bouncing ideas off each other. Additionally, you now have multiple financial statements on which to rely and an entity that usually survives if one of the partners dies or leaves.

In terms of liability, though, you're raising the stakes, because each partner becomes liable for the obligations incurred by other partners in the course of doing business. This *doctrine of ostensible authority* works like this: Suppose one of your partners enters a contract on behalf of the partnership, purchasing certain goods from a supplier. That partner has just bound the partnership to make good on a contract even if the rest of the partners knew nothing about it. The one major exception is that personal debts of an individual partner cannot attach to the rest of the partners.

On the positive side, each partner uses any property owned by the partnership and shares in the profits and losses of the partnership unless otherwise stated in the partnership agreement. Partners don't have to share equally in the profits and losses. Ownership in the partnership can be divided in any manner the partners choose. The biggest issue with partnerships is that they often are fraught with conflict in much the same way as family businesses. However, when you think about it, any business that includes a team of entrepreneurs, whether a corporation or limited liability company, has similar issues. The partnership agreement, therefore, becomes important from the beginning.

Forming a partnership

You don't have to have a written agreement when forming a partnership; a simple oral agreement works. In fact, in some cases, the conduct of the parties involved implies a partnership.

Accepting a share of the profits of a business is *prima facie* (legally sufficient) evidence that you are a partner in the business, meaning that you may also be liable for its losses.

Partnerships come in several flavors. In most partnerships, entrepreneurs are general partners, meaning they share in the profits, losses, and responsibilities, and are personally liable for actions of the partnership. But other types of partners have more limited liability, including the following:

- ✔ **Limited partners:** These partners' liability generally is limited to the amount of their investment.

- ✔ **Secret partners:** These partners are active in the ventures but are unknown to the public.

- ✔ **Silent partners:** These partners are usually inactive with only a financial interest in the partnership.

The partnership agreement

It's hard to overstate the importance of a partnership agreement. Many a prospective partner says things like, "We've been the best of friends for years; we know what we're doing," or "How can I ask my father to sign a partnership agreement?" Well, how can you not? You must separate business from friendship and family, at least when it comes to structuring your company. This is a serious deal. No matter how well you know your partner, you probably haven't worked with him or her in this particular kind of situation. You have no way of predicting all the things that can cause a disagreement with your partner. The partnership agreement gives you an unbiased mechanism for resolving disagreements or dissolving the partnership, if it comes to that.

Consulting an attorney is necessary when drawing up an agreement, so that you're not inadvertently causing yourself further problems by the way a phrase is worded in the agreement or leaving something important out. The partnership agreement addresses the following:

- ✔ The legal name of the partnership.

- ✔ The nature of your business.

- ✔ How long the partnership is to last. As with any contract, it needs a stop date.

- ✔ What each of the partners is contributing to the partnership — capital, in-kind goods, services, and so forth. This is the *initial capitalization*.

- ✔ Any sales, loans, or leases to the partnership.

✔ Who is responsible for what — the management of the partnership.

✔ The sale of a partnership interest. This clause restricts a partner's right to sell his or her interest to third parties. It provides, however, a method by which a partner can divest his or her interest in the partnership.

✔ How the partnership can be dissolved.

✔ What happens if a partner leaves or dies.

✔ How disputes will be resolved.

If you don't execute a partnership agreement, all partners are equal under the law.

Going for the Gold: The Corporation

A *corporation* is a legal entity under the law and has continuity of life. Chartered or registered by the state in which it resides, a corporation can survive the death or separation of all of its owners. It can also sue, be sued, acquire and sell real property, and lend money.

Corporation owners are called *stockholders*. They invest capital into the corporation and receive shares of stock, usually proportionate to the level of their investment. Much like limited partners, shareholders are not responsible for the debts of the corporation (unless they have personally guaranteed them), and their investment is the limit of their liability.

This chapter covers two major types of corporations: the C Corporation (closely held, close, and public) and the S Corporation. Most corporations are C Corporations and are closely held, which means stock is held privately by a few individuals. A closely held corporation operates as any type of corporation — general, professional, or nonprofit. But in a close corporation, the number of shareholders you may have is restricted, usually to between 30 and 50 shareholders. In addition, holding directors' meetings is not required. Such meetings are a requirement for an S Corporation. The C Corporation is not available in every state and does not permit you to conduct an initial public offering. Basically, a close corporation operates much like a partnership.

Doctors, lawyers, accountants, and other professionals who previously were not allowed to incorporate use professional corporations. This vehicle now lets professionals enjoy tax-free and tax-deferred fringe benefits. You should be aware that only members of the specific profession can be shareholders in the corporation.

In a professional corporation, all the shareholders are liable for negligent or wrongful acts of any shareholder.

By contrast, in a public corporation, stock is traded on a securities exchange like the New York Stock Exchange, and the company generally has thousands (in some cases, millions) of shareholders. For space concerns, and because most people starting a business choose the C Corporation type over the S, the focus here is on C Corporations.

Three groups of individuals — shareholders, directors, and officers — make up the corporate structure. Shareholders own the corporation but they don't manage it. Shareholders exert influence through the directors they elect to serve and represent them on the board. The board of directors, in turn, manages the affairs of the corporation at a policy level and hires and fires the officers who are responsible for the day-to-day decisions of the company.

Public corporations in most states in the U.S. require only one director, but in some states, the number of shareholders you have determines the number of directors. However, you can always have more directors for many different reasons. If you are forming a corporation in a country other than the U.S., check with the local government to find out the requirements for boards of directors. The rules differ from country to country.

What is surprising for many is in the U.S., corporations comprise a small minority of all businesses, yet they generate most of the sales. Part of this surprising picture is attributable to the fact that most entrepreneurs who intend to grow their companies choose the corporate form for its many benefits.

Enjoying the benefits of a corporation

The advantages of a corporate form definitely outweigh the disadvantages. For one, the owners enjoy limited liability to the extent of their investment (the one important exception is payroll taxes that haven't been paid to the IRS). By selecting the corporate form, you also can do the following:

- Raise capital through the sale of stock in the company.

- Own a corporation without the public being aware of your involvement. So, if you want anonymity, it's the way to go.

- Create different classes of stock to help you meet the various needs of investors. For example, you may want to issue nonvoting, preferred stock to conservative investors wanting to be first to recoup their investment in the event the business fails. Most stock issued is *common* stock, the owners of which enjoy voting rights and share in the profits after the preferred stock has been paid.

- Easily transfer ownership. In a private corporation, you want assurances that your shareholders can't sell their stock to just anyone. In other words, you want to know who owns your stock. You can protect yourself by including a buy-sell clause in the stockholder's agreement. Usually, this clause specifies that the stock must first be offered to the corporation at an agreed-upon price.

✔ Enter into corporate contracts and sue or be sued without the signatures of the owners.

✔ Enjoy more status in the business world than other legal forms because corporations survive apart from their owners.

✔ Enjoy the benefits of setting up retirement funds, Keogh and defined-contribution plans, profit sharing, and stock option plans. The corporation deducts these fringe benefits as expenses that are not taxable to the employee.

Weighing the risks

Every legal form has disadvantages and risks, and the corporation is no exception. Here are risks worth considering when contemplating using the corporate form.

✔ Corporations are much more complex, cumbersome, and expensive to set up.

✔ Corporations are subject to more government regulation.

✔ A corporation pays taxes on profits regardless of whether they are distributed as dividends to stockholders.

✔ Shareholders of C Corporations do not receive the tax benefits of company losses.

✔ By selling shares of stock in your corporation, you're effectively giving up a measure of control to a board of directors. The reality, however, is that the entrepreneur determines who sits on that board of directors in privately held corporations.

✔ You must keep your personal finances and the corporation's finances completely separate. You must conduct directors' meetings, and maintain minutes from those meetings. If you don't, you may leave your company open to what is known as piercing the corporate veil, which makes you and your officers liable personally for the company.

Where and how to incorporate

You create a corporation by filing a certificate of incorporation with the state in which you do business and issue stock, making your company a *domestic* corporation. If you incorporate in a state other than the one in which you do business, your company is a *foreign* corporation.

In general, you want to incorporate in the state where you're planning to locate the business so that you don't find yourself working under the regulations of two states. When deciding where to incorporate, consider the following:

1. **The cost difference of incorporating in your home state versus doing business as a foreign corporation in another state.**

   In general, if you're doing business mostly in your home state, incorporating there won't subject you to taxes and annual report fees from both states.

2. **The advantages and disadvantages of the other state's corporate laws and tax structure.**

   For example, in some states, a corporation pays a minimum state tax regardless of whether it makes a profit, whereas other states have no minimum state tax. Likewise, if you're incorporating anywhere other than your home state and find yourself defending a lawsuit in the state of incorporation, you may incur the expense of travel back and forth during that time.

Book II

Planning
for Your
Business

Looking for Flexibility: The S Corporation, the LLC, and the Nonprofit Corporation

A number of different legal organizational forms offer flexibility for entrepreneurs in a variety of ways. This section looks at three: the S Corporation, the LLC, and the nonprofit. All the criteria used for making a decision about which form to choose apply to these as well.

Sizing up the S Corporation

An S Corporation is a corporation that elects and is eligible to choose S Corporation status, and shareholders at the time consent to the corporation's choice. In general, an S Corporation does not pay any income tax. Instead, the corporation's income and deductions are passed through to its shareholders. The shareholders must then report the income and deductions on their own income tax returns.

An S Corporation can provide employee benefits and deferred compensation plans. To qualify for S Corporation status, you must

1. Form your corporation with no more than 100 shareholders, none of whom may be nonresident aliens.

2. Issue only one class of stock.

3. Ensure no more than 25 percent of the corporate income is derived from passive investments like dividends, rent, and capital gains.

In addition, your S Corporation cannot be a financial institution, a foreign corporation, or a subsidiary of a parent corporation. If you elect to change from an S Corporation to a C Corporate form, you cannot go back to being an S Corporation form for five years.

In general, S Corporations work best

✔ When you expect to experience a loss in the first year or two, and owners have other income they can shelter with that loss.

✔ Where shareholders have low tax brackets (lower than the corporate rate), so the profits can be distributed as dividends without double taxation.

✔ Where your business may incur an accumulated earnings penalty tax for failure to pay out its profits as dividends.

Comparing the S Corporation with the LLC

The Limited Liability Company (LLC) is the newest legal form of business organization, and although gaining in popularity for many entrepreneurs, it confuses the many choices they already face in structuring their companies. The LLC combines the best of partnerships (pass-through earnings) with the best of the corporate form (limited liability). LLCs have grown in popularity because they

✔ Limit liability for business debts up to the amount invested.

✔ Offer flexible management structure that allows the *members* (the equivalent of shareholders in a corporation) or *nonmembers* they hire to manage the organization.

✔ Allow the choice of being treated as a partnership with the benefits of pass-through earnings or as a corporation, whichever provides the lowest tax liability.

✔ Enable flexible distribution of profits and losses, meaning that you can divide them up any way you want among the members.

So what are the differences between between an LLC and an S Corporation? Why would you choose one over the other?

✔ An LLC provides for an unlimited number of owners, whereas the S Corporation limits you to 100.

✔ An LLC permits you to include nonresident aliens, pension plans, partnerships, and corporations as members, whereas the S Corporation does not.

✔ LLCs can have different classes of stock, whereas an S Corporation is generally limited to one class.

The members of an LLC are analogous to partners in a partnership or shareholders in a corporation. If the members self-manage, then the members act more like partners than shareholders, because they have a direct say in what happens within the organization. Stock in an LLC is known as *interest*.

If you're looking for more flexibility in what you're able to do in the long term, you would probably choose an LLC over an S Corporation.

Book II

Planning for Your Business

Making profits in a nonprofit organization

Let's dispel the biggest myth about nonprofit organizations first. You *can* make a profit in a nonprofit company; in fact, doing so is a good idea. What you can't do is distribute those profits in the form of dividends the way other legal forms do. A nonprofit (or not-for-profit corporation) is formed for charitable, public (in other words, scientific, literary, or educational), religious, or mutual benefit (as in trade associations).

Like the C Corporation, the nonprofit is a legal entity with a life of its own and offers its members limited liability. Profits that it generates from its nonprofit activities are not taxed as long as the company meets the state and federal requirements for exemption from taxes under IRS 501(c)(3). When you form a nonprofit, you actually give up proprietary interest in the corporation and dedicate all the assets and resources to tax-exempt activities. If you choose to dissolve the corporation, you must distribute those assets to another tax-exempt organization — you can't take them with you. Any profits you make from for-profit activities are taxed the same as any other corporation.

Nonprofit organizations derive their revenues from a variety of sources. They receive donations from corporations (which are tax deductible to the corporation) and others, conduct activities to raise money, or sell services (a for-profit activity). As entrepreneurs, founders of nonprofit, tax-exempt corporations can pay themselves a good salary, provide themselves with cars, and generally do the kinds of things you would do within a normal corporation — except distribute profits.

Most entrepreneurs who start nonprofits do so for reasons other than money — for example, a driving need to give back to the community. James Blackman founded the Civic Light Opera of South Bay Cities, Redondo Beach, California, providing a cultural arts center for the community. The opera became the third-largest musical theater in California and has won many awards. Blackman's company also provides opportunities for physically and mentally challenged children to experience music and the theater.

Benchmarking Your Best Choice

Now that you've gotten a good overview of what's available, Figure 6-2 offers a strategy for choosing the best legal form for your new business. Starting with the first question, work your way down, mapping an easy way to find your alternatives and organize your business.

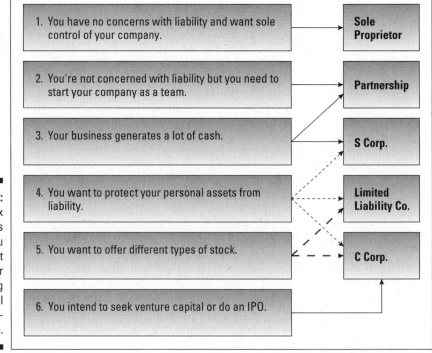

Figure 6-2: Six questions point you in the right direction for choosing your legal organization.

1. You have no concerns with liability and want sole control of your company. → **Sole Proprietor**

2. You're not concerned with liability but you need to start your company as a team. → **Partnership**

3. Your business generates a lot of cash. → **S Corp.**

4. You want to protect your personal assets from liability. → **Limited Liability Co.**

5. You want to offer different types of stock. → **C Corp.**

6. You intend to seek venture capital or do an IPO.

Book III
Managing Your Finances

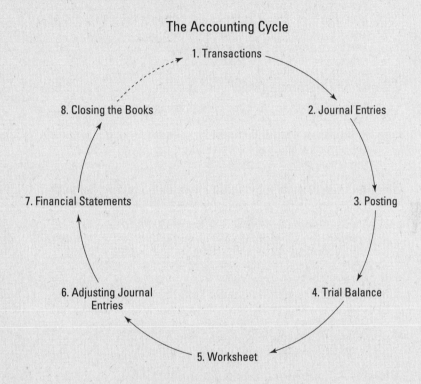

The Accounting Cycle

1. Transactions

2. Journal Entries

3. Posting

4. Trial Balance

5. Worksheet

6. Adjusting Journal Entries

7. Financial Statements

8. Closing the Books

Contents at a Glance

Chapter 1: Setting Up the Books 237

Bookkeepers: The Record Keepers of the Business World 238
Wading through Basic Bookkeeping Lingo 239
Pedaling through the Accounting Cycle 241
Tackling the Big Decision: Cash-Basis or Accrual Accounting 243
Seeing Double with Double-Entry Bookkeeping 245
Differentiating Debits and Credits 247
Outlining Your Financial Roadmap with a Chart of Accounts 248
Starting with the Balance Sheet Accounts 250
Tracking the Income Statement Accounts 256
Setting Up Your Chart of Accounts 260

Chapter 2: Understanding Your P&L 263

Getting Intimate with Your Profit and Loss Report 264
Measuring and Reporting Profit and Loss 268
Presenting the P&L Report for Your Business 273
Breaking Through the Breakeven Barrier 281
Improving Profit 282

Chapter 3: Working with Cash Flow and Staying Solvent 287

Sorting Out Your Sources of Cash 288
Avoiding Confusion Between Profit and Its Cash Flow 290
Deciding How to Have Cash Flow Information Reported to You 291
Introducing the Statement of Cash Flows 296
Summing Up the Critical Importance of Cash Flow from Profit 303
Liquidity and Business Solvency 303
Business Solvency Measurements Tools 307
Liquidity Measurements Tools 309
Liquidity Traps 311
Untapped Sources of Liquidity 316
Financial Leverage: The Good, the Bad, and the Ugly 320

Chapter 4: Controlling Costs and Budgeting 321

Getting in the Right Frame of Mind 322
Getting Down to Business 322
Looking into Cost of Goods Sold Expense 336
Focusing on Profit Centers 339
Reducing Your Costs 341
Deciding Where the Budgeting Process Starts 341
Honing In on Budgeting Tools 343
Preparing an Actual Budget or Forecast 347
Understanding Internal versus External Budgets 350
Creating a Living Budget 351
Using the Budget as a Business-Management Tool 354
Using Budgets in Other Ways 355

Chapter 5: Satisfying the Tax Man 357

Tax Reporting for Sole Proprietors 357
Filing Tax Forms for Partnerships 358
Paying Corporate Taxes 359
Taking Care of Sales Taxes Obligations 361

Chapter 1

Setting Up the Books

· ·

In This Chapter

▶ Keeping business records

▶ Navigating the accounting cycle

▶ Choosing between cash-basis and accrual accounting

▶ Deciphering double-entry bookkeeping

▶ Introducing the Chart of Accounts

▶ Reviewing the types of accounts that make up the chart

▶ Creating your own Chart of Accounts

· ·

*A*ll businesses need to keep track of their financial transactions — that's why bookkeeping and bookkeepers are so important. Without accurate records, how can you tell whether your business is making a profit or taking a loss?

The first part of this chapter covers the key parts of bookkeeping by introducing you to the language of bookkeeping, familiarizing you with how bookkeepers manage the accounting cycle, and showing you how to understand the most difficult type of bookkeeping — double-entry bookkeeping.

Can you imagine the mess your checkbook would be if you didn't record each check you wrote? You've probably forgotten to record a check or two on occasion, but you certainly learn your lesson when you realize that an important payment bounces as a result. Yikes!

Keeping the books of a business can be a lot more difficult than maintaining a personal checkbook. Each business transaction must be carefully recorded to make sure it goes into the right account. This careful bookkeeping gives you an effective tool for figuring out how well the business is doing financially.

As a bookkeeper, you need a roadmap to help you determine where to record all those transactions. This roadmap is called the Chart of Accounts. The second half of this chapter tells you how to set up the Chart of Accounts, which includes many different accounts. It also reviews the types of transactions you enter into each type of account in order to track the key parts of any business — assets, liabilities, equity, revenue, and expenses.

Bookkeepers: The Record Keepers of the Business World

Bookkeeping, the methodical way in which businesses track their financial transactions, is rooted in accounting. *Accounting* is the total structure of records and procedures used to record, classify, and report information about a business's financial transactions. Bookkeeping involves the recording of that financial information into the accounting system while maintaining adherence to solid accounting principles.

Bookkeepers are the ones who toil day in and day out to ensure that transactions are accurately recorded. Bookkeepers need to be very detail oriented and love to work with numbers because numbers and the accounts they go into are just about all these people see all day. A bookkeeper is not required to be a certified public accountant (CPA).

Many small business people who are just starting up their businesses initially serve as their own bookkeepers until the business is large enough to hire someone dedicated to keeping the books. Few small businesses have accountants on staff to check the books and prepare official financial reports; instead, they have bookkeepers on staff who serve as the outside accountants' eyes and ears. Most businesses do seek an accountant with a CPA certification.

In many small businesses today, a bookkeeper enters the business transactions on a daily basis while working inside the company. At the end of each month or quarter, the bookkeeper sends summary reports to the accountant who then checks the transactions for accuracy and prepares financial statements.

In most cases, the accounting system is initially set up with the help of an accountant in order to be sure it uses solid accounting principles. That accountant periodically stops by the office and reviews the system's use to be sure transactions are being handled properly.

Accurate financial reports are the only way you can know how your business is doing. These reports are developed using the information you, as the bookkeeper, enter into your accounting system. If that information isn't accurate, your financial reports are meaningless. As the old adage goes, "Garbage in, garbage out."

Wading through Basic Bookkeeping Lingo

Before you can take on bookkeeping and start keeping the books, the first things you must get a handle on are key accounting terms. The following is a list of terms that all bookkeepers use on a daily basis.

Accounts for the balance sheet

Here are a few terms you'll want to know:

✔ **Balance sheet:** The financial statement that presents a snapshot of the company's financial position (assets, liabilities, and equity) as of a particular date in time. It's called a balance sheet because the things owned by the company (assets) must equal the claims against those assets (liabilities and equity).

On an ideal balance sheet, the total assets should equal the total liabilities plus the total equity. If your numbers fit this formula, the company's books are in balance.

✔ **Assets:** All the things a company owns in order to successfully run its business, such as cash, buildings, land, tools, equipment, vehicles, and furniture.

✔ **Liabilities:** All the debts the company owes, such as bonds, loans, and unpaid bills.

✔ **Equity:** All the money invested in the company by its owners. In a small business owned by one person or a group of people, the owner's equity is shown in a Capital account. In a larger business that's incorporated, owner's equity is shown in shares of stock. Another key Equity account is *Retained Earnings,* which tracks all company profits that have been reinvested in the company rather than paid out to the company's owners. Small, unincorporated businesses track money paid out to owners in a Drawing account, whereas incorporated businesses dole out money to owners by paying *dividends* (a portion of the company's profits paid by share of common stock for the quarter or year).

Accounts for the income statement

Here are a few terms related to the income statement that you'll want to know:

- **Income statement:** The financial statement that presents a summary of the company's financial activity over a certain period of time, such as a month, quarter, or year. The statement starts with Revenue earned, subtracts out the Costs of Goods Sold and the Expenses, and ends with the bottom line — Net Profit or Loss.

- **Revenue:** All money collected in the process of selling the company's goods and services. Some companies also collect revenue through other means, such as selling assets the business no longer needs or earning interest by offering short-term loans to employees or other businesses.

- **Costs of goods sold:** All money spent to purchase or make the products or services a company plans to sell to its customers.

- **Expenses:** All money spent to operate the company that's not directly related to the sale of individual goods or services.

Other common terms

Some other common terms include the following:

- **Accounting period:** The time for which financial information is being tracked. Most businesses track their financial results on a monthly basis, so each accounting period equals one month. Some businesses choose to do financial reports on a quarterly basis, so the accounting periods are three months. Other businesses only look at their results on a yearly basis, so their accounting periods are 12 months. Businesses that track their financial activities monthly usually also create quarterly and *annual reports* (a year-end summary of the company's activities and financial results) based on the information they gather.

- **Accounts Receivable:** The account used to track all customer sales that are made by store credit. *Store credit* refers not to credit card sales but rather to sales in which the customer is given credit directly by the store and the store needs to collect payment from the customer at a later date.

- **Accounts Payable:** The account used to track all outstanding bills from vendors, contractors, consultants, and any other companies or individuals from whom the company buys goods or services.

✔ **Depreciation:** An accounting method used to track the aging and use of assets. For example, if you own a car, you know that each year you use the car its value is reduced (unless you own one of those classic cars that goes up in value). Every major asset a business owns ages and eventually needs replacement, including buildings, factories, equipment, and other key assets.

✔ **General Ledger:** Where all the company's accounts are summarized. The General Ledger is the granddaddy of the bookkeeping system.

✔ **Interest:** The money a company needs to pay if it borrows money from a bank or other company. For example, when you buy a car using a car loan, you must pay not only the amount you borrowed but also additional money, or interest, based on a percent of the amount you borrowed.

✔ **Inventory:** The account that tracks all products that will be sold to customers.

✔ **Journals:** Where bookkeepers keep records (in chronological order) of daily company transactions. Each of the most active accounts, including cash, Accounts Payable, and Accounts Receivable, has its own journal.

✔ **Payroll:** The way a company pays its employees. Managing payroll is a key function of the bookkeeper and involves reporting many aspects of payroll to the government, including taxes to be paid on behalf of the employee, unemployment taxes, and workmen's compensation.

✔ **Trial balance:** How you test to be sure the books are in balance before pulling together information for the financial reports and closing the books for the accounting period.

Book III

Managing Your Finances

Pedaling through the Accounting Cycle

As a bookkeeper, you complete your work by completing the tasks of the accounting cycle. It's called a cycle because the workflow is circular: entering transactions, manipulating the transactions through the accounting cycle, closing the books at the end of the accounting period, and then starting the entire cycle again for the next accounting period.

The accounting cycle has eight basic steps, which you can see in Figure 1-1.

1. **Transactions:** Financial transactions start the process. Transactions can include the sale or return of a product, the purchase of supplies for business activities, or any other financial activity that involves the exchange of the company's assets, the establishment or payoff of a debt, or the deposit from or payout of money to the company's owners. All sales and expenses are transactions that must be recorded.

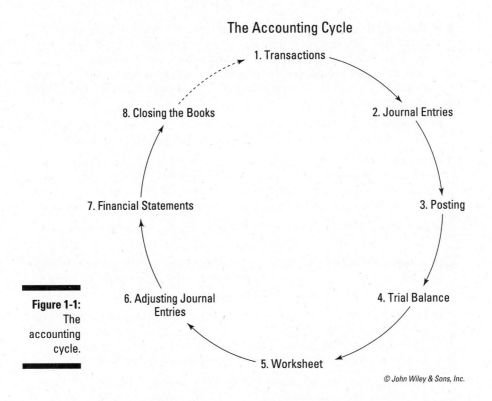

Figure 1-1: The accounting cycle.

2. **Journal entries:** The transaction is listed in the appropriate journal, maintaining the journal's chronological order of transactions. (The journal is also known as the "book of original entry" and is the first place a transaction is listed.)

3. **Posting:** The transactions are posted to the account that it impacts. These accounts are part of the General Ledger, where you can find a summary of all the business's accounts.

4. **Trial balance:** At the end of the accounting period (which may be a month, quarter, or year depending on your business's practices), you calculate a trial balance.

5. **Worksheet:** Unfortunately, many times your first calculation of the trial balance shows that the books aren't in balance. If that's the case, you look for errors and make corrections called *adjustments,* which are tracked on a worksheet. Adjustments are also made to account for the depreciation of assets and to adjust for one-time payments (such as insurance) that should be allocated on a monthly basis to more accurately match monthly expenses with monthly revenues. After you make and record adjustments, you take another trial balance to be sure the accounts are in balance.

6. **Adjusting journal entries:** You post any corrections needed to the affected accounts once your trial balance shows that the accounts will be balanced after the adjustments needed are made to the accounts. You don't need to make adjusting entries until the trial balance process is completed and all needed corrections and adjustments have been identified.

7. **Financial statements:** You prepare the balance sheet and income statement using the corrected account balances.

8. **Closing:** You close the books for the revenue and expense accounts and begin the entire cycle again with zero balances in those accounts.

As a businessperson, you want to be able to gauge your profit or loss on month by month, quarter by quarter, and year by year bases. To do that, Revenue and Expense accounts must start with a zero balance at the beginning of each accounting period. In contrast, you carry over Asset, Liability, and Equity account balances from cycle to cycle because the business doesn't start each cycle by getting rid of old assets and buying new assets, paying off and then taking on new debt, or paying out all claims to owners and then collecting the money again.

Tackling the Big Decision: Cash-Basis or Accrual Accounting

Before starting to record transactions, you must decide whether to use cash-basis or accrual accounting. The crucial difference between these two processes is in how you record your cash transactions.

Waiting for funds with cash-basis accounting

With *cash-basis accounting,* you record all transactions in the books when cash actually changes hands, meaning when cash payment is received by the company from customers or paid out by the company for purchases or other services. Cash receipt or payment can be in the form of cash, check, credit card, electronic transfer, or other means used to pay for an item.

Cash-basis accounting can't be used if a store sells products on store credit and bills the customer at a later date. There is no provision to record and track money due from customers at some time in the future in the cash-basis accounting method. That's also true for purchases. With the cash-basis accounting method, the owner only records the purchase of supplies or goods that will later be sold when he actually pays cash. If he buys goods on credit to be paid later, he doesn't record the transaction until the cash is actually paid out.

Depending on the size of your business, you may want to start out with cash-basis accounting. Many small businesses run by a sole proprietor or a small group of partners use cash-basis accounting because it's easy. But as the business grows, the business owners find it necessary to switch to accrual accounting in order to more accurately track revenues and expenses.

Cash-basis accounting does a good job of tracking cash flow, but it does a poor job of matching revenues earned with money laid out for expenses. This deficiency is a problem particularly when, as it often happens, a company buys products in one month and sells those products in the next month. For example, you buy products in June with the intent to sell them, and you pay $1,000 cash for those products. You don't sell the products until July, and that's when you receive cash for the sales. When you close the books at the end of June, you have to show the $1,000 expense with no revenue to offset it, meaning you have a loss that month. When you sell the products for $1,500 in July, you have a $1,500 profit. So, your monthly report for June shows a $1,000 loss, and your monthly report for July shows a $1,500 profit, when in actuality you had revenues of $500 over the two months.

This chapter concentrates on the accrual accounting method. If you choose to use cash-basis accounting, you'll still find most of the bookkeeping

Making the switch to accrual accounting

Changing between the cash-basis and accrual basis of accounting may not be simple, and you should check with your accountant to be sure you do it right. You may even need to get permission from the IRS, which tests whether you're seeking an unfair tax advantage when making the switch. You might be required to complete and file the IRS form Change in Accounting Method (Form 3115) in advance of the end of the year for which you make this change. In certain circumstances, IRS approval of change is automatic, but you should still file Form 3115 with the affected year's tax return. For example, if you started as a service business and shifted to a business that carries inventory, permission for the accounting method change should be automatically granted.

Businesses that generally should not use cash-basis accounting include

- Businesses that carry an inventory if sales exceed $1 million per year.

- Businesses that incorporated as a C Corporation (more on incorporation in Chapter 6 of Book II).

- Businesses with gross annual sales that exceed $5 million.

information here useful, but you don't need to maintain some of the accounts listed, such as Accounts Receivable and Accounts Payable, because you aren't recording transactions until cash actually changes hands. If you're using a cash-basis accounting system and sell things on credit, though, you had better have a way to track what people owe you.

Recording right away with accrual accounting

With *accrual accounting*, you record all transactions in the books when they occur, even if no cash changes hands. For example, if you sell on store credit, you record the transaction immediately and enter it into an Accounts Receivable account until you receive payment. If you buy goods on credit, you immediately enter the transaction into an Accounts Payable account until you pay out cash.

Like cash-basis accounting, accrual accounting has its drawbacks. It does a good job of matching revenues and expenses, but it does a poor job of tracking cash. Because you record revenue when the transaction occurs and not when you collect the cash, your income statement can look great even if you don't have cash in the bank. For example, suppose you're running a contracting company and completing jobs on a daily basis. You can record the revenue upon completion of the job even if you haven't yet collected the cash. If your customers are slow to pay, you may end up with lots of revenue but little cash.

Many companies that use the accrual accounting method also monitor cash flow on a weekly basis to be sure they have enough cash on hand to operate the business. If your business is seasonal, such as a landscaping business with little to do during the winter months, you can establish short-term lines of credit through your bank to maintain cash flow through the lean times.

Book III

Managing Your Finances

Seeing Double with Double-Entry Bookkeeping

All businesses, whether they use the cash-basis accounting method or the accrual accounting method (see the section "Tackling the Big Decision: Cash-Basis or Accrual Accounting" for details), use *double-entry bookkeeping* to keep their books. A practice that helps minimize errors and increases the chance that your books balance, double-entry bookkeeping gets its name because you enter all transactions twice.

When it comes to double-entry bookkeeping, the key formula for the balance sheet (Assets = Liabilities + Equity) plays a major role.

In order to adjust the balance of accounts in the bookkeeping world, you use a combination of *debits* and *credits*. You may think of a debit as a subtraction because you've found that debits usually mean a decrease in your bank balance. On the other hand, you've probably been excited to find unexpected credits in your bank or credit card that mean more money has been added to the account in your favor. Now, forget everything you ever learned about debits or credits. In the world of bookkeeping, their meanings aren't so simple.

The only definite thing when it comes to debits and credits in the bookkeeping world is that a *debit* is on the left side of a transaction, and a credit is on the *right* side of a transaction. Everything beyond that can get very muddled.

Here's an example of the practice in action. Suppose you purchase a new desk that costs $1,500 for your office. This transaction actually has two parts: You spend an asset — cash — to buy another asset — furniture. So, you must adjust two accounts in your company's books: the Cash account and the Furniture account. Here's what the transaction looks like in a bookkeeping entry:

Account	Debit	Credit
Furniture	$1,500	
Cash		$1,500

To purchase a new desk for the office

In this transaction, you record the accounts impacted by the transaction. The debit increases the value of the Furniture account, and the credit decreases the value of the Cash account. For this transaction, both accounts impacted are asset accounts, so, looking at how the balance sheet is affected, you can see that the only changes are to the asset side of the balance sheet equation:

Assets = Liabilities + Equity

Furniture increase = No change to this side of the equation

Cash decrease

In this case, the books stay in balance because the exact dollar amount that increases the value of your Furniture account decreases the value of your Cash account. At the bottom of any journal entry, you should include a brief explanation that explains the purpose for the entry. In the first example, "To purchase a new desk for the office" indicates this entry.

To show you how you record a transaction if it impacts both sides of the balance sheet equation, here's an example that shows how to record the purchase of inventory. Suppose you purchase $5,000 worth of widgets on credit. (Haven't you always wondered what widgets are? They're just commonly used in accounting examples to represent something that's purchased.) These new widgets add value to your Inventory Asset account and also add value to your Accounts Payable account. (Remember, the Accounts Payable account is a Liability account where you track bills that need to be paid at some point in the future.) Here's how the bookkeeping transaction for your widget purchase looks:

Account	Debit	Credit
Inventory	$5,000	
Accounts Payable		$5,000

To purchase widgets for sale to customers

Here's how this transaction affects the balance sheet equation:

Assets = Liabilities + Equity

Inventory increases = Accounts Payable increases = No change

Book III

Managing Your Finances

In this case, the books stay in balance because both sides of the equation increase by $5,000.

You can see from the two example transactions how double-entry bookkeeping helps to keep your books in balance — as long as you make sure each entry into the books is balanced. Balancing your entries may look simple here, but sometimes bookkeeping entries can get very complex when more than two accounts are impacted by the transaction.

Differentiating Debits and Credits

Because bookkeeping's debits and credits are different from the ones you're used to encountering, you're probably wondering how you're supposed to know whether a debit or credit will increase or decrease an account. Believe it or not, identifying the difference will become second nature as you start making regular bookkeeping entries. But to make things easier, Table 1-1 is a chart that's commonly used by all bookkeepers and accountants.

Copy Table 1-1 and post it at your desk when you start keeping your own books. It will help you keep your debits and credits straight.

Table 1-1	How Credits and Debits Impact Your Accounts	
Account Type	*Debits*	*Credits*
Assets	Increase	Decrease
Liabilities	Decrease	Increase
Income	Decrease	Increase
Expenses	Increase	Decrease

Outlining Your Financial Roadmap with a Chart of Accounts

The *Chart of Accounts* is the roadmap that a business creates to organize its financial transactions. After all, you can't record a transaction until you know where to put it! Essentially, this chart is a list of all the accounts a business has, organized in a specific order; each account has a description that includes the type of account and the types of transactions that should be entered into that account. Every business creates its own Chart of Accounts based on how the business is operated, so you're unlikely to find two businesses with the exact same Charts of Accounts.

However, some basic organizational and structural characteristics are common to all Charts of Accounts. The organization and structure are designed around two key financial reports: the *balance sheet,* which shows what your business owns and what it owes, and the *income statement,* which shows how much money your business took in from sales and how much money it spent to generate those sales.

The Chart of Accounts starts with the balance sheet accounts, which include

✔ **Current Assets:** Includes all accounts that track things the company owns and expects to use in the next 12 months, such as cash, accounts receivable (money collected from customers), and inventory

✔ **Long-term Assets:** Includes all accounts that track things the company owns that have a lifespan of more than 12 months, such as buildings, furniture, and equipment

✓ **Current Liabilities:** Includes all accounts that track debts the company must pay over the next 12 months, such as accounts payable (bills from vendors, contractors, and consultants), interest payable, and credit cards payable

✓ **Long-term Liabilities:** Includes all accounts that track debts the company must pay over a period of time longer than the next 12 months, such as mortgages payable and bonds payable

✓ **Equity:** Includes all accounts that track the owners of the company and their claims against the company's assets, which include any money invested in the company, any money taken out of the company, and any earnings that have been reinvested in the company

The rest of the chart is filled with income statement accounts, which include

✓ **Revenue:** Includes all accounts that track sales of goods and services as well as revenue generated for the company by other means

✓ **Cost of Goods Sold:** Includes all accounts that track the direct costs involved in selling the company's goods or services

✓ **Expenses:** Includes all accounts that track expenses related to running the businesses that aren't directly tied to the sale of individual products or services

When developing the Chart of Accounts, you start by listing all the Asset accounts, the Liability accounts, the Equity accounts, the Revenue accounts, and finally, the Expense accounts. All these accounts come from two places: the balance sheet and the income statement.

This chapter reviews the key account types found in most businesses, but this list isn't cast in stone. You should develop an account list that makes the most sense for how you operate your business and the financial information you want to track. In the discussion of the Chart of Accounts here, you can see how the structure may differ for different businesses.

The Chart of Accounts is a money-management tool that helps you track your business transactions, so set it up in a way that provides you with the financial information you need to make smart business decisions. You'll probably tweak the accounts in your chart annually and, if necessary, you may add accounts during the year if you find something for which you want more detailed tracking. You can add accounts during the year, but it's best not to delete accounts until the end of a 12-month reporting period.

Book III

Managing Your Finances

Starting with the Balance Sheet Accounts

The first part of the Chart of Accounts is made up of balance sheet accounts, which break down into the following three categories:

- **Asset:** These accounts are used to track what the business owns. Assets include cash on hand, furniture, buildings, vehicles, and so on.

- **Liability:** These accounts track what the business owes, or, more specifically, claims that lenders have against the business's assets. For example, mortgages on buildings and lines of credit are two common types of liabilities.

- **Equity:** These accounts track what the owners put into the business and the claims owners have against assets. For example, stockholders are company owners that have claims against the business's assets.

The balance sheet accounts, and the financial report they make up, are so-called because they have to *balance* out. The value of the assets must be equal to the claims made against those assets. (Remember, these claims are liabilities made by lenders and equity made by owners.)

This section examines the basic components of the balance sheet, as reflected in the Chart of Accounts.

Tackling assets

First on the chart are always the accounts that track what the company owns — its assets: current assets and long-term assets.

Current assets

Current assets are the key assets that your business uses up during a 12-month period and will likely not be there the next year. The accounts that reflect current assets on the Chart of Accounts are:

- **Cash in Checking:** Any company's primary account is the checking account used for operating activities. This is the account used to deposit revenues and pay expenses. Some companies have more than one operating account in this category; for example, a company with many divisions may have an operating account for each division.

✔ **Cash in Savings:** This account is used for surplus cash. Any cash for which there is no immediate plan is deposited in an interest-earning savings account so that it can at least earn interest while the company decides what to do with it.

✔ **Cash on Hand:** This account is used to track any cash kept at retail stores or in the office. In retail stores, cash must be kept in registers in order to provide change to customers. In the office, petty cash is often kept around for immediate cash needs that pop up from time to time. This account helps you keep track of the cash held outside a financial institution.

✔ **Accounts Receivable:** If you offer your products or services to customers on store credit (meaning *your* store credit system), then you need this account to track the customers who buy on your dime.

Accounts Receivable isn't used to track purchases made on other types of credit cards because your business gets paid directly by banks, not customers, when other credit cards are used.

✔ **Inventory:** This account tracks the products on hand to sell to your customers. The value of the assets in this account varies depending on how you decide to track the flow of inventory in and out of the business.

✔ **Prepaid Insurance:** This account tracks insurance you pay in advance that's credited as it's used up each month. For example, if you own a building and prepay one year in advance, each month you reduce the amount that you prepaid by 1/12 as the prepayment is used up.

Depending upon the type of business you're setting up, you may have other current asset accounts that you decide to track. For example, if you're starting a service business in consulting, you're likely to have a Consulting account for tracking cash collected for those services. If you run a business in which you barter assets (such as trading your services for paper goods), you may add a Barter account for business-to-business barter.

Long-term assets

Long-term assets are assets that you anticipate your business will use for more than 12 months. This section lists some of the most common long-term assets, starting with the key accounts related to buildings and factories owned by the company:

✔ **Land:** This account tracks the land owned by the company. The value of the land is based on the cost of purchasing it. Land value is tracked separately from the value of any buildings standing on that land because land isn't depreciated in value, but buildings must be depreciated. *Depreciation* is an accounting method that shows an asset is being used up.

Book III

Managing Your Finances

- **Buildings:** This account tracks the value of any buildings a business owns. As with land, the value of the building is based on the cost of purchasing it. The key difference between buildings and land is that the building's value is depreciated, as discussed in the previous bullet.

- **Accumulated Depreciation – Buildings:** This account tracks the cumulative amount a building is depreciated over its useful lifespan.

- **Leasehold Improvements:** This account tracks the value of improvements to buildings or other facilities that a business leases rather than purchases. Frequently when a business leases a property, it must pay for any improvements necessary in order to use that property the way it's needed. For example, if a business leases a store in a strip mall, it's likely that the space leased is an empty shell or filled with shelving and other items that may not match the particular needs of the business. As with buildings, leasehold improvements are depreciated as the value of the asset ages.

- **Accumulated Depreciation – Leasehold Improvements:** This account tracks the cumulative amount depreciated for leasehold improvements.

The following are the types of accounts for smaller long-term assets, such as vehicles and furniture:

- **Vehicles:** This account tracks any cars, trucks, or other vehicles owned by the business. The initial value of any vehicle is listed in this account based on the total cost paid to put the vehicle in service. Sometimes this value is more than the purchase price if additions were needed to make the vehicle usable for the particular type of business. For example, if a business provides transportation people with physical disabilities and must add additional equipment to a vehicle in order to serve the needs of its customers, that additional equipment is added to the value of the vehicle. Vehicles also depreciate through their useful lifespan.

- **Accumulated Depreciation – Vehicles:** This account tracks the depreciation of all vehicles owned by the company.

- **Furniture and Fixtures:** This account tracks any furniture or fixtures purchased for use in the business. The account includes the value of all chairs, desks, store fixtures, and shelving needed to operate the business. The value of the furniture and fixtures in this account is based on the cost of purchasing these items. These items are depreciated during their useful lifespan.

- **Accumulated Depreciation – Furniture and Fixtures:** This account tracks the accumulated depreciation of all furniture and fixtures.

✔ **Equipment:** This account tracks equipment that was purchased for use for more than one year, such as computers, copiers, tools, and cash registers. The value of the equipment is based on the cost to purchase these items. Equipment is also depreciated to show that over time it gets used up and must be replaced.

✔ **Accumulated Depreciation – Equipment:** This account tracks the accumulated depreciation of all the equipment.

The following accounts track the long-term assets that you can't touch but that still represent things of value owned by the company, such as organization costs, patents, and copyrights. These are called *intangible assets,* and the accounts that track them include

✔ **Organization Costs:** This account tracks initial start-up expenses to get the business off the ground. Many such expenses can't be written off in the first year. For example, special licenses and legal fees must be written off over a number of years using a method similar to depreciation, called *amortization,* which is also tracked.

✔ **Amortization – Organization Costs:** This account tracks the accumulated amortization of organization costs during the period in which they're being written off.

✔ **Patents:** This account tracks the costs associated with *patents,* grants made by governments that guarantee to the inventor of a product or service the exclusive right to make, use, and sell that product or service over a set period of time. Like organization costs, patent costs are amortized. The value of this asset is based on the expenses the company incurs to get the right to patent the product.

✔ **Amortization – Patents:** This account tracks the accumulated amortization of a business's patents.

✔ **Copyrights:** This account tracks the costs incurred to establish copyrights, the legal rights given to an author, playwright, publisher, or any other distributor of a publication or production for a unique work of literature, music, drama, or art. This legal right expires after a set number of years, so its value is amortized as the copyright gets used up.

✔ **Goodwill:** This account is only needed if a company buys another company for more than the actual value of its tangible assets. Goodwill reflects the intangible value of this purchase for things like company reputation, store locations, customer base, and other items that increase the value of the business bought.

Book III

Managing Your Finances

If you hold a lot of assets that aren't of great value, you can also set up an "Other Assets" account to track them. Any asset you track in the Other Assets account that you later want to track individually can be shifted to its own account.

Laying out your liabilities

After you cover assets, the next stop on the bookkeeping highway is the accounts that track what your business owes to others. These "others" can include vendors from which you buy products or supplies, financial institutions from which you borrow money, and anyone else who lends money to your business. Like assets, liabilities are lumped into two types: current liabilities and long-term liabilities.

Current liabilities

Current liabilities are debts due in the next 12 months. Some of the most common types of current liabilities accounts that appear on the Chart of Accounts are

- ✔ **Accounts Payable:** Tracks money the company owes to vendors, contractors, suppliers, and consultants that must be paid in less than a year. Most of these liabilities must be paid 30–90 days from billing.

- ✔ **Sales Tax Collected:** You may not think of sales tax as a liability, but because the business collects the tax from the customer and doesn't pay it immediately to the government entity, the taxes collected become a liability tracked in this account. A business usually collects sales tax throughout the month and then pays it to the local, state, or federal government on a monthly basis.

- ✔ **Accrued Payroll Taxes:** This account tracks payroll taxes collected from employees to pay state, local, or federal income taxes as well as Social Security and Medicare taxes. Companies don't have to pay these taxes to the government entities immediately, so depending on the size of the payroll, companies may pay payroll taxes on a monthly or quarterly basis.

- ✔ **Credit Cards Payable:** This account tracks all credit card accounts to which the business is liable. Most companies use credit cards as short-term debt and pay them off completely at the end of each month, but some smaller companies carry credit card balances over a longer period of time. Because credit cards often have a much higher interest rate than most lines of credits, most companies transfer any credit card debt they can't pay entirely at the end of a month to a line of credit at a bank. When it comes to your Chart of Accounts, you can set up one Credit Card Payable account, but you may want to set up a separate account for each card your company holds to improve tracking credit card usage.

How you set up your current liabilities and how many individual accounts you establish depend on how detailed you want to track each type of liability. For example, you can set up separate current liability accounts for major vendors if you find that approach provides you with a better money management tool. For example, suppose that a small hardware retail store buys most of the tools it sells from Snap-on. To keep better control of its spending with Snap-on, the bookkeeper sets up a specific account called Accounts Payable – Snap-on, which is used only for tracking invoices and payments to that vendor. In this example, all other invoices and payments to other vendors and suppliers are tracked in the general Accounts Payable account.

Long-term liabilities

Long-term liabilities are debts due in more than 12 months. The number of long-term liability accounts you maintain on your Chart of Accounts depends on your debt structure. The two most common types are

- ✔ **Loans Payable:** This account tracks any long-term loans, such as a mortgage on your business building. Most businesses have separate Loans Payable accounts for each of their long-term loans. For example, you could have Loans Payable – Mortgage Bank for your building and Loans Payable – Car Bank for your vehicle loan.

- ✔ **Notes Payable:** Some businesses borrow money from other businesses using *notes,* a method of borrowing that doesn't require the company to put up an asset, such as a mortgage on a building or a car loan, as collateral. This account tracks any notes due.

In addition to any separate long-term debt you may want to track in its own account, you may also want to set up an account called "Other Liabilities" that you can use to track types of debt that are so insignificant to the business that you don't think they need their own accounts.

Eyeing the equity

Every business is owned by somebody. *Equity accounts* track owners' contributions to the business as well as their share of ownership. For a corporation, ownership is tracked by the sale of individual shares of stock because each stockholder owns a portion of the business. In smaller companies that are owned by one person or a group of people, equity is tracked using Capital and Drawing Accounts. Here are the basic equity accounts that appear in the Chart of Accounts:

- ✔ **Common Stock:** This account reflects the value of outstanding shares of stock sold to investors. A company calculates this value by multiplying the number of shares issued by the value of each share of stock. Only corporations need to establish this account.

- **Retained Earnings:** This account tracks the profits or losses accumulated since a business was opened. At the end of each year, the profit or loss calculated on the income statement is used to adjust the value of this account. For example, if a company made a $100,000 profit in the past year, the Retained Earnings account would be increased by that amount; if the company lost $100,000, then that amount would be subtracted from this account.

- **Capital:** This account is only necessary for small, unincorporated businesses. The Capital account reflects the amount of initial money the business owner contributed to the company as well as owner contributions made after initial start-up. The value of this account is based on cash contributions and other assets contributed by the business owner, such as equipment, vehicles, or buildings. If a small company has several different partners, then each partner gets his or her own Capital account to track his or her contributions.

- **Drawing:** This account is only necessary for businesses that aren't incorporated. It tracks any money that a business owner takes out of the business. If the business has several partners, each partner gets his or her own Drawing account to track what he or she takes out of the business.

Tracking the Income Statement Accounts

The income statement is made up of two types of accounts:

- **Revenue:** These accounts track all money coming into the business, including sales, interest earned on savings, and any other methods used to generate income.

- **Expenses:** These accounts track all money that a business spends in order to keep itself afloat.

The bottom line of the income statement shows whether your business made a profit or a loss for a specified period of time. This section examines the various accounts that make up the income statement portion of the Chart of Accounts.

Recording the money you make

First up in the income statement portion of the Chart of Accounts are accounts that track revenue coming into the business. If you choose to offer discounts or accept returns, that activity also falls within the revenue grouping. The most common income accounts are

- ✔ **Sales of Goods or Services:** This account, which appears at the top of every income statement, tracks all the money that the company earns selling its products, services, or both.

- ✔ **Sales Discounts:** Because most businesses offer discounts to encourage sales, this account tracks any reductions to the full price of merchandise.

- ✔ **Sales Returns:** This account tracks transactions related to returns, when a customer returns a product because he or she is unhappy with it for some reason.

When you examine an income statement from a company other than the one you own or are working for, you usually see the following accounts summarized as one line item called Revenue or Net Revenue. Because not all income is generated by sales of products or services, other income accounts that may appear on a Chart of Accounts include

- ✔ **Other Income:** If a company takes in income from a source other than its primary business activity, that income is recorded in this account. For example, a company that encourages recycling and earns income from the items recycled records that income in this account.

- ✔ **Interest Income:** This account tracks any income earned by collecting interest on a company's savings accounts. If the company loans money to employees or to another company and earns interest on that money, that interest is recorded in this account as well.

- ✔ **Sale of Fixed Assets:** Any time a company sells a fixed asset, such as a car or furniture, any revenue from the sale is recorded in this account. A company should only record revenue remaining after subtracting the accumulated depreciation from the original cost of the asset.

Tracking the Cost of Sales

Before you can sell a product, you must spend some money to either buy or make that product. The type of account used to track the money spent is called a Cost of Goods Sold account. The most common are:

- **Purchases:** Tracks the purchases of all items you plan to sell.

- **Purchase Discount:** Tracks the discounts you may receive from vendors if you pay for your purchase quickly. For example, a company may give you a 2 percent discount on your purchase if you pay the bill in 10 days rather than wait until the end of the 30-day payment allotment.

- **Purchase Returns:** If you're unhappy with a product you've bought, record the value of any returns in this account.

- **Freight Charges:** Charges related to shipping items you purchase for later sale. You may or may not want to keep track of this detail.

- **Other Sales Costs:** This is a catchall account for anything that doesn't fit into one of the other Cost of Goods Sold accounts.

Acknowledging the money you spend

Expense accounts take the cake for the longest list of individual accounts. Any money you spend on the business that can't be tied directly to the sale of an individual product falls under the expense account category. For example, advertising a storewide sale isn't directly tied to the sale of any one product, so the costs associated with advertising fall under this category.

The Chart of Accounts mirrors your business operations, so it's up to you to decide how much detail you want to keep in your expense accounts. Most businesses have expenses that are unique to their operations, so your list will probably be longer than the one presented here. However, you also may find that you don't need some of these accounts.

On your Chart of Accounts, the expense accounts don't have to appear in any specific order. Here they're listed alphabetically. The most common are as follows:

- **Advertising:** Tracks expenses involved in promoting a business or its products. Money spent on newspaper, television, magazine, and radio advertising is recorded here, as well as any money spent to print flyers and mailings to customers. For community events such as cancer walks or craft fairs, associated costs are tracked in this account as well.

✔ **Bank Service Charges:** This account tracks any charges made by a bank to service a company's bank accounts.

✔ **Dues and Subscriptions:** This account tracks expenses related to business club membership or subscriptions to magazines.

✔ **Equipment Rental:** This account tracks expenses related to renting equipment for a short-term project. For example, a business that needs to rent a truck to pick up some new fixtures for its store records that truck rental in this account.

✔ **Insurance:** Tracks any money paid to buy insurance. Many businesses break this down into several accounts, such as Insurance – Employees Group, which tracks any expenses paid for employee insurance, or Insurance – Officers' Life, which tracks money spent to buy insurance to protect the life of a key owner or officer of the company. Companies often insure their key owners and executives because an unexpected death, especially for a small company, may mean facing many unexpected expenses in order to keep the company's doors open. In such a case, insurance proceeds can be used to cover those expenses.

✔ **Legal and Accounting:** This account tracks any money that's paid for legal or accounting advice.

✔ **Miscellaneous Expenses:** This is a catchall account for expenses that don't fit into one of a company's established accounts. If certain miscellaneous expenses occur frequently, a company may choose to add an account to the Chart of Accounts and move related expenses into that new account by subtracting all related transactions from the Miscellaneous Expenses account and adding them to the new account. With this shuffle, it's important to carefully balance out the adjusting transaction to avoid any errors or double counting.

✔ **Office Expense:** This account tracks any items purchased in order to run an office. For example, office supplies such as paper and pens or business cards fit in this account. As with miscellaneous expenses, a company may choose to track some office expense items in their own accounts. For example, if you find your office is using a lot of copy paper and you want to track that separately, you set up a Copy Paper expense account. Just be sure you really need the detail because the number of accounts can get unwieldy and hard to manage.

✔ **Payroll Taxes:** This account tracks any taxes paid related to employee payroll, such as the employer's share of Social Security and Medicare, unemployment compensation, and workmen's compensation.

✔ **Postage:** Tracks money spent on stamps and shipping. If a company does a large amount of shipping through vendors such as UPS or Federal Express, it may want to track that spending in separate accounts for each vendor. This option is particularly helpful for small companies that sell over the Internet or through catalog sales.

Book III

Managing Your Finances

- ✔ **Rent Expense:** Tracks rental costs for a business's office or retail space.

- ✔ **Salaries and Wages:** This account tracks any money paid to employees as salary or wages.

- ✔ **Supplies:** This account tracks any business supplies that don't fit into the category of office supplies. For example, supplies needed for the operation of retail stores are tracked using this account.

- ✔ **Travel and Entertainment:** This account tracks money spent for business purposes on travel or entertainment. Some businesses separate these expenses into several accounts, such as Travel and Entertainment – Meals, Travel and Entertainment – Travel, and Travel and Entertainment – Entertainment, to keep a close watch.

- ✔ **Telephone:** This account tracks all business expenses related to the telephone and telephone calls.

- ✔ **Utilities:** Tracks money paid for utilities (electricity, gas, and water).

- ✔ **Vehicles:** Tracks expenses related to the operation of company vehicles.

Setting Up Your Chart of Accounts

You can use the lists upon lists of accounts provided in this chapter to get started setting up your business's own Chart of Accounts. There's really no secret — just make a list of the accounts that apply to your business.

Don't panic if you can't think of every type of account you may need for your business. It's very easy to add to the Chart of Accounts at any time. Just add the account to the list and distribute the revised list to any employees that use it. (Even employees not involved in bookkeeping need a copy of your Chart of Accounts if they code invoices or other transactions and indicate to which account those transactions should be recorded.)

The Chart of Accounts usually includes at least three columns:

- ✔ **Account:** Lists the account names

- ✔ **Type:** Lists the type of account — Asset, Liability, Equity, Income, Cost of Goods Sold, or Expense

- ✔ **Description:** Contains a description of the type of transaction that should be recorded in the account

Many companies also assign numbers to the accounts, to be used for coding charges. If your company is using a computerized system, the computer automatically assigns the account number. Otherwise, you need to plan out your own numbering system. The most common number system is:

- ✔ Asset accounts: 1,000 to 1,999
- ✔ Liability accounts: 2,000 to 2,999
- ✔ Equity accounts: 3,000 to 3,999
- ✔ Sales and Cost of Goods Sold accounts: 4,000 to 4,999
- ✔ Expense accounts: 5,000 to 6,999

This numbering system matches the one used by computerized accounting systems, making it easy at some future time to automate the books using a computerized accounting system. A number of different Charts of Accounts have been developed. When you get your computerized system, whichever accounting software you use, all you need to do is review the chart options for the type of business you run included with that software, delete any accounts you don't want, and add any new accounts that fit your business plan.

If you're setting up your Chart of Accounts manually, be sure to leave a lot of room between accounts to add new accounts. For example, number your Cash in Checking account 1,000 and your Accounts Receivable account 1,100. That leaves you plenty of room to add other accounts to track cash.

Figure 1-2 is a Chart of Accounts from QuickBooks 2014. Asset accounts are first, followed by Liability, Equity, Income, and Expense accounts.

Book III

Managing Your Finances

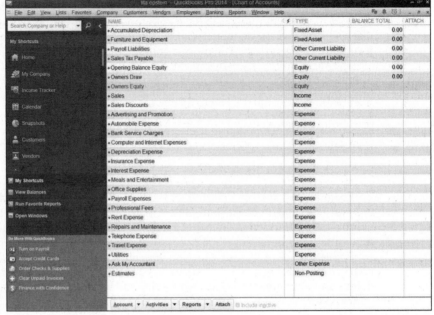

Figure 1-2:
The top
portion of
a sample
Chart of
Accounts.

Chapter 2

Understanding Your P&L

In This Chapter

▶ Getting better acquainted with your P&L

▶ Matching up the P&L with your business model

▶ Being clear on profit and loss issues

▶ Analyzing profit performance

▶ Exploring ways of improving your profit performance

*S*mall business owners must know whether they're earning a profit. You need to make a steady profit to survive and thrive, after all. So, you'd think that the large majority of small business owners would be pretty good at understanding and analyzing their profit performance.

The evidence suggests just the opposite. They generally know that profit information comes out of their accounting system. But accounting reports are in a foreign language to many start-up business owners. They don't do much more than glance at the bottom line. And a quick peek at the bottom line is no way to keep your business profitable and growing.

Profit is a financial measure for a period of time — one quarter (three months) and one year are the two most common periods for which profit is determined. At the end of the period, your accountant (often called a *controller*) prepares a financial statement, known as the *P&L (profit and loss)* statement, which reports the amount of profit or loss you made and the components of your profit or loss.

A good part of this chapter explains this profit performance financial statement. You should thoroughly understand this accounting report. You can't afford to be fuzzy on this financial statement. There's no other way to know your profit performance and understand how to improve your profit.

You can't look at your cash balance to track profit performance. Your cash balance may be going down even though you're making a profit. Or your cash balance may be going up even though you're suffering a loss. You can't smell profit in the air; you can't feel it in your bones. You have to read the newspaper to learn the news. Likewise, you have to read your P&L report to discover your profit news.

This chapter concentrates on the fundamentals of profit accounting and the basic design of the financial statement that reports your profit performance.

Getting Intimate with Your Profit and Loss Report

One main function of accounting is to measure your periodic profit or loss and to prepare a financial statement that reports information about how you made a profit or loss. *Periodic* means for a period of time, which can be one calendar quarter (three months), one year, or some other stretch of time.

Inside most businesses, as already mentioned, this key financial statement is called the P&L report. In the formal financial statements released outside the business (to creditors and nonmanagement owners), it's called the *income statement, earnings statement,* or *operating statement.* The P&L report is also called a *statement,* or sometimes a *sheet.*

Your controller is the P&L *scorekeeper* for your business, although owners generally have a lot to say regarding the methods and estimates used to measure profit and loss.

Your business may sell products, which are also known as *goods* or *merchandise.* Your basic business model is to sell a volume of products at adequate markups over their costs to cover operating expenses so that you generate a satisfactory profit after your interest and income tax expenses. As a matter of fact, this basic business model fits a wide variety of businesses that sell products — from Walmart to your local bookstore or shoe store.

The information content and layout of your P&L report should follow your business model. Figure 2-1 presents an illustrative P&L report that reflects your business model. The P&L statement is designed so that you can see the actual results of your business model for the period. Hypothetical dollar amounts are entered in this illustrative P&L report to make calculations easy to follow.

Here are important points to keep in mind when you read a P&L report, such as the one shown in Figure 2-1:

> ✔ **Where the information comes from:** The Source column on the right side of Figure 2-1 isn't really part of the P&L report; only what's inside the box is in a P&L report. The source column in Figure 2-1 is included to call your attention to where the dollar amounts come from. Account(s)

Your Business Name P&L Report For Year Ended December 31, 2015			Source
Sales revenue		$1,000,000	Account(s)
Cost of goods sold expense		$600,000	Account(s)
Gross margin		$400,000	Calculation
Operating expenses:			
Salaries, wages, commissions and benefits	$185,000		Account(s)
Advertising and sales promotion	$30,000		Account(s)
Depreciation	$35,000		Account(s)
Other expenses	$35,000		Account(s)
Total operating expenses		$285,000	Calculation
Operating profit		$115,000	Calculation
Interest expense		$30,000	Account(s)
Earnings before income tax		$85,000	Calculation
Income tax expense		none	Not applicable
Net income		$85,000	Calculation

Figure 2-1: An illustrative small business P&L report.

© John Wiley & Sons, Inc.

Book III

Managing Your Finances

means that the dollar amount for this line of information comes from one or more accounts maintained in the business's accounting system. For example, the business keeps several accounts for recording sales revenue. These several sales accounts are added together to get the $1,000,000 total sales revenue amount reported in the P&L.

✔ **Amounts from accounts versus amounts from calculations:** Several dollar amounts in a P&L aren't from accounts; rather, these figures are *calculated amounts.* For example, the P&L statement reports *gross margin,* which is equal to sales revenue less cost of goods sold expense. (This important number is also called *gross profit.*) In Figure 2-1, the $400,000 gross margin amount is calculated by deducting the $600,000 cost of goods sold expense amount from the $1,000,000 sales revenue amount. A business doesn't keep an account for gross margin (or for any of the calculated amounts in the P&L report).

✔ **The business entity and income tax:** Note the income tax expense line in the P&L (see Figure 2-1). In the source column, you see *not applicable.* What's this all about? Figure 2-1 is for a business entity that doesn't pay income tax itself as a separate entity. The business is organized legally as a so-called *pass-through* entity. Its annual taxable income is passed through to its owners, and they include their proportionate share of the business's taxable income in their income tax returns for the year. (For more on different legal types of business forms, see Book II Chapter 6.)

✔ **GAAP assumption:** GAAP stands for *generally accepted accounting principles.* GAAP refers to the body of authoritative accounting and financial reporting standards that has been established by the accounting profession over many years. Today, the main source of new pronouncements on GAAP is the Financial Accounting Standards Board (FASB). The GAAP rulebook has become exceedingly complex, and some persons compare it with the Internal Revenue Code and Regulations. Presently, the FASB is looking into giving small businesses some relief from its more technical pronouncements, but don't hold your breath.

In short, these accounting standards should be used by all businesses no matter their size. Unless a financial statement makes clear that different accounting methods are being used, the reader is entitled to assume that GAAP are used to measure profit and to present financial condition. You should assume that the business is using *accrual-basis accounting,* not a cash-basis method. See Book III Chapter 1 for an introduction to these methods and setting up your books.

✔ **Markup in the P&L:** The first step in your business model is to sell a lot of products at adequate markups over their costs. The first three lines in the P&L provide feedback information on how well you did in this regard. In Figure 2-1, sales generated $1,000,000 *revenue,* or total income, total inflow, or total increases of assets, during the year. Cost of goods (products) sold is $600,000, so the business's total markup for the year is $400,000, which is reported on the third line in the P&L. This amount is called *gross margin* (or *gross profit*).

In P&L reports, accountants don't use the term *markup.* Gross margin equals profit before other expenses are taken into account. In accounting, the word *gross* simply means before other expenses are deducted. Indeed, your profit or loss depends on the size of the other expenses.

✔ **Reporting operating expenses:** Practices aren't uniform regarding how many operating expense lines are reported in P&L statements — except that interest and income tax expenses are almost always reported on separate lines. Even a fairly small business keeps more than 100 expense accounts. In filing its annual federal income tax return, a business has to disclose certain expenses (advertising, repairs and maintenance, salaries and wages, rents, and so on). Of course, a business should keep these basic expense accounts. But this categorization isn't necessarily ideal for reporting operating expenses to business owners. (By the way, it's not a bad idea for the small business owner to read the first page of the annual federal income tax return of the business, which is the P&L reported to the IRS.)

Figure 2-1 shows four operating expense lines below the gross margin profit line. Operating expenses encompass the various costs of running a business. Typically salaries, wages, and commissions (plus benefits) make up the lion's share of operating expenses. Many small businesses have substantial advertising and other sales promotion costs. The cost of using its long-term operating assets (building, machines, trucks, and equipment) is recorded as depreciation expense. This particular expense is usually reported in a P&L (though not always).

The various operating costs that aren't included in the first three expenses just explained are collected in a catchall expense account. Total operating expenses are $285,000 in Figure 2-1. This total is deducted from gross margin to arrive at the $115,000 *operating profit* amount. (This measure of profit is also called *operating earnings* or *earnings before interest and income tax.*)

✔ **Interest expense:** This expense is separated from operating expenses because it's a financial cost that depends on the amount of debt used by the business (and interest rates, of course). In the P&L statement shown in Figure 2-1, the business uses a fair amount of debt because its interest expense is $30,000 for the year. Assuming an annual interest rate of 8 percent, its interest expense amount indicates that the business used $375,000 interest-bearing debt during the year:

$375,000 debt × 8%= $30,000 interest

✔ **Income tax expense (maybe):** A business may be organized as an entity that is subject to paying federal income tax. If so, the amount of its income tax is reported as the last expense in its P&L report, after interest expense. Interest is deductible to determine annual taxable income (just like other business expenses). Thus, it makes sense to put income tax expense below the interest expense line. In contrast, many small businesses are organized as pass-through entities that don't pay income tax. Instead, this type of business entity passes through its taxable income for the year to its owners. In the example shown in Figure 2-1, the business is a pass-through tax entity, so it has no income tax expense. Nevertheless, the income tax expense line is shown in the illustrative P&L to show how it would be reported.

Book III

Managing
Your
Finances

What's the bottom line? This question refers to the last, or "bottom" line of the P&L report, which is called *net income.* It is also called *net earnings,* or just *earnings.* The term *profit* is generally avoided. The business earned $85,000 net income for the year. So, the business model was executed successfully: The business made sales that generated enough gross margin to cover its operating expenses and had $85,000 profit after interest expense.

You may very well ask how successful the business's profit performance was. This question crosses the border from the accounting function to the financial management function. Accountants provide information; managers interpret and judge the information and take action for the future. As the owner/manager, would you be satisfied with the profit performance for the business example presented in Figure 2-1?

A quick primer on accrual-basis accounting

Simple cash-basis service businesses may use *cash-basis accounting,* which means they don't do much more bookkeeping than keeping a checkbook. If a business sells products, however, cash-basis accounting isn't always acceptable and, in fact, this method of accounting may not be permitted for income tax purposes. A business that sells products must keep track of its inventory of products and can't record the cost of products to expense until the products are actually sold to customers. Until sold, the cost of products is recorded in an asset account called *inventory.* This is one basic element of *accrual-basis accounting.*

Accrual-basis accounting can be viewed as economic reality accounting. Businesses that sell products (and hold an inventory of products awaiting sale), sell on credit, make purchases on credit, and own long-lived operating assets (buildings, trucks, tools, equipment, and so on) use accrual-basis accounting to measure their profit and to record their assets and liabilities. Basically, accrual-basis accounting recognizes the assets and liabilities of selling and buying on credit and spreads the cost of long-term operating assets over the years of their useful lives, which is called *depreciation.* See Book III Chapter 1 for more on these two accounting methods.

Measuring and Reporting Profit and Loss

Many small business owners read their P&L reports only on a superficial level. They don't have a deep enough understanding of the information presented in this important financial statement. One result is that they make false and misleading interpretations of the information in the P&L report. For example, they think sales revenue equals cash inflow from customers during the period. However, if the business sells on credit (which is typical for business to business sales), actual cash collections from customers during the year can be significantly lower than the sales revenue amount reported in the P&L statement.

Furthermore, many small business owners tend to think that an expense equals cash outflow. But in fact, the cash payment for an expense during the year can be significantly more (or less) than the amount of the expense in the P&L statement. The confusion of amounts reported in the P&L with cash flows is common.

In addition to the confusion over the cash flows of revenue and expenses, small business owners should be aware of several other issues, outlined in the following sections, in measuring and reporting profit.

Accounting for profit isn't an exact science

Many estimates and predictions must be made in recording revenue and expenses. Most are arbitrary and subjective to some degree. For one example, a business has to estimate the useful lives of its *fixed,* or long-term, operating assets in order to record depreciation expense each year. Predicting useful lives of fixed assets is notoriously difficult and ends up being fairly arbitrary.

Here's another example. At the end of the year, a business may have to record an expense caused by the loss in value of its inventory because some of its products will have to be sold at a price below cost, or the products may not be salable at all. Determining the loss in inventory value is notoriously difficult. Inventory write-down is subject to abuse by businesses that want to minimize their taxable income for the year.

Your accounting records may have errors

The financial statements prepared from the accounting records of a business, including the P&L, of course, are no better than the accounting system that generates the information for the financial statements. The reliability of your accounting system depends first of all on hiring a competent accountant to put in charge of your accounting system. Bigger businesses have an advantage on this score. They hire more experienced and generally more qualified accountants.

If at all possible, you should hire a trained and competent *accountant* to be put in charge of your accounting system and given the title *controller,* assuming that she has adequate accounting education and experience. To save money, many small businesses also hire a *bookkeeper* who knows record-keeping procedures but whose accounting knowledge may be limited. If you employ a bookkeeper (instead of a better-educated and more experienced accountant), you should consider using an independent CPA to periodically review the adequacy of your accounting system and appropriateness of your accounting methods.

Additionally, every business should enforce internal accounting controls to prevent or at least minimize errors and fraud. As a practical matter, errors can and do sneak into accounting records, and employees or others may have committed fraud against the business. In order to conceal theft or embezzlement, they prevent the recording of the loss in your accounting records.

Ideally, your accounting system should capture and record all your transactions completely, accurately, and in a timely manner. Furthermore, any losses from fraud and theft should be rooted out and recorded. You have to be vigilant about the integrity of your accounting records. Avoid taking your accounting records for granted; use good internal accounting controls; and be ever alert for possible fraud. Trust, but verify.

Selecting the accounting methods for recording revenue and expenses

Sales revenue can be recorded sooner or later, and likewise expenses can be recorded sooner or later. Some accounting methods record revenue and expenses as soon as possible; alternative methods record these profit transactions as late as possible. *Remember that profit is a periodic measure.* Expenses for the period are deducted from sales revenue for the period to measure profit for the period. This state of affairs is like having different speed limits for a highway. How fast do you want to drive?

In short, accounting standards permit different methods regarding when to record revenue and expenses. Take cost of goods sold expense, for example (one of the largest expenses of businesses that sell products). You can use three alternative, but equally acceptable, methods. Someone has to decide which method to use. You should take the time to discuss the selection of accounting methods with your controller. As the owner, you can call the shots. You shouldn't get involved in all the technical details, but you should decide whether to use conservative (slow) or liberal (fast) methods for recording revenue and expenses.

Once the die is cast — in other words, after you have decided on which specific accounting methods to adopt — you have to stick with these methods year after year. For all practical purposes, accounting methods have to be used consistently and can't be changed year to year. For one thing, the IRS insists on this consistency in filing your annual income tax returns. (A pass-through business tax entity must file an information return with the IRS.) For management purposes, a business should keep its accounting methods consistent. Otherwise, it would be next to impossible to compare profit performance one year to the next.

Recording unusual, nonrecurring gains and losses

The P&L report focuses on the regular, recurring sales revenue and expenses of your business. In addition to these ongoing profit-making activities, most businesses experience certain types of gains and losses now and then that are incidental to their normal operations. For example, your business may sell a building you no longer need at a sizable gain (or loss). Or, you may lose a major lawsuit and have to pay substantial damages to the plaintiff. These special, nonrecurring events are called *extraordinary gains and losses.* They're reported separately in the P&L. You don't want to intermingle them with your regular revenue and expenses.

Keeping the number of lines in your P&L relatively short

For practical purposes, you need to keep a P&L report to one page — perhaps on one computer screen. By its very nature, the P&L is a *summary-level* financial statement. Figure 2-1, for example, includes only one line for all sales. As the owner, you're very interested in the total sales revenue. You also want to know a lot more information about your sales — by customers, by products, by locations (if you have more than one), by size of order, and so on. The best approach is to put detailed information in separate schedules. Use supporting schedules for further detail and don't put too much information in the main body of your P&L.

The P&L is just the headline page of your profit story. You need to know more detailed information about your sales and expenses than you can cram into a one-page P&L report. For example, you need to know the makeup of the total $30,000 advertising and sales promotion expense (see Figure 2-1). How much was spent on each type of advertising? How much was spent on special rebates? You need to keep on top of many details about your expenses. The place to do so is not in the main body of the P&L but in supporting schedules. In short, the P&L gives you the big picture. Reading the P&L is like reading the lead paragraph in a newspaper article. For details, you have to read deeper.

Book III

Managing Your Finances

Profit-neutral business transactions

Many business transactions don't affect revenue or expenses. You probably already know this fact, but it's a good point to be very clear on. Only transactions that affect profit — in other words, ones that increase revenue or expense — are reported in the P&L. A business carries on many transactions over the course of the year that aren't reported in its P&L.

For example, during the year, the business shown in Figure 2-1 borrowed a total of $450,000 from its bank and later in the year paid back $100,000 of the borrowings. These borrowings and repayments aren't reported in the

P&L — although the interest expense on the debt is included in the P&L. Likewise, the business invested $575,000 in long-term operating assets (land and building, forklift truck, delivery truck, computer, and so on). These *capital expenditures* aren't reported in the P&L — although the depreciation expense on these fixed assets is included in the P&L report.

The business shown in Figure 2-1 purchased $630,000 of products during the year. This cost was recorded in its inventory asset account at the time of purchase. When products are sold, their cost is removed from the inventory asset account and recorded in cost of goods sold expense. The business started the year with a stock of products (inventory) that cost $120,000. Therefore, the cost of products available for sale was $750,000. The total cost of goods sold during the year is $600,000. Therefore, the cost of unsold inventory at the end of the year is $150,000. This additional information about beginning inventory, purchases, and ending inventory is not presented in the P&L report in Figure 2-1, but it could have been, as the next section explains.

Including more information on inventory and purchases

Traditionally, internal P&L reports and external income statements include the following information (using the example from Figure 2-1):

Beginning inventory	$120,000	
Purchases	$630,000	
Available for sale	$750,000	
Ending inventory	$150,000	
Cost of goods sold expense		$600,000

The P&L report presented in Figure 2-1 includes only the cost of goods sold expense line. You can ask your accountant/controller to include all the preceding information, but do you really need this additional information in your P&L report?

You can easily find the beginning and ending inventory balances in your *balance sheet.* This financial statement is a summary of your assets and liabilities at the beginning and end of the period. The only real gain of information is your total purchases during the year. Do you want/need to know this amount? This question reveals the core issue in preparing the P&L and other financial statements: *What information should be included in the statement?* What does the business owner need to know from each financial statement? Basically, it's your call; you should tell your controller what you want in your financial statements.

For internal reporting, owners can ask for as much or as little information as they need and want. A business owner has only so much time to read and ponder the information in the financial statements he receives. So, the accountant should keep in mind how long the owner has available to digest information included in the P&L and other financial statements. The financial statements included in external financial reports that circulate outside the business are bound by standards of minimum disclosure. For example, Book III Chapter 3 presents a formal balance sheet that follows the rules of disclosure for external financial reporting.

Presenting the P&L Report for Your Business

Small business owners have certain questions on their minds after the close of the year. "How did I do during the year just ended? Did I do better or worse than last year? Did I make a profit or a loss?" Sounds odd, doesn't it, to say, "make a loss," but that's what happens.

Figure 2-2 presents a comparative P&L for the year just ended (December 31, 2015) and the preceding year (December 31, 2014) using the same format used for Figure 2-1. However, the P&L format is modified slightly to omit the income tax expense line, and the *Change* column is added. Recall that this business is organized legally as a pass-through entity for income tax.

Book III

Managing Your Finances

Your bottom line for 2014 reveals a $166,270 loss for the year. A loss is not good news of course. But it doesn't necessarily mean that you're on the edge of bankruptcy and will have to shortly terminate the business. In fact, you made improvements and your bottom line for the year just ended shows $95,651 profit — see Figure 2-2. This is a $261,921 improvement!

By the way, you should notice one thing in the Change column in Figure 2-2. A change from a negative number (the loss in 2014) to a positive number (the profit in 2015) can't be expressed as a percent. Therefore, the dollar amounts of the changes in operating profit and the bottom line are given in Figure 2-2.

Maintaining *solvency* (being able to pay liabilities on time) is a distinct financial function. You have to control your solvency in order to keep your business afloat and free from interruptions by your creditors. Book III Chapter 3 discusses solvency management — in good times and in bad times. Solvency depends in part on cash flow from profit or loss. That chapter also explains the important topic of cash flow from profit or loss and covers the broader function of managing solvency.

Your Business Name
P&L Report
For Year Ended December 31

	2014	2015	Change
Sales revenue	$2,286,500	$2,920,562	27.7%
Cost of goods sold expense	$1,411,605	$1,693,926	20.0%
Gross margin	$874,895	$1,226,636	40.2%
Operating expenses:			
Salaries, wages, commissions and benefits	$624,590	$662,400	6.1%
Advertising and sales promotion	$158,900	$192,550	21.2%
Depreciation	$93,250	$88,950	-4.6%
Other expenses	$116,800	$137,079	17.4%
Total operating expenses	$993,540	$1,080,979	8.8%
Operating profit (loss)	($118,645)	$145,657	$264,302
Interest expense	$47,625	$50,006	5.0%
Net income (loss)	($166,270)	$95,651	$261,921

© John Wiley & Sons, Inc.

Figure 2-2:
Presenting your P&L report for year just ended and preceding year.

When you get the P&L report (see Figure 2-2), what should you do? Well, obviously, you didn't panic and start firing employees and slashing expenses following your loss in 2014. This reaction would have only worsened your situation. You should analyze the main reasons for your turnaround from a loss last year to a respectable profit in 2015. Maybe you could do more of the same and improve profit in 2016.

Here are a few questions to ask yourself:

✔ **What about your salary?** Notice the $624,590 salaries, wages, commissions and benefits expense for 2014 in your P&L (Figure 2-2). Here's a question: Is your salary included in this amount, and if so, is your salary a reasonable amount? Of course, the bottom line depends on the size of expenses deducted from sales revenue. Small businesses are unusual in one particular respect — the owner sets his or her salary with little or no overview by anyone else. Suppose your salary and benefits were $350,000 for the year (don't you wish). In this case, the loss for the year is due to your lofty compensation. Or putting it another way, your sales revenue was not enough to justify this level of compensation.

Of course, the small business owner deserves a reasonable compensation for his or her time, talents, and capital invested in the business. There's no debate about that. But, what exactly is a *reasonable* amount of compensation? There's no clear-cut way to answer this question. You could attempt to compare your compensation with other small business owners, but that information is hard to come by.

Perhaps you have joined a national trade association that compiles compensation information on the owners and principal managers of their members, which you could use as a benchmark. You could troll through government statistics for small businesses put out by the Department of Commerce (www.commerce.gov) and the Internal Revenue Service (www.irs.gov). You could ask your CPA or banker for general compensation guidelines for small business owners. These are helpful sources of information. But in the end, the compensation you decide on is a fairly arbitrary amount. In many cases, the new business owner limits his or her compensation until the business turns the profit corner. The example presented here assumes that your compensation is reasonable in amount.

✔ **Are you cheating in any way?** Many small businesses are pretty much under the control of one person — the owner of the business. It's just a fact that many small businesses engage in dishonest or illegal activities that distort the P&L report. (*Note:* The "you" in the following points is someone else, because you certainly would never think of doing any of the following things.) Some of these nefarious tactics include the following:

- **Sales skimming:** Instead of recording sales and putting the money in the business's cash account, you put the money directly in your pocket and don't record the sales. Diverting sales revenue directly to you rather than letting it flow through the business is called *skimming*. However, the cost of products (goods) sold is paid by the business. The result is that the sales revenue amount in the P&L is too low. The expense of the products sold is included in cost of goods sold. Therefore, gross margin is too low, and all the profit lines below gross margin are too low. People skim sales revenue to make income that they don't report on their income tax returns, to evade income tax. Be advised that the IRS is very aware that sales skimming goes on.

- **Expense padding:** Many small business owners use the business to pay their personal expenses, which aren't expenses of the business. For example, the business pays the monthly lease for the auto driven by the spouse of the owner. The car is never used for business, but the business absorbs the cost of the auto. The owner takes a personal pleasure trip and conducts no business while on the trip, yet the business pays for the trip. Often, the spouse goes along on the trip. The owner may have substantial repairs and improvements done on her private residence and runs the cost through the business as repair and maintenance expense. The result is that the expenses of the business are too high, and profit is too low.

Book III

Managing Your Finances

- **Income shifting:** In many cases, the owner of a small business has other business interests and investments. Suppose, for example, that you own a building, and your business signs a lease agreement with the landlord (you). You could set the monthly rent too high or too low so as to shift income between your building investment and your business. Setting the rent too high makes the return on your building investment look better. But your business's profit ends up being too low because its rent is artificially high. Being the landlord of the building your business rents space in is just one example of how revenue and expenses can be shifted between the different business interests of a person.

- **Patently illegal activities:** To reduce expenses, a business (small or large) may knowingly pay employees less than the amounts they're legally entitled to under minimum wage laws or overtime laws. To save building maintenance costs, a business may violate building safety codes. You may bribe the building inspector. The number of laws and regulations affecting every business — small and large — is truly staggering. It's one thing to unknowingly violate an obscure law or a highly technical regulation. It's quite another thing to be aware of a major law or regulation and knowingly disregard it.

Illegal behavior has a way of eventually catching up with a business. You've heard the expression *keeping one step ahead of the law?* That appears to sum up the strategy of unethical businesses. The eventual costs of illegal activities are impossible to account for as the business goes along — and generally aren't recorded until the day of reckoning. In summary, your P&L doesn't include the potential fines and other costs that may eventually result from illegal activities.

The rest of this chapter assumes you don't skim sales revenue, you don't pad expenses, you don't shift income from or to your business, and you don't engage in illegal activities. Therefore, the revenue and expense amounts in your P&L report are fair and square and aren't misleading.

Figuring out the reasons for your profit improvement

Referring back to Figure 2-1's P&L, what were the main reasons for the big improvement from the loss in 2014 to the profit in 2015? You would want build on these factors in trying to improve profit in 2016. No obvious answers jump off the page and grab you by the throat. A glib answer is that your sales revenue increased more than your expenses for the year. That's just another way of saying that your profit improved $261,921. It offers little insight into what caused the profit increase and how you can improve things to make a bigger profit next year.

You should notice the 27.7 percent increase in sales revenue compared with the 20 percent increase in cost of goods sold expense (see Figure 2-2). Therefore, your 2015 gross margin benefited — jumping 40.2 percent over 2014. You increased your markups on product costs in 2015, which helps gross margin and bottom-line profit of course.

You should also notice the changes in expenses in 2015 over 2014. Are your expenses under control? You were probably reasonably careful, maybe downright tight-fisted with your expenses. It's possible that you were careless about your costs, but this analysis assumes not. You didn't put your brother-in-law on the payroll with nothing to do, just to help the family. You didn't spend any more on your computer system than you really needed. You didn't spend too much on rent or advertising. In short, there's really no flab in any of your expenses — although it's always a good idea to scrutinize all your costs to make sure.

Looking at the sales capacity provided by operating expenses

A very useful way to look at operating expenses is that these costs provide *sales capacity.* For example, you rent a building for your retail, warehouse, and office space. Your retail space is 12,000 square feet. For your line of products, one square foot of retail space can accommodate $300 sales per year. (You can find benchmark information for sales in publications of trade associations, state business agencies, and university business research bureaus.) Thus, your annual sales capacity based on your retail space is $3,600,000:

> 12,000 square feet retail space × $300 annual sales per square foot = $3,600,000 annual sales

Your $2,920,562 sales revenue for 2015 (see Figure 2-2) falls short of this standard for retail sales space. However, the shortfall indicates that you have enough retail space to accommodate an increase in sales next year.

Looking at sales revenue needed per employee

Here's another dimension that illustrates how operating expenses provide sales capacity. You employ ten full-time people — salespersons, yourself, office staff, a warehouse worker, and a truck driver. Your workforce provides the people power to make and support sales. In your line of business, you need at least $300,000 annual sales per employee — not just from sales employees, but all employees. Sales revenue pays the costs of your employees. This point

Book III

Managing Your Finances

goes back to your basic business model — to sell a volume of products at high enough markups over cost to cover your operating costs.

Your basic pricing policy is to mark up product cost to earn 45 percent gross margin on sales revenue. For $100 sales revenue, you aim for $45 gross margin on product cost of $55. (Your markup on cost is about 82 percent: ($45 markup ÷ $55 product cost = 81.1% markup on product cost.) Using this benchmark, $300,000 annual sales yields $135,000 gross margin per employee ($300,000 sales × 45 percent gross margin rate on sales = $135,000 gross margin). Out of this $135,000, you have to pay the employee's salary or wages, employment taxes, workers' compensation insurance, and benefits. Also, you have a lot of marketing and business overhead costs to pay, not to mention interest expense.

In summary, you need $3,000,000 total annual sales revenue to support ten employees: $300,000 per employee × 10 employees = $3,000,000 sales revenue. Your actual $2,920,562 sales revenue for 2015 (see Figure 2-2) is close to this sales benchmark for sales per employee. The small gap between your benchmark annual sales revenue and your actual annual sales revenue could signal that stepping up sales volume next year means that you may have to hire another person or two.

As for _annual sales per square foot of retail space_ and _annual sales per employee,_ you'd better darn well know these two benchmarks for your line of business. You can find this information from trade association publications for your industry, from talking with bankers, CPAs, and business consultants, and from statistics for small businesses published by the Department of Commerce. You can talk with other business owners in the same line of business at weekly service club meetings and at local Chamber of Commerce meetings.

Looking at marketing expenses

Now for the advertising and sales promotion expense in your P&L report (refer, once again, to Figure 2-2). How much sales bang should you get for your marketing buck? This question isn't easy to answer. There are no handy yardsticks you can easily refer to. Nevertheless, you should try to develop a benchmark to judge this expense. Look to data published by the trade associations and talk with other business owners and managers in your line of business. As the old chestnut goes, half of advertising expense is wasted, but nobody knows which half. There's a lot of truth in that.

You don't have to be a rocket scientist to see that a small business owner should develop techniques for tracking the sales effects of advertising and sales promotion costs. Customers often indicate whether they have responded to your advertising and sales promotions. You can watch the sales response to special advertising and promotion campaigns. You might even hire a marketing consultant. (See the chapters in Book V for a lot more about using marketing and promotion in your business.)

Knowing how your expenses behave

There's an undercurrent below the water line of the expenses reported in the P&L statement (back in Figure 2-2). In analyzing profit, you should understand how expenses behave relative to sales revenue. Some expenses are higher when sales are higher and lower when sales are lower. These are called *variable* expenses. In the business example (Figure 2-2), you pay your sales staff 5 percent commission on sales. The sales commission is a good example of a variable expense. Packing and shipping costs also vary with the total quantity of products sold.

On the other hand, many expenses remain the same whether sales are high or low. As you may guess, these expenses are *fixed*. For example, you sign a building lease for the coming year; the monthly rents are a fixed expense. You buy a computer system. The annual depreciation charged off is a fixed expense. Most employees are paid a fixed amount of wages or salaries. Employee compensation is a fixed cost for the year, unless you lay off someone or change the number of hours worked. The annual fixed expenses of many small businesses are a large part of their total operating expenses.

In a P&L statement for a business that sells products, the cost of goods sold expense is the first expense deducted from sales revenue, to determine gross margin. (Refer to the P&L report in Figure 2-2 again.) Cost of goods sold varies with sales revenue. In other words, when sales go up, this expense goes up; when sales go down, this expense goes down. However, cost of goods sold doesn't necessarily move in strict lockstep with changes in sales revenue.

In the example in Figure 2-2, you were able to increase sales prices in 2015, even though your product costs per unit didn't increase. (Of course, product costs don't always stay the same from year to year.) Selling additional units at the higher sales prices pushed up your sales revenue by a larger percent than the increase in cost of goods sold (at the same product costs). Alternatively, a business may have to reduce its markups by cutting sales prices even though its product costs remain the same. Selling additional units at the lower markups would cause sales revenue to increase by a smaller percent than the increase in cost of goods sold.

Your controller can put your operating expenses in two piles — *fixed* and *variable*. Depreciation expense is a fixed cost; a certain amount of depreciation expense is recorded each year regardless of the actual sales volume in the year. The annual compensation of the janitor is a fixed cost. Sales commissions are a prime example of a variable cost. The segregation between fixed and variable costs is important in analyzing past profit performance and in developing plans for improving profit in the future.

The P&L report presented in Figure 2-2 shows the typical format, or configuration, of this profit performance financial statement. If you visited 100 businesses and looked at their quarterly and annual P&L reports, the large majority of the profit reports would look pretty much like Figure 2-2. The number of expense lines would vary from business to business. Otherwise, you would find significant deviations from the basic format shown in Figure 2-2.

The standard format of the P&L has one flaw, or limitation: It does not differentiate between variable and fixed operating expenses. You can ask your accountant to prepare a second version of the P&L that does classify between fixed and variable operating expenses. (As a matter of fact, preparing a second version of the P&L isn't difficult; you can export the original P&L to an Excel spreadsheet and then rearrange the data.)

Figure 2-3 presents an alternative format for your P&L that classifies operating expenses between fixed and variable. Of course, your bottom-line profit (or loss) for each year is the same as in Figure 2-2. Notice the *contribution margin*

Your Business Name
P&L Classified By Expense Behavior
For Years Ended December 31

	2014		2015	
Sales revenue	$2,286,500	100.0%	$2,920,562	100.0%
Variable expenses:				
Cost of goods sold	$1,411,605		$1,693,926	
Operating costs	$114,325		$146,028	
Total variable expenses	$1,525,930	66.7%	$1,839,954	63.0%
Contribution margin	$760,570	33.3%	$1,080,608	37.0%
Fixed expenses:				
Operating costs	$879,215		$934,951	
Interest	$47,625		$50,006	
Total fixed expenses	$926,840		$984,957	
Profit (Loss)	($166,270)		$95,651	
Breakeven sales revenue =	$2,786,357		$2,662,046	

Figure 2-3:
P&L that separates fixed and variable expenses.

© John Wiley & Sons, Inc.

line in this alternative format P&L report. Contribution margin equals sales revenue minus all variable expenses. In other words, contribution margin is profit before fixed expenses are deducted. In this example, the contribution margin equals 33.3 percent of sales revenue in 2014 and 37 percent in 2015. In other words, in 2015, you had 37 cents from each dollar of sales for covering your fixed expenses, compared with only 33.3 cents per dollar in 2014.

Breaking Through the Breakeven Barrier

One way to explain your profit improvement in 2015 over 2014 (see Figure 2-3) is that you broke through your breakeven barrier in 2015, which you failed to do in 2014.

You probably have heard about *breakeven*. It's the mythical sales level at which your bottom line is exactly zero — no profit and no loss. A business doesn't try to just break even, of course. The breakeven point is just an *estimate* of what would happen if sales revenue were a certain amount and expenses behaved exactly as predicted. Nevertheless, the breakeven point is a valuable point of reference for profit analysis.

Determining the breakeven point requires that you, or more accurately that your controller, distinguish between your fixed and variable operating expenses. Cost of goods sold is a variable expense. Generally, interest expense is treated as a fixed expense for purposes of breakeven analysis.

To illustrate the application of breakeven analysis, assume that your accountant determines that in 2014, your $993,540 total operating expenses (see Figure 2-2) were as follows: fixed operating expenses = $879,215; variable operating expenses = $114,325. (Don't take these two amounts as precise numbers; your controller takes some expedient shortcuts in coming up with these numbers.)

Your breakeven sales level for 2014 is $2,786,357 (see Figure 2-3). The 2014 breakeven point is computed as follows:

> $926,840 total fixed expenses for year ÷ 33.3% contribution margin on sales = $2,786,357 breakeven sales revenue

Your actual sales for 2014 were lower than your breakeven sales level, so you had a loss (see Figure 2-3). You needed about $500,000 additional sales in 2014 just to hit your breakeven point. Alternatively, you needed a contribution margin ratio higher than 33.3 percent.

Book III

Managing Your Finances

In 2015, you made a profit for the year, so you know that you exceeded your breakeven sales level for the year. Pay close attention to your contribution margin ratio as a percent of sales revenue for 2015. Your contribution margin ratio in 2015 improved to 37 percent, which is a marked improvement over the 33.3 percent in 2014 — see Figure 2-3.

Why did your contribution margin ratio increase in 2015? You were able to improve your markup. Notice from Figure 2-2 that your sales revenue increased 27.7 percent, but your cost of goods sold increased only 20 percent. Your product costs per unit remained the same in 2015 (which isn't always true in many situations, of course). This news is really good. You sold 20 percent more volume at higher sales prices, which is no small accomplishment. (Perhaps you had underpriced your products in 2014 and remedied this problem in 2015).

Breakeven analysis is important because it focuses attention on the *incremental,* or *marginal* profit earned by additional units sold. For example, if you had sold more units and sales revenue had been $100,000 higher in 2015, you would have increased your bottom line $37,000, which is a substantial gain over your actual profit for the year (see Figure 2-3):

$100,000 additional sales revenue × 37.0% contribution margin ratio on sales = $37,000 additional profit

Breakeven analysis offers another important advantage: It focuses attention on fixed expenses, which are like an albatross hanging around the neck of your business. Your 2014 fixed operating expenses were $879,215 (see Figure 2-3), which is a big chunk of change. The bulk of these fixed operating costs are salaries and wages. This amount also includes depreciation, rent, licenses and fees, and several other costs. Interest is a fixed expense. Sometimes, the total amount of fixed expenses for the year is called "the nut" of the business, and it's a tough nut to crack. On the other hand, fixed costs buy sales capacity — the space and workforce to make sales.

Improving Profit

Yes, you did earn a profit in 2015, but you shouldn't be satisfied with your profit performance. For one thing, in the example in Figure 2-2, your 2015 profit is only 3 percent of annual sales revenue, and the normal profit for your industry is in the 7 to 10 percent range. For another thing, your relatively small profit for the year severely limited the amount of cash distribution from profit to you and the other owners of the business. Therefore, assume that you set a goal of earning at least $250,000 profit next year. Now comes the hard part: How are you going to improve profit next year?

Basically, your options for improving profit boil down to four areas:

- ✔ **Increase the markup ratio on sales revenue:** Through a combination of sales price increases, product cost decreases, and a richer mix of sales, improve your overall markup ratio on sales revenue.

- ✔ **Increase sales volume:** Sell new products and sell more units of old products.

- ✔ **Reduce variable costs:** Scale down the cost per dollar or the cost per unit of making sales.

- ✔ **Tighten down fixed costs:** Downsize fixed costs to match the sales capacity you actually need (which means eliminating the costs related to idle capacity you're not using), and lower other fixed costs if you can.

The most realistic ways to improve profit are found mainly in the first two options — increasing markup and sales volume. Most operating costs are victims of irresistible cost inflation pressures. Small business owners can't do much about general cost inflation trends. It goes without saying that a small business owner should ruthlessly scrutinize all operating costs and weed out wasteful expenditures. Most small business owners (though not all) are pretty good at expense control. Furthermore, they don't take on more fixed operating costs than are justified by their level of sales — though you should always be alert for the cost of idle sales capacity that you don't need.

Therefore, improving your markup and increasing sales volume are the two most realistic paths for stepping up your profit performance.

A very useful technique for analyzing profit-improvement alternatives is to prepare *what-if scenarios* for next year. What if you sell 10 percent more volume next year? What if your markup ratio improves to 40 percent next year? This approach is quite practical using Microsoft Excel. Using a spreadsheet program takes the drudgery out of the process. Your 2015 profit performance is the point of reference for testing different scenarios for improving profit next year.

Book III

Managing Your Finances

Improving markup

Recall that your basic business model is to sell a volume of products at adequate markups over their costs to cover your marketing and operating expenses in order to generate satisfactory profit after interest expense. In 2015, your markup (gross margin) equals 42 percent (refer to Figure 2-2 for data):

$1,226,636 gross margin ÷ $2,920,562 sales revenue = 42% markup ratio on sales

Recall that your objective is to set sales prices high enough so that you earn a 45 percent markup on sales. Therefore, you fell short of this goal in 2015. During the year, you made price concessions on some sales; you didn't always hold to list prices that are based on your 45 percent markup rule. In other words, you discounted sales prices for certain customers. A logical what-if profit scenario to look at is one in which you hadn't discounted any sales prices.

To earn 45 percent gross margin on sales revenue, your cost of goods sold expense has to be 55 percent of sales revenue. Holding cost of goods sold the same, your sales revenue for 2015 should have been $3,079,865, which is calculated as follows (see Figure 2-3 for data):

$1,693,926 cost of goods sold ÷ 55% cost of goods sold as percent of sales revenue = $3,079,865 sales revenue needed to earn 45% gross margin on sales

Figure 2-4 shows the what-if scenario for the case in which you can set sales prices higher so that you'd earn gross margin equal to 45 percent of sales revenue. In this scenario, sales volume isn't changed; only sales prices are higher. Also, all other factors are held the same. In other words, the sales price factor is isolated; this is the only profit factor that is changed in the what-if scenario.

In the higher sales prices scenario shown in Figure 2-4, notice that the variable operating costs increase in proportion with the sales revenue increase. You pay your sales staff 5 percent commissions on sales, so the

Your Business Name
P&L Comparing Actual With Higher Sales Prices Scenario
For Year Ended December 31, 2015

	Actual 2015		Higher Sales Prices	
Sales revenue	$2,920,562	100.0%	$3,079,865	100.0%
Variable expenses:				
Cost of goods sold	$1,693,926		$1,693,926	
Operating costs	$146,028		$153,993	
Total variable expenses	$1,839,954	63.0%	$1,847,919	60.0%
Contribution margin	$1,080,608	37.0%	$1,231,946	40.0%
Fixed expenses:				
Operating costs	$934,951		$934,951	
Interest	$50,006		$50,006	
Total fixed expenses	$984,957		$984,957	
Profit	$95,651		$246,989	

Figure 2-4: P&L showing the what-if scenario for higher sales prices.

© John Wiley & Sons, Inc.

larger amount of sales revenue makes this expense larger. The cost of goods sold expense and your fixed expenses remain the same in this scenario, and sales volume (the total number of products sold) doesn't change.

The higher sales prices would have improved your profit significantly, from $95,651 to $246,989 (see Figure 2-4). Increasing your sales prices 5.5 percent (from $2,920,562 total sales revenue to $3,079,865 total sales revenue) would have resulted in a very large percent increase in profit. This example illustrates the power of even relatively small changes in sales prices on the bottom line. If you could have sold products for just 5.5 percent higher prices than you actually did in 2015, your profit would have been almost $250,000.

In many cases, customers are very sensitive to sales prices. Even a seemingly small sales price increase could lead to a serious decline in demand. You, the owner of the small business, have the difficult job of figuring out the reaction of your customers to sale price increases and decreases. The purpose in showing the higher sales prices scenario is to demonstrate the powerful effect of increasing sales prices on the bottom line.

Improving sales volume

Suppose you had sold 10 percent more volume in 2015 than you actually sold. For every 100 units actually sold, you actually sold 110 units. (Presume that your *sales mix,* the proportion of each product sold in total sales volume, would have been the same.) How much higher would your profit be in this scenario? Can you hazard a guess? Well, not really; you have to crank the numbers.

Figure 2-5 presents the P&L for the 10 percent higher sales volume scenario in 2015. Sales revenue, cost of goods sold expense, variable operating expenses, and contribution margin all increase 10 percent. The additional amount of sales revenue causes sales commissions expense to increase proportionally, which is the only variable operating cost in the business example shown in Figure 2-5. (A business may have other variable operating costs that depend on the number of units sold, such as delivery costs and packing and shipping costs.)

So, contribution margin is 10 percent higher in the 10 percent higher sales volume scenario (data from Figure 2-5):

$1,188,669 contribution at higher sales volume – $1,080,608 contribution at actual sales level = $108,061 contribution margin increase

$108,061 increase ÷ $1,080,608 contribution at actual sales level = 10% increase

		Actual 2015		Higher Sales Volume	
		Actual 2015		**Higher Sales Volume**	
Sales revenue		$2,920,562	100.0%	$3,212,618	100.0%
Variable expenses:					
Cost of goods sold		$1,693,926		$1,863,319	
Operating costs		$146,028		$160,631	
Total variable expenses		$1,839,954	63.0%	$2,023,950	63.0%
Contribution margin		$1,080,608	37.0%	$1,188,669	37.0%
Fixed expenses:					
Operating costs		$934,951		$934,951	
Interest		$50,006		$50,006	
Total fixed expenses		$984,957		$984,957	
Profit		$95,651		$203,712	

Your Business Name
P&L Comparing Actual With Higher Sales Volume Scenario
For Year Ended December 31, 2015

© John Wiley & Sons, Inc.

Figure 2-5:
P&L
showing
the what-if
scenario for
10 percent
higher sales
volume.

At this juncture, you encounter a serious question: Would your fixed expenses be higher at the 10 percent higher sales volume level? They might. Suppose your actual 2015 sales volume stretched your sales capacity to the limit. Additional sales volume may require renting larger retail space or hiring more employees. Figure 2-5 shows results based on the assumption that your fixed costs remain the same at the higher sales volume. But your fixed costs may have to be higher, and you should keep this point in mind.

In any case, notice that the profit improvement in the 10 percent higher sales volume scenario is less — that's right, is *less* — than in the 5.5 percent higher sales prices scenario shown in Figure 2-4. Sales price increases generally are more powerful than sales volume increases for improving profit. On the other hand, increasing sales volume may be the only avenue for increasing profit when you can't really bump up sales prices.

Chapter 3

Working with Cash Flow and Staying Solvent

In This Chapter

▶ Differentiating cash flow and bottom-line profit

▶ Deciding how you want cash flow from profit information reported to you

▶ Exploring the statement of cash flows

▶ Understanding and measuring liquidity and business solvency

▶ Watching for liquidity traps

▶ Tapping sources of liquidity for your business

▶ Keying in on financial leverage

*S*uppose your business earned $250,000 net income for the year just ended. How do you know this fact? Well, you read your P&L statement, of course. The P&L reports sales revenue and expenses for the year, leading down to $250,000 bottom-line profit (also called *net income* and *earnings*). Book III Chapter 2 explains the P&L statement in detail. But now, a different question: What's your *cash flow* for the year from the $250,000 profit you earned?

You probably had other sources of cash during the year. You increased the amount borrowed from the bank, and the owners (including you) invested additional capital in the business. The question here focuses only on profit, not your other sources of cash during the year.

Did your cash balance increase $250,000 because of your profit for the year? The answer is no: The amount of cash flow from profit is almost certainly higher or lower than the amount of profit. For the large majority of businesses, profit and cash flow from profit are virtually never the same amount.

Your accountant or controller (the chief accounting officer of your business) prepares a *statement of cash flows* that summarizes your cash sources and uses for the period. The first section reports cash flow from profit, which is called *cash flow from operating activities.* Unfortunately, the design of the first section isn't particularly user-friendly. Even CPAs can have trouble reading this section. It's far too technical. Therefore, this chapter doesn't start with the statement of cash flows. That waits till later in the chapter. First comes a more user-friendly explanation of cash flow from profit.

All businesses, at one point or another, have most likely experienced some sort of financial pain when it comes to keeping the doors open and the bills paid. From suppliers demanding payments on outstanding invoices to customers providing every excuse in the book as to why they need extended payment terms, businesses must constantly manage financial resources to ensure that capital is readily available to support their ongoing operations.

The concept of keeping a business *solvent,* on the surface, would appear to be relatively simple from the standpoint of making sure that *enough capital is available to meet its current obligations and commitments.* Though this statement isn't entirely untrue, the problem with business solvency isn't so much based in managing short-term financial issues and obligations but rather managing a long-term business plan and making sure that the appropriate amount and type of capital is *readily* available. As most businesses will attest, economic as well as business cycles come and go, so the real key lies in being able to properly position your company during the cycles to always ensure that adequate solvency and liquidity are maintained.

When times are good, businesses tend to have more than enough capital available from both internal sources and external partners (for example, a bank providing a loan) because everyone wants to jump on the bandwagon and share in the success. It's when the times turn, profits suddenly become losses, and internal financial pressures mount that you find your financial partners may not be all they promised and begin to demand that "you perform before they commit." This situation, of course, represents the ultimate catch-22, because before your business can perform, you need them to commit! Implementing proper business-planning efforts becomes the foundation to ensuring that your business will always remain solvent and have ample liquidity to manage through both good times and bad.

The latter half of this chapter focuses on providing a better understanding of business solvency and liquidity, as well as the necessary tools to properly measure it. It also covers helping your business avoid falling into liquidity traps, and if you do, what strategies, resources, and/or "tricks of the trade" may be available to assist you with getting out of a real mess.

Sorting Out Your Sources of Cash

One immutable law for keeping a business going is *thou shall not run out of cash.* If your cash balance drops to zero, you can't meet your payroll or pay creditors on time. Your employees may quit, and your creditors may pull the plug on your business. You simply can't afford cash flow surprises. Quite clearly, you (or someone in your business) has to manage cash flows. You can't put cash flows on automatic pilot.

To start a business, you need to raise money to invest in the assets needed to support sales and to carry on day-to-day operations. Making profit starts with making sales, and making sales requires investing in a variety of assets. Every business needs some assets, and many businesses need a lot of assets to make sales and carry on operations. Usually, a business taps both debt and equity (ownership) sources of capital for money needed to get the business up and running. (Book II Chapter 2 explores raising capital from different sources.)

An ongoing business needs ongoing capital to finance its operations — both equity and debt capital (unless the business eschews borrowing money). And an ongoing business depends on a third source of cash flow — *profit*. Profit is called an *internal source* of capital because the business doesn't have to go to outside, external sources of capital for this money. Profit is one of the three main tributaries of a business's cash flow river.

Cash flow from profit is the source for making distributions to owners. These distributions compensate the owners for their capital investment in the business. As you know, interest is compensation for the use of debt capital. In like manner, cash distributions from profit to owners provide compensation, or payment, for the use of owners' equity capital.

Instead of making distributions to owners, you can retain cash flow from profit and keep it in the business. To grow the sales of your business, you usually have to expand the assets you need to operate at the higher level of activity — you need higher levels of receivables and inventory, for example. You use the cash flow from profit plus money provided from debt and equity sources of capital to expand the assets of the business. See Figure 3-3 (a balance sheet example), later in this chapter, for the types of assets you need to operate a business.

Speaking very broadly — approximately as wide as the Mississippi — making a profit generates positive cash flow, and making a loss causes negative cash flow. However, cash flows run on a different timetable than recording revenue and expenses. When you sell on credit, the actual cash inflow takes place weeks after recording the sales revenue. The actual payments of many expenses don't happen until weeks after recording the expenses (like when you use a credit card for your personal expenses). Furthermore, some costs are paid before being recorded as expenses.

Book III

Managing Your Finances

Avoiding Confusion Between Profit and Its Cash Flow

Business managers don't think like accountants (and many argue that's a good thing). Say "sales revenue" to a business manager, and he thinks of collecting money from customers. Say "expenses" to a business manager, and she thinks of writing checks for the costs of operating the business. In short, business managers are cash flow thinkers. So, when business managers read their P&L reports, they tend to think they're reading cash flow information. However, the sales revenue and expense information in the P&L statement has been recorded on the accrual-basis of accounting. The sales revenue amount in your P&L statement is different than the total cash collections from customers during the year (unless you make only cash sales). And, the expense amounts in your P&L statement are different than the total amounts actually disbursed for these costs during the year.

In short, when discussing profit and cash flow from profit, you're talking about two different things — apples and oranges, as it were.

Here are two rather extreme examples that illustrate the divergence of cash flow and profit. Suppose that a business records $3,000,000 sales revenue and $2,750,000 total expenses for the year. So, its profit is $250,000 for the year.

 ✔ **Scenario 1:** Suppose that the business didn't collect a dime of its sales revenue; it extended long-term credit terms to its customers, and none of its customers made any payments to the business by the end of the year. Assume, however, that the business paid all its expenses during the year. Therefore, cash in equals zero, and cash out equals $2,750,000; cash flow from profit is a *negative* $2,750,000 for the year, despite a profit of $250,000!

 ✔ **Scenario 2:** Suppose that the business collected all its sales revenue for the year. However, it didn't pay a dime of expenses; its vendors and suppliers, as well as its employees, agreed to wait for payment until next year (most unlikely, of course). Therefore, cash in equals $3,000,000, and cash out equals zero; cash flow from profit is a *positive* $3,000,000 despite profit of only $250,000!

Of course, you don't find such extreme examples in the real world of business. But the examples bring out a valid point: Cash flow from profit depends on when sales revenue is collected and when expenses are paid. When you ask about cash flow from profit, you're inquiring about whether cash collections from customers during the year are different than sales revenue and whether cash payments for expenses during the year are different than the expense amounts that are recorded to measure profit for the year.

A loss is bad news from the cash flow point of view. In most cases, a loss sucks money out of the business. There is no money to expand the business or to provide for cash distributions to owners (the shareholders or partners of the business who provide its owners' equity capital). The amount of cash drain caused by a loss can be significantly higher, or significantly lower, than the bottom line amount of loss reported in the P&L for the year. It's possible that a business could report a big loss in its P&L, and yet realize a *positive* cash flow from the loss. Isn't this an odd state of affairs?

Deciding How to Have Cash Flow Information Reported to You

You can't afford to ignore cash flow from profit. Knowing your cash flow performance is as important as knowing your profit performance. There's no question that your accountant should determine the cash flow from profit (operating activities) for each quarter and for each year (perhaps monthly as well). But, there certainly is a question regarding how cash flow information should be reported to you, the owner/manager of the small business. Your basic alternatives are the following three:

Book III

Managing Your Finances

- ✔ **Report just cash flow:** Tell your accountant to include the amount of cash flow from profit for the period with your P&L. It's only one more line of information and can fit easily at the end of the statement. Just the amount of cash flow is reported, with no details indicating why it's more or less than profit for the period.

- ✔ **Report differences between cash flows and sales revenue and expenses in the P&L:** Tell your accountant to add an additional column of information in your regular P&L statement that reports the differences between cash flow and sales revenue and cash flows and expenses. You can skim over relatively minor differences and pay attention to significant variances between cash flow and your profit factors.

- ✔ **Try to read the first section of the statement of cash flows:** The statement of cash flows is one of the three primary financial statements that are prepared for external reporting to creditors and outside owners of a business. Because this cash flow statement has to be prepared anyway, use it for your cash flow information. In a sense, you get double duty out of the statement — for both external financial reporting and for internal managerial uses.

The middle option is good — including cash flow differences from sales revenue and expenses in the P&L statement. The first option doesn't give you much information. Reading the first section of the statement of cash flows is like reading the owner's manual that comes with an electronic gadget. The decision is up to you.

Next up: discussing each of the three ways for having cash flow information reported to you. Remember, you're the boss; don't be intimidated by your accountant.

Appending cash flow to your P&L report

You may prefer not to analyze cash flow from profit in detail. In that case, you may decide on the first option mentioned in the preceding section: Just have the amount of cash flow from profit tacked on at the end of your P&L report without further details.

Figure 3-1 shows the 2015 P&L report of the business example introduced in Book III Chapter 2. That chapter explains the P&L statement in detail. (See

Your Business Name
P&L Report Including Cash Flow From Net Income
For Year Ended December 31, 2015

	2015
Sales revenue	$2,920,562
Cost of goods sold expense	$1,693,926
Gross margin	$1,226,636
Operating expenses:	
Salaries, wages, commissions and benefits	$662,400
Advertising and sales promotion	$192,550
Depreciation	$88,950
Other expenses	$137,079
Total operating expenses	$1,080,979
Operating profit (loss)	$145,657
Interest expense	$50,006
Net income	$95,651
Cash flow from net income (operating activities)	$133,141

Figure 3-1: P&L report that also includes the cash flow from profit figure.

© John Wiley & Sons, Inc.

Figure 2-2 in Book III Chapter 2 for its P&L statement.) You don't need to have read that chapter before this chapter, although you may want to refer to it if you don't have a basic understanding of the P&L statement.

In Figure 3-1, your eye is drawn to the difference between the business's $95,651 net income for the year and its $133,141 cash flow from profit. The business earned $95,651 profit for the year based on proper accounting methods. But, at the same time, the business had $133,141 net cash flow from its profit-making activities. Its cash increased $133,141 — not from increasing its debt and not from its owners investing more money in the business. This money was available for use as the owner/manager thinks is best for the business.

The rather obvious limitation of reporting only the final amount of cash flow from profit is that this one figure offers no clues regarding why the cash flow was more than profit. You're at a loss to know whether the excess of cash flow over profit is the normal state of affairs or not. Reporting only the final amount of cash flow from profit provides rather skimpy information, but it's better than no information at all.

Reporting differences of cash flows from sales revenue and expenses in the P&L

It's good to include cash flow information with your P&L report. Figure 3-2 presents the business's P&L statement with additional cash flow statement for the year ending December 31, 2015. You'll notice the new column on the right side of the P&L statement that reports the negative or positive cash flow differences from sales revenue and expenses in the P&L statement.

Figure 3-2 separates depreciation expense from the total of other operating expenses. As an aside, note that operating expenses are presented many different ways. Looking below the gross margin line in P&L reports, you'd see that expenses are reported in a variety of ways from business to business.

The purpose of combining the P&L and cash flow information (see Figure 3-2) is to call attention to the difference in cash flow actually generated from the stated sales revenue and the difference in the cash flow actually used in paying the stated expenses. In this example, cash collections from customers are $12,550 less than sales revenue for the year. Cash payments for products sold by the business were $50,555 more than cost of goods sold expense for the year. Both are negative cash flow factors. A negative cash flow difference means that cash inflow is less or cash outflow is more than the corresponding amount in the P&L statement.

Your Business Name
P&L Report and Cash Flow Differences
For Year Ended December 31, 2015

P&L		Cash Flow Difference*
Sales revenue	$2,920,562	($12,550)
Cost of goods sold expense	$1,693,926	($50,555)
Gross margin	$1,226,636	
Operating expenses:		
Salaries, wages, commissions and benefits	$662,400	
Advertising and sales promotion	$192,550	
Other expenses	$137,079	
Operating expenses excluding depreciation	$992,029	$10,380
Depreciation expense	$88,950	$88,950
Total operating expenses	$1,080,979	
Operating profit	$145,657	
Interest expense	$50,006	$1,265
Net income	$95,651	
Net cash flow difference		$37,490
Cash flow from profit (operating activities)	$133,141	

* Positive = More cash inflow or less cash outflow than amount in P&L
(Negative) = Less cash inflow or more cash outflow than amount in P&L

© John Wiley & Sons, Inc.

Figure 3-2: P&L report that includes cash flow differences from sales revenue and expenses.

The combined P&L and cash flow information report shown in Figure 3-2 would be new to your accountant/controller. Including cash flow information along with sales revenue and expenses isn't done in most businesses. You have to instruct your accountant to prepare this statement for you. Being a new report, your accountant would face a learning curve in getting up to speed on the report. Computer accounting programs don't include a module for generating a report like this one. Therefore, your accountant has to export data from your accounting database to an Excel spreadsheet to prepare the report. (Your accountant probably already uses this procedure in preparing other reports that aren't included in the computer accounting program.)

Here are brief explanations for each of the five cash flow differences reported in Figure 3-2:

> ✔ **Sales revenue:** You collected $12,550 less cash from customers during the year than the amount of sales revenue for the year, which appears as an increase in your *accounts receivable* asset account during the year.

✔ **Cost of goods sold expense:** You paid $50,555 more cash to vendors during the year than the amount of cost of goods sold expense for the year. You increased your store of products being held for sale, which is recorded in your *inventory* asset account, which is seen as an increase in your inventory asset account during the year. Also, you increased the amount you owe vendors, which is recorded in the *accounts payable* liability account, which is seen in the increase of your *accounts payable* liability account during the year. The net effect of increasing your inventory and accounts payable is that you wrote checks for $50,555 more than your cost of goods sold expense for the year.

✔ **Operating expenses (excluding depreciation):** Certain operating expenses (for example, insurance) are prepaid before being recorded as an expense; these advance payments are recorded in your *prepaid expenses* asset account. Other operating expenses are paid after being recorded as an expense; the liabilities for these expenses are recorded either in your *accounts payable* and *accrued expenses payable* liability accounts. The net cash flow effect is a positive $10,380 amount for the year. In other words, your actual cash payments were $10,380 less than the total amount of operating expenses (excluding depreciation). Your accountant uses changes in your prepaid expense asset account and the two liability accounts to determine the net cash flow effect.

✔ **Depreciation expense:** Over the years, you've invested in long-term operating assets, including land and a building, delivery trucks, a computer system, office furniture, warehouse equipment, tools, and so on. Although these fixed assets last more than one year, they wear out or lose their economic usefulness over the years. Therefore, the cost of a fixed asset (except land) is allocated to each year of the estimated useful life of the fixed asset. Each year is charged with a certain amount of *depreciation expense.* Recording depreciation expense doesn't involve any further cash outlay. You already spent money when you bought the fixed assets. Therefore, depreciation expense is a positive cash flow difference. There was zero cash outlay for this expense during the year.

During the year, you collected most (though not quite all) of your sales revenue in cash — total cash collections from customers during the year were just $12,550 less than your $2,920,562 sales revenue for the year (see Figure 3-2). Sales revenue reimburses the business for its expenses. In other words, the business sets sales prices high enough to recover its expenses and leave a little for profit. Most expenses are paid in cash sooner or later. But depreciation is unique. Depreciation expense is embedded in the cost of the fixed asset, and the cost is paid for when the business acquires the fixed asset. Therefore, the cash collections from sales each year pay, back the business for the use of its fixed assets. In this way, depreciation generates cash flow to the business.

Book III

Managing Your Finances

✔ **Interest expense:** You paid $1,265 less interest to the bank on your loans than the amount of interest recorded in the year. Interest expense is recorded as it accrues month to month, but typically interest is paid *in arrears,* or at the end of the period. The lag in paying interest is recorded in an accrued expense payable account. This liability account increased $1,265 during the year, which means you paid less cash than the amount of expense for the year.

The net cash flow difference from net income is $37,490 for the year — see Figure 3-2. The cash flow from depreciation is the biggest positive factor. The cash flow for building up your inventory is the biggest negative factor. Did you really need to build up your inventory? Assuming that you did, you should definitely understand that doing so required a $50,555 cash outlay.

The $133,141 cash flow from profit (net income) for the year, plus your other sources of cash during the year, was the total amount of cash at your disposal. Presumably, you made good use of this money. Usually, a business faces several demands on its available cash — in particular, for growing the business and for making distributions from profit to owners.

Introducing the Statement of Cash Flows

An external financial report of a business to its creditors and shareowners includes three primary *financial statements:*

✔ **Income statement:** *Income statement* is the name for the P&L statement when it's reported outside the business. It's not called a P&L statement outside the business; it may be called the *earnings statement* or *operating statement.* Its purpose is to summarize the sales revenue (and other income) and the expenses (and losses) of the business for a period of time, and ends with the net income (or net loss) for the period. Public corporations also report earnings *per share* in their income statements.

✔ **Balance sheet:** This statement presents the assets, liabilities, and sources of owners' equity of the business at the close of business on the last day of the income statement period. It's also called the *statement of financial position* or *statement of financial condition.* It allows the reader to examine the composition of the business's assets, compare its liabilities against its assets, and evaluate profit performance relative to the total capital invested in assets that is being used to make profit.

✔ **Statement of cash flows:** This statement is prepared for the same period of time as the income statement. It summarizes the sources and uses of cash during the period so that the reader can determine where the business got its cash during the period and what it did with the money. For example, you can see whether the business distributed some of its profit to owners during the year.

To get a complete financial picture of a business, you have to read all three of its financial statements. One tells you whether it made a profit or not, one tells you about its financial condition at the end of the profit period, and the third tells you about its cash flows during the period.

Figure 3-3 presents the business's balance sheets at the end of 2014 and 2015. The changes in the business's assets, liabilities, and owners' equity accounts are the building blocks of its statement of cash flows.

Your Business Name
Balance Sheet
At December 31

	2014	2015	Changes
Assets			
Cash	$347,779	$584,070	$236,291
Accounts receivable	$136,235	$148,785	$12,550
Inventory	$218,565	$250,670	$32,105
Prepaid expenses	$65,230	$61,235	($3,995)
Total current assets	$767,809	$1,044,760	
Property, plant and equipment	$774,600	$896,450	$121,850
Accumulated depreciation	($167,485)	($256,435)	($88,950)
Cost less depreciation	$607,115	$640,015	
Total assets	$1,374,924	$1,684,775	
Liabilities and Owners' Equity			
Accounts payable	$286,450	$261,430	($25,020)
Accrued expenses payable	$67,345	$81,565	$14,220
Short-term notes payable	$100,000	$200,000	$100,000
Total current liabilities	$453,795	$542,995	
Long-term notes payable	$300,000	$400,000	$100,000
Owners' equity:			
Invested capital	$500,000	$525,000	$25,000
Retained earnings	$121,129	$216,780	$95,651
Total owners' equity	$621,129	$741,780	
Total liabilities and owners' equity	$1,374,924	$1,684,775	

Figure 3-3: Presenting the balance sheet for business example.

Book III

Managing Your Finances

Running down the balance sheet from the cash flow point of view

If you sell products, you probably sell them both at retail to consumers and to other businesses. You extend short-term credit to your business customers. Over the years, you have invested in various long-term operating assets (called *fixed assets*) that you need to conduct the activities of the business — a parcel of land and a building, computers, trucks, office furniture, cash registers, and so on. Your business borrows money from two banks. Yours is not the only business model in the world of course. But it's a good comprehensive model to look at; one that captures most cash flow factors.

Here's a rundown on the items reported in your balance sheet (see Figure 3-3), paying particular attention to cash flow aspects:

- ✔ **Cash:** This item includes cash on hand (coins and currency) and money on deposit in checking accounts. Sooner or later, every transaction goes through the cash account, and it's the *sooner or later* that you should understand.

- ✔ **Accounts receivable:** You extend credit to your business customers; this asset account holds the amount of customers' receivables that should be collected in the near term. The balance of this account is the amount of money not yet collected from customers. It's been recorded as sales revenue, but it hasn't been received in cash as of the balance sheet date.

- ✔ **Inventory:** You stockpile products and hold them for sale and make immediate delivery to customers when sold; this asset account holds the cost of goods not yet sold, but that should be sold in the near term. The balance in your inventory asset account is the cost value of products held for sale. This amount has not been recorded as expense yet.

- ✔ **Prepaid expenses:** You prepay some expenses, such as insurance, property taxes, a store of office and shipping supplies, and so on. This asset account holds the cost of these prepaid costs that will not be charged to expense until time passes. You've paid cash for these things, but their cost hasn't yet been recorded to expense.

- ✔ **Property, plant, and equipment (fixed assets):** The balance in this account is the cost of long-term operating resources that your business has bought. Acquiring these assets required major cash outlays, most of which occurred in previous years.

- ✔ **Accumulated depreciation:** This *contra account* is deducted from the original cost of your property, plant, and equipment asset account; the recording of depreciation expense each year increases the balance in this account, thus decreasing the *book value* of your fixed assets. Recording depreciation expense doesn't involve a cash outlay. The cash outlay was made when the fixed assets were bought.

✔ **Accounts payable:** You purchase products for inventory and buy many things on credit, which means that their costs aren't paid immediately. This liability account holds the total cost of these credit purchases until the amounts are paid. No cash has been paid out yet for these purchases. Of course, that's why they're a liability at the end of the year.

✔ **Accrued expenses payable:** Before being paid, certain expenses are recorded based on calculations and estimates of costs as they accrue, or accumulate, during the period. Examples include accrued vacation pay, property taxes to be paid later, and accrued interest on notes payable. This liability account holds the costs of the expenses until they're paid. Like accounts payable, no cash has been paid out yet for these liabilities.

✔ **Notes payable:** The amount of money borrowed from your banks is reported in this liability account. Actually, the total amount borrowed is divided into the current (short-term) portion, and the remainder is put in the long-term category (see Figure 3-3). Debt is a major source of money for most businesses.

✔ **Owners' equity — invested capital:** The amount of money invested in the business by its owners is recorded in this account. The exact title of the account depends on how the business entity is organized legally. For example, a business corporation issues capital stock shares to its owners, so the account is called *capital stock*. Owners' equity is a major source of money to a business.

✔ **Owners' equity — retained earnings:** The amount of annual profit earned by a business is recorded in this account to recognize the increase in owners' equity and to separate this source of owners' equity from money invested in the business by the owners. The balance in this account equals the cumulative total of annual profits over the years, minus any annual losses that occurred, and minus distributions to owners from profit.

Book III

Managing Your Finances

Doing a quick calculation of cash flow from profit

In the sample business's two-year balance sheet (see Figure 3-3), note that its short-term and long-term notes payable increased $200,000 during the year, which provided $200,000 cash to the business. Also, note that Owners' equity — invested capital increased $25,000; the owners put $25,000 additional money in the business during the year.

So, the business raised $225,000 from debt and equity sources during the year. It spent $121,850 on capital expenditures (see Figure 3-3) for purchases of fixed assets. The net increase in cash from securing $250,000 from debt and equity sources less the $121,850 capital expenditures is, therefore, $103,150:

> ($225,000 from debt and equity – $121,850 capital expenditures = $103,150 cash increase)

The business's balance sheet reports that its cash balance increased $236,291 (see Figure 3-3). So, there's another $133,141 of cash increase to explain:

> ($236,291 increase in cash balance during year – $103,150 net cash increase explained by debt and equity sources minus capital expenditures = $133,141 to be explained)

There's only one other source of cash — *profit*. Therefore, the cash flow from profit for the year is a positive $133,141. After you account for increases in cash from debt and equity sources during the year and deduct the amount spent on capital expenditures, the remaining amount of the cash increase during the year must be attributable to cash flow from profit.

Classifying cash flows in the statement of cash flows

In the statement of cash flows, a business's flows of money during the year are classified into three types: *operating* activities, *investing* activities, and *financing* activities. Note the *changes* column in the balance sheet (see Figure 3-3). Each change is put into one of the three categories — except the increase in cash itself. One purpose of the statement of cash flows is to explain the reasons for the increase (or decrease) of cash during the year. The broader purpose is to present an overview of the business's cash flows, which are separated into three classes of activities.

The term *operating activities* refers to making sales and incurring expenses, or in other words, the transactions a business engages in to make profit. The term *investing activities* refers to making expenditures for the long-term operating assets (long-lived tangible and intangible resources). Investments in new long-term operating assets are also called *capital expenditures,* to emphasize the investment of capital in these assets for relatively long periods. This category includes proceeds from the disposal of previously owned fixed assets. In the example, the business didn't dispose of any fixed assets during the year.

The term *financing activities* refers to borrowing and repaying money from debt sources of capital. Financing activities also includes raising capital from equity sources of capital and distributions from profit to them, as well as the return of capital to them. In the example, the business increases its short-term and long-term debt during the year, which are positive cash flows. Also, its owners invested additional equity capital in the business during the year. The business didn't make any distributions from profit to its owners during the year (though it probably could have).

Presenting the statement of cash flows

The Financial Accounting Standards Board (FASB) is the authoritative body that makes pronouncements on *generally accepted accounting principles* (GAAP) in the United States. For many years, the accounting profession had been criticized for not requiring disclosure of cash flows in business financial reports. Finally, in 1975, the FASB issued an edict regarding how to report cash flow information. It decided on a basic format for the statement of cash flows. Accordingly, the 2015 statement of cash flows for the business example is presented in Figure 3-4.

The first section in the statement of cash flows begins with the business's $95,651 net income for the year — see Figure 3-4. Following net income, positive and negative adjustments are made to net income to determine the $133,141 cash flow from operating activities. (Note the use of the term *cash flow from profit* instead of the official phraseology *cash flow from operating activities,* which doesn't emphasize what is being emphasized here.) For example, the increase in accounts receivable during the year is a negative adjustment to net income. The depreciation expense amount is a positive adjustment to net income.

The first section of the statement of cash flows has proven difficult for non-accountants to understand. Frankly, this part of the statement seems designed for other accountants rather than for business managers and other users of financial reports. As the younger generation would say, the section sucks.

As shown in Figure 3-2, including cash flow differences from sales revenue and expenses in the regular P&L report seems a more user-friendly way to present cash flow information to business managers (and probably to investors and creditors as well). Most accountants probably would not agree. In any case, you should feel free to instruct your accountant to report information on cash flow from profit to you in the most understandable way and not to be constrained in the GAAP straitjacket. Remind your accountant that GAAP were developed for *external* financial reporting, and that these rules don't govern the reporting of financial information inside a business.

Your Company Name
Statement of Cash Flows
For Year Ending December 31, 2015

Cash Flow From Operating Activities

Net income from income statement		$95,651	
Accounts receivable increase	($12,550)		
Inventory increase	($32,105)		
Prepaid expenses decrease	$3,995		
Depreciation	$88,950		
Accounts payable decrease	($25,020)		
Accrued expenses payable increase	$14,220	$37,490	$133,141

Cash Flow From Investing Activities

Expenditures for property, plant and equipment	($121,850)

Figure 3-4:
Presenting the statement of cash flows for business example.

Cash Flow From Financing Activities

Increase in short-term debt	$100,000	
Increase in long-term debt	$100,000	
Additional capital invested by owners	$25,000	$225,000
Increase in cash during year		$236,291
Cash balance at start of year		$347,779
Cash balance at end of year		$584,070

© John Wiley & Sons, Inc.

Small business owners/mangers should find easier going in reading the investing and financing sections of the statement of cash flows — in most cases. Please read these two sections in Figure 3-4. It's a good bet that you understand the information in these two parts of the statement for this business example. However, reading the investing and financial sections for many businesses (especially large companies) can be a real challenge.

WARNING!

Financing activities can be quite complicated (stock options, financial derivatives, and so on). A business can have many purchases, construction projects, and disposals of fixed assets in the year. Summarizing all these investing activities in the statement of cash flows can be a bit much. A business may have extraordinary (nonrecurring) losses and gains during the year that add further detail to the statement. The upshot is that the statement of cash flows often is crowded with many details, which works against the readability of the financial statement of course. Many public companies report 40 to 50 lines of information in their statement of cash flows, if you can believe it.

Summing Up the Critical Importance of Cash Flow from Profit

The financial sustainability of a business depends foremost on its capability to generate a steady stream of cash flow from profit. Without a doubt, you should have a good grip on the factors that drive cash flow from profit. Profit is the mainstream of cash for every business. You should be very clear on the factors that control cash flow from profit. Financial and investment analysts pay a great deal of attention to cash flow from profit, for good reason.

Generally, the big three factors governing cash flow from profit are changes in accounts receivable and inventory and depreciation. Changes in accounts payable and other short-term operating liabilities are important factors in some situations — but first look to the big three factors.

Suppose you forecast minor changes in your accounts receivable and inventory for the coming year. In that case, you can simply add depreciation to profit for the coming year, which gives a good estimate of cash flow. On the other hand, when your business is growing or if your business is in a cyclical industry, you should forecast changes in your accounts receivable and inventory for the coming year. These changes will have a definite impact on cash flow from profit for the year.

Projecting cash flow from profit for the coming year is the critical first step in developing your master financial plan for the coming year. You start with how much internal cash you'll generate during the coming year from making profit, and then you build your overall financial plan based on this foundation. A successful business plan includes a carefully thought-out forecast of cash flow from profit. Budgeting cash flow from profit is a big plus in securing loans from banks and raising equity capital. In fact, if you don't include a convincing projection of cash flow from profit, it will appear that you don't know what you're doing.

Book III

Managing Your Finances

Liquidity and Business Solvency

To truly understand whether a business is solvent, the concept of liquidity must be addressed. *Solvency* is best defined from a balance sheet perspective in terms of evaluating a company's assets and liabilities. If assets are greater than liabilities, then a business would appear to be *solvent*. If assets are less than liabilities, then a business would appear to be *insolvent* (not enough assets are available to satisfy all liabilities). This rather simplistic definition represents a sound basis on which to evaluate a company's solvency — but you must look past just the balance sheet to gain a complete understanding of whether a business is *really* solvent.

Business solvency is best described by evaluating a business's financial position at a point in time. To illustrate the concept of liquidity versus solvency, Figure 3-5 summarizes the financial results of XYZ Wholesale, Inc., for three years. By applying business solvency measurement tools (see the section "Business Solvency Measurement Tools," later in this chapter), you may conclude that XYZ, Wholesale, Inc., is basically insolvent as of 12/31/13. The company's current ratio is less than one to one and stands at .68 to 1; only $118,000 of cash is available; the company realized a loss of $1,066,000 during the year; and only $335,000 of equity remains compared to total liabilities of $3,747,000. All are relatively poor signs (no doubt) to an external party attempting to understand the financial performance of the company and evaluate whether XYZ Wholesale, Inc., has a chance to survive.

But this type of situation is where business solvency measurements stop and business liquidity measurements start. Business liquidity looks at not only the current financial position of a company (which looks bleak for XYZ

XYZ WHOLESALE, INC.
UNAUDITED FINANCIAL STATEMENTS — COMPARISON

Summary Balance Sheet	Year End 12/31/11	Year End 12/31/12	Year End 12/31/13
Current Assets:			
Cash & Equivalents	$94,929	$123,214	$117,632
Trade Receivables, Net	$1,272,083	$1,743,750	$1,271,875
Inventory	$1,383,391	$1,916,381	$867,188
Total Current Assets	$2,750,403	$3,783,345	$2,256,695
Fixed & Other Assets:			
Property, Plant, & Equipment, Net	$1,250,000	$1,500,000	$1,750,000
Other Assets	$75,000	$75,000	$75,000
Total Fixed & Other Assets	$1,325,000	$1,575,000	$1,825,000
Total Assets	$4,075,403	$5,358,345	$4,081,695
Current Liabilities:			
Trade Payables	$1,037,543	$2,682,934	$2,601,563
Accrued Liabilities	$51,877	$134,147	$195,117
Line of Credit Borrowings	$0	$100,000	$200,000
Current Portion of Long-Term Liabilities	$300,000	$300,000	$300,000
Total Current Liabilities	$1,389,420	$3,217,080	$3,296,680
Long-Term Liabilities:			
Notes Payable, Less Current Portion	$900,000	$600,000	$300,000
Other Long-Term Liabilities	$125,000	$140,000	$150,000
Total Long-Term Liabilities	$1,025,000	$740,000	$450,000
Total Liabilities	$2,414,420	$3,957,080	$3,746,680
Equity:			
Common and Preferred Equity, $1 Per Share	$500,000	$500,000	$500,000
Retained Earnings	$750,000	$1,160,983	$901,265
Current Earnings	$410,983	($259,718)	($1,066,250)
Total Equity	$1,660,983	$1,401,265	$335,015
Total Liabilities & Equity	$4,075,403	$5,358,345	$4,081,694

Figure 3-5:
Liquidity versus solvency.

Summary Income Statement	Year End 12/31/11	Year End 12/31/12	Year End 12/31/13
Revenue	$15,265,000	$16,740,000	$13,875,000
Costs of Goods Sold	$11,067,125	$13,140,900	$10,406,250
Gross Profit	$4,197,875	$3,599,100	$3,468,750
Gross Margin	27.50%	21.50%	25.00%
Selling, General, & Administrative Expenses	$3,001,000	$3,525,000	$3,060,000
Depreciation Expense	$250,000	$300,000	$350,000
Interest Expense	$72,000	$68,000	$75,000
Other (Income) Expenses	$212,000	$125,000	$1,050,000
Net Profit Before Tax	$662,875	($418,900)	($1,066,250)
Income Tax Expense (Benefit)	$251,893	($159,182)	$0
Net Profit (Loss)	$410,983	($259,718)	($1,066,250)

Summary Cash Flow Statement	Year End 12/31/11	Year End 12/31/12	Year End 12/31/13
Operating Cash Flow:			
Net Income (Loss)	$410,983	($259,718)	($1,066,250)
Depreciation Expense	$250,000	$300,000	$350,000
Net Operating Cash Flow	$660,983	$40,282	($716,250)
Working Capital:			
(Increase) Decrease in Trade Receivables	($250,000)	($471,667)	$471,875
(Increase) Decrease in Inventory	($150,000)	($532,991)	$1,049,194
Increase (Decrease) in Trade Payables	$350,000	$1,645,391	($81,371)
Increase (Decrease) in Accrued Liabilities	$25,000	$82,270	$60,971
Increase (Decrease) in Current Debt	$0	$100,000	$100,000
Net Working Capital Cash Flow	($25,000)	$823,003	$1,600,668
Financing Capital:			
Equity Contributions	$0	$0	$0
Additions to Long-Term Debt	$0	$0	$0
Deletions to Long-Term Debt	($300,000)	($300,000)	($300,000)
Fixed Asset Additions	($500,000)	($550,000)	($600,000)
Change to Other Long-Term Assets	$0	$0	$0
Change to Other Long-Term Liabilities	$0	$15,000	$10,000
Net Financial Capital Cash Flow	($800,000)	($835,000)	($890,000)
Beginning Cash	$258,946	$94,929	$123,214
Ending Cash	$94,929	$123,214	$117,632

Book III

Managing Your Finances

Figure 3-5: *Continued.*

© John Wiley & Sons, Inc.

Wholesale, Inc.) but captures financial information and data that isn't clearly presented in the basic financial statements. *Liquidity* is best defined by evaluating the total resources available to a company in relation to meeting its total obligations. A company may appear to be insolvent, but if resources are available to meet its obligations, then the business has enough liquidity to support its continued operations.

For XYZ Wholesale, Inc., the following additional company information needs to be evaluated to determine whether enough liquidity is available to survive:

- ✔ XYZ Wholesale, Inc., has structured a loan agreement that allows the company to borrow up to 80 percent of eligible trade receivables and 50 percent of inventory. As of 12/31/13, the company can borrow a total of roughly $1.4 million (80 percent of $1,272,000 of receivables plus 50 percent of $867,000 of inventory) compared to an outstanding balance of just $200,000 (the current balance outstanding on the line of credit borrowings). After subtracting the current amount of $200,000 borrowed from the total amount available to borrow of $1,400,000, an additional $1,200,000 of borrowing capacity remains to support the company's operations.

- ✔ XYZ Wholesale, Inc., has successfully secured extended payment terms with its vendors and suppliers. The primary shareholder of the company has provided a personal guarantee to key vendors and suppliers, which has allowed the company to move its payment terms for net 30 days to net 90 days. The personal guarantee was accepted by the vendors and suppliers due to the shareholder's high personal net worth. These terms can be extended to 120 days.

- ✔ XYZ Wholesale, Inc.'s financial performance for 2012 was negatively impacted by the company's decision to expand its product offerings into a high volume, low price/profitability product line. Although sales increased (but below management's expectations), gross margins suffered significantly because too much of the product was purchased and thus sold at discounted prices (to move the inventory). In addition, the company increased its sales, general, and administrative expenses too much in anticipation of supporting the higher sales volumes that did not materialize. By 2013, the company's "sins" finally were addressed by management as the product line was discontinued. This decision drove sales lower but allowed gross margin to recover from 21 percent to 25 percent (as well as reducing sales, general, and administrative expenses). However, the company had to take a one-time write-down of $1 million (reflected in other expenses) related to obsolete inventory with the product line that could not be sold. By cleaning house and refocusing the company's efforts in 2013, XYZ Wholesale, Inc., had to sacrifice its current financial statements to position the company for future growth.

Although the company's struggles over the last two years have negatively impacted its current business solvency, XYZ Wholesale, Inc., has secured additional capital to ensure that it has enough liquidity to survive and prosper in the coming years. Also, note that no income tax expense or benefit is present in 2013 because the company used up its income tax benefit from losses in 2012 by "carrying" them back to 2011 and receiving a refund for prior taxes paid. The company used up all of its income tax carry-back benefits in 2012, so nothing is left to be realized in 2013 (the bad news). The good news is that if the company can generate future profits, it will be able to carry forward roughly $1 million of losses to offset the future profits and reduce income tax liabilities.

You need to understand both business solvency and liquidity measurement concepts when managing your business. Solvency measurements, by themselves, don't often tell a company's entire story and whether it has the capability to survive. In Figures 3-5 through 3-7, the company appears to be insolvent. But upon review of the company's operations, it was determined that the company has additional liquidity to operate the business and has implemented operational changes to support its return to profitability. Conversely, the example could just as easily been a company that is highly profitable with strong solvency measurements but, as a result of poor planning, has run out of cash (with no borrowing facilities structured to support continued growth) and has pushed its vendors and suppliers to the limit. Due to the lack of understanding of liquidity and poor planning, this company may even be at greater risk of failing (as the vendors and suppliers may cut off the flow of products to sell, thus causing a chain reaction of events that ultimately cause the company to implode).

Business Solvency Measurements Tools

Business solvency measurements tend to evaluate data as of a point in time, such as the fiscal year end. This data is then subjected to numerous analyses to evaluate how well a company is performing, as well as how strong financially it is (including measuring the businesses solvency). Figure 3-6 presents basic business solvency measurement tools that all business executives should clearly understand.

Needless to say, this list of business solvency measurements is by no means complete, as Wall Street would attest. However, the following measurements represent the basics in understanding business solvency:

- **Net working capital:** Total current assets less total current liabilities equals the *net working capital* of a business. Generally speaking, a positive figure should be present for most businesses.

- **Current ratio:** Total current assets divided by total current liabilities equals a company's *current ratio*. A ratio of greater than one to one should be present.

XYZ WHOLESALE, INC.
BUSINESS SOLVENCY RATIO ANALYSIS

Ratio	Year End 12/31/11	Year End 12/31/12	Year End 12/31/13
Net Working Capital:			
Total Current Assets	$2,750,403	$3,783,345	$2,256,695
Total Current Liabilities	$1,389,420	$3,217,080	$3,296,680
Net Working Capital	$1,360,983	$566,265	($1,039,985)
Current Ratio:			
Total Current Assets	$2,750,403	$3,783,345	$2,256,695
Total Current Liabilities	$1,389,420	$3,217,080	$3,296,680
Current Ratio	1.98	1.18	0.68
Quick or Acid Test Ratio:			
Total Current Assets	$2,750,403	$3,783,345	$2,256,695
Less: Inventory & Other Current Assets	$1,383,391	$1,916,381	$867,188
Net Current Assets	$1,367,012	$1,866,964	$1,389,507
Current Liabilities	$1,389,420	$3,217,080	$3,296,680
Quick or Acid Test Ratio	0.98	0.58	0.42
Debt to Equity Ratio:			
Total Liabilities	$2,414,420	$3,957,080	$3,746,680
Total Equity	$1,660,983	$1,401,265	$335,015
Debt to Equity Ratio	1.45	2.82	11.18
Days Sales O/S in Trade Receivables:			
Total Trade Receivables	$1,272,083	$1,743,750	$1,271,875
Average Monthly Sales	$1,272,083	$1,395,000	$1,156,250
Days Sales O/S in Trade Receivables	30	37.5	33
Days Costs of Goods Sold O/S in Inventory:			
Total Inventory	$1,383,391	$1,916,381	$867,188
Average Monthly Costs of Sales	$922,260	$1,095,075	$867,188
Days Costs of Goods Sold O/S in Inventory	45	52.5	30
Debt Service Coverage Ratio:			
Net Income (Loss)	$410,983	($259,718)	($1,066,250)
Interest Expense	$72,000	$68,000	$75,000
Depreciation Expense	$250,000	$300,000	$350,000
Adjusted Debt Service Cash Flow	$732,983	$108,282	($641,250)
Interest Expense	$72,000	$68,000	$75,000
Note Payable Principal Payments Due, 1 Yr.	$300,000	$300,000	$300,000
Current Balance of Line of Credit, Due in 1 Yr.	$0	$100,000	$200,000
Total Debt Service Payments, 1 Yr.	$372,000	$468,000	$575,000
Debt Service Coverage Ratio	1.97	0.23	–1.12

© John Wiley & Sons, Inc.

Figure 3-6:
Basic business solvency measurement tools.

✔ **Quick or acid-test ratio:** Total current assets is reduced by inventory and other current assets (such as prepaid expenses, deposits, and so on) and then divided by total current liabilities to produce the *quick or acid-test ratio*. The higher the ratio, the better, but having a ratio of less than one to one is often common, especially for companies with significant levels of inventory.

✔ **Debt-to-equity ratio:** Total debt (current and long term) divided by the total equity of the company equals the *debt-to-equity ratio*. Higher ratios indicate that the company has more financial leverage (see the last section of this chapter), which translates into more risk being present.

✔ **Days sales outstanding in trade accounts receivable:** Trade receivables divided by average monthly sales multiplied by 30 days produces the *days sale outstanding in trade accounts receivable* figure. Lower numbers with this calculation are usually positive because it indicates a company is doing a good job of managing this asset and not consuming excess capital.

Be careful when using average monthly sales, because companies that are growing rapidly or that have significant seasonal sales want to use an average monthly sales figure that is more representative of recent business activity.

✔ **Days costs of goods sold outstanding in inventory:** Inventory divided by average monthly costs of goods sold multiplied by 30 days produces the *days costs of goods sold outstanding in inventory* figure. Lower numbers with this calculation are usually positive because it indicates a company is doing a good job of managing this asset and not consuming excess capital.

As with *days sale outstanding in trade accounts receivable,* be careful when using average monthly costs of goods sold, because companies that are growing rapidly or that have significant seasonal sales want to use an average monthly costs of sales figure that is more representative of recent business activity.

✔ **Debt service coverage ratio:** Interest and depreciation expense are added back to the net income (or loss) of a company, which is then divided by the current *debt service* (defined as interest expense plus the current portion of long-term debt plus any outstanding balance with a current line of credit facility termed out over a reasonable period) to produce the *debt service coverage ratio*. A ratio of greater than one to one is desired and indicates that a company generates enough free cash flow to cover its debt service.

Book III

Managing Your Finances

Liquidity Measurements Tools

Business liquidity measurements are meant to evaluate a business's total liquidity by using both data as presented at a point in time, as well as resources available to a business (but not necessarily presented in the basic financial statements) either today or in the future. Following are liquidity measurement tools (see Figure 3-7):

✔ **Available current working capital:** Takes the current net working capital of the company and adds available capital that can be accessed during the next 12 months. This figure then needs to be adjusted to account for any other factors, such as extended vendor terms that impact the company's liquidity.

XYZ WHOLESALE, INC.
BUSINESS LIQUIDITY RATIO ANALYSIS

Ratio	Year End 12/31/11	Year End 12/31/12	Year End 12/31/13
Available Current Liquidity:			
Net Working Capital	$1,360,983	$566,265	($1,039,985)
Available Borrowing Capacity	$1,709,362	$1,753,191	$1,251,094
Extended Vendor Terms Benefit	$0	$0	$1,500,000
Available Current Liquidity	$3,070,345	$2,319,455	$1,711,109
Cash Burn Rate:			
Net Income (Loss)	$410,983	($259,718)	($1,066,250)
Depreciation Expense	$250,000	$300,000	$350,000
Monthly Cash Burn Rate	$55,082	$3,357	($59,688)
Liquidity Availability Analysis:			
Trade Receivables	$1,272,083	$1,743,750	$1,271,875
Borrowing Rate	80%	80%	80%
Available Liquidity	$1,017,667	$1,395,000	$1,017,500
Inventory, Net of Obsolete Items	$1,383,391	$916,381	$867,188
Borrowing Rate	50%	50%	50%
Available Liquidity	$691,695	$458,191	$433,594
Total Available Liquidity	$1,709,362	$1,853,191	$1,451,094
Current Borrowings — Line of Credit	$0	$100,000	$200,000
Net Available Liquidity	$1,709,362	$1,753,191	$1,251,094
Fixed Assets, @ Cost	$2,000,000	$2,550,000	$3,150,000
Maximum Loan Value Available	60%	40%	30%
Total Available Potential Liquidity	$1,200,000	$1,020,000	$945,000
Current Borrowings — Note Payable	$1,200,000	$900,000	$600,000
Potential Net Available Liquidity	$0	$120,000	$345,000
Total Potential & Actual Available Liquidity	$2,909,362	$2,873,191	$2,396,094
Total Borrowings, All Types	$1,200,000	$1,000,000	$800,000
Net Potential & Actual Available Liquidity	$1,709,362	$1,873,191	$1,596,094
Current Borrowing Utilization Rate	41%	35%	33%
Available Borrowing Capacity Rate	59%	65%	67%

© John Wiley & Sons, Inc.

Figure 3-7:
Liquidity
measure-
ment tools.

✔ In Figure 3-7, two points should be noted. First, in 2012, the available borrowing capacity was reduced to account for $1 million of obsolete inventory. In this example, the bank became concerned about the value of this inventory and decided to eliminate it from the company's capability to borrow. Second, in 2013, $1.5 million was added back to account for the fact that the company was able to secure extended payment terms from vendors for the coming year. In effect, the company has secured a "permanent" source of capital for the year from the vendors providing extended terms (and thus providing more capital to operate the business).

✔ **Cash burn rate:** Calculates the average *negative cash flow* (defined as net income or loss plus depreciation expense) the company is experiencing on a periodic basis (usually monthly). Burn rates represent key data points for investors attempting to understand how long a company will take until it becomes cash flow positive. This figure then drives how much capital is needed to support the company during the negative cash burn periods. For XYZ Wholesale, Inc., the company's cash burn rate was approximately $60,000 a month in 2013. The equation to calculate this would be to take the annual net loss of the company, add back depreciation expense, and then divide it by 12 to calculate the monthly burn rate.

> ✔ **Liquidity availability analysis:** The concept with this analysis is to calculate the potential available liquidity that can be tapped from company assets and compare it to the total current outstanding debt (secured with the assets). The idea is to evaluate whether any "untapped" sources of capital are available on the balance sheet. In Figure 3-7, roughly $1.5 million of potential and actual liquidity is available (even though the solvency measurements paint a much more difficult situation).

The three liquidity measurement tools provided represent just a small sample of the entire list of potential liquidity measurements tools available. Unlike the business solvency measurements noted in the preceding section, liquidity measurements tend to be customized for specific company and industry issues in order to properly manage and understand liquidity at any point in time. The key concept, however, remains the same because you must always have a clear understanding of what capital and liquidity is available to your company (at any time) in order to properly manage your business interests.

Liquidity Traps

Sometimes businesses get into trouble and unintentionally find themselves in liquidity traps. *Liquidity traps* come in a variety of shapes, sizes, and forms and, to a certain extent, result from business or industry-specific factors. However, when the liquidity traps are viewed from a generalized perspective, the primary sources (of liquidity traps) are centered in one of three areas, described in the following sections.

The volume and complexity of liquidity traps are extensive and vary from business to business. You'd be amazed at how many liquidity traps there are and how quickly they can consume your business. One day everything is fine, and then 180 days later, the markets turned, new product releases have been delayed, sales have softened, and the banks are all over you. It's probably not a matter of *if* you will have to manage a liquidity trap but rather *when,* so the better prepared you are in dealing with liquidity traps (and understanding their primary causes), the better you'll be at managing the problem.

Having access to capital (whether debt or equity) represents one of the most important elements of executing a business plan. This point especially holds true when a business is turning the corner and is ready to grow rapidly, because that's when the demand for capital will be the greatest. Not managing liquidity traps or positioning a business to pursue new market opportunities often leads to one of the largest losses a company will ever realize (but never see): lost market opportunity!

Asset investment

As everyone knows, a company needs assets so that it can execute its business plan and generate revenue. Some assets are highly liquid and represent attractive vehicles on which to secure financing (think trade accounts receivables that a bank may use as collateral to extend a loan, new equipment that a leasing company may use as collateral to provide a long-term lease, and so on).

Other assets, though, such as certain inventory, prepaid expenses, intangible assets, and the like, aren't nearly as attractive to a lender, because the lender can't liquidate the asset (and repay the loan) if the company can't survive. The more liquidation value the asset has, the more likely lenders will provide financing.

The following list of asset investment liquidity traps are examples of when "Good Assets Go Bad":

- **Trade receivables:** Trade receivables, in general, are usually very liquid assets that can be utilized to secure financing. Certain trade receivables, however, aren't as attractive to financing sources. For example, trade receivables that are 90 days past due will often be excluded by a lender from being able to borrow against because the age of the receivable "indicates" that the business is having trouble paying its bills. Although this situation may or may not be the case, the lender usually assumes the worst and excludes the trade receivable from being able to borrow against.

  In addition to old trade account receivables, other receivables can create problems, including receivables generated from foreign customers, governmental entities, and related parties/entities. Also (and as strange as it may sound), receivable concentration issues may produce problems; if too much of your company's trade receivables are centered in too few accounts, again the lender will get nervous (as its logic is now that if one big customer tanks, the entire company may go down).

   Make sure that you have a complete understanding of what comprises your trade accounts receivable balance so you have a clear understanding of what is available to borrow against at any point in time. Although the balance sheet may state that your company has $1,000,000 (which the company can borrow 80 percent of, or $800,000), you may find that $400,000 of the receivables are "ineligible" — the receivables can't be borrowed against — which leaves only $600,000 of good receivables to borrow against (meaning only $480,000 of financing is available).

✔ **Inventory:** Similar to trade accounts receivables, inventory can often represent the basis of a sound asset on which to secure financing; if you already have a readily available market for a company's product, you should have no problem liquidating the products in case the worst should happen, right? No. Financing sources tend to be very nervous and skittish with lending against inventory because if the worst should happen, all kinds of problems are produced by taking possession of the inventory and then attempting to sell or liquidate it. Financing sources aren't prepared to handle this function. When all potential liquidation factors are considered with inventory, including identifying and disposing of obsolete items, paying a liquidator to sell the inventory, watching the market hammer the value of the inventory as it becomes available (for example, the going-out-of-business sale), the lender will be lucky to receive 40 to 50 percent on the dollar. Hence, lenders tend to shy away from extending loans against inventory, and when they do, lending rates are usually well below 50 percent.

Excessive inventory levels can create problems on numerous fronts. First, for every dollar of inventory increase, a lending source may only provide 40 percent of the cash necessary to support the added investment (leaving 60 percent to be supported by internal resources). Second, the risk of inventory obsolescence increases; the slower the inventory moves, the older it becomes, which generally forces the company into taking inventory write-off "hits" on the financial statements. As most business owners know, in today's rapidly changing market, inventory can become obsolete in as little as three months. And third, excessive inventory is expensive to maintain because it must be stored, insured, tracked, protected from theft, and so on. Quite often, inventory maintenance expenses can run up to 10 percent of the inventory's cost on an annual basis.

✔ **Property, equipment, and other fixed assets:** The concept of consuming liquidity in fixed assets is based on the same concept as when you purchase a new car (but even worse). That is, the day you purchase a new car and drive it off the lot, the car loses up to 25 percent of its value. For fixed assets, this concept also applies, but tends to be even more severe. Once new equipment, computers, furniture, fixtures, and so on are purchased, within 90 days, their value is now based on a "used" status (and you will be lucky to get 50 percent on the dollar). Compounding this problem is that if you do need to secure financing against the fixed assets (which are now used), the financing will be expensive (meaning higher interest rates) compared to acquiring the fixed assets when new.

The time to obtain financing with fixed assets is at the point of purchase when the asset value is the highest and the most financing sources are available to obtain competitive pricing and terms. Once the equipment becomes used, the market for financing sources becomes much more expensive, with far fewer choices available.

Book III

Managing Your Finances

Inappropriate use of debt

The second major liquidity trap is centered in not keeping your balance sheet in balance. This is when short-term debt, such as a line of credit structured to support trade accounts receivables, is utilized to finance a purchase of a long-term asset. This scenario can create significant problems for a company.

For example, say a company has structured a line of credit financing agreement or loan where it could borrow up to 80 percent of eligible or qualified receivables. The company is growing quickly and had increased its trade accounts receivables to roughly $2 million in total, of which 90 percent were eligible to borrow against. In total, the company borrowed $1.4 million, which was within the financing agreements limit ($2 million of total accounts receivables, of which $200,000 were ineligible to borrow against, leaving a net borrowing base balance of $1.8 million, producing a total borrowing capacity of $1.44 million). Of the $1.4 million, $400,000 was used to purchase fixed assets and $1 million used to support the trade accounts receivables.

Within six months, the company's trade accounts receivables decreased to $1.5 million, while at the same time the ineligible percent increased to 20 percent (as a result of certain trade accounts receivables becoming 90 days past due). The change in accounts receivables reduced the company's capability to borrow to $960,000 ($1.5 million of trade accounts receivables times 80 percent eligible times 80 percent advance rate). Unfortunately, the company used the cash generated from the $500,000 decrease in trade accounts receivables to reduce trade payables and cover operating losses (as well as pay down the loan). The company was able to pay down the loan only by $200,000, leaving an outstanding balance of $1.2 million against a borrowing available of $960,000.

Needless to say, the financing source requested the company "cure" this over-advanced position, which the company couldn't (leading to a very interesting round of discussions and additional financing source restrictions being placed on the company). By not properly financing the fixed asset purchase (which the financing source showed little sympathy in addressing, especially given the losses the company had recently incurred), the company fell into a very common and painful liquidity trap.

The exact opposite can happen as well. For example, say a loan payable, which has a repayment term of three years, is used to support a current asset (such as trade accounts receivables). Though the asset (or trade accounts receivable) may be growing as a result of increased sales, the debt is being reduced over a three-year period. Just when the company needs capital to finance growth, capital is flowing out of the organization to repay debt.

It's imperative that a proper balance of capital to asset type be maintained to better manage the balance sheet. The following three simple rules can help you match capital or financing sources with asset investments:

✔ **Finance current assets with current debt.** Current assets, such as trade accounts receivables or inventory, should be financed with current debt, such as trade vendors or suppliers and a properly structured lending facility.

✔ **Finance long-term assets with long-term debt.** Fixed assets, such as equipment, furniture, computers, technology, and so on, should be financed with longer-term debt, such as term notes payables (a five-year repayment period), operating or capital leases, and so. The general concept here is that a fixed asset will produce earnings or cash flow over a period of greater than one year, and as such, the cash flow stream should be matched with the financing stream.

✔ **Debt-financing sources provide capital for tangible assets and don't like to finance losses or "soft" assets.** Other asset types (including intangibles such as patents or trademarks, certain investments, and prepaid expenses) and company net losses need to be supported from equity capital sources, including the internal earnings of the company.

Excessive growth rates

The most common, but least understood liquidity trap is when your business experiences excessive growth rates. That sounds like a nice problem to have, but a rapidly growing business requires significant amounts of capital to support ongoing operations. As revenue (and hopefully profitability) levels grow, so do assets and the need to finance the assets.

The problems rapidly growing companies run into is that they get caught up in the fact that new market opportunities seem almost endless and, as such, the company "invests" earnings from profitable operations into the expansion of new operations (which tend to lose money during the startup phase). This strategy, if properly managed, can be very effective as long as management keeps a keen eye on the distribution of earnings between supporting new operations versus strengthening the balance sheet. Although no set rule dictates how much of your earnings should be used to reinvest in new operations versus strengthening the balance sheet, the real key lies in the capability to keep your debt-to-equity ratio manageable so that if the company does hit a speed bump, resources are available through the difficult times.

Book III

Managing Your Finances

Pushing your company to the limit by leveraging every asset with debt financing and reinvesting internal earnings in new operations is a recipe for failure. Businesses must constantly manage the growth-versus-available-capital tradeoff issue to ensure that their interests aren't exposed to unnecessary risks that quite often carry extremely expensive outcomes.

Untapped Sources of Liquidity

If you've run out of cash and can't borrow any more, it's up to the executive management team to identify sources of capital to work through the troubled times. Fortunately, potential capital sources are available, described in the following sections, which can assist your business in times of need.

Asset liquidations

Liquidating assets is often targeted by management as a quick and easy method to raise capital. This philosophy would appear to make sense if a company has unneeded or underutilized assets; selling them may help ease a cash crunch.

Although liquidating assets does represent a viable alternative, be careful of the following pitfalls with this strategy:

✔ **Values received:** If you plan on moving older, slow-moving inventory in bulk or selling old, unused equipment, be prepared to sell the assets at well below cost. Although the cash received is great, remember that you'll have to explain the losses to investors, lending sources, and the like.

✔ **Collateral support:** Certain assets represent collateral for loans extended to the company. If you liquidate the assets, not only may you be violating your loan agreement, you may also be reducing your capability to borrow (because as the asset base is reduced, so is your borrowing capacity).

✔ **Future growth:** Liquidating assets that are unnecessary in the short term but that you'll eventually need can be very expensive.

✔ **Management time:** Liquidating assets often takes much more time and effort than anticipated, which means that the parties responsible for this function are distracted from their regular duties.

Lending sources

Your company's primary lending sources, such as banks, asset-based lenders, leasing companies, and the like, represent a potential source of quick capital if needed. The key in approaching these sources is to have solid information available for review and a clear action plan on how the capital will be repaid in a reasonable time frame. There is no question that these groups want to see your business survive, so being able to leverage the relationship can provide some added liquidity.

The following three examples demonstrate how you can squeeze capital from these sources:

- ✔ **Loan advance rates:** Lenders provide borrowing capacity based on the value of the asset they're secured by. For example, a bank may advance 80 percent on eligible trade account receivables. During a particular tight period, such as during increased seasonal demand, you may be able to get the lender to advance 85 to 90 percent of the eligible receivables so that you can free up capital.

  If your bank doesn't want to work with you, then an asset-based lender may be a better financial partner. Asset-based lenders offer more aggressive loan facilities in exchange for higher rates and tighter reporting to compensate for the higher risk present. Asset-based lenders understand the importance of having access to capital in relation to businesses operating in challenging times.

- ✔ **Asset sale lease-back:** Although asset sales may represent a source of quick capital to your business, they come with a number of potential problems. You may want to consider executing an *asset sale lease-back* where you sell the asset to a leasing company that in turn immediately leases it back to you. You achieve your goal of freeing up short-term liquidity, and the leasing company doesn't have to worry about finding a new lessee for the asset.

  Similar to working with an asset-based lender, leasing companies that support these types of transactions are more expensive.

- ✔ **Restructure notes payable:** You may want to consider restructuring any long-term notes payable with the lender to lengthen the repayment period (thus reducing the current monthly payment) or move it to an interest-only note for a short period (for example, six months). The goal is to reduce the capital outflow with the note agreement to better match it with the capability for your company to generate internal cash flows to service the debt.

If you find that your company has to work with financing sources that are more expensive than traditional banks and low-risk leasing companies, you can expect to be charged higher interest rates and more fees. Although there are no set rules, on average you can expect to pay at least 3 percent more in overall interest costs (which can quickly reach 5 percent). If the bank is charging you Prime Rate plus 1 percent, you can expect to pay at least Prime Rate plus 4 percent.

If the difference between your business making money and losing money is 3 percent points, then you probably have bigger problems than just a short-term liquidity squeeze. Access to the capital is the key, so paying 3 percent more on the capital should be far cheaper than the alternatives, which include lost business growth opportunities or, worse yet, a failed business.

Unsecured creditors

You can tap your vendors, suppliers, and yes, even your customers, from time to time to help manage potential liquidity issues. These parties are already in bed with you and stand to lose the most if your company fails. In addition, they stand to gain quite a bit if your business continues to grow and prosper (which means more business for everyone).

Having customers step up with an advance payment, deposit on a large project, and so on can help ease a liquidity squeeze. Also, you can provide customers with incentives, such as a 1 percent discount if paid within ten days, to pay more quickly. If a customer has ample cash resources available and it's earning a measly 4 percent, why not offer an incentive that provides a chance to save three times this much? Of course, this strategy has some pitfalls, but in certain situations, customers can be leveraged to accelerate payment delivery. An example of a pitfall is that certain large customers may still take the discount offered but not pay within the shorter time period. Although you could pursue the larger customer for the discount, you would then risk alienating the customer. Large companies tend to dictate payment terms based on their criteria and not yours.

In addition, vendors and suppliers offer a relatively cheap and easily accessible source of capital to your company. Various strategies are available and range from requesting extended payment terms during a high sales period to *terming out* a portion of the balance due the vendors to be repaid over a longer period — in other words, instead of paying the entire balance in 60 days, see whether you can pay it over 12 months in equal installments with a nominal interest rate attached.

When needed, you can also evaluate your internal employees to determine whether you can secure added liquidity. In tight times, you may choose to defer a portion of your compensation, which will then be paid when the company hits certain milestones. Also, if you have paid commissions on sales when they're booked, you may want to restructure this program to pay commissions when payment for sales are actually received (in cash) to better match cash outflows with cash inflows.

You must remember to be careful when using customers, vendors, and suppliers to provide additional capital resources. It's one thing to push these sources within the normal course of business, but you don't want to appear desperate. You may actually find that payment terms tighten up and customers get nervous (thus delaying orders), which then produces the exact opposite of what you were trying to achieve.

Equity and off-balance sheet sources

A number of external capital sources are also available to provide additional liquidity during a bind:

- ✓ **Owner personal financial strength:** Business owners have been asked (on more than one occasion) to step up and provide additional capital to support their business. If your lenders, vendors, suppliers, customers, and employees are all on board, why not the owners of the business? Business owners with ample personal wealth are often asked to pledge some of it for the benefit of the company.

- ✓ **Family, friends, and close business associates:** This group is a natural source to secure capital for a business, as well as during a liquidity squeeze when they may be able to provide a bridge loan to get the company through a tight period. Although nobody likes to ask family members for money, when your business life depends on it, you may have no other choice.

- ✓ **Off-balance sheet assets:** You may have various assets that relate to the business, but aren't included in the balance sheet or are restricted in nature. For example, the building your company leases may actually be owned by a group of investors (including the owners of the company) with close ties to the company. Over a period of time, the building may have appreciated in value and may be refinanced with the proceeds then loaned to your company from the legal entity that owns the building. Conversely, if the legal entity that owns the building has the resources, the lease payments from your company may be reduced or deferred for a period of time to free up cash.

Business owners have the most to gain if a business succeeds and the most to lose if it fails. Stepping up on the capital front provides for much more than simply helping with a liquidity squeeze. Rather, it displays creditability to other parties that the business owners believe in the business and are willing to stand behind it (in good times and in bad).

See Book II Chapter 2 for more on finding funding for your business.

Book III

Managing Your Finances

Financial Leverage: The Good, the Bad, and the Ugly

Financial leverage is best measured by the business solvency debt-to-equity ratio (see the section "Business Solvency Measurement Tools"). That is, the higher the amount of debt your company has in relation to your equity, the higher the ratio will be that indicates your company is operating with a greater degree of financial risk. As such, financial leverage can be broken down into the Good, the Bad, and the (outright) Ugly:

- **The Good:** If properly managed, financial leverage can enhance your company's profitability and improve earnings per share. This approach allows the company to secure less equity-based capital (since the appropriate amount and type of debt-based capital is secured), providing the business owners with greater ownership control of the entity.

    To achieve the good, you must remember to keep the balance sheet in balance and avoid leveraging your assets too high. Companies always need to remember to keep a war chest available to manage both business problems and opportunities. The challenge is to find the ideal balance between equity and debt capital sources.

- **The Bad:** Financial leverage can often produce a certain amount of business and personal stress during the down times. The creditors of your company tend to be more interested in getting repaid during the down times instead of providing additional capital to support a new growth opportunity. Companies that have strong equity levels and that can afford some missteps along the way will have more leeway in pursuing new markets than companies operating under heavy debt loads. Although you may survive a down period and manage to get your company's debt under control, a stronger competitor may have seized the moment and captured new market opportunities that you didn't have the resources to pursue.

- **The Ugly:** The ugly is when financial leverage is so excessive (or high), that you've tapped out every asset and have nothing left to work with or your debt financing sources push the company into bankruptcy or an involuntary liquidation. Basically, you reach a point of no hope of the company repaying the debt and turning around its operations. The remaining option is to lose control of your company and watch others dismantle it to settle the obligations due.

Chapter 4

Controlling Costs and Budgeting

· ·

In This Chapter

▶ Getting the right perspective on controlling costs using your P&L

▶ Comparing your P&L with your balance sheet

▶ Focusing on profit centers

▶ Becoming familiar with the budgeting process and CART and SWOT

▶ Understanding flash reports

▶ Preparing your first budget and applying advanced techniques

▶ Using the budget as a business management tool

· ·

*W*hat's the first thing that comes to mind when you hear *cost control?* Cutting costs, right? Well, it may come as a surprise, but slashing costs is not the main theme of this chapter. Cost control is just one element in the larger playing field of profit management. The best, or optimal, cost is not always the lowest cost.

A knee-jerk reaction is that costs should be lower. Don't rush to judgment. In some situations, increasing costs may be the best path to increasing profits. It's like coaching sports: You have to play both defense and offense. You can't play on just one side of the game. Making sales is the offense side of business; defense is keeping the costs of making sales and operating the business less than sales revenue.

The planning process includes numerous elements, ranging from obtaining current market information to evaluating personnel resources to preparing budgets or forecasts. The first part of this chapter focuses on one of the most critical elements of the planning process: preparing a budget.

Budgets aren't based on the concept of "How much can I spend this year?" Rather, budgets are more comprehensive in nature and are designed to capture all relevant and critical financial data, including revenue levels, costs of sales, operating expenses, fixed asset expenditures, capital requirements, and the like. All too often, budgets are associated with expense levels and management, which represent just one element of the entire budget.

The budgeting process doesn't represent a chicken and egg riddle. From a financial perspective, the preparation of budgets, forecasts, projections, proformas, and the like represent the end result of the entire planning process. Hence, you must first accumulate the necessary data and information on which to build a forecasting model prior to producing projected financial information (for your company). There is no point in preparing a budget that does not capture your company's true economic structure.

Getting in the Right Frame of Mind

Of course, you shouldn't waste money on excessive or unnecessary costs. If possible, you should definitely save a buck here and there on expenses. There's no argument on this point. Small business owners don't particularly need tutorials on shaving costs. Rather, they need to stand back a little and rethink the nature of costs and realize that costs are pathways to profit. If you had no costs, you'd have no revenue and no profit. You need costs to make profit. You have to spend money to make money.

The crucial test of a cost is whether it contributes to generating revenue. If a cost has no value whatsoever in helping a business bring in revenue, then it's truly money down the rat hole. The key management question about costs is whether the amounts of the costs are in alignment with the amount of revenue the business is generating. A business owner should ask: Are my expenses the appropriate amounts for the revenue of my business?

Getting Down to Business

Controlling costs requires that you evaluate your costs relative to your sales revenue. Suppose your business's salaries and wages expense for the year is $225,000. Is this cost too high? There's no way in the world you can answer this question, except by comparing the cost against your sales revenue for the year. The same goes for all your expenses.

In an ideal world, your customers are willing to pay whatever prices you charge them. You could simply pass along your costs in sales prices and still earn a profit. Your costs would be under control no matter how high your costs might be. Because you earn a profit, your costs are under control and need no further attention.

The real world is very different, of course. But this ideal world teaches a lesson. Your costs are out of control when you can't set sales prices high enough to recover your costs and make a profit.

It's hardly news to you that small businesses face price resistance from their customers. Customers are sensitive to sales prices and changes in sales prices for the products and services sold by small businesses. In setting sales prices, you have to determine the maximum price your customers will accept before turning to lower price alternatives, or not buying at all. If the price resistance point is $125 for a product, you have to figure out how to keep your costs below $125 per unit. In other words, you have to exercise cost control.

Putting cost control in its proper context

Cost control is part of the larger management function of revenue/cost/profit analysis. So, the best place to focus is your P&L report. (Book III Chapter 2 explains the P&L report.) This profit performance statement summarizes your sales revenue based on the sales prices in effect during the year and your expenses for the year based on the amounts recorded for the expenses. (There are some issues regarding the accounting methods for recording certain expenses, discussed in the upcoming section "Selecting a cost of goods sold expense method.")

Suppose your business is a pass-through income tax entity, which means it doesn't pay income tax itself but passes its taxable income through to its shareholders, who then include their shares of the business's annual taxable income in their personal income tax returns for the year.

Figure 4-1 presents the P&L report of a hypothetical business (you can say it's yours) for the year just ended and includes the prior year for comparison (which is standard practice). This P&L report includes the percents of expenses to sales revenue. It also breaks out a *facilities expense* — the cost of the space used by the business — and reports it on a separate line.

Facilities expense includes expenditures for leases, building utilities, real estate taxes, and insurance on your premises. Depreciation isn't included in facilities expense; depreciation is an unusual expense and it's best to leave it in an expense by itself.

In this case, the business moved out of the red zone (loss) in 2014 into the black zone (profit) in 2015. Making a profit, however, doesn't necessarily mean your costs are under control. Dealing with the issue of cost control requires closer management analysis.

Book III

Managing Your Finances

	2014		2015		Change Over 2014	
	% of Sales Revenue		% of Sales Revenue		Amount	%
Sales revenue		$2,286,500		$2,920,562	$634,062	27.7%
Cost of goods sold expense	61.7%	$1,411,605	58.0%	$1,693,926	$282,321	20.0%
Gross margin	38.3%	$874,895	42.0%	$1,226,636	$351,741	40.2%
Operating expenses:						
Salaries, wages, commissions and benefits	27.3%	$624,590	22.7%	$662,400	$37,810	6.1%
Advertising and sales promotion	6.9%	$158,900	6.6%	$192,550	$33,650	21.2%
Depreciation	4.1%	$93,250	3.0%	$88,950	($4,300)	-4.6%
Facilities expense	3.9%	$89,545	3.2%	$94,230	$4,685	5.2%
Other expenses	1.2%	$27,255	1.5%	$42,849	$15,594	57.2%
Total operating expenses	43.5%	$993,540	37.0%	$1,080,979	$87,439	8.8%
Operating profit (loss)	–5.2%	($118,645)	5.0%	$145,657	$264,302	
Interest expense	2.1%	$47,625	1.7%	$50,006	$2,381	5.0%
Net income (loss)	–7.3%	($166,270)	3.3%	$95,651	$261,921	

Your Business Name
P&L Report
For Years Ended December 31

Figure 4-1:
Your P&L
report for
cost control
analysis.

© John Wiley & Sons, Inc.

You can attack cost control on three levels:

- ✔ Your *business as a whole* in its entirety
- ✔ The separate *profit centers* of your business
- ✔ Your specific costs item by item

Figure 4-1 is the P&L for your business as a whole. At this level, you look at the forest and not the trees. It's helpful to divide your business into separate parts called profit centers. Basically, a *profit center* is an identifiable, separate stream of revenue to a business. At this level, you examine clusters or stands of trees that make up different parts of the forest.

For example, Starbucks sells coffee, sure — but also coffee beans, cupware, food, CDs, and other products. Each is a separate profit center. For that matter, each Starbucks store is a separate profit center, so you have profit centers within profit centers. Last, you can drill down to particular, individual costs. At this level, you look at specific trees in the forest.

Beginning with sales revenue change

You increased sales $634,062 in 2015 (refer to Figure 4-1). This is good news for profit, but only if costs don't increase more than sales revenue, of course. For revenue/cost/profit analysis, it's extremely useful to know how much of your sales revenue increase is due to change in volume (total quantity sold) versus changes in sales prices. Unfortunately, measuring sales volume can be a problem.

An auto dealer can keep track of the number of vehicles sold during the year. A movie theater can count the number of tickets sold during the year, and a brewpub can keep track of the number of barrels of beer sold during the year. On the other hand, many small businesses sell a very large number of different products and services. A clothing retailer may sell several thousand different items. A hardware store in Boulder claims to sell more than 100,000 different items.

Exactly how your business should keep track of sales volume depends on how many different products you sell and how practical it is to compile sales volume information in your accounting system. In many situations, a small business can't do more than keep count of its sales transactions — number of sales rung up on cash registers, number of invoices sent to customers, customer traffic count, or something equivalent. If nothing else, you should make a rough count of the number of sales you make during the year.

In the example portrayed in Figure 4-1, you increase sales volume 20 percent in 2015 over the prior year, which is pretty good by any standard. You made much better use of the sales capacity provided by your workforce and facilities in 2015. You increased sales per employee and per square foot in 2015 — see the later sections "Analyzing employee cost" and "Looking at facilities expense." The 20 percent sales volume increase is very important in analyzing your costs in 2015. A key question is whether changes in your costs are consistent with the sales volume increase.

The example portrayed in Figure 4-1 is for a situation in which product costs remain the same in both years. Therefore, cost of goods sold expense increases exactly 20 percent in 2015 because sales volume increases 20 percent over the previous year. (Of course, product costs fluctuate from year to year in most cases.)

Sales revenue, in contrast, increases more than 20 percent because you were able to increase sales prices in 2015. In Figure 4-1, note that sales revenue increases more than the 20 percent sales volume increase. Ask your accountant to calculate the average sales price increase. In the example, your sales prices in 2015 are 7.7 percent higher than the previous year.

You did not increase sales prices exactly 7.7 percent on every product you sold; that situation would be quite unusual. The 7.7 percent sales price increase is an average over all the products you sold. You should know the reasons for and causes of the average sales price increase. The higher average sales price may be due to a shift in your sales mix toward higher priced products. (*Sales mix* refers to the relative proportions that each source of sales contributes to total sales revenue.) Or perhaps your sales mix remained constant and you bumped up prices on most products.

Book III

Managing Your Finances

In any case, what's the bottom line (or maybe top line, for sales revenue)? In 2015, you had $634,062 additional sales revenue to work with compared with the prior year. More than half of the incremental revenue is offset by increases in costs. But $261,921 of the additional revenue ended up in profit. How do you like that? More than 41 percent of your additional revenue goes toward profit (see Figure 4-1 for data):

> $261,921 profit increase ÷ $634,062 additional sales revenue = 41.3% profit from additional revenue

This scenario may seem almost too good to be true. Well, you should analyze what happened to your costs at the higher sales level to fully understand this profit boost. Could the same thing happen next year if you increase sales revenue again? Perhaps, but maybe not.

Focusing on cost of goods sold and gross margin

For businesses that sell products, the first expense deducted from sales revenue is *cost of goods sold.* (You could argue that it should be called cost of products sold, but you don't see this term in P&L statements.) As mentioned in Book III Chapter 2, this expense is deducted from sales revenue to determine *gross margin.* Gross margin is also called *gross profit;* it's profit before any other expense is deducted from sales revenue. Cost of goods sold is a *direct variable* expense, which means it's directly matched against revenue and varies with sales volume.

This expense may appear straightforward, but it's more entangled than you may suspect. It's anything but simple and uncomplicated. In fact, a later section ("Looking into Cost of Goods Sold Expense") in this chapter explains this expense in more detail. For the moment, step around these issues and focus on the basic behavior of the expense. In the example in Figure 4-1, your business's product costs are the same as last year. Of course, in most situations, product costs don't remain constant very long. But it makes for a much cleaner analysis to keep product costs constant at this point in the discussion.

The 20 percent jump in sales volume increases your cost of goods sold expense 20 percent — see Figure 4-1 again. Pay special attention to the change in your gross margin ratio on sales. Book III Chapter 2 explains that your basic sales pricing strategy is to mark up product cost to earn 45 percent gross margin on sales. For example, if a product cost is $55, you aim to sell it for $100 to yield $45 gross margin. However, your gross margin is only

42.0 percent in 2015. You gave several customers discounts from list prices. But you did improve your average gross margin ratio over last year, which brings up a very important point.

How is it that your sales volume increases 20.0 percent and your sales prices increase 7.7 percent in 2015, but your gross margin increases 40.2 percent? The increase in gross margin seems too high relative to the percent increases in sales volume and sales prices, doesn't it? What's going on? Figure 4-2 analyzes how much of the $351,741 gross margin gain is attributable to higher sale prices and how much to the higher sales volume.

Figure 4-2:
Analyzing your gross margin increase.

2014			Change in 2015			
$2,286,500	Sales revenue	×	7.7%	Sales price increase	=	$176,762
$874,895	Gross margin	×	20.0%	Sales volume increase	=	$174,979
				Total increase in gross margin	=	$351,741

© John Wiley & Sons, Inc.

Note that the 7.7 percent increase in sales prices causes more gross margin increase than the 20.0 percent sales volume increase. That's because of the *big base effect;* the smaller sales prices percent increase applies to a relatively large base (about $2.3 million) compared with the volume gain, which is based on a much smaller amount (about $.9 million).

Suppose you want to increase gross margin $100,000 next year. Assume that your 42.0 percent gross margin ratio on sales remains the same. If sales prices remain the same next year, then your sales volume would have to increase 8.15 percent:

> $100,000 gross margin increase goal ÷ $1,226,636 gross margin in 2015 = 8.15% sales volume increase

If your sales volume remains the same next year, then your sales prices on average would have to increase just 3.42 percent:

> $100,000 gross margin increase goal ÷ $2,920,562 sales revenue in 2015 = 3.42% sales price increase

In short, a 1 percent sales price increase has more profit impact than a 1 percent sales volume increase.

Book III

Managing Your Finances

Analyzing employee cost

As the owner of a small business, your job is to judge whether the ratio of each expense to sales revenue is acceptable. Is the expense reasonable in amount? Your salaries, wages, commissions, and benefits expense equals 22.7 percent of sales revenue in 2015 (refer to Figure 4-1). In other words, your employee cost absorbs $22.70 of every $100.00 of sales revenue. This expense ratio is lower than it was last year, which is good, of course. But the fundamental question is whether it should be an even smaller percent of sales. This question strikes at the essence of cost control. It's not an easy question to answer. But, as they say, that's why you earn the big bucks — to answer such questions.

It's tempting to think first of reducing every cost of doing business. It would have been better if your employee cost had been lower — or would it? Could you have gotten by with one less employee? One less employee may have reduced your sales capacity and prevented the increase in sales revenue. In the example, you have ten full-time employees on the payroll both years. Book III Chapter 2 explains that for your line of business, the benchmark is $300,000 annual sales per employee. In 2015, your sales per employee is $292,056 (see Figure 4-1 for sales revenue):

> $2,920,562 annual sales revenue ÷ 10 employees = $292,056 sales revenue per employee

Summing up, your employee cost looks reasonable for 2015, assuming your sales per employee benchmark is correct. This doesn't mean that you couldn't have squeezed some dollars out of this expense during the year. Maybe you could have furloughed employees during the slow time of year. Maybe you could have fired one of your higher-paid employees and replaced him or her with a person willing to work for a lower salary. Maybe you could have cut corners and not have paid overtime rates for some of the hours worked during the busy season. Maybe you could have cut health care and vacation benefits during the year.

Business owners get paid to make tough and sometimes ruthless decisions. This is especially true in the area of cost control. If your sales prices don't support the level of your costs, what are your options? You can try to get more sales out of your costs. In fact, you did just this with employee costs in 2015 compared with 2014. Your sales revenue per employee increased significantly in 2015. But you may be at the end of the line on this course of action. You may have to hire an additional employee or two if you plan to increase sales next year.

Analyzing advertising and sales promotion costs

The total of your advertising and sales promotion costs in 2015 is just under 7 percent of sales revenue, which is about the same it was in 2014. As you probably have observed, many retail businesses depend heavily on advertising. Others don't do more than put a sign on the building and rely on word of mouth. You can advertise and promote sales a thousand different ways (see the chapters in Book V for a lot more on marketing and promotion).

Maybe you give away free calendars. Maybe you put an insertion in the yellow pages. You can place ads in local newspapers. Maybe you make a donation to your local public radio or television station. Or perhaps you place ads on outdoor billboards or bus benches.

Like other costs of doing business, you need a benchmark or reference point for evaluating advertising and sales promotion costs. For the business example, the ratio is around 7 percent of annual sales. This ratio is in the typical range of the advertising and sales promotion expense of many small businesses. Of course, your business may be different. Retail furniture stores, for example, spend a lot more than 7 percent of sales revenue on advertising. Locally owned office-supply stores, in contrast, spend far less on advertising.

You should keep watch on which particular advertisements and sales promotions campaigns work best and have the most impact on sales. The trick is to find out which ads or promotions your customers respond to and which they don't. Keeping the name of your business on the customer's mind is a high marketing priority of most businesses, although measuring how your name recognition actually affects customers' purchases is difficult. Nevertheless, you should develop some measure or test of how your marketing expenses contribute to sales.

Of course, you can keep an eye on your competitors, but they aren't likely to tell you which sales promotion techniques are the most effective. You increased your advertising and sales promotion costs more than $30,000 in 2015, which is more than 20 percent over last year (see Figure 4-1). Sales revenue went up by an even larger percent, so the ratio of the expense to sales revenue actually decreased. Nevertheless, you should determine exactly what the extra money was spent on. Perhaps you bought more newspaper ads and doubled the number of flyers distributed during the year.

Appreciating depreciation expense

Depreciation expense is the cost of owning fixed assets. The term *fixed assets* includes land and buildings, machinery and equipment, furniture and fixtures, vehicles and forklift trucks, tools, and computers. These long-term operating resources aren't held for sale; they're used in the day-to-day operations of the business. Except for land, the cost of these long-term operating resources is allocated over the estimated useful lives of the assets. (Land is viewed as a property right that has perpetual life and usefulness, so its cost is not depreciated; the cost stays on the books until the land is disposed of.)

As a practical matter, the useful life estimates permitted in the federal income tax law are the touchstones used by most small businesses. Instead of predicting actual useful lives, businesses simply adopt the useful lives spelled out in the income tax law to depreciate their fixed assets. The useful life guidelines are available from the IRS at www.irs.gov/publications. Probably the most useful booklet is Publication 946 (2013), *How To Depreciate Property.* Your accountant should know everything in this booklet.

You should understand the following points about the depreciation expense:

- ✔ The two basic methods for allocating the cost of a fixed asset over its useful life are the *straight-line method* (an equal amount every year) and an *accelerated method,* by which more depreciation expense in recorded in the earlier years than in the later years; the straight-line method is used for buildings, and either method can be used for other classes of fixed assets.

- ✔ Businesses generally favor an accelerated depreciation method in order to reduce *taxable income* in the early years of owning fixed assets; but don't forget that taxable income will be higher in the later years when less depreciation is recorded.

- ✔ In recording depreciation expense, a business *does not set aside money* in a fund for the eventual replacement of its fixed assets restricted only for this purpose. (A business could invest money in a separate fund for this purpose, of course, but no one does.)

- ✔ Recording depreciation expense *does not require a decrease to cash* or an increase in a liability that will be paid in cash at a later time; rather the fixed asset accounts of the business are written down according to a systematic method of allocating the original cost of each fixed asset over its estimated useful life. (Book III Chapter 3 explains the cash-flow analysis of profit.)

- ✔ Even though the *market value of real estate* may appreciate over time, the cost of a building owned by the business is depreciated (generally over 39 years).

✔ The *eventual replacement costs* of most fixed assets will be higher than the original cost of the assets due to inflation; depreciation expense is based on original cost, not on the estimated future replacement cost.

✔ The *estimated useful lives of fixed assets for depreciation are shorter* than realistic expectations of their actual productive lives to the business; therefore, fixed assets are depreciated too quickly, and the book values of the assets in the balance sheet (original cost less accumulated depreciation to day) are too low.

✔ Depreciation expense is a real cost of doing business because fixed assets wear out or otherwise lose their usefulness to the business — although a case can be made for not recording depreciation expense on a building whose market value is steadily rising. Generally accepted accounting principles require that the cost of all fixed assets (except land) must be depreciated.

One technique used in the fields of investment analysis and business valuation focuses on EBITDA, which equals earnings before interest, tax (income tax), depreciation, and amortization. *Amortization* is similar to depreciation. Amortization refers to the allocating the cost of *intangible* assets over their estimated useful lives to the business. By and large, small businesses do not have intangible assets, so they're not discussed here.

One last point about depreciation expense: Note in Figure 4-1 that your depreciation expense is lower in 2015 than the prior year. Yet sales revenue and all other expenses are higher than the prior year. The drop in depreciation expense is an aberrant effect of accelerated depreciation; the amount of depreciation decreases year to year. You have a year-to-year built-in gain in profit because depreciation expense drops year to year. The aggregate effect on depreciation expense for the year depends on the mix of newer and older fixed assets. The higher depreciation on newer fixed assets is balanced by the lower depreciation on older fixed assets. One advantage of the straight-line method is that the amount of depreciation expense on a fixed asset is constant year to year, so you don't get fluctuations in depreciation expense year to year that are caused by the depreciation method being used.

Book III

Managing Your Finances

Ask your accountant to explain the year-to-year change in depreciation expense in your annual P&L. In particular, ask the accountant whether a decrease in the depreciation expense is due to your fixed assets getting older, with the result that less depreciation is recorded by an accelerated depreciation method.

Looking at facilities expense

The P&L report shown back in Figure 4-1 includes a separate line for facilities expense. Book III Chapter 2 argues that you should definitely limit the number of expense lines in your P&L. But this particular expense deserves separate reporting. Basically, this expense is your cost of physical space — the square footage and shelter you need to carry on operations plus the costs directly associated with using the space. (You may prefer the term *occupancy expense* instead.)

Most of the specific costs making up facilities expense are *fixed commitments* for the year. Examples are lease payments, utilities, fire insurance on contents and the building (if owned), general liability insurance premiums, security guards, and so on. You could argue that depreciation on the building (if owned by the business) should be included in facilities expense. However, it's best to put depreciation in its own expense account.

In this example, your business uses 12,000 square feet of space, and you've determined that a good benchmark for your business is $300 annual sales per square foot. Accordingly, your space could support $3,600,000 annual sales. In 2015, your annual sales revenue is short of this reference point. Therefore, you presumably have space enough for sales growth next year. These benchmarks are no more than rough guideposts. Nevertheless, benchmarks are very useful. If your actual performance is way off base from a benchmark, you should determine the reason for the variance. Based on your own experience and in looking at your competitors, you should be able to come up with reasonably accurate benchmarks for sales per employee and sales per square foot of space.

In the business example portrayed in Figure 4-1, you use the same amount of space both years. In other words, you did not have to expand your square footage for the sales growth in 2015. The relatively modest increase in facilities expense (only 5.2 percent, as shown in Figure 4-1) is due to inflationary cost pressures. Sooner or later, however, continued sales growth will require expansion of your square footage. Indeed, you may have to relocate to get more space.

Looking over or looking into other expenses

In your P&L report (refer to Figure 4-1), the last expense line is the collection of residual costs that aren't included in another expense. A small business has a surprising number of miscellaneous costs — annual permits, parking meters, office supplies, postage and shipping, service club memberships, travel, bad debts, professional fees, toilet paper, signs, to name just a handful. A business keeps at least one account for miscellaneous expenses. You should draw the line on how large an amount can be recorded in this catchall expense account. For example, you may instruct your accountant that no outlay over $250 or $500 can be charged to this account; any expenditure over the amount has to have its own expense account.

The cost control question is whether it's worth your time to investigate these costs item by item. In 2015, these assorted costs represented only 1.5 percent of your annual sales revenue. Most of the costs, probably, are reasonable in amount — so, why spend your valuable time inspecting these costs in detail?

On the other hand, these costs increase $15,594 in 2015 (see Figure 4-1), and this amount is a relatively large percent of your profit for the year:

> $15,594 increase in other expenses ÷ $95,651 net income for year = 16.3% of profit for year

Ask the accountant to list the two or three largest increases. You may see some surprises. Perhaps an increase is a one-time event that will not repeat next year. You have to follow your instincts and your experience in deciding how deep to dive into analyzing these costs. If your employees know you never look into these costs, they may be tempted to use one of these expense accounts to conceal fraud. So, it's generally best to do a quick survey of these costs, even if you don't spend a lot of time on them. It's better to give the impression that you're watching the costs like a hawk, even if you're not.

Running the numbers on interest expense

Interest expense is a financial cost — the cost of using debt for part of the total capital you use in operating the business. It's listed below the operating profit line in the P&L report (see Figure 4-1). Putting interest expense beneath the operating profit line is standard practice, for good reason. *Operating profit* (also called *operating earnings,* or *earnings before interest and income tax*) is the amount of profit you squeeze out of sales revenue before you consider how your business is financed (where you get your capital) and income tax.

Obviously, interest expense depends on the amount of debt you use and the interest rates on the debt. Figure 4-3 shows the balance sheets of your business at the end of the two most recent years. At the end of 2014, which is the start of 2015, you had $400,000 of interest bearing debt ($100,000 short-term and $300,000 long-term). Early in 2015, you increased your borrowing and ended the year with $600,000 debt ($200,000 short-term and $400,000 long-term). Based on the $600,000 debt level, your interest expense for the year is 8.3 percent.

Because you negotiated the terms of the loans to the business, you should know whether this interest rate is correct. By the way, the interest expense in your P&L may include other costs of borrowing, such as loan origination fees and other special charges in addition to interest. If you have any question about what's included in interest expense, ask your accountant for clarification.

Book III

Managing Your Finances

Your Business Name
Balance Sheet
At December 31

	2014	2015
Assets		
Cash	$347,779	$584,070
Accounts receivable	$136,235	$148,785
Inventory	$218,565	$250,670
Prepaid expenses	$65,230	$61,235
Total current assets	$767,809	$1,044,760
Property, plant and equipment	$774,600	$896,450
Accumulated depreciation	($167,485)	($256,435)
Cost less depreciation	$607,115	$640,015
Total assets	$1,374,924	$1,684,775
Liabilities and Owners' Equity		
Accounts payable	$286,450	$261,430
Accrued expenses payable	$67,345	$81,565
Short-term notes payable	$100,000	$200,000
Total current liabilities	$453,795	$542,995
Long-term notes payable	$300,000	$400,000
Owners' equity:		
Invested capital	$500,000	$525,000
Retained earnings	$121,129	$216,780
Total owners' equity	$621,129	$741,780
Total liabilities and owners' equity	$1,374,924	$1,684,775

© John Wiley & Sons, Inc.

Figure 4-3: Your year-end balance sheets.

Comparing your P&L with your balance sheet

You should compare your P&L numbers with your balance sheet numbers. Basically, you should ask whether your sales and expenses for the year are in agreement with your assets and liabilities. Every business, based on its experience and its operating policies, falls into ruts regarding the sizes of its assets and liabilities relative to its annual sales revenue and expenses. If one of these normal ratios is out of kilter, you should find out the reasons for the deviation from normal.

A small business owner should definitely know the proper sizes of assets and liabilities relative to the sizes of the business's annual sales revenue and expenses.

Three critical tie-ins between the P&L and balance sheet are the following:

- **Accounts receivables/Sales revenue from sales on credit:** Your ending balance of accounts receivable (uncollected credit sales) should be consistent with your credit terms. So, if you give customers 30 days credit, then your ending balance should equal about one month of credit sales.

- **Inventory/Cost of goods sold expense:** Your ending inventory depends on the average time that products spend in your warehouse or on your retail shelves before being sold. So, if your inventory turns six times a year (meaning products sit in inventory about two months on average before being sold), your ending inventory should equal about two months of annual cost of goods sold.

- **Operating liabilities/Operating costs:** Your ending balances of accounts payable and accrued expenses payable should be consistent with your normal trade credit terms from vendors and suppliers and the time it takes to pay accrued expenses. So, if your average credit terms for purchases are 30 days, your ending accounts payable liability balance should equal about 30 days of purchases.

Book III

Managing Your Finances

You should instruct your accountant to do these calculations and report these P&L/balance sheet ratios so that you can keep tabs on the sizes of your assets and liabilities.

A business can develop solvency problems. One reason is that the owner keeps a close watch on the P&L but ignores what was going on in the balance sheet. Assets and liabilities were getting out of hand, but the owner thought that everything was okay because the P&L looked good. Book III Chapter 3 discusses solvency problems and cures.

One additional purpose for comparing your P&L with your balance sheet is to evaluate your profit performance relative to the amount of capital you're using to make the profit. Your 2015 year-end balance sheet reports that your owners' equity is $741,780 (see Figure 4-3). This amount includes the capital the owners (you and any other owners) put in the business (invested capital), plus the earnings plowed back into the business (retained earnings). Theoretically, the owners could have invested this $741,780 somewhere else and earned a return on the investment. For 2015, your business earned 12.9 percent return on owners' equity:

$95,651 net income for 2015 ÷ $741,780 2015 year-end owners' equity = 12.9% return on owners' equity capital

Keep in mind that the business is a pass-through tax entity. So, the 12.9 percent return on capital is before income tax. Suppose that the average income tax bracket of the owners is 25 percent (it may very well be higher). Taking out 25 percent for income tax, the return on owners' equity is 9.7 percent. You have to decide whether this percentage is an adequate return on capital for the owners (you, but also any other owners). And don't forget that the business did not pay cash dividends during the year. All the profit for the year is retained; the owners did not see any cash in their hands from the profit.

Looking into Cost of Goods Sold Expense

Small business owners have a tendency to take cost amounts reported by accountants for granted — as if the amount is the actual, true, and only cost. In contrast, small business owners are pretty shrewd about dealing with other sources of information. When listening to complaints from employees, for example, business owners are generally good at reading between the lines and filling in some aspects that the employee is not revealing. And then there's the legendary response from a customer who hasn't paid on time: The check's in the mail. Business owners know better than to take this comment at face value. Likewise, you should be equally astute in working with the cost amounts reported for expenses.

Everyone agrees that there should be uniform accounting standards for financial reporting by businesses. Yet the accounting profession hasn't reached agreement on the best method for recording certain expenses. The earlier section "Appreciating depreciation expense" explains that a business can choose between a straight-line and an accelerated method for recording depreciation expense. And a business can choose between two or three different methods for recording cost of goods sold expense.

Selecting a cost of goods sold expense method

The cost of goods sold expense is the largest expense of businesses that sell products, typically more than 50 percent of the sales revenue from the goods sold. In the business example, cost of goods sold is 58 percent of sales revenue in the most recent year (refer to Figure 4-1). You would think that the accounting profession would have settled on one uniform method to record cost of goods sold expense. This isn't the case, however. Furthermore, the federal income tax law permits different cost of goods sold expense methods for determining annual taxable income. A business has to stay with the same method year after year (although a change is permitted in very unusual situations).

This chapter is directed to small business owners, not accountants. There's no reason for a small business owner to get into the details of the alternative cost of goods sold expense methods. Your time is too valuable. Like other issues that you deal with in running a small business, the basic question is: What difference does it make? Generally, the method doesn't make a significant difference in your annual cost of goods sold expense — assuming that you don't change horses in the middle of the stream (in other words, that you keep with the same method year after year). Instruct your accountant to give you a heads up if your accounting method causes an unusual, or abnormal impact, on cost of goods expense for the year.

Your cost of goods sold expense accounting method affects the *book value of inventory,* which is the amount reported in the balance sheet. Under the *first-in, first out* (FIFO) accounting method, the inventory amount is based on recent costs. For example, refer to the balance sheet in Figure 4-3. Inventory at year-end 2015 is reported at $250,670. Under the FIFO method, this amount reflects costs of products during two or three months ending with the balance sheet date. Instead of using FIFO or LIFO, a business can split the difference as it were and use the *average cost* method. The average cost accounting method reaches back a little further in time compared to the FIFO method; the cost of ending inventory is based on product costs from throughout the year under the average cost method.

Book III

Managing Your Finances

If you use the last-in, first-out (LIFO) accounting method, the cost value of your year-end inventory balance could reach back many years, depending on how long you have been using this method and when you accumulated your inventory layers. For this reason, businesses that use the LIFO method disclose the current replacement cost of their ending inventories in a footnote to their financial statements to warn the reader that the balance sheet amount is substantially below the current cost of the products.

Which cost of goods sold expense method should you use, then? You might start by looking at your sales pricing policy. What do you do when a product's cost goes up? Do you wait to clear out your existing stock of the product before you raise the sales price? If so, try the first-in, first-out (FIFO) method, because this method keeps product costs in sync with sales prices. On the other hand, sales pricing is a complex process, and sales prices aren't handcuffed with product cost changes. To a large extent, your choice of accounting method for cost of goods sold expense depends on whether you prefer a conservative, higher-cost method (generally LIFO) — or a liberal, lower-cost method (generally FIFO).

Dealing with inventory shrinkage and inventory write-downs

Deciding which cost of goods sold expense accounting method to use isn't the main concern of many small businesses that carry a sizable inventory of products awaiting sale. The more important issues to them are losses from *inventory shrinkage* and from *write-downs of inventory* caused by products that they can't sell at normal prices. These problems are very serious for many small businesses.

Inventory shrinkage stems from theft by customers and employees, damages caused by the handling, moving, and storing of products, physical deterioration of products over time, and errors in recording the inflow and outflow of products through the warehouse. A business needs to take a *physical inventory* to determine the amount of inventory shrinkage. A physical inventory refers to inspecting and counting all items in inventory, usually at the close of the fiscal year. This purpose is to discover shortages of inventory. The cost of the missing products is removed from the inventory asset account and charged to expense. This expense is painful to record because the business receives no sales revenue from these products. A certain amount of inventory shrinkage expense is considered to be a normal cost of doing business, which can't be avoided.

Also, at the close of the year, a business should do a *lower of cost or market test* on its ending inventory of products. Product costs are compared against the current replacement costs of the products and the current market (sales) prices of the products. This is a twofold test of product costs. If replacement costs have dropped or if the products have lost sales value, your accountant should make a year-end adjusting entry to write down your ending inventory to a lower amount, which is below the original costs you paid for the products.

Recording inventory shrinkage expense caused by missing products is cut and dried. You don't have the products. So, the cost of the products is removed from the asset account — that's all there is to it. In contrast, writing down the costs of damaged products (that are still salable at some price) and determining replacement and market values for the lower of cost or market test is not so clear-cut.

A business may be tempted to write down its inventory too much in order to minimize its taxable income for the year. You're on thin ice if you do this, and you better pray that the IRS won't audit you.

In recording the expense of inventory shrinkage and inventory write-down under the lower of cost of market test, your accountant has to decide which expense account to charge and how to report the loss in your P&L. Generally, the loss should be included in your cost of goods sold expense in the P&L because the loss is a normal expense that sits on top of cost of goods sold. However, when an abnormal amount of loss is recorded, your accountant should call the loss to your attention — either on a separate line in the P&L report or in a footnote to the statement.

Focusing on Profit Centers

A business consists of different revenue streams, and some are more profitable than others. It would be very unusual if every different source of sales were equally profitable. A common practice is to divide the business into separate *profit centers,* so that the profitability of each part of the business can be determined. For example, a car dealership is separated into new car sales, used car sales, service work, and parts sales. Each profit center's sales revenue may be further subdivided. New vehicle sales can be separated into sedans, pickup trucks, SUVs, and other models. In the business example used in this and the two preceding chapters, you sell products both at retail prices to individual consumers and at wholesale prices to other businesses. Quite clearly, you should separate your two main sources of sales and create a profit center for each.

Determining how to partition a business into profit centers is a management decision. The first question is whether the segregation of sales revenue into distinct profit centers helps you better manage the business. Generally, the answer is yes. The information helps you focus attention and effort on the sources of highest profit to the business. Comparing different profit centers puts the spotlight on sources of sales that don't generate enough profit, or even may be losing money.

Generally, a business creates a profit center for each major product line and for each location (or territory). There are no hard-and-fast rules, however. At one extreme, each product can be defined as a profit center. As a matter of fact, businesses keep records for every product they sell. Many owners want a very detailed report on sales and cost of goods sold for every product they sell. This report can run many, many pages. A hardware store in Boulder sells more than 100,000 products. Would you really want to print out a report that lists the sales and cost of goods of more than 100,000 lines? The more practical approach is to divide the business into a reasonable number of profit centers and focus your time on the reports for each profit center.

A profit center is a fairly autonomous source of sales of a business, like a tub standing on its own feet. For example, the Boulder hardware store sells outdoor clothing, which is quite distinct from the other products it sells. Does the hardware store make a good profit on its outdoor clothing line of products? The first step is to determine the gross margin for the outdoor clothing department. The cost of goods sold is deducted from sales revenue for the outdoor clothing line of products. Is outdoor clothing a high gross margin source of sales? The owner of the hardware store certainly should know.

The report for a profit center doesn't stop at the gross profit line. One key purpose of setting up profit centers is, as far as possible, to match direct operating costs against the sales revenue of the profit center. *Direct operating costs* are those that can be clearly assigned to the sales activity of the profit center. Examples of direct operating costs of a profit center are the following:

✔ Commissions paid to salespersons on sales of the profit center

✔ Shipping and delivery costs of products sold in the profit center

✔ Inventory shrinkage and write-downs of inventory in the profit center

✔ Bad debts from credit sales of the profit center

✔ The cost of employees who work full-time in a profit center

✔ The cost of advertisements for products sold in the profit center

Assigning direct operating costs to profit centers doesn't take care of all the costs of a business. A business has many *indirect* operating costs that benefit all, or at least two or more profit centers. The employee cost of the general manager of the business, the cost of its accounting department, general business licenses, real estate taxes, interest on the debt of the business, and liability insurance are examples of general, business-wide operating costs. Accountants have come up with ingenious methods for allocating indirect operating costs to profit centers. In the last analysis, however, the allocation methods have flaws and are fairly arbitrary. The game may not be worth the candle in allocating indirect operating costs to profit centers. Generally, there is no gain in useful information. You have all the information you need by ending the profit center report after direct operating costs.

The bottom line of a profit center report is a measure of profit before general business operating costs and interest expense (and income tax expense, if applicable) are taken into account. The bottom line of a profit center is more properly called *contribution* toward the aggregate profit of the business as a whole. The term *profit* is a commonly used label for the bottom line of a profit center report, but keep in mind that it doesn't have the same meaning as the bottom line of the P&L statement for the business as a whole.

Reducing Your Costs

This section covers a few cost-reduction tactics. It's not an exhaustive list, to be sure, but you may find one or two of these quite useful:

- ✔ Have your accountant alert you to any expense that increases more than a certain threshold amount, or by a certain percent.

- ✔ Hire a cost control specialist. Many of these firms work on a contingent fee basis that depends on how much your expense actually decreases. These outfits tend to specialize in certain areas such as utility bills and property taxes, to name just two.

- ✔ Consider outsourcing some of your business functions, such as payroll, security, taking inventory, and maintenance.

- ✔ Put out requests for competitive bids on supplies you regularly purchase.

- ✔ Make prompt payments of purchases on credit to take advantage of early payment discounts. Indeed, offer to pay in advance if you can gain an additional discount.

- ✔ Keep all your personal and family costs out of the business.

- ✔ Keep your assets as low as possible so that the capital you need to run the business is lower, and your cost of capital will be lower.

- ✔ Set priorities on cost control, putting the fastest rising costs at the top.

- ✔ Ask your outside CPA for cost control ideas she or he has observed in other businesses.

Book III

Managing Your Finances

Deciding Where the Budgeting Process Starts

Accounting represents more of an art than a science. This concept also holds true with the budgeting process, as it helps to be creative when preparing projections. Before creating your first budget, you should prepare by taking the following four steps:

1. **Delve into your business's financial history.**

   To start, you should have a very good understanding of your company's prior financial and operating results. This history doesn't stretch back very far when you're starting out (obviously), but the key concept is that sound information not only should be readily available but it should be clearly understood. There is no point in attempting to prepare a budget if the party completing the work doesn't understand the financial information.

Remember that although the history of a company may provide a basic foundation on which to develop a budget, it by no means is an accurate predictor of the future.

2. **Involve your key management.**

The budgeting process represents a critical function in most companies' accounting and financial departments — and rightfully so, because these are the people who understand the numbers the best. If you have other managers looking after different departments or sections of your business, be sure to get them involved. Although the financial and accounting types produce the final budget, they rely on data that comes from numerous parties, such as marketing, manufacturing, and sales. Critical business data comes from numerous parties, all of which must be included in the budgeting process to produce the most reliable information possible.

3. **Gather reliable data.**

The availability of quality market, operational, and accounting data represents the basis of the budget. A good deal of this data often comes from internal sources. For example, when a sales region is preparing a budget for the upcoming year, the sales manager may survey the direct sales representatives on what they feel their customers will demand as far as products and services in the coming year. With this information, you can determine sales volumes, personnel levels, wages rates, commission plans, and so on.

Although internal information is of value, it represents only half the battle because external information and data is just as critical to accumulate. Having access to quality and reliable external third-party information is absolutely essential to the overall business planning process and the production of reliable forecasts. Market forces and trends may be occurring that can impact your business over the next 24 months but aren't reflected at all in the previous year's operating results.

4. **Coordinate the budget timing.**

From a timing perspective, most companies tend to start the budgeting process for the next year in the fourth quarter of their current calendar year. This way, they have access to recent financial results on which to support the budgeting process moving forward. The idea is to have a sound budget to base the next year's operations on. On the timeline front, the following general rule should be adhered to: The nearer the term covered by the projection means more detailed information and results should be produced. That is, if you're preparing a budget for the coming fiscal year, then monthly financial statement forecasts are expected (with more detailed support available). Looking two or three years out, you could produce quarterly financial statement projections (with more summarized assumptions used).

The concept of *garbage in, garbage out* definitely applies to the budgeting process. If you don't have sound data and information, the output produced will be of little value to the owners. The data and information used to prepare your company's budgets must be as complete, accurate, reliable, and timely as possible. Though you can't be 100 percent assured that the data and information accumulated achieves these goals (because, by definition, you're attempting to predict the future with a projection), proper resources should be dedicated to the process to avoid getting bit by large information black holes.

Finally, keep in mind that the projections prepared must be consistent with the overall business plans and strategies of the company. Remember, the budgeting process represents a living, breathing thing that constantly must be updated and adapted to changing market conditions. What worked two years ago may not provide management with the necessary information today on which to make appropriate business decisions.

Honing In on Budgeting Tools

Book III

Managing Your Finances

After you have solid historical data in hand, you're ready to produce an actual projection model. To help start the process, you can use three simple acronyms as tools to accumulate the necessary information to build the projection model.

CART: Complete, Accurate, Reliable, and Timely

Complete, Accurate, Reliable, and Timely (CART) applies to all the data and information you need to prepare for the projection model. It doesn't matter where the information is coming from or how it's presented; it just must be complete, accurate, reliable, and timely:

✔ **Complete:** Financial statements produced for a company include a balance sheet, income statement, and a cash flow statement. All three are needed in order to understand the entire financial picture of a company. If a projection model is incorporating an expansion of a company's manufacturing facility in a new state, for example, all information related to the new facility needs to be accumulated to prepare the budget. This data includes the cost of the land and facility, how much utilities run in the area, what potential environmental issues may be present, whether a trained workforce is available, and if not, how much will it cost to train them, and so on. Although overkill is not the objective, having access to all material information and data is.

✔ **Accurate:** Incorporating accurate data represents the basis for preparing the initial budget. Every budget needs to include the price your company charges for the goods or services it sells, how much you pay your employees, what the monthly office rent is, and so on. The key to obtaining accurate information is ensuring that your accounting and financial information system is generating accurate data.

✔ **Reliable:** The concepts of reliability and accuracy are closely linked but also differ as well. It may be one thing to obtain a piece of information that is accurate, but is it reliable? For example, you may conduct research and find that the average wage for a paralegal in San Diego is $24 per hour. This figure may sound accurate, but you may need a specialist paralegal who demands $37 per hour.

✔ **Timely:** The information and data accumulated must be done in a timely fashion. It's not going to do a management team much good if the data and information that is needed is provided six months after the fact. Companies live and die by having access to real-time information on which to make business decisions and change course (and forecasts) if needed.

SWOT: Strengths, Weaknesses, Opportunities, and Threats

Don't be afraid to utilize a Strengths, Weaknesses, Opportunities, and Threats (SWOT) analysis, which is an effective planning and budgeting tool used to keep businesses focused on key issues. The simple SWOT analysis (or matrix) in Figure 4-4 shows you how this process works.

A SWOT analysis is usually broken down into a matrix containing four segments. Two of the segments are geared toward positive attributes, such as your strengths and opportunities, and two are geared toward negative attributes, such as your weaknesses and threats. In addition, the analysis differentiates between internal company source attributes and external, or outside of the company source attributes. Generally, the SWOT analysis is meant to ensure that critical conditions are communicated to management for inclusion in the budget.

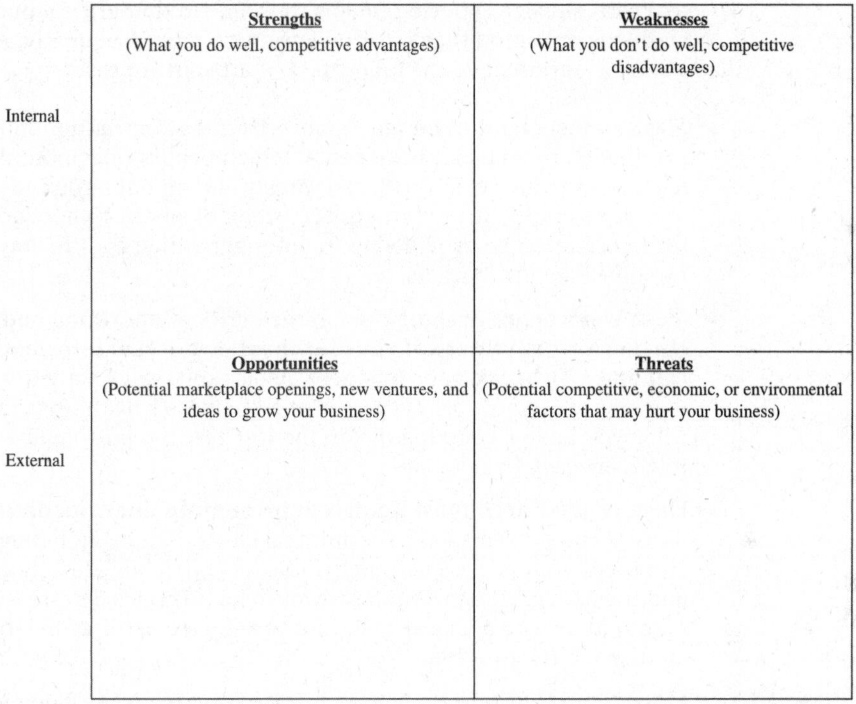

	Strengths	Weaknesses
Internal	(What you do well, competitive advantages)	(What you don't do well, competitive disadvantages)
External	**Opportunities** (Potential marketplace openings, new ventures, and ideas to grow your business)	**Threats** (Potential competitive, economic, or environmental factors that may hurt your business)

© John Wiley & Sons, Inc.

Figure 4-4:
A basic
SWOT
analysis.

As an owner of a business, you must be able to understand the big picture and your company's key economic drivers in order to prepare proper business plans, strategies, and ultimately, forecasts. The ability to understand and positively affect the key economic drivers of your business and empower the team to execute the business plan represents the end game. Getting lost in the forest of "Why did you spend an extra $500 on the trip to Florida?" is generally not the best use of the owner's time.

Flash reports

Flash reports are a quick snapshot of critical company operating and financial data, which is then used to support the ongoing operations of the business. All types of flash reports are used in business, and they range from evaluating a book-to-bill ratio on a weekly basis, to reporting daily sales activity during the holiday season, to looking at weekly finished goods inventory levels.

The goal with all flash reports remains the same in that critical business information is delivered to you for review much more frequently. As such, flash reports tend to have the following key attributes present:

- ✔ **Flash reports tend to be much more frequent in timing.** Unlike the production of financial statements (which occurs on a monthly basis), flash reports are often produced weekly and, in numerous cases, daily. In today's competitive marketplace, small business owners are demanding information be provided more frequently than ever to stay on top of rapidly changing markets.

- ✔ **Flash reports are designed to capture critical operating and financial performance data of your business or the real information that can make or break your business.** As a result, sales activities and/or volumes are almost always a part of a business's flash reporting effort. Once you have a good handle on the top line, the bottom line should be relatively easy to calculate.

- ✔ **Flash reports aren't just limited to presenting financial data.** Flash reports can be designed to capture all kinds of data, including retail store foot volume (or customer traffic levels), labor utilization rates, and the like. Although you may want to know how sales are tracking this month, the store manager will want to keep a close eye on labor hours incurred in the process.

- ✔ **Flash reports obtain their base information from the same accounting and financial information system that produces periodic financial statements, budgets, and other reports.** Though the presentation of the information may be different, the source of the information should come from the same transactional basis (of your company).

- ✔ **Flash reports are almost exclusively used for internal management needs and are rarely delivered to external parties.** The information contained in flash reports is usually more detailed in nature and tends to contain far more confidential data than, say, audited financial statements, and are almost never audited.

- ✔ **Flash reports are closely related to the budgeting process.** For example, if a company is experiencing a short-term cash flow squeeze, the owner will need to have access to a rolling 13-week cash flow projection to properly evaluate cash inflows and outflows on a weekly basis. Each week, the rolling 13-week cash flow projection is provided to the owner for review in the form of a flash report, which is always being updated to look out 13 weeks.

Flash reports should act more to "reconfirm" your company's performance rather than representing a report that offers "original" information. Granted, though a flash report that presents sales volumes for the first two weeks of February compared to the similar two-week period for the prior year is reporting new sales information, the format of the report and the presentation of the information in the report should be consistent. Thus, you should be able to quickly decipher the results and determine whether the company is performing within expectations and what to expect on the bottom line for the entire month.

Preparing an Actual Budget or Forecast

The best way to dive into preparing a budget, after all the necessary information has been accumulated, is to begin by building a draft of the budget that is more summary in nature and is focused on the financial statement, which is most easily understood and widely used. The reason more summarized budgets are developed at first is to create a general format or framework that captures the basic output desired by the parties using the budget. Offering a summarized visual version of the budget allows for reviews and edits to be incorporated into the forecasting model before too much effort is expended in including detail that may not be needed. Once the desired output reports and data points of the budget are determined, it can be expanded and adjusted to incorporate the correct level of detail. The best way to prepare a summarized budget that is both flexible and adaptable is to build the forecasting model in software such as Excel, which is relatively easy to use and widely accepted by most businesses.

On the financial statement front, for most companies, the forecasting process tends to starts with producing a projected income statement for three primary reasons. First, this financial statement tends to be the one that is most widely used and easily understood by the organization. Questions such as how much revenue can the company produce, what will the gross margin be, and how much profit will be generated are basic focal points of almost every business owner. The balance sheet and cash flow statements aren't nearly as easy to understand and produce.

Second, the income statement often acts as a base data point to produce balance sheet and cash flow statement information. For example, if sales volumes are increasing, it's safe to say that the company's balance in trade accounts receivable and inventory would increase as well.

And third, the majority of the information and data accumulated to support the budgeting process is generally centered in areas associated with the income statement, such as how many units can be sold, at what price, how many sales persons will you need, and so on.

Book III

Managing Your Finances

Remember also that most budgets are prepared in a consistent format with that of the current internally produced financial statements and reports utilized by your company. This achieves the dual goal of information conformity (for ease of understanding) and capturing your business's key economic drivers. To illustrate, Figure 4-5 presents a summarized budget for XYZ Wholesale, Inc., for the coming year.

A budget is shown for the year ending 12/31/14 for XYZ Wholesale, Inc. The basic budget shown in Figure 4-5 is fairly simplistic but also very informative. It captures the macro level economic structure of the company in terms of where it is today and where it expects to be at the end of next year. When reviewing the figure, notice the following key issues:

- ✔ **The most recent year-end financial information has been included in the first column to provide a base reference point to work from.** Gaining a thorough understanding of your company's historical operating results to forecast into the future is important. Also, by having this base information, you can develop a consistent reporting format for ease of understanding.

- ✔ **The projections are "complete" from a financial statement perspective.** That is, the income statement, balance sheet, and statement of cash flows have all been projected to assist management with understanding the entire financial picture of the company. The forecasts prepared for XYZ Wholesale, Inc., indicate that the line of credit will be used extensively through the third quarter to support working capital needs. By the end of the fourth quarter, borrowings on the line of credit are substantially lower as business slows and cash flows improve (used to pay down the line of credit).

- ✔ **The projections have been presented with quarterly information.** You might use projections for the next fiscal year, prepared on a monthly basis to provide you with more frequent information. However, this chapter uses prepared quarterly information.

- ✔ **The projections have been prepared and presented in a "summary" format.** That is, not too much detail has been provided, but rather groups of detail have been combined into one line item. For example, if your business has more than one location, individual budgets are prepared to support each location, but when a company-wide forecast is completed, all the sales are rolled up onto one line item. Budgets prepared in a summary format are best suited for review by external parties and managers.

XYZ WHOLESALE, INC.
UNAUDITED FINANCIAL STATEMENT — QUARTERLY PROJECTIONS
CONFIDENTIAL

Summary Balance Sheet	Actual Year End 1/1/15	Forecast Quarter End 4/1/15	Forecast Quarter End 7/1/15	Forecast Quarter End 10/1/15	Forecast Quarter End 1/1/16	Forecast Year End 1/1/16
Current Assets:						
Cash & Equivalents	$117,632	$11,364	$26,263	$38,200	$24,313	$24,313
Trade Receivables, Net	$1,271,875	$1,213,333	$1,646,667	$2,253,333	$1,610,000	$1,610,000
Inventory	$867,188	$886,667	$1,132,400	$1,248,000	$856,800	$856,800
Total Current Assets	$2,256,695	$2,111,364	$2,805,330	$3,539,533	$2,491,113	$2,491,113
Fixed & Other Assets:						
Property, Plant, & Equipment, Net	$1,750,000	$1,725,000	$1,700,000	$1,675,000	$1,650,000	$1,650,000
Other Assets	$75,000	$75,000	$75,000	$75,000	$75,000	$75,000
Total Fixed & Other Assets	$1,825,000	$1,800,000	$1,775,000	$1,750,000	$1,725,000	$1,725,000
Total Assets	$4,081,695	$3,911,364	$4,580,330	$5,289,533	$4,216,113	$4,216,113
Current Liabilities:						
Trade Payables	$2,601,563	$2,340,800	$2,547,900	$2,808,000	$1,965,600	$1,965,600
Accrued Liabilities	$195,117	$234,080	$254,790	$280,800	$196,560	$196,560
Line of Credit Borrowings	$200,000	$500,000	$1,000,000	$1,100,000	$250,000	$250,000
Current Portion of Long-Term Liabilities	$300,000	$300,000	$300,000	$300,000	$300,000	$300,000
Total Current Liabilities	$3,296,680	$3,374,880	$4,102,690	$4,488,800	$2,712,160	$2,712,160
Long-Term Liabilities:						
Notes Payable, Less Current Portion	$300,000	$225,000	$150,000	$75,000	$0	$0
Other Long-Term Liabilities	$150,000	$150,000	$150,000	$150,000	$150,000	$150,000
Total Long-Term Liabilities	$450,000	$375,000	$300,000	$225,000	$150,000	$150,000
Total Liabilities	$3,746,680	$3,749,880	$4,402,690	$4,713,800	$2,862,160	$2,862,160
Equity:						
Common and Preferred Equity, $1 Per Share	$500,000	$500,000	$500,000	$500,000	$1,000,000	$1,000,000
Retained Earnings	$901,265	($164,985)	($164,985)	($164,985)	($164,985)	($164,985)
Current Earnings	($1,066,250)	($173,531)	($157,375)	$240,719	$518,938	$518,938
Total Equity	$335,015	$161,484	$177,640	$575,734	$1,353,953	$1,353,953
Total Liabilities & Equity	$4,081,695	$3,911,364	$4,580,330	$5,289,534	$4,216,113	$4,216,113

Summary Income Statement	Actual Year End 1/1/15	Forecast Quarter End 4/1/15	Forecast Quarter End 7/1/15	Forecast Quarter End 10/1/15	Forecast Quarter End 1/1/16	Forecast Year End 1/1/16
Revenue	$13,875,000	$2,800,000	$3,800,000	$5,200,000	$4,200,000	$16,000,000
Costs of Goods Sold	$10,406,250	$2,128,000	$2,831,000	$3,744,000	$3,024,000	$11,727,000
Gross Profit	$3,468,750	$672,000	$969,000	$1,456,000	$1,176,000	$4,273,000
Gross Margin	25.00%	24.00%	25.50%	28.00%	28.00%	26.71%
Selling, General, & Administrative Expenses	$3,060,000	$700,000	$800,000	$900,000	$750,000	$3,150,000
Depreciation Expense	$350,000	$100,000	$100,000	$100,000	$100,000	$400,000
Interest Expense	$75,000	$20,531	$27,844	$32,906	$22,781	$104,063
Other (Income) Expenses	$1,050,000	$25,000	$25,000	$25,000	$25,000	$100,000
Net Profit Before Tax	($1,066,250)	($173,531)	$16,156	$398,094	$278,219	$518,938
Income Tax Expense (Benefit)	$0	$0	$0	$0	$0	$0
Net Profit (Loss)	($1,066,250)	($173,531)	$16,156	$398,094	$278,219	$518,938

Summary Cash Flow Statement	Actual Year End 1/1/15	Forecast Quarter End 4/1/15	Forecast Quarter End 7/1/15	Forecast Quarter End 10/1/15	Forecast Quarter End 1/1/16	Forecast Year End 1/1/16
Operating Cash Flow:						
Net Income (Loss)	($1,066,250)	($173,531)	$16,156	$398,094	$278,219	$518,938
Depreciation Expense	$350,000	$100,000	$100,000	$100,000	$100,000	$400,000
Net Operating Cash Flow	($716,250)	($73,531)	$116,156	$498,094	$378,219	$918,938
Working Capital:						
(Increase) Decrease in Trade Receivables	$471,875	$58,542	($433,333)	($606,667)	$643,333	($338,125)
(Increase) Decrease in Inventory	$1,049,194	($19,479)	($245,733)	($115,600)	$391,200	$10,388
Increase (Decrease) in Trade Payables	($81,371)	($260,763)	$207,100	$260,100	($842,400)	($635,963)
Increase (Decrease) in Accrued Liabilities	$60,971	$38,963	$20,710	$26,010	($84,240)	$1,443
Increase (Decrease) in Current Debt	$100,000	$300,000	$500,000	$100,000	($850,000)	$50,000
Net Working Capital Cash Flow	$1,600,668	$117,263	$48,743	($336,157)	($742,107)	($912,257)
Financing Capital:						
Equity Contributions	$0	$0	$0	$0	$500,000	$500,000
Additions to Long-Term Debt	$0	$0	$0	$0	$0	$0
Deletions to Long-Term Debt	($300,000)	($75,000)	($75,000)	($75,000)	($75,000)	($300,000)
Fixed Asset Additions	($600,000)	($75,000)	($75,000)	($75,000)	($75,000)	($300,000)
Change to Other Long-Term Assets	$0	$0	$0	$0	$0	$0
Change to Other Long-Term Liabilities	$10,000	$0	$0	$0	$0	$0
Net Financial Capital Cash Flow	($890,000)	($150,000)	($150,000)	($150,000)	$350,000	($100,000)
Beginning Cash	$123,214	$117,632	$11,364	$26,263	$38,200	$117,632
Ending Cash	$117,632	$11,364	$26,263	$38,200	$24,312	$24,312

Figure 4-5:
A quarterly forecast.

Book III

Managing
Your
Finances

✔ **Certain key or critical business economic drivers have been highlighted in the projection model.** First, the company's gross margin has been called out as it increases from 24 percent in the first quarter to 28 percent in the first half of the year. The increase was the result of the company moving older and obsolete products during the first six months of the year to make way for new merchandise and products to be sold at higher prices starting in the third quarter (and then accelerating in the fourth quarter during the holidays). Second, the company's pretax net income, for the entire year, has improved significantly. This increase occurred because the company's fixed overhead and corporate infrastructure (expenses) did not need to increase nearly as much to support the higher sales (as a result of realizing the benefits of economies of scale). In addition, the company didn't have to absorb an inventory write-off of $1 million (as with 2013).

✔ **A couple of very simple, but extremely important, references are made at the top and bottom of the projections.** At the top, the company clearly notes that the information prepared is confidential in nature. At the bottom, the company notes that the information is unaudited. In today's business world, information that is both confidential and that hasn't been audited by an external party should clearly state so.

The best way to prepare your first budget is to simply dive in and give it a go. There is no question that your first draft will undergo significant changes, revisions, and edits, but it's much easier to critique something that already exists than create it from scratch. The hard part is preparing the first budget. After that, the budget can then be refined, expanded, and improved to provide your organization an even more valuable tool in managing everyday challenges, stress, and growing pains.

Understanding Internal versus External Budgets

Information prepared for and delivered to external users (a financing source, taxing authorities, company creditors, and so on) isn't the same as information prepared for and utilized internally in the company. Not only does this fact apply to historically produced information, but it applies to financial information you forecast as well. The following examples show how a business can basically utilize the same information, but for different objectives:

✔ **The internal sales-driven budget:** You never see a budget prepared based on sales and marketing information that is more conservative than a similar budget prepared based on operations or accounting information. By nature, sales and marketing personnel tend to be far more optimistic in relation to the opportunities present than other segments of the business (which, of course, includes the ultra-conservative nature of accountants). So, rather than attempt to have these two groups battle it out over what forecast model is the most accurate, it's a good idea to simply prepare two sets of projections. Companies often have more than one set of projections. You can use the marketing- and sales-based projection as a motivational tool to push this group but use a more conservative projection for delivery to external financing sources, which provides a "reasonable" projection so that the company isn't under enormous pressure to hit aggressive plans. Granted, this strategy has to be properly managed (and kept in balance) because one forecast shouldn't be drastically different than another.

✔ **Drilling down into the detail:** When information is delivered to external parties, the level of detail is far less than what is utilized internally on a daily basis. This concept holds true for the budgeting process as well. The level and amount of detail that is at the base of the projection model will often drill down to the core elements of your business. For example, the summary projected in Figure 4-5 displays corporate overhead expenses as one line item. This one line item could, in fact, be the summation of more than 100 lines of data and capture everything from the cost of personnel in the accounting department to the current year's advertising budget (for the company). Again, an outside party should not (and does not want to) see that level of detail because it tends to only confuse them and lead to more questions being asked than are needed. However, by being able to drill down into the detail at any given time (and provide real support for financial information presented in the budget), you can kill two birds with one stone. Internally, you have the necessary detail to hold team members responsible for expense and cost control. Externally, you can provide added confidence and creditability to your partners (for example, a financing source) that the business is being tightly managed.

Creating a Living Budget

A *living budget* is based on the idea that in today's fiercely competitive marketplace, business models change much quicker than they did a decade ago (see Book I Chapter 3 for more on business models). Although the budget prepared in the fourth quarter of the previous year looked good, six months later the story may change. Any number of factors, such as losing a key sales rep, having a competitor go out of business, or experiencing a significant increase in the price of raw materials to produce your products, may cause the best prepared budgets to be useless by midyear. So, you may want to keep in mind the following terminology when preparing budgets to ensure that the process doesn't become stagnant during the year:

✔ **What ifs:** A what-if analysis is just as it sounds. That is, if this happens to my business or in the market, what will be the impact on my business? If I can land this new account, what additional costs will I need to incur and when to support the account? Utilizing what-if budgeting techniques is a highly effective business-management strategy that you can apply to all levels of the budgeting process. Figure 4-6 presents a company's original budget alongside two other scenarios, one of which is a low-case scenario and the other a best-case scenario. By completing what-if budgeting, XYZ Wholesale, Inc., has provided itself with a better understanding of what business decisions need to be made in case either the low-case or high-case scenarios are realized.

✔ **Recasts:** When you hear the term *recast,* it generally means a company is going to update its original budgets or forecasts during some point of the year to recast the information through the end of the year. Companies are constantly under pressure to provide updated information on how they think the year will turn out. Everyone wants updated information, so at the end of select periods (for example, month end or quarter end), the actual results for the company through that period are presented with recast information for the remainder of the year to present recast operating results for the entire year (a combination of actual results and updated projected results). Having access to this type of information can greatly assist business owners so that they can properly direct the company and adapt to changing conditions, not to mention provide timely updates to key external parties (on how the company is progressing).

Nobody likes surprises (more exactly, nobody likes bad ones), and nothing will get an external party, such as a bank or investor, more fired up than a business owner not being able to deliver information on the company's performance.

✔ **Rolling forecasts:** *Rolling forecasts* are similar to preparing recast financial results with the exception that the rolling forecast is always looking out over a period of time (for example, the next 12 months) from the most recent period end. For example, if a company has a fiscal year end of 12/31/14 and has prepared a budget for the fiscal year end 12/31/15, an updated rolling 12-month forecast may be prepared for the period of 4/1/15 through 3/31/16 once the financial results are known for the first quarter ending 3/31/15. This way, you always have 12 months of projections available to work with.

Rolling forecasts tend to be utilized in companies operating in highly fluid or uncertain times that need to always look out 12 months. However, more and more companies are utilizing rolling forecasts to better prepare for future uncertainties.

XYZ WHOLESALE, INC.
UNAUDITED FINANCIAL STATEMENT — COMPARATIVE

CONFIDENTIAL

Summary Balance Sheet	Actual Year End 1/1/15	Forecast — Low Year End 1/1/16	Forecast — Med Year End 1/1/16	Forecast — High Year End 1/1/16
Current Assets:				
Cash & Equivalents	$117,632	$56,515	$24,313	$48,265
Trade Receivables, Net	$1,271,875	$1,550,000	$1,610,000	$2,000,000
Inventory	$867,188	$825,000	$856,800	$1,000,000
Total Current Assets	$2,256,695	$2,431,515	$2,491,113	$3,048,265
Fixed & Other Assets:				
Property, Plant, & Equipment, Net	$1,750,000	$1,600,000	$1,650,000	$1,700,000
Other Assets	$75,000	$75,000	$75,000	$75,000
Total Fixed & Other Assets	$1,825,000	$1,675,000	$1,725,000	$1,775,000
Total Assets	$4,081,695	$4,106,515	$4,216,113	$4,823,265
Current Liabilities:				
Trade Payables	$2,601,563	$1,900,000	$1,965,600	$1,750,000
Accrued Liabilities	$195,117	$190,000	$196,560	$210,000
Line of Credit Borrowings	$200,000	$700,000	$250,000	$550,000
Current Portion of Long-Term Liabilities	$300,000	$300,000	$300,000	$300,000
Total Current Liabilities	$3,296,680	$3,090,000	$2,712,160	$2,810,000
Long-Term Liabilities:				
Notes Payable, Less Current Portion	$300,000	$0	$0	$0
Other Long-Term Liabilities	$150,000	$150,000	$150,000	$150,000
Total Long-Term Liabilities	$450,000	$150,000	$150,000	$150,000
Total Liabilities	$3,746,680	$3,240,000	$2,862,160	$2,960,000
Equity:				
Common and Preferred Equity, $1 Per Share	$500,000	$1,000,000	$1,000,000	$1,000,000
Retained Earnings	$901,265	($164,985)	($164,985)	($164,985)
Current Earnings	($1,066,250)	$31,500	$518,938	$1,028,250
Total Equity	$335,015	$866,515	$1,353,953	$1,863,265
Total Liabilities & Equity	$4,081,695	$4,106,515	$4,216,113	$4,823,265

Summary Income Statement	Actual Year End 1/1/15	Forecast — Low Year End 1/1/16	Forecast — Med Year End 1/1/16	Forecast — High Year End 1/1/16
Revenue	$13,875,000	$14,250,000	$16,000,000	$18,500,000
Costs of Goods Sold	$10,406,250	$10,687,500	$11,727,000	$13,597,500
Gross Profit	$3,468,750	$3,562,500	$4,273,000	$4,902,500
Gross Margin	25.00%	25.00%	26.71%	26.50%
Selling, General, & Administrative Expenses	$3,060,000	$3,000,000	$3,150,000	$3,250,000
Depreciation Expense	$350,000	$350,000	$400,000	$450,000
Interest Expense	$75,000	$81,000	$104,063	$74,250
Other (Income) Expenses	$1,050,000	$100,000	$100,000	$100,000
Net Profit Before Tax	($1,066,250)	$31,500	$518,938	$1,028,250
Income Tax Expense (Benefit)	$0	$0	$0	$0
Net Profit (Loss)	($1,066,250)	$31,500	$518,938	$1,028,250

Summary Cash Flow Statement	Actual Year End 1/1/15	Forecast — Low Year End 1/1/16	Forecast — Med Year End 1/1/16	Forecast — High Year End 1/1/16
Operating Cash Flow:				
Net Income (Loss)	($1,066,250)	$31,500	$518,938	$1,028,250
Depreciation Expense	$350,000	$350,000	$400,000	$450,000
Net Operating Cash Flow	($716,250)	$381,500	$918,938	$1,478,250

Figure 4-6:
What-if
forecasts.

Book III

Managing
Your
Finances

(continued)

Working Capital:				
(Increase) Decrease in Trade Receivables	$471,875	($278,125)	($338,125)	($728,125)
(Increase) Decrease in Inventory	$1,049,194	$42,188	$10,388	($132,813)
Increase (Decrease) in Trade Payables	($81,371)	($701,563)	($635,963)	($851,563)
Increase (Decrease) in Accrued Liabilities	$60,971	($5,117)	$1,443	$14,883
Increase (Decrease) in Current Debt	$100,000	$500,000	$50,000	$350,000
Net Working Capital Cash Flow	$1,600,668	($442,617)	($912,257)	($1,347,617)
Financing Capital:				
Equity Contributions	$0	$500,000	$500,000	$500,000
Additions to Long-Term Debt	$0	$0	$0	$0
Deletions to Long-Term Debt	($300,000)	($300,000)	($300,000)	($300,000)
Fixed Asset Additions	($600,000)	($200,000)	($300,000)	($400,000)
Change to Other Long-Term Assets	$0	$0	$0	$0
Change to Other Long-Term Liabilities	$10,000	$0	$0	$0
Net Financial Capital Cash Flow	($890,000)	$0	($100,000)	($200,000)
Beginning Cash	$123,214	$117,632	$117,632	$117,632
Ending Cash	$117,632	$56,515	$24,312	$48,265

Figure 4-6:
Continued.

Using the Budget as a Business-Management Tool

The real key to a budget lies in you, as the business owner, being able to understand the information and then act on it. This section reviews some of the most frequently relied upon outcomes from the budgeting process.

The *variance report* is nothing more than taking a look at the budget and comparing it to actual results for a period of time. Figure 4-7 presents a variance report for XYZ Wholesale, Inc., and compares the budgeted results for the quarter ending 3/31/15 against the company's actual results.

Of keen importance is the increase in the company's gross margin, which helped the company break even during the quarter compared to a projected loss of $174,000. Obviously, you need to understand what caused the gross margin to increase. Was it from higher sales prices or lower product costs? Of more importance, however, is that you need to act on the information. If the market is supporting higher prices in general, then you may want to revisit pricing strategies for the second through fourth quarters to take advantage of conditions that may allow the company to further improve its annual financial performance.

Another use of the budget is to support the implementation of specific plans and action steps. For example, if your second dry cleaning store is set to open in the third quarter of the year, then you need to secure the staff to support this store in the middle of the second quarter and then train them to ensure that they're ready when the new store opens. Yes, all this data should have been accumulated and incorporated into the original budget prepared for the new store, but the idea is to turn the budget into a proactive working document (easily accessible for reference) rather than a one-time effort left on the shelf to die.

XYZ WHOLESALE, INC.
UNAUDITED FINANCIAL STATEMENT — VARIANCE ANALYSIS

Summary Income Statement	Forecast Qtr. End 4/1/15	Actual Qtr. End 4/1/15	Variance Qtr. End 4/1/15
Revenue	$2,800,000	$2,865,000	$65,000
Costs of Goods Sold	$2,128,000	$2,018,500	$109,500
Gross Profit	$672,000	$846,500	$174,500
Gross Margin	24.00%	29.55%	
Selling, General, & Administrative Expenses	$700,000	$705,000	($5,000)
Depreciation Expense	$100,000	$100,000	$0
Interest Expense	$20,531	$20,000	$531
Other (Income) Expenses	$25,000	$18,500	$6,500
Net Profit Before Tax	($173,531)	$3,000	$172,469
Income Tax Expense (Benefit)	$0	$0	$0
Net Profit (Loss)	($173,531)	$3,000	$172,469

© John Wiley & Sons, Inc.

Figure 4-7: Variance analysis.

Using Budgets in Other Ways

When preparing budgets, you must remember that you can use the base data and information accumulated to support other business planning and management functions as well. For example, you can use a well-developed budget to not only prepare forecast financial statements but to prepare the estimated taxable income or loss of a company. For some companies, the difference between book and tax income is small. However for others, the difference can be significant, as the following example illustrates.

A large provider of personnel services elects to implement a strategy to self-fund its worker's compensation insurance costs. The preliminary analysis indicates that an average annual savings of 30 percent or more can be achieved if properly managed. At the end of the third year of the self-funded worker's compensation insurance program, the company had established an accrued liability for more than $1 million to account for potential future claims (to properly reflect the fact that claims made under the program through the end of the year would eventually cost the company $1 million). For book purposes, the $1 million represented an expense recorded in the financial statements, which resulted in the company producing net income of roughly zero dollars. For tax purposes, the IRS would not allow the expense until the claims were actually paid, so the taxable income of the company was $1 million (resulting in a tax liability of $400,000). If the company didn't properly budget for this business event, it may have been in for a rude surprise because, per the books, the company made nothing, yet owed $400,000 in taxes. You can be assured that this is not the type of surprise an executive business owner wants to experience on short notice.

Budgets also play a critical role in developing a business plan, especially when a company is attempting to secure capital to execute its strategy. Financial forecasts act as a visual or numeric display of your vision and outlook of where the company is headed. Effectively presented, financial forecasts can enhance the creditability of the management team and basis of the business plan, which, in turn, provides for fewer barriers to acceptance from potential funding sources. In effect, the financial forecasts must clearly present the "story" of the business.

You can also use the budget for other purposes as well, such as preparing information for specialized needs from external parties to training a new store manager on the basic economics of how his store should perform to ensuring that the vision of the company is properly aligned with your direct actions.

The better a budget is designed and structured from the beginning, the more uses and value it will provide your business down the road.

Chapter 5

Satisfying the Tax Man

In This Chapter

▶ Filing sole proprietor taxes

▶ Reporting taxes on partnerships

▶ Filing taxes for corporations

▶ Reporting and paying sales taxes

*P*aying taxes and reporting income for your company are very important jobs, and the way in which you complete these tasks properly depends on your business's legal structure. From sole proprietorships to corporations and everything in between, this chapter explains how taxes are handled for each type. You also get some instruction on collecting and transmitting sales taxes on the products your company sells. (See Book II Chapter 6 for in-depth information on what's what with all the different forms of business structure and for choosing the right legal structure for your business.)

Go to www.irs.gov to see the latest and greatest versions of the federal tax forms discussed in this chapter.

Tax Reporting for Sole Proprietors

The federal government doesn't consider sole proprietorships to be separate and distinct legal entities, so they're not taxed as such. Instead, sole proprietors report any business earnings on their individual tax returns — that's the only financial reporting they must do for income tax purposes.

Most sole proprietors file their business tax obligations as part of their individual 1040 tax return using the additional two-page form *Schedule C, Profit or Loss from Business.* On the first page of Schedule C, you report all the company's income and expenses and answer a few questions about your business. The second page is where you report information about Cost of Goods Sold and any vehicles used as part of the business.

Sole proprietors must also pay both the employee and the employer sides of Social Security and Medicare (self-employment tax) — that's double what an employee would normally pay, because the employer matches what is withheld from the employee's wages. Table 5-1 shows the drastic difference in these types of tax obligations for sole proprietors.

Table 5-1	Comparison of Tax Obligations for Sole Proprietors	
Type of Tax	*Amount Taken from Employees*	*Amount Paid by Sole Proprietors*
Social Security	6.2%	12.4%
Medicare	1.45%	2.9%

Social Security and Medicare taxes are based on the net profit of the small business, not the gross profit, which means that you calculate the tax after you've subtracted all costs and expenses from your revenue. To help you figure out the tax amounts you owe on behalf of your business, use IRS form *Schedule SE, Self-Employment Tax.* On the first page of this form, you report your income sources, and on the second page, you calculate the tax due.

As the bookkeeper for a sole proprietor, you're probably responsible for pulling together the income, Cost of Goods Sold, and expense information needed for this form. In most cases, you then hand off this information to an accountant to fill out all the required forms.

Filing Tax Forms for Partnerships

If your business is structured as a partnership (which, by definition, has more than one owner), your business doesn't pay taxes. Instead, all money earned by the business is split up (passed through) among the partners — who then pay personal income taxes.

The bookkeeper for a partnership or an LLC choosing to be taxed as a partnership needs to provide the financial data necessary to prepare *Form 1065 U.S. Return of Partnership Income.* Typically an accurate income statement and balance sheet are all that is necessary. These financial statements should be provided to the company's accountant, who prepares Form 1065.

The partnership's income and expenses from Form 1065 are used to generate a *Schedule K-1 (Form 1065), Partner's Share of Income, Deductions, Credits, etc.* for each partner. The partnership's tax results will "pass through" to the individual partners based on the partnership agreement. The Schedule

K-1 reports to each partner his or her respective share of the partnership's tax results. Using the K-1 information, each partner is then required to report the tax results on his or her tax returns.

Individuals use page 2 of *Form 1040 Schedule E Supplemental Income and Loss* to report the K-1 information on their Form 1040. Note that Schedule E is used for other reporting purposes such as income rental real estate, income from S Corporations, and so on. Your accountant can help you with preparing Schedule E as well as making the passive and non-passive distinctions.

Paying Corporate Taxes

Corporations come in two varieties, S Corporations and C Corporations; as you may expect, each has unique tax requirements and practices. In fact, not all corporations pay taxes. Some smaller corporations have elected to be taxed as S Corporations and pass their earnings through to their stockholders. Both C and S Corporations have the same legal requirements and protections; they only vary in tax treatment.

Check with your accountant to determine whether incorporating your business makes sense for you. Tax savings isn't the only issue you have to think about; operating a corporation also increases administrative, legal, and accounting costs. Be sure that you understand all the costs before incorporating.

Book III

Managing Your Finances

Reporting for an S Corporation

An *S Corporation* must have 100 stockholders or fewer, have only one class of stock, and only have shareholders who are individuals, certain trusts, and estates. (See a professional for other, less common eligibility requirements.) An S Corporation functions like a partnership but gives owners more legal protection from lawsuits than traditional partnerships do. S Corporations still file a corporate tax return, on Form 1120S. However, the tax return is for informational purposes only, with the income on each shareholder's Form K-1 passing through to the individual's tax return on Schedule E of Form 1040, just as in the previous partnership example.

Reporting for a C Corporation

The type of corporation that's considered a separate legal entity for tax purposes is the *C Corporation.* A C Corporation is a legal entity that has been formed specifically for the purpose of running a business.

The biggest disadvantage of structuring your company as a C Corporation is that your profits are taxed twice — as a corporate entity and based on dividends paid to stockholders. If you're the owner of a C Corporation, you can be taxed twice, but you can also pay yourself a salary and therefore reduce the earnings of the corporation. Corporate taxation is very complicated, with lots of forms to be filled out, so it's impossible to go into sufficient detail here about how to file corporate taxes. However, Table 5-2 shows you the tax rates C Corporations are subject to. Note that each tax rate/income bracket is incremental. For example, income is taxed at the 15 percent rate up to $50,000, and only income in excess of $50,000 (up to the next bracket) is taxed at 25 percent.

Table 5-2	C Corporation Tax Rates
Taxable Income	*C Corporation Tax Rate*
$0–$50,000	15%
$50,001–$75,000	25%
$75,001–$100,000	34%
$100,001–$335,000	39%
$335,001–$10,000,000	34%
$10,000,001–$15,000,000	35%
$15,000,001–$18,333,333	38%
Over $18,333,333	35%

You may think that C Corporation tax rates look a lot higher than personal tax rates, but in reality, many corporations don't pay tax at all or pay taxes at much lower rates than you do. As a corporation, you have plenty of deductions and tax loopholes to use to reduce your tax bites. So even though you, the business owner, may be taxed twice on the small part of your income that's paid in dividends, with a corporation, you're more likely to pay less in taxes overall.

Reporting for Limited Liability Companies (LLC)

As noted in earlier chapters, LLCs, or Limited Liability Companies, are now being used extensively in business. LLCs can elect or choose their tax classification, such as being taxed as a C Corporation or as a partnership. LLCs have the same reporting requirements and file the same tax returns discussed earlier in this section, depending on their chosen classification.

Taking Care of Sales Taxes Obligations

Even more complicated than paying income taxes is keeping up-to-date on local and state tax rates and paying your business's share of those taxes to the government entities. Because tax rates vary from county to county, and even city to city in some states, managing sales taxes can be very time-consuming.

Things get messy when you sell products in multiple locations. For each location, you must collect from customers the appropriate tax for that area, keep track of all taxes collected, and pay those taxes to the appropriate government entities when due. In many states, you have to collect and pay local (for the city or county governments) and state taxes.

An excellent website for data about state and local tax requirements is the Federation of Tax Administrators (`www.taxadmin.org/fta/link/default.php?lnk=2`). This site has links for state and local tax information for every state.

States require you to file an application to collect and report taxes even before you start doing business in that state. Be sure that you contact the departments of revenue in the states you plan to operate stores before you start selling and collecting sales tax.

All sales taxes collected from your customers are paid when you send in the Sales and Use Tax Return for your state — you must have the cash available to pay this tax when the forms are due. Any money you collected from customers during the month should be kept in an account called Accrued Sales Taxes, which is actually a Liability account on your balance sheet because it's money owed to a governmental entity.

Book III

Managing Your Finances

Book IV

Managing Your Business

Five steps to better interviewing

Every interview consists of five key steps:

1. **Welcome the applicant.** Greet your candidates warmly and chat with them informally to help loosen them up. Questions about the weather, the difficulty of finding your offices, or how they found out about your position are old standbys.

2. **Summarize the position.** Briefly describe the job, the kind of person you're looking for, and the interview process you use.

3. **Ask your questions (and then listen).** Questions should be relevant to the position and should cover the applicant's work experience, education, and other related topics. Limit the amount of talking you do as an interviewer. Many interviewers end up trying to sell the job to an applicant instead of probing whether a candidate is a good fit.

4. **Probe experience and discover the candidate's strengths and weaknesses.** The best predictor of future behavior is past behavior, which is why exploring applicants' past experience can be so helpful to see what they did and how they did it! And although asking your candidates to name their strengths and weaknesses may seem clichéd, the answers can be very revealing.

5. **Conclude the interview.** Allow your candidates the opportunity to offer any further information that they feel is necessary for you to make a decision, and to ask questions about your firm or the job. Thank them for their interest and let them know when they can expect your firm to contact them.

You'll find some handy tips for new managers at
www.dummies.com/extras/startingabusinessaio.

Contents at a Glance

Chapter 1: Tackling the Hiring Process 365

Starting with a Clear Job Description 366
Defining the Characteristics of Desirable Candidates 367
Finding Good People 368
Becoming a Great Interviewer 372
Evaluating Your Candidates 376
Hiring the Best (and Leaving the Rest) 379

Chapter 2: Setting Goals 383

Knowing Where You're Going 384
Identifying SMART Goals 386
Setting Goals: Less Is More 388
Communicating Your Vision and Goals to Your Team 389
Juggling Priorities: Keeping Your Eye on the Ball 391
Using Your Power for Good: Making Your Goals Reality 393

Chapter 3: Embracing Corporate Social Responsibility 395

Understanding Socially Responsible Practices 396
Doing the Right Thing: Ethics and You 400

Chapter 4: Managing with Technology 405

Weighing the Benefits and Drawbacks of Technology
  in the Workplace 406
Using Technology to Your Advantage 409
Getting the Most Out of Company Networks 413

Chapter 5: Developing Employees Through
Coaching and Mentoring 415

Why Help Develop Your Employees? 416
Getting Down to Employee Development 418
Coaching Employees to Career Growth and Success 422
Finding a Mentor, Being a Mentor 429

Chapter 6: Delegating to Get Things Done 431

Delegating: The Manager's Best Tool 431
Debunking Myths about Delegation 433
Taking the Six Steps to Delegate 437
Sorting Out What to Delegate and What to Do Yourself 438

Chapter 1

Tackling the Hiring Process

In This Chapter

▶ Determining your needs

▶ Recruiting new employees

▶ Following interviewing do's and don'ts

▶ Evaluating your candidates

▶ Making the big decision

Finding and hiring the best candidate for a job has never been easy. The good news about all the streamlining, downsizing, and rightsizing going on in business nowadays is that a lot of people are looking for work. The bad news, though, is that few of them have the exact qualifications you're looking for.

Added to that, the Baby Boom generation that has dominated most organizations for the past couple of decades is beginning to retire. Between 2010 and 2020, 32 million jobs will be vacated, and 20 million new jobs will be created. This means 52 million jobs in the United States will need to be filled; however, the projected available labor force will be only 29 million. This leaves a gap of 23 million jobs, which is having a huge impact on recruiting, training, succession planning, transfer of knowledge, retaining, and leading. Three conditions — an aging workforce, a shrinking labor pool, and a projected population peak — are converging to create one of the most competitive marketplaces ever. It's up to business owners and other business leaders to address these issues soon or risk falling behind the competition.

Your challenge as a business owner is to figure out how to not just find the best candidates for your job openings, but also to convince them that your company is the best place to work. This chapter guides you through both sides of that challenge.

Starting with a Clear Job Description

Is the position new, or are you filling an existing one? In either case, before you start the recruiting process, you need to ask yourself some questions. Do you know exactly what standards you're going to use to measure your candidates? Do you have a designated pay range for this position? The clearer you are about what you need and the boundaries you need to work within, the easier and less arbitrary your selection process becomes.

If you're filling an existing position, you probably already have a detailed job description available. Review it closely and make changes where necessary. Again, ensure that the job description reflects exactly the tasks and requirements of the position. When you hire someone new to fill an existing position, you start with a clean slate. For example, you may have had a difficult time getting a former employee to accept certain new tasks — say, taking minutes at staff meetings or filing travel vouchers. By adding these new duties to the job description before you open recruitment, you make the expectations clear and you don't have to struggle with your new hire to do the job.

If the job is new, now is your opportunity to design your ideal candidate. Draft a job description that fully describes all the tasks and responsibilities of the position and the minimum necessary qualifications and experience. If the job requires expertise in addition and subtraction, for example, say so. You're not going to fill the position with the right hire if you don't make certain qualifications a key part of the job description. The more work you put into the job description now, the less work you have to do after you bring in your new hire.

Finally, before you start recruiting, use the latest-and-greatest job description to outline the most important qualities you're seeking in your new hire. Consult and compare notes with other owners of similar businesses to get input on your descriptions, and ask employees for their feedback as well. Use this outline to guide you in the interview process. Keep in mind, however, that job descriptions may give you the skills you want, but they don't automatically give you the kind of employee you want — finding the right person is much more difficult (and is the reason you spend so much time recruiting in the first place).

Making an *interview outline* carries an additional benefit: You can easily document why you didn't hire the candidates who didn't qualify for your positions. An interview outline is your personal summary of your impressions of the candidate — a memory trigger, based on your notes taken before, during, and after the interview. Pay close attention here. If a disgruntled job candidate ever sues you for not hiring him — and such lawsuits are more common than you may suspect — you'll be eternally thankful that you did your homework in this area of the hiring process. One more thing: Don't make notes on the résumé — your comments could be used in a lawsuit.

Defining the Characteristics of Desirable Candidates

Employers look for many qualities in candidates. The following list gives you an idea of the qualities employers consider most important when hiring new employees. Other characteristics may be particularly important to you, your company, and the job you're looking to fill. This list gives you a good start in identifying them:

- ✔ **Hard working:** Hard work can often overcome a lack of experience or training. You want to hire people who are willing to do whatever it takes to get the job done. Conversely, no amount of skill can make up for a lack of initiative or work ethic. Although you won't know for sure until you make your hire, carefully questioning candidates can give you some idea of their work ethic (or, at least, what they want you to believe about their work ethic). Of course, hard work alone isn't always the end-all, be-all of hiring. People can generate a lot of work, but if the work doesn't align with your business's strategies or isn't within the true scope of their role, then it's wasted effort. Be careful to note the difference as you assess your candidates.

- ✔ **Good attitude:** Although what constitutes a "good" attitude differs for each person, a positive, friendly, willing-to-help perspective makes life at the office much more enjoyable and makes everyone's job easier. When you interview candidates, consider what they'll be like to work with for the next five or ten years. Skills are important, but attitude is even more important. This is the mantra for the success of Southwest Airlines: "Hire for attitude, train for success."

- ✔ **Experienced:** Some candidates may naively think they should be hired immediately based on the weight of their institution's diploma. However, they may lack a critical element that's so important in the hiring process: experience. An interview gives you the opportunity to ask pointed questions that require your candidates to demonstrate that they can do the job.

- ✔ **Self-starter:** Candidates need to demonstrate an ability to take initiative to get work done. Initiative ranks as a top reason employees are able to get ahead where they work.

✔ **Team player:** Teamwork is critical to the success of today's organizations that must do far more with far fewer resources than their predecessors. The ability to work with others and to collaborate effectively is a definite must for employees today.

✔ **Smart:** Smart people can often find better and quicker solutions to the problems that confront them. In the world of business, work smarts are more important than book smarts (present book excepted, of course).

✔ **Responsible:** You want to hire people who are willing to take on the responsibilities of their positions. Questions about the kinds of projects your candidates have been responsible for and the exact roles those projects played in their success can help you determine this important quality. Finer points, like showing up for the interview and remembering the name of the company they're interviewing for, can also be key indicators of your candidates' sense of responsibility.

✔ **Flexible/resilient:** Employees who are able to multitask and switch direction if necessary in a seamless manner are real assets to any organization in today's fast-changing world.

✔ **Cultural fit:** Every business has its own unique culture and set of values. The ability to fit into this culture and values is key to whether candidates can succeed within a particular business (assuming that they already have the technical skills).

✔ **Stable:** You don't want to hire someone today and then find out he's already looking for the next position tomorrow. No business can afford the expense of hiring and training a new employee, only to have that person leave six months later. You can get some indication of a person's potential stability (or lack thereof) by asking pointed questions about how long candidates worked with a previous employer and why they left. Be especially thorough and methodical as you probe this particular area.

Hiring the right people is one of the most important tasks business owners face. You can't have a great organization without great people. Unfortunately, business owners traditionally give short shrift to hiring, devoting as little time as possible to preparation and the actual interview process. As in much of the rest of your life, the results you get from the hiring process are usually in direct proportion to the amount of time you devote to it.

Finding Good People

People are the heart of every business. The better people you hire, the better business you'll have. Some people are just meant to be in their jobs. You may know such individuals — someone who thrives as a receptionist or someone who lives to sell. Think about how great your organization would be if you staffed every position with people who lived for their jobs.

Likewise, bad hires can make working for an organization an incredibly miserable experience. The negative impacts of hiring the wrong candidate can reverberate both inside and outside an organization for years. If you, as a business owner, ignore the problem, you put yourself in danger of losing your good employees — and clients, business partners, and vendors. Would you rather spend a few extra hours up front to find the best candidates, or later devote countless hours trying to straighten out a problem employee?

Of course, as important as the interview process is to selecting the best candidates for your jobs, you won't have anyone to interview if you don't have a good system for finding good candidates. So, where can you find the best candidates for your jobs? The simple answer is *everywhere*.

Take a long-term view of the hire: a broad search and long hiring cycle that involves other employees in the process. The short-term, "We've gotta have somebody right away" approach often results in selecting an applicant who is the lesser of a number of evils — and whose weaknesses soon become problems for the organization.

Going through traditional recruiting channels

Your job is to develop a recruitment system that helps you find the kinds of people you want to hire. Here are some of the best ways to find candidates for your positions:

- ✔ **Internal candidates:** In most organizations, the first place to look for candidates is within the organization. If you do your job training and developing employees, you probably have plenty of candidates to consider for your job openings. Only after you exhaust your internal candidates should you look outside your organization. Not only is hiring people this way less expensive and easier, but you also get happier employees, improved morale, and new hires who are already familiar with your organization.

- ✔ **Personal referrals:** Whether from co-workers, professional colleagues, friends, relatives, or neighbors, you can often find great candidates through referrals. Who better to present a candidate than someone whose opinion you already value and trust? You get far more insight about the candidates' strengths and weaknesses from the people who refer them than you ever get from résumés alone. Not only that, but research shows that people hired through current employees tend to work out better, stay with the company longer, and act happier. When you're getting ready to fill a position, make sure you let people know about it. Your employees and co-workers may well mount their own Twitter and Facebook campaigns for you, getting the word out to a wide audience.

- **Temporary agencies:** Hiring *temps,* or temporary employees, has become routine for many companies. When you simply have to fill a critical position for a short period of time, temporary agencies are the way to go — no muss, no fuss. And the best part is that when you hire temps, you get the opportunity to try out employees before you buy them. If you don't like the temps you get, no problem. Call the agency, and it sends replacements before you know it. But if you like your temps, most agencies allow you to hire them at a nominal fee or after a minimum time commitment. Either way, you win. One more point: If you're using temps, you can complete your organization's necessary work while you continue looking for the right full-time employee. This buys you more time to find the best person for the job without feeling pressure to hire someone who doesn't really meet all your needs.

- **Professional associations:** Most professions have their accompanying associations that look out for their interests. Whether you're a doctor (and belong to the American Medical Association) or a truck driver (and belong to the Teamster's Union), you can likely find an affiliated association for whatever you do for a living. Associations even have their own associations. Association newsletters, magazines, websites, blogs, and social networking sites are great places to advertise your openings when you're looking for specific expertise, because your audience is already prescreened for you.

- **Employment agencies:** If you're filling a particularly specialized position, are recruiting in a small market, or simply prefer to have someone else take care of recruiting and screening your applicants, employment agencies are a good, albeit pricey alternative (with a cost of up to a third of the employee's first-year salary, or more). Although employment agencies can usually locate qualified candidates in lower-level or administrative positions, you may need help from an executive search firm or *headhunter* (someone who specializes in recruiting key employees away from one firm to place in a client's firm) for your higher-level positions.

- **Want ads:** Want ads can be relatively expensive, but they're an easy way to get your message out to a large cross-section of potential candidates. You can choose to advertise in your local paper, in nationally distributed publications such as *The Wall Street Journal,* or on popular job-search websites (see the next section for suggestions). On the downside, you may find yourself sorting through hundreds or even (gulp) thousands of unqualified candidates to find a few great ones.

Leveraging the power of the Internet

Every day, more businesses discover the benefits of using the Internet as a hiring tool. The proliferation of job search tools, corporate web pages, and online employment agencies has brought about an entirely new dimension in recruiting. Your own website lets you present almost unlimited amounts and kinds of information about your business and your job openings — in text, audio, graphic, and video formats. Your site works for you 24 hours a day, 7 days a week.

Consider a few of the best ways to leverage the power of the Internet in your own hiring efforts:

- ✓ **Websites and blogs:** If you don't already have a great recruiting page on your company website, you should. In addition to this baseline item, also consider setting up company blogs where employees can describe what they do and how they do it. This gives prospective job candidates insight into your organization, helping them decide for themselves whether yours is the kind of organization they want to actively pursue. Be sure to include a function where people can supply their e-mail address or sign up for an RSS feed to be updated as new positions open. Prices to set up a website or blog vary from free to a few thousand dollars a year, depending on how many bells and whistles you require.

- ✓ **E-mail campaigns:** If you set up the e-mail function on your website just mentioned, you'll soon collect a large number of addresses from potential job candidates. Don't just sit there — use them! Be sure to e-mail an announcement to everyone on your list every time you have a job opening. Even if the people who receive your e-mail message aren't interested, they may know someone who is and may forward your announcement.

- ✓ **Social networking sites:** Two, in particular, deserve your attention if you hope to broaden your search for good candidates: Facebook (www.facebook.com) and LinkedIn (www.linkedin.com). Many millions of people have established accounts at both of these sites; however, LinkedIn was specifically designed to help job seekers network with one another to find new job opportunities. This makes it a particularly effective way for you to get the word out about your open positions. Although Facebook isn't specifically set up for job networking, you can set up a fan page there and use it as an effective recruiting platform. There's no charge to set up and use a Facebook or LinkedIn account.

- ✓ **Twitter:** Many organizations today are using Twitter (www.twitter.com) as a real-time platform for getting out information to anyone interested in getting it. This includes prospective job applicants. The variety of information you can send out to the world is limited only by your imagination — and by the 140-character limit for individual tweets. There's no charge to set up and use your Twitter account.

✔ **Traditional job-hunting sites:** A number of job-hunting sites have become popular with people looking for new positions. This makes them good platforms from which to pitch your own job openings. Popular ones include Career Builder (www.careerbuilder.com), Indeed (www.indeed.com), Simply Hired (www.simplyhired.com), Monster (www.monster.com), and Beyond (www.beyond.com). You'll likely have to pay to post your jobs on these sites — prices vary. For a free option, don't forget your local Craigslist (www.craigslist.com).

Becoming a Great Interviewer

After you narrow the field to the top three or five applicants, the next step is to start interviewing. What kind of interviewer are you? Do you spend several hours preparing for interviews — reviewing résumés, looking over job descriptions, writing and rewriting questions until each one is as finely honed as a razor blade? Or are you the kind of interviewer who, busy as you already are, starts preparing for the interview when you get the call from your receptionist that your candidate has arrived?

The secret to becoming a great interviewer is to be thoroughly prepared for your interviews. Remember how much time you spent preparing to be interviewed for a job you really wanted? You didn't just walk in the door, sit down, and get offered the job, did you? You probably spent hours researching the company, its products and services, its financials, its market, and other business information. You probably brushed up on your interviewing skills and may have even done some role-playing with a friend or in front of a mirror. Don't you think you should spend at least as much time getting ready for the interview as the people you're going to interview?

Asking the right questions

More than anything else, the heart of the interview process is the questions you ask and the answers you get in response. You get the best answers when you ask the best questions. Lousy questions often result in lousy answers that don't really tell you whether the candidate is right for the job.

A great interviewer asks great questions. According to Richard Nelson Bolles, author of the perennially popular job-hunting guide *What Color Is*

Your Parachute?, you can categorize all interview questions under one of the following four headings:

✔ **Why are you here?** Why is the person sitting across from you going to the trouble of interviewing with you today? You have just one way to find out — ask. You may assume that the answer is because he or she wants a job with your firm, but what you find may surprise you.

Consider the story of the interviewee who forgot that he was interviewing for a job with Hewlett-Packard. During the entire interview, the applicant referred to Hewlett-Packard by the name of one of its competitors. He didn't get the job.

✔ **What can you do for us?** Always an important consideration! Of course, your candidates are all going to dazzle you with their incredible personalities, experience, work ethic, and love of teamwork — that almost goes without saying. However, despite what many job seekers seem to believe, the question is not, "What can your firm do for me?" — at least, not from your perspective. The question that you want an answer to is, "What can you do for us?"

✔ **What kind of person are you?** Few of your candidates will be absolute angels or demons, but don't forget that you'll spend a lot of time with the person you hire. You want to hire someone you'll enjoy being with during the many work hours, weeks, and years that stretch before you — and the holiday parties, company picnics, and countless other events you're expected to attend. You also want to confirm a few other issues: Are your candidates honest and ethical? Do they share your views regarding work hours, responsibility, and so forth? Are they responsible and dependable employees? Would they work well in your company culture? Of course, all your candidates will answer in the affirmative to mom-and-apple-pie questions like these. So how do you find the real answers?

You might try to "project" applicants into a typical, real-life scenario and then see how they'd think it through. For example, ask the prospect what she would do if a client called at 5 p.m. with an emergency order that needed to be delivered by 9 a.m. the next morning. This way, there's no "right" answer and candidates are forced to expose their thinking process: what questions they'd ask, what strategies they'd consider, which people they'd involve, and so forth. Ask open-ended questions and let your candidates do most of the talking.

✔ **Can we afford you?** It does you no good to find the perfect candidate but, at the end of the interview, discover that you're so far apart in pay range that you're nearly in a different state. Keep in mind that the actual wage you pay to workers is only part of an overall compensation package. You may not be able to pull together more money for wages for particularly good candidates, but you may be able to offer them better benefits, a nicer office, the option of working from home, extra time off, a more impressive title, or a key to the executive sauna.

Following interviewing do's

So what can you do to prepare for your interviews? The following handy-dandy checklist gives you ideas on where to start:

- ✓ **Review the résumés of each interviewee the morning before interviews start.** Not only is it extremely poor form to wait to read your interviewees' résumés during the interview, but you miss out on the opportunity to tailor your questions to those little surprises you invariably discover in the résumés.

- ✓ **Become intimately familiar with the job description.** Are you familiar with all the duties and requirements of the job? Surprising new hires with duties that you didn't tell them about — especially when they're major duties — isn't a pathway to new-hire success.

- ✓ **Draft your questions before the interview.** Make a checklist of the key experience, skills, and qualities that you seek in your candidates, and use it to guide your questions. Of course, one of your questions may trigger other questions that you didn't anticipate. Go ahead with such questions, as long as they give you additional insights into your candidate and help illuminate the information you're seeking with your checklist.

- ✓ **Select a comfortable environment for both of you.** Your interviewee will likely be uncomfortable regardless of what you do. You don't need to be uncomfortable, too. Make sure that the interview environment is well ventilated, private, and protected from interruptions. You definitely don't want your phone ringing off the hook or employees barging in during your interviews. You get the best performance from your interviewees when they aren't thrown off track by distractions.

As you have no doubt gathered by now, interview questions are one of your best tools for determining whether a candidate is right for your company. Although some amount of small talk is appropriate to help relax your candidates, the heart of your interviews should focus on answering the questions just listed. Above all, don't give up. Keep asking questions until you're satisfied that you have all the information you need to make your decision.

Take lots of notes as you interview your candidates. Don't rely on your memory when it comes to interviewing candidates for your job. If you interview more than a couple of people, you can easily forget who said exactly what, as well as what your impressions were of their performances. Not only are your written notes a great way to remember who's who, but they're an important tool to have when you're evaluating your candidates.

And try to avoid the temptation to draw pictures of little smiley faces or that new car you've been lusting after. Write the key points of your candidates' responses and their reactions to your questions. For example, if you ask why your candidate left her previous job, and she starts getting really nervous, make a note about this reaction. Finally, note your own impressions of the candidates:

- ✔ *Top-notch performer — the star of her class.*

- ✔ *Fantastic experience with developing applications in a client/server environment. The best candidate yet.*

- ✔ *Geez, was this one interviewing for the right job?*

Avoiding interviewing don'ts

If you've gone through the hiring process a few times already, you know that you can run into tricky situations during an interview and that certain questions can land you in major hot water if you make the mistake of asking them.

Some interviewing don'ts are merely good business practice. For example, accepting an applicant's invitation for a date is probably not a good idea. Believe it or not, it happens. After a particularly drawn-out interview at a well-known high-tech manufacturer, a male candidate asked out a female interviewer. The interviewer considered her options and declined the date; she also declined to make Prince Charming a job offer.

Avoid playing power trips during the course of the interview. Forget the old games of asking trick questions, turning up the heat, or cutting the legs off their chairs (yes, some people still do this game playing) to gain an artificial advantage over your candidates. Get real — it's the 21st century.

Some blunders are the major legal type — the kind that can land you and your company in court. Interviewing is one area of particular concern in the hiring process as it pertains to possible discrimination. For example, although you can ask applicants whether they are able to fulfill job functions, in the United States, you can't ask them whether they have disabilities. Because of the critical nature of the interview process, you must know the questions that you absolutely should never ask a job candidate. Here is a brief summary of the kinds of topics that may get you and your business into trouble, depending on the exact circumstances:

- ✔ Age

- ✔ Arrest and conviction record

- ✔ Debts

- ✔ Disability

Book IV

Managing Your Business

- ✔ Height and weight
- ✔ Marital status
- ✔ National origin
- ✔ Race or skin color
- ✔ Religion (or lack thereof)
- ✔ Sex
- ✔ Sexual orientation

Legal or illegal, the point is that none of the preceding topics is necessary to determine applicants' ability to perform their jobs. Therefore, ask questions that directly relate to the candidates' ability to perform the tasks required. To do otherwise can put you at definite legal risk. In other words, what *does* count is job-related criteria — that is, information that's directly pertinent to the candidate's ability to do the job (you clearly need to decide this *prior* to interviewing!).

Evaluating Your Candidates

Now comes the really fun part of the hiring process — evaluating your candidates. If you've done your homework, then you already have an amazing selection of candidates to choose from, you've narrowed your search to the ones showing the best potential to excel in your position, and you've interviewed them to see whether they can live up to the promises they made in their résumés. Before you make your final decision, you need a bit more information.

Checking references

Wow! What a résumé! What an interview! What a candidate! Would you be surprised to find out that this shining employee-to-be didn't really go to Yale? Or that he really wasn't the account manager on that nationwide marketing campaign? Or that his last supervisor wasn't particularly impressed with his analytical skills?

A résumé and interview are great tools, but a reference check is probably the only chance you have to find out before you make a hiring decision whether your candidates are actually who they say they are. Depending on your organization, you may be expected to do reference checks. Or maybe your human resources department takes care of that task.

Depending on your industry and level of security consciousness, you may want to run a background check on your prospects before hiring them. The legal and privacy implications of doing so vary from state to state. You can check out www.privacyrights.org/small-business-owner-background-check-guide for an overview of the process of doing a background check. But you should definitely consult a lawyer licensed to practice in your state before doing your first background check.

The twin goals of checking references are to verify the information that your candidates have provided and to gain some candid insight into who your candidates really are and how they behave in the workplace. When you contact a candidate's references, limit your questions to topics related to the work to be done. As in the interview process, asking questions that can be considered discriminatory to your candidates isn't appropriate.

Here are some of the best ways to do your reference checking:

- ✔ **Check academic references.** A surprising number of people exaggerate or tell outright lies when reporting their educational experience. Start your reference check here.

- ✔ **Call current and former supervisors.** Getting information from employers is getting more difficult. Many businesspeople are rightfully concerned that they may be sued for libel or defamation of character if they say anything negative about current or former subordinates. Still, it doesn't hurt to try. You get a much better picture of your candidates if you speak directly to their current and former supervisors instead of to their company's human resources department — especially if the supervisors you speak to have left their firms. The most you're likely to get from the HR folks is a confirmation that the candidate worked at the company during a specific period of time.

- ✔ **Check your network of associates.** If you belong to a professional association, union, or similar group of like-minded careerists, you have the opportunity to tap into the rest of the membership to get the word on your candidates. For example, if you're a certified public accountant (CPA) and want to find out about a few candidates for your open accounting position, you can check with the members of your professional accounting association to see whether anyone knows anything about them.

- ✔ **Do some surfing.** On the web, that is. Google your candidate's name, perhaps along with the name of the company where the person last worked or the city where she lives. Or do a search for your candidate on Facebook (www.facebook.com) or LinkedIn (www.linkedin.com). You might be surprised by how much information you can uncover about a job candidate — good and bad — doing just a few simple web searches. But be careful. Many people have the same name. Make sure you have the right person!

Book IV

Managing Your Business

Reviewing your notes

You did take interview notes, didn't you? Now's the time to drag them back out and look them over. Review the information package for each candidate — one by one — and compare your findings against your predetermined criteria. Take a look at the candidates' résumés, your notes, and the results of your reference checks. How do they stack up against the standards you set for the position? Do you see any clear winners at this point? Any clear losers? Organize your candidate packages into the following stacks:

- ✔ **Winners:** These candidates are clearly the best choices for the position. You have no hesitation in hiring any one of them.

- ✔ **Potential winners:** These candidates are questionable for some reason. Maybe their experience isn't as strong as that of other candidates, or perhaps you weren't impressed with their presentation skills. Neither clear winners nor clear losers, you hire these candidates only after further investigation or if you can't hire anyone from your pool of winners.

- ✔ **Losers:** These candidates are clearly unacceptable for the position. You simply don't consider hiring any of them.

Conducting a second (or third) round

When you're a busy business owner, you have pressure to get things done as quickly as possible, and you're tempted to take shortcuts to achieve your goals. It seems that everything has to be done yesterday — or maybe the day before. When do you have the opportunity to really spend as much time as you want to complete a task or project? Time is precious when you have ten other projects crying for your attention. Time is even more valuable when you're hiring for a vacant position that's critical to your organization and needs to be filled right now.

Hiring is one area of business where you must avoid taking shortcuts. Remember, hire slowly and fire quickly (but within the rules). Finding the best candidates for your vacancies requires an investment of time and resources. Your company's future depends on it. Great candidates don't stay on the market long, though, so don't allow the process to drag on too long. Make sure the candidates know your required time frame, and stick to it.

Depending on your organization's policies or culture, or if you're undecided on the best candidate, you may decide to bring candidates in for several rounds of interviews. But keep in mind that the timeline for an offer differs depending on the job you're interviewing for. Lower-level job hunters cannot afford to be unemployed (if they are) for long, and they often get and accept job offers quickly. A higher-level position — say, a general manager — gives you more time.

The ultimate decision on how many rounds and levels of interviews to conduct depends on the nature of the job itself, the size of your company, and your policies and procedures. If the job is simple or at a relatively low level in the company, a single phone interview may be sufficient to determine the best candidate. However, if the job is complex or at a relatively high level in the organization, you may need several rounds of testing and personal interviews to determine the best candidate.

Checking employment eligibility

With today's increased emphasis on national security and immigration status, employers are required to take some steps to verify the eligibility of employees to work in the U.S. You should obtain USCIS Form I-9 (Employment Eligibility Verification) from prospective employees. This form is used to collect information on the employee and document the verification steps. Be aware: An employer can be fined for failing to follow the process. In addition, there is a relatively new program called E-Verify, which allows employers to verify an applicant's work status online. You can obtain Form I-9 and related information from the U.S. Citizenship and Immigration Services (USCIS) website at www.uscis.gov. The E-Verify program is free, and you can find out more about it at www.uscis.gov/e-verify.

Immigrants can be a good source of workers, and you may be able to sponsor employees through various programs. For example, there are H-1B visas for specialty occupations, such technical or scientific workers. The USCIS website mentioned in the preceding paragraph has additional information about these and other employer-sponsored worker visas.

You should be aware of possible federal tax credits available for hiring certain targeted workers. For example, the American Taxpayer Relief Act of 2012 extended the Work Opportunity Tax Credit, which provided tax credits for hiring qualified veterans. Congress is considering extending these types of credits. You can find current information at www.irs.gov.

Book IV

Managing Your Business

Hiring the Best (and Leaving the Rest)

Rank your candidates within the groups of winners and potential winners that you established during the evaluation phase of the hiring process. You don't need to bother ranking the losers because you wouldn't hire them anyway — no matter what. The best candidate in your group of winners is first, the next best is second, and so on. If you've done your job thoroughly and well, the best candidates for the job are readily apparent at this point.

The next step is to get on the phone and offer your first choice the job. Don't waste any time — you never know whether your candidate has interviewed with other employers. It would be a shame to invest all this time in the hiring process only to find out that your top choice accepted a job this morning with one of your competitors. If you can't come to terms with your first choice in a reasonable amount of time, go on to your second choice. Keep going through your pool of winners until you either make a hire or exhaust the list of candidates.

The following sections give you a few tips to keep in mind as you rank your candidates and make your final decision.

Being objective

In some cases, you may prefer certain candidates because of their personalities or personal charisma, regardless of their abilities or work experience. Sometimes the desire to like these candidates can obscure their shortcomings, while a better qualified, albeit less socially adept, candidate may fade in your estimation.

Be objective. Consider the job to be done, as well as the skills and qualifications that being successful requires. Do your candidates have these skills and qualifications? What would it take for your candidates to be considered fully qualified for the position?

Don't allow yourself to be unduly influenced by your candidates' looks, champagnelike personalities, high-priced hairstyles, or fashion-forward clothing ensembles. None of these characteristics can tell you how well your candidates will actually perform the job. The facts are present for you to see in your candidates' résumés, interview notes, and reference checks. If you stick to the facts, you can still go wrong, but the chances are diminished.

One more thing: Diversity in hiring is positive for any organization. Check your bias at the door.

Trusting your gut

Sometimes you're faced with a decision between two equally qualified candidates, or with a decision about a candidate who is marginal but shows promise. In such cases, you have weighed all the objective data and given the analytical side of your being free rein, but you still have no clear winner. What do you do in this kind of situation?

Listen to yourself. Although two candidates may seem equal in skills and abilities, do you have a feeling that one is better suited to the job? If so, go with it. As much as you may want your hiring decision to be as objective as possible, whenever you introduce the human element into the decision-making process, a certain amount of subjectivity is naturally present.

In reality, rarely are two candidates equally qualified, although often one or more people seem to have more to bring to the job than anticipated (for example, industry focus, fresh ideas, previous contacts, and so forth). This is again where your pre-work can be so valuable in keeping you focused. Can they both do the job? If so, the bonus traits can tip the scale.

Other options:

- ✔ Give them each a nonpaid assignment and see how they do.
- ✔ Try them each on a paid project.

Keep in touch with other top candidates as additional needs arise or in case your first choice doesn't work out.

Revisiting the candidate pool

What do you do if, heaven forbid, you can't hire anyone from your group of winners? This unfortunate occurrence is a tough call, but no one said hiring is an easy task. Take a look at your stack of potential winners. What would it take to make your top potential winners into winners? If the answer is as simple as a training course or two, then give these candidates serious consideration — with the understanding that you can schedule the necessary training soon after hiring. Perhaps a candidate just needs a little more experience before moving into the ranks of the winners. You can make a judgment call on whether you feel that someone's current experience is sufficient until that person gains the experience you're looking for. If not, you may want to keep looking for the right candidate. After all, this person may be working with you for a long time — waiting for the best candidate only makes sense.

If you're forced to go to your group of almost-winners and no candidate really seems up to the task, don't hire someone simply to fill the position. If you do, you're probably making a big mistake. Hiring employees is far easier than unhiring them. The damage that an inappropriate hire can wreak — on co-workers, your customers, and your organization (not to mention the person you hired) — can take years and a considerable amount of money to undo. Not only that, but it can be a big pain in your neck! Other options are to redefine the job, reevaluate other current employees, or hire on a temporary basis to see whether a risky hire works out.

Chapter 2

Setting Goals

In This Chapter

▶ Linking goals to your vision

▶ Creating SMART goals

▶ Concentrating on fewer goals

▶ Publicizing your goals

▶ Following through with your employees

▶ Determining sources of power

*I*f you created a list of the most important duties of management, "setting goals" would likely be near the top of the list. In most small and startup companies, the owner sets the overall purpose — the vision — of the organization. The owner then has the job of developing goals and plans for achieving that vision. Owners and employees work together to set goals and develop schedules for attaining them.

As a business owner, you're probably immersed in goals — not only for yourself, but also for your employees and your organization. This flood of goals can cause stress and frustration as you try to balance the relative importance of each one.

Should I tackle my goal of improving turnaround time first, or should I get to work on finishing the budget? Or maybe the goal of improving customer service is more important. Well, I think I'll just try to achieve my own personal goal of setting aside some time to eat lunch today.

Sometimes having too many goals is as bad as not having any goals. This chapter helps you understand why setting strong, focused goals is essential to your success and that of your employees. It also guides you in communicating visions and goals and keeping both you and your employees on track to meet established goals.

Goals provide direction and purpose. Don't forget, if you can see it, you can achieve it. Goals help you see where you're going and how you can get there. And the *way* you set goals can impact how motivating they are to others.

Knowing Where You're Going

Believe it or not, Lewis Carroll's classic book *Alice's Adventures in Wonderland* offers lessons that can enhance your business relationships. Consider the following passage, in which Alice asks the Cheshire Cat for advice on which direction to go.

"Would you tell me, please, which way I ought to go from here?"

"That depends a good deal on where you want to go," said the Cat.

"I don't much care where —," said Alice.

"Then it doesn't matter which way you go," said the Cat.

" — so long as I get *somewhere*," Alice added as an explanation.

"Oh, you're sure to do that," said the Cat, "if you only walk long enough."

It takes no effort at all to get *somewhere*. Just do nothing, and you're there. (In fact, everywhere you go, there you are.) However, if you want to get somewhere meaningful and succeed as a business owner, you first have to know where you want to go. And after you decide where you want to go, you need to make plans for how to get there. This practice is as true in business as in your everyday life.

For example, suppose that you have a vision of starting up a second dry cleaning store in a nearby suburb so that you can grow your business. How do you go about achieving this vision? You have three choices:

- An unplanned, non-goal-oriented approach
- A planned, goal-oriented approach
- A hope and a prayer

Which choice do you think is most likely to get you to your goal? Go ahead, take a wild guess. If you guessed the unplanned, non-goal-oriented approach to reaching your vision, shame on you. Please report to study hall. Your assignment is to write 500 times: *A goal is a dream with a deadline.*

If you guessed the planned, goal-oriented approach, you've earned a big gold star.

Following are the main reasons to set goals whenever you want to accomplish something significant:

- **Goals provide direction.** To get something done, you have to set a definite vision — a target to aim for and to guide the efforts of you and your organization. You can then translate this vision into goals that take you where you want to go. Without goals, you're doomed to waste countless hours going nowhere. With goals, you can focus your efforts and your team's efforts on only the activities that move you toward where you're going — in this case, opening another dry cleaning location.

- **Goals tell you how far you've traveled.** Goals provide milestones to measure how effectively you're working toward accomplishing your vision. If you determine that you must accomplish several specific milestones to reach your final destination and you complete a few of them, you know exactly how many remain. You know right where you stand and how far you have yet to go.

- **Goals help make your overall vision attainable.** You can't reach your vision in one big step — you need many small steps to get there. If, again, your vision is to open a second dry cleaning location, you can't expect to proclaim your vision on Friday and walk into a fully staffed and functioning store on Monday. You must accomplish many goals — from shopping for business space, to hiring staff, to getting the word out via advertising — before you can attain your vision. Goals enable you to achieve your overall vision by dividing your efforts into smaller pieces that, when accomplished individually, add up to big results.

- **Goals clarify everyone's role.** When you discuss your vision with your employees, they may have some idea of where you want to go but no idea of how to go about getting there. As your well-intentioned employees head off to help you achieve your vision, some employees may duplicate the efforts of others, some employees may focus on the wrong strategies and ignore more important tasks, and some employees may simply do something else altogether (and hope that you don't notice the difference). Setting goals with your team clarifies what the tasks are, who handles which tasks, and what is expected from each employee and, ultimately, from the entire team.

- **Goals give people something to strive for.** People are typically more motivated when challenged to attain a goal that's beyond their normal level of performance — this is known as a *stretch goal*. Not only do goals give people a sense of purpose, but they also relieve the boredom that can come from performing a routine job day after day. Be sure to discuss the goal with them and seek feedback where appropriate to gain their commitment and buy-in.

For goals to be effective, they have to link directly to the owner's final vision. To stay ahead of the competition — or simply to maintain their current position in business — business owners create compelling visions, and then they and their employees work together to set and achieve the goals to reach those visions.

When it comes to goals, the best ones

- ✔ Are few in number but very specific and clear in purpose.

- ✔ Are stretch goals. They're attainable, but they aren't too easy or too hard.

- ✔ Involve people. When you involve others in a collaborative, team-based process, you get buy-in so it becomes their goal, not just yours.

Identifying SMART Goals

You can find all kinds of goals in all types of organizations. Some goals are short term and specific ("Starting next month, we will increase production by two units per employee per hour"); others are long term and vague ("Within the next five years, we will become a learning organization"). Employees easily understand some goals ("Line employees will have no more than 20 rejects per month"), but other goals can be difficult to measure and subject to much interpretation ("All employees are expected to show more respect to each other in the next fiscal year"). Still other goals can be accomplished relatively easily ("Reception staff will always answer the phone by the third ring"), whereas others are virtually impossible to attain ("All employees will master the five languages that our customers speak before the end of the fiscal year").

How do you know what kind of goals to set? The whole point of setting goals, after all, is to achieve them. It does you no good to go to the trouble of calling meetings, hacking through the needs of your organization, and burning up precious time only to end up with goals that aren't acted on or completed. Unfortunately, this scenario describes what far too many business owners do with their time.

The best goals are *smart* goals — actually, SMART goals is the acronym to help you remember them. SMART refers to a handy checklist for the five characteristics of well-designed goals:

- ✔ **Specific:** Goals must be clear and unambiguous; broad and fuzzy thinking has no place in goal setting. When goals are specific, they tell employees exactly what's expected, when, and how much. Because the goals are specific, you can easily measure your employees' progress toward their completion.

✓ **Measurable:** What good is a goal that you can't measure? If your goals aren't measurable, you never know whether your employees are making progress toward their successful completion. Not only that, but your employees may have a tough time staying motivated to complete their goals when they have no milestones to indicate their progress.

✓ **Attainable:** Goals must be realistic and attainable by average employees. The best goals require employees to stretch a bit to achieve them, but they aren't extreme. That is, the goals are neither out of reach nor set too low. Goals that are set too high or too low become meaningless, and employees naturally come to ignore them.

✓ **Relevant:** Goals must be an important tool in the grand scheme of reaching your company's vision and mission. You may have heard that 80 percent of workers' productivity comes from only 20 percent of their activities. You can guess where the other 80 percent of work activity ends up. This relationship comes from Italian economist Vilfredo Pareto's 80/20 rule. This rule, which states that roughly 80 percent of effects come from 20 percent of causes, has been applied to many other fields. Relevant goals address the 20 percent of workers' activities that has such a great impact on performance and brings your organization closer to its vision, thereby making it, and you, a success.

✓ **Time-bound:** Goals must have starting points, ending points, and fixed durations. Commitment to deadlines helps employees focus their efforts on completing the goal on or before the due date. Goals without deadlines or schedules for completion tend to be overtaken by the day-to-day crises that invariably arise in the workplace.

SMART goals make for smart businesses. In our experience, many owners and managers neglect to work with their employees to set goals together. And for the ones that do, goals are often unclear, ambiguous, unrealistic, immeasurable, uninspiring, and unrelated to the organization's vision. By developing SMART goals with your employees, you can avoid these traps while ensuring the progress of your business and your team.

Although the SMART system of goal setting provides guidelines to help you frame effective goals, you have additional considerations to keep in mind. The following considerations help you ensure that anyone in your organization can easily understand and act on the goals you and your employees agree on.

✓ **Ensure that goals are related to your employees' role in the business.** Pursuing an organization's goals is far easier for employees when those goals are a regular part of their jobs and they can see how their contributions support the company. For example, suppose that you set

Book IV

Managing Your Business

a goal for employees who solder circuit boards to raise production by 2 percent per quarter. These employees spend almost every working moment pursuing this goal, because the goal is an integral part of their job. However, if you give the same employees a goal of "improving the diversity of the organization," what exactly does that have to do with your line employees' role? Nothing. The goal may sound lofty and may be important to your business, but because your line employees don't make the hiring decisions, you're wasting both your time and theirs with that particular goal.

✔ **Whenever possible, use values to guide behavior.** What's the most important value in your organization? Honesty? Fairness? Respect? Whatever it is, ensure that you and any other leaders in the business model this behavior and reward employees who live it.

✔ **Simple goals are better goals.** The easier your goals are to understand, the more likely the employees are to work to achieve them. Goals should be no longer than one sentence; make them concise, compelling, and easy to read and understand.

Goals that take more than a sentence to describe are actually multiple goals. When you find multiple-goal statements, break them into several individual, one-sentence goals. Goals that take a page or more to describe aren't really goals; they're books. File them away and try again.

Setting Goals: Less Is More

Big businesses love to plan. When the last planning meetings are over, the managers often congratulate each other over their collective accomplishment and go back to their regular office routines. Before long, the goals they hammered out together are forgotten, and the pages they were recorded on are neatly folded and stored away in someone's file cabinet. Meanwhile, business goes on as usual, and the long-range planning effort goes into long-term hibernation. You probably don't have this problem, but the lesson is there for you to learn all the same, because even in a small business, it can be tempting to create goals and then let them slide as you resume your normal day-to-day work.

Don't let all your hard work be in vain. When you go through the exercise of setting goals, keep them to a manageable number that can realistically be followed up on. And when you finish one goal, move on to the next.

The following guidelines can help you select the right goals — and the right number of goals — for your business:

✔ **Pick two to three goals to focus on.** You can't do everything at once — at least not well — and you can't expect your employees to, either. Attempt to complete only a few goals at any one time. Setting too many goals dilutes the efforts of you and your staff and can result in a complete breakdown in the process.

✔ **Pick the goals with the greatest relevance.** Certain goals bring you a lot closer to attaining your vision than do other goals. Because you have only so many hours in your workday, it clearly makes sense to concentrate your efforts on a few goals that have the biggest payoff rather than on a boatload of goals with relatively less impact to the business.

✔ **Focus on the goals that tie most closely to your organization's mission.** You may be tempted to take on goals that are challenging, interesting, and fun to accomplish but that are far removed from your organization's mission. Don't do it.

✔ **Regularly revisit the goals and update them as necessary.** Business is anything but static, and regularly assessing your goals is important in making sure that they're still relevant to the vision you want to achieve. Put in quarterly or midyear review schedules. If the goals remain important, great — carry on. If not, meet with your employees to revise the goals and the schedules for attaining them.

Avoid creating too many goals in your zeal to get as many things done as quickly as you can. Too many goals can overwhelm you — and they can overwhelm your employees, too. You're far better off setting a few significant goals and then concentrating your efforts on attaining them. Don't forget that your management skill isn't measured by one huge success after another. Instead, it involves successfully meeting daily challenges and opportunities — gradually but inevitably improving the business in the process.

Communicating Your Vision and Goals to Your Team

Having goals is great, but how do you get the word out to your employees? As you know, goals should align with your vision for your business. Establishing goals helps you ensure that employees focus on achieving the vision in the desired time frame and with the desired results. You have many possible ways to communicate goals to your employees, but some ways are better than others. In every case, you must communicate goals clearly, the receiver must understand the goals, and the relevant parties must follow through on achieving the goals.

Communicating your organization's vision is as important as communicating specific goals. You can communicate the vision in every way possible, as often as possible, throughout your organization and to significant others such as clients, customers, suppliers, and so forth.

When you communicate vision and goals, do it with energy and a sense of urgency and importance. You're talking about the future of your business and your employees, not the score of last night's game. If your team doesn't think that you care about the vision, why should they? Simply put, they won't.

Companies usually announce their visions to employees — and the public — in ways that are designed to maximize the impact. Companies commonly communicate their vision in these ways:

- By conducting employee rallies where the vision is unveiled in an inspirational presentation

- By branding their vision on anything possible — business cards, letterhead stationery, posters hung in the break room, employee name tags, and more

- By proudly emblazoning their vision statements within company websites; on Facebook fan pages; and via electronic media campaigns, Twitter tweets, and other Internet-enabled methods of communication

- By mentioning the corporate vision in newspaper, radio, television, and other media advertising

- By encouraging managers to "talk up" the vision in staff meetings or other verbal interactions with employees and during recruiting

To avoid a cynical "fad" reaction from employees who may be suspicious of management's motives when unveiling a new initiative, making consistent, casual, and genuine reference to it is much more effective than hosting a huge, impersonal event. Again, in this case, less is often better.

Unlike visions, goals are much more personalized to the department or individual employees, and you must use more formal and direct methods to communicate them. The following guidelines can help:

- **Write down your goals.**

- **Conduct one-on-one, face-to-face meetings with your employees to introduce, discuss, and assign goals.**

  If you can't conduct a face-to-face meeting, conduct your meeting over the phone. The point is to make sure that your employees hear the goals, understand them and your expectations, and have the opportunity to ask for clarifications.

✔ **Call your team together to introduce team-related goals.**

You can assign goals to teams instead of solely to individuals. Get the team together and explain the role of the team and each individual in the successful completion of the goal. Make sure that all team members understand exactly what they are to do and whether a leader or co-leaders are ultimately responsible for the goals' completion. Get employee buy-in and try to make the goals resonate with each person. (Book IV Chapter 5 discusses teams in more detail.)

✔ **Gain the commitment of your employees, whether individually or on teams, to work toward the successful accomplishment of their goals.**

Ask your employees to prepare and present plans and milestone schedules explaining how they can accomplish the assigned goals in the agreed-upon timeline. After your employees begin working on their goals, regularly monitor their progress to ensure that they're on track, and collaborate with them to resolve any problems.

Juggling Priorities: Keeping Your Eye on the Ball

After you've decided what goals are important to you and your organization, you come to the difficult part. How do you, the owner, maintain the focus of your employees — and yourself, for that matter — on achieving the goals you've set?

The process of goal setting can generate excitement and engage employees in the inner workings of the business, whether the goals are set individually or by function. This excitement can quickly evaporate, though, when employees return to their desks. You, the owner, must take steps to ensure that the organization's focus remains centered on the agreed-upon goals, not on other matters (which are less important but momentarily more pressing). Of course, this task is much easier said than done.

Book IV

Managing Your Business

Staying focused on goals can be extremely difficult — particularly when you're a busy person and the goals compound your regular responsibilities. Think about situations that demand your attention during a typical day at work:

✔ How often do you sit down at your desk in the morning to prioritize your day, only to have your priorities completely changed five minutes later when you get a call from an angry customer?

✔ How many times has an employee unexpectedly come to you with a problem?

✔ Have you ever gotten caught in a so-called quick meeting that lasts for hours?

In unlimited ways, you or your employees can get derailed and lose the focus you need to get your organization's goals accomplished. One of the biggest problems employees face is confusing activity with tangible results. Do you know anyone who works incredibly long hours — late into the night and on weekends — but never seems to get anything done? These employees always seem busy, but they're working on the wrong things. This is called the *activity trap,* and it's easy for you and your employees to fall into.

Remember the 80/20 rule? The flip side is when you consider that only 20 percent of workers' productivity comes from 80 percent of their activity. This statistic illustrates the activity trap at work. What do you do in an average day? More important, what do you do with the 80 percent of your time that produces so few clear results? You can get out of the activity trap and take control of your schedules and priorities. However, you have to be tough, and you have to single-mindedly pursue your goals.

Achieving your goals is all up to you. No one can make it any easier for you to concentrate on achieving your goals. You have to take charge and find an approach that works for you. If you aren't controlling your own schedule, you're simply letting everyone else control your schedule for you.

Following are some tips to help you and your employees get out of the activity trap:

✔ **Complete your top-priority task first.** With all the distractions that compete for your attention, with the constant temptation to work on the easy stuff first and save the tough stuff for last, and with people dropping into your office just to chat or to unload their problems on you, concentrating on your top-priority task is always a challenge. However, if you don't do your top priority first, you're almost guaranteed to find yourself caught in the activity trap. That is, you'll find the same priorities on your list of tasks to do day after day, week after week, and month after month. If your top-priority task is too large, divide it into smaller chunks and focus on the most important piece first.

✔ **Get organized.** Getting organized and managing your time effectively are both incredibly important pursuits for anyone in business. If you're organized, you can spend less time trying to figure out what you should be doing and more time just doing it.

✔ **Just say no.** If someone tries to make his or her problems your problems, just say no. If you're a small business owner, you probably like nothing more than taking on new challenges and solving problems. However, the conflict arises when solving somebody else's problems interferes with your own work. You have to fight the temptation to lose control of your day. Always ask yourself, "How does this help me achieve my goals?"

Using Your Power for Good: Making Your Goals Reality

After you create a set of goals with your employees, how do you make sure they get done? How do you turn your priorities into your employees' priorities? The best goals in the world mean nothing if they aren't achieved. You can choose to leave this critical step to chance or you can choose to get involved.

You have the power to make your goals happen.

Power has gotten a bad rap lately. In reaction to the highly publicized leadership styles that signified greed and unethical behavior in American corporations, employees have increasingly demanded — and organizations are recognizing the need for — management that is principle centered and has a more compassionate, human face.

Nothing is inherently wrong with power — everyone has many sources of power within. Not only do you have power, but you also exercise power to control or influence people and events around you on a daily basis (hopefully in a positive way). Generally, well-placed power is a positive thing. However, power can be a negative thing when abused or when someone acts in only self-interest. Manipulation, exploitation, and coercion have no place in the modern workplace.

You can use your positive power and influence to your advantage — and to the advantage of the people you lead — by tapping into it to help achieve your organization's goals. People and systems often fall into ruts or nonproductive patterns of behavior that are hard to break. Power properly applied can redirect people and systems and move them in the right direction — the direction that leads to the accomplishment of goals.

Everyone has five primary sources of power, as well as specific strengths and weaknesses related to these sources. Recognize your strengths and weaknesses and use them to your advantage. As you review the five sources of power that follow, consider your own personal strengths and weaknesses.

- ✔ **Personal power:** This is the power that comes from within your character. Your passion for greatness, the strength of your convictions, your ability to communicate and inspire, your personal charisma, and your leadership skills all add up to personal power.

- ✔ **Relationship power:** Everyone has relationships with people at work. These interactions contribute to the relationship power that you possess in your organization. Sources of relationship power include close friendships with top executives, partners, owners, people who owe you favors, and co-workers who provide you with information and insights that you wouldn't normally receive.

- ✔ **Knowledge power:** To see knowledge power in action, just watch what happens the next time your organization's computer network goes down. You'll see who really has the power in your organization — in this case, your computer network administrator. Knowledge power comes from the special expertise and knowledge gained during the course of your career. Knowledge power also comes from obtaining academic degrees (think MBA) or special training.

- ✔ **Task power:** Task power is the power that comes from the job or process you perform at work. As you've probably witnessed, people can facilitate or impede the efforts of their co-workers and others by using their task power. For example, when you submit a claim for payment to your insurance company and months pass with no action ("Gee, we don't seem to have your claim in our computer — are you sure you submitted one? Maybe you should send us another one just to be safe!"), you're on the receiving end of task power.

- ✔ **Position power:** This kind of power derives strictly from your rank or title in the organization and is a function of the authority that you wield to command human and financial resources. Whereas the position power of the receptionist in your organization may be low, the position power of you, the owner, is at the top of the position power chart. But the best leaders seldom rely on position power to get things done today.

If you identify weakness in certain sources of power, you can strengthen them. For example, work on your weakness in relationship power by making a concerted effort to know your employees better. Instead of passing on the invitations to get together after work, join them once in a while — have fun and strengthen your relationship power at the same time. (Just never forget you're the boss. Try to keep such social gatherings as low-key as you can. If things start getting a little loose and rowdy, it's likely time for your departure.)

Be aware of the sources of your power and use your power in a positive way to help you and your employees accomplish the goals of your organization. For getting things done, a little power can go a long way.

Chapter 3

Embracing Corporate Social Responsibility

In This Chapter

▶ Understanding corporate social responsibility

▶ Creating a CSR strategy

▶ Behaving ethically

Corporate social responsibility — CSR, for short — is a way of doing business that's rapidly gaining in popularity both in the United States and around the world. *Corporate social responsibility* is conducting your business in a way that has a positive impact on the communities you serve. CSR affects many different aspects of operating a business — from recycling, to ethics, to environmental laws, and much more.

Ethics and office politics are powerful forces in any organization. *Ethics* is the framework of values that employees use to guide their behavior. You've seen the devastation that poor ethical standards can lead to — witness the string of business failures attributed to less than sterling ethics in more than a few large, seemingly upstanding businesses. Today more than ever, business owners are expected to model ethical behavior, to ensure that their employees follow in their footsteps, and to purge employees who refuse to align their own standards with your standards.

This chapter looks at adopting a corporate social responsibility strategy, building an ethical organization, and determining the nature and boundaries of your political environment.

Understanding Socially Responsible Practices

CSR has been gaining traction within businesses of all kinds in recent years. At one time, CSR was the sole province of socially progressive companies like ice cream maker Ben & Jerry's and organic yogurt manufacturer Stonyfield Farm, but this is no longer the case. Today even small, local, startup companies have adopted CSR practices and strategies.

Depending on the exact approach you take and how you implement it, you may have to spend a significant amount of money to conduct your business in a socially responsible way, but the benefits nearly always outweigh the costs. The consumer is changing. People want to buy products and services from companies that are socially responsible and that are making a positive impact on their communities. What's more, they want to *work for* companies that are socially responsible and that are making a positive impact on their communities. Finally, becoming a socially responsible company can actually reduce costs. For these reasons and others like them, CSR has taken the business world by storm.

Figuring out how you can employ CSR

As mentioned, CSR involves conducting your business in a way that has a positive impact on the communities you serve. But what exactly does that look like in the real world? Consider some of the traits of a socially responsible business:

- Takes responsibility for the conditions in which its products are manufactured, whether in this country or internationally, and whether by the company itself or by subcontractors.

- Promotes recycling, environmental responsibility, and natural resources used in more efficient, productive, and profitable ways.

- Views employees as assets instead of costs and engages them in their jobs by involving them in decision making. In the event of layoffs or job eliminations, it is viewed as a company that treats people fairly.

- Is committed to diversity in hiring and selection of vendors and employees.

- Adopts strong internal management and financial controls.

- Meets or exceeds all applicable social and environmental laws and regulations.

✓ Supports its communities through volunteerism, philanthropy, and local hiring.

✓ Promotes sustainability — that is, meeting the needs of the present without compromising the ability of future generations to meet their needs.

As a business owner, you will develop or lead the development of your company's CSR goals. The exact goals you select must be aligned with both your company's core business objectives and its core competencies. Some of the traits in the preceding list may or may not fit with your company's culture, objectives, or competencies. To be effective, your approach to CSR must make sense for your company and its employees, customers, and other stakeholders.

Consider for a moment the six Guiding Principles that coffee purveyor Starbucks embraces. The company's CSR strategy strongly influences these Guiding Principles:

✓ Provide a great work environment and treat each other with respect and dignity.

✓ Embrace diversity as an essential component in the way we do business.

✓ Apply the highest standards of excellence to the purchasing, roasting, and fresh delivery of our coffee.

✓ Develop enthusiastically satisfied customers all the time.

✓ Contribute positively to our communities and our environment.

✓ Recognize that profitability is essential to our future success.

Enjoying net benefits of socially responsible practices

The best corporate social responsibility is tightly integrated into a company's business operations; this strong connection can have a positive impact on the bottom line. Many CSR activities can reduce the cost of doing business while drawing new customers into the company's orbit, increasing the top line. The younger generation of employees now entering the workplace wants to make a difference in the world, too. Companies that practice CSR are more attractive to these talented men and women, who will remain loyal to their employers as long as they continue to have an opportunity to make a difference.

Book IV

Managing Your Business

Starbucks presents a strong business case for adopting a corporate social responsibility strategy in its Corporate Social Responsibility Annual Report:

✓ **Attracting and retaining our partners (employees):** We believe Starbucks's commitment to CSR contributes to overall retention and higher-than-usual levels of partner satisfaction and engagement. The company's comprehensive benefits package also motivates partners to stay at Starbucks.

✓ **Customer loyalty:** Studies have revealed that customers prefer to do business with a company they believe to be socially responsible, when their other key buying criteria are met. We surveyed our customers and found that 38 percent associate Starbucks with good corporate citizenship. The vast majority (86 percent) of customers surveyed indicated being extremely or very likely to recommend Starbucks to a friend or family. Our customers' loyalty has been instrumental to the company's ability to grow.

✓ **Reducing operating costs:** Many environmental measures, such as energy-efficient equipment or lighting, involve initial investments but deliver long-term environmental and cost-saving benefits.

✓ **Creating a sustainable supply chain:** We have made significant investments in our supply chains, with the long term in mind. Our focus has been to ensure that our suppliers of today will have the capacity to supply Starbucks business tomorrow. Their sustainability is critically linked to our growth and success. This is especially true of those who supply our core products or ingredients, such as coffee, tea, and cocoa.

✓ **License to operate:** Having a strong reputation as a socially responsible company makes it more likely we will be welcomed into a local community. In a recent customer survey, nearly half of the respondents indicated extremely or very positive attitudes about having a Starbucks in their neighborhood, while only 7 percent expressed negative attitudes.

Long story short, adopting socially responsible business practices is a net benefit to the companies that adopt them. Why not try them in your organization and see what happens?

Developing a CSR strategy for implementation

Adopting CSR in an effective manner requires developing a strategy for its implementation. The spectrum of possible CSR initiatives available to a company is mind boggling. You can start with a barebones approach — say, replacing disposable (and environmentally unfriendly) Styrofoam coffee cups with washable and infinitely reusable porcelain coffee mugs — or you can go all the way to a multiphase international CSR strategy that touches every part of your organization and has a direct and significant impact on the world.

Kellie McElhaney is the faculty director of the Center for Responsible Business at the Haas School of Business, University of California, Berkeley. In her book *Just Good Business: The Strategic Guide to Aligning Corporate Social Responsibility and Brand* (Berrett Koehler), Kellie describes seven rules to consider when developing an effective CSR strategy:

- ✔ **Know thyself.** Your CSR strategy must be authentic and must ring true for your organization. The best way to ensure that this is the case is to closely match it to your company's mission, vision, and values. Employees, customers, and others will know when it's not authentic, and your CSR strategy won't have the desired effect.

- ✔ **Get a good fit.** The goals you select for your CSR strategy must fit your company and its products and services. For example, if your business is a boutique selling women's clothing, then actively supporting breast cancer research is a good fit.

- ✔ **Be consistent.** Be sure that everyone in your organization knows what your CSR strategy and goals are and that everyone can express them consistently to one another — and to the general public. Your CSR efforts are multiplied when everyone in your company has a clear understanding of his or her role and is completely aligned with the program.

- ✔ **Simplify.** In developing and implementing a CSR strategy, simpler is usually better. Organic yogurt maker Stonyfield Farm's mantra is simple: "Healthy food, healthy people, healthy planet." Anyone can understand what the company is committed to accomplishing, and customers feel tremendous brand loyalty because they want to be a part of what Stonyfield is doing.

- ✔ **Work from the inside out.** Your CSR strategy isn't worth the paper it's written on if you haven't engaged your employees in the process of developing and implementing it. Instead of forcing a CSR strategy on your employees, invite their active participation in creating it and then rolling it out. You'll get better results and your employees will be pleased that you thought highly enough about them to involve them in the process.

- ✔ **Know your customer.** When developing a CSR strategy, it's better to address the immediate needs of your customers before you try to solve all the problems of the world. These customer needs often boil down to the most basic of human needs: safety, love and belonging, self-esteem, and self-actualization. If you can address these customer needs, you'll have a customer for life.

Book IV

Managing Your Business

✔ **Tell your story.** When you have your CSR strategy in place, don't be afraid to publicize your efforts to be socially responsible along with your successes. Again, many people (including prospective customers, clients, and employees) are attracted to companies that operate in a socially responsible way. If you don't get out the word about your programs, you'll lose this powerful advantage. So tell your story — as often as you can — to your employees and to the general public. Use company newsletters and brochures, your website, and online social media such as Twitter, Facebook, LinkedIn, and YouTube.

Above all, don't spend hours, days, or weeks laboring over a CSR strategy, only to file it away and forget all about it. Integrate your strategy into your everyday business operations. In this way, you'll gain the full benefit of corporate social responsibility — a benefit that can give you a distinct competitive advantage in the marketplace.

Doing the Right Thing: Ethics and You

Each year or two, the leaders of some company somewhere trigger a huge scandal due to some ethical lapse. These lapses are often so egregious that you wonder whether people in charge know the difference between right and wrong — or, if they do know the difference, whether they care.

Despite appearances to the contrary, many business leaders do know the difference between right and wrong. Now more than ever, businesses and the leaders who run them are trying to do the right thing, not just because the right thing is politically correct, but because it's good for the bottom line.

Defining ethics on the job

Do you know what ethics are? In case you're a bit rusty on the correct response, the long answer is that *ethics* are standards of beliefs and values that guide conduct, behavior, and activities — in other words, a way of thinking that provides boundaries for your actions. The short answer is that ethics are simply doing the right thing.

Although all people come to a job with their own sense of ethical values — based on their own upbringing and life experiences — organizations and leaders are responsible for setting clear ethical standards.

When you have high ethical standards on the job, you generally exhibit some or all of the following personal qualities and behaviors:

- ✔ Accountability
- ✔ Dedication
- ✔ Fairness
- ✔ Honesty
- ✔ Impartiality
- ✔ Integrity
- ✔ Loyalty
- ✔ Responsibility

Ethical behavior starts with you. As the owner, you're the leader of your organization, and you set an example — both for any managers you have reporting to you and for the many workers who are watching your every move. When others see you behaving unethically, you're sending the message loud and clear that ethics don't matter. The result? Ethics won't matter to them, either.

However, when you behave ethically, others follow your example and behave ethically, too. And if you practice ethical conduct, it also reinforces and perhaps improves your own ethical standards. Small business owners have a responsibility to try to define, live up to, and improve their own set of personal ethics.

Creating a code of ethics

Although most people have a pretty good idea about which kinds of behavior are ethical and which aren't, ethics are somewhat subjective and open to interpretation by the individual employee. For example, one worker may think that making unlimited personal phone calls from the office is okay, whereas another worker may consider that to be inappropriate.

So what's the solution to ethics that vary from person to person in an organization? A code of ethics. By creating and implementing a code of ethics, you clearly and unambiguously spell out for all employees — from the very top to the very bottom — your organization's ethical expectations. A code of ethics isn't a substitute for company policies and procedures; the code complements them. Instead of leaving your employees' definition of ethics on the job to chance — or someone's upbringing — you clearly spell out that stealing, sharing trade secrets, sexually harassing a co-worker, and engaging in other unethical behavior is unacceptable and may be grounds for dismissal. And when you require your employees to read and sign a copy acknowledging their acceptance of the code, your employees can't very well claim that they

Book IV

Managing Your Business

didn't know what you expected of them. The ethics policy should be reviewed and agreed to annually so that it remains top-of-mind for all employees.

Four key areas form the foundation of a good code of ethics:

✔ Compliance with internal policies and procedures

✔ Compliance with external laws and regulations

✔ Direction from organizational values

✔ Direction from individual values

Of course, a code of ethics isn't worth the paper it's printed on if it doesn't address some very specific issues, as well as generic ones. The following are some of the most common issues addressed by typical codes of ethics:

✔ Conflicts of interest

✔ Diversity

✔ Employee health and safety

✔ Equal opportunity

✔ Gifts and gratuities

✔ Privacy and confidentiality

✔ Sexual harassment

In addition to working within an organization, a well-crafted code of ethics can be a powerful tool for publicizing your company's standards and values to people outside your organization, including vendors, clients, customers, investors, potential job applicants, the media, and the general public. Your code of ethics tells others that you value ethical behavior and that it guides the way you and your employees do business.

Of course, simply having a code of ethics isn't enough. You and your employees must also live it. Even the world's best code of ethics does you no good if you file it away and never use it.

Making ethical choices every day

You may have a code of ethics, but if you never behave ethically in your day-to-day business transactions and relationships, what's the purpose of having a code in the first place? Ethical challenges abound in business — some are spelled out in your company's code of ethics, or in its policies and procedures, and some aren't. For example, what would you do in these situations?

- ✔ One of your favorite employees gives you tickets to a baseball game.

- ✔ An employee asks you not to write her up for a moderate infraction of company policies.

- ✔ You sold a product to a client that you later found out to be faulty, but the client seems unaware of the problem.

- ✔ You find out that your star employee actually didn't graduate from college, as he claimed in his job application.

- ✔ You know that a product you sell doesn't actually do everything your company claims it does.

We all make ethical choices on the job every day — how do you make yours? Consider this framework comprising six keys to making better ethical choices:

- ✔ **Evaluate** circumstances through the appropriate filters. (Filters include culture, laws, policies, circumstances, relationships, politics, perception, emotions, values, bias, and religion.)

- ✔ **Treat** people and issues fairly within the established boundaries. *Fair* doesn't always mean *equal.*

- ✔ **Hesitate** before making critical decisions.

- ✔ **Inform** those affected of the standard or decision that has been set.

- ✔ **Create** an environment of consistency for yourself and your working group.

- ✔ **Seek** counsel when you have any doubt (but from those who are honest and whom you respect).

Chapter 4

Managing with Technology

· ·

In This Chapter

▶ Using technology to help you

▶ Understanding the pros and cons of technology

▶ Improving efficiency and productivity

▶ Networking your organization

▶ Developing a technology plan

· ·

You've gotta love technology. Unfortunately, like everything else in life, technology has its good and bad points. On the upside, computers make our work lives much easier and more efficient (right?). As long as your computer doesn't crash, it remembers everything you've done and makes completing repetitive tasks (like merging a letter with a 1,000-person mailing list) a snap. On the downside, computers can be an enormous waste of time. Instead of working, some people spend a significant portion of their work-days checking their Facebook accounts, watching cat videos on YouTube, and keeping track of the latest celebrity gossip.

You may automatically assume that your employees are more productive because they have computers at their fingertips, but are you (and your fledg-ling business) really getting the most out of this innovative and expensive technology? Given how much money most startups invest in their informa-tion technology (IT) systems, hardware, and software, that can be an expen-sive question.

This chapter explains how to harness IT — technology used to create, store, exchange, and use information in its various forms. It examines the technology edge and considers how technology can help or hinder a new organization. It looks at how technology can improve efficiency and produc-tivity, and how to get the most out of it. Finally, it describes how to create a technology plan.

Weighing the Benefits and Drawbacks of Technology in the Workplace

Think for a moment about the incredible progress of information technology just in your lifetime. With so many tools at your fingertips, can you believe that, only about three decades ago, the personal computer hadn't yet been introduced commercially? Word processing used to mean a typewriter and a lot of correction fluid or sheets of messy carbon paper; computers have revolutionized the way businesspeople can manipulate text, graphics, and other elements in their reports and other documents. Mobile phones, fax machines, the Internet, broadband wireless connections, and other business technology essentials are all fairly recent innovations.

You can't turn back the clock on technology. To keep up with the competition — and beat it — you must keep pace with technology and adopt tools that can make your employees more productive, while improving products and services, customer service, and the bottom line. You really have no other choice.

Making advances, thanks to automation

IT can have a positive impact on your business in two important ways, both related to the practice of automation:

- **Automating processes:** Not too many years ago, business processes were manual. For example, your bookkeeper may have calculated payroll entirely by hand with the assistance of only a ten-key adding machine. What used to take hours, days, or weeks can now be accomplished in minutes or even seconds. Other processes that are commonly automated are inventory tracking, customer service, call analysis, and purchasing.

- **Automating personal management functions:** More people than ever are moving their calendars and personal planners onto computers. Although paper-based planners aren't going to die completely, many folks are finding that computers are much more powerful management tools than their unautomated counterparts. Small business owners use computers to schedule meetings, track projects, analyze numbers, manage business contact information, conduct employee performance evaluations, and more.

Before you run off and automate everything, keep this piece of information in mind: If your manual system is inefficient or ineffective, simply automating the system isn't necessarily going to make your system perform any better. In fact, automating it can make your system perform worse than the manual version.

When you automate, review the process in detail. Cut out any unnecessary steps and make sure your system is optimized for the new, automated environment. The time you take now to improve your processes and functions is going to pay off when you automate.

Improving efficiency and productivity

The explosion of IT accompanies the shift in business from old-school standards, such as cigar stores, video rental shops, and shoe repair outfits, to those producing web design, app development, and online retail products and services. The personal computer industry, still in its infancy three decades ago, has quickly grown into a market worth many billions of dollars in annual sales.

The idea that businesspeople who best manage information have a competitive advantage in the marketplace seems obvious enough. The sooner you receive information, the sooner you can act on it. The more effectively you handle information, the easier you can access that information when and where you need it. The more efficiently you deal with information, the fewer expenses you incur for managing and maintaining your information.

New business owners often cite the preceding reasons, and others like them, as justification for running up huge start-up costs to buy computers, install e-mail and voice-mail systems worthy of much larger organizations, and train employees to use these new tools of the Information Age. But have all these expenditures made your own workers more productive? If not, perhaps you aren't taking the right approach to implementing IT within your business.

Before spending the money, a business owner should take time to identify the questions that need an answer:

- ✔ Who needs the answer? (customer, supplier, employee, owner)
- ✔ How fast do they need the answer? (real time, one minute, one hour, one day)
- ✔ How frequently do they need the answer? (daily, weekly, monthly)

When the answers to these questions become clear, you have a rational basis for evaluating alternate technologies based on how well they meet the criteria needed for your "answers." A lot of technology seems to be designed to provide a real-time answer to a question that may need to be asked only once a month.

Book IV

Managing Your Business

When planned and implemented wisely, IT can improve an organization's efficiency and productivity. Recent studies are beginning to show a relationship between the implementation of IT and increased productivity. Examples like the following bear out this relationship:

- ✔ Implementing a computerized inventory-management system at Warren, Michigan–based Duramet Corporation — a manufacturer of powdered metal and now a part of the Cerametal Group — helped the company double sales over a three-year period without hiring a single new salesperson.

- ✔ By using IT to provide employees with real-time information about orders and scheduling that cuts through the traditional walls within the organization, M.A. Hanna, a manufacturer of polymers that merged with Geon Company to form PolyOne Corporation, reduced its working capital needs by a third to achieve the same measure of sales.

- ✔ At Weirton Steel Corporation — now Mittal Steel USA, based in Weirton, West Virginia — the company found that it needed only 12 people to run the hot mill that once required 150 people to operate, all because of the efficiencies gained as a result of new technology installed in the production line.

Although evidence is beginning to swing toward productivity gains, studies indicate that merely installing computers and other IT doesn't automatically lead to gains in employee efficiency. As a business owner, you must take the time to improve your work processes before you automate them. If you don't, office automation can actually lead to decreases in employee efficiency and productivity. Instead of the usual lousy results that you get from your manual, unautomated system, you end up with something new: garbage at the speed of light. Don't let your organization make the same mistake.

Taking steps to neutralize the negatives

Just as information technology can help a business, it can also hinder it. Consider a few examples of the negative side of IT:

- ✔ Widespread worker abuse of Internet access has reduced worker productivity by 10 to 15 percent. According to Forrester Research, 20 percent of employee time on the Internet at work doesn't involve their jobs. A recent study by Nucleus Research found that employee use of Facebook at work causes a 1.5 percent decrease in employee productivity all by itself.

- ✔ Hackers have sent periodic waves of computer viruses and malicious attacks through the business world, leaving billions of dollars of damage and lost productivity in their wake.

 ✔ E-mail messages can be unclear and confusing, forcing workers to waste time clarifying their intentions or covering themselves in case of problems.

 ✔ Employees are forced to wade through spam and junk e-mail messages.

 ✔ The slick, animated, and sound-laden, computer-based, full-color presentations so common today can take longer to prepare than the simple text and graphs that were prevalent a few years ago — especially if you're not technologically savvy.

You have to take the bad with the good. But don't take the bad lying down. You can maximize the positives of IT while minimizing the negatives:

 ✔ **Stay current on the latest information innovations and news.** You don't need to become an expert on how to install a network server or configure your voice-mail system, but you do need to become conversant in the technology behind your business systems.

 ✔ **Hire experts.** Although you must have a general knowledge of IT, plan to hire experts to advise you in the design and implementation of critical IT–based systems.

 ✔ **Manage by walking around.** Make a habit of dropping in on employees — wherever they're located — and observe how they use your organization's IT. Solicit their feedback and suggestions for improvement. Research and implement changes as soon as you discover the need.

Using Technology to Your Advantage

Information technology is all around us today, and it touches every aspect of our lives — at home and at work. Computers and telecommunications technology are essential tools for any business. Even the most defiant, old-school entrepreneurs can now be seen glued to their smartphones. IT can give you and your business tremendous advantages. As an owner, you must capitalize on them — before your competition does.

Before you act, you must become technology savvy. The next sections recommend the four basic ways for doing just that.

Know your business

Before you can design and implement IT in the most effective way, you have to completely understand how your business works. What work is being done? Who's doing it? What do employees need to get their work done?

One way to know your business is to approach it as an outsider. Pretend you're a customer and see how your company's people and systems handle you. Do the same with your competitors to see how their people and systems handle you. What are the differences? What are the similarities? How can you improve your own organization using IT as a result of what you've discovered?

Create a technology-competitive advantage

Few business owners understand how technology can become a competitive advantage for their businesses. They may have vague notions of potential efficiency gains or increased productivity, but they're clueless when dealing with specifics.

Information technology can create real and dramatic competitive advantages over other businesses in your markets, specifically by doing the following:

- ✔ Competing with large companies by marketing on a level playing field (the Internet)
- ✔ Helping to build ongoing, loyal relationships with customers
- ✔ Connecting with strategic partners to speed up vital processes, such as product development and manufacturing
- ✔ Linking with everyone in the company, as well as with necessary sources of information both inside and outside the organization
- ✔ Providing real-time information on pricing, products, and so forth to vendors, customers, and original equipment manufacturers (OEMs)

Now is the time to create advantages over your competition. Keep in mind that the winner isn't the company that *has* the most data, but the company that *manages* that data best.

Develop a plan

If you're serious about using IT as an edge, you must have a plan for its implementation. When it comes to the fast-changing area of technology, having a *technology plan* — a plan for acquiring and deploying IT — is a definite must. Many businesses buy bits and pieces of computer hardware, software, and other technology without considering the technology that they already have in place and without looking very far into the future. Then when they try to hook everything together, they're surprised that their thrown-together system doesn't work.

Business owners who take the time to develop and implement technology plans aren't faced with this problem, and they aren't forced to spend far more money and time fixing the problems with their systems.

Technology is no longer an optional expense; it's a strategic investment that can help push your company ahead of the competition. And every strategic investment requires a plan. In their book *eBusiness Technology Kit For Dummies* (John Wiley & Sons, Inc.), Kathleen Allen and Jon Weisner recommend that you take the following steps in developing your technology plan:

1. **Write down your organization's core values.**

   For example, core values might be to provide customers with the very best customer service possible, or to always act ethically and honestly.

2. **Picture where you see your business ten years from now. Don't limit yourself.**

   Will you be in the same location or perhaps some new ones? What products and services will you offer, and to whom will you offer them? How many employees will you have? 1? 10? 50?

3. **Set a major one-year goal for the company that is guided by your vision.**

   This goal might be to create a system that tracks customer service complaints and gets them in front of you in real time.

4. **List some strategies for achieving the goal.**

   A strategy to achieve the preceding one-year goal might be to hire a consultant to develop a set of recommended solutions within three months.

5. **Brainstorm some tactics that can help you achieve your strategies.**

   Specific tactics to achieve the preceding strategy might include assigning responsibility for the project to a specific employee or vendor, and setting milestones and deadlines for completion and reporting of results.

6. **Identify technologies that support your strategies and tactics.**

   Provide some guidance by bounding the technologies to use in achieving the one-year goal, strategies, and tactics. For example, you may require that any new system work with existing systems or that the new system be web based.

Gather your thoughts — and your employees' thoughts — and write them down. Create a concise document, perhaps no more than five to ten pages, that describes your IT strategies as simply and exactly as possible. After you

Book IV

Managing Your Business

create your plan, screen and select vendors that can help you implement your plan. Close out the process by monitoring performance and adjusting the plan as needed to meet the needs of your organization and employees, and to produce optimal performance.

Keep the following points in mind as you navigate the planning process:

- **Don't buy technology just because it's the latest and greatest thing.** It's always fun shopping for the latest whiz-bang gizmo. Unfortunately, just because an item is new, has lots of flashing lights, and makes cool noises doesn't mean it's right for your business. It could be too big or too small, too fast or too slow, too expensive or too cheap. Or it might not even be compatible with the systems you've already got. Be sure that whatever technology you include in your plan makes sense for your business.

- **Check in with your IT guru.** It's important to make sure your planned purchase will be compatible with existing systems. You also want to find out whether the program you're thinking of buying will be obsolete within a couple months.

- **Plan for the right period of time.** Different kinds of businesses require different planning *horizons,* the time periods covered by their plans. If you're in a highly volatile market such as smartphone app development, your planning horizon may be only six months or so out. If you're in a stable market such as plumbing or garage door repair, your planning horizon may extend three to five years into the future.

- **Consider the benefits of outsourcing.** You may be able to save significant amounts of money by outsourcing appropriate functions to further streamline systems and create efficiencies.

- **Make the planning process a team effort.** You're not the only one who's going to be impacted by all this new technology that you bring into your company. Make employees, customers, and vendors a part of your planning team. If you take time to involve them in the process and get their buy-in ahead of time, your technology rollout will go much more smoothly.

Get some help

If you're a fan of technology and pretty knowledgeable in it, that's great — you have a head start on the process. But if you're not, get help from people who are experts in IT. Are any of your employees knowledgeable about IT? Can you hire a technician or technology consultant to fill in the gaps? Whatever you do, don't try it alone. Even if you're a full-fledged techno-geek, recruit others for your cause. Technology is changing incredibly fast and on every front. No one person can be an expert in every aspect of the IT necessary to run and grow your business.

Windows versus Mac

Only a few years ago, business managers took the question of whether to buy a "PC" (IBM-compatible personal computer) or an Apple computer very seriously. Although Apple's products — with their intuitive and easy-to-learn operating interface, graphical icons, and computer mouse — were once vastly superior to their PC rivals, Microsoft Windows software changed all that. PCs using Microsoft Windows have nearly caught up with their Apple equivalents in ease of use, and they generally cost less, to boot.

Although Apple almost crashed and burned some years ago, the return of Steve Jobs to the company led to a resurgence both in Apple and in the popularity of its products. And although the Mac has always been the standard for applications such as video, graphics and design, and musical composition, the Mac is increasingly finding its way back into business — especially now that Apple prices its machines much more competitively than it did in past years.

You can, and probably will, end up having both. Your accounting employees can be blazing away on Windows while the graphics department happily designs and creates on their Macs.

Who says that we can't all coexist peacefully?

Getting the Most Out of Company Networks

The personal computer began revolutionizing business a decade ago, shifting the power of computing away from huge mainframes and onto the desks of individual users. Now computer networks are bringing about a new revolution in business. Although the personal computer is a self-sufficient island of information, when you link these islands in a network, individual computers have the added benefit of sharing with every computer on the network.

So does networking have any benefits? You bet it does. See what you think about these reasons:

✔ **Networks improve communication:** Computer networks allow anyone in an organization to communicate with anyone else quickly and easily. With the click of a button, you can send messages to individuals or groups of employees. You can send replies just as easily. Furthermore, employees on computer networks can access financial, marketing, and product information to do their jobs from throughout the organization.

Book IV

Managing Your Business

✔ **Networks save time and money:** In business, time is money. The faster you can get something done, the more tasks you can complete during the course of your business day. E-mail allows you to create messages, memos, and other internal communications and files and send them instantaneously to as many co-workers as you want. Even better, these co-workers can be located across the hall or out in the marketplace making account calls.

✔ **Networks improve market vision:** Information communicated via computer networks is, by nature, timely and direct. In the old world of business communication, many layers of employees filtered, modified, and slowed the information as it traveled from one part of the organization to another. With direct communication over networks, no one filters, modifies, or slows the original message. What you see is what you get. The sooner you get the information that you need and the higher its quality is, the better your market vision can be.

Chapter 5

Developing Employees Through Coaching and Mentoring

In This Chapter

▶ Understanding what makes a coach

▶ Developing basic coaching skills

▶ Identifying turning points in coaching

▶ Making career development plans

▶ Understanding the power of mentoring

As a business owner, if you have employees, you are by definition a manager. That may not be your goal when you first imagine starting your own business, but unless you can do everything yourself, you need people to help get the work done. Managing people can be tricky, and the ways in which it's been successfully accomplished through the years have changed dramatically.

One recurring theme of today's new management reality is the new role of managers as people who support and encourage their employees instead of telling them what to do (or, worse, simply expecting them to perform). The best managers take time to develop their employees by staying actively involved in employee progress and development, helping to guide them along the way. The best managers also are *coaches* — that is, individuals who guide, discuss, and encourage others on their journey. With the help of coaches, employees can achieve outstanding results and organizations can perform better than ever.

Employee development doesn't just happen. Managers and employees must make a conscious, concerted effort. The best employee development is ongoing and requires that you support and encourage your employees' initiative. Recognize, however, that all development is self-development. You can really develop only yourself. You can't force your employees to develop; they have to want to develop themselves. You can, however, help set an environment that makes it more likely that they will want to learn, grow, and succeed. This chapter guides you through employee development, coaching, and mentoring, pointing to the large and small things you can do to help improve your employees' performance and position them for future success.

As the maxim goes . . .

> Tell me . . . I forget.
>
> Show me . . . I remember.
>
> Involve me . . . I learn.

Why Help Develop Your Employees?

Many good reasons exist for helping your employees develop and improve themselves. Perhaps the number one reason is that they'll perform more effectively in their current jobs. However, despite all the good reasons, development boils down to one important point: As a manager, you're the one person in the best position to provide your employees with the support they need to develop in your organization. You can provide them with not only the time and money required for training, but also unique on-the-job learning opportunities and assignments, mentoring, team participation, and more. Besides, you'll need *someone* capable of running things when you go on a vacation, right? Employee development involves a lot more than just going to a training class or two. In fact, approximately 90 percent of development occurs on the job.

The terms *training* and *development* can have two distinctly different meanings. *Training* usually refers to teaching workers the short-term skills they need to know right now to do their jobs. *Development* usually refers to teaching employees the kinds of long-term skills they'll need in the future as they progress in their careers. For this reason, employee development is often known as *career development*.

Now, in case you're still not sure why developing your employees is a good idea, the following list provides just a few reasons:

> ✔ **You may be taking your employees' knowledge for granted.** Have you ever wondered why your employees continue to mess up assignments that you know they can perform? Believe it or not, your employees may not know how to do those assignments. Have you ever actually seen your employee perform the assignments in question?

Suppose you give a pile of numbers to your assistant and tell him you want them organized and totaled within an hour. But instead of presenting you with a nice, neat computer spreadsheet, your employee gives you a confusing mess. No, your assistant isn't necessarily incompetent; he may not know how to put together a spreadsheet on his computer. Find out! The solution may be as simple as walking through your approach to completing the assignment with your employee and then having him give it a try.

✔ **Employees who work smarter are better employees.** Simply put, smarter employees are better employees. If you could help your employees develop and begin to work smarter and more effectively — and doubtless you can — why wouldn't you? No one in your organization knows everything there is to know. Find out what your employees don't know about their jobs and then make plans for getting them help with what they need to know. When your employees have achieved their development goals, they'll work smarter, your business will reap the benefits in greater employee efficiency and effectiveness, and you'll sleep better at night — all good things when you're a small-business owner.

✔ **Someone has to be prepared to step into your shoes.** Do you ever plan to take a vacation? Or do you need to travel for your business, to seek new suppliers or attend conferences? How are you going to go anywhere or do anything outside the office if you don't prepare your employees to take on the higher-level duties that are part of your job? Some owners are so worried about what's going on at the office when they're on vacation that they call in for a status update several times a day. No matter where they are, they spend more time worrying about the office than they do enjoying themselves.

The reason many business owners *don't* have to call their offices when they're on vacation is that they make it a point to develop their employees to take over when they're gone. You can do the same, too. The future of your company depends on it — really.

✔ **Your employees win, and so does your business.** When you allocate funds to employee development, your employees win by learning higher-level skills and new ways of viewing the world — and your company wins because of increased employee motivation and improved work skills. When you spend money for employee development, you actually double the effect of your investment because of this dual effect. Most important, you prepare your employees to fill the roles your business will need them to move into in the future.

✔ **Your employees are worth your time and money.** New employees cost a lot of money to recruit and train. You have to consider the investment not only in dollars, but also in time.

Book IV

Managing Your Business

When you have a trained employee, you must do everything to keep that person. Constantly training replacements can be disruptive and expensive.

When employees see that you have their best interests at heart, they're likely to want to work for you and learn from you. As a result, your business will attract talented people. Invest in your employees now, or waste your time and money finding replacements later. The choice is yours.

✔ **The challenge stimulates your employees.** Face it, not every employee is fortunate enough to have the kind of exciting, jet-setting, make-it-happen job you have. Right? For this reason, some employees occasionally become bored, lackadaisical, and otherwise indisposed. Employees constantly need new challenges and new goals to maintain interest in their jobs. And if you don't challenge your employees, you're guaranteed to end up with either an unmotivated, low-achievement workforce or employees who jump at offers from employers who will challenge them. Which option do you prefer?

Getting Down to Employee Development

Employee development doesn't just happen all by itself. It takes the deliberate and ongoing efforts of employees with the support of their supervisor — you. If either employees or you drop the ball, employees don't develop and your business suffers the consequences of employees who aren't up to the challenges of the future. This outcome definitely isn't good. As a business owner, you want your company to be ready for the future the moment it arrives, not always trying to catch up to it.

The employees' role is to identify areas where development can help make them better and more productive workers and then to relay this information to their managers. After identifying further development opportunities, managers and employees can work together to schedule and implement them.

As a business owner who directly supervises employees, your role is to be alert to the development needs of your employees and to keep an eye out for potential development opportunities. You're also the one who determines where the organization will be in the next few years. Armed with that information, you're responsible for finding ways to ensure that employees are available to meet the needs of the future organization. Your job is then to provide the resources and support required to develop employees so that they're able to fill your company's needs.

Taking a step-by-step approach

To develop your employees to meet the coming challenges within your business, follow these steps:

1. **Meet with an employee about her career.**

   After you assess your employee, meet with her to discuss where you see her in the organization and also to find out where in the organization she wants to go. This effort has to be a joint one. Having elaborate plans for an employee to rise up the company ladder in sales management doesn't do you any good if she hates the idea of leaving sales to become a manager of other salespeople.

2. **Discuss your employee's strengths and weaknesses.**

   Assuming that, in the preceding step, you discover that you're on the same wavelength as your employee, the next step is to have a frank discussion regarding her strengths and weaknesses. Your main goal here is to identify areas the employee can leverage — that is, strengths she can develop to continue her upward progress in the organization and to meet the future challenges your business faces. Focus most of your development efforts and dollars on these opportunities.

   Most important, you need to spend more time developing her strengths than improving her weaknesses. She can excel in an area that comes easy to her, resulting in more value for you and your organization than if you forced her to be merely adequate at tasks others excel in.

3. **Assess where your employee is now.**

   The next step in the employee-development process is to determine the current state of your employee's skills and talents. Does Jane show potential for supervising other warehouse employees? Which employees have experience in doing customer demos? Is the pool of line cooks and expediters adequate enough to accommodate a significant upturn in business? If not, can you develop internal candidates, or will you have to hire new employees from outside the organization? Assessing your employees provides you with an overall road map to guide your development efforts.

4. **Create career development plans.**

   A career development plan is an agreement between you and your employee that spells out exactly what formal support (tuition, time off, travel expenses, and so on) she'll receive to develop her skills and when she'll receive it. Career development plans include milestones.

5. **Follow through on your agreement, and make sure your employee follows through on hers.**

   Don't break the development plan agreement! Provide the support that you agreed to provide. Make sure that your employee upholds her end of the bargain, too. Check on her progress regularly. If she misses a schedule because of other priorities, reassign her work as necessary to ensure that she has time to focus on her career development plans.

So when is the best time to sit down with your employees to discuss career planning and development? The sooner the better. Unfortunately, many organizations closely tie career discussions to annual employee performance appraisals. On the plus side, doing so ensures that a discussion about career development happens at least once a year; on the minus side, development discussions become more of an afterthought than the central focus of the meeting. Because of that limitation, along with the current rapid changes in competitive markets and technology, once a year just isn't enough to keep up.

Conducting a career development discussion twice a year with each of your employees is definitely not too frequent, and quarterly is even better. Include a brief assessment in each discussion of the employee's development needs. Ask your employee what she can do to fulfill them. If those needs require additional support, determine what form of support the employee needs and when to schedule the support. Career development plans are best adjusted and resources best redirected as necessary.

Creating career development plans

The career development plan is the heart and soul of your efforts to develop your employees. Unfortunately, many business owners don't take the time to create development plans with their employees. Instead, they trust that, when the need arises, they can find training to accommodate that need. This kind of reactive thinking ensures that you're always playing catch-up to the challenges your organization will face in the years to come.

Why wait for the future to arrive before you prepare to deal with it? Are you really so busy that you can't spend a little of your precious time planting the seeds that your business will harvest years from now? No! Although you do have to take care of the seemingly endless crises that arise in the here and now, you also have to prepare yourself and your employees to meet the challenges of the future. To do otherwise is an incredibly shortsighted and ineffective way to run your company.

All career development plans must contain at least the following key elements:

- ✔ **Specific learning goals:** When you meet with an employee to discuss development plans, you identify specific *learning goals.* And don't forget, every employee in your organization can benefit from having learning goals. Don't leave anyone out.

- ✔ **Resources required to achieve the designated learning goals:** After you identify your employee's learning objectives, you have to decide how he will reach them. Development resources include a wide variety of opportunities that support the development of your employees. Continuing education classes, job shadowing, *stretch assignments* (assignments that aren't too easy or too hard and that involve some learning and discomfort), formal training, and more may be required. Formal training may be conducted by outsiders, by internal trainers, or perhaps in a self-guided series of learning modules. If the training requires funding or other resources, identify those resources and make efforts to obtain them.

- ✔ **Employee responsibilities and resources:** Career development is the joint responsibility of an employee and his manager. A business can and does pay for training and development opportunities, but so can employees (as any employee who has paid out of her own pocket to get a college degree can attest). A good career development plan should include what the employee is doing on her own time.

- ✔ **Required date of completion for each learning goal:** Plans are no good without a way to schedule the milestones of goal accomplishment and progress. Each learning goal must have a corresponding date of completion. Don't select dates that are so close that they're difficult or unduly burdensome to achieve, or so far into the future that they lose their immediacy and effect. The best schedules for learning goals allow employees the flexibility to get their daily tasks done while keeping ahead of the changes in the business environment that necessitate the employees' development in the first place.

- ✔ **Standards for measuring the accomplishment of learning goals:** For every goal, you must have a way to measure its completion. Normally, the manager assesses whether the employees actually use the new skills they've been taught. Whatever the individual case, make sure that the standards you use to measure the completion of a learning goal are clear and attainable and that both you and your employees are in full agreement with them.

Book IV

Managing Your Business

Easy ways to develop employees

Although you can develop employees in many different ways, some are definitely better than others. Here are some of the best — and easiest:

1. Give employees opportunities to learn and grow.

2. Be a mentor to an employee.

3. Let an employee fill in for you sometimes, starting with some non-critical task.

4. Allow employees to pursue and develop any idea they have.

5. Give employees more say in how they do their jobs.

6. Send an employee to a seminar on a new topic.

7. Bring an employee with you when you call on customers.

8. Give employees special assignments.

9. Allow an employee to shadow you during your workday.

Coaching Employees to Career Growth and Success

Coaching plays a critical part in the learning process for employees who are developing their skills, knowledge, and self-confidence. Your employees don't learn effectively when you simply tell them what to do. In fact, they usually don't learn at all.

With the right guidance, anyone can be a good coach. This section considers what effective coaches do and how they do it so that you can coach your employees toward successful results.

Serving as both manager and coach

Even if you have a pretty good sense of what it means to be a manager, do you really know what it means to be a coach? A coach is a colleague, counselor, and cheerleader, all rolled into one. Based on that definition, are you a coach? Why or why not?

Surely you're familiar with the role of coaches in other realms. A drama coach, for example, is almost always an accomplished actor or actress. The drama coach's job is to conduct auditions for parts, assign roles, schedule rehearsals, train and direct cast members throughout rehearsals, and support and encourage the actors and actresses during the final stage production. These roles aren't all that different from the roles managers perform in a business, are they?

Coaching a team of individuals isn't easy, and certain characteristics make some coaches better than others. Fortunately, as with most other business skills, you can discover, practice, and improve the traits of good coaches. You can always find room for improvement, and good coaches are the first to admit it. Following are key characteristics and tasks for coaches:

- ✔ **Coaches set goals.** Whether a small business's vision is to become the leading pizza franchise in the city, to increase revenues by 20 percent a year, or simply to get the break room walls painted this year, coaches work with their employees to set goals and deadlines for completion. They then go away and allow their employees to determine how to accomplish the goals.

- ✔ **Coaches support and encourage.** Employees — even the best and most experienced — can easily become discouraged from time to time. When employees are learning new tasks, when a long-term account is lost, or when business is down, coaches are there, ready to step in and help the team members through the worst of it. "That's okay, Kim. You've learned from your mistake, and I know that you'll get it right next time!"

- ✔ **Coaches emphasize team success over individual success.** The team's overall performance is the most important concern, not the stellar abilities of a particular team member. Coaches know that no one person can carry an entire team to success; winning takes the combined efforts of all team members. The development of teamwork skills is a vital step in an employee's progress in a company.

- ✔ **Coaches can quickly assess the talents and shortfalls of team members.** The most successful coaches can quickly determine their team members' strengths and weaknesses and, as a result, tailor their approach to each. For example, if one team member has strong analytical skills but poor presentation skills, a coach can concentrate on providing support for the employee's development of better presentation skills. "You know, Mark, I want to spend some time with you to work on making your viewgraph presentations more effective."

- ✔ **Coaches inspire their team members.** Through their support and guidance, coaches are skilled at inspiring their team members to the highest levels of human performance. Teams of inspired individuals are willing to do whatever it takes to achieve their organization's goals.

- ✔ **Coaches create environments that allow individuals to succeed.** Great coaches ensure that their workplaces are structured to let team members take risks and stretch their limits without fear of retribution if they fail.

Book IV

Managing Your Business

Coaches are available to advise their employees or just to listen to their problems, as needed. "Carol, do you have a minute to discuss a personal problem?"

✔ **Coaches provide feedback.** Communication and feedback between coach and employee is a critical element of the coaching process. Employees must know where they stand in the company — what they're doing right and what they're doing wrong. Equally important, employees must let their coaches know when they need help or assistance. And both parties need this dialogue in a timely manner, on an ongoing basis — not just once a year in a performance review.

Firing someone doesn't constitute effective feedback. Unless an employee has engaged in some sort of intolerable offense (such as physical violence, theft, or intoxication on the job), a manager needs to give the employee plenty of verbal and written feedback before even considering termination. Giving employees several warnings offers them opportunities to correct deficiencies that they may not be able to see.

Identifying a coach's tools

Coaching is not a one-dimensional activity. Because every person is different, the best coaches tailor their approach to their team members' specific, individualized needs. If one team member is independent and needs only occasional guidance, recognize where she stands and provide that level of support. This support may consist of an occasional, informal progress check while making the rounds of the office. On the other hand, if another team member is insecure and needs more guidance, the coach must recognize this employee's position and assist as needed. In this case, support may consist of frequent, formal meetings with the employee to assess progress and provide advice and direction as needed.

Although you have your own coaching style, the best coaches employ certain techniques to elicit the greatest performance from their team members:

✔ **Make time for team members.** Managing is primarily a people job. Part of being a good manager and coach is being available to your employees when they need your help. If you're not available, your employees may seek out other avenues to meet their needs — or simply stop trying to work with you. Always keep your door open to your employees and remember that they are your first priority. Manage by walking around. Regularly get out of your office and visit your employees at their workstations. "Do I have a minute, Elaine? Of course, I always have time for you and the other members of my staff."

✔ **Provide context and vision.** Instead of simply telling employees what to do, effective coaches explain the why. Coaches provide their employees with context and a big-picture perspective. Instead of spouting long lists of do's and don'ts, they explain how a system or procedure works and then define their employees' parts in the scheme of things. "Chris, you have a very important part in the financial health and vitality of our company. By ensuring that our customers pay their invoices within 30 days after we ship their products, we're able to keep our cash flow on the plus side, and we can pay our obligations such as rent, electricity, and your paycheck on time."

✔ **Transfer knowledge and perspective.** A great benefit of having a good coach is the opportunity to learn from someone who has more experience than you do. In response to the unique needs of each team member, coaches transfer their personal knowledge and perspective. "We faced this exact situation about five years ago, Dwight. I'm going to tell you what we did then, and I want you to tell me whether you think it still makes sense today."

✔ **Be a sounding board.** Coaches talk through new ideas and approaches to solving problems with their employees. Coaches and employees can consider the implications of different approaches to solving a problem and role-play customer or client reactions before trying them out for real. By using active listening skills, coaches can often help their employees work through issues and come up with the best solutions themselves. "Okay, Priscilla, you've told me that you don't think your customer will buy off on a 20 percent price increase. What options do you have to present the price increase, and are some more palatable than others?"

✔ **Obtain needed resources.** Sometimes coaches can help their employees make the jump from marginal to outstanding performance simply by providing the resources those employees need. These resources can take many forms: money, time, staff, equipment, or other tangible assets. "So, Gene, you're confident that we can improve our cash flow if we throw a couple more clerks into collections? Okay, we'll give it a try."

✔ **Offer a helping hand.** For an employee who is learning a new job and is still responsible for performing her current job, the total workload can be overwhelming. Coaches can help workers through this transitional phase by reassigning current duties to other employees, authorizing overtime, or taking other measures to relieve the pressure. "Phoebe, while you're learning how to troubleshoot that new network server, I'm going to assign your maintenance workload to Rachel. We can get back together at the end of the week to see how you're doing."

Book IV

Managing Your Business

Teaching through show-and-tell coaching

Besides the obvious coaching roles of supporting and encouraging employees in their quest to achieve an organization's goals, managers as coaches also teach their employees how to achieve an organization's goals. Drawing from your experience, you lead your workers step by step through work processes or procedures. After they discover how to perform a task, you delegate full authority and responsibility for its performance to them.

For the transfer of specific skills, you can find no better way of teaching, and no better way of learning, than the *show-and-tell* method. Developed by a post–World War II American industrial society desperate to quickly train new workers in manufacturing processes, show-and-tell is beautiful in its simplicity and effectiveness.

Show-and-tell coaching has three steps:

1. **You do, you say.** Sit down with your employees and explain the procedure in general terms while you perform the task.

2. **They do, you say.** Now have the employees do the same procedure as you explain each step in the procedure.

3. **They do, they say.** Finally, as you observe, have your employees perform the task again as they explain to you what they're doing.

As you go through these steps, have employees create a "cheat sheet" of the new steps to refer to until they become habit.

Making turning points big successes

Despite popular impressions to the contrary, 90 percent of management isn't the big event — the blinding flash of brilliance that creates markets where none previously existed, the magnificent negotiation that results in unheard-of levels of union-management cooperation, or the masterful stroke that catapults the firm into the big leagues. No, 90 percent of a manager's job consists of the daily chipping away at problems and the shaping of talents.

The best coaches are constantly on the lookout for *turning points* — the daily opportunities to succeed that are available to all employees.

The big successes — the victories against competitors, the dramatic surges in revenues or profits, the astounding new products — are typically the result of building a foundation of countless small successes along the way. Making a phone-prompt system more responsive to your customers' needs, sending an employee to a seminar on time management, writing a great sales agreement, conducting a meaningful performance appraisal with an employee, meeting a prospective client for lunch — all are turning points in the average business day. Although each event may not be particularly spectacular on its own, when aggregated over time, they can add up to big things.

This is the job of a coach. Instead of using dynamite to transform the business in one fell swoop (and taking the chance of destroying their business, their employees, or themselves in the process), coaches are like the ancient stonemasons who built the great pyramids of Egypt. The movement and placement of each individual stone may not have seemed like a big deal when considered as a separate activity. However, each was an important step in achieving the ultimate result — the construction of awe-inspiring structures that have withstood thousands of years of war, weather, and tourists.

Incorporating coaching into your day-to-day interactions

Coaches focus daily on spending time with employees to help them succeed — to assess their progress and to find out what they can do to help the employees capitalize on the turning points that present themselves every day. Coaches complement and supplement the abilities and experience of their employees by bringing their own abilities and experience to the table. They reward positive performance and help their employees learn important lessons from making mistakes — lessons that, in turn, help the employees improve their future performance.

For example, suppose you have a young and inexperienced, but bright and energetic, sales trainee on your staff. Your employee has done a great job of contacting customers and making sales calls, but she hasn't yet closed her first deal. When you talk to her about this, she confesses that she's nervous about her own personal turning point: She's worried that she may become confused in front of the customer and blow the deal at the last minute. She needs your coaching.

The following guidelines can help you, the coach, handle any employee's concerns:

- ✔ **Meet with your employee.** Make an appointment with your employee as soon as possible for a relaxed discussion of the concerns. Find a quiet place free of distractions, and put your phone on hold or forward it to voice-mail.

- ✔ **Listen!** One of the most motivating things one person can do for another is to listen. Avoid instant solutions or lectures. Before you say a word, ask your employee to bring you up-to-date with the situation, her concerns, and any possible approaches or solutions she's considered. Let her do the talking while you do the listening.

- ✔ **Reinforce the positive.** Begin by pointing out what your employee did right in the particular situation. Let your employee know when she's on the right track. Give her positive feedback on her performance.

- ✔ **Highlight areas for improvement.** Point out what your employee needs to do to improve and tell her what you can do to help. Agree on the assistance you can provide, whether your employee needs further training, an increased budget, more time, or something else. Be enthusiastic about your confidence in the employee's ability to do a great job.

- ✔ **Follow through.** After you determine what you can do to support your employee, do it! Notice when she improves. Periodically check up on the progress your employee is making and offer your support as necessary.

Above all, be patient. You can't accomplish coaching on your terms alone. At the outset, understand that everyone is different. Some employees catch on sooner than others and some employees need more time to develop. Differences in ability don't make certain employees any better or worse than their co-workers — they just make them different. Just as you need time to build relationships and trust in business, your employees need time to develop skills and experience.

Top five coaching websites

Here are five places on the web where you can learn a lot more about coaching:

- ✔ The Coaching and Mentoring Network: www.coachingnetwork.org.uk

- ✔ International Coach Federation: www.coachfederation.org

- ✔ The Coaching Connection: http://coachingconnection.wordpress.com

- ✔ *Fast Company* magazine: www.fastcompany.com/27412/coaching-resources

- ✔ Find a Mentor: http://findamentor.com

Finding a Mentor, Being a Mentor

Someone who's already been there and seen what it takes to succeed and who takes a special interest in helping someone else learn what you should and shouldn't do as you work your way up is called a *mentor*. As a new business owner, you may want to find an established business owner to advise you. And as you become established, you may want to help out someone else who is just starting out.

Isn't a manager supposed to be a mentor? No. A mentor is most typically not someone's boss. A manager's job is clearly to coach and help guide employees. Although managers certainly *can* act as mentors for their own employees, mentors most often act as confidential advisers and sounding boards to their chosen employees and, therefore, aren't typically in the employee's direct chain of command.

The day that a mentor takes you under his wing is a day for you to celebrate. Why? Not everyone is lucky enough to find a mentor. And someday you'll be in the position to be a mentor to someone else. When that day comes, don't be so caught up in your busy business life to neglect to reach out and help someone else find his way up in the business.

Here are some of the things mentors do:

- ✔ **Mentors explain how the business really works.** Mentors are a great way to find out what's really going on. There is often a difference between what's formally announced to employees and what really goes on in the business. A mentor can convey that knowledge (at least, the knowledge that isn't confidential).

- ✔ **Mentors teach by example.** A mentor has likely already seen it all and can help an employee discover the most effective and efficient ways to get things done. Why reinvent the wheel or get beaten up by the powers-that-be when you don't have to? This aspect of mentoring is particularly relevant if you choose to seek out an established business owner to be your mentor.

- ✔ **Mentors provide growth experiences.** A mentor can help guide someone to activities above and beyond formal career development plans that are helpful to growth as an employee. For example, a mentor may strongly suggest joining a group such as Toastmasters, to improve public-speaking skills. A mentor makes this suggestion because he knows that public-speaking skills are important to future career growth.

Book IV

Managing Your Business

> ✓ **Mentors provide career guidance and discussion.** A mentor knows which career paths are dead ends and which offer the most rapid advancement. This knowledge can be incredibly important to an employee's future when making career choices. The advice a mentor gives can be invaluable.

Within a business, the mentoring process often happens when a more experienced employee takes a professional interest in a new or inexperienced employee. Employees can also initiate the mentoring process by engaging the interest of potential mentors while seeking advice or working on projects together. Recognizing the potential benefits for the development of their employees, many organizations have formalized the mentoring process and made it available to a wider range of employees than the old informal process ever could. You may want consider doing the same in your business.

Chapter 6

Delegating to Get Things Done

In This Chapter

▶ Managing through delegation

▶ Debunking the myths about delegation

▶ Putting delegation to work

▶ Choosing which tasks to delegate

*O*nce you grow beyond a one-person shop, the power of your business comes not from your efforts alone, but from the sum of all the efforts of your employees. If you're responsible for only a few employees, with extraordinary effort, you perhaps can do the work of your entire group if you so desire — and if you want to be a complete stranger to your friends and family. When you're talking about more than a few employees, you simply can't do all the work if you tried. Besides, you don't want to be known as a *micromanager* who gets too involved in the petty details of running things. And your employees may take less responsibility for their work because you're always there to do it (or check it) for them. They will be less engaged in their work, and morale will plummet. Why should they bother trying to do their best job if you don't trust them enough to do it?

Managers — even ones who are also business owners — assign responsibility for completing tasks through *delegation*. But simply assigning tasks and then walking away isn't enough. To delegate effectively, you must also give employees authority and ensure that they have the resources necessary to complete tasks effectively. You must also monitor the progress of their employees, if they have direct reports of their own, toward meeting their assigned goals.

Delegating: The Manager's Best Tool

As a business owner, you're required to develop skills in many different areas. You need good technical, analytical, and organizational skills, but most important, you also must have good people skills. Of all the people skills, the one skill that can make the greatest difference in your effectiveness is the *ability to delegate well.* Delegating is the number one management tool, and the inability to delegate well is the leading cause of management failure.

Why do you have a hard time delegating? A variety of possible reasons exist:

- ✔ You're too busy and just don't have enough time.
- ✔ You don't trust your employees to complete their assignments correctly or on time.
- ✔ You're afraid to let go.
- ✔ You're concerned that you'll no longer be the center of attention.
- ✔ You have no one to delegate to (lack of resources).
- ✔ You don't know how to delegate effectively.

Consider these reasons why you must let go of your preconceptions and inhibitions and start delegating today:

- ✔ **Your success depends on it.** Business owners who can successfully manage team members — each of whom has specific responsibilities for a different aspect of the team's performance — are the ones who enjoy the most success.

- ✔ **You can't do it all.** No matter how great a manager you are, shouldering the entire burden of achieving your goals isn't in your best interest unless you want to work yourself into an early grave. Besides, wouldn't it be nice to see what life is like outside the four walls of your office?

- ✔ **You have to concentrate on the jobs that you can do and your staff can't.** You're the manager — not a software programmer, truck driver, accounting clerk, or customer service representative. Do your job, and let your employees do theirs.

- ✔ **Delegation gets workers more involved.** When you give employees the responsibility and authority to carry out tasks — whether individually or in teams — they respond by becoming more involved in the day-to-day operations of the organization. Instead of acting like drones with no responsibility or authority, they become vital to the success of the business. And if your employees succeed, you succeed.

- ✔ **Delegation gives you the chance to develop your employees.** If you make all the decisions and come up with all the ideas, your employees never learn how to take initiative and see tasks through to successful completion. And if they don't learn, guess who's going to get stuck doing everything forever? (Hint: Take a look in the mirror.) In addition, doing everything yourself robs your employees of a golden opportunity to develop their work skills. Today's employees increasingly report learning and development opportunities as one of the top motivators.

Suppose, for example, that you're running a health care consulting firm. When the firm had only a few employees and sales of $100,000 a year, it was no problem for you to personally bill all your customers, cut checks to vendors, run payroll, and take care of the company's taxes every April. However, now you've grown to 20 employees and sales are at $3 million a year. Face it, you can't even pretend to do it all — you don't have enough hours in the day. You now have specialized employees who take care of accounts payable, accounts receivable, and payroll, and you have farmed out the completion of income tax work to a CPA.

Each employee that you've assigned to a specific work function has specialized knowledge and skills in a certain area of expertise. If you've made the right hiring decisions (see Book IV Chapter 1), each employee is a talented and specialized pro in a specific field. Sure, you could personally generate payroll if you had to, but you've hired someone to do that job for you. (By the way, your payroll clerk is probably a lot better and quicker at it than you are.)

On the other hand, you're uniquely qualified to perform numerous responsibilities in your organization. These responsibilities may include developing and monitoring your operations budget, conducting performance appraisals, and helping to plan the overall direction of your company's acquisitions. The section "Sorting Out What to Delegate and What to Do Yourself," later in this chapter, suggests which tasks to delegate to your employees and which ones to retain.

Debunking Myths about Delegation

Admit it, you may have many different rationalizations for why you can't delegate work to your employees. Unfortunately, these reasons have become part of the general folklore of being a manager. And they're guaranteed to get in the way of your ability to be effective.

You can't trust your employees to be responsible

If you can't trust your employees, whom can you trust? Assume that you're responsible for hiring at least a portion of your staff. Now, forgetting for a moment the ones you didn't personally hire, you likely went through quite an involved process to recruit your employees. Remember the mountain of résumés you had to sift through and then divide into winners, potential winners, and losers? After hours of sorting and then hours of interviews, you selected the best candidates — the ones with the best skills, qualifications, and experience for the job.

You selected your employees because you thought they were the most talented people available and deserved your trust. Now your job is to give them that trust without strings attached.

You usually reap what you sow. Your staff members are ready, willing, and able to be responsible employees — you just have to give them a chance. Sure, not every employee is going to be able to handle every task you assign. If that's the case, find out why. Does someone need more training? More time? More practice? Maybe you need to find a task that's better suited to an employee's experience or disposition. Or perhaps you simply hired the wrong person for the job. If that's the case, face up to the fact and fire or reassign the employee before you lose even more time and money. To get responsible employees, you have to give responsibility.

You'll lose control of a task and its outcome

If you delegate correctly, you don't lose control of the task or its outcome. You simply lose control of the way the outcome is achieved. Picture a map of the world. How many different ways can a person get from San Francisco to Paris? One? One million? Some ways are quicker than others. Some are more scenic, and others require a substantial resource commitment. Do the differences in these ways make any of them inherently wrong? No.

In business, getting a task done doesn't mean following only one path. Even for tasks that are spelled out in highly defined steps, you can always leave room for new ways to make a process better. Your job is to describe to your employees the outcomes that you want and then let them decide how to accomplish the tasks. Of course, you need to be available to coach and counsel them so that they can learn from your past experience, if they want, but you need to let go of controlling the *how* and instead focus on the *what* and the *when*.

You're the only one with all the answers

You're joking, right? As talented as you may be, unless you're the only employee, you can't possibly have the only answer to every question in your organization.

On the other hand, a certain group of people deals with an amazing array of situations every day. The group talks to your customers, your suppliers, and each other — day in and day out. Who are these people? They are your employees.

Your employees have a wealth of experience and knowledge about your business contacts and the intimate, day-to-day workings of the organization. They are often closer to the customers and problems of the company than you are. They've seen things you haven't. To ignore their suggestions and advice is not only disrespectful, but also shortsighted and foolish. Don't ignore this resource. You're already paying for it, so use it.

You can do the work faster by yourself

You may think that you're completing tasks faster when you do them than when you assign them to others, but this belief is merely an illusion. Yes, discussing a task and assigning it to one of your employees may require more of your time when you first delegate that task, but if you delegate well, you'll spend significantly less time the next time you delegate that same task.

What else happens when you do it yourself instead of delegating it? When you do the task yourself, you're forever doomed to doing the task — again and again and again. When you teach someone else to do the task and then assign that person the responsibility for completing it, you may never have to do it again. Your employee may even come to do it faster than you can. Who knows? That employee may actually improve the way that you've always done it, perhaps reducing costs or increasing customer satisfaction.

Delegation dilutes your authority

Delegation does the exact opposite of what this myth says — it actually *extends* your authority. You're only one person, and you can do only so much by yourself. Now imagine all 5, 10, 20, or 100 members of your team working toward your common goals. You still set the goals and the timetables for reaching them, but each employee chooses her own way of getting there.

Do you have less authority because you delegate a task and transfer authority to an employee to carry out the task? Clearly, the answer is no. What do you lose in this transaction? Nothing! Your authority is extended, not diminished. The more authority you give to employees, the better able your employees are to do the jobs you hired them to do.

As you grant others authority, you gain an efficient and effective workforce — employees who are truly empowered, feel excited by their jobs, and work as team players. You also gain the ability to concentrate on the issues that deserve your undivided attention.

You relinquish the credit for doing a good job

Letting go of this belief is one of the biggest difficulties in the transition from being a doer to being a manager of doers. When you're a doer, you're rewarded for writing a great report, developing an incredible market analysis, or programming an amazing piece of computer code. When you're a manager, the focus of your job shifts to your performance in reaching an overall company or project goal through the efforts of others. The skills required are quite different, and your success is a result of the indirect efforts of others and your behind-the-scenes support.

Wise managers know that when their employees shine, they shine, too. The more you delegate, the more opportunities you give your employees to shine. Give your workers the opportunity to do important work — and do it well. And when they do well, make sure you tell everyone about it. If you give your employees credit for their successes publicly and often, they'll more likely want to do a good job for you on future assignments. Don't forget, when you own a business that employs others, your business's success is primarily measured on your employees' performance, not what you're personally able to accomplish.

Delegation decreases your flexibility

When you do everything yourself, you have complete control over the progress and completion of tasks, right? Wrong! How can you, when you're balancing multiple priorities at the same time and dealing with the inevitable crisis (or two or three) of the day? Being flexible is pretty tough when you're doing everything yourself. Concentrating on more than one task at a time is impossible. While you're concentrating on that one task, you put all your other tasks on hold. Flexibility? Not!

The more people you delegate to, the more flexible you can be. As your employees take care of the day-to-day tasks necessary to keep your business running, you're free to deal with those surprise problems and opportunities that always seem to pop up at the last minute.

Taking the Six Steps to Delegate

Delegation can be scary, at least at first. But as with anything else, the more you do it, the less scary it gets. When you delegate, you're putting your trust in another individual. If that individual fails, you're ultimately responsible — regardless of whom you give the task to. When you delegate tasks, you don't automatically abdicate your responsibility for their successful completion.

As a part of this process, you need to understand your employees' strengths and weaknesses. For example, you probably aren't going to delegate a huge task to someone who has been on the job for only a few days. As with any other task that you perform as a manager, you have to work at delegating — and keep working at it. Ultimately, delegation benefits both workers and managers when you do it correctly.

Follow these six steps for effectively delegating:

1. **Communicate the task.**

   Describe exactly what you want done, when you want it done, and what end results you expect. Ask for any questions your employee might have.

2. **Furnish context for the task.**

   Explain why the task needs to be done, its importance in the overall scheme of things, and possible complications that may arise during its performance.

3. **Determine standards.**

   Agree on the standards you plan to use to measure the success of a task's completion. Make these standards realistic and attainable.

4. **Grant authority.**

   You must grant employees the authority to complete the task without constant roadblocks or standoffs with other employees.

5. **Provide support.**

   Determine the resources necessary for your employee to complete the task, and then provide them. Successfully completing a task may require money, training, or the ability to check with you about progress or obstacles as they arise.

6. **Get commitment.**

   Make sure your employee has accepted the assignment. Confirm your expectations and your employee's understanding of and commitment to completing the task.

Book IV

Managing Your Business

Sorting Out What to Delegate and What to Do Yourself

In theory, you can delegate anything you're responsible for to your employees. Of course, if you delegate all your duties, what are you going to do? The point is, there are some things you are better able to do, and some things your employees are better able to do. As a result, some tasks you make an effort to delegate to your employees and other tasks you retain for yourself.

When you delegate, begin with simple tasks that don't substantially impact the business if they aren't completed on time or within budget. As your employees gain confidence and experience, delegate higher-level tasks. Carefully assess the level of your employees' expertise and assign tasks that meet or slightly exceed that level. Set schedules for completion and then monitor your employees' performance against them. This is a good opportunity to see if an employee isn't being challenged or is bored. When you get the hang of it, you'll find that you have nothing to be afraid of when you delegate.

Pointing out appropriate tasks for delegation

Certain tasks naturally lend themselves to being delegated. Take every opportunity to delegate the following kinds of work to your employees.

Detail work

As a business owner, you have no greater time-waster than getting caught up in details — you know, tasks such as double-checking pages, spending days troubleshooting a block of computer code, or personally auditing your employees' timesheets. The Pareto Principle holds that 20 percent of the results come from 80 percent of the work. You can no doubt run circles around almost anyone on those detailed technical tasks that you used to do all the time.

But now that you're the owner, your duty is to orchestrate the workings of a team of workers toward a common goal — not just to perform an individual task. So leave the details to your employees, but hold them accountable for the results. Concentrate your efforts on tasks that have the greatest payoff and that allow you to most effectively leverage the work of all your employees.

Information gathering

Browsing the web for information about your competitors, spending hours poring over issues of *Fortune* magazine, and moving into your local library's reference stacks for weeks on end isn't an effective use of your time. Still, many business owners can get sucked into the trap. Not only is reading newspapers, reports, books, magazines, and the like fun, but it also gives you an easy way to postpone the more difficult tasks of managing your company. Your responsibility is to look at the big picture — to gather a variety of inputs and make sense of them. You can work so much more efficiently when someone else gathers needed information, freeing you to take the time you need to analyze the inputs and devise solutions to your problems.

Repetitive assignments

What a great way to get routine tasks done: Assign them to your employees. Many of the jobs in your company arise again and again; checking inventory levels and placing orders for more product, reviewing your biweekly report of expenditures versus budget, and approving your monthly phone bill are just a few examples. Your time is much too important to waste on routine tasks that you mastered years ago.

If you find yourself involved in repetitive assignments, first take a close look at their particulars. How often do the assignments recur? Can you anticipate the assignments in sufficient time to allow an employee to successfully complete them? What do you have to do to train your employees in completing the tasks? When you figure all this out, develop a schedule and make assignments to your employees.

Surrogate roles

Do you feel that you have to be everywhere all the time? Well, you certainly can't be everywhere all the time — and you shouldn't even *try*. Every day, your employees have numerous opportunities to fill in for you. Presentations, conference calls, client visits, and meetings are just a few examples. In some cases, you may be required to attend. However, in many other cases, whether you attend personally or send someone to take your place really doesn't matter.

The next time someone calls a meeting and requests your attendance, send one of your employees to attend in your place. This simple act benefits you in several different ways. Not only do you have an extra hour or two in your schedule, but also your employee can present you with only the important outcomes of the meeting. In any case, your employee has the opportunity to take on some new responsibilities, and you have the opportunity to spend the time you need on your most important tasks. Your employee may even discover something new in the process.

Future duties

As a business owner, you must always be on the lookout for opportunities to train your staff in their future job responsibilities. For example, one of your key duties may be to develop your annual budget. By allowing one or more of your employees to assist you — perhaps in gathering basic market or research data, or analyzing trends in previous-year budgets — you can give your employees a taste of what goes into putting together a budget.

Don't fall into the trap of believing that the only way to train your employees is to sign them up for an expensive class taught by someone with a slick color brochure who knows nothing about *your* business. Opportunities to train your employees abound within your own business. An estimated 90 percent of all development occurs on the job. Not only is this training free, but also by assigning your employees to progressively more important tasks, you build their self-confidence and help pave their way to progress in the organization.

Knowing what tasks should stay with you

Some tasks are part and parcel of the job of being the owner. By delegating the following work, you fail to perform your basic management duties.

Long-term vision and goals

Your position at the top provides you with a unique perspective on the organization's needs. One of the key functions of management is vision. Although employees at any level can give you input and make suggestions that help shape your perspectives, developing the business's long-term vision and goals is up to you. Employees can't collectively decide the direction in which you should move. An organization is much more effective when everyone moves together in the same direction.

Positive performance feedback

Rewarding and recognizing employees when they do good work is an important job for every manager. If this task is delegated to lower-level employees, however, the workers who receive it won't value the recognition as much as if it came from the owner. The impact of the recognition is therefore significantly lessened.

Performance appraisals, discipline, and counseling

In a busy small business, a strong relationship between owner and employee is often hard to come by. Most owners are probably lucky to get off a quick "Good morning" or "Good night" between the hustle and bustle of a typical workday. Given everyone's hectic schedules, you may have times when you don't talk to one or more of your employees for days at a time.

However, sometimes you absolutely have to set time aside for your employees. When you discipline and counsel your employees, you're giving them the kind of input that only you can provide. You set the goals for your employees, and you set the standards by which you measure their progress. Inevitably, you decide whether your employees have reached the marks you've set or whether they've fallen short. You can't delegate away this task effectively — everyone loses as a result.

Politically sensitive situations

Some situations are just too politically sensitive to assign to your employees. For example, auditing the expenses for your business. The results of your review show that someone has gone to way too many lunches on company funds. Do you assign a worker the responsibility of reporting this explosive situation? No! You're in the best position to deal with this information.

Not only do such situations demand your utmost attention and expertise, but placing your employee in the middle of the line of fire in a potentially explosive situation is also unfair. Being the owner may be tough sometimes, but you're paid to make the difficult decisions and to take the political heat that your work generates.

Confidential or sensitive circumstances

You're privy to information that your staff isn't, such as wage and salary figures, proprietary data, and personnel assessments. Releasing this information to the wrong individuals can be damaging to a business. For example, salary information should remain confidential. Similarly, if your competitors get their hands on some secret process that your company has spent countless hours and money to develop, the impact on your organization and employees can be devastating. Unless your staff has a compelling need to know, retain assignments involving these types of information.

Book IV

Managing Your Business

Book V
Marketing and Promotion

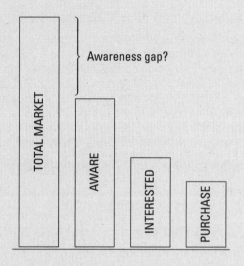

Awareness gap?

TOTAL MARKET

AWARE

INTERESTED

PURCHASE

Contents at a Glance

Chapter 1: Optimizing Your Marketing Program...............445

Know Yourself, Know Your Customer.................................445
Finding Your Marketing Formula.....................................453
Controlling Your Marketing Program...............................456
Refining Your Marketing Expectations.............................457
Revealing More Ways to Maximize Your Marketing Impact............459

Chapter 2: Strengthening Your Marketing Strategy..............461

Finding and Riding a Growth Wave..................................461
Growing with a Market Expansion Strategy..........................463
Specializing with a Market Segmentation Strategy..................465
Developing a Market Share Strategy................................467
Designing a Positioning Strategy..................................471
Considering Other Core Strategies.................................473
Selling Innovative Products.......................................475
Writing Down and Regularly Reviewing Your Strategy................476

Chapter 3: Taking Stock of Your Business Image 477

Making First Impressions..477
Auditing the Impressions Your Business Makes......................488

Chapter 4: Forging Your Brand.................................491

What Brands Are and What They Do..................................491
Building a Powerful Brand...493
Your Market Position: The Birthplace of Your Brand................496
Conveying Your Position and Brand through Taglines................498
Balancing Personal and Business Brands............................500
Maintaining and Protecting Your Brand.............................501

Chapter 5: Creating Marketing Communications That Work 507

Starting with Good Objectives.....................................508
Developing Effective Marketing Communications.....................514
Making Media Selections...518
The Making of a Mass Media Schedule...............................521
Evaluating Your Efforts...523

Chapter 6: Social Marketing: Facebook, Pinterest, Twitter, and Blogs.................................525

Developing a Business Presence on Facebook........................526
Sharing Your Images with Pinterest................................531
Building a Fan Base with Twitter..................................532
Using Your Blog for Profit . . . and Fun..........................534

Chapter 1

Optimizing Your Marketing Program

In This Chapter

▶ Succeeding by understanding your customers — and yourself

▶ Formulating a winning marketing strategy

▶ Leveraging your marketing program with focus and control

▶ Figuring out what to realistically expect from your program

▶ Maximizing the appeal of your product, service, or business

*M*arketing is all the activities that contribute to building ongoing, profitable relationships with customers to grow your business. The traditional goal of marketing is to bring about healthy sales through advertising, brand development, and other activities. A more long-term goal is to become increasingly useful or valuable to a growing number of customers so as to ensure your future success. Watch both short-term sales and long-term development of value to make your organization a growing success.

Your *marketing program* is the right mix of products or services, pricing, promotions, branding, sales, and distribution that will produce immediate sales and also help you grow over time. You'll know when you've found the right mix for you and your organization because it will produce profitable sales and enough demand to allow you to grow at a comfortable rate.

This chapter serves as a jumping-off point into the world of marketing. By reading it, you can begin to design a marketing program that works for you. The rest of the chapters in Book V can help you refine the program that meets your needs.

Know Yourself, Know Your Customer

To make your marketing program more profitable and growth-oriented, think about how to reach and persuade more of the right customers. When you understand how your customers think and what they like, you may find better ways to make more sales. The next sections help you get better acquainted with what you have to offer and start communicating those offerings to your customers.

Asking the right question

Traditional marketers ask just one key question:

What do we need to tell customers to make the sale?

Then they flood the environments (both virtual and actual) with competing claims, trying to outdo each other in their efforts to prove that they have what customers want. This barrage of noisy advertising and one-up sales-manship is inefficient, wasteful, and, to many, an unfortunate source of social pollution.

A better initial question to ask is this:

What do I/we have uniquely to offer?

When you start right off by examining yourself in the mirror and identifying your genuine, honest-to-yourself strength(s), you're many laps ahead of most marketers, whether you're selling something as simple as your résumé, as complex as a new high-tech product, or anything in between. Your unique strengths form the core of your offering, and you should keep building your strengths in ways that are true to your identity.

Whether you're marketing yourself (perhaps you're a consultant or someone else who offers individualized services) or a business, you can't make consis-tent and efficient headway by deceiving yourself and trying to deceive others. The more true to your core the marketing message is, the more effective it is. If you can't find any unique qualities to advertise, postpone those media purchases and work on self-improvement or product development. (Perhaps you simply need to listen harder to what your customers say and make sure they're so happy that they recruit new customers!) Then come back to your program with a stronger set of claims that any customer can clearly see are of benefit — that is, unique benefit, not just a run-of-the-mill, everybody-does-it-that-way benefit.

 If you draw a large enough circle around your market, you'll probably encom-pass competitors who are better than you. There are so many people out there, working hard and innovating, just like you. So as you work to improve your offerings and become ever more unique and special, draw that circle appropriately. It's the equivalent of your bar, so don't set it too high. Perhaps you should try to be the best distributor of alternative, organic, and local foods in just one city. After you have that city sewed up, expand to the next closest market. Don't, however, try to advertise and distribute across a ten-state area right out of the starting block. Knowing yourself means knowing your limitations as well as your strengths.

Marketing programs communicate *benefits*. Benefits are the qualities that your customers value. For example, your product may offer benefits such as convenience, ease of use, brand appeal, attractive design, local sourcing, healthiness, or a lower price than the competition. A service business, or an individual who provides services like consulting, may list benefits such as expertise, friendliness, and availability. The right mix of benefits can make your product or service particularly appealing to the group of customers who value those benefits. Make your list now: What are your core benefits, things that you can honestly say you're good at and that customers may value?

Even if you're better from a logical or rational perspective, customers may still choose the competition. Say your new cola scores better in blind taste tests or is made of organic ingredients. So what? Who wants to buy an unknown cola rather than the brand they know and love? No, this trust issue isn't rational, but it still affects the purchase — which is why you absolutely must take a look at the emotional reasons people may or may not buy from you. Is your brand appealing? Do you use an attractive design for your packaging? Is your presentation professional and trustworthy? Do people know you or your business and look upon you favorably? Positive image isn't hard to build for free when you market locally or regionally; you just need to show up consistently in ways that demonstrate your concern for the community.

Image isn't everything in marketing, but it *is* just about everything when it comes to the emotional impact you make. So pay close attention to your image when you're looking for ways to boost sales. To truly know your customers, you also need to explore the answers to these two questions:

- ✔ **What do customers think about my product?** Do they understand it? Do they think its features and benefits are superior to the competition and can meet their needs? Do they feel that my product is a good value given its benefits and costs? Is it easy for them to buy the product when and where they need it?

- ✔ **How do customers feel about my product?** Does it make them feel good? Do they like its personality? Do they like how it makes them feel about themselves? Do they trust me?

To answer these questions, find something to write on and draw a big *T* to create two columns. Label the left column "What Customers Know About," and put the name of your brand, company, or product in the blank. Label the right column "How Customers Feel About," and fill in as much as you can from your own knowledge before asking others to give you more ideas. Keep working on this table until you're sure you have an exhaustive list of both the logical thoughts and facts and the emotional feelings and impressions that customers have.

If you have access to a friendly group of customers or prospective customers, tell them you're holding an informal focus group with complimentary drinks and snacks (doing so helps with your recruiting) and ask them to help you understand your marketing needs by reviewing and commenting on your table. The goal is to see whether your lists of what customers know and feel about your product agree with theirs. Do they concur with how you described their emotional viewpoint and/or their factual knowledge base?

Filling the awareness gap

Are prospective customers even aware that you exist? If not, then you need to bump up your marketing communications and get in front of them somehow to reduce or eliminate the *awareness gap,* which is the percentage of people in your target market who are unaware of your offerings and their benefits. (How? That's what the rest of this Book is about, so keep reading!) If only one in ten prospective customers knows about your brand, then you have a 90 percent awareness gap and need to get the word out to a lot more people.

If you need to communicate with customers more effectively and often, you have some options for bumping up the impact of your marketing communications and reducing the awareness gap:

- ✔ **You can put in more time.** For example, if customers lack knowledge about your product, more sales calls can help fill this awareness gap.

- ✔ **You can spend more money.** More advertisements help fill your awareness gap, but of course, they cost money.

- ✔ **You can communicate better.** A strong, focused marketing program with clear, consistent, and frequent communications helps fill the awareness gap with information and a positive brand image, which then allows interest and purchase levels to rise significantly. See Figure 1-1 for a graphic that illustrates the awareness gap, and consider creating your own graph in the same format to see how big your awareness gap is. (Communicating better is usually the best approach, because it substitutes to some degree for time and money.)

- ✔ **You can become more popular.** Sometimes you can create a buzz of talk about your product. If people think it's really cool or exciting, they may do some of the communicating for you, spreading the news by word of mouth and via social media (this is sometimes referred to as *viral marketing*). If your customers are active on any social media, then you need to be, too.

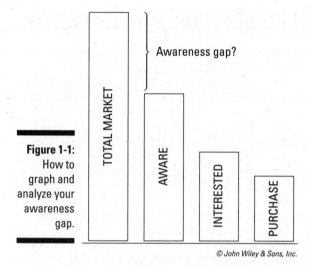

Figure 1-1:
How to graph and analyze your awareness gap.

© John Wiley & Sons, Inc.

Focusing on your target customer

Your *target customer* is the person for whom you design your product and marketing program. If you don't already have a clear profile of your target customer, make one now; otherwise, your marketing program will be adrift in a sea of less-than-effective options.

To craft your target customer profile, assemble any and all facts about your target customer on a large piece of poster paper: age, employer, education level, income, family status, hobbies, politics (if relevant), favorite brand of automobile, or anything else that helps you focus on this person. Also list your target customer's motivations: what he or she cares about in life and how you can help him or her achieve those goals. Finally, cut and paste one to three pictures out of magazine ads to represent the face or faces of your target customer. This is the audience you have to focus your marketing program on. Everything from product design or selection to the content, timing, and placement of ads must specifically target these people.

You can further increase your focus on your target customer by deciding whether he or she prefers marketing that takes a rational, information-based approach; an emotional, personality-based approach; or a balanced mix of the two. By simply being clear about whom to target and whether to market to them in an informational or emotional manner, you ensure that your marketing program has a clear focus.

Identifying and playing up your strengths

One of the best steps you can take as a marketer is to find your chief strengths and build on them so you can add an additional degree of focus and momentum to your marketing program. The key is to always think about what you do well for the customer (don't get hung up on shortcomings) and make sure you build on your strengths in everything you do.

For example, imagine that customers say your pricing isn't as good as larger competitors, and you also feel that your brand name isn't very well known. That's the bad news, but the good news is that existing customers are loyal because they like your product and service. The thing to do here is build on this strength by creating a loyalty program for customers, asking for and rewarding referrals, and including testimonials in your marketing materials and on your website. Also, remind customers and prospects that you are the local alternative. "Shop Locally to Support Your Community" may be a good phrase to sneak into every marketing communication, whether on paper, signs, your vehicles, or the web. Building on your strength in this manner can help you overcome the weaknesses of your higher pricing and lesser name recognition.

Focus on your strengths by clearly and succinctly defining what your special strength or advantage is. Grab a piece of paper and a pen and start your sentence like this: "My product (or service) is special because . . . ." Take a minute to think about what makes your firm or product special and why customers have been attracted to you in the past. Then make sure you talk about your strengths or show them visually whenever you communicate with customers. (Some marketers call the resulting statement of what makes you special a *unique selling proposition,* or USP. As its name implies, it ought to be unique to your product, to help differentiate it from your competitors.)

Discovering the best way to find customers

Another aspect of your customer focus is deciding whether you want to emphasize attracting new customers or retaining and growing existing customers. One or the other may need to dominate your marketing program, or perhaps you need to balance the two. Marketing to new prospects is usually a different sort of challenge from working with existing customers, so knowing which goal is most important helps you improve the focus of your marketing.

"What's your best way to attract customers?" Here are some of the most common answers — things that marketers often say are most effective at bringing them customers:

✔ **Referrals:** Your customers may be willing to help you sell your product.

✔ **Social media:** Your presence as a provider of helpful or interesting content can't be underestimated in its potential impact on brand development and as a source of customer leads, so try to get ever more comfortable with blogging, Twitter, Facebook, and similar options (see Book V Chapter 6 for more on marketing and social media).

✔ **Trade shows and professional association meetings:** Making contacts and being visible in the right professional venue may be a powerful way to build your business.

✔ **Sales calls:** Salespeople sell products, so make more calls yourself, or find a way to put commissioned salespeople or sales representatives to work for you.

✔ **Advertising:** Advertising sells the product, but only if you do it consistently and frequently, whether in print, on radio and TV, outdoors, or on the web.

✔ **Product demonstrations, trial coupons, or distribution of free samples:** If your product is impressive, let it sell itself.

✔ **Placement and appearance of buildings/stores:** Location is still one of the simplest and best formulas for marketing success.

As the preceding list indicates, every business has a different optimal formula for attracting customers. However, in every case, successful businesses report that one or two methods work best. Their programs are therefore dominated by one or two effective ways of attracting customers. They put between one-third and two-thirds of their marketing resources into their primary way of attracting customers and then use other marketing methods to support their most effective method.

To find your business's most effective way of reaching out to customers, you need to ask yourself this important question: What's my best way to attract customers, and how can I focus my marketing program to take fuller advantage of it? You can't look up the answer in a book, but you can take heart from the fact that, with persistence, you'll eventually work out what your winning formula is, and then you may have to make only minor changes from year to year to keep your program working well.

When you answer this question, you're taking yet another important step toward a highly focused marketing program that leverages your resources as much as possible. Your marketing program can probably be divided into four tiers of activities:

✔ Major impact

✔ Helpful; secondary impact

✔ Minor impact

✔ Money loser; very low impact

If you reorganize last year's budget into these categories, you may find that your spending isn't concentrated near the top of your list. If that's the case, then you can try to move up your focus and spending. Cut the bottom tier, where your marketing effort and spending isn't paying off. Reduce the next level of spending and shift your spending to one or two activities with the biggest impact.

This is the *marketing pyramid.* Marketers should try to move their spending up the pyramid so their marketing resources are concentrated near the top (which reflects the most effective activities). Ideally, the pyramid gets turned upside down, with most of the spending on the top floor rather than the bottom. What does your marketing pyramid look like? Can you move up it by shifting resources and investments to higher-impact marketing activities? Ideally, your marketing pyramid should have clear distinctions between the primary, secondary, and tertiary activities so you know where to concentrate your resources for best effect.

If you haven't done much marketing yet, go forth and ask nosey questions. Find marketers who sell something at least remotely similar to what you plan to sell, and ask them what activities bring them customers. First, draw out a list of at least six different things they do to find or close customers. Then ask them which are the most and least effective. Combine all this data into a speculative marketing pyramid, and begin to get quotes on and experiment with the methods yourself. Hopefully, the benchmark information you gathered will get you closer to an effective program the first time around, but plan on testing and refining your methods. Each marketer's winning formula is unique. There is no one sure-fire marketing plan that everybody can use.

Embracing sustainability

Sustainable marketing is the thoughtful selection or modification of methods, materials, and technologies to make your marketing, and your organization in general, more sustainable environmentally as well as economically. You may not have heard the term, but it's a good bet that you will in the future, because sustainability is looming as the greatest long-term challenge ahead for society and business in general. Innovators who seek to make marketing more local, more low-impact, more natural, and less wasteful (of time and tangible resources) will be seen as leaders in their field in the future — a fact that makes sustainable marketing an interesting frontier to think about as you design your next marketing program.

Finding Your Marketing Formula

Book V

Marketing and Promotion

A marketing program should be based on a *marketing strategy,* which is the big-picture idea driving your success (if you don't have one yet, check out Book V, Chapter 2). The marketing program is all the coordinated activities that together make up the tactics to implement that strategy. To make both strategy and program clear, write them up in a *marketing plan.*

For example, a general contractor (builder) may choose the strategy of renovating and building residential homes close to downtown areas in appealing smaller cities and larger suburbs in their region to take advantage of a trend where professional couples are moving out of the suburbs and back to revitalized downtowns. Stating this strategy clearly is a great way to bring focus to the marketing program. You now know what kinds of projects to talk about in blogs and to local media and acquaintances and to show in your website portfolio. And you know who your customers are and will soon be brainstorming ways to find more of them (for example, by networking to local realtors who help relocate them).

You don't have to get fully into the technicalities of strategies and plans right now. This chapter goes over a lot of simpler, quicker actions you can take to leverage your marketing activities into a winning program. The following sections require you to think about and write down some ideas, so get out your pencil and paper or tablet to jot down notes while you're reading.

Analyzing your Five P's

What really matters in marketing are the points of contact between the customer and your communications, products, and people. These customer interactions (or *influence points*) with you constitute your marketing program. To make a list of your own influence points, use the following Five *P*'s of marketing for your categories.

Product

Determine which aspects of the *product* itself are important and have an influence on customer perception and purchase intentions. List all tangible features plus intangibles, such as personality, look and feel, and packaging — these are the aspects (both rational features and emotional impressions) of your product that influence customer perception.

First impressions are important for initial purchase, but performance of the product over time is more important for repurchase and referrals.

Price

List the aspects of *price* that influence customer perception. What does it cost the customer to get and use your product? The list price is often an important element of the customer's perception of price, but it isn't the only one. Discounts and special offers belong on your list of price-based influence points, too. And don't forget any extra costs the customer may have to incur, like the cost of switching from another product to yours; extra costs can really affect a customer's perception of how attractive your product is. (If you can find ways to make switching from the competitor's product to yours easier or cheaper, you may be able to charge more for your product and still make more sales.)

Placement

List the aspects of *placement* or distribution (in both time and space) that influence the accessibility of your product. When and where is your product available to customers? Place is a big influence, because most of the time, customers aren't actively shopping for your product. Nobody runs around all day every day looking for what you want to sell her. When someone wants something, she's most strongly influenced by what's available to her. Getting the place and timing right is a big part of success in marketing and often very difficult.

The web allows you to define your market narrowly and locally, or globally, or (and this is the really exciting idea that many businesses haven't yet picked up on) in local markets other than your physical one. For example, if you have a bookstore specializing in children's and young adult titles, then you would do best to be present in the local areas where there are the most children and young adult readers. The web can narrowly target the top five cities for your product.

Promotion

List all the ways you have to *promote* your offering by communicating with customers and prospects. Do you have a website? Do you routinely update your blog, Facebook page, and Pinterest boards? Do you advertise? Send mailings? Hand out brochures? What about the visibility of signs on buildings or vehicles? Do distributors or other marketing partners also communicate with your customer? If so, include their promotional materials and methods in your marketing program, because they help shape the customer's perception, too. And what about other routine elements of customer communication, like bills? They're yet another part of the impression your marketing communications make.

The web hasn't finished revolutionizing promotion, and you can innovate to get messages out creatively and inexpensively in a lot of ways (see Book V Chapter 6 for details).

People

The fifth *P* is perhaps the most important one, because without *people,* you can't have a marketing program. List all the points of human contact that may be important to the success of your program. If you run a small business, this list may just be a handful of people, but even so, include this list in your planning and think about ways each person can help make a positive impression and encourage a sale.

The web has also revolutionized the process of making connections with people. Your professional and business Facebook pages, your blogs (which should be pulled into your Facebook page and your website), your tweets, your Pinterest boards, and so forth are all opportunities to build followers and friendships.

Refining your list of possibilities

You need to find efficient, effective ways to positively influence customer perception. You want to use elements of your marketing program to motivate customers to buy and use your product (service, firm, whatever). The list of your current influence points for each of your Five *P*'s (see the previous related sections) is just a starting point on your journey to an optimal marketing program.

Now ask yourself the following questions: What can be subtracted because it isn't working effectively? What can be emphasized or added? Think about each of the Five *P*'s and try to add more possible influence points. Look to competitors or successful marketers from outside your product category and industry for some fresh ideas. The longer your list of possibilities, the more likely you are to find really good things to include in your marketing program. But in the end, don't forget to focus on the handful of influence points that give you the biggest effect.

To craft your own winning formula, think of one or more new ways to reach and influence your customers and prospects in each of the Five *P*'s and add them to your list as possibilities for your next marketing program.

Avoiding the pricing trap

Don't be tempted to make price the main focus of your marketing program. Many marketers emphasize discounts and low prices to attract customers. But price is a dangerous emphasis for any marketing program because you're buying customers rather than winning them. That's a very, very hard way to make a profit. So unless you actually have a sustainable cost advantage (a rare thing in business), don't allow low prices or coupons and discounts to dominate your marketing program. Price reasonably, use discounts and price-off coupons sparingly, and look for other tactics to focus on in your marketing program.

Controlling Your Marketing Program

Little details can and do make all the difference in closing a sale. Does your marketing program display inconsistencies and miss opportunities to get the message across fully and well? If so, you can increase your program's effectiveness by eliminating these pockets of inconsistency to prevent out-of-control marketing.

Consider the numerous eBay sellers who fail to take and post high-quality photographs of the products they're trying to sell and then wonder why they get few bidders and have to sell for low prices. These sellers can easily upgrade their photography, but they fail to recognize the problem, so they allow this critical part of their marketing mix to remain poorly managed.

Given the reality that some of your influence points may be partially or fully uncontrolled right now, draw up a list of inconsistent and/or uncontrolled elements of your marketing program. You'll likely find some inconsistencies in each of the Five *P*'s of your program (don't worry, though, that's common!). If you can make even one of your marketing elements work better and more consistently with your overall program and its focus, you're improving the effectiveness of your marketing. Answer the questions in Table 1-1 to pinpoint elements of your marketing mix that you need to pay more attention to.

Table 1-1	Getting a Grip on Your Marketing Program
Customer Focus	
Define your customers clearly: Who are they? Where and when do they want to buy?	
Are they new customers, existing customers, or a balanced mix of both?	
Understand what emotional elements make customers buy: What personality should your brand have? How should customers feel about your product?	
Understand what functional elements make customers buy: What features do they want and need? What information do they need to see to make their decision?	

Product Attraction

What attracts customers to your product?

What's your special brilliance that sets you apart in the marketplace?

Do you reflect your brilliance throughout all your marketing efforts?

Most Effective Methods

What's the most effective thing you can do to attract customers?

What's the most effective thing you can do to retain customers?

Which of the Five *P*'s (product, price, placement, promotion, and people) is most important in attracting and retaining customers?

Controlling Points of Contact

What are all the ways you can reach and influence customers?

Are you using the best of these right now?

Do you need to increase the focus and consistency of some of these points of contact with customers?

What can you do to improve your control over all the elements that influence customer opinion of your product?

Action Items

Draw up a list of things you can do based on this analysis to maximize the effectiveness of your marketing program.

Refining Your Marketing Expectations

When you make improvements to your marketing program, what kind of results can you expect? As a general rule, the percentage change in your program will at best correspond with the percentage change you see in sales. For example, if you change only 5 percent of your program from one year to the next, you can't expect to see more than a 5 percent increase in sales. Check out the next sections for help refining what to expect from your marketing plan.

Projecting improvements above base sales

Base sales are what you can reasonably count on if you maintain the status quo in your marketing. If, for example, you've seen steady growth in sales of 3 to 6 percent per year (varying a bit with the economic cycle), then you may reasonably project sales growth of 4 percent next year, presuming every-thing else stays the same. But things rarely do stay the same, so you may want to look for threats from new competitors, changing technology, shifting customer needs, and so on. Also, be careful to adjust your natural base downward if you anticipate any such threats materializing next year. If you don't change your program, your base may even be a negative growth rate, because competitors and customers tend to change even if you don't.

After you have a good handle on what your base may be for a status quo sales projection, you can begin to adjust it upward to reflect any improve-ments you introduce. Be careful in doing this, however, because some of the improvements are fairly clearly linked to future sales, whereas others aren't. If you've tested or tried something already, then you have some real experi-ence upon which to project its impact. If you're trying something that's quite new to you, be cautious and conservative about your projections until you have your own hard numbers and real-world experience to go on.

Preparing for (ultimately successful) failures

Start small with new ideas and methods in marketing so you can afford to fail and gain knowledge from the experience; then adjust and try again. Effective marketing formulas are developed through a combination of planning and experimentation, not just from planning alone. In marketing, you don't have to feel bad about making mistakes, as long as you recognize the mistakes and take away useful lessons.

What can go wrong, will go wrong . . . and you'll be fine. Try to avoid being too heavily committed to any single plan or investment. Keep as much flex-ibility in your marketing programs as you can. For example, don't buy ads too far in advance even though that would be cheaper, because if sales drop, you don't want to be stuck with the financial commitment to a big ad campaign. Monthly commissions for salespeople and distributors is preferable because then their pay is variable with your sales and goes down if sales fall — so you don't have to be right about your sales projections.

Flexibility, cautious optimism, and contingency planning give you the knowl-edge that you can survive the worst. That knowledge, in turn, gives you the confidence to be a creative, innovative marketer and the courage to grow your business and optimize your marketing program. And you can afford to profit from your mistakes.

Revealing More Ways to Maximize Your Marketing Impact

You can improve a marketing program and increase your business's sales and profits in an infinite number of ways. Following are just some of the ideas you may be able to put to use; keep searching for more ideas and implement as many good ones as you can.

✔ **Talk to some of your best customers.** Do they have any good ideas for you? (Ignore the ideas that are overly expensive, however. You can't count on even a good customer to worry about your bottom line.)

✔ **Thank customers for their business.** A friendly "thank you" and a smile, a card or note, or a polite cover letter stuffed into the invoice envelope — all are ways to tell customers that you appreciate their business. People tend to go where they're appreciated.

✔ **Change your marketing territory.** Are you spread too thin to be visible and effective? If so, narrow your focus to your core region or customer type. But if you have expansion potential, try broadening your reach bit by bit to grow your territory.

✔ **Get more referrals.** Spend time talking to and helping out folks who can send customers your way. And make sure you thank anyone who sends you a lead. Positive reinforcement increases the behavior.

✔ **Make your marketing more attractive (professional, creative, polished, clear, well written, and well produced).** You can often increase the effectiveness of your marketing programs by upgrading the look and feel of all your marketing communications and other components. (Did you know that the best-dressed consultants get paid two to five times as much as the average in their fields?)

✔ **Smile to attract and retain business.** Make sure your people have a positive, caring attitude about customers. If they don't, their negativity is certainly losing you business. Don't let people work against your marketing program. Spend time making sure they understand that they can control the success of the program, and help them through training and good management so they can take a positive, helpful, and productive approach to all customer interactions.

✔ **Offer a memorable experience for your customer or client.** Make sure doing business with you is a pleasant experience. Also, plan to do something that makes it memorable (in a good way, please!).

✔ **Know what you want to be best at and invest in being the best.** Who needs you if you're ordinary or average? Success comes from being clearly, enticingly better at something than any other company or product. Even if it's only a small thing that makes you special, know what it is and make sure you keep polishing that brilliance. It's why you deserve the sale.

✔ **Try to cross-sell additional products (or related services) to your customer base.** Increasing the average size of a purchase or order is a great way to improve the effectiveness of your marketing program. But keep the cross-sell soft and natural. Don't sell junk that isn't clearly within your focus or to your customer's benefit.

✔ **Take advantage of the increasingly local options for advertising on the web.** Don't think of the web as worldwide. Google ads can be tailored to customers in your region who are looking for services or products like yours. Now, that's incredibly local, and often an inexpensive way to get leads. There are lots of ways to localize your reach on the web.

✔ **Debrief customers who complain or who desert you.** Why are they unhappy? Can you do something simple to retain them? (But ignore the customers who don't match your target customer profile, because you can't be all things to all people.)

Every time you put your marketing hat on, seek to make at least a small improvement in how marketing is done in your organization and for your customers.

Chapter 2

Strengthening Your Marketing Strategy

In This Chapter

▶ Taking advantage of market growth and targeting specific customer groups

▶ Competing to grow your market share

▶ Positioning your brand in consumers' minds

▶ Adjusting your approach as the market matures

▶ Sharing your strategic vision

Most people don't know what a marketing strategy is. So how important can they be? Very important, actually. A *marketing strategy* is a way to achieve success. There are only a dozen or so main ways to achieve success in marketing.

This chapter explains what the different marketing strategies are and helps you select the right one for your business. It also shows you how to use strategic thinking to make your marketing program more effective and profitable than most.

Finding and Riding a Growth Wave

The simplest and most reliable marketing strategy you can adapt for your business or product is to go where the growth is. Find it and ride the *growth wave* — an opportunity to sell something with increasing demand — for as long as you can. Doing so is important because growing and prospering when selling into a growing market is much easier than when facing stagnant or shrinking demand.

The following sections help you determine what the growth rate of your market is and evaluate other markets to find one that's growing. With this information, you can make sure you're focused on growth opportunities.

Measuring the growth rate of your market

At any point in time, some markets are growing rapidly. However, most markets are growing at a slow pace, and some markets are shrinking. Knowing how quickly or slowly your market is growing is vital because it's a key driver of your sales growth and profits. Take a moment to evaluate the current growth rate and future growth potential of *your* market. If it's not fast enough, then find a new and faster market to target (check out the next section for how to find a growing market). Your market ought to be experiencing at least 5 percent overall annual growth; a 10 percent or better growth rate is preferable. Anything slower than 5 percent makes it hard to grow your own business.

To assess your market's growth potential, think of one or several simple indicators of your market's overall growth rate and use them to gauge market growth. These indicators include the year-to-year trend in industry-wide sales, the trend in number of customers, and the trend in type and size of purchases per customer. If you find that the market is shrinking or static, then you need to look for a growth opportunity.

Sometimes, finding a direct measure of your market's size and growth rate is difficult. For example, if you sell office equipment and furniture in the greater Chicago area, your market is the dollar value of all office furniture purchased in that area. Can you find out what that figure is? Not very easily, if at all, so you need to find indirect indicators of your market's growth rate that you can use instead. Statistics on business employment in Chicago are useful because as business employment grows, so does the need for furniture. If corporate headquarters are leaving the downtown area or laying off workers, then you can assume that the overall market for office furniture is shrinking.

Responding to a flat or shrinking market

When faced with a declining market, you might want to eliminate low-margin products from your line so you can survive in a slow market. Other ideas would include looking for other places to sell your product or finding another product line to sell that offers more growth potential. (See the chapters in Book I for more on choosing a business.)

Don't waste your time trying to grow and prosper in an unhealthy market. By keeping a regular eye on market growth rates and focusing on selling into growth markets, you simultaneously ensure that you can grow your sales and increase the ease of operating at a profit. Slow-growth and no-growth markets are brutally competitive. To win sales in either case, you often have to slash prices, ruining your profit margins. That's why smart marketers (and smart business owners doing their own marketing) make a strategic point of focusing on growth markets. They also keep careful track of the growth rate in their market so as to be alert to a slowdown that may indicate a need to move on again.

To identify the best market for your future growth, ask yourself where growth is. Some types of customers may be increasing in number while others are declining (for instance, the United States has a lot of consumers in their 20s, so some marketers are shifting away from older consumers and targeting the newer ones). Furthermore, certain types of businesses are expanding (such as health care businesses), so a business-to-business marketer can grow by providing specific products or services to them. Also, geographic areas vary in their economic health and strength, so if you're willing to relocate or expand into new markets, you can target cities or states with relatively strong economies.

Growing with a Market Expansion Strategy

Market expansion is the most common strategy in marketing. The idea is to start selling to new groups of prospective customers. If you find a way to get in front of more prospects than last year, you should be able to make more sales than last year, too.

Two powerful ways to expand your market (and business) involve introducing more products into the market, which can give you access to multiple new customer bases, and taking advantage of a product that's especially popular, which allows you to piggyback sales of other products when customers are drawn in by your bestseller. The sections that follow highlight how you can go about accomplishing both.

Offering more products

Introducing new products is a strong way to expand your share of a particular market — eventually. If you sold only 10 products last year, and you offer 20 this year, you just may find that your sales double, too. Of course, it's quite likely that the new products won't sell as well as your old ones at first, but if you persist, you should be able to ramp up their sales over the course of a few years.

When looking to offer more products, you have two options:

- Add new products simply by reselling or distributing products that complement your current line and meet some need of your current customer base.

- Innovate to create one or more new products that nobody else sells.

Either way, you have the twofold challenge of informing customers that you have something new to offer and convincing them to take a look. That's why being especially visible and persistent in the first few months of your campaign to open a new market is so crucial. A concentrated blast of marketing communications is the key to opening a new market successfully.

Create visibility by showing people your brand or product often and in a consistent, professional manner. You can do this through advertising, direct mail, e-mail blasts, paid placement of your web address for key-term searches, signage (such as billboards and transit ads), sales calls, or presence at conferences and trade shows. Plan to use at least three of these or similar methods in the beginning of your campaign to open a new market.

Risks and costs increase when you experiment with new products — defined as anything you're not accustomed to making and marketing. Consequently, you should discount your first year's sales projections for a new market by some factor to reflect the degree of risk. A good general rule is to cut back the sales projections by 20 to 50 percent, depending on your judgment of how new and risky the product is to you and your team. It may also cost you double the time and money to make each sale when entering a new market, because your new prospects won't be familiar with your brand, and you likely won't have a well-defined marketing formula at the start. Budget accordingly.

Riding a bestseller to the top

If you have a *bestseller* on your hands — in other words, a product that outsells your other products by a multiple, which means it ought to sell at least three times as much as anything else — why not make the most of it? Some marketing experts look for bestsellers to achieve sales that are at least ten times the norm; outstanding bestsellers can achieve a hundred or more times the normal level of sales for a product in their category. If you have just one bestseller in your line, growing your revenues and profits is a piece of cake.

How do you create a bestselling product? First, look for one. Don't be content with products that sell moderately well. Keep looking for something that has more excitement and potential. Test many alternatives. When you find one that seems to have momentum (you'll know it has momentum when early sales figures surprise you by their rapid growth), quickly refocus your marketing efforts on that product. Make it the heart of sales calls and ads, feature it at the top of your website's home page, talk to the media about it, and offer specials for new customers who try it. Bestsellers are found and made by marketers who believe in them. Be a believer!

When you have a product with bestseller potential, your marketing strategy should be to ride it as hard and far as you can. Write a marketing plan that puts the majority of your budget and efforts behind the bestseller and gives the rest of your product line as minimal a budget as you think you can get away with. The bestseller will tend to lift all sales by attracting customers, so don't worry about the rest of your products.

After you have a bestseller, you should see your profits grow. Use some of these profits to look for the next bestseller. Why? Because eventually your bestseller will lose its momentum. Your best bet is to find another bestseller, which may take a while, so you can have it ready and waiting in the wings. Test ideas and options, and be patient. If you can't find another bestseller, switch to another marketing strategy. You don't have to have a bestseller to succeed, but it sure is nice if you can find a product that fits this strategy.

Specializing with a Market Segmentation Strategy

A *market segmentation strategy* is a strategy in which you target and cater to (or specialize in) just one narrow type or group of customer. The object of this approach is to be so well suited to that specialized customer that you become the top seller in your segment. The main way to develop a segmentation strategy is to look at your current customers and identify one particular type that seems most profitable for you right now. Or if a subset of your customers is growing faster than the rest, consider specializing in those types of customers to gain more of their business. (And you don't have to limit yourself to just one segment. If you see several with potential, adjust your product, pricing, promotion, or distribution for each, and, in essence, operate several parallel marketing programs that have enough synergy, such as through a common core product, to be economical and easy to manage.)

The advantage of a segmentation strategy is that it allows you to tailor your product and your entire marketing effort to a clearly defined group with uniform, specific characteristics. For example, the consulting firm that targets only the health care industry knows that prospective clients can be found at a handful of health care industry conferences and that they have certain common concerns around which consulting services can be focused. Many smaller consulting firms target a narrowly defined market segment to compete against larger, less specialized consulting firms.

If you're in the consulting business, you can specialize in nonprofits, for example, instead of trying to be a consultant to all businesses. If you sell office furniture, you can decide whether to focus on corporate sales, small businesses, government offices, schools, or home offices. Each segment has different needs and buying patterns, and at any particular time, one of these segments is going to be easier for you to dominate (and it may be growing faster, too). As an added bonus, marketing is usually easier and less expensive when you're highly specialized because you know exactly where to find your customers.

The next sections explain how to determine whether a market segmentation strategy is right for you and how to expand your business by focusing on more than one specific target customer base.

Gauging whether specializing is a good move

Specializing in a specific market segment can give you the momentum you need to power past your competition, but it may not always be the right approach for your operation. The segmentation strategy may work well for you if

- ✔ You think your business can be more profitable by specializing in a more narrowly defined segment than you do now.
- ✔ You face too many competitors in your broader market and can't seem to carve out a stable, profitable customer base of your own.
- ✔ It takes better advantage of things you're good at.
- ✔ You're too small to be one of the leaders in your overall market or industry. Maybe you can be the leader in a specific segment of your market.

Adding a segment to expand your market

If you're running out of customers and market and need to expand (see the earlier "Growing with a Market Expansion Strategy" section), one way to do so is to decide to target a new segment. For example, the consulting firm specializing in coaching health care executives can decide to start offering a similar service to nonprofits. A different approach and marketing program may be needed, because the two industries are different in many ways and have only partial overlap (some hospitals are nonprofits, but many nonprofits aren't hospitals). By specializing in two segments rather than just one, the firm may be able to grow its total sales significantly while still maintaining a grasp in niche markets that gives it an edge over the competition.

Developing a Market Share Strategy

The bigger you are in comparison to your competitors, the more profitable you'll be. Scale helps. That's why trying to be relatively big is a good idea. A powerful strategy is to increase your market share through your marketing activities. In essence, that means taking some business from your competitors. *Market share* is, very simply, your sales as a percentage of total sales for your product category in your market (or in your market segment if you use a segmentation strategy). If you sell $2 million worth of shark teeth and the world market totals $20 million per year, then your share of the global shark teeth market is 10 percent. It's that simple. Or is it?

To help you comprehend how increasing your market share can be beneficial for you and your business, the following sections provide some basics on this strategy and how you can implement it.

Choosing a unit

Before you can completely determine your market share, you must know which *unit* (what you're measuring sales in) you're going to reference. Dollars, pesos, containers, or grams are fine — as long as you use the same unit throughout. Just pick whatever seems to make sense for your product and the information you have access to.

Estimating market share

To effectively increase your market share, you must have an accurate picture of how large your market is and what your current share of it is. Take a look at this simple method for estimating market size and share (you can even sketch it out on the back of a napkin if you don't have the time or money for fancier approaches):

1. **Estimate the number of customers in your market.**

   For instance, guess how many people in your country are likely to buy toothpaste or how many businesses in your city buy consulting services.

2. **Estimate how much each customer buys a year, on average.**

   Does each customer buy six tubes of toothpaste? Fifteen hours of consulting services? You can check your sales records or ask some people what they do to make your estimate as accurate as possible.

3. **Multiply the two figures together to get the total size of the annual market and then divide your unit sales into it to get your share.**

For example, if you import fine English teas to the U.S. market and wholesale them to grocery stores, specialty shops, and the growing number of online specialty tea stores (such as www.theteaspot.com), you can look up U.S. tea wholesalers by visiting www.census.gov (where the latest U.S. Census data is posted). Hover your cursor over the Topics tab and then over Economy in the drop-down list that appears; choose Economic Census from the drop-down list. Doing so brings up the economic census data, which includes data from 2002, 2007, and 2012. There will be a way to look up your category or industry and find the code number for it; this code number acts as a key to tables of relevance to you.

If you were to research tea sales, code 4244901, you may find out that there were 98 tea wholesalers with a total of $3.886 million in annual sales. If your sales of tea are $525,000, then your market share is 0.525 ÷ 3.886, or 13.5 percent. (The numbers may be out of date by the time you read this, but the source — the industry series of the U.S. Census — is a great place for all sorts of market statistics. Check it out.)

Alternatively, you may estimate that three-quarters of the wholesalers handle low-cost, inexpensive teas and therefore don't compete directly with you. In that case, you can calculate your market share of the quarter of total sales that are similar specialty teas as 0.525 ÷ (0.25 × 3.886), which gives you 54 percent. That's a much larger share based on a narrower definition of the market. Estimating your market share helps you determine which market share numbers are correct.

Understanding where your product fits in the market

To create a market share strategy, you need to clearly identify and define your product and where it fits into your market. In other words, you need to know your *product category:* the general grouping of competitive products to which your product belongs (be it merchandise or a service). Knowing your product category is extremely important. If you don't know where your product fits into the market, you can't begin to develop a strategy to build on and increase your existing market share. For example, if you sell specialty teas, are you competing with mass-market brands? Should you count their sales in your market calculations and try to win sales from them? Or, if you've noted the rise in specialty tea suppliers who are online and don't have physical stores, do you want to segment by focusing on the faster-growing online category? If so, should you sell as a wholesaler still or leap in as a retailer who does all your own sourcing from overseas?

To get an accurate picture of your product category, you really need to get feedback from your customers. Doing so helps you create goals to drive your planning, as explained in the following sections.

Ask your customers

Your customers can provide you with valuable information and help you determine exactly where your product fits in the market. What matters is *customer perception:* how the customer sees the category. So watch your customers or ask them to find out what their purchase options are. Get a feel for how they view their choices. Then include all the likely or close choices in your definition of the market.

To stick with the tea example, are they choosing among all the tea options or just some of them? With specialty teas, you may find that a majority of consumers sometimes drink the cheaper mass-market brands, too. You may also find that you, as a wholesaler, must fight the mass-market brands for shelf space in grocery stores and mentions on restaurant menus. So you probably do need to use total market sales as your base, not just specialty sales.

On the other hand, you compete more closely against other specialty teas, so you may want to track this smaller market share number also and set a secondary goal for it. A wholesale tea importer's strategic goals may therefore look something like this:

✔ Increase dollar sales of our products to U.S.-end tea consumers from 13.5 percent to 15 percent.

✔ Protect our share of the specialty tea market by keeping it at 54 percent or higher.

✔ Differentiate ourselves even more from mass-market tea brands by emphasizing what makes our tea special to avoid having to compete directly against much larger marketers.

Make a plan

To achieve your market share goals, you must plan accordingly and look at what you need to do to get the market share you want. For starters, a wholesaler needs retail shelf space, so you may need to push to win a larger share of shelf space from retailers. And to earn the right to this shelf space, you may need to do some consumer advertising or publicity, provide the stores with good point-of-purchase displays or signs, improve your product packaging, or do other things to help ensure that consumers take a stronger interest in buying your products.

This plan needs to revolve around the goal of increasing your share of tea sales by 1.5 percentage points. Each point of share is worth roughly $40,000 in annual sales (one percent of the total sales in the market), so a plan that involves spending, say, an extra $25,000 to win a 1.5 percent share gain can provide an extra $60,000 if it works. But will it work? To be cautious, you, as the owner/marketer, may want to discount this projection of $60,000 in additional sales by a risk factor of, say, 25 percent, which cuts your projected gain back to $45,000.

Then consider timing. Remember that the plan can't achieve the full gain in the first month of the year. A sales projection starting at the current level of sales in the first month and ramping up to the projected increase by, say, the sixth month may be reasonable. Dividing $45,000 by 12 to find the monthly value of the risk-discounted 1.5 share point increase gives you $3,750 in extra monthly sales for the sixth month and beyond. Lower increases apply to earlier months when the program is just starting to kick in. But the marketing expenses tend to be concentrated in the early months, reflecting the need to invest in advance to grow your market share.

Knowing your competitors

So what if your competitors have more market share than you? Don't fear them; use them instead! Study your closest and/or most successful competitors to figure out how you're going to gain market share. The better you understand your competitors, the more easily you can take customers away from them.

Ask yourself what your competitors do well, how they take business from you now, and what new initiatives they're trying this year. Talk to customers, suppliers, distributors, and anyone else with good knowledge of your competitors' practices and gather any online information about them from their websites. Also, collect their marketing materials and brochures and keep track of any information you come across on how they market. For example, if they're picking up good business by having a booth at a trade show you don't attend, consider getting a booth next time to make sure you're able to compete against them there. Also find out what your competitors do badly. Those things are the chinks in their market share armor where you can easily succeed by being better!

Studying market trends and revising if need be

Market share gives you a simple way of comparing your progress to your competitors from period to period. If your share drops, you're losing; if your share grows, you're winning. It's that simple. Consequently, most marketing programs are based at least partly on a *strategic market share goal,* which is the percentage of sales you want to win during a specific period, such as a year. For example, you can say, "Increase share from 5 percent to 7 percent by introducing a product upgrade and increasing our use of trial-stimulating special offers," which is a clear goal.

You also need to study the market and see how your products compare year to year and against your competition. The postmortem on last year's program should always be based on an examination of what market share change accompanied it. (If you don't already do routine *reviews* — careful analyses of what happened and why it differed positively or negatively from your plans — you should.) If the past period's program doubled your market share, seriously consider replicating it. But if your market share stayed the same or fell, you're ready for something new. *Note:* Whether you make share gain the focus of your marketing program or not, at least keep it in mind and try not to lose any share.

Designing a Positioning Strategy

A *positioning strategy* takes a psychological approach to marketing. It focuses on getting customers or prospects to see your product in a favorable light and think of it before competitors' offerings. The positioning goal you articulate for this kind of strategy is the position your product holds in the customer's mind. The following sections break down how to find your position and craft your positioning strategy.

Your positioning strategy can be as simple as saying that you want your brand to be the easiest to buy, or as complex as saying your brand is easier to purchase, more affordable, hipper, and more contemporary than the competition. Just make sure your claims are truthful and believable.

Envisioning your position: An exercise in observation and creativity

Good positioning means your product has a prime parking space in customers' minds thanks to its strong, clear image. People recognize your brand and know immediately what it stands for. If you're in a fairly new or uncompetitive market, standing out in customers' minds should be easy. But if a lot of other businesses are involved, as in older, well-established markets, chances are they've already used positioning strategies and secured their places in customers' minds. That's why it's important not to get hung up on what you *want* your positioning to be. Instead, focus on what it *needs* to be to resonate and stick.

To help you figure out your position compared to other brands, start by drawing a simple, two-line graph. The two lines represent the range, from high to low, of the two core dimensions of your positioning strategy. You find these dimensions by asking yourself — and ideally some talkative customers, too — what the main differences between products are. The differences may be price and quality, or any number of other possible variables, depending on the product in question. Map all the major competitors and look for a space where you can fit your brand.

For example, if you're marketing soap, your dimensions can be how gentle or harsh the soaps are as well as how natural they are. A brand that claims to be all natural and as gentle as the rain is obviously in the gentle and natural quadrant. Another brand that claims to be tough on dirt and germs is going to score low on the all-natural scale and high on the harsh scale, placing it squarely in the opposite quadrant. If the owners/marketers of these two brands consistently communicate their different positions, the two brands won't compete directly. Consumers who want a gentle, natural soap buy one brand, whereas consumers who want a strong soap that kills germs buy the other. Both businesspeople can succeed by virtue of their unique positioning strategies.

Writing a positioning strategy: The how-to

After you're clear on what the consumer values most, position your product in relation to that. For example, if your customers say in a survey that they're desperate for low prices on your best-selling product or service, then your advertising can focus on a discounted introductory offer. To refine your positioning strategy and make sure it gets incorporated into all your marketing communications, you need to write down a positioning statement. Fortunately, writing a positioning statement is pretty easy. Just follow these two simple steps:

1. **Answer the following questions:**

    • What type of customer do you target?

    • What attribute does the customer value most?

    • What do you do for that customer with respect to that attribute?

    • How do you fulfill your customer's wants and needs?

    • Why do you do it better than the competition?

2. **Fill in the following with your own words:**

    • Our product offers the following benefit (which the customer values):

    • To the following customers (describe target segment):

- Our product is better than competitors' in the following manner:

- We can prove we're the best because of (provide evidence/ differences):

Here are some of the common approaches for a positioning strategy:

- ✔ **You may position against a competitor.** "Our service calls cost less than XYZ's." (This tactic is a natural in a mature product category, where the competitive strategy applies.)

- ✔ **You may emphasize a distinctive benefit.** "The only peanut butter cookie with no harmful trans fats."

- ✔ **You can affiliate yourself with something the customer values.** "The toothpaste most often recommended by dentists." (Doing so allows some of the virtues of this other thing to rub off on your brand.) A celebrity endorser, an image of a happy family playing on the beach, a richly appointed manor house set in beautiful gardens, a friendly giant: All have been used to position products favorably in consumers' minds.

Write your positioning strategy in big print and post it above your desk to make sure you stay focused on its execution. Handing out copies of it to your ad agency, distributor, salespeople, and anyone else who works on or in your marketing program also pays off.

Considering Other Core Strategies

Are there other winning marketing strategies? Certainly. In fact, strategy, like everything in marketing, is limited only by your imagination and initiative. If you can think of a better approach to strategy, go for it. The following sections present a few examples of other proven marketing strategies. Perhaps one of them may work for you.

Simplicity marketing

With *simplicity marketing,* you position your business as simpler, easier to understand, and easier to use or work with than the competition. Some customers are willing to pay a premium to avoid complexity and make purchase decisions simply and quickly. Can this approach be useful to customers in your market? Look for technologies or processes that can make your customers' lives simpler and easier. For example, try making it easy to reorder on your website by storing information about what customers last purchased so they don't have to search through many options to find the right item.

Quality strategies

Most marketers grossly underrate quality. All else being anywhere near equal, a majority of customers choose the higher-quality option. But be careful to find out what your customers think the word *quality* means. They may have a different view from you. Also, be careful to integrate your quality-based marketing messages with a genuine commitment to quality in all aspects of your business.

You can't just say you're better than the competition; you really have to deliver. But if customers see you as superior on even one dimension of quality — then by all means emphasize that in your marketing. Quote customer testimonials praising your quality, describe your commitment to quality in your marketing materials, and make trial usage easy for prospective customers so they can experience your quality, too. And make sure your pricing is consistent with a high-quality image. Don't advertise cheap prices or deep discounts, which signal cheapness, not quality.

Reminder strategies

A reminder strategy is good when you expect that people will buy your product if they think of it — but they may not without a reminder. A lot of routine purchases benefit from this strategy (for example, "Got milk?").

Point-of-purchase (POP) marketing is often an effective way to implement the reminder strategy. *Point-of-purchase marketing* simply means doing whatever advertising is necessary to sway the consumer your way at the time and place of his purchase. For retail products, this often means a clever in-store display or sign to remind the consumer about your product. For the rest of us, it may mean a pop-up couponlike special offer on Facebook (which is easy enough to do and can be targeted at your friends or a certain population).

Wenger NA promotes its Swiss Army knife product line in jewelry and knife stores by offering it in attractive, attention-getting countertop display cases. Although the pocketknife market has been mature for decades, POP displays remind consumers about the option of buying a Swiss Army knife as a gift — for someone else or even for themselves.

Innovative distribution strategies

Sometimes the most important feature of a purchase is when and where people can buy it. With *innovative distribution strategies,* you can capture sales from your competitors by being more convenient or available than other options.

For example, can you recall the brand of gas you purchased the last time you stopped at a highway rest stop? Probably not, because it didn't matter. Whatever brand was offered, you bought it because you needed gas, and highway rest stops offer only one or two options. The gas station owner who manages to secure one of the slots at a rest stop is using a distribution strategy. As the old saying goes, the three secrets of success in retail are location, location, and location. (Funny how this turns out to be true online, too! If you aren't on the first page of the search engine list, you're in trouble, so use Google ads, daily social media activity linked to your site, rich content, and lots of website babysitting to make sure you have a good location when someone searches online.)

The three rules of success actually hold true in all businesses, not just in retail. Always consider what you can do to be more present and convenient for your buyers. The Internet offers opportunities for innovative distribution, and many businesses are building online stores that make it easy to shop at midnight from the comfort of your own bed, or whenever and wherever you please.

Selling Innovative Products

Every product category has a limited life. At least in theory — and usually in all-too-real reality — some new type of product comes along to displace the old one. The result is called *the product life cycle,* a never-ending cycle of birth, growth, and decline, fueled by the endless inventiveness of competing businesses. Product categories arise, spread through the marketplace, and ultimately decline as replacements arise and begin their own life cycles. If you're marketing an innovative product that's just beginning to catch on (in what marketers call the growth phase of the life cycle), you can expect rapid growth in sales and profits. Fast-growing products are every marketer's and business-owner's dream.

As a strategic marketer, you need to keep a sharp eye on your product line and weed out any fading old products before they drag you down with them. Keep looking for adding hot new ones, so your marketing efforts will be supplemented by the natural growth of exciting new options.

Some businesses do hardcore product development and regularly file patents on their inventions. However, if you don't, that's okay. Most businesses source their products from elsewhere and resell them. That's fine, but don't forget to keep looking for new, better options. Make a strategic point of upgrading your product line (or services if you don't sell products) to stay on the growth curve. Don't let innovation pass you by.

Writing Down and Regularly Reviewing Your Strategy

What's your marketing strategy? Is it a pure version of one of the strategies reviewed in this chapter, or is it a variant (or even a combination) of more than one of them? Whatever it is, take some time to write it down clearly and thoughtfully. Put it in summary form in a single sentence. (If you must, add some bullet points to explain it in more detail.) After you write it down, don't put it away in a drawer and forget about it. Keep it close by and review it on a regular basis.

Write a strategy that's a clear statement of the direction you want your business's or product's marketing to take. This statement needs to be a big-picture game plan. With this strategy on paper, you can work on designing good products and packaging, friendly services, and impressive ads that communicate your quality to consumers. Here's what one company's marketing strategy looks like:

> Our strategy is to maximize the quality of our security alarm products and services through good engineering and to grow our share of a competitive market by communicating our superior quality to high-end customers.

After you develop a marketing strategy, be sure to follow it and make it obvious in all that you do. In fact, do some formal planning to figure out exactly how you'll implement your strategy in all aspects of your marketing program. After you adopt a specific marketing strategy, you must actually read it from time to time and check that you're following it. Everyone involved in your organization's marketing needs to understand how his or her work ties to the strategy.

Outside vendors you work with need to be aware of your marketing strategy, too. When you interact with a graphic designer, web designer, ad rep, list broker, or tech support person from any of the big online web environments (Google and Facebook being great examples of where to purchase well-focused web ads), tell him or her your strategy. Start with "We are trying to . . . " and finish the sentence with whatever is appropriate for you, such as "attract serious collectors of antiquarian books," "let people know that they don't have to feed their families grocery store food with low nutritional value and many contaminants," or "bring broadband interfaces to every trade show display."

Your strategic imagination is the only limitation to your growth, but make sure you share your vision with everyone who contributes to your marketing.

Chapter 3

Taking Stock of Your Business Image

· ·

In This Chapter

▶ Taking steps to ensure that your business makes a consistent, positive impression

▶ Compiling an inventory of the impressions your business makes

▶ Assessing and strengthening your marketing communications

· ·

Right now, even if you're not doing much marketing, your business is making an impression. Somewhere, someone is encountering your ad, seeing your logo, calling your company, visiting your website, reading a review or article about your business, or walking through your door. Maybe someone is driving by the sign on your locked-up shop at night or running across your business name in a web search.

As a result, right now people are drawing conclusions about your business. Based on what they're seeing or hearing, they're deciding whether your business looks like a top-tier player, an economical alternative, or a struggling startup — all based on impressions that you may not even be aware that you're making.

This chapter is about where and when your business makes impressions and how you can align your communications so that people form the opinion you want them to have.

Making First Impressions

You've heard the saying a thousand times: "You never get a second chance to make a first impression." The advice is self-evident and sounds easy enough to follow until you realize that your business most often makes its first impressions when you're nowhere to be found. In your stead is your website, your Facebook page, your voicemail message, your ad or direct mailing, your business sign, your employees, some customer's review or rating, or maybe your logo on the back of a Little League player's uniform.

Ask yourself the following questions as you assess whether the impressions you're making on customers represent you well:

- ✔ When people receive multiple impressions of your business, do they see and hear evidence of a consistent, reliable, well-managed, successful enterprise?

- ✔ Do your communications look and sound like they all represent the same company?

- ✔ Does your logo always look the same? What about your use of typestyles and color scheme? How about the sound and smell of your business? And the tone or voice of your communications? People form impressions through all senses. Be sure you're consistent through all encounters.

- ✔ If you use a tagline or slogan, is it always the same or does it change from one presentation to the next?

- ✔ Do search engines deliver results that are consistent with the image you want customers to see and believe about your business?

To evaluate what kinds of impressions you're making, begin by tracking the ways in which customers approach your business. Then work backward to determine what marketing efforts led to their arrivals. After that, work forward to determine what kinds of impressions customers form when they actually "meet" your business, whether that first contact is made in person, over the phone, or online.

Encountering your business through online searches

What customers see online is fundamental to their impressions of what you and your business are and offer. Book V Chapter 6 is all about connecting with customers online. This section is about assessing what customers see when they search online and whether their search results align with what you want them to believe about your business.

Study search results for your name and the name of your company and products. First, Google your name, and then search with Bing, DuckDuckGo, and other search engines. Here's what to look for:

✔ Does the name you're searching for appear prominently in the first few pages of results — which is as far as most people look?

✔ Are you happy with what you see? Do links to your name lead to sites with information that's relevant to the brand image you want to project (see Book V Chapter 4 for more on your brand image)?

✔ Do top results lead straight to your business website or to a map or phone number for your company?

✔ When you search your name in online images and video, are you happy with what you see or are results inconsistent with the image you want your business to project?

Google+ Local: Your key to being found through Google

If you serve a local market, your customers are searching for you online. Improve your position in their search results by establishing a free Google My Business listing that will appear to consumers as a Google+ Local page. Google+ Local pages integrate business-provided information with information from other Google properties such as Search, Maps, Zagat ratings, and reviews and recommendations from friends, family, and colleagues. What's more, Local pages are indexed by Google to appear in search results and maps, and customers can reach them through the Local tab on their Google+ pages.

Start by going to `http://www.google.com/business` to claim and create your free listing, following these tips:

✔ **Be sure your listing is complete, with your business name, street address, city, state, zip code, phone number, email address, website address, and 200-character description.**

✔ **Enhance your listing to improve search results by adding photos, videos, a list of services (such as free parking), and** coupons or offers. Be sure all visuals on your page are titled using relevant keywords and are tagged with descriptive words that people searching online might use.

✔ **Optimize your page title by including frequently searched keywords so long as they're part of your business name.** For example, Patient Paul's Bait Shop can feature "bait shop" in its page title because those words are actually part of the business name. But another shop can't just add "bait shop" to its title without being penalized by search engines for keyword stuffing.

✔ **Use keywords in your business description.** In your free, 200-character description, include the keywords customers are likely to search for when looking for businesses or products like yours, but don't duplicate keywords presented by your business name. The business description for Patient Paul's Bait Shop shouldn't repeat "bait shop" but may include "fly-fishing trips" or "fly-tying classes" if customers typically seek those offerings. It might also

(continued)

(continued)

include the business location if it serves a local market area (for example, "offering the freshest bait in Charleston"). Use the free Google AdWords Keyword Planner (`https://adwords.google.com/KeywordPlanner`) to see which terms on your website are most frequently searched globally and locally. The findings can help you determine which keywords to feature in your description.

✔ **Create a page for each location of your business, and always use street addresses because Google often rejects P.O. box addresses.**

✔ **Encourage customers to add reviews.** Reviews, especially if they're spaced to appear from time to time rather than all at once, help your page appear more prominently in results. Just be sure not to offer reviewers incentives, which Google considers a conflict of interest.

✔ **Establish listings in other online directories.** Those listings make your business more findable online and therefore improve your position in search results.

From time to time, log on to your Google Places page to study which keywords users are searching and how many clicks your site received as a result. Also, visit `http://support.google.com/business` to get the latest tips. You can also stay on top of ongoing changes by following the official Google blog at `http://googleblog.blogspot.com`.

Arriving at your website

To people shopping online, your website *is* your business. To everyone else, it's a gateway to your business. Here are some quick points to keep in mind as you develop an online presence that supports your business image:

✔ **You have to work to be found online.** With the web already hosting at least a trillion pages, and the number of URLs or site addresses increasing by more than 150,000 a day, any business in this day and age needs the following:

- A website with its own name in the site address

- Social media pages

- A network of online links that point web users to the business site

- A commitment to optimizing the site's visibility in search engine results

- A communication effort that features links to all major online locations in all ads and marketing materials

✔ **People arriving at your site may not know where they are.** They may be coming from search engine results or online links that send them to an internal page of your site, so be sure that every page features your name or logo, along with a link to your home page.

✔ **Realize that most customers are channel agnostics.** They migrate between online and offline encounters and expect continuity as they travel. Whether they see your Facebook page, your website or blog, your traditional media ads, your display windows, or you and your staff members in person, they expect a single business image. Be sure your online identity meshes with your offline identity, right down to the style of typeface you use, the kinds of messages you present, and the way you display your business name and logo.

Don't ignore the fact that more than eight out of ten smartphone owners search from their phones while they're shopping, traveling, or otherwise away from their computers, even when they're in their own homes. Be sure to create a simplified mobile version of your website (see Book II Chapter 5 for more on creating a mobile version of your site).

Managing email impressions

Sometime in the late 1990s (in other words, ancient history), the number of email messages eclipsed the volume of traditional letters sent by businesses. By 2010, 294 billion emails were sent daily, amounting to more than 100 trillion a year, a quarter of which were sent by businesses.

Yet while businesses routinely format, proofread, print, and file traditional correspondence, they send email messages spontaneously, often with no standard policy and rarely with a company record for future referral. Such an informal approach to email is fine for thank-you notes or quick updates to customers, but what if the message includes a fee estimate or a notice that client-requested changes will result in an additional thousand dollars of expense? And what if the staff member who sent the email is no longer with your company when the customer questions the bill?

For the sake of your business, set a few email guidelines:

✔ **Unify all company emails by use of a common signature.** A *signature* or *sig* is a few lines of text that appear at the end of every email message. The signature usually includes

- The name of the person sending the message
- Your business logo
- A tagline that tells what your business does
- Your business address, phone number, and website URL
- Often a promotional message or offer

You can create a signature in almost any email program. Go to the help function for instructions.

- ✔ **Set a tone and style for email messages.** In well-managed businesses, traditional letters go out on company letterhead, use a consistent typeface and style, and employ clear, professional language. Consider email a dressed-down version of your formal correspondence. It can be more relaxed and more spontaneous, and it can (and should) be more to the point — but it can't be impolite or unprofessional.

- ✔ **Respond to email within 4 hours, even if your response is simply a one-line note that offers a complete answer within days.** An email that isn't answered promptly falls into the same category as phone calls that are placed on endless hold or long, slow-moving lines at the cash register. The customer service impact is devastating.

- ✔ **Back up email messages so they're accessible should an employee quit or not be available when a customer questions a pricing, delivery, or other promise made through email communications.**

- ✔ **Consider establishing business-wide email standards.** Keep email messages short, encourage the use of greetings and standard punctuation, and limit the use of emoticons. Also avoid colored backgrounds or graphics that make messages slow to download on customer computers or mobile devices.

Arriving by telephone

Often, with no prompting at all, callers will tell you how they found your number. "John Jones suggested I call," or, "I'm curious about the new whatchamacallits I see in your ad," or, "I was on your website, but I couldn't tell whether your business is open Sundays." If the conversation doesn't naturally disclose how the person obtained your phone number, take a few seconds (but only a few seconds) to ask something like, "I'm glad you called us. We're always working to improve our communications, and I'd love to note how you got our phone number."

The responses help you see what is and isn't working to generate phone calls. They also help you determine which first impression points bring qualified prospects into your business and which ones reel in people who are "just looking." In the latter case, realize that the problem is rarely with the caller and most often with the impression point.

Here's an example: A real estate brokerage that specializes in high-end residential properties continuously fields calls from shoppers trying to buy homes in a much lower price tier than those listed by the realty company. Upon questioning, the real estate agents discover that most of the mismatched callers found the phone number in a regional real estate guide in which the company's ad read, "We have your dream home." The agents realize that their ad message is appealing to the wrong target market. As a result, they amend their ad to read, "Specialists in fine properties and estate homes."

To get the right prospects to call your business, be sure to target your communications carefully, help customers understand what you offer, make your phone number appropriately large and bold, give people a reason to dial it, and then be ready to treat every call as a valuable business opportunity.

All marketing communications — whether through advertising, direct mail, email, networking, presentations, social media, or website visits — aim to achieve a single goal: a personal contact and the opportunity to make a sale.

When the hard-won call comes, don't fumble the opportunity:

- ✓ **Answer calls promptly.** Pick up after the first or second ring whenever possible. Even if you have a receptionist, train others to serve as back-ups, answering any call that reaches a third ring.

- ✓ **Transfer calls as quickly as you answer them.** Be prompt about getting the caller to the appropriate person in your business. If that person isn't available, say so immediately. Offer to take a message, put the caller through to voicemail, or find someone else to help.

  On hold is a dangerous and costly place to leave valuable prospects.

- ✓ **Get everyone in your company to answer the phone in a consistent and professional manner.** "Hello, this is John" is an appropriate business greeting only when the caller is specifically calling John. Otherwise, answer with the business name in addition to a personal name.

- ✓ **Keep voicemail messages brief and friendly.** Use wording that conveys your business purpose and personality and offer no more than three options so callers can quickly jump to the option they seek. For example:

  - • "Thank you for calling 20/20 Vision. We're focusing on eye exams and frame selections right now, but please press 1 for our hours and location or press 2 to leave a message. We promise to call you back within the hour."

- ✓ **Ask your phone company to monitor and report on your hang-up rate.** Multiple rings, lengthy hold times, and voicemail responses are reasons for callers to abandon their efforts to reach your business.

Consider placing mirrors near the phones if your business relies heavily on telephone contact. People instinctively smile at themselves in mirrors because it makes them look more attractive, and a smile also makes a voice more attractive — more natural, friendly, and enthusiastic. You'll be able to hear the difference, and so will the person on the other end of the line.

Book V

Marketing and Promotion

Making your voicemail more personal

A personal greeting, a meaningful message, and a commitment to prompt, personal follow-up are all it takes to turn voicemail from a personality-free and sometimes annoying fact of life to a pleasant and efficient means to present yourself and your message. Follow these tips:

✔ Record a greeting that accurately reflects your company's image, update it regularly, and check for messages faithfully.

✔ Make sure that your greeting includes your company name (or your own name if it's a personal phone), indicates when you'll return the call, and invites the caller to leave a message.

✔ Encourage detailed messages. "Please leave a message of up to three minutes, and we'll get back to you by day's end." If you encourage a lengthy message, the caller is more likely to convey complete information, reducing the need for telephone tag after the call.

✔ If possible, include the option of pressing zero to speak with a real, live person.

✔ If you can't fully respond to the caller's request within the specified time period, call with a polite explanation and tell when you'll have a response.

✔ Voicemailboxes have limited storage capacity. Delete messages regularly to ensure that new messages can be stored.

✔ Regularly call your own voicemail to see that it's working and that the message is current.

The minute that your voicemail starts to sound like that of a big, faceless corporation, move quickly to put your small business personality back into it. Customers choose small businesses in large part for their personal touch. Don't let voicemail or other systems encroach on that small business advantage.

Approaching your business in person

If a person walks into your business, looks around, and asks, "What kind of a business is this?" you can make an educated guess that the drop-in was unplanned and triggered only by a look at your signage or window displays. (You may want to improve these impression points to better address this obvious question.)

Many businesses boast that their signage is their most effective means of attracting first-time visitors. But before banking on your sign to draw people in, realize that when people respond only to your signage, they're making spur-of-the-moment, drop-in visits — perhaps at a time when they're short on both time and money. Instead, work to achieve *destination visits* by making impressions and cultivating interest well in advance of prospects noticing your sign and walking through your door.

Leading people to your business

If your business relies on consumer visits, convey directions on your website and in ads, mailings, and other advance communications. Build a mobile version of your website to quickly help on-the-go customers reach your location. Invest in directional road signs or billboards if appropriate. Establish a Google+ Local page, a free Google service that helps your business appear in local search results along with a map showing your location (see the sidebar earlier in this chapter, "Google+ Local: Your key to being found through Google"). Also, be sure that when visitors arrive at your business, whether you're located in a high-rise building or a home office, they see a sign with your business name and instructions on how to reach your front door.

Parking

Is your business's parking area clean, well marked, well lit, and capable of making a good impression? If a parking fee is involved, do you have a validation program that customers know about in advance? Have you saved the nearest spots for customers rather than for your car or your employees' cars? (How many times have you driven into a parking lot only to see the spot nearest to the door marked "Reserved for Manager"? And what do those three simple words tell you about your standing as a customer?)

Nearing your front door

As a prospect approaches your entrance, does your business look open and inviting? Here's a list of questions to consider:

- ✔ Is your signage visible, clean, and professional?

- ✔ Do signs and window displays clearly indicate what your business does?

- ✔ Is your business well lit?

- ✔ Is the entrance easy to find?

- ✔ Is your entryway signage welcoming or is it papered with negatives such as "No UPS," "No Smoking," "Deliveries Use Back Door," or "No Outside Food or Beverages"? With just a little editing, you can state your rules in a positive way. "Let us hold your umbrella and packages while you shop" sure beats "No backpacks."

- ✔ If your business success relies on foot traffic, do your windows have show-stopping capacity? Stand back and look hard. If necessary, adjust lighting to improve visibility or to cut glare. Replace small objects with big, bold items that are magnets for attention. Use mirrors to slow people down and also to help them adjust their dispositions (remember, people automatically put on a friendly face when they look in the mirror), both of which are likely to benefit your business.

The moment of arrival

Walk through the process of approaching and entering your business. Forget for a minute that this is *your* business. Imagine how it feels to a stranger. Does it convey the right set of impressions? Consider the following:

- ✔ Is your entry area impeccably clean?

- ✔ Is the entry area decorated to make a strong statement about the nature of your business, its customers, and its products?

- ✔ Do your surroundings present and promote *your* company, or do they inadvertently promote other companies whose logos happen to appear on calendars, posters, coffee cups, and other items that sneak their way into your environment? Rather than making your lobby a display for others, turn it into a showcase of your own products, your clients, or your staff. If you want customers to be proud to associate with your business, proudly spotlight your offerings.

- ✔ Does your business have a clear "landing area" — a place where a visitor can pause upon entry and receive a good first impression?

- ✔ Does your business offer an obvious greeting, either by a person or a welcoming display?

- ✔ If you have a customer waiting area, do people head straight for it, or do they pause and look for an invitation before entering? In some businesses, a coffeemaker, a stack of logo ID cups, and a welcoming sign are all it takes to break the ice. Other times, you may need to remodel or at least redecorate to break down obstacles and enhance the sense of welcome.

  If customers consistently stop in a certain area or study a particular display, consider that area as prime marketing real estate and think of ways that you can enhance it to deliver the strongest possible statement on behalf of your business.

What it's like to be a customer in your business

In designing your business environment, balance your operations and internal needs against the wants and needs of your most important asset: your customers. Follow the path that customers take through your business to figure out where you need to make adjustments to improve their experience. Take the following steps, and then repeat the process in fact-finding visits to a few of your competitors, if such visits are possible:

- ✔ **Stop where customers stop.** Stand in an inconspicuous spot and watch what people do when they enter your business.

  - How long do they wait until someone greets them?

  - Do they look around for a clue regarding what to do next?

- If you're a retailer, do they see a bottleneck at the cash register as their first impression?

- How many people make a U-turn and leave before they make a purchase, and where do they seem to most frequently lose interest?

✔ **Shop like they shop.** Study what it's like to purchase your product. How many different people or departments do customers deal with, and does each contribute value rather than require an annoying duplication of customer input? Where do points of concern or resistance arise? How can you eliminate obstacles that hinder your customers' decisions to buy or their ability to enjoy dealing with your business?

- If you have a service business and customers want to know how your charges add up, be ready with answers. Create a brochure or handout describing your services and fee structure.

- If they want to touch the merchandise, build appropriate displays.

- If they need to try before they buy, offer samples, fitting rooms, before-and-after photos, or other ways to experience your product.

- If they want to browse, display products at eye level and give them room to stop and shop, realizing that narrow aisles and tight spaces drive people — especially women — right out the door.

✔ **Wait where they wait and for as long.** Test your customer service from a customer's viewpoint. Look at how customers react to the way your company serves and treats them.

- Have you provided chairs in areas where they end up waiting?

- In areas where customers pause, have you placed displays that move them toward buying decisions?

- If spouses, children, or friends accompany customers, have you created entertainment areas and appropriate diversions?

- If their visits consistently last longer than an hour, do you provide some form of refreshment?

- Watch for nonverbal complaints about a lack of attentiveness. Do customers glance at their watches or fidget while waiting for employees to handle phone calls, deal with other customers, or complete paperwork? Be aware that customers use waiting time as the single most important factor in gauging your customer service, so plan accordingly.

Auditing the Impressions Your Business Makes

The only way you can be sure you're making consistently good impressions in your marketplace is to take inventory and assess every contact with prospects, customers, and others who deal with your business.

Surveying your marketing materials and communications

Start by pulling samples of stationery, ads, signs, brochures, coffee cups, T-shirts, online communications, and any other items that represent your business. Line them all up and evaluate them using these questions:

- ✔ Does your business name and logo look the same every time you make an impression?
- ✔ Do you consistently use the same colors?
- ✔ Do you consistently use the same typeface?
- ✔ Do your marketing materials present a consistent image in terms of look, quality, and message?

Study your samples and isolate those that don't fit with the others, perhaps because they use outdated or inaccurate versions of your name or logo. Or maybe the colors are wrong or the tone is inconsistent. Possibly the message is witty or silly when the rest of your communications are fact-filled and serious. Or the caliber may be unprofessional compared to the rest of your materials.

Cull the inappropriate items and then look at what's left.

- ✔ **Does the consistent portion of your marketing materials accurately reflect your business?**
- ✔ **Do your marketing materials adequately appeal to your target market?**
    - For example, if you know that your customers value top quality, do your marketing materials convey a top-quality company? Do your ads convey quality? Do you apply your logo only to prestigious advertising items? If you're a retailer, are your shopping bags the finest you can afford? If you're a service company, do you present your proposals in a manner that reinforces the caliber of your firm while affirming your customer's taste level?

- If your customers value economy, do your materials look too upscale? If so, they may telegraph the wrong message.

- If your customers choose you primarily for convenience, do your materials put forth that assurance? Or, if customers value your reliability, do you convey that attribute through a flawless commitment to a reliably consistent projection of your identity?

In forming opinions about your company, your market relies on the impressions it gets from your communications.

Creating an impression inventory

Your business makes impressions in person, online, in ads and marketing materials, in correspondence . . . the list goes on and on. Every contact is capable of contributing to or detracting from the image you want people to hold in their minds about your business. Try the following tips:

- ✔ **Define your company's impression points.** Using the provided entries, check all impression points that apply to your business, and add any additional ways your business comes into contact with customers and prospective customers. No item is too small to include. If your ad is a work of art but your proposal cover is flimsy, the negative impact of one cancels out the positive impact of the other. Every impression counts.

- ✔ **Define the target market for each impression point.** Is it to develop a new prospect or to communicate with an existing customer — or maybe a little bit of both? If your business has a number of customer types or product lines, you may want to get even more specific. For instance, one ad for an insurance brokerage may target property insurance prospects and another may target life insurance prospects. By defining the different purposes, the brokerage is able to gauge how much it invests in the development of each product line.

- ✔ **Rate the quality of each impression your business makes.** Give each of your communication vehicles a grade of Good, Average, or Poor, based on your assessment of how well it conveys your business image, message, look, and style.

- ✔ **Who's in charge of each impression point?** Many impressions that affect a company's image are made by those who don't think of themselves as marketers. Nine times out of ten, no one is thinking about marketing when a cost estimate is presented, a bill is sent, or a purchase order is issued. The key is to think about the marketing impact far in advance so that you create materials, processes, and systems that advance a positive image for your company.

✔ **Evaluate the costs involved.** What does each communication cost in terms of development, media, printing, or other expenses? After you know the answer, you can add up what you're spending on business development, customer retention, and marketing of each product line. You may be surprised to find that you're over-supporting some functions and under-supporting others, and you can adjust accordingly.

Improving the impressions you're making

Ask yourself the following questions to assess the quality and effectiveness of the impressions your business makes:

✔ **Are you allocating your efforts well?** Are you spending enough on efforts to keep current customers happy, or are your efforts too heavily weighted toward getting new people through the door — or vice versa?

✔ **Do your communications fit your image and objectives?** Answer this question for every item, whether it's an ad or a logo-emblazoned coffee cup. Be sure that each contributes to the image you're trying to etch in your marketplace rather than to some decision made long ago based on the powerful presentation by a sales representative.

✔ **Is your image consistent, professional, and well suited to the audiences that matter most to your business?**

Use your inventory as you fine-tune your communications. Keep it on hand. If you ever decide to change your name, logo, or overall look, this list will remind you of all the items that you need to update.

Use your impression inventory to guide changes as you strengthen the image you project to your market. Work to phase out and replace any impression points you rate as poor and to adjust and improve the quality of any impression points you rate as average.

Chapter 4

Forging Your Brand

In This Chapter

▶ Defining what brands are and why they're important

▶ Beginning to build your brand

▶ Positioning your brand in your market

▶ Using taglines to enhance your brand

▶ Developing your brand message, creative strategy, and consistent style

"*W*e're just a small business," you may be thinking. "We're not Coca-Cola or Nike, with a bazillion-dollar ad budget and a global market. We're just 12 people trying to build a half million dollars in sales. We hardly need a brand."

Guess what? A brand isn't some mysterious, expensive treasure available only to the rich and famous. And it isn't just for mega-marketers, though they all have one.

Branding simply (well, maybe not all *that* simply) involves developing and consistently communicating a set of positive characteristics that consumers can relate to your name. If those characteristics happen to fill a meaningful and available position in their minds — a need they've been sensing and trying to fill — then you just scored a marketing touchdown, and that half-million-dollar sales goal will be way easier to reach.

What Brands Are and What They Do

Keep in mind two facts about what brands are and aren't:

✔ A brand is a set of beliefs. It's a promise that customers believe.

✔ A brand isn't a logo. A logo is a symbol that identifies a brand. When people see your logo or hear your name, a set of images arises. Those images define your brand in their minds.

Your brand isn't what *you* think it is. Your brand is whatever mental image those in your target audience automatically unlock when they encounter your name or logo. Your brand is what they believe about you based on everything they've ever seen or heard — whether good or bad, true or false.

If you make impressions in your marketplace, whether proactively or unconsciously, you're building your brand. In fact, you're likely building two brands at once — a business brand for your company and a personal brand for yourself, a brand balancing act featured in a section later in the chapter.

Something as basic as your street or online address contributes to how people perceive your brand. For that matter, customers, prospective customers, job applicants, reporters, bankers, suppliers, and those who refer people to you and your business form impressions every time they walk through your front door, visit your website, meet an employee, see your ad, or scan an online review or search results.

All those impressions accumulate to become your brand image in your customer's mind, which is where brands live.

Unlocking the power and value of a brand

If you need a motivating fact to boot you into branding action, here it is: Branding makes selling easier because people want to buy from those they know and like, and those they trust will deliver on commitments. A good brand puts forth that promise.

With a well-managed brand, your company hardly needs to introduce itself. Within your target market, people will already know your business, its personality, and the promise it makes to customers — all based on the positive set of impressions you've made and they've stored in their minds.

Without a well-managed brand, you'll spend a good part of every sales opportunity trying to introduce your business, while some well-known brand down the street can spend that time actually making the sale.

Brands fuel success in three ways:

- ✔ Brands lead to name awareness, which sets your business apart from all the contenders your audience has never heard of.
- ✔ Brands prompt consumer selection because people prefer to work with those they've heard of and heard good things about.
- ✔ Brands unlock profitability because people pay premium prices for products (or, in the case of personal brands, for people) that they trust will deliver higher value than lesser-known alternatives.

As a result of the advantages they deliver, brands increase the odds of business success, which makes them especially valuable in a world where half of all businesses fail in the first five years, nine out of ten products don't make it to their second anniversary, and too many people are vying for the same jobs, sales, and opportunities.

Tipping the balance online

Without a brand, you have to build the case for your business before every sale. Doing that is tough work in person and even tougher online, because you can't be there to make introductions, inspire confidence, counter resistance, or break down barriers.

Brands are essential to online and offline success for very different reasons.

✔ **For those who sell online, brands are necessary for credibility.**

People buy everything online — from contact lenses to cars — all without the benefit of personal persuasion, hands-on evaluation, or test drives. Why? Because customers arrive at websites with confidence in the brands they buy. When they see a brand they know and like, they check the price and terms, click to buy, and move on to checkout. If your business takes place primarily online, your brand is your key to sales.

✔ **For those who sell offline, brands are necessary for findability.**

Anymore, nearly every brand needs to be findable, prominent, and credible online. The rare exceptions are those that serve a target market that never goes online and that's never influenced by those that do. For every other brand, Chris Anderson, author of *The Long Tail* (Hachette Books) and *Wired* magazine editor, says, "Your brand is what Google says it is." If customers can't find your business in an online search, they conclude that you either don't exist or aren't a top player in your arena.

Branding facilitates sales and spurs success, whether your cash register is online or on Main Street.

Building a Powerful Brand

Your small business will probably never have a globally recognized "power brand" simply because you don't have (and for that matter don't need) the marketing muscle that would fuel that level of awareness.

But you *can* be the most powerful brand in your target market. All it takes is the following:

- ✔ Knowing the brand image that you want to project
- ✔ Developing a distinct point of difference that's relevant and beneficial to your target audience
- ✔ Having commitment and discipline to project your brand well
- ✔ Spending what's necessary to get your message to your target market
- ✔ Managing your marketing so that it makes consistent impressions that etch your desired brand image into the mind of your target prospect

Being consistent to power your brand

To build a strong brand, project a consistent look, tone, and level of quality through each point of customer contact, whether in person or through marketing and whether online or offline.

Then stick with the brand you build. People in your target audience are exposed to thousands of images every day. To manage the marketing clutter, they filter out all but the messages and images that are relevant and familiar. The quickest route to making your brand image one they recognize and trust is to present it consistently — without fail.

Don't try to change your brand image unless you're certain that it's no longer appropriate for the market. (And if that's the case, you'd better be prepared to change your business, because your brand is the public representation of your business.) Imagine how tired the people at Campbell's Soup must be of their label, but imagine what would happen to their sales if they abandoned it simply because a fickle marketing manager said, "Let's try something new." Remember "New Coke"?

Consistency builds brands, and brands build business.

Taking six brand-management steps

Building a well-managed brand follows certain steps:

1. **Define why you're in business.**

   What does your business do? Or, if you're building a personal brand, what do you do? How do you do it better than anyone else? Put into writing the reason that your business exists and the positive change you aim to achieve.

2. **Consider what you want people to think when they hear your name.**

   What do you want current and prospective employees to think about your business? What do you want prospects, customers, suppliers, associates, competitors, and friends to think?

   You can't be different things to each of these groups and still have a well-managed brand. For example, you can't have an internal company mind-set that says "economy at any price" and expect consumers to believe that no one cares more about product quality and customer service than you do.

   Figure out what you want people to think when they hear your name. Then ask yourself whether that brand image is believable to each of the various groups with whom you communicate. If it isn't, decide how you need to alter your business to make achieving your brand image possible.

3. **Think about the words you want people to use when defining your business.**

   Ask your employees, associates, and customers this question: When people hear our name, what images do you think come into their minds? If everyone says the same thing, and if those words are the words you *want* associated with your name, you have a well-managed brand. If gaps occur, you have your brand-management work cut out for you.

   List words that you want people to link to your business and be certain that you live up to that desired image. Then lead people to the right conclusions by presenting those characteristics — that brand image — consistently and repeatedly in your marketing communications. Choose messages and graphic symbols that support the image you want to project. For example, to etch its image as a brand for middle America, Conseco Insurance features a daisy rather than a rose, a golden retriever rather than a poodle, and a comfortable loafer rather than a stiletto heel. Rolex maintains its luxury brand image by featuring a crown as its logo and by giving its signature watch collection the name *Oyster*.

4. **Pinpoint the advantages you want people to associate with your business.**

   Figuring out these distinctions leads to your definition of the position you want to own in consumer minds.

5. **Define your brand.**

   Look at your business through a customer's or prospect's eyes as you define your brand. What do people say and think about your company and the unique benefits they count on it to deliver? Why do they choose your business and prefer to buy from you again and again? How would they define your brand and the promise it makes?

Boil your findings down to one concept — one brand definition — that you honestly believe you can own in the minds of those who deal with your business. The following are examples of how three widely known brands are generally perceived by the public:

- Volvo: The safest car
- CNN: The middle-of-the-road, all-news channel
- Google: The top Internet search engine

6. **Build your brand through every impression that you make.**

   Flip back to Book V Chapter 3 for advice on auditing your brand's impression points. Rate whether each impression enhances or detracts from the brand you're building, depending on how well it projects your brand with clarity and consistency.

Your Market Position: The Birthplace of Your Brand

Brands live in consumer minds. But just like you need to find an empty lot if you want to build a home to live in, you need to find an empty mind space if you want to embed your brand in your customer's brain.

Positioning involves figuring out what meaningful and available niche in the market — and in your customer's head — your business is designed to fill, and then filling it and performing so well that people have no reason to allow anyone else into the space in their minds they hold for your brand.

Seeing how positioning happens

When people learn about your business, they subconsciously slot you into a business hierarchy composed of the following:

- ✔ **Me-too businesses:** If the mind slot — or position — that you want for your business is already taken, you have to persuade consumers to switch allegiances on your behalf, and that's a tough job. The best advice for a "me-too" business is to find a way to become a "similar-but-different" business by targeting an unserved market niche or providing a differentiating benefit.

- ✔ **Similar-but-different businesses:** These businesses market a meaningful difference in a crowded field. Depending on the nature of your business, your positioning distinction may be based on pricing, inventory, target market, service structure, or company personality. For example, instead of simply opening your town's umpteenth pizza shop, open the only one in a trendy new neighborhood, the only one that offers New York–style pizza by the slice, or the only one that uses recipes from Southern Italy in a trattoria setting. Your distinction had better be compelling, though, because you have to convince people the difference is worth hearing about, sampling, and changing for.

✔ **Brand-new offerings:** If you can be the first to fill a market's needs, you have the easiest positioning task of all. Just don't expect that marketing to seize that brand-new position will be a cakewalk. First-in-market businesses need to educate consumers about what the new offering is and why they should care. Then they have to promote skillfully and forcefully before competitors enter the fray.

First-in-a-market businesses and first-of-a-kind products have to market fast and fastidiously because, in the end, being first isn't as important as being first to seize a positive position in the consumer's mind.

Determining your positioning strategy

The simplest way to figure out what position you hold is to determine what your business offers that your customers would have a hard or impossible time finding elsewhere. Some questions that will lead to your positioning statement include the following:

✔ How is our offering unique or at least difficult to copy?

✔ Is our unique offering something that consumers really want?

✔ Is our offering compatible with economic and market trends?

✔ How is our offering different — and better — than available options?

✔ Is our claim believable?

Don't aim for a position that requires the market to make a leap of faith on your behalf. If a restaurant is known for the best burgers in town, it can't suddenly decide to try to jump into the position of "the finest steakhouse in the state." Leapfrogging doesn't work well when the game is positioning.

Develop your position around the distinct attributes that have made your business successful to date. Here are a few positioning examples:

✔ Skyliner is a community offering families the finest view in town.

✔ Treetops is an inn hosting the most pampered ski vacationers in the East.

✔ *Starting a Business All-in-One For Dummies* is a friendly guide packed with advice and tools to help small business leaders achieve success by planning, launching, and managing their businesses.

See how it works? A positioning statement is easy to construct — just apply the formula you see in Figure 4-1.

Figure 4-1:
This formula helps you build a positioning statement.

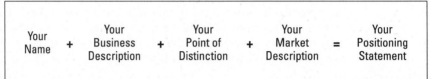

| Your Name | + | Your Business Description | + | Your Point of Distinction | + | Your Market Description | = | Your Positioning Statement |

© John Wiley & Sons, Inc.

As you write your statement, avoid these traps:

✔ **Don't try to duplicate a position in an already crowded category.** Opening the third shoe repair shop in a small town requires more than a location and announcement. You need to convince customers who are already committed to the other shops that your store is better — because of its location, service, or other distinguishing attributes.

✔ **Don't base your distinction on a pricing or quality difference that a competitor can take from you.** For instance, you're only egging on your competitors if you position yourself as "the lowest priced" or "the most creative." With effort, a competitor can beat you on either front.

✔ **Don't hang your hat on a factor you can't control.** Too many resorts have ended up red-faced after positioning themselves as "the region's only five-star resort," only to lose a star or have a competitor gain one. Instead, communicate distinctions that matter to your customers and then back them up with definitions and promises. For example, instead of making a vague promise about "best service," Alaska Air says it's the first major U.S. airline with a 20-minute baggage service guarantee.

✔ **Don't settle for a generic positioning statement.** Be sure you can answer no to this question: Could another business say the same thing?

Conveying Your Position and Brand through Taglines

Your *tagline* or *slogan* is a quick, memorable phrase that helps consumers link your name to your business brand and position. Your positioning statement tells the unique market niche and mind space you aim to occupy. Your tagline converts that statement to a line that matters to consumers.

You need a tagline if your brand name benefits from some explanation. For instance, Jiffy Lube doesn't need a tagline but BMW does, because if you'd never heard of BMW, its name alone wouldn't tell you what it is and does.

For some tagline inspiration, go to www.adslogans.co.uk and click the Hall of Fame link for a list of famous taglines compiled by the Advertising Slogan Hall of Fame.

As you develop a tagline for your brand, follow some advice from Eric Swartz, who calls himself a *verbal branding professional* and *master wordslinger,* and who lives up to his self-description on both counts. He's created thousands of brand expressions, including corporate taglines, city mottoes, campaign slogans, company and product names, headlines, and other short-form messages.

His business, TagLine Guru (www.taglineguru.com), is summed up by the tagline, "It's your brand on the line." Here's what he says you need to know as you write a tagline for your brand:

- ✔ **A tagline should say something essential about who you are, what makes you special, and why the world should care.** It should confer marquee value on your brand and illustrate the value and appeal of your organization. Think of your tagline as a final exclamation point that wraps up your 30-second elevator pitch.

- ✔ **Because taglines aren't written in stone, you can easily update or replace them if your organization or message undergoes a shift.** Use your tagline to reflect a change in positioning, launch a marketing or brand-awareness campaign, forge a relationship with a new audience, define a new direction, or highlight a key benefit or attribute.

Swartz lists the following 12 characteristics of great taglines:

- ✔ **Original:** Make it your own
- ✔ **Believable:** Keep it real
- ✔ **Simple:** Make it understandable
- ✔ **Succinct:** Get to the point
- ✔ **Positive:** Elevate their mood
- ✔ **Specific:** Make it relevant
- ✔ **Unconventional:** Break the mold
- ✔ **Provocative:** Make them think

✔ **Conversational:** Make it personable

✔ **Persuasive:** Sell the big idea

✔ **Humorous:** Tickle their funny bone

✔ **Memorable:** Make a lasting impression

Not all taglines incorporate all 12 characteristics — obviously, a legal or accounting firm wouldn't aim to convey humor — but this list can help during the tagline brainstorming process.

After you adopt a tagline, include it in all marketing communications so that when people see your brand name, they also see the tagline that translates your brand promise into a descriptive and memorable phrase.

Balancing Personal and Business Brands

Most people build two brands at once: one for their business and one for themselves, personally. Between the two, you need to maintain balance.

To rate your personal/business brand balance, answer these questions:

✔ Online and within your personal and business community, is one of your brands — your personal brand or your business brand — significantly more visible and credible than the other?

✔ If you sold your business or left your current position tomorrow, is your personal brand strong enough to transport you into new business opportunities?

✔ If you own your business, is your business brand strong enough to survive without the weight of your personal brand behind it?

Based on your answers, you can take one of two steps:

✔ **Strengthen your personal brand if it's weak in comparison to your business brand.** Especially if you own your company, your personal brand helps you humanize your business and take it places where only people go, such as into networking events and community or industry leadership positions.

   • Follow the six brand management steps in this chapter to develop your personal brand in addition to your business brand.

   • Develop heightened personal-brand awareness within your business, industry, and community, and especially online, which is where most brand research starts.

- Create and maintain a personal online home base — your own website, a blog, or pages on social networks. (See Book V Chapter 6 for help with this step.)

✔ **Strengthen your business brand if it's eclipsed by your personal brand.** This is especially important if you hope to one day sell your business or develop it into an enterprise that can survive without you.

  - If your business doesn't have a website, get one (see Book II Chapter 5 for advice). And if it doesn't rank well in search results, broaden its online presence to improve its visibility.

  - If your personal brand is monopolizing your business image, make way for others on your team to get more visible with clients, on projects, in media, and within your community and industry. Online, instead of personally representing your business, create separate social media accounts for yourself and your company. Then invite members of your team to add their voices (with guidance) to your business blog and social media pages so people view your company as an enterprise larger than one visible person.

  - Make a conscious effort to direct interest in you, personally, to your business. Feature your business prominently in your personal communications and introductions. Even consider using your business logo instead of a personal photo on your personal online pages, where business contacts may be searching.

 Especially if you're planning to grow or sell your business, strengthen your business brand. If you want to pursue personal career opportunities or to humanize your business, strengthen your personal brand. In between, the best approach is to keep your two brands nicely in balance.

Maintaining and Protecting Your Brand

For something so powerful, brands are surprisingly vulnerable. They thrive with consistency and they wither under the attack of zigs and zags in message, experience, and management. The best way to grow a healthy brand is to follow two steps:

✔ Establish your brand message and creative strategy.

✔ Put controls in place to protect your brand and ensure its consistent presentation.

Staying consistent with your brand message and creative strategy

Your *creative strategy* is the plan that directs the development of all your marketing communications. It defines

- Your target market
- The believable and meaningful benefit you offer to your market
- The way you present your personality in your communications

Writing your creative strategy

You can write your creative strategy in three sentences that define the purpose, approach, and personality that will guide the creation of your marketing communications, following this formula:

1. **"The purpose of our marketing communications is to convince** [insert a brief description of your target market] **that our product is the most** [describe the primary benefit you provide to customers]."

2. **"We will prove our claim by** [insert a description of why your distinct benefit is believable and how you'll prove it in your marketing]."

3. **"The mood and tone of our communications will be** [insert a description of the personality that your communications will convey]."

Following is a sample strategy for a fictitious business:

Glass Houses, a window-washing service: The purpose of our marketing communications is to convince affluent homeowners in our hometown that our service is the easiest and most immediately gratifying way to beautify their homes. We will prove our claim by guaranteeing same-week and streak-free service, by promising four-month callback reminders, and by offering special, three-times-a-year rates so that homeowners never have to think about window cleaning after their first call to us. The mood and tone of our communications will be straightforward and clean — like our service.

Using your creative strategy

Every time you create an ad, a mailer, a voicemail recording, or even a business letter or an employee uniform or dress code, be 100 percent certain that your communication is consistent with the creative strategy that you've established to guide your business personality. Here are some ways to do so:

✓ **Use your creative strategy to guide every representation of your business — and your brand.** Start by looking around your business to see that your physical space projects the tone and develops the image you want for your business. If your creative strategy stipulates a discreet image for your business, you don't want prospects to encounter a rowdy atmosphere with music blaring when they walk into or call your business. Carry that same discipline into every marketing communication.

✓ **Create each new marketing communication with your creative strategy in mind.** Whether you're developing a building sign, a website, or a major ad campaign, insist that the final product adheres to your creative strategy.

✓ **Fine-tune your creative strategy annually.** Review your creative strategy. You may decide to reach out to a different target market or to present a different marketing message based on your assessment of market opportunities. But hold tight to your definition of the mood and tone of your communications. (Flip back to the section "Being consistent to power your brand" for a reminder of why your look and tone need to be reliable indicators of your brand image.)

Controlling your brand presentation

Well-branded organizations have rules — called *style guidelines* — that determine how their logos may be presented, what typestyles and colors may be used in marketing materials, how certain words are used, and when and how taglines, copyrights, and trademark indicators apply.

Create style guidelines to protect the consistency of your brand image, too. Then, before a print shop, specialty-advertising producer, staff designer, outside marketing firm, or any other supplier creates marketing materials on your behalf, share your style guidelines to steer the outcome of their efforts.

Managing your logo presentation

Your logo is the face of your business on marketing materials. Ensure that it's presented cleanly and without unnecessary alteration by asking and answering the following questions in your style guidelines:

✓ When your logo appears in black ink, what color backgrounds may be used?

✓ When your logo appears in white ink (called a *reverse*), what color backgrounds may be used?

✓ When your logo appears in color, what ink color or colors may be used?

✓ What's the smallest size that can be used for your logo?

Indicate in your guidelines that your logo must be reproduced from original artwork or a professionally produced reproduction and never from a photocopy or previously printed piece, because the quality will be inferior. If a professional designed your logo, be sure to request the EPS or vector art files. JPG and PNG files may look fine online, but they appear fuzzy when stretched for large-scale use. Also, get professional guidance on which colors to use, whether your logo translates well in reverse treatments, and other presentation advice.

Deciding on your typestyle

A quick way to build consistency is to limit the typestyles you use in your ads, web pages, brochures, signs, and all other communications. Choose one typeface (also called a *font*) for headlines and one for ad copy. If your company prints technical materials (instruction guides, warranties, operating or assembly instructions, or other copy-intensive pieces), you might designate a third, easy-to-read font for small print and long-text applications or for online use where your selected brand fonts may not display well.

When choosing fonts for your marketing materials, aim to reflect your brand's personality. If you want to convey an old-fashioned or traditional tone, you probably need a *serif* type, which is also the best choice for use in large bodies of type. But if you want your materials to appear informal or very clean and straightforward, *sans serif* type is an appropriate choice.

In addition to specifying fonts, you may want to define usage preferences, taking the following points into consideration:

- ✔ Type featuring both uppercase and lowercase letters is easier to read than copy printed in all capital letters. For legibility, avoid using all capital letters unless the headline or copy block is extremely short and easy for the eyes to track.

- ✔ If your target market has aging vision, keep text or body copy no smaller than 10 points in size. (This is 8-point type. This is 10-point type.)

- ✔ Avoid reversed type — white type on black or dark backgrounds — if you expect people to read your words easily. If, for design purposes, you decide to reverse type, keep the type size large.

- ✔ Use only two fonts in any single marketing piece, unless you're trying through your design to create a cluttered look.

Establishing copy guidelines

Copy refers to the words, text, or content of your marketing materials. As you establish style guidelines, also define how you want your copy prepared, taking these points into consideration:

✔ If certain words in your marketing materials require copyright (©), trademark (™), or registered trademark (®) symbols, list these words in your style guidelines.

✔ Indicate in your guidelines whether you want your marketing materials to carry a copyright notice in small (usually 6-point) type. For example: © 2015 John Doe. (Go to www.copyright.gov for more information.)

✔ If you plan to send printed materials over national borders, ask your attorney whether you need to include a line reading "Printed in U.S.A." If so, include the instructions in your guidelines.

✔ Decide which words you prefer to have capitalized. For example, perhaps your style preference is to say your business is located in "Southern California" and not "southern California." Or maybe you want your business to be "The Candy Factory" and not "the Candy Factory."

✔ Determine whether you want to ban certain words. For example, a real estate developer may prohibit the word *lots* in favor of the word *home-sites*. A public relations firm may insist that the term *PR* be spelled out to read *public relations*. A business with a down-to-earth image might rule out any word that ends in "-ize," saying "see" instead of "visualize" or "make the most of" instead of "maximize."

Chapter 5

Creating Marketing Communications That Work

In This Chapter

▶ Defining your marketing objectives

▶ Generating marketing communications that get results

▶ Figuring out which media channel(s) to tap into

▶ Balancing the reach, frequency, and timing of your ads

▶ Monitoring your ads' effectiveness

C reative. The very word turns confident people queasy and rational people giddy. It prompts marketers to say such outrageous things as "Let's dress up like chickens" or such well-intended but pointless things as "Let's cut through the noise" or "Let's think outside the box." Far less often will you hear the conversation turn strategic, with statements like "Let's talk in terms that matter to our customers" or "Let's define what we're trying to accomplish."

This chapter helps you set communication objectives and steer past the mistakes that shoot too many ad efforts into the great abyss, where wasted dollars languish.

Note: The first three sections of this chapter apply to small business owners doing your own marketing, whether you present your marketing communications in person, online, with print or broadcast ads, or through direct mail. If you place ads in traditional mass media outlets such as newspapers, magazines, and broadcast stations, stick with this chapter to the end for information on scheduling and evaluating your ads. For info on using digital communications, including social media, turn to Book V Chapter 6.

Starting with Good Objectives

Copywriters and designers are talented and creative, but they're rarely telepathic. They can't create marketing materials that meet specific objectives if their instructions don't include what they're expected to accomplish.

So who is supposed to define the objective, set the strategy, and steer the creative process? Well, get ready, because that task falls to the person responsible for marketing, which is probably, well, *you.*

Defining what you want to accomplish

You can hit your marketing target almost every time if you take careful aim. Consider the following examples of creative instructions and note the differences:

> **Example 1:** "We need to build sales. Let's run some ads."

> **Example 2:** "We need a campaign to convince teenagers that by shopping after school on weekdays they'll enjoy our best prices in a club atmosphere because we feature live music, two-for-one cafe specials, and weekday-only student discounts."

Example 1 forces those creating the ad to guess what message to project — and toward whom. It'll likely lead to round after round of revisions as the creative team makes best guesses about the target market, promotional offer, and creative approach.

Example 2 tells the ad creators precisely which consumers to target, what message and offer to project, and what action to prompt. It guides the project toward an appropriate concept and media plan — probably on the first try.

As the business owner, it's your job to give those who produce your marketing communications the information they need to do the job right the first time.

An old saying among marketers concludes that half of all ad dollars are wasted, but no one knows which half. You can move the dividing line between what works and what doesn't by avoiding three wasteful errors:

- ✔ **Mistake #1:** Producing marketing materials without first defining your marketing objectives, leading to materials that address neither the target prospect nor the marketing objective.

- ✔ **Mistake #2:** Creating messages that are too "hard-sell" — asking for the order without first reeling in the prospect's attention and interest.

✔ **Mistake #3:** Creating self-centered communications that focus more on what your business wants to say about itself than on the benefits that matter to a prospective customer.

A good ad can inform, persuade, sell, or connect with consumers, but it can't do all those things at once. Nor is it likely to move the right target audience to the desired consumer action if the audience and objective aren't clearly established before ad creation begins.

Before you undertake any marketing effort, define the audience you aim to influence, the action you're working to inspire, the message you want to promote, and the way that you'll measure effectiveness, whether by leads, web or store traffic, inquiries, social media likes or follows, or other actions you can prompt and monitor.

When setting the objective for your marketing communication, use the following template by inserting the appropriate text in the brackets.

> *This* [ad/brochure/sales call/speech/trade booth display] *will convince* [describe the target market for this communication] *that by* [describe the action that you intend to prompt] *they will* [describe the benefit the target audience will realize] *because* [state the facts that prove your claim, which form the basis of the message you want the communication to convey].

Putting creative directions in writing

Your communication objective defines *what* you're trying to accomplish. A *creative brief* provides the instructions for *how* you'll get the job done.

Answer the following seven questions, and your briefing instructions will be complete.

Who is your target audience for this communication?

Start with everything you know about your prospective customers and then boil down your knowledge into a one-sentence definition that encapsulates the geographic location, the lifestyle facts, and the purchasing motivators of those you want to reach.

Here's an example:

> The target audience is comprised of Montana residents, age 40+, married with children living at home, with professional careers, upper-level income, and an affinity for travel, outdoor recreation, status brands, and high levels of service.

What does your target audience currently know or think about your business and offering?

Use research findings (if available), your own instincts, and input from your staff and colleagues to answer the following questions:

✔ Have prospects heard of your business?

✔ Do they know what products or services you offer?

✔ Do they know where you're located or how to reach you?

✔ Do they see you as a major player? If they were asked to name three suppliers of your product or service, would you be among the responses?

✔ How do they rate your service, quality, pricing, accessibility, range of products, and reputation?

✔ Do you have a clear brand and market position or a mistaken identity in their minds?

Be candid with your answers. Only by acknowledging your real or perceived shortcomings can you begin to address them through your marketing efforts. If your prospects haven't heard of your business, you need to develop awareness. If they're clueless about your offerings, you need to present meaningful facts. If they hold inaccurate impressions, you need to persuade them to think differently.

Here's an example:

> The majority of those in our target audience aren't aware of our existence, but among those familiar with our name, we're known to provide an experience competitive with the best contenders in our field. We need to reinforce the opinions of our acquaintances while also developing awareness and credibility with prospective customers and especially with opinion leaders whose recommendations are most valued by our affluent and socially connected target market.

What do you want your target audience to think and do?

Don't get greedy. In each communication, present one clear idea and chances are good that you'll *convey* one clear idea. If you try to present two or three messages, you'll likely communicate nothing at all.

Four out of five consumers read only your headline, absorb no more than seven words off of a billboard, and take only one idea away from a broadcast ad — provided they don't tune out or skip over the ad altogether.

What single idea do you want prospects to take away from this particular marketing effort? As you answer, follow this process:

1. **Step out of your own shoes and stand in those of your prospect.**

2. **Think about what your prospect wants or needs to know.**

3. **Develop a single sentence describing what you want people to think and what motivating idea you want them to take away from this communication.**

Here's the desired outcome for a computer retailer targeting senior citizens:

> We want senior citizens to know that they're invited to our Computer 101 open houses every Wednesday afternoon this month, where they can watch computer and Internet demonstrations, receive hands-on training, and learn about our special, first-time computer owner packages.

 Be careful what you ask for. Be sure that you're prepared for the outcome you say you desire. If you aren't geared up to handle the online traffic, answer the phone, manage the foot traffic, or fulfill the buying demand that your ad generates, you'll fail strategically even though you succeeded — wildly — on the advertising front.

Consider this example: A one-man painting company decides to rev up business by placing a series of clever, small-space newspaper ads touting impeccable service, outstanding quality, affordable estimates, and prompt response. The ads win attention, action, and advertising awards. The problem is, the painter can't keep up with the phone calls, the estimates, or the orders. Prospects — who had been inspired by the great ads — end up signing contracts with the painter's competitors instead.

The moral of the story is to expect a miracle from good advertising and to be prepared to get what you ask for.

Why should people believe you and take the proposed action?

To be believable, your marketing materials need to make and support a claim.

- ✔ **The easy way** is to list features: the oldest moving company in the East, under new management, the only manufacturer featuring the X2000 widget, the winner of our industry's top award, yada yada yada.

- ✔ **The effective way** is to turn those features into benefits that you promise to your customers. The difference between features and benefits is that features are facts and benefits are personal outcomes.

Table 5-1 shows you exactly what this crucial difference means.

Table 5-1	Features versus Benefits		
Product	*Feature*	*Benefit*	*Emotional Outcome*
Diet soda	One calorie	Lose weight	Look and feel great
Flower arrangements	Daily exotic imports	Send unique floral presentations	Satisfaction that your gift stands out and draws attention
Automobile	Best crash rating	Reduce risk of harm in accidents	Security that your family is safe
Miniature microwave	1.5 cubic feet in size	Save dorm room space	Make room for the floor's only big-screen TV

Every time you describe a *feature* of your product or service, you're talking to yourself. Every time you describe the *benefit* that your product or service delivers, you're talking to your prospect. Consumers don't buy the feature — they buy what the feature does for them. Here are some examples:

- ✔ Consumers don't buy V-8 engines. They buy speed.
- ✔ They don't buy shock-absorbing shoes. They buy walking comfort.
- ✔ They don't buy the lightest tablet computer. They buy the freedom to get online wherever they want.

Follow these steps to translate features into benefits:

1. **State your product or business feature.**
2. **Add the phrase "which means."**
3. **Complete the sentence by stating the benefit.**

For example, a car has the highest safety rating (that's the feature), *which means* you breathe a little easier as you hand the keys over to your teenager (that's the benefit).

What information must your communication convey?

Be clear about your must-haves. Those who create ads, websites, mailers, and other communications call it "death by a thousand cuts" when marketers respond to every creative presentation with, "Yes, but we also have to include. . . ."

If you know that you need to feature a certain look, specific information, or artwork, say so upfront — not after you see the first creative presentation. And keep the list of requirements as short as possible. Here are some guidelines:

- **Must-have #1:** Every communication has to advance your brand image (refer to Book V Chapter 4 for help with defining your image). Provide your image style guide whenever you assign a staff person or outside professional to help with the development of marketing materials.

- **Must-have #2:** Be sparing with all other "musts." Every time you start to say, "We have to include . . ." check yourself with this self-test:

  - Is this element necessary to protect our brand?

  - Is it necessary to protect our legal standing?

  - Is it necessary to prompt the marketing action we want to achieve?

  - Is it necessary to motivate the prospect?

  Let necessity — not history — guide your answers. Any ad designer will tell you that less is more. The more stuff you try to jam into an ad, the less consumer attention it draws. Include no more information than is necessary to arouse interest and lead people to the next step in the buying process.

How will you measure success?

Small business leaders are critical of their marketing efforts — after the fact. Instead, before creating any marketing communication, set your expectations and define your measurement standard in your creative brief.

After an ad has run its course, you'll hear such criticism as, "That ad didn't work, it didn't make the phone ring, and it sure didn't create foot traffic." Yet if you examine the ad, you'll often find that it includes no reason to call, no special offer, a phone number that requires a magnifying glass, and no address whatsoever.

What's your time frame and budget?

Know the specifications of your job before you start producing it, especially if you assign the production task to others.

- **Set and be frank about your budget.** Small business owners often worry that if they divulge their budgets, the creative team will spend it all — whether it needs to or not. But the never-reveal-the-budget strategy usually backfires. If suppliers *don't* know the budget, they *will* spend it all — and then some — simply because no one gave them a not-to-exceed figure to work within. The solution is to hire suppliers you trust, share your budget with them (along with instructions that they can't exceed the budget without your prior approval), and count on them to be partners in providing a cost-effective solution.

- ✓ **Know and share deadlines and material requirements.** If you've already committed to a media buy, attach a media rate card to your creative brief so your designer can obtain the specifications directly rather than through your translation.

- ✓ **Define the parameters of nonmedia communication projects.** For example, if you ask for speechwriting assistance, know the length of time allocated for your speech. If you request materials for a sales presentation, know the audio-visual equipment availability and the number of handouts you want to distribute.

What the creative team doesn't know can cost you dearly in enthusiasm and cost overruns if you have to retrofit creative solutions to fit production realities. Communicate in advance for the best outcome.

Whether you're creating an ad, writing a speech, making a sales presentation, planning a brochure, posting on an online network, or composing an important business letter, start by running through the questions on the creative brief to focus your thinking. For all major projects — or for any project that you plan to assign to a staff member, freelance professional, vendor, or advertising agency — take the time to put your answers in writing. Pass them along so they can serve as a valuable navigational aid. Then monitor success by counting inquiries, click-throughs to landing pages, coupon redemptions, or other measurable actions prompted by your communications — and share your findings so your creative team can benefit from the knowledge of what worked well.

Developing Effective Marketing Communications

Whether delivered in person, through promotions, or via traditional media, direct mail, or email, all marketing communications need to accomplish the same tasks:

- ✓ Grab attention.

- ✓ Impart information the prospect wants to know.

- ✓ Present offers that are sensitive to how and when the prospect wants to take action.

- ✓ Affirm why the prospect would want to take action.

  ✔ Offer a reason to take action.

  ✔ Launch a relationship, which increasingly means fostering interaction and two-way communication between you and your customer.

Good communications convince prospects and nudge them into action without any apparent effort. They meld the verbiage with the visual and the message with the messenger so the consumer receives a single, inspiring idea.

Creative types will tell you that making marketing communications look easy takes a lot of time and talent, and they're right. If you're spending more than $10,000 on an advertising effort or developing a major marketing vehicle such as a website, ad campaign, or product package, bring in pros to help you out.

Steering the creative process toward a "big idea"

After you establish your objectives and prepare your creative brief (see the earlier "Putting creative directions in writing" section), it's time to develop your creative message.

No matter which target audience you're reaching out to, the people in that audience are busy and distracted by an onslaught of competing messages. That's why great communicators know that they need to project big ideas to be heard over the marketplace din.

The *big idea* is to advertising what the brake, gas pedal, and steering wheel are to driving. (See why they call it *big?*) Here's what the big idea does:

  ✔ It stops the prospect.

  ✔ It fuels interest.

  ✔ It inspires prospects to take the desired action.

Advertising textbooks point to Volkswagen's "Think Small" ad campaign as a historic example of a big idea. Volkswagen used it to stun a market into attention at a time when big-finned, lane-hogging gas guzzlers ruled the highways. "Think Small" — two words accompanied by a picture of a squat, round Volkswagen Beetle miniaturized on a full page — stopped consumers, changed attitudes, and made the Bug chic.

More recently, "Got Milk?" was a big idea that juiced up milk sales, and "Smell like a man" worked like magic for Old Spice.

But big ideas aren't just for big advertisers. In Portland, Oregon, quirky Voodoo Doughnut's big idea that "The magic is in the hole" has gained international appeal for a five-outlet (though expanding) enterprise.

Big ideas are

- ✔ Appealing to your target market
- ✔ Attention-getting
- ✔ Capable of conveying the benefit you promise
- ✔ Compelling
- ✔ Memorable
- ✔ Persuasive

An idea qualifies as a big idea only if it meets *all* the preceding qualifications. Many advertisers quit when they hit on an attention-getting and memorable idea. Think of it this way: A slammed door is attention-getting and memorable, but it's far from appealing, beneficial, compelling, or persuasive.

Brainstorming

Brainstorming is an anything-goes group process for generating ideas through free association and imaginative thinking with no grandstanding, no idea ownership, no evaluation, and definitely no criticism.

The point of brainstorming is to put the mind on automatic pilot and see where it leads. You can improve your brainstorming sessions by doing some research in advance:

- ✔ Study websites and magazines for inspiration. Pick up copies of *Advertising Age*, *Adweek*, or *Communication Arts* (available at newsstands and in most libraries) for a look at the latest in ad trends. Also include fashion magazines, which are a showcase for big ideas and image advertising.

- ✔ Check out competitors' ads and ads for businesses that target similar audiences to yours. If you sell luxury goods, look at ads for high-end cars, jewelry, or designer clothes. If you compete on price, study ads by Target and Walmart.

- ✔ Look at your own past ads.

- ✔ Think of how you can turn the most unusual attributes of your product or service into unique benefits.

✔ Doodle. Ultimately, great marketing messages combine words and visuals. See where your pencil leads your mind.

✔ Widen your perspective by inviting a customer or a front-line staff person to participate in the brainstorming session.

If you're turning your marketing project over to a staff member or to outside professionals, you may or may not decide to participate in the brainstorming session. If you do attend, remember that a brainstorming session has no boss, and every idea is a good idea. Bite your tongue each time you want to say, "Yes, but . . ." or, "We tried that once and . . ." or, "Get real, that idea is just plain dumb."

At the end of the brainstorm, gather up and evaluate the ideas:

✔ Which ideas address the target audience and support the objectives outlined in your creative brief?

✔ Which ones best present the consumer benefit?

✔ Which ones can you implement with strength and within the budget?

Any idea that wins on all counts is a candidate for implementation.

Following simple advertising rules

The following rules apply to *all* ads, regardless of the medium, the message, the mood, or the creative direction:

✔ Know your objective and stay on strategy.

✔ Be honest.

✔ Be specific.

✔ Be original.

✔ Be clear and concise.

✔ Don't overpromise or exaggerate.

✔ Don't be self-centered or, worse, arrogant.

✔ Don't hard-sell.

✔ Don't insult, discriminate, or offend.

✔ Don't turn the task of ad creation over to a committee.

Committees are great for brainstorming, but when it comes to developing headlines, they round the edges off of strong ideas. They eliminate any nuance that any committee member finds questionable, and they crowd messages with details that matter more to the marketers than to the market. An old cartoon popular in ad agencies is captioned, "A camel is a horse designed by committee."

Making Media Selections

Even back in the day when advertisers chose from among three TV networks, a couple of local-market AM radio stations, and a single hometown newspaper, deciding where to place ads was a nail-biting proposition.

Now add in cable TV channels, dozens of radio stations in even the smallest market areas, 7,500 consumer magazines (and another 7,500 online magazines), countless alternative newspapers, and constantly emerging online advertising options, and you can see why placing ads sometimes feels like a roll of the dice.

The upcoming two sections help tip the odds in your favor with an overview of today's advertising channels and advice about how to select the best vehicles for your advertising messages.

Selecting from the media menu

Marketing communications are delivered in one of two ways:

- *Mass media* channels, which reach many people simultaneously.
- *One-to-one marketing* tools, which reach people individually, usually through direct mail or email.

When people talk about *media,* it's usually mass media they're talking about, which traditionally has been divided into three categories, with a new category recently added:

- **Print media:** Includes newspapers, magazines, and print directories.
- **Broadcast media:** Includes TV and radio.
- **Outdoor media:** Includes billboards, transit signs, murals, and signage.
- **Digital media:** A few years ago, the digital-media category was usually called "new media," but it's not new anymore, and its usage, popularity, and effectiveness increase almost by the moment. Exactly as its name

implies, digital media includes any media that's reduced to digital data that can be communicated electronically. That means Internet advertising, webcasts, web pages, mobile and text ads, and interactive media, including social media networks.

Each mass-media channel comes with its own set of attributes and considerations, which are summarized in Table 5-2.

Table 5-2	Mass Media Comparisons	
Media Channel	*Advantages*	*Considerations*
Newspapers, which reach a broad, geographically targeted market	Involve short timelines and low-cost ad production	You pay to reach the total circulation, even if only a portion fits your prospect profile
Magazines, which reach target markets that share characteristics and interests	Good for developing awareness and credibility through strong visual presentations	Require long advance planning and costly production; ads are viewed over long periods of time
Directories, which reach people at the time of purchase decisions	Increasingly available for free in digital versions; good for prompting selection over unlisted competitors	Print versions are impossible to update between editions and increasingly eclipsed by digital directories
Radio, which reaches targeted local audiences (if they're tuned in)	Cost is often negotiable; good for building immediate interest and response	You must air ads repeatedly to reach listeners; airtime is most expensive when most people are tuned in
TV, which reaches broad audiences of targeted viewers (if they're tuned in)	Well-produced ads engage viewer emotions while building awareness and credibility	Ad production is costly; reaching large audiences is expensive; ads must be aired repeatedly; options such as DVD, Tivo, and Hulu erode effectiveness
Digital media, which reaches people on-demand via any digital device	Allows two-way communication with customers; allows convergence of content by linking among digital sources; low cash investment	Requires targeting of customers and keywords and a significant time investment to create, monitor, and evaluate online visibility and interaction

Deciding which media vehicles to use and when

Face it: Sorting through pitches from local newspapers, local radio stations, daily-deal coupon sites, and industry-specific publications can consume entire days if you let it. Plus there's the elephant in the room — social media (see Book V Chapter 6).

Your media options are seemingly infinite, but your time and budget aren't. So before considering media proposals for any given communication or campaign, answer the following questions:

✔ **What do you want this marketing effort to accomplish?**

If you want to develop general, far-reaching awareness and interest, use mass-media channels that reach a broad and general market. If you want to talk one-to-one with targeted prospective customers, bypass mass media in favor of targeted online communications and direct mail or other one-to-one communication tools.

✔ **Where do the people you want to reach turn for information?**

When it comes to purchasing ad space and time, trying to be all-inclusive is a bankrupting proposition. The more precisely you can define your prospect, the more precisely you can determine which media that person uses and, therefore, which media channels you should consider for your marketing program.

When in doubt, ask customers how they like to be reached with marketing messages. Ask whether they read the local newspaper, tune in to local broadcast stations, or notice transit or outdoor ads. Ask whether they use social media networks and which ones. Ask whether they like or dislike marketing messages sent by text message or email. Talking directly with customers is your great advantage as a small business. Ask directly if you can or use the free survey tools available through sites like SurveyMonkey (www.surveymonkey.com) and Zoomerang (www.zoomerang.com) to poll customers.

By finding out the media habits of your established customers, you get a good idea of the media habits of your prospective customers because they likely fit a very similar customer profile. After you're clear about who your customers are and how they use media, you'll know which media channels to target.

✔ **What information do you want to convey and when do you want to convey it?**

Be clear about your message urgency and content, and then refer to Table 5-2 to match your objectives with media channels. For example:

- If you're promoting an offer with a close deadline, such as a one-week special event, you obviously want to steer away from monthly magazines that are in circulation long after your offer is history.

- If you want to show your product in action, you want to feature video in TV ads or on your website or YouTube channel, to which you can lead customers by including the link in your promotional materials, ads, and social media posts.

✓ **How much money is in your media budget?**

Set your budget before planning your media buy. Doing so forces you to be realistic with your media choices and saves you an enormous amount of time because you don't have to listen to media sales pitches for approaches that are outside your budget range.

The Making of a Mass Media Schedule

When advertising on all mass media except digital media, the amount of money you spend and how you spend it depends on how you balance three scheduling considerations: *reach, frequency,* and *timing*.

Balancing reach and frequency

Your ad schedule needs to achieve enough reach (that is, your message needs to get into the heads of enough readers or viewers) to generate a sufficient number of prospects to meet your sales objective. It also needs to achieve enough frequency to adequately impress your message into those minds — and that rarely happens with a single ad exposure.

✓ *Reach* is the number of individuals or homes exposed to your ad. In print media, reach is measured by circulation counts. In broadcast media, reach is measured by *gross rating points*.

✓ *Frequency* is the number of times that an average person is exposed to your message.

If you have to choose between frequency and reach — and nearly every small business works with a budget that forces that choice — limit your reach to carefully selected target markets and then spend as much as you can on achieving frequency within that area.

The case for frequency

Ad recall studies prove that people remember ad messages in direct proportion to the number of times they encounter them. Here are some facts about frequency:

- ✔ **One-shot ads don't work, unless you opt to spend more than three million dollars to air an ad during the Super Bowl.** Even then, part of the audience will be away from the tube, replenishing the guacamole dish or grabbing a beer from the refrigerator.

- ✔ **On most broadcast channels, you need to place an ad as many as nine times to reach a prospect even once.** That means you need to place it as many as 27 times in order to make contact three times — the number of exposures it takes before most ad messages sink in. If your ad airs during a program that people tune into with regular conviction, the placement requirement decreases, but especially in the case of radio ads, the 27-time schedule generally holds true.

  Why? Because each time your ad airs, a predictably large percentage of prospects aren't present. They're either tuned out or distracted, or maybe your creative approach or offer failed to grab their attention.

- ✔ **Multiple exposures to your ad results in higher advertising effectiveness.** By achieving frequency, you increase the number of people who see your ad, resulting in increased recognition for your brand, increased consumer reaction to your message, and increased responsiveness to your call to action.

Reach creates awareness, but frequency changes minds.

The case for limiting reach by using only a few media channels

Frequency and limited-reach, concentrated ad campaigns go hand in hand. A *concentrated campaign* gains exposure using only a few media outlets.

Instead of running an ad one time in each of six magazines that reach your target market, a concentrated campaign schedules your ad three times each in two of the publications. Or instead of running a light radio schedule and a light newspaper schedule, a concentrated campaign bets the full budget on a strong schedule that builds frequency through one medium or the other.

A concentrated ad campaign offers several benefits:

- ✔ It allows you to take advantage of media volume discounts.

- ✔ It can give you dominance in a single medium, which achieves a perception of strength and clout in the prospect's mind.

- ✔ It allows you to limit ad production costs.

- ✔ It ensures a higher level of frequency.

Timing your ads

No small business has enough money to sustain media exposure 52 weeks a year, 24/7. Instead, consider the following mass media scheduling concepts:

- **Flighting:** Create and sustain awareness by running ads for a short period, then go dormant before reappearing with another *flight* of ads.

- **Front-loading:** Announce openings, promote new products, and jump-start sales by running a heavy schedule of ads before pulling back to a more economical schedule that aims to maintain awareness.

- **Heavy-up scheduling:** Synchronize ad schedules with seasonal business or market activity using schedules that include heavy buys several times a year during what's called *ad blitzes*.

- **Pulsing:** Maintain visibility with an on-and-off schedule that keeps your ad in media channels on an intermittent basis with no variations.

After setting your schedule, leverage your buy by using email and social media to alert customers to watch for your ads, or post the ad on your website and pages to make your investment go further.

Evaluating Your Efforts

Armchair quarterbacking is a popular and pointless after-the-ad-runs activity. Instead, set objectives and plan your evaluation methods early on — not after the play has taken place.

The quickest way to monitor ad effectiveness is to test a couple of great headlines online and measure the clicks they generate. The next-easiest way to monitor ad effectiveness is to produce ads that generate responses and then track how well they do, following this advice:

- Give your target audience a time-sensitive invitation to take action, a reason to respond, and clear, easy instructions to follow. For example, if you're measuring phone calls, make your phone number large in your ad and be ready for call volume; if you're measuring website visits, present an easy-to-enter site address that leads to a landing page tied to your ad message.

- Measure media effectiveness by assessing the volume of responses that each media channel generates compared to the investment you made in that channel. Also measure ad effectiveness by tracking the volume of responses to various ad headlines.

✔ Produce your ads to make tracking possible by including a *key,* which is a code used to differentiate which ads produce an inquiry or order. Here are ways to key your ads:

- Direct calls to a unique phone extension keyed to indicate each medium or ad concept. Train those who answer the phone to record the responses to each extension so you can monitor media and ad effectiveness.

- Add a key to coupons that you include in print ads and direct mailers. For direct mailers, the key might indicate the mailing list from which the inquiry was generated. For print ads, the code could match up with the publication name and issue date. For example, BG0214 might be the key for an ad that runs on Valentine's Day in *The Boston Globe.*

- Feature different post office box numbers or email addresses on ads running in various media channels. When receiving responses, attach the source as you enter names in your database so you can monitor not only the number of responses per medium but also the effectiveness of each medium in delivering prospects that convert to customers.

✔ Test headline or ad concepts by placing several ads that present an identical offer. Track responses to measure which ads perform best.

✔ Compare the cost effectiveness of various media buys by measuring the number of responses against the cost of the placement.

Chapter 6

Social Marketing: Facebook, Pinterest, Twitter, and Blogs

In This Chapter

▶ Exploring marketing opportunities for entrepreneurs on Facebook

▶ Setting up an e-commerce "kiosk" on Facebook

▶ Boosting your visibility with Pinterest images

▶ Using Twitter to build and hold a fan base

▶ Promoting yourself by creating a blog

*N*o longer a novelty, sites like Facebook and Twitter are now a part of the daily lives of millions of people around the world. Facebook has gone public. Pinterest is helping businesses improve visibility — not by spreading the word but by spreading images. The idea that businesses can and should promote themselves through social media is a given.

But let's back up a moment. What exactly is "social networking"? If it's social rather than commercial, how can it help you and your business? E-commerce business and more traditional kinds of business are built on concepts such as trust, brands, and reputation. The better you can brand yourself and prove that you are either an authority in your field or someone who sells desirable merchandise, the more successful you'll be. By soliciting customers on social networking sites, you go out and actively find them rather than wait for them to find your storefront.

Social networking is simply the practice of connecting with people online at venues that have been specially created for that purpose. When the venues become especially popular, they become practical places to build a brand and spread the word about yourself and your business. You can even post items for sale through a social networking site or, at the very least, advertise them online. This chapter describes business uses for social networking sites like Facebook, Pinterest, and Twitter, and your own social networking venue: an online blog.

Developing a Business Presence on Facebook

Back in the early days of the Internet, the way to find customers was to create a website and then list your site on directories with names like Site of the Day. You sat back and hoped you would be noticed through your merchandise or your company name. As any established businessperson will tell you, the "sit back and wait" approach just won't fly these days. You've got to go out and find customers where they hang out — and increasingly, that's on social networking sites like Facebook.

One attractive thing about Facebook is its "opt in" nature. You get content from a person or an organization only if you decide to "friend" that person or indicate that you "like" an organization or a brand. You can set up seven different kinds of "pages" on Facebook:

- ✔ **A personal profile:** This is where you connect with family, friends, old school chums, and anyone who mutually agrees to be your Facebook "friend."

- ✔ **A page for a local business or place:** If you have a brick-and-mortar store (alone or in addition to an online business), choose this option.

- ✔ **A page for a company, organization or institution:** This is the best option for an online-only business, which doesn't have a physical presence.

- ✔ **A page promoting a brand or product:** Businesses that want to connect with customers regularly choose this option.

- ✔ **A page for an artist, band, or public figure:** Fans can connect, and performers or politicians can get the word out about what they're up to.

- ✔ **A page for entertainment:** This might be a book, a television show, a sporting event, a movie, and so on.

- ✔ **A cause or community page:** This can be a page about a cause, an organization, or a business. Individuals connect to such a page by clicking a link to show they "like" it. The organization can then communicate with those who "like" it by sending out announcements.

You're probably interested in the second, third, or fourth option. Starting a company or organization page is easy, as long as you have a Facebook account. First, go to the Facebook home page (www.facebook.com). If you don't have an account, fill out the form on the right side of the home page under the heading Sign Up. After you sign up, you create a business page by going to www.facebook.com/pages and clicking Your Pages➪Create Page.

Do some prep work before creating your page. Decide on

- ✔ The name of your page.
- ✔ The purpose of your page.
- ✔ What thumbnail image you'll post along with your page. (If you have a business logo, this is the perfect place for it. If you are selling your professional services, include a thumbnail image of yourself.)
- ✔ A short (two- to three-paragraph) description of yourself, your business, or your place ready to post.

When you're ready, click "Local Business or Place" or "Company, Organization or Institution," whichever best fits your situation. Fill out the form shown in Figure 6-1 and click Get Started.

Book V

Marketing and Promotion

Figure 6-1: Make the name of your Facebook page easy to remember.

Source: Facebook.com

The "local business or place" is a good option if you sell a particular product or service and you have a physical location. Check the categories in both the local business and company page options for a category that matches what you do.

Attracting "likers" to your Facebook page

As a businessperson, your job is to encourage Facebook members to "like" you. But first, they've got to find you on Facebook. You should definitely include a link to your Facebook page on your business website and as part of the signature file at the bottom of your e-mail messages.

There are other ways to attract fans to your page. One is shown in Figure 6-2. The venerable business 1-800-FLOWERS offers a discount: If you click the Fan Offer! link, a code appears that gives you a discount when you order flowers from the company.

Figure 6-2: Give visitors a reason to return to your site, such as a discount, game, or freebie.

Source: 1-800-FLOWERS.com

Anything that keeps visitors on your site and gives them an incentive to return makes it more likely they'll purchase something.

Getting your customers excited

When you look at the 1-800-FLOWERS site, you immediately see another, perhaps even bigger benefit: You get to interact with individual customers and get feedback on how they deal with your site. On the Wall for the site, some folks leave comments about company postings, as they would about any information on Facebook; others simply indicate that they "like" a promotion or announcement. (On Facebook, in case you don't know, "liking" is essentially a way of giving the thumbs-up gesture without actually saying anything.) Some of the comments are complaints, but the fact that they are on Facebook gives your staff person who is assigned to manage the page a chance to respond personally and perform some positive customer-relations work.

Other feedback on the page is enthusiastic: comments from people who are happy with the flowers they ordered and who are true "likers" of the company. Such interaction not only builds loyalty and lets customers feel empowered, but also gives 1-800-FLOWERS personal comments about packages that are well received and deals that generate interest. You would have to conduct expensive and time-consuming focus groups to get the same sort of feedback.

The Info tab, which is available on Facebook business pages, allows you to put out basic information about your company and make a link to your website.

The Shop tab, which is not typically available on Facebook pages, lets customers shop for and purchase floral arrangements. Such a utility requires a programmer to create a Facebook storefront using the Facebook application programming interface. You need a programmer to create such a Sales tab yourself or an account with a company that provides that service.

Creating a Facebook "kiosk"

An innovative marketplace called ArtFire (www.artfire.com) has developed a Facebook sales system for members who sign up and pay their monthly subscription fee.

The Facebook kiosk is available to all ArtFire members. At this writing, an account costs $20 per month.

After you create a storefront with ArtFire and list works of art or other items for sale in a catalog, you set up a page for your store on Facebook. Then you install the kiosk, which "grabs" your store logo and a selection of merchandise for sale and groups them in a format that those who "like" you will find easy to browse. You can also make purchases directly from the kiosk without ever having to log out of Facebook and go to another site.

Kharisma Ryantori, who sells handmade jewelry through an ArtFire store called Popnicute, has a page for her business on Facebook, shown in Figure 6-3.

Click one of the items shown for sale in the kiosk to view a close-up image of the item. You can select it by clicking the Add To Cart button shown in Figure 6-4. You then click the Checkout Now button to complete the purchase.

Figure 6-3:
ArtFire
members
set up
a sales
"kiosk" as
part of a
business
page.

Source: Artfire.com

Figure 6-4:
Close-up
photos and
Add To Cart
buttons
make
shopping on
Facebook
easy.

Source: Artfire.com

Sharing Your Images with Pinterest

You may be used to sharing short messages with Twitter and Facebook; it's not a great leap to start sharing images as well. That's the purpose of Pinterest: It allows you to post content that your customers and fans can then repost around the Internet.

Suppose you have a brand-new rhinestone dog leash that your pet supply business has just developed. After announcing it on Facebook, Twitter, your blog, and your website, you "pin" it to your pinboard on Pinterest. Those of your customers who are already on Pinterest will see it and share it with their pet-loving friends. The result: viral marketing for free, with a positive personal endorsement included as a built-in extra.

Pinterest, a relative newcomer in the social marketing field, has grown by leaps and bounds since it was launched in 2010. That's probably because the web is such a visual medium, not to mention the adage that a picture is worth a thousand words. Take a look at what Society43 does on Pinterest. In Figure 6-5, you can see that it has pinned 104 images, and that 55 individuals are "following" them on Pinterest. Best of all, from Society43's standpoint, three people have repinned its images and told their friends about them.

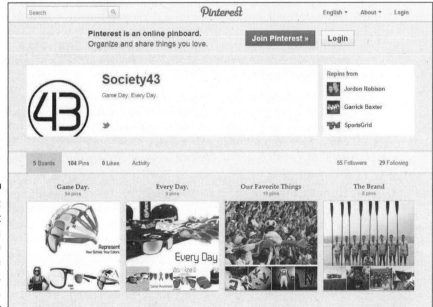

Figure 6-5:
Pinterest helps you manage your online image, literally.

Source: Pinterest.com

To take advantage of Pinterest, make sure you do the following:

- ✔ Sign up for a business account with Pinterest (`business.pinterest.com`); it's free.

- ✔ Get a "Pin" button that you can add to your website next to your Facebook "Like" icon and Twitter "tweet" icon.

- ✔ Check out any businesses on Pinterest that are similar to yours for ideas about the sorts of images they pin.

Building a Fan Base with Twitter

Twitter (`www.twitter.com`) is one of those social networking sites that you hear about and then scratch your head, saying, "What's the purpose of *that?*" At first glance, you might not think a site that lets you post 140-character messages would have a business purpose. But look around at businesses that are using Twitter, and you realize that yes, Twitter can play a huge role in keeping up with customers, building brand visibility, and promoting your own identity or that of your organization.

Lots of individuals use Twitter for fun, journalists use it to spread the news, and celebrities use it to make a point about a cause or issue. Big corporations such as the following use Twitter for a variety of business-related purposes:

- ✔ **Ford Motor Company:** Through its FordService Twitter feed (`twitter.com/FordService`), Ford fields complaints, spam, and occasional useful feedback from customers.

- ✔ **Popeyes Chicken:** The company (`twitter.com/popeyeschicken`) jokes with customers about its food selections, announces sales, and occasionally responds with offers to personally address customer concerns with comments like this: *Sorry about your experience. Direct Mail me your e-mail & phone number and our Manager of Guest Relations will give you a call.*

- ✔ **Starbucks:** The coffee giant has a Twitter site called MyStarbucksIdea (`twitter.com/mystarbucksidea`) where the company listens to customer suggestions and implements many of them. At this writing, one Twitter posting boasted that 50 suggestions originally voiced via Twitter had been implemented.

- ✔ **H & R Block:** The tax-preparation service (`twitter.com/HRBlock`) responds to customer questions, either by email or phone.

Of course, one social networking forum can be used to point to another one. The Kodak CB feed (`twitter.com/kodakCB`) is used to publicize new posts on the Kodak Corporate Blog. The blog, in turn (`1000words.kodak.com`), has links to the Kodak website, the Kodak Facebook page, the Kodak YouTube feed . . . get the idea?

For businesses small and large, Twitter plays a role in the overall online marketing effort. To build prominence on search engine results and word-of-mouth publicity, you need to set up a web of connections from one site to another. By chatting with your customers, even if it seems as though you are giving your knowledge away and answering questions that don't lead to immediate sales, you are building loyalty and good relations. Those benefits to others lead to sales for you.

Setting up a Twitter presence

It's easy to start posting on Twitter. As on Facebook, the challenge is to come up with a plan for promoting your business with Twitter postings (called *tweets*). Before you sign up, answer a few simple questions:

✔ What are your business goals for being on Twitter? Who will read your tweets?

✔ Do you have a cause or issue you want people to pay attention to?

✔ What action do you want people to take after reading a tweet? Do you want them to visit your website, read your blog, or shop in your sales catalog?

✔ How will people find you easily? What's a one- or two-word name that you can assign to your Twitter page?

✔ Who will post tweets? Should this be a team effort, to keep postings flowing to Twitter on a regular basis?

✔ Do you have special sales or promotions you can offer?

That last part is especially important if you sell items from a catalog. Twitter denizens are used to getting special details or notices of items on sale from sites like DellOutlet (`www.twitter.com/delloutlet`).

Signing up and posting

After you have a Twitter communications plan in place, you can sign up for the service and set up your Twitter feed. Go to `www.twitter.com`. enter a name, email address, and password, and then click the Sign Up for Twitter button.

After filling out a simple form to create an account comes the real work: remembering to post and updating your posts regularly. Being limited to 140 characters per tweet is a relief to many. But because tweets are so short, the convention is to keep them coming at least once a day or even several times a day.

Twitter is perfect if you have a smartphone with a keyboard and you like to type text messages. Twitter offers an official app for iPhones, iPads, and Android devices, too, and there are also even fancier third-party Twitter apps.

Using Your Blog for Profit . . . and Fun

You are probably familiar with blogs as online diaries whose owners record thoughts and observations and share them with anyone who cares to read them. There are millions of blogs in the world; in fact, at the time of this writing, there are an estimated 190 million+ blogs in the world.

Many blogs are just casual chatter. A few, though, make money for their creators. You, too, can use a blog to spread the word about you, your company, and what you sell, and maybe make a few extra bucks as well.

Choosing a host with the most for your posts

One of the many nice things about blogging is that you don't have to invent the wheel. Some sites set you up with a graphic look and a mechanism for posting, editing your posts, and receiving comments. Two of these are especially popular:

- ✔ WordPress (`www.wordpress.com`)
- ✔ Blogger (`www.blogger.com`)

Of these two, WordPress is far more popular because it offers more features than Blogger. For its part, Blogger (which is owned by Google) has been around a while and is free. WordPress is also free, but it offers a Premium version that adds features such as a custom domain, extra storage, and the capability to add a feature called VideoPress to your postings. You can also buy premium themes to give your site a professional-looking design.

If you are more technically minded and like to control your website and your blog, consider Movable Type (`www.movabletype.org`). Instead of hosting your blog on someone else's site, you post this blogging software on a server that you either own or on which you rent space. Movable Type is free for individuals but costs $595 for a five-user Pro version license.

Adding ads to your blog

The most obvious and common way to make money from a blog is to sell ads on it. This becomes practical, however, only if you are already attracting a substantial number of visitors to your blog. Advertisers aren't going to pay to place ads on a blog that has only 300 visitors a month. One that has 3,000 visitors per month has a chance of gaining some ad revenue. The most common ad sources include the following:

- ✓ **AdSense:** This service from Google allows you to choose advertisers whose products and services are related to your own content.

- ✓ **BlogAds:** This service does the "matchmaking," pairing up bloggers with advertisers and taking a fee for its work.

- ✓ **Affiliate ads:** As an affiliate, you advertise someone else's products. You sign up for a program such as the popular affiliate program run by Amazon. com. Suppose you review a book on your blog and include a link to the book's description in the Amazon.com marketplace. If someone clicks your ad to Amazon and then buys the book, you get paid an affiliate fee.

A blog is essentially a website in its own right — one to which you add the primary content on a regular basis. Although many blogs generate income, they also provide financial benefits because they save money for their owners. You can set one up for no money at all, as long as you have it hosted for free and are willing to take photos and write content yourself.

Achieving other business benefits

Blogs give customers and potential clients a place to gather so that they can find out more about you and your company. The more time they spend with you, the greater your chances of making a sale to them. A blog also gives you a forum for developing a credible reputation. Besides that, blogs are fun. They can take on a life of their own, especially when people start posting comments and you engage in dialog with them.

Marketing yourself

Many blogs exist to give the creator a place to demonstrate his or her knowledge and expertise in a chosen field. Even if your blog isn't specifically about you, consider including some biographical information so your visitors can find out something about your background, your knowledge of your field, and your trustworthiness. You might include the following:

- ✓ The basics about your qualifications: why you started your blog and why you went into business

✔ Any certifications, honors, or titles related to your business

✔ Something about your business philosophy: your goals and objectives, and why you enjoy what you do

For many professionals, a blog is a place to promote and manage an image. When the famous golfer Tiger Woods was involved in legal controversy, he used his website (www.tigerwoods.com) to issue statements. The site includes a blog where he periodically posts about his tours and activities.

You don't have to include a photo with your blog if you want to maintain your privacy. A photo would make your blog seem more friendly and personal, however. Don't include your personal phone number or email address unless you want to be especially open to your customers. Many CEOs do include email addresses on their blogs and websites so that they can give personal attention to customer inquiries.

Selling your products instead of yourself

You don't have to get personal with your blog. Some of the most successful blogs are roundups of software, gadgets, or other consumer goods. Some businesspeople advertise their products right within their blog.

Index

• A •

academic references, 377
accelerated method, 330
Account column, in Chart of
    Accounts, 260
accountants, 183–184, 269
accounting cycle, 241–243
accounting methods, 188–190, 270
accounting period, 240
accounts payable, 240, 254, 299
accounts receivable, 240, 251, 298
accrual-basis accounting, 189, 244,
    245, 268
accrued expenses payable, on statement
    of cash flows, 299
Accrued Payroll Taxes account, 254
accumulated depreciation
    buildings account, 252
    equipment account, 253
    furniture and fixtures account, 252
    leasehold improvements account, 252
    on statement of cash flows, 298–299
    vehicles account, 252
acid-test ratio, 308
action plan, 102
activity trap, 392
actual budgeting, 347–350
adjusting journal entries, as step in
    accounting cycle, 242, 243
adjustments, 242
Adobe Dreamweaver, 199–200, 215
AdSense, 535
advertising
    adding to blogs, 535
    analyzing costs of, 329
    finding customers with, 451
    simple rules of, 517–518
    timing, 523
Advertising account, 258
Advertising Age (magazine), 516

Adweek (magazine), 516
affiliate ads, 535
Affordable Care Act (2010), 171, 181
airline industry, 68–69
Allen, Kathleen (author)
    *eBusiness Technology Kit
    For Dummies,* 411
alternate sites, for franchises, 138–139
Amazon, 55, 62, 175, 535
American Recovery and Reinvestment
    Act (ARRA, 2009), 180
American Stock Exchange (AMEX), 128
American Taxpayer Relief Act (2012), 379
Americans with Disabilities Act, 159
Amgen, 60
amortization
    defined, 331
    organization costs account, 254
    patents account, 254
analyzing
    advertising costs, 329
    employee cost, 328
    influence points, 453–455
    sales promotion cost, 329
    shortfalls, 423
    talents, 423
anatomy, of business plans, 101–104
angels, finding, 120–121
Angie's List, 74
annual reports, 240
answering phones, 483
anticipated upsell business model, 51
appearance of buildings/stores, finding
    customers with, 451
appendixes, in business plan, 103
Apple Computer, 56, 61, 62, 65, 72,
    175, 413
Applebee's, 85
approving plans, 125
area development agreement, 89–91
area representatives, 92

arrival, at your business, 486
ArtFire, 529–530
The Art of War (Sun Tzu), 47
Ask (website), 19
asset investment, as liquidity
    trap, 312–313
asset sale lease-back, 317
asset-based lenders, 130–131
assets
  about, 250
  current, 248, 250–251
  defined, 239
  liquidating, 316
  long-term, 248, 251–254
Astro Events of America, 166
at-home sites, for franchises, 138, 139–140
Attainable characteristic, of SMART
    goals, 387
attitude, good, as job candidate
    characteristic, 367
audiences, 108. *See also* target audiences
auditing business image, 488–490
Aussie Pet Mobile, 165
authority, delegation and, 435–436
automation, 406–407
available current working capital, 309–310
average cost method, 337
A&W, 85, 140
awareness gap, 448–449

• *B* •

back of the house, 157–158
backgrounds
  choosing, 207–208
  tile images in, 207–208
backing up email messages, 482
"bad apple" franchises, 95
balance sheets
  about, 189, 250, 296
  assets, 250–254
  from cash flow point of view, 298–299
  comparing with P&L, 334–336
  defined, 239
  equity, 255–256
  liabilities, 254–255
Bank Service Charge account, 259

bankers, consulting before starting
    home-based businesses, 184
Barkoff, Rupert (businessman), 151
Barron's (magazine), 67
base sales, projecting improvements
    above, 457–458
Beginning HTML5 & CSS3 For Dummies
    (Tittel and Minnick), 204
benchmarking, 234, 332
benefit plans, as a consideration before
    leaving day job, 180
benefits
  communicated by marketing
    programs, 447
  of products, 512
Berkus Technology Ventures, 121
Best Buy, 75
bestseller, 464–465
Beyond (website), 372
Bezos, Jeff (entrepreneur), 175
big base effect, 327
big idea, 515–516
BigBelly Solar, 54
Bing (website), 19
BlackBerry, 61
Blakely, Sara (entrepreneur), 176
Blockbuster Video, 49
BlogAds, 535
Blogger (website), 534
blogs
  about, 216–218, 534
  adding ads, 535
  benefits of, 535–536
  for finding employees, 371
bonus money, as a consideration
    before leaving day job, 180
book value, 299, 337
bookkeepers, 238, 269
bookkeeping
  about, 237
  accounting cycle, 241–243
  accrual-basis accounting, 244, 245
  balance sheet accounts, 250–256
  bookkeepers, 238, 269
  cash-basis accounting, 243–245
  Chart of Accounts, 248–249, 260–262
  credits, 247–248

debits, 247–248
double-entry, 189, 245–247
income statement accounts, 256–260
terminology for, 239–241
bootstrap, 119
Boston stock exchange, 129
brainstorming
about, 32–33, 516–517
boosting creativity, 36
idea blender, 33–35
inspiring team creativity, 36–38
tweaking ideas, 38
within work environment, 39–40
brand
about, 491
balancing personal and business,
500–501
building, 493–496
conveying through taglines, 498–500
determining positioning strategy,
497–498
in franchising, 81–82
maintaining, 501–505
managing, 494–496
market position, 496–498
online, 493
power of, 492–493
protecting, 501–505
reasons for, 491–492
value of, 492–493
brand loyalty, as threat to new
entrants, 13
brand penetration, 87
branded location, 93
brand-new offerings, 497
breakeven, 281–282
bricks and clicks business model, 50
broadcast media, 518
budgeting. *See also* cost control
about, 321–322
actual, 347–350
as business-management tool, 354–355
external, 350–351
forecasting, 347–350
frame of mind for, 322
internal, 350–351
living budget, 351–354
for marketing communications, 513–514

other uses for, 355–356
process of, 341–343
tools for
CART (Complete, Accurate, Reliable,
and Timely), 343–344
flash reports, 345–347
SWOT (Strengths, Weaknesses,
Opportunities, and Threats), 344–345
building
brand, 493–496
locations, 148–149
buildings account, 252
Bureau of Labor Statistics (website), 20
Burger King, 57–58
business. *See also specific topics*
about, 7
defining market niche, 20–23
feasibility analysis, 8–11
industry
about, 11–12
entry strategy, 15
framework of structure, 12–14
researching, 15–20
knowing your, 409–410
products, 23–25
business associates, NDAs and, 133
business concept, 9
business consultants, consulting before
starting home-based businesses, 184
business environment, in business
plan, 102
business format franchising, 82, 83–84
business ideas
about, 27
brainstorming, 32–40
identifying business opportunities,
40–41
power of good, 27–32
reality checks, 42–43
testing, 41
business image
about, 477
auditing, 488–490
first impressions
about, 477–478
email, 481–482
online searches, 478–480
in person, 484–487

business image *(continued)*
  telephone, 482–484
  website, 480–481
business interruption insurance, for
    home-based businesses, 188
business model
  about, 45
  common aspects of, 47–49
  evolution of, 46
  examples of, 49–53
  finding success with, 53–62
  importance of, 46
  simple, 49
  who needs a, 47
business names, choosing, 186–187
business networking group, as a
    resource, 113
business opportunity, 40–41, 165–166
business plan
  developing, 182–183
  writing
    about, 99
    anatomy of, 101–104
    establishing time frame, 109–111
    identifying key messages, 107–109
    identifying target audiences, 107–109
    planning, 99–101
    planning objectives, 106–107
    preparing for real world, 111–113
    starting position, 104–106
business school, as a resource, 112
business solvency, 303–309
Business Week (magazine), 67
business-management tool, budgeting
    as, 354–355
buyer bargaining power, threats from, 14
buyer switching costs, as threat to new
    entrants, 13
buyers, NDAs and, 133
buying
  competitor's products, 18
  goods from franchisor, 151

● *C* ●

C Corporations
  about, 185–186, 223, 228
  tax reporting for, 359–360

calculated amounts, 265
California Cedar Company, 57
calls, transferring, 483
Camp Bow Wow, 54
Capital account, 256
capital expenditures, 272
capital requirements, as threat to new
    entrants, 13
Career Builder (website), 372
career development, 416
Career Documents, 176
carrying capacity, 12
cash
  sources of, 288–289
  on statement of cash flows, 298
cash accounting, 189
cash burn rate, 310
cash flow
  about, 287–288
  appending to P&L report, 292–293
  classifying, 300–301
  compared with profit, 290–291
  reporting, 291–296
  sources of cash, 288–289
cash flow from operating activities, 287
cash flow from profit, 299–300, 301, 303
Cash in Checking account, 250
Cash in Savings account, 251
Cash on Hand account, 251
cash-basis accounting, 243–245, 268
cash-flow projections, 189–190
central business district (CBD), 138
certificates of occupancy, 148
chamber of commerce, 31, 113, 190
Change in Accounting Method
    (Form 3115), 244
characteristics, of ideal job candidates,
    367–368
Chart of Accounts
  about, 248–249
  setting up, 260–262
cheap chic business model, 50, 58–59
Cheat Sheet (website), 3
classifying cash flows, 300–301
*Clicking: 17 Trends That Drive Your
    Business - And Your Life* (Popcorn), 67
clip art, for websites, 209–210
Clip Art Universe (website), 210

Clipart.com (website), 210
Clorox Company, 71
ClosetMaid, 166
closing, as step in accounting cycle, 242, 243
cloud computing, 168
Coach, 70, 75–76
coaching
  about, 422
  getting started, 418–421
  identifying tools for, 424–425
  incorporating into day-to-day interactions, 427–428
  managing and, 422–424
  show-and-tell, 426
  successes of, 426–427
  websites for, 428
The Coaching and Mentoring Network (website), 428
The Coaching Connection (website), 428
Coca-Cola, 82, 83
code of ethics, creating, 401–402
CoffeeCup HTML Editor, 210
collective business model, 51
college library, as a resource, 112
color, for websites, 207
Comet, 71
comments, inviting from customers, 214–219
commercial banks, 130
commercial finance companies, 130
committing to schedules, 110
Common Stock account, 255
communication. *See also* marketing communications
  evaluating, 488–489
  networks and, 413
  of your vision, 389–391
Communication Arts (magazine), 516
community centers, for franchises, 136–137
company description, in business plan, 102
company networks, 413–414
company overview, in business plan, 102
company strategy, in business plan, 102

competition
  business models and, 58–59
  buying products from, 18
  evaluating, 31–32
competitive advantage
  considerations about, 59
  enhancing, 61–62
  obtaining your, 59–60
competitive benefits, of franchise ownership, 93
competitive edge, addressed in business model, 48
competitive intelligence, 17–20
competitive strategy, addressed in business model, 48
The Competitive Intelligence Guide (website), 19
complementary products, addressed in business model, 48
Complete, Accurate, Reliable, and Timely (CART), 343–344
complexity, 12
Computer Renaissance, 85
concentrated campaign, 522
conducting
  multiple interviews, 378–379
  self-appraisals, 43
confidential circumstances, delegating, 441
consideration, 133
consistency, in brand, 494, 502–503
Consolidated Omnibus Budget Reconciliation Act (COBRA, 1985), 180
consulting outside professionals, 183–184
content, creating to attract customers to websites, 195–206
context, provided by coaches, 425
continuity, for enhancing competitive advantage, 62
contra account, 298–299
contractors, selecting, 149
contracts, 132
contribution, 340
contribution margin, 280–281
control, loss of, after delegation, 434
controller, 263, 269
conversion franchising, 84

conveying brand and position through taglines, 498–500

cooperatives, buying goods through, 153

copy guidelines, 504–505

copyright (©) symbol, 505

copyrights account, 254

corporate social responsibility (CSR)
about, 395
benefits of, 397–398
developing strategy for implementation, 398–400
employing, 396–397
ethics, 400–403
socially responsible practices, 396–400

corporations
about, 185–186, 228–229
benefits of, 229–230
incorporating process, 230–231
risks of, 230
tax reporting for, 359–360

cost control. *See also* budgeting
about, 321–322, 322–323
analyzing advertising and sales promotion costs, 329
analyzing employee cost, 328
comparing P&L and balance sheet, 334–336
context of, 323–324
cost of goods sold, 326–327, 336–339
depreciation expense, 330–331
expenses, 332–333
facilities expense, 331–332
frame of mind for, 322
gross margin, 326–327
interest expense, 333–334
profit centers, 339–340
reducing costs, 341
sales revenue change, 324–326

cost leadership, 59–60

cost of goods sold
about, 295
on Chart of Accounts, 249
cost control and, 326–327, 336–339
defined, 240
inventory shrinkage, 338–339
inventory write-downs, 338–339
selecting methods, 336–338

cost superiority, 15

The Costly Myths That Entrepreneurs, Investors, and Policy Makers Live By (Shane), 64

costs
advertising, 329
employee, 328
with market expansion strategy, 464
reducing, 341
sales promotion, 329

counseling, delegating, 440–441

Courtyard by Marriott, 84

Covel (website), 212

Craigslist (website), 372

creating
business model
about, 45
common aspects of, 47–49
evolution of, 46
examples of, 49–53
finding success with, 53–62
importance of, 46
simple, 49
who needs a, 47
career development plans, 420–421
code of ethics, 401–402
content to attract customers to websites, 195–206
deals, 126
Facebook kiosk, 529–530
impression inventory, 489–490
logos, 213
mass media schedule, 521–523
sustainable supply chain, 398
technology-competitive advantages, 410
websites
about, 191–192
attracting customers with content, 195–206
creating a web presence, 219–220
establishing visual identities, 206–213
Feng Shui, 192–195
inviting comments from customers, 214–219

creative brief, 509

creative strategy, 502–503

creativity, 36–38

Credit Cards Payable account, 254
creditors, unsecured, 318–319
credits, 246–248
crowdsourcing business model, 52
Crowdspring.com, 54
CSR. *See* corporate social
responsibility (CSR)
cultural fit, as job candidate
characteristic, 368
current assets
accounts, 250–251
on Chart of Accounts, 248
current liabilities
accounts, 254–255
on Chart of Accounts, 249
current ratio, 307
customer loyalty, 398
customer perception, 469
customer segments
for enhancing competitive advantage, 61
evaluating attractiveness of, 64
customers
analysis of, 10
determining attractiveness of, 74–76
finding, 450–452
inviting comments from, 214–219
knowing your, 445–452, 470
listening to, 40
prospective, talking to, 31
putting yourself in shoes of, 486–487
cut out the middle man business model, 52

• *D* •

dafont (website), 208
data, trolling for at government
websites, 20
day job, leaving your, 180–181
daypart, 140
days costs of goods sold outstanding, in
inventory, 309
days sales outstanding, in trade accounts
receivable, 309
dealing with failure, 130
deals, crafting, 126
debenture, 130
debits, 246–248

debt service coverage ratio, 309, 314–315
Debt Zero LLC, 166
debt-to-equity ratio, 308
delegating
about, 431–432
appropriate tasks for, 438–440
appropriate tasks to keep, 440–441
myths about, 433–436
reasons for, 432–433
steps in, 437
deliveries, receiving, 155
Demko, Alexis (entrepreneur), 176
Demko Demolition Warehouse, 176
dental insurance, as a consideration before
leaving day job, 180
Department of Commerce (website), 275
depreciation
about, 268, 295
accumulated, 252, 253, 298–299
cost control and, 330–331
defined, 241
Description column, in Chart of
Accounts, 260
detail work, delegating, 438
developing
business plan, 182–183
CSR strategy for implementation, 398–400
effective marketing communications,
514–518
employees. *See* employee development
marketing plans, 190
a niche strategy, 23
technology plans, 410–412
development, 416
differentiation, 15, 54, 60
digital media, 518, 519
direct sales business model, 52
direct selling, with home-based
business, 165
direct variable expense, 326
direction, provided by goals, 385
directories, 519
direct-unit franchises, 87–88
discipline, delegating, 440–441
discussion areas, on websites, 218–219
distribution and delivery, as category of
business possibilities, 40

distribution strategies, 474–475
dividends, 239
doctrine of ostensible authority, 226
Dollarshaveclub.com, 54
Domino's Pizza, 53
Dorotik, Dan (entrepreneur), 176
dots per inch (dpi), 195, 212
double-entry bookkeeping, 189, 245–247
Drawing account, 256
Dreamweaver (Adobe), 199–200, 215
drive time, evaluating for franchises, 144
Drugstore.com (website), 118
dry storage, 157
dual branding, 140
DuckDuckGo (website), 19
due diligence, doing, 125
Dues and Subscriptions account, 259
Dummies (website), 3
Dunkin Donuts, 83
DuraFlame, 57

• **E** •

earnings, 267
earnings before interest and income tax.
    See operating expenses
earnings statement. *See* income statement
eBay (website), 220
eBusiness Technology Kit For Dummies
    (Allen and Weisner), 411
e-commerce, funding for, 118–119
EcommerceBytes (website), 218
economies of scale, as threat to new
    entrants, 13
eCRATER (website), 220
Edwards, Paul (author)
  Finding Your Perfect Work, 164
Edwards, Sarah (author)
  Finding Your Perfect Work, 164
efficiency, improving, 407–408
80/20 rule, 392
Electric Library (website), 19
elevator pitch, 9
e-mail
  campaigns, for finding employees, 371
  first impressions from, 481–482
email feedback, 214–215

employee development
  about, 415–416
  coaching, 422–428
  reasons for, 416–418
employees
  analyzing cost of, 328
  developing. *See* employee development
  finding good, 368–372
  listening to, 428
  meeting with, 427
  sales revenue needed per, 277–278
  trust of, 433–434
employment agencies, for job
    candidates, 370
employment eligibility, checking, 379
enabling comments on web pages, 217
encouragement, from coaches, 423
encroachment, 87, 145–147
end user, 22–23
entrants, threats to new, 13–14
Entrepreneur (magazine), 177
Entrepreneur Media (website), 166
entry strategy, 15
envisioning your position, 471–472
equipment account, 253
Equipment Rental account, 259
equity
  about, 250
  accounts, 255–256
  on Chart of Accounts, 249
  defined, 239
equity sources, 319
errors, in accounting records, 269–270
errors-and-omissions insurance, for
    home-based businesses, 188
estimating market share, 467–468
ethics
  about, 400
  creating a code of, 401–402
  daily choices, 402–403
  on the job, 400–401
evaluating
  communications, 488–489
  competition, 31–32
  drive times for franchises, 144
  job candidates, 376–379
  marketing materials, 488–489

mass media efforts, 523–524
target market, 63–64
whether to use a market segmentation
strategy, 466
eventual replacement costs, 331
E-Verify program (website), 379
evolution, of business models, 46
examples, of business models, 49–53
excessive growth rates, as liquidity
trap, 315–316
executive summary, 8, 102
expense accounts, 258–260
expense padding, 275
expenses
about, 256
behavior of, 279–281
on Chart of Accounts, 249
cost control and, 332–333
defined, 240
recording, 270
reporting differences of cash flows from,
293–296
experience, as job candidate
characteristic, 367
expert advice, seeking, 113
extended coverage, for home-based
businesses, 187
external budgets, 350–351
external image, 203
extraordinary gains and losses,
recording, 270–271
eXtropia.com (website), 219
ExxonMobil, 140

● **F** ●

Facebook
about, 526–527
attracting "likers," 527–528
creating Facebook kiosk, 529–530
getting customers excited, 528–529
website, 19, 219, 371, 377, 526
facilities expense, 323, 331–332
failures
dealing with, 130
preparing for, 458

family
funding from, 119–120
NDAs and, 133
FAQ, business plan, 103–104
FASB (Financial Accounting Standards
Board), 266, 301
Fast Company (magazine), 428
feasibility analysis
about, 8
business concept, 9
executive summary, 8
feasibility decision, 11
financial analysis, 10
genesis or founding team analysis, 10
industry analysis, 9
market/customer analysis, 10
product/service development analysis, 10
timeline to launch, 11
features, of products, 512
Federal Business Opportunities
(website), 190
Federation of Tax Administrators
(website), 361
FedEx, 56
FedWorld (website), 20
feedback
email, 214–215
provided by coaches, 424
Feng Shui, for your website, 192–195
fickleness, of investors, 123–124
Financial Accounting Standards Board
(FASB), 266, 301
financial analysis, 10
financial leverage, 320
financial review, in business plan, 102
financial statements, as step in accounting
cycle, 242, 243
financing
for e-commerce, 118–119
a traditional business, 116–117
financing activities, 301
Find a Mentor (website), 428
finding
angels, 120–121
assistance, 190
best industries, 66–67

finding *(continued)*
business ideas within work environment, 39–40
changes leading to new opportunities, 40–41
customers, 450–452
expert advice, 113
good people as employees, 368–372
goods, 154
informative resources, 112–113
marketing formula, 453–456
mentors, 429–430
success with a business model, 53–62
suppliers, 154
target market
about, 63
customer attractiveness, 74–76
determining industry attractiveness, 64–69
gauging, 63–64
industry value chain, 76–78
niche attractiveness, 69–74
underserved markets, 73–74
unserved markets, 73–74
your place on industry value chain, 76–78
Finding Your Perfect Work (Edwards and Edwards), 164
fire insurance, for home-based businesses, 187
Firehouse Subs, 85
first impressions
about, 477–478
email, 481–482
online searches, 478–480
in person, 484–487
telephone, 482–484
website, 480–481
first mover advantage, as way to gain differentiation, 60
first-in, first-out (FIFO) accounting method, 337
first-stage funding, 117
Five Guys, 70
fixed assets, 298
fixed costs, 279–280, 283
flat fee business model, 53
flat market, 462–463

flexibility
delegation and, 436
as job candidate characteristic, 368
flighting, 523
floor plan, of location, 149
focus, 60
focusing on target customers, 449
Folgers, 77
follow through, 428
font, 504
Font Squirrel's Webfont Generator (website), 208
foot traffic, 485
Ford Motor Company, 83, 532
forecasting budgeting, 347–350
Form 1040 Schedule E Supplemental Income and Loss, 359
Form 1065 U.S. Return of Partnership Income, 358
form fields, 216
Form I-9, 379
forming partnerships, 226–227
forms, 216
Forrester (website), 67
founding team, analysis of, 10
franchise agreement, 79, 144, 145–147
franchise business model, 51
franchise fee, 80
franchisee, 79, 84–87
franchising
about, 79–80, 135
brands in, 81–82
conversion, 84
effects of, 80
encroachment, 145–147
franchisees, 79, 84–87
franchisors, 79, 84–87, 142–144, 151, 153, 169
as a home-based business, 165
location options, 135–140
maintaining inventory, 156–159
master, 91–92
merchandise, 149–154
pros and cons of, 92–96
receiving merchandise, 154–156
relationships, 87–92
researching locations for, 141–144

securing a location, 147–149
success of, 80
supplies, 149–154
taxes and, 96
training, 159–162
types of franchises, 82–84
franchisor
about, 79, 142–144, 169
buying goods from, 151
buying products authorized by, 153
roles and goals of, 84–87
Free Edgar (website), 19
FreeFind (website), 205
freemium business model, 52
Freight Charges account, 258
frequency, balancing with reach, 521–522
friends
funding from, 119–120
NDAs and, 133
front of the house, 158–159
front-loading, 523
Fuller Brush Company, 165
full-time jobs, leaving for part-time
business, 168–169
funding
about, 115
finding angels, 120–121
from friends and family, 119–120
growth, 130–131
guarding interests, 132–133
IPOs, 126–130
planning for, 116–119
venture capital, 122–126
furniture and fixtures account, 252
future duties, delegating, 440

• *G* •

garbage in, garbage out concept, 343
Gartner (website), 67
General Ledger, 241
General Motors, 61
generally accepted accounting principles
(GAAP), 266, 301
genesis team, analysis of, 10
Getting, Ivan (physicist), 61
GIF format, 213, 214

gigs, turning into businesses, 29–30
goal-setting
about, 383–384
by coaches, 423
communicating goals and vision, 389–391
directions for, 384–386
identifying SMART goals, 386–388
juggling priorities, 391–393
making goals reality, 393–394
number of goals, 388–389
goodwill account, 254
Goodyear Tires, 83
Google (website), 19
Google AdWords Keyword Planner
(website), 480
Google blog (website), 480
Google Images (website), 203, 208
Google+ Local, 479–480, 485
Google My Business, 479–480
Google Places (website), 480
gosmallbiz (website), 166
government
legal requirements, for home-based
businesses, 187
regulations, as threat to new entrants, 13
trolling for data on websites, 20
GPS system, 61
Green Irene, 165
Greenfield, Jeff (author)
*Negotiating Commercial Leases &
Renewals For Dummies,* 147
gross margin. *See* gross profit margin
gross profit, 265, 266
gross profit margin, 17, 265, 266, 326–327
Groupon (website), 194
growth, funding, 130–131
growth opportunity, planning to seize, 106
growth wave, 461–462
guarding interests, 132–133
guestbook, 217
Gustin, Abe (business owner), 85
gut instinct, in hiring process, 380–381

• *H* •

H & R Block, 532
Häagen Dazs, 70

hard working, as job candidate
  characteristic, 367
headings, for websites, 200
health insurance
  as a consideration before leaving day
    job, 180
  for home-based businesses, 167, 187
heavy-up scheduling, 523
`height` attribute, 203
help
  finding, 190
  with information technology (IT), 412
  offered by coaches, 425
Hewlett, Bill (entrepreneur), 175
Hewlett-Packard, 175
H.H. Gregg, 55
hiring process
  about, 365
  defining desirable characteristics,
    367–368
  evaluating candidates, 376–379
  finding good people, 368–372
  hiring the best, 379–381
  interviewing, 372–376
  job description, 366–367
  professional website creators, 220
hobbies, turning into businesses, 29–30
Holden, Greg (author)
  *Starting an Online Business For
    Dummies,* 198
Hollis, Jack (business owner), 85
home page, 192–193
home-based business
  about, 163
  basics of, 164–169
  benefits of, 169–170
  disadvantages of, 170–171
  examples of successful, 175–176
  opportunities for, 177
  process for starting, 181–190
  quiz for, 172–174
  starting from scratch, 174–178
  transitioning into, 178–190
  types of, 164
homeowner's policy, for home-based
  businesses, 188

Hoover's Online (website), 19
hosts, for websites, 195
hotel california business model, 52
HotHotHot (website), 207
HouseWall, 83
The Huffington Post, 54

● *I* ●

icons, explained, 2–3
idea blender, 33–35
ideas, tweaking, 38. *See also* business ideas
identifying
  business opportunities, 40–41
  coach's tools, 424–425
  key messages, 107–109
  SMART goals, 386–388
  strengths, 450
  target audiences, 107–109
images
  enhancing text on websites with, 203–204
  sharing with Pinterest, 531–532
impression inventory, 489–490
impressions, improving, 490
improving
  competitive advantage, 61–62
  creativity, 36
  efficiency, 407–408
  impressions, 490
  marketing strategy
    about, 461
    designing positioning strategy, 471–473
    developing market share strategy,
      467–471
    growth wave, 461–463
    innovative distribution strategies,
      474–475
    market expansion, 463–465
    market segmentation, 465–466
    quality strategies, 474
    reminder strategies, 474
    reviewing strategies, 476
    selling innovative products, 475
    simplicity marketing, 473
    writing down strategies, 476
markup, 283–295

markup ratio, 283
productivity, 407–408
profit, 282–286
sales volume, 283, 285–286
website text with images, 203–204
in person, first impressions from, 484–487
Inc. (magazine), 67
Inc 500 (website), 19
income expectations, with franchise
    ownership, 95
income shifting, 276
income statement
    about, 256, 264, 296
    accounts for, 240
    defined, 240
    expenses, 258–260
    recording money, 257
    tracking cost of sales, 258
income tax expense, on P&L, 267
incorporating coaching into day-to-day
    interactions, 427–428
Indeed (website), 372
independence, loss of, with franchise
    ownership, 94
individual success, compared with team
    success, 423
industry
    about, 11–12
    analysis of, 9
    compared with market, 66
    determining attractiveness of, 64–69
    differing business models in same, 57–58
    evaluating attractiveness of, 64
    finding best, 66–67
    framework of structure, 12–14
    hostility, as threat to new entrants, 14
    researching
        about, 15–16
        checking status, 16–17
        competitive intelligence, 17–20
        defining market niche, 20–23
industry niche, evaluating
    attractiveness of, 64
industry symposium, as a resource, 112
industry trade associations, 20
industry trade journal, as a resource, 112

industry value chain, finding your place
    on, 76–78
inelasticity, with franchise ownership, 95
influence points, analyzing, 453–455
information gathering, delegating, 439
information technology (IT)
    about, 405
    automation, 406–407
    company networks, 413–414
    developing technology plans, 410–412
    help with, 412
    improving efficiency, 407–408
    improving productivity, 407–408
    neutralizing negatives, 408–409
    using to your advantage, 409–412
informative resources, locating, 112–113
innovation, for enhancing competitive
    advantage, 61
innovative products, 475
inserting images on websites, 210–213
insolvent, 303
insurance, for home-based businesses,
    187–188
Insurance account, 259
insurance agents/brokers, consulting
    before starting home-based
    businesses, 184
intangible assets, 331
intellectual property, as way to gain
    differentiation, 60
interest expenses
    about, 296
    cost control and, 333–334
    on P&L, 267
Interest Income account, 257
interests, 132–133, 241
internal budgets, 350–351
internal candidates, as job candidates, 369
Internal Revenue Service (website), 275,
    330, 357, 379
International Coach Federation
    (website), 428
International Council of Shopping Centers
    (website), 141
International Franchise Association
    (IFA), 80

Internet
  for finding employees, 371–372
  researching job candidates on, 377
  as a resource, 112
interviewing
  about, 372
  dont's, 375–376
  do's, 374–375
  questions to ask, 372–373
inventions, licensing, 25
inventor
  becoming an, 24
  teaming up with an, 24–25
inventory
  days costs of goods sold outstanding
    in, 309
  defined, 241
  as liquidity trap, 313
  maintaining, 156–159
  on P&L, 272–273
  on statement of cash flows, 298
Inventory account, 251
inventory shrinkage, 338–339
inventory write-downs, 338–339
inverted razor and blades business
    model, 50
investing activities, 300
investors, fickleness of, 123–124
inviting comments from customers,
    214–219
invoices, verifying, 156
iPad, 70
IPOs, 126–130
IT. *See* information technology (IT)
iTunes, 55

Jani-King, 165
Jazzercise, 165
Jell-O, 73
job candidates
  evaluating, 376–379
  revisiting pool of during hiring
    process, 381
job description, 366–367

Jobs, Steven (entrepreneur), 175, 413
John Deere, 83
journal entries, 242, 243
journals, 241
JPEG format, 213, 214
juggling priorities, 391–393
*Just Good Business: The Strategic Guide to
  Aligning Corporate Social Responsibility
  and Brand* (McElhaney), 399

• K •

key messages, identifying, 107–109
KFC, 85, 140
Kindle, 55
KISS principle, 196–197
Kleenex, 73
knowledge
  as source of power, 394
  transferring from coaches, 425
Kodak CB feed, 533
Komodo Edit, 207
Kroger, 77

• L •

LaFontaine, David (author)
  Mobile Web Design For Dummies, 194
land account, 251
landlords, 145
last-in, first-out accounting (LIFO)
    method, 337
lawyers, consulting before starting home-
    based businesses, 183
layout, of location, 149
LCS system, 37
leading people to your business, 485
leasehold improvements account, 252
leases, signing, 147
Legal and Accounting account, 259
legal issues, 167, 375–376
legal structure
  about, 221
  benchmarking, 234
  choosing, 184–186, 222–224
  corporation, 228–231

limited liability company (LLC), 185, 223, 232–233, 260
   nonprofit, 233–234
   partnership, 185, 226–228, 358–359
   S corporation, 186, 228, 231–233, 359
   sole proprietorship, 184–185, 223–226, 357–358
lending sources, 317–318
LEXUS/NEXUS, 112
liabilities
   about, 250
   accounts, 254–255
   current, 254–255
   defined, 239
   long-term, 255
liability insurance, for home-based businesses, 188
license to operate, 398
licensing inventions, 25
lifestyle centers, for franchises, 137
"likers," attracting to Facebook page, 527–528
limited liability company (LLC)
   about, 185, 223
   compared with S Corporation, 232–233
   tax reporting for, 360
limited partnership, 185, 227
LinkedIn (website), 371, 377
links, for websites, 202–203
liquidating assets, 316
liquidity
   about, 303–307
   measurements tools for, 309–311
   traps, 311–316
   untapped sources of, 316–319
liquidity availability analysis, 311
listening
   to customers, 40
   to employees, 428
lists, for websites, 201
living budget, 351–354
loan advance rates, 317
Loans Payable account, 255
locations
   building, 148–149
   options for franchises, 135–140

   researching for franchises, 141–144
   securing for franchises, 147–149
   as way to gain differentiation, 60
logic, of niche markets, 72
logos
   choosing, 186
   creating, 213
   managing presentation of, 503–504
   typestyle for, 504
Long John Silvers, 85, 140
long tail business model, 52
Longaberger, 165
long-term assets
   accounts, 251–254
   on Chart of Accounts, 248
long-term liabilities, 249, 255
long-term vision and goals, delegating, 440
losers, as job candidate category, 378
loss leader business model, 51
loss of control, after delegation, 434
lower of cost or market test, 338

• *M* •

Macs, 413
magazines, 519
`mailto` link, 215
maintaining
   brands, 501–505
   inventory, 156–159
malicious mischief coverage, for home-based businesses, 188
malls, for franchises, 136
managing
   brand presentation, 503–504
   coaching and, 422–424
   logo presentation, 503–504
   marketing program, 456–457
   money, 166–167
market exclusivity, 90
market expansion strategy
   about, 463
   bestseller, 464–465
   offering more products, 463–464
market niche, defining, 20–23
market position, brand and, 496–498

market segment, addressed in business model, 48
market segmentation strategy
  about, 465–466
  adding segments, 466
  evaluating whether to use a, 466
market share, estimating, 467–468
market share strategy
  about, 467
  choosing units, 467
  estimating market share, 467–468
  knowing customers, 470
  market trends, 470–471
  product category, 468–470
market trends, 470–471
market value of real estate, 330
marketing
  considering expenses, 278–279
  evaluating materials, 488–489
  finding formula for, 453–456
  refining expectations, 457–458
  yourself, 535–536
marketing communications
  about, 507
  creating mass media schedules, 521–523
  developing effective, 514–518
  evaluating efforts, 523–524
  making media selections, 518–521
  objectives for, 508–514
marketing plans
  about, 453
  in business plan, 102
  developing, 190
marketing program
  controlling, 456–457
  finding marketing formula, 453–456
  maximizing impact of, 459–460
  refining marketing expectations, 457–458
marketing pyramid, 452
marketing strategy
  about, 453, 461
  designing positioning strategy, 471–473
  developing market share strategy, 467–471
  growth wave, 461–463
  innovative distribution strategies, 474–475

market expansion, 463–465
market segmentation, 465–466
quality strategies, 474
reminder strategies, 474
reviewing strategies, 476
selling innovative products, 475
simplicity marketing, 473
writing down strategies, 476
markets
  analysis of, 10
  compared with industries, 66
  narrowing your, 21–23
  splitting, 71–73
markup, 266, 283–295
markup ratio, increasing, 283
Mary Kay, Inc., 165
mass media
  creating schedule for, 521–523
  evaluating efforts, 523–524
mass media channels, 518
master franchise fee, 91
master franchising, 91–92
maximizing impact of marketing program, 459–460
Mazero, Joyce G. (attorney), 146
McDonald's, 57–58, 70
McDonnell, Tom (business owner), 85
McElhaney, Kellie (author)
  Just Good Business: The Strategic Guide to Aligning Corporate Social Responsibility and Brand, 399
McKenna, Jim (businessman), 142
McKenna Associates, Corp., 142
Measurable characteristic, of SMART goals, 387
measuring
  growth rate of market, 462
  profit and loss, 268–273
  real cost of money, 123–124
  success, 513
media selections, 518–521
medical insurance, as a consideration before leaving day job, 180
meeting, with employees, 427
Meineke, 81
mentoring
  being a mentor, 429–430

finding mentors, 429–430
getting started, 418–421
merchandise
about, 149–150, 264
receiving, 154–156
who to buy from, 150–153
message, 108–109
me-too business, 496
Microloan program, 131
micromanager, 431
Microsoft Clip Gallery Live, 210
Microsoft Expression Web (website), 201
milestones, 110–111
Minnick, Chris (author)
Beginning HTML5 & CSS3 For Dummies, 204
Minority Business Development Agency (website), 190
Miscellaneous Expenses account, 259
mobile versions, of websites, 194
Mobile Web Design For Dummies (Warner and LaFontaine), 194
Money (magazine), 67
money, managing, 166–167
Monster (website), 372
Motorola, 61
Movable Type (website), 534
multilevel marketing business model, 50, 165
multi-unit development agreement, 89–91
myths, delegation, 433–436

narrowing your market, 21–23
NASA, 61
NASDAQ (National Association of Securities Dealers Automated Quotation), 128
National Business Incubation Association (website), 190
National Market System, 128–129
navigation, for websites, 197–200
negative cash flow, 310
negatives, neutralizing in IT, 408–409

Negotiating Commercial Leases & Renewals For Dummies (Willerton and Greenfield), 147
negotiation, rules of, 122
neighborhood centers, for franchises, 136
net earnings, 267
net income, 267
net working capital, 307
network effect business model, 52
network effects, addressed in business model, 49
networking, 20
networks, company, 413–414
neutralizing negatives of IT, 408–409
New York Stock Exchange (NYSE), 128
New York Times (newspaper), 112
newspapers, 112, 519
niche markets, 72
niche strategy, 15, 23
niches
determining attractiveness, 69–74
power of, 69
unlimited, 70
nickel and dime business model, 53
Nike, 65
NoChar, 56
non-disclosure agreements (NDAs), 132–133
nonprofit organization, 233–234
notes payable, on statement of cash flows, 299
Notes Payable account, 255
NSAS QuickLaunch licensing tool (website), 25

Obamacare, 171
objectives, of marketing communications, 508–514
objectivity, in hiring process, 380
obtaining your competitive advantage, 59–60
off-balance sheet sources, 319
Office Expenses account, 259
off-street sites, for franchises, 138–139

On the Run, 83, 140
1-800-FLOWERS, 528–529
one-to-one marketing, 518
online auctions business model, 52
online branding, 493
online media, using for researching
    industries, 19
online searches, first impressions though,
    478–480
Oogles n Googles, 85
operating activities, 300
operating costs, reducing, 398
operating earnings. *See* operating expenses
operating expenses
    about, 295
    reporting, 266–267
    sales capacity provided by, 277
operating system. *See* income statement
organization costs account, 254
Other Income account, 257
Other Sales Costs account, 258
outdoor media, 518
outside professionals, consulting, 183–184
outsourcing, 168
over-dependence, with franchise
    ownership, 94–95
owners' equity - invested capital, on
    statement of cash flows, 299
owners' equity - retained earnings, on
    statement of cash flows, 299

• *P* •

Pacific Exchange, 129
Packard, David (entrepreneur), 175
The Pampered Chef, 165
Panera Bread Company, 70, 85
parking, 485
partners
    about, 223
    addressed in business model, 48
    attracting, 398
    retaining, 398
partnerships
    about, 185, 226
    forming, 226–227

partnership agreement, 227–228
    tax reporting for, 358–359
passion, compared with profitability, 28–29
pass-through entity, 265
patently illegal activities, 276
patents account, 254
patronage dividends, 153
payroll, 241
Payroll Taxes account, 259
performance appraisals, delegating, 440–
    441
periodic, 264
permits, 148
personal brands, balancing with business
    brands, 500–501
personal management functions,
    automating, 406
personal power, as source of power, 394
personal referrals, for job candidates,
    369–370
perspective, transferring from coaches, 425
Pinterest, 19, 531–532
pixels, 212
Pizza Hut, 85, 140
placement of buildings/stores
    finding customers with, 451
    as influence point, 454
planning
    to address changing conditions, 106
    with business plan, 99–101
    for businesses, 30
    for funding, 116–119
    to seize growth opportunity, 106
    for solo business, 105
    for startup, 105
planning objectives, 106–107
plans, approving, 125
playing up strengths, 450
plugins, 216
PNG format, 214
point-of-purchase (POP) marketing, 474
politically sensitive situations,
    delegating, 441
Popcorn, Faith (author)
    *Clicking: 17 Trends That Drive Your
        Business - And Your Life,* 67

Popeyes Chicken, 532
position
  conveying through taglines, 498–500
  in market, 496–498
position power, as source of power, 394
positioning strategy
  about, 471
  determining, 497–498
  envisioning your position, 471–472
  writing a, 472–473
positive, reinforcing, 428
positive performance feedback,
    delegating, 440
Postage account, 259
posting
  as step in accounting cycle, 242
  on Twitter, 533–534
potential profits, for enhancing
    competitive advantage, 62
potential winners, as job candidate
    category, 378
power, of brands, 492–493
power centers, 137
Power Presentations, 129
premium business model, 53
pre-opening benefits, of franchise
    ownership, 93–94
prepaid expenses, on statement of cash
    flows, 298
Prepaid Insurance account, 251
presence, 191
pricing, 62, 454
pricing trap, 455–456
primary offering, 127
print media, 518
priorities, juggling, 391–393
privacy rights, 377
problems, addressed in business
    model, 47, 48
processes, automating, 406
product demonstrations, finding
    customers with, 451
product development
  analysis of, 10
  becoming an inventor, 24
  teaming up with an inventor, 24–25
product distribution franchising, 82–83

product liability coverage, for home-based
    businesses, 188
product life cycle, 475
productivity, improving, 407–408
productization of services business model,
    51
products
  about, 264
  buying from competitors, 18
  category for market share strategy,
    468–470
  finding, 154
  as influence point, 453
  offering more, 463–464
  selling, 475, 536
products for sale, as category of business
    possibilities, 39
professional associations
  finding customers with, 451
  for job candidates, 370
  as resources, 113
professional liability insurance, for
    home-based businesses, 188
professional service corporation, 186
profit
  accounting for, 269
  cash flow from, 299–300
  compared with cash flow, 290–291
  defined, 289
  improving, 282–286
  reasons for improvement in, 276–279
Profit and Loss (P&L) statement
  about, 189, 263–264
  appending cash flow to, 292–293
  breakeven barrier, 281–282
  comparing with balance sheet, 334–336
  components of, 264–267
  improving profit, 282–286
  measuring and reporting on, 268–273
  presenting, 273–281
  reporting differences of cash flows
      from sales revenue and expenses
      on, 293–296
profit centers, 324, 339–340
profit sharing, as a consideration before
    leaving day job, 180
profitability, compared with passion, 28–29

profit-neutral business transactions, 270–272

ProfNet (website), 19

projecting improvements above base sales, 457–458

promotion, as influence point, 454

proof of concept, 8

property, plant, and equipment (fixed assets), 298, 313

proprietary factors
  of business models, 55–57
  as threat to new entrants, 13
  as way to gain cost leadership, 60

prospective customers, talking to, 31

protected market, 86–87

protected territory, 86–87

protecting brands, 501–505

public companies
  checking information on, 19
  selling stock to the, 126–130

Publication 946 (2013), *How To Depreciate Property,* 330

pulsing, 523

Pump It Up, 83

Purchase Discount account, 258

Purchase Returns account, 258

purchases, on P&L, 272–273

Purchases account, 258

• *Q* •

quality strategies, 474

quick ratio, 308

quick service restaurants (QSRs), 139

Quicken, 68–69

Quiznos, 85

• *R* •

radio, 519

Rally's, 60, 70

razor and blades business model, 50

reach, balancing with frequency, 521–522

real cost of money, calculating, 123–124

real world, preparing for, 111–113

reality, of goals, 393–394

reality checks, carrying out, 42–43

recasts, 352

recording
  expenses, 270
  revenue, 270
  unusual, nonrecurring gains and losses, 270–271

recruiting channels, traditional, 369–370

red herring, 128

Red Robin, 70

reducing
  costs, 341
  fixed costs, 283
  operating costs, 398
  variable costs, 283

references, checking, 376–377

referrals
  finding customers with, 451
  personal, for job candidates, 369–370

refining marketing expectations, 457–458

refrigerated storage, 158

registered trademark (®) symbol, 505

reinforcing positive, 428

relationship power, as source of power, 394

relationships, franchise, 87–92

Relevant characteristic, of SMART goals, 387

Remember icon, 3

reminder strategies, 474

Rent Expense account, 260

Rent-A-Center, 75

repetitive assignments, delegating, 439

reporting
  cash flow, 291–296
  operating expenses, 266–267
  profit and loss, 268–273
  on taxes for corporations, 359–360
  on taxes for partnerships, 358–359
  on taxes for sole proprietorships, 357–358

researching
  businesses, 31
  industry
    about, 15–16
    checking status, 16–17
    competitive intelligence, 17–20
    defining market niche, 20–23
    locations for franchises, 141–144

resiliency, as job candidate characteristic, 368
resolution, for website images, 212
responding to email messages, 482
responsibility
  of employees, 433–434
  as job candidate characteristic, 368
retained earnings
  account, 256
  defined, 239
retaining partners, 398
retirement, for home-based businesses, 167
revenue
  account, 256
  on Chart of Accounts, 249
  recording, 270
revenue model
  addressed in business model, 48
  defined, 240
reviewing
  marketing strategies, 476
  notes about job candidates, 378
revisiting candidate pool in hiring process, 381
risks, with market expansion strategy, 464
rivalry, among existing firms, 14
road show, 129
rolling forecasts, 352
royalty, 80

● *S* ●

S Corporations
  about, 186, 223, 228, 231–232
  compared with limited liability company (LLC), 232–233
  tax reporting for, 359
SafeAuto, 55
Salaries and Wages account, 260
salary, on P&L, 273–275
Sale of Fixed Assets account, 257
sales calls, finding customers with, 451
sales capacity, provided by operating expenses, 277
Sales Discounts account, 257
sales mix, 325
Sales of Goods or Services account, 257

sales promotion cost, analyzing, 329
Sales Returns account, 257
sales revenue
  changing, 324–326
  expense, 294
  needed per employee, 277–278
  reporting differences of cash flows from, 293–296
sales skimming, 275
sales tax, 361
Sales Tax Collected account, 254
sales volume, 283, 285–286
samples, free, finding customers with, 451
Save It Now, 85
SBA 7(a) loans, 131
SBA Express, 131
scale, 60
scams, for home-based businesses, 167
Schedule C, Profit or Loss from Business, 357
Schedule K1 (Form 1065), Partner's Share of Income, Deductions, Credits, etc., 358
Schedule SE, Self-Employment Tax, 358
schedules, committing to, 110
Script Archive (website), 219
search and research company, as a resource, 112
search boxes, 204–205
search engines, for researching industries, 18–19
searchability, of websites, 204–205
SEC (Securities and Exchange Commission), 19, 127, 128–129
second opinion, 42–43
second-stage funding, 117
secret partners, 227
securing locations for franchises, 147–149
Securities and Exchange Commission (SEC), 19, 127, 128–129
self-appraisals, conducting, 43
self-starter, as job candidate characteristic, 367
selling
  ability to sell, for enhancing competitive advantage, 62
  innovative products, 475
  products, 536
  stock to the public, 126–130

sensitive circumstances, delegating, 441
serif typefaces, 209, 504
Service Corps of Retired Executives (SCORE) (website), 190
service development, analysis of, 10
ServiceMaster Clean, 165
services for hire, as category of business possibilities, 39
servitization of products business model, 51
setting goals
  about, 383–384
  communicating goals and vision, 389–391
  directions for, 384–386
  identifying SMART goals, 386–388
  juggling priorities, 391–393
  making goals reality, 393–394
  number of goals, 388–389
Shaklee, 165
Shane, Scott A. (author)
  The Costly Myths That Entrepreneurs, Investors, and Policy Makers Live By, 64
sharing images with Pinterest, 531–532
Shop tab (Facebook), 529
shopping areas, for franchises, 138
shortfalls, assessing, 423
show-and-tell coaching, teaching through, 426
shrinking market, 462–463
signage, 485
signature, email, 481
signing leases, 147
signing up, on Twitter, 533–534
silent partners, 227
similar-but-different business, 496–497
simplicity marketing, 473
Simply Hired (website), 372
single entry accounting, 189
single-level marketing, 165
single-unit franchises, 87–88
site map, 205–206
SiteMiner (website), 205
SKS, 55
Skyliner, 497
slogan. *See* taglines
small business, 163

Small Business Administration (SBA), 112, 131, 182
Small Business Development Centers (website), 190
SMART goals, identifying, 386–388
smartness, as job candidate characteristic, 368
Snap-on Tools, 165
social marketing
  about, 525
  blog
    about, 534
    adding ads, 535
    benefits of, 535–536
  Facebook
    about, 526–527
    attracting "likers," 527–528
    creating Facebook kiosk, 529–530
    getting customers excited, 528–529
    website, 19, 219, 371, 377, 526
  Pinterest, 19, 531–532
  Twitter
    about, 532–533
    for finding employees, 371–372
    posting, 533–534
    setting up a presence, 533
    signing up, 533–534
    website, 19, 219, 532
social media, finding customers with, 451
social networking. *See* social marketing
socially responsible practices. *See* corporate social responsibility (CSR)
Society43, 531
Soft Scrub, 71
software industry, 68–69
sole proprietorships
  about, 184–185, 223, 224–225
  advantages of, 225
  disadvantages of, 225–226
  tax reporting for, 357–358
solo business, planning for, 105
solvency, 303–307
sounding boards, coaches as, 425
Southwest Airlines, 54, 56, 68–69
spam, 215
Spanx, 176

Specific characteristic, of SMART goals, 386–387

splitting markets, 71–73

stability, as job candidate characteristic, 368

Standard Industrial Classification Index (website), 16

standards, email, 482

Stanford University Office of Technology Licensing (website), 25

Starbucks, 59, 60, 70, 76, 77, 398, 532

Starting an Online Business For Dummies (Holden), 198

starting position, established with business plan, 104–106

startup, planning for, 105

statement of cash flows
  about, 287–288, 296–297
  balance sheet from cash flow point of view, 298–299
  business solvency, 303–309
  cash flow from profit, 299–300
  classifying cash flows, 300–301
  financial leverage, 320
  liquidity, 303–311
  liquidity traps, 311–316
  presenting, 301–302
  untapped sources of liquidity, 316–319

status, of industry, 16–17

Steak 'n Shake, 70

stock, selling to the public, 126–130

stockholders, 228

straight-line method, 330

strategic market share goal, 470

strengths, 450

Strengths, Weaknesses, Opportunities, and Threats (SWOT), 344–345

stretch goal, 385

strikingly (website), 198

string value proposition, 74

style, for email messages, 482

style guidelines, 503

subfranchisees, 91

subscription model, 51

substitute products/services, threats from, 14

success
  of coaching, 426–427
  finding with a business model, 53–62
  measuring, 513

Sun Tzu (author)
  The Art of War, 47

superior branding, as way to gain differentiation, 60

supervisors, checking references with, 377

suppliers, finding, 154

supplies
  about, 149–150
  who to buy from, 150–153

Supplies account, 260

support, from coaches, 423

support services, for home-based businesses, 167

surrogate roles, delegating, 439

SurveyMonkey (website), 520

sustainable marketing, 452

sustainable supply chain, creating, 398

Swartz, Eric (verbal branding professional), 499–500

• T •

table of contents, in business plan, 102

Taco Bell, 85, 140

TagLine Guru (website), 499

taglines, conveying brand and position through, 498–500

Taiwan Semiconductor, 60

talents, assessing, 423

Target, 58–59

target audiences
  current knowledge of, 510
  focusing on, 449
  identifying, 107–109
  knowing who they are, 509
  what you want them to know, 510–511

target market
  about, 63
  customer attractiveness, 74–76
  determining industry attractiveness, 64–69
  gauging, 63–64

target market *(continued)*
  industry value chain, 76–78
  niche attractiveness, 69–74
Taser, 62
task power, as source of power, 394
taxable income, 330
taxes
  about, 357
  franchising and, 96
  paying for home-based businesses, 167
  reporting for corporations, 359–360
  reporting for partnerships, 358–359
  reporting for sole proprietors, 357–358
  sales tax, 361
teaching, through show-and-tell
    coaching, 426
team
  coaches making time for, 424
  communicating your vision to your,
    389–391
  inspiring creativity in, 36–38
team player, as job candidate
    characteristic, 368
team success, compared with individual
    success, 423
Technical Stuff icon, 3
technological leverage, as way to gain cost
    leadership, 60
technology. *See* information
    technology (IT)
The Tech Coast Angels, 121
telephone, first impressions from, 482–484
Telephone account, 260
temporary agencies, for job candidates,
    370
term sheets, 118
terminology, bookkeeping, 239–241
Tesla, 54, 60
test drive, business planning as a, 109
testing business ideas, 41
text, enhancing on websites with images,
    203–204
theft coverage, for home-based businesses,
    188
third-stage funding, 117

Thomas, Dave (business owner), 85
threats
  from buyers' bargaining power, 14
  to new entrants, 13–14
  from substitute products/services, 14
thumbnail, 203
tile images, in background, 207–208
time frame
  establishing, 109–111
  for marketing communications, 513–514
Time-bound characteristic, of SMART
    goals, 387
timeline to launch, 11
timing ads, 523
Tip icon, 3
<title> tag, 202
titles, for web pages, 202
Tittel, Ed (author)
  *Beginning HTML5 & CSS3 For
    Dummies,* 204
tombstone, 128
tone
  for email messages, 482
  for website, 197
tools, for budgeting
  CART, 343–344
  flash reports, 345–347
  SWOT, 344–345
Toyota, 53, 55
tracking venture capital process, 124–126
trade accounts receivable, days sales
    outstanding in, 309
trade receivables, as liquidity trap, 312
trade shows, 112
trademark (™) symbol, 505
traditional business, financing a, 116–117
traditional job-hunting sites, for finding
    employees, 372
traditional recruiting channels, 369–370
training, 159–162, 416
transactions, 241–242, 271–272
transferring calls, 483
transitioning, into home-based businesses,
    178–190
Travel and Entertainment account, 260

Treetops, 497

trends, market, 470–471

trial balance, 241, 242

trial coupons, finding customers with, 451

trolling for data at government websites, 20

Trout, Jack (author)
The 22 Immutable Laws of Marketing, 73

trust, for employees, 433–434

TV, 519

tweaking ideas, 38

tweets, 533

The 22 Immutable Laws of Marketing (Trout), 73

Twitter
about, 532–533
for finding employees, 371–372
posting, 533–534
setting up a presence, 533
signing up, 533–534
website, 19, 219, 532

Type column, in Chart of Accounts, 260

typefaces, for websites, 208–209

typestyle, for logo, 504

• *U* •

uncertainty, 12

underserved markets
finding, 73–74
working in, 67–68

underwriters, choosing, 128

Uniform Franchise Offering Circular (UFOC), 150, 162

unique supplier relationship, as way to gain differentiation, 60

United Parcel Service (website), 207

units, choosing for market share strategy, 467

university library, as a resource, 112

unlimited niches, 70

unsecured creditors, 318–319

unserved markets
finding, 73–74
working in, 67–68

unusual, nonrecurring gains and losses, recording, 270–271

U.S. Census Bureau (website), 20, 468

U.S. Department of Commerce (website), 20

U.S. Patent and Trademark Office (website), 190

U.S. Postal Service (website), 207

U-Save Auto Rental, 85

users as experts business model, 52

Utilities account, 260

• *V* •

value, of brands, 492–493

value chain, 48, 76–78

value proposition, addressed in business model, 48

vandalism coverage, for home-based businesses, 188

variable costs, reducing, 283

variable expenses, 279–280

variance report, 354

variances, 148

vehicle insurance, for home-based businesses, 188

vehicles account, 252, 260

Vendstar, 166

venture capital, 117, 122–126

vertical integration, as way to gain cost leadership, 60

vision
communicating your, 389–391
provided by coaches, 425

vision insurance, as a consideration before leaving day job, 180

Vistaprint, 55, 65, 69

visual identities, establishing, 206–213

voicemail messages, 483, 484

Volkswagen, 515

VooDoo Doughnut, 516

• *W* •

Walk-In Lab, 54

Wall Street Journal (newspaper), 112, 370

Walmart, 53, 55, 58–59, 72
want ads, for job candidates, 370
Warner, Janine (author)
  Mobile Web Design For Dummies, 194
Warning icon, 3
Waste Management, 65
web pages, 202,216
WebAward Competition (website), 206
Webby Awards (website), 206
websites
  Affordable Care Act (2010), 171, 181
  Ask, 19
  Barron's (magazine), 67
  Beyond, 372
  Bing, 19
  Blogger, 534
  Bureau of Labor Statistics, 20
  Business Week (magazine), 67
  Career Builder, 372
  Cheat Sheet, 3
  clip art for, 209–210
  Clip Art Universe, 210
  Clipart.com, 210
  for coaching, 428
  The Coaching and Mentoring
    Network, 428
  The Coaching Connection, 428
  color for, 207
  The Competitive Intelligence Guide, 19
  Covel, 212
  Craigslist, 372
  creating
    about, 191–192
    attracting customers with content,
      195–206
    creating a web presence, 219–220
    establishing visual identities, 206–213
    Feng Shui, 192–195
    inviting comments from customers,
      214–219
  dafont, 208
  Department of Commerce, 275
  discussion areas on, 218–219
  Drugstore.com, 118
  DuckDuckGo, 19

Dummies, 3
eBay, 220
EcommerceBytes, 218
eCRATER, 220
Electric Library, 19
Entrepreneur (magazine), 177
Entrepreneur Media, 166
E-Verify program, 379
eXtropia.com, 219
Facebook, 19, 219, 371, 377, 526
Fast Company (magazine), 428
Federal Business Opportunities, 190
Federation of Tax Administrators, 361
FedWorld, 20
Find a Mentor, 428
for finding employees, 371
first impressions from, 480–481
Font Squirrel's Webfont Generator, 208
Forrester, 67
Free Edgar, 19
FreeFind, 205
Gartner, 67
Google, 19, 479
Google AdWords Keyword Planner, 480
Google blog, 480
Google Images, 203, 208
Google Places, 480
gosmallbiz, 166
Groupon, 194
headings for, 200
Hoover's Online, 19
HotHotHot, 207
Inc., 67
Inc 500, 19
Indeed, 372
Internal Revenue Service, 275, 330,
  357, 379
International Coach Federation, 428
International Council of Shopping
  Centers, 141
LinkedIn, 371, 377
links for, 202–203
lists for, 201
Microsoft Expression Web, 201

Minority Business Development
    Agency, 190
mobile versions of, 194
Money, 67
Monster, 372
Movable Type, 534
National Business Incubation
    Association, 190
NSAS QuickLaunch licensing tool, 25
online specialty tea stores, 468
Pinterest, 19, 532
privacy rights, 377
ProfNet, 19
SBA (Small Business Administration), 131
Script Archive, 219
searchability of, 204–205
Service Corps of Retired Executives
    (SCORE), 190
Simply Hired, 372
site map, 205–206
SiteMiner, 205
SKS, 55
Small Business Development
    Centers, 190
Standard Industrial Classification
    Index, 16
Stanford University Office of Technology
    Licensing, 25
strikingly, 198
SurveyMonkey, 520
TagLine Guru, 499
taglines, 499
Twitter, 19, 219, 371, 532, 533
typefaces for, 208–209
United Parcel Service, 207
U.S. Census Bureau, 20, 468
U.S. Chamber of Commerce, 190
U.S. Department of Commerce, 20
U.S. Patent and Trademark Office, 190
U.S. Postal Service, 207
U.S. Securities & Exchange
    Commission, 19
WebAward Competition, 206
Webby Awards, 206
Woods, Tiger (golfer), 536

WordPress, 534
Yahoo, 19
Yelp, 19
Zoomerang, 520
Weisner, Jon (author)
    *eBusiness Technology Kit For
        Dummies,* 411
Weissman, Jerry (management
    consultant), 129
Wendy's, 57–58, 70, 81, 83, 152
what-if analysis, 283, 352, 353–354
White Castle, 70
width attribute, 203
Willerton, Dale (author)
    *Negotiating Commercial Leases &
        Renewals For Dummies,* 147
Windows (Microsoft), 413
Wing Zone, 83
winners, as job candidate category, 378
Woods, Tiger (golfer), 536
WordPress (website), 534
workers' compensation, for home-based
    businesses, 188
worksheet, as step in accounting c
    ycle, 242
Wozniak, Stephen (entrepreneur), 175
write-downs of inventory, 338–339
writing
  business plan
    about, 99
    anatomy of, 101–104
    establishing time frame, 109–111
    identifying key messages, 107–109
    identifying target audiences, 107–109
    planning, 99–101
    planning objectives, 106–107
    preparing for real world, 111–113
    starting position, 104–106
creative strategy, 502
  marketing strategies down, 476
  a positioning strategy, 472–473

Xerox, 56, 73

Yahoo (website), 19
Yelp (website), 19
yourself
  knowing, 445–452
  marketing, 535–536
Yum! Brands, 140

• Z •

Zappos.com, 53
Zipcar, 54
Zoomerang (website), 520

Notes

Notes

Notes

Notes

About the Authors

Kathleen R. Allen, PhD: Dr. Allen is an authority on entrepreneurship and small business technology and is the author of *The Complete MBA For Dummies* (with Peter Economy), *eBusiness Technology Kit For Dummies* (with Jon Weisner), *Entrepreneurship and Small Business Management, Launching New Ventures,* and *Growing and Managing an Entrepreneurial Business*, as well as several other books. She has also written for popular business magazines and newspapers (*Inc., Los Angeles Times, Los Angeles Business Journal,* and *The New York Times*) and is called upon by *The Wall Street Journal,* CNN, CNBC, and a variety of other media for expert opinion in the field of entrepreneurship.

Peter Economy is a home-based business author, ghostwriter, and publishing consultant, and the author or coauthor of more than 50 books, including *Why Aren't You Your Own Boss?* with Paul and Sarah Edwards (Three Rivers Press), *Managing For Dummies,* 2nd Edition, and *Consulting For Dummies,* 2nd Edition, with Bob Nelson (Wiley), and *Writing Children's Books For Dummies* with Lisa Rojany Buccieri (Wiley). Peter is also associate editor for the Apex Award-winning magazine *Leader to Leader.* Peter invites you to visit his Web site at www.petereconomy.com.

Paul and Sarah Edwards are award-winning authors of 17 books with over two million books in print. Sarah, a licensed clinical social worker with a PhD in ecopsychology, and Paul, a licensed attorney, are recognized as pioneers in the working-from-home field. With the emergence of a global economy that challenges the environment and everyone's personal, family, and community well-being, they are focusing their efforts on finding pathways to transition to a sustainable Elm Street economy in which home business plays a vital role. Paul and Sarah write a quarterly column for *The Costco Connection.* They hosted the *Working From Home* show on HGTV and have been regular commentators on CNBC. Paul and Sarah provide a wealth of ongoing information, resources, and support at www.pathwaystotransition.com.

Lita Epstein, who earned her MBA from Emory University's Goizueta Business School, enjoys helping people develop good financial, investing, and tax planning skills. While getting her MBA, Lita worked as a teaching assistant for the financial accounting department and ran the accounting lab. After completing her MBA, she managed finances for a small nonprofit organization and for the facilities management section of a large medical clinic. She designs and teaches online courses on topics such as accounting and bookkeeping and starting your own business. She's written more than 35 books, including *Bookkeeping For Dummies, Reading Financial Reports for Dummies, Trading For Dummies, The Business Owner's Guide to Reading and Understanding Financial Statements,* and *Financial Decision Making.*

Alex Hiam helps organizations (including nonprofits and government agencies) think through their branding and marketing strategies and their leadership development programs. He has served on the boards of directors of a variety of organizations and also as an instructor in the Isenberg School of Management at UMass Amherst. Alex earned his BA from Harvard and his MBA in marketing and strategic planning from the Haas School at U.C. Berkeley. He has led creative retreats for top consumer and industrial firms to facilitate innovative thinking about strategic plans, branding, naming, and product ideas. He also writes novels and believes that all good writing (including advertising) is, at heart, good storytelling. Alex is the coauthor of the bestseller *The Portable MBA in Marketing* (Wiley) as well as numerous other books and training programs. His most recent book is *Business Innovation For Dummies*.

Greg Holden started the small business Stylus Media, which is a group of editorial, design, and computer professionals who produce both print and electronic publications. The company's name comes from the recording stylus, which reads the traces left on a disk by voices or instruments and translates those signals into electronic data that can be amplified and enjoyed by listeners. Greg has been a freelance writer since 1996, and is also a novelist. A former PowerSeller on eBay, he is now embarking on a new hobby — beekeeping. (Visit Greg's blog, www.gregholden.com, for more about his activities and for links to his fiction.) The first edition of *Starting an Online Business For Dummies* was the ninth of Greg's more than 45 computer books, and he authored *eBay PowerUser's Bible* for Wiley Publishing. Over the years, he has been a regular contributor to CNET and to EcommerceBytes. He received a Master of Arts degree in English from the University of Illinois at Chicago, and he writes general-interest books, short stories, and poetry.

Peter Jaret has written for *The New York Times, Newsweek, National Geographic, Health, Reader's Digest,* and dozens of other magazines. He is the author of seven books, including *In Self-Defense, From the Frontlines of Global Public Health, Nurse: A World of Care,* and *Active Living Every Day.* He has developed written materials for the Electric Power Research Institute, Lucas Arts, The California Endowment, WebMD, BabyCenter, Stanford University, Collabria, Home Planet Technologies, and others. In 1992, he received the American Medical Association's first-place award for medical reporting. In 1997 and again in 2007, he won James Beard Awards for food and nutrition writing. He holds degrees from Northwestern University and the University of Virginia.

Jim Muehlhausen, JD: Like most entrepreneurs, Jim Muehlhausen has an eclectic background, ranging from CPA to franchisee, attorney, business owner, consultant, franchisor, public speaker, university professor, and book author. While still attending the Indiana University School of Law, he became the youngest franchisee in Meineke Discount Muffler history (1987–1991). After successfully selling that business, Jim founded an automotive aftermarket manufacturing concern. During his nine-year tenure with that business, the company achieved recognition from Michael Porter of the Harvard Business School and *Inc.* magazine in the IC 100 Fastest Growing Businesses. In 2009, he founded the Business Model Institute, which is devoted to the innovation and study of business models. Jim writes several articles for the Institute each year as well as contributing to publications such as *Inc., The Small Business Report, Entrepreneur, BusinessWeek,* and various business journals.

Bob Nelson, PhD is president of Nelson Motivation Inc., a management training and consulting company that specializes in helping organizations improve their management practices, programs, and systems. Dr. Nelson has sold more than 3.5 million books on management and motivation, which have been translated in more than 35 languages, including *1001 Ways to Reward Employees* (now in its 55th printing), *The 1001 Rewards & Recognition Fieldbook, 1001 Ways to Energize Employees, 1001 Ways to Take Initiative at Work, Keeping Up in a Down Economy, Ubuntu: An Inspiring Story of an African Principle of Teamwork and Collaboration,* and (with Peter Economy) *The Management Bible* and *Consulting For Dummies,* 2nd Edition. He has appeared extensively in the media, including on CBS's *60 Minutes,* CNN, MSNBC, PBS, and National Public Radio, and has been featured in *The New York Times, The Wall Street Journal, The Washington Post, BusinessWeek, Fortune,* and *Inc.* magazines to discuss how to best motivate today's employees. Dr. Nelson holds an MBA in organizational behavior from UC Berkeley and received his PhD in management with Dr. Peter F. Drucker at the Drucker Graduate Management School of Claremont Graduate University. For more information about available products or services offered by Nelson Motivation Inc., including registration for Dr. Nelson's free Tip of the Week, visit www.nelson-motivation.com.

Steven Peterson is founder and CEO of Strategic Play, a management training company specializing in software tools designed to enhance business strategy, business planning, and general management skills. He's the creator of the Protean Strategist, a business simulation that reproduces a dynamic business environment where participant teams run companies and compete against each other in a fast-changing marketplace. He is coauthor, along with Paul Tiffany, of *Business Plans For Dummies,* which was nominated as one of the best business books of the year by the *Financial Times.* He holds advanced degrees in mathematics and physics and received his doctorate from Cornell University. For more information, visit www.StrategicPlay.com.

Barbara Findlay Schenck has spent her career helping business owners start, grow, market, and brand their companies. She's worked internationally in community development, served as a college administrator and instructor in Hawaii, and cofounded an advertising agency in Oregon. She writes marketing advice columns for MSN and participates in programs that help businesses adapt to their ever-changing media and consumer markets. She is the author of *Small Business Marketing Kit For Dummies* and *Selling Your Business For Dummies* and is coauthor of *Branding For Dummies* and *Business Plans Kit For Dummies.* For more information on her background, books, and business advice, visit her website at www.bizstrong.com.

Michael Seid is founder and Managing Director of Michael H. Seid & Associates (MSA), the nation's leading consulting firm specializing in franchising and other methods of distribution. During his 25+ years in franchising, Michael has been a Senior Operations and Financial Executive or Consultant for companies within the franchise, retail, hospitality, restaurant, and service industries. He has also been a franchisee. Michael is the past Chairman of the International Franchise Association (IFA) Supplier Forum, a former member of the IFA's Executive Committee, and the first supplier ever directly elected to the IFA's Board of Directors. Michael is a CFE (Certified Franchise Executive) and a very nonpracticing CPA. Michael is a noted author of numerous articles on franchising, an oft-quoted expert in the field, and a frequent lecturer on the subject of franchising. For more information on the services offered by MSA, including speaking or consulting services, visit MSA's website at www.msaworldwide.com.

Dave Thomas began his lifelong career in the restaurant industry at the age of 12, working the counter at the Regas Restaurant in Knoxville, Tennessee. There, he fell in love with the restaurant business and learned that he could be anything he wanted to be if he worked hard and had a burning desire to succeed. Dave passed away in 2002. Dave was a franchisee of Kentucky Fried Chicken (KFC) until 1968, when at the age of 35 the restaurants were sold back to KFC and Dave became a millionaire. In 1969, Dave opened the first Wendy's Old Fashioned Hamburgers restaurant in downtown Columbus, Ohio. By 1973, Dave began franchising Wendy's, and today, more than 6,700 Wendy's restaurants dot the globe. For more information about Dave Thomas and Wendy's, visit the website at www.wendys.com.

John A. Tracy is Professor of Accounting, Emeritus, at the University of Colorado in Boulder. Before his 35-year tenure at Boulder, he was on the business faculty for four years at the University of California at Berkeley. He served as staff accountant at Ernst & Young and is the author of several books on accounting and finance, including *Accounting For Dummies, Accounting Workbook For Dummies, The Fast Forward MBA in Finance,* and *How to Read a Financial Report,* and is coauthor with his son, Tage, of *How to Manage Profit and Cash Flow.* Dr. Tracy received his B.S.C. degree from Creighton University and earned his MBA and PhD degrees from the University of Wisconsin. He is a CPA (inactive) in Colorado.

Tage C. Tracy is the principal owner of TMK & Associates, an accounting, financial, and strategic business planning consulting firm focused on supporting small- to medium-sized businesses since 1993. Tage received his baccalaureate in accounting in 1985 from the University of Colorado at Boulder with honors. Tage began his career with Coopers & Lybrand (now merged into PricewaterhouseCoopers). More recently, Tage coauthored *How to Manage Profit and Cash Flow* with his father, John Tracy.

Publisher's Acknowledgments

Acquisitions Editor: Stacy Kennedy

Compilation Editor: Corbin Collins

Project Manager and Editor:
Christine Meloy Beck

Technical Editor: Terrance J. Sullivan,
Certified Public Accountant,
www.tjsullivancpa.com

Art Coordinator: Alicia B. South

Production Editor: Selvakumaran Rajendiran

Cover Image: © iStock.com/mrdoomits

ple & Mac

d For Dummies,
Edition
8-1-118-72306-7

one For Dummies,
Edition
8-1-118-69083-3

cs All-in-One
Dummies, 4th Edition
8-1-118-82210-4

X Mavericks
Dummies
8-1-118-69188-5

ogging & Social Media

cebook For Dummies,
Edition
8-1-118-63312-0

cial Media Engagement
Dummies
8-1-118-53019-1

rdPress For Dummies,
Edition
8-1-118-79161-5

siness

ck Investing
Dummies, 4th Edition
8-1-118-37678-2

esting For Dummies,
Edition
8-0-470-90545-6

Personal Finance
For Dummies, 7th Edition
978-1-118-11785-9

QuickBooks 2014
For Dummies
978-1-118-72005-9

Small Business Marketing
Kit For Dummies,
3rd Edition
978-1-118-31183-7

Careers

Job Interviews
For Dummies, 4th Edition
978-1-118-11290-8

Job Searching with Social
Media For Dummies,
2nd Edition
978-1-118-67856-5

Personal Branding
For Dummies
978-1-118-11792-7

Resumes For Dummies,
6th Edition
978-0-470-87361-8

Starting an Etsy Business
For Dummies, 2nd Edition
978-1-118-59024-9

Diet & Nutrition

Belly Fat Diet For Dummies
978-1-118-34585-6

Mediterranean Diet
For Dummies
978-1-118-71525-3

Nutrition For Dummies,
5th Edition
978-0-470-93231-5

Digital Photography

Digital SLR Photography
All-in-One For Dummies,
2nd Edition
978-1-118-59082-9

Digital SLR Video &
Filmmaking For Dummies
978-1-118-36598-4

Photoshop Elements 12
For Dummies
978-1-118-72714-0

Gardening

Herb Gardening
For Dummies, 2nd Edition
978-0-470-61778-6

Gardening with Free-Range
Chickens For Dummies
978-1-118-54754-0

Health

Boosting Your Immunity
For Dummies
978-1-118-40200-9

Diabetes For Dummies,
4th Edition
978-1-118-29447-5

Living Paleo For Dummies
978-1-118-29405-5

Big Data

Big Data For Dummies
978-1-118-50422-2

Data Visualization
For Dummies
978-1-118-50289-1

Hadoop For Dummies
978-1-118-60755-8

Language & Foreign Language

500 Spanish Verbs
For Dummies
978-1-118-02382-2

English Grammar
For Dummies, 2nd Edition
978-0-470-54664-2

French All-in-One
For Dummies
978-1-118-22815-9

German Essentials
For Dummies
978-1-118-18422-6

Italian For Dummies,
2nd Edition
978-1-118-00465-4

 **Available in print and e-book formats.**

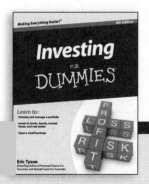

Available wherever books are sold. **For more information or to order direct visit www.dummies.com**

Math & Science

Algebra I For Dummies,
2nd Edition
978-0-470-55964-2

Anatomy and Physiology
For Dummies, 2nd Edition
978-0-470-92326-9

Astronomy For Dummies,
3rd Edition
978-1-118-37697-3

Biology For Dummies,
2nd Edition
978-0-470-59875-7

Chemistry For Dummies,
2nd Edition
978-1-118-00730-3

1001 Algebra II Practice
Problems For Dummies
978-1-118-44662-1

Microsoft Office

Excel 2013 For Dummies
978-1-118-51012-4

Office 2013 All-in-One
For Dummies
978-1-118-51636-2

PowerPoint 2013
For Dummies
978-1-118-50253-2

Word 2013 For Dummies
978-1-118-49123-2

Music

Blues Harmonica
For Dummies
978-1-118-25269-7

Guitar For Dummies,
3rd Edition
978-1-118-11554-1

iPod & iTunes
For Dummies, 10th Edition
978-1-118-50864-0

Programming

Beginning Programming
with C For Dummies
978-1-118-73763-7

Excel VBA Programming
For Dummies, 3rd Edition
978-1-118-49037-2

Java For Dummies,
6th Edition
978-1-118-40780-6

Religion & Inspiration

The Bible For Dummies
978-0-7645-5296-0

Buddhism For Dummies,
2nd Edition
978-1-118-02379-2

Catholicism For Dummies,
2nd Edition
978-1-118-07778-8

Self-Help & Relationships

Beating Sugar Addiction
For Dummies
978-1-118-54645-1

Meditation For Dummies,
3rd Edition
978-1-118-29144-3

Seniors

Laptops For Seniors
For Dummies, 3rd Edition
978-1-118-71105-7

Computers For Seniors
For Dummies, 3rd Edition
978-1-118-11553-4

iPad For Seniors
For Dummies, 6th Edition
978-1-118-72826-0

Social Security
For Dummies
978-1-118-20573-0

Smartphones & Tablets

Android Phones
For Dummies, 2nd Edition
978-1-118-72030-1

Nexus Tablets
For Dummies
978-1-118-77243-0

Samsung Galaxy S 4
For Dummies
978-1-118-64222-1

Samsung Galaxy Tabs
For Dummies
978-1-118-77294-2

Test Prep

ACT For Dummies,
5th Edition
978-1-118-01259-8

ASVAB For Dummies,
3rd Edition
978-0-470-63760-9

GRE For Dummies,
7th Edition
978-0-470-88921-3

Officer Candidate Tests
For Dummies
978-0-470-59876-4

Physician's Assistant Exam
For Dummies
978-1-118-11556-5

Series 7 Exam For Dummies
978-0-470-09932-2

Windows 8

Windows 8.1 All-in-One
For Dummies
978-1-118-82087-2

Windows 8.1 For Dummies
978-1-118-82121-3

Windows 8.1 For Dummies
Book + DVD Bundle
978-1-118-82107-7

Available in print and e-book formats.

Available wherever books are sold. **For more information or to order direct visit www.dummies.com**

Take Dummies with you everywhere you go!

Whether you are excited about e-books, want more from the web, must have your mobile apps, or are swept up in social media, Dummies makes everything easier.

For Dummies is the global leader in the reference category and one of the most trusted and highly regarded brands in the world. No longer just focused on books, customers now have access to the For Dummies content they need in the format they want. Let us help you develop a solution that will fit your brand and help you connect with your customers.

Advertising & Sponsorships

Connect with an engaged audience on a powerful multimedia site, and position your message alongside expert how-to content.

Targeted ads • Video • Email marketing • Microsites • Sweepstakes sponsorship

Custom Publishing

Reach a global audience in any language by creating a solution that will differentiate you from competitors, amplify your message, and encourage customers to make a buying decision.

Apps • Books • eBooks • Video • Audio • Webinars

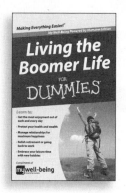

Brand Licensing & Content

Leverage the strength of the world's most popular reference brand to reach new audiences and channels of distribution.

For more information, visit www.Dummies.com/biz

FOR DUMMIES

A Wiley Brand

Dummies products make life easier!

- DIY
- Consumer Electronics
- Crafts
- Software
- Cookware
- Hobbies
- Videos
- Music
- Games
- and More!

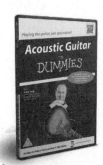

For more information, go to **Dummies.com** and search the store by category.

DUMMIES

A Wiley Bra